VOLUME ONE
SIXTH EDITION

THE CREATIVE IMPULSE
AN INTRODUCTION TO THE ARTS

DENNIS J. SPORRE

Custom Edition for University of Phoenix

Pearson Custom Publishing

Prentice Hall

Taken from:

The Creative Impulse: An Introduction to the Arts, Sixth Edition
by Dennis J. Sporre

A Pearson Education Company
Upper Saddle River, New Jersey 07458

This special edition published in cooperation with Pearson Custom Publishing.

Published in the United States of America

10 9 8 7 6 5 4 3 2

Please visit our web site at www.pearsoncustom.com

ISBN 0–536–67924-X

BA 995045

Pearson Custom Publishing

PEARSON CUSTOM PUBLISHING
75 Arlington Street, Suite 300, Boston, MA 02116
A Pearson Education Company

Contents

3 Greek Classicism and Hellenism *74*

4 The Roman Period *110*

5 Judaism and Early Christianity *140*

6 Byzantium and the Rise of Islam *174*

7 The Early Middle Ages: *The Monastic and Feudal Romanesque Period* *206*

Picture Credits and Literary Acknowledgments

Picture Credits

The author, the publishers, and Laurence King Publishing Ltd wish to thank the museums, galleries, collectors, and other owners who have kindly allowed their works to be reproduced in this book. Every effort has been made to contact the copyright holders, but should there be any errors or omissions, Laurence King Publishing would be pleased to insert the appropriate acknowledgment in any subsequent printing of this publication. In general, museums have supplied their own photographs; other sources are listed below:

Ansell Adams Publishing Rights Trust/Corbis: 17.24; AKG London: 1.3 (Erich Lessing), 1.5 (Erich Lessing), 1.6, 3.2 (Joseph Martin), 5.4 (detail) and 5.10 (Erich Lessing), 5.11, 7.5, 9.2, 9.5, 10.10, 10.24, 10.16, 10.19, 10.28, 10.29, 10.30, 10.31, 11.1, 11.5, 11.9, 11.14, 11.20, 11.35, 12.2, 12.3, 12.11, 12.12, 12.14, 12.15, 12.16, 12.18, 12.22, 12.24, 12.25, 13.4, 13.6, 17.35 (Cameraphoto); Wayne Andrews, Chicago: 14.22; © Araldo De Luca, Rome: 4.3; Arcaid, London: 16.40; The Architectural Association, London: 17.27, 18.35, 18.40; Archivi Alinari, Florence: 10.6; The Art Archive, London: 9.21, 17.40 (Dagli Orti); Ancient Art & Architecture Collection, London: 4.29 (C.M. Dixon), 5.5 (C.M. Dixon), 8.10, 13.29; James Austin, Cambridge: 10.8; Alan Bedding: 17.36; Bibliothèque Nationale, Paris: 6.9, 6.10, 7.4 (detail) and 7.24 (Bridgeman Art Library), 7.23, 8.4, 8.7, 8.23, 9.3; Bildarchiv Foto Marburg, Germany: 3.28, 5.15, 5.29, 14.38, 14.39; Bildarchiv Preusisscher Kulturbesitz, Berlin: 14.35; Bodleian Library, Oxford: 8.8; Bridgeman Art Library, London: 9.8, 11.10, 12.6, 14,13, 15.5, 16.8; British Library, London: 6.11, 6.12, 7.6, 7.11, 8.9, 9.22, 11.6, 14.23; British Museum, London: 1.4, 3.14. 4.31, 5.4, 7.12, 9.4, 16.21; CNMHS/SPADEM, Paris: 7.22; Trudy Lee Cohen © 1986, Philadelphia: 16.34; Colorphoto Hans Hinz, Allschwil, Switzerland: 1.1, 1.5; Corbis: 7.17, 12.19 (Bettmann), 17.32; Courtauld Institute of Art, London: 13.22; © Donald Cooper/Photostage: 17.39, 18.46; James Davis Travel Photography: 18.44; Jean Dieuzaide, Toulouse: 7.18; Deutsches Archäologisches Institut, Rome: 4.33; Esto Photographics, Inc., New York: 18.36; Mary Evans Picture Library: 9.23, 11.33, 12.4, 12.5, 13.7; Fotomas Index, London: 15.4; Alison Franz, Princeton, New Jersey: 3.26, 6.4; Sonia Halliday Photographs: 3.1, 6.29, 6.33, 8.2, 8.24, 8.26; Robert Harding Picture Library, London: 11.36, 13.28; Clive Hicks, London: 7.13; 8.22, 8.23; Hirmer Fotoarchiv, Munich: 1.11, 1.19, 2.3, 2.19, 3.10, 3.19, 3.25, 6.7, 6.8, 6.13, 6.35, 8.16, 17.38; Perry Hoberman © Canal Street Communications, New York: 18.45; Angelo Hornak, London: 16.39; Hulton Archive, London, 6.25, 12.23, 14.34, 17.29, 17.30; Jahns/SOA Photo Agency & Gallery: 18.43; A.F. Kersting: 3.21, 3.24, 8.1, 8.18, 9.14, 9.15, 9.16, 9.18, 11.26, 11.27, 11.30, 13.1, 13.36, 13.38, 14.19, 15.13; Lauros-Giraudon/Bridgeman Art Library, London: 8.25, 8.27, 8.28, 13.12; Ralph Liebermann, North Adams, MA: 16.31, 17.28, 18.38; Louvre Musée, Paris. Photo RMN (Hervé Lewandowski): 2.11; Paul M.R. Maeyaert, Mont de l'Enclus (Orroir), Belgium: 4.28, 7.14, 17.41; Mansell Collection: 3.8, 3.12, 3.13, 4.15, 4.16, 4.19, 4.25, 4.27, 9.9, 10.4 (detail) and 10.13, 10.17, 10.22, 10.25, 10.26, 11.11, 13.19; Craig & Marie Mauzy, Athens: 3.3; Jean Mazenod, L'Art de l'Ancienne Rome, Editions Mazenod, Paris: 4.12; Gérard Monico, Saint-Denis, France: 8.13; Peter Moore © The Estate of Peter Moore: 18.3 and 18.29; Musei Capitolini, Rome/Barbara Malter: 4.30; © National Commission for Museums & Monuments, Lagos/Laurence King Publishing; National Film Archive, London: 16.38; New York Public Library: 12.21 (Cia Fornaroli Collection); Courtesy of the Oriental Institute, University of Chicago: 1.8; Josephine Powell, Rome: 6.6; Prestel Verlag, Munich: 18.23; Richardson & Kailas Icons, London/Bridgeman Art Library, London: 6.3; Rijksmuseum Foundation, Amsterdam: 13.2; © Photo RMN-Arnaudet: 17.2; © RMN-Gérard Blot: 13.3; © Photo RMN-Hervé Lewandowski: 6.15, 6.16, 7.25, 13.9, 14.12, 17.3; Eric Robertson, New York: 17.20; Peter Sanders Photography: 6.5; Scala, Florence: 1.2, 2.1, 5.1, 5.13, 6.1, 7.1, 9.1, 9.2 , 9.7, 9.11, 10.11, 10.20, 11.13, 11.16, 11.18, 11.32, 11.39, 11.40, 11.43, 11.44, 13.8, 13.11, 13.23, 13.27; Bob Schalkwijk, Mexico City: 17.19; Science Photo Library, London: 18.4 (Hank Morgan); Holly Solomon Gallery, New York: 18.3 (detail) and 18.29; Edwin Smith, Saffron Walden: 14.36, 14.37; Spectrum Colour Library: 8.17; © Steffans/SOA Photo Agency, London: 7.27; © Studio Fotografico Quattrone, Florence: 7.2, 10.4, 10.9, 11.4, 11.22, 11.23, 13.18, 17.34; Wim Swaan: 9.17; Tate Picture Library, London: 10.2; Telegraph Colour Library, London: 12.26 (T. Yamada); Ullstein-Margaret Schulz: 16.2; Ullstein Bilt: 17.4; Vatican Museums: 11.37; Roger Viollet: 9.13; Weidenfeld & Nicolson, London: 14.20; Yale Center for British Art, Paul Mellon Collection, USA/Bridgeman Art Library, London: 15.1.

Literary Acknowledgments

Every effort has been made to contact copyright holders, but should there be any errors or omissions, Laurence King Publishing would be pleased to insert the appropriate acknowledgment in any subsequent printing of this publication. The author, the publishers, and Laurence King Publishing Ltd wish to thank the following for permission to use copyright material:

Alfred A. Knopf, a division of Random House Inc. for "The Negro Speaks of Rivers" by Langston Hughes, from *The Collected Poems of Langston Hughes* (1994), © 1994 The Estate of Langston Hughes

American Indian Studies Center, UCLA for "Recuerdo" by Paul Gunn Allen, from *Shadow Country* (1982), © 1982 Regents of the University of California

Bantom Doubleday Dell for "Der Erlkonig" by Johann Wolfgang von Goethe, trs. Philip L. Miller, from *The Ring of Words: An Anthology of Song Texts* (1963)

University of Chicago Press for an extract from *Hecuba* by Euripides, from *Complete Greek Tragedies*, ed. David Grene and Richmond Lattimore (1982)

W.W. Norton & Company Inc. for extracts from *Agamemnon* and *Prometheus Bound* by Aeschylus, from *Three Greek Plays*, trs. Edith Hamilton, © 1937 W.W. Norton, Inc., renewed © 1965 Doris Fielding Reid

PREFACE

This edition, the sixth, maintains *The Creative Impulse*'s overall focus and intent—that is, to present an overview of the arts in the Western tradition in the contexts of the philosophy, religion, aesthetic theory, economics, and politics surrounding them. The text remains an historical introduction to the humanities from which the reader will gain a basic familiarity with major styles and their implications as well as a sense of the historical development of individual arts disciplines. The major focus of the text is the arts, and one of the changes in this edition is an attempt to make that focus clearer, and the organization of each chapter more transparent, by dividing each chapter into two major divisions: 1) Contexts and Concepts; and 2) The Arts.

Another emphasis fundamental to the book remains, and that is an emphasis, by example, on formal analysis of works of art to supplement discussion about them. Not every work illustrated herein is analyzed, but analysis occurs frequently enough that, with a little encouragement from the instructor, students can infer how to see and hear and put into words what makes a particular work of art tick, so to speak. Developing confidence in relating and responding to works of art—verbally and viscerally—is critical if students are to carry an interest in the arts beyond the confines of the classroom and the timeframe of the course, into the rest of their lives. That lifelong relationship with art, hopefully, is the purpose of humanities and introductory art courses. When encountering an artwork for the first time—whether in a museum, a theatre, a concert hall, or on the street—we usually do not have access to biographical or contextual materials. We have only the artwork and the ability to confront it, either with or without confidence. Thus, the analyses, which examine how artworks work in terms of line, form, color, melody, plot, and so on, teach a means by which artworks can be approached, responded to, and shared in an on-the-spot manner; the way works of art are encountered in real life.

Also new to this edition are three features. The first comprises a chapter-opening exploration of "The Way Art Works." In these features, basic concepts are defined, illustrated, and related to the material of the text. The second feature occurs throughout the body of the text, and it comprises hyperlinks, or URLs, to connect with websites for additional examples. The third feature, likewise, involves the World Wide Web. Each chapter closes with a "Cybersources" section for further study of examples and materials concerning the periods discussed in the preceding chapter.

Finally, it should be clear that a book such as this depends upon a multitude of sources other than the general knowledge of its author. In the interest of readability and in recognition of the generalized purpose of this text, copious footnoting has been avoided. I hope the method chosen for presentation and documentation of the works of other authors meets the needs of both responsibility and practicality. The Further Reading section at the end of the book comprises the works used in the preparation of this text. I am indebted to these authors and to scores of colleagues around the country who have assisted in one way or another in the preparation of this book over the six editions of its existence.

Dennis J. Sporre

Getting Started and Understanding and Evaluating the Arts

OUTLINE

0.1 Antonio Canova, *Perseus Holding the Head of Medusa*, 1804–08. Marble, 7 ft 2⁵⁄₈ ins (2.20 m) high. The Metropolitan Museum of Art, New York (Fletcher Fund) 1967.

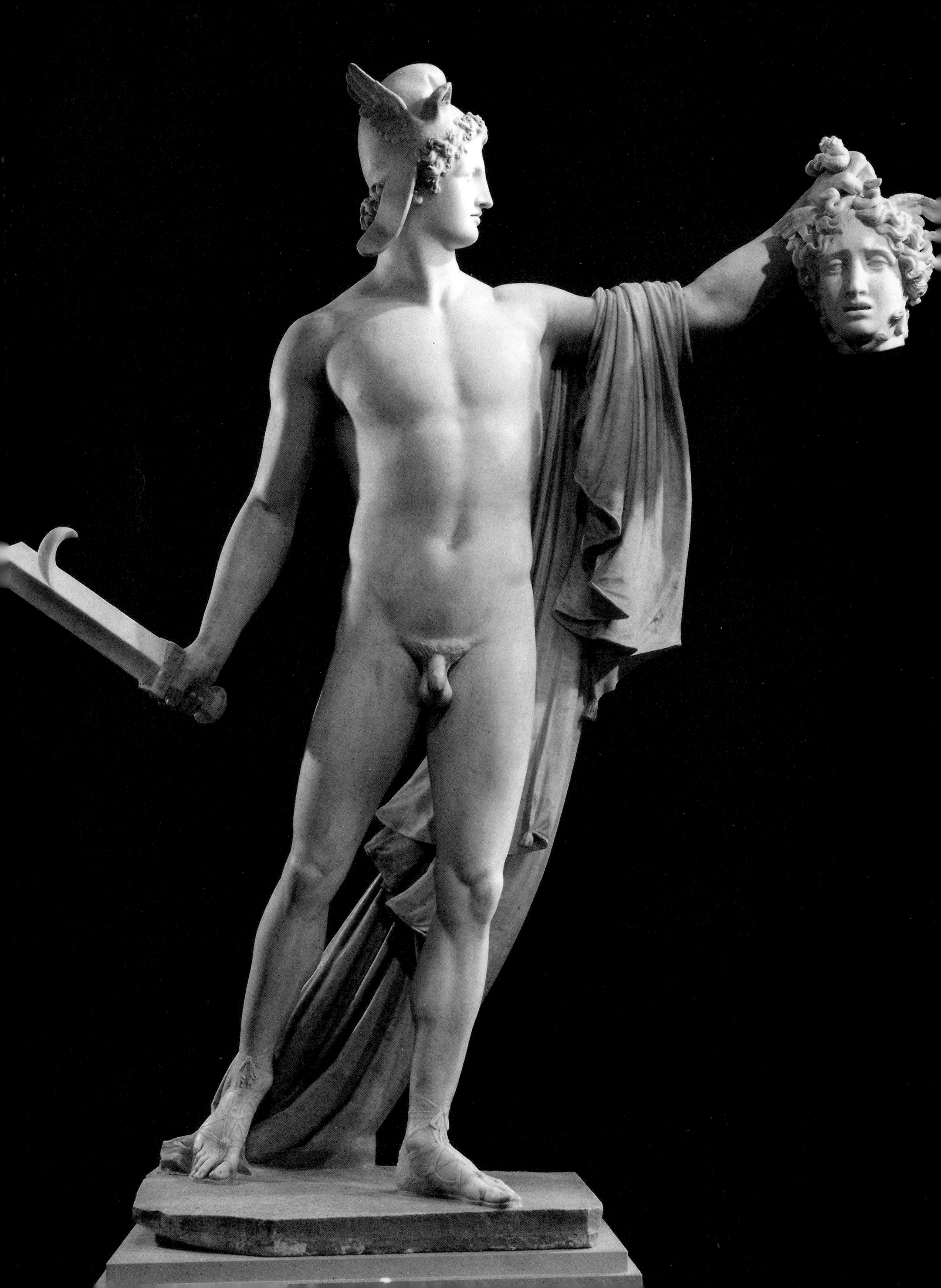

GETTING STARTED

Two-Dimensional Art | Sculpture | Architecture | Music | Theatre | Literature | Film | Dance | Features

Getting Started takes us into the land of basic terminology and fundamental artistic concepts. In other words, we are about to sample some of the things that will help us to identify and communicate important characteristics appropriate to the works of two-dimensional art, sculpture, music, theatre, dance, literature, and film that are presented later in the text.

Although it may not seem so on first reading, the terms and concepts discussed here represent only a fraction of what we might study. The terms are technical, and, undoubtedly, you will want to return to this section as you encounter works of art in the chapters that follow, especially when you seek to describe and compare paintings, musical selections, and so on, using accurate terminology.

Two-Dimensional Art

Two-dimensional art consists of paintings, drawings, prints, and photographs, which differ from each other primarily in the technique of their execution. Probably, our initial response to all four is a response to content—that is, we first notice what the painting, drawing, print, or photogaph seems to be about. Such recognition usually triggers an emotional and intellectual response that leads us into the work's meaning. Beyond the recognition of content, however, lie the technical elements chosen by artists to make their vision appear the way they wish it to appear, and these include **media** and **composition**.

Media

The media of the two-dimensional arts are paintings, drawings, prints, and photography. Paintings and drawings can be executed with oils, watercolors, tempera, acrylics, ink, and pencils, to name just a few of the more obvious. Each physical medium has its own particular characteristics. As an example, let us look at *oils.*

Oils, developed around the beginning of the fifteenth century, offer artists a broad range of color possibilities; they do not dry quickly and can, therefore, be reworked; they present many options for textural manipulation; and they are durable. Look at the texture in the brushwork of Van Gogh's (van-GOH or van GAHK) *Harvest at La Crau* (see Fig. **16.20**). This kind of manipulation is a characteristic of oil. Whatever the physical medium—that is, painting, drawing, print, or photograph—we can find identifiable characteristics that shape the final work of art. Had the artist chosen a different physical medium, the work—all other things being equal—would not look the same.

Composition

The second area that we can isolate and respond to involves artists' use of the *elements* and *principles of composition.* These make up the building blocks of two-dimensional works of art. Among others, these elements and principles include **line**, **form**, **color**, **repetition**, and **balance**.

Elements

The primary element of composition is line. In Joan Miró's (hoh-AHN mee-ROH) *Composition* (Fig. **0.2**) we see amorphous shapes. Some of these are like cartoon

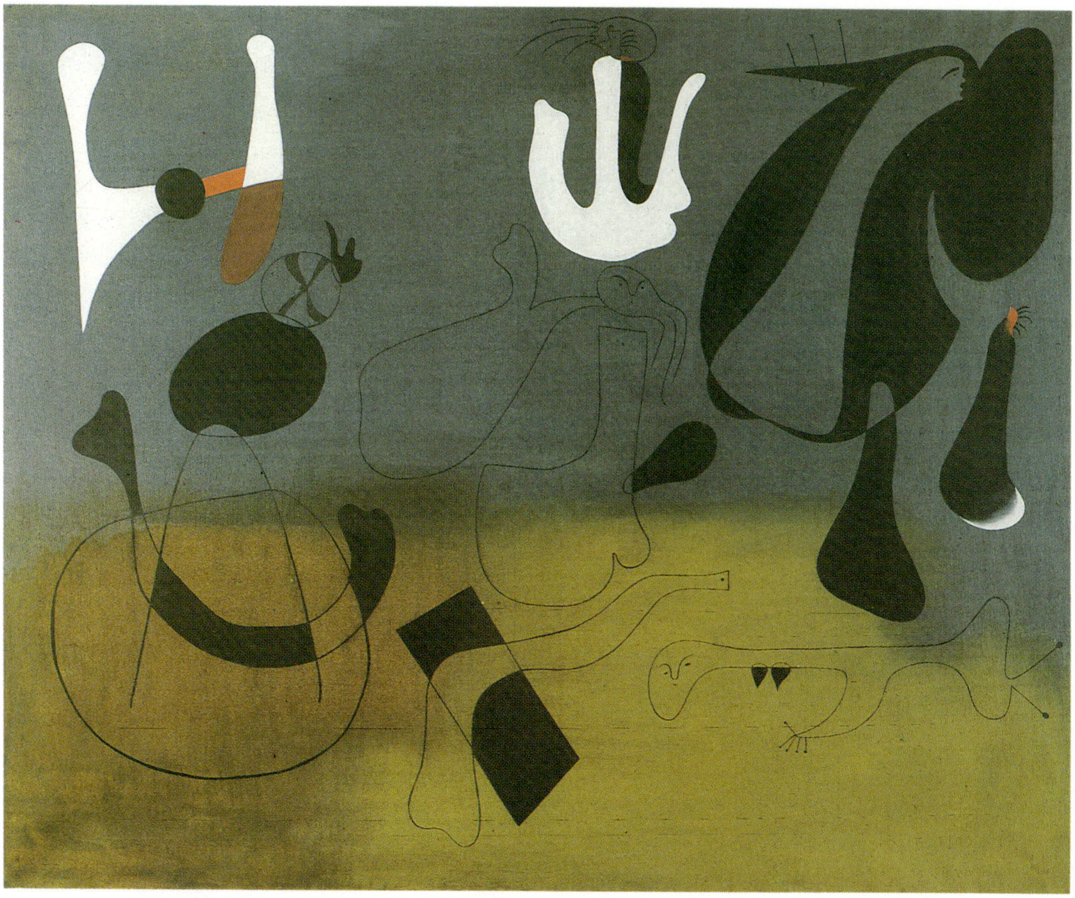

0.2 Joan Miró, *Composition*, 1933. Oil on canvas, 51⅜ × 64 ins (130.5 × 165 cm). Wadsworth Atheneum, Hartford, Connecticut. © ADAGP, Paris and DACS, London 2001.

figures—identifiable because of their outline—but the other shapes also exemplify line, and they do so because they create boundaries between areas of color and between other shapes or forms. Essentially, line is either curved or straight, and it is used by artists to control our vision and to create unity, emotional value, and, ultimately, meaning.

Form and line are closely related. Form as a compositional element is the **shape** of an object. It is the space described by line. A building is a form. So is a tree. We perceive them as buildings or trees, and we perceive their individual details, because of the line by which they are composed. *Color* is a somewhat complex compositional element. The word **hues** is used to describe the basic colors of the spectrum (Fig. **0.3**). The apparent whiteness or grayness of a color is its **value** (Fig. **0.4**). When we observe a work of art, we can, among other aspects of color, identify, respond to, and describe the breadth of the *palette*—how many different hues and values the artist has used—and the way the artist has used those hues and values.

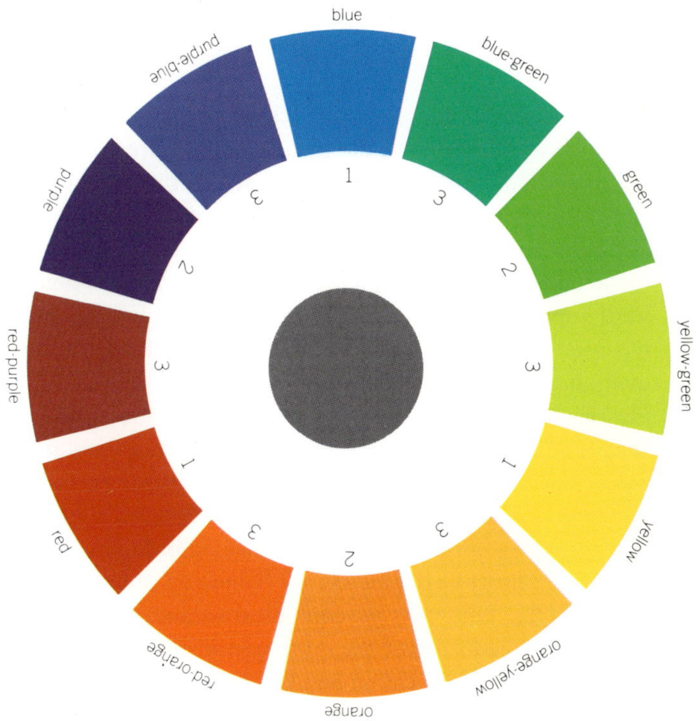

0.3 Color wheel.

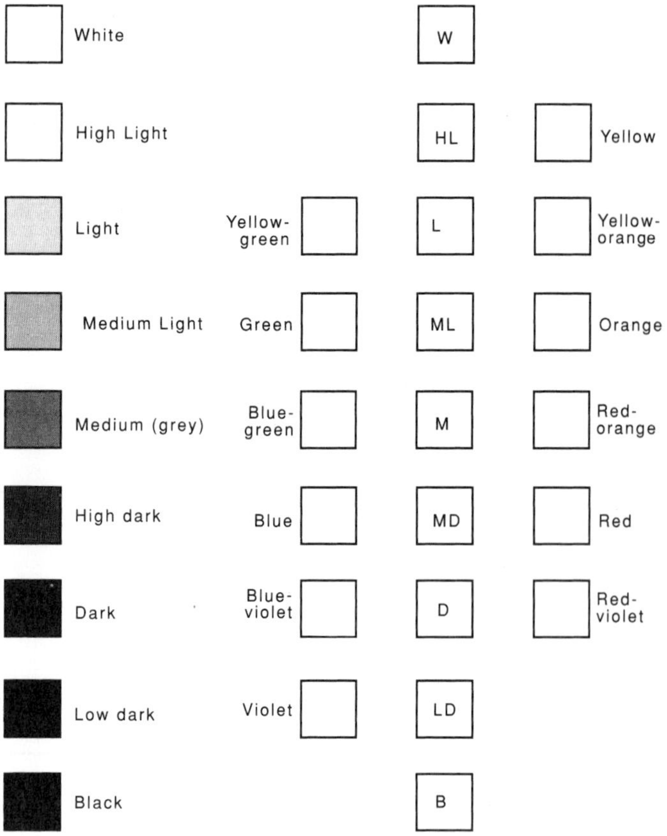

0.4 Value scale.

TECHNIQUES
Linear Perspective

Throughout the text, we will witness how two-dimensional artists utilize "deep space"—that is, the illusion of depth in their works. One of the methods for creating deep space that appears rational or **naturalistic** is the use of **linear perspective** (Fig. **0.5**). Very simply, *linear perspective* is the creation of the illusion of distance in a two-dimensional artwork through the convention of line and foreshortening— that is, the illusion that parallel lines come together in the distance. Linear perspective is also called *scientific, mathematical one-point*, or *Renaissance perspective* and was developed in fifteenth-century Italy (see Chapter 10). It uses mathematical formulas to construct illusionistic images in which all elements are shaped by imaginary lines called *orthogonals* that converge in one or more *vanishing points* on a *horizon line*. Linear perspective is the system most people in the Euro-American cultures think of as perspective, because it is the visual code they are accustomed to seeing.

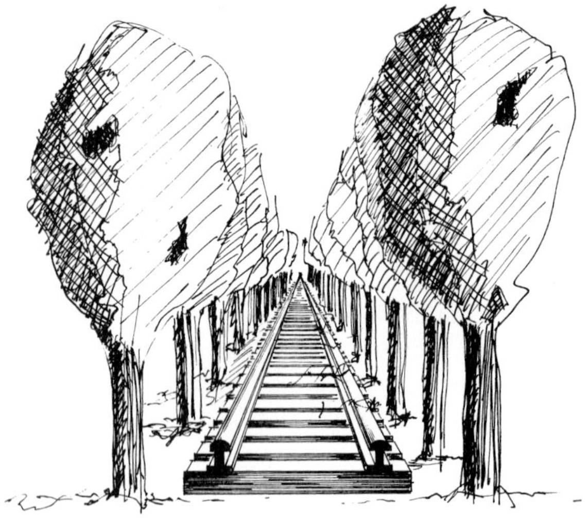

0.5 Linear perspective.

Principles

The principles of composition include *repetition* (the way in which the elements of the picture are repeated or alternated) and *balance* (the way in which the picture stands on its axes). In Picasso's (pee-KAH-soh) *Girl Before a Mirror* (Fig. **0.6**), the artist has ordered the recurrence of elements in a regular manner. He has placed hard angles and soft curves side by side, and, in addition, has used two geometric forms, the oval and the diamond, over and over again to build up the forms of the work. He also has balanced the picture with nearly identical shapes on each side of the central axis. When shapes and colors that are identical appear on either side of the axis, it creates a condition called **symmetry**. Balance achieved by using unequal shapes, as demonstrated in Figures **0.2** and **0.6**, indicates asymmetry, the balancing of unlike objects—also known as psychological balance. If the repeated elements are of the same size or importance, then the repetition is called regular. If they are of differing size and/or importance, then the repetition is called irregular.

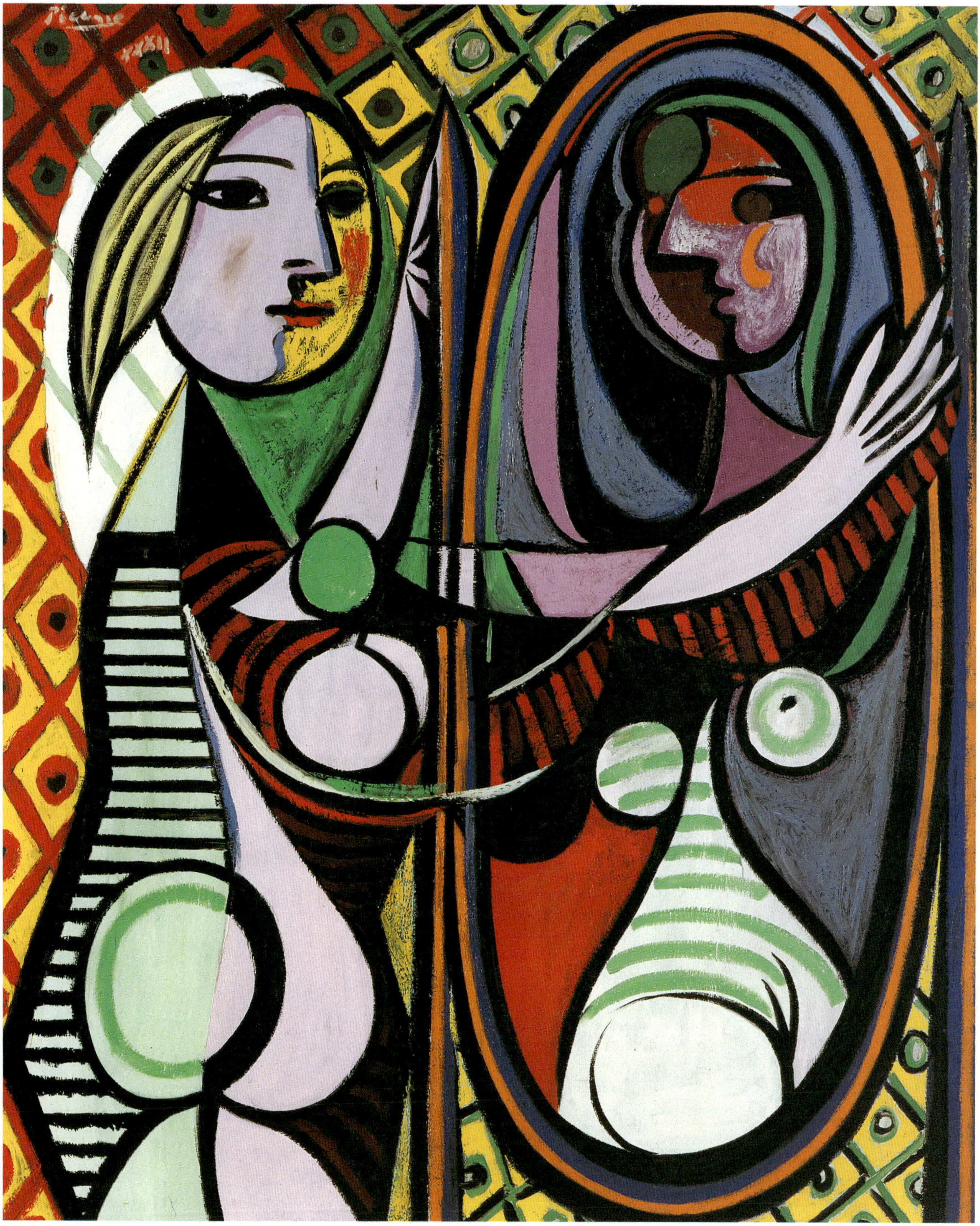

0.6 Pablo Picasso, *Girl Before a Mirror*, 1932. Oil on canvas, 64 × 51¼ ins (162.3 × 130.2 cm). Collection, Museum of Modern Art, New York (Gift of Mrs. Simon Guggenheim). Photo: © 1998 The Museum of Modern Art, New York. © Succession Picasso/DACS 2001.

Sculpture

Sculpture is a medium of three dimensions. Thus, in addition to those qualities of composition just noted, we can approach sculpture by another element of composition called **mass:** the size, shape, and volume of the forms. Sculpture appeals to us by how large or small it is and by the appearance of weight and density in its materials.

Dimensionality

As we have noted, sculpture defines actual space. Sculpture may be **full-round**, **relief**, or **linear**. Full-round works are freestanding and fully three-dimensional. They are meant to be viewed from any angle. Relief sculpture projects from a background and cannot be seen from all sides. It maintains a two-dimensional quality, as compared to full-rounded sculpture. Linear sculpture emphasizes construction with thin, tubular items such as wire or neon tubing.

Texture

The surface treatment (called texture) of a work of sculpture is as important as its dimensionality. Michelangelo carved *David* (see Fig. **11.24**) from marble, but he made the stone seem alive and warm like living flesh by giving it a lustrous, polished texture.

TECHNIQUES

LOST-WAX CASTING

The **lost-wax** technique, sometimes known by the French term *cire-perdue*, is a method of casting sculpture in which the basic mold is created by using a wax model, which is then melted to leave the desired spaces in the mold. The technique probably began in Egypt. By 200 B.C.E., the technique was used in China and ancient Mesopotamia, and it was used soon after that by the Benin people of Africa. It spread to Greece sometime in the late sixth century B.C.E.

The drawings indicated in Figure **0.7** illustrate the steps Benin sculptors would have utilized. A heat-resistant "core" of clay—approximately the shape of the sculpture—was covered by a layer of wax approximately the thickness of the final work. The sculptor carved the details in the wax. Rods and a pouring cup made of wax were attached to the model, and then the model, rods, and cup were covered with thick layers of clay. When the clay was dry, the mold was heated to melt the wax. Molten metal could then be poured into the mold. When the molten metal had dried, the clay mold was broken and removed, which meant that the sculpture could not be duplicated.

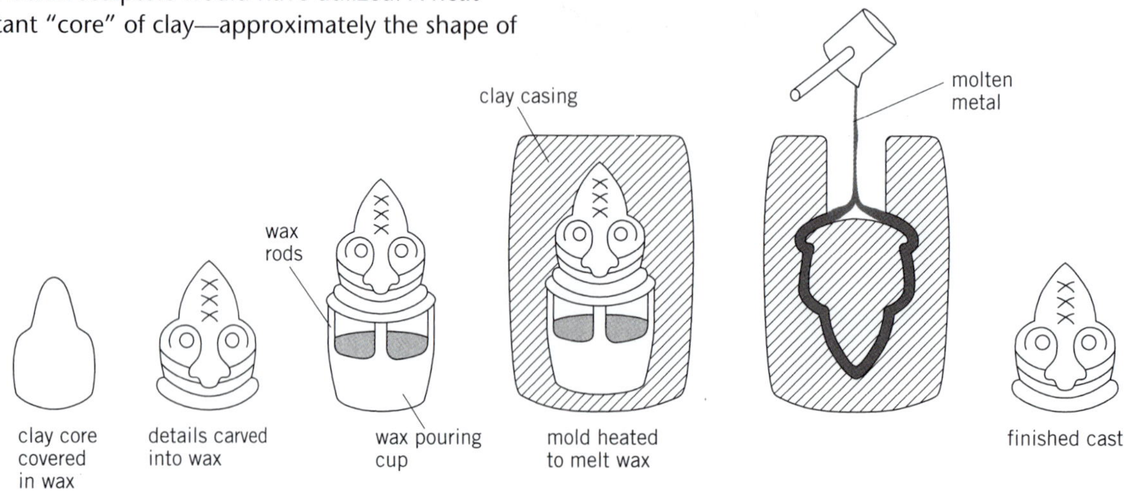

0.7 Lost-wax process.

Architecture

Architecture is often described as the art of sheltering, and it is the one art form that combines aesthetic considerations with intensely practical ones. Our formal responses to architecture often involve the purpose of the building: a church, an office building, a residence, and so on. The way architects merge interior function with exterior form provides much of our encounter with works of architecture.

Although a variety of fundamental technical elements exist in architecture, we will only discuss one: *structure*.

Structure

Architecture contains many systems of structure. As we travel through the centuries in our examination of human creativity, we will see examples of **post-and-lintel, cantilever, arch**, bearing wall, and skeleton frame structures. Laying horizontal pieces (**lintels**) across vertical supports (posts) gives us one of our oldest structural systems—that is, post-and-lintel (see Fig. **4.22**). When unimpeded interior space became an architectural necessity, the arch gave architects an additional means of solving the practical problems involved. Whether it was used in **vaults** (arches joined end to end) or in domes (concentric arches), as we shall see in the great Gothic cathedrals of the Middle Ages or the dome of the Pantheon (see Fig. **4.21**), the arch opened interior space to usable proportions. When vaults cross at right angles, they create a **groin vault** (Fig. **0.8**). The protruding masonry that indicates a diagonal juncture of arches in a tunnel vault is a **ribbed vault** (Fig. **0.9**). Cantilever, as exemplified in the Zarzuela (zahr-ZWAY-luh) Race Track (Fig. **0.10**), provided architects with dramatic means for expression, for here, unsupported, overhanging precipices define space.

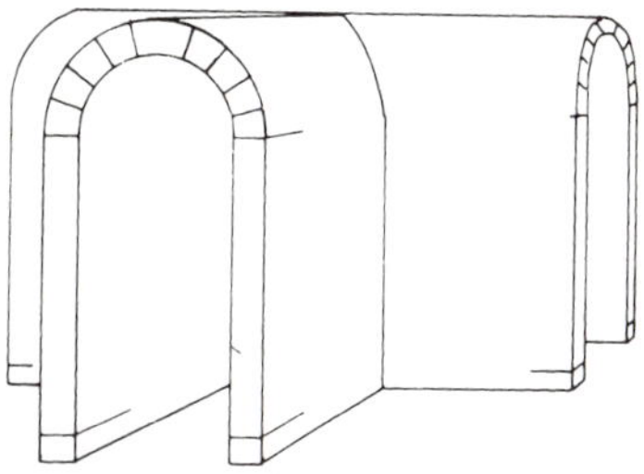

0.8 Groin vault.

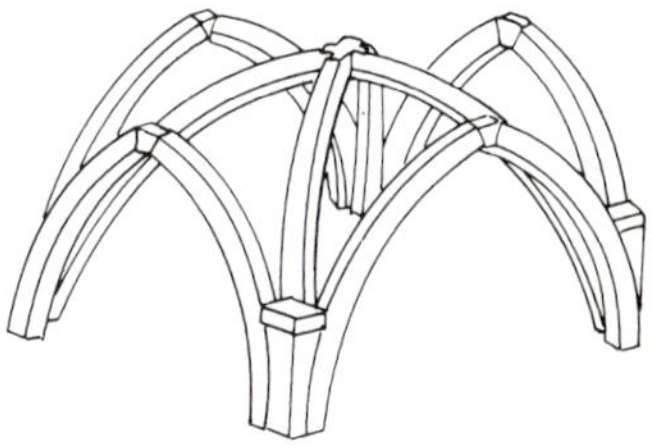

0.9 Ribbed vault.

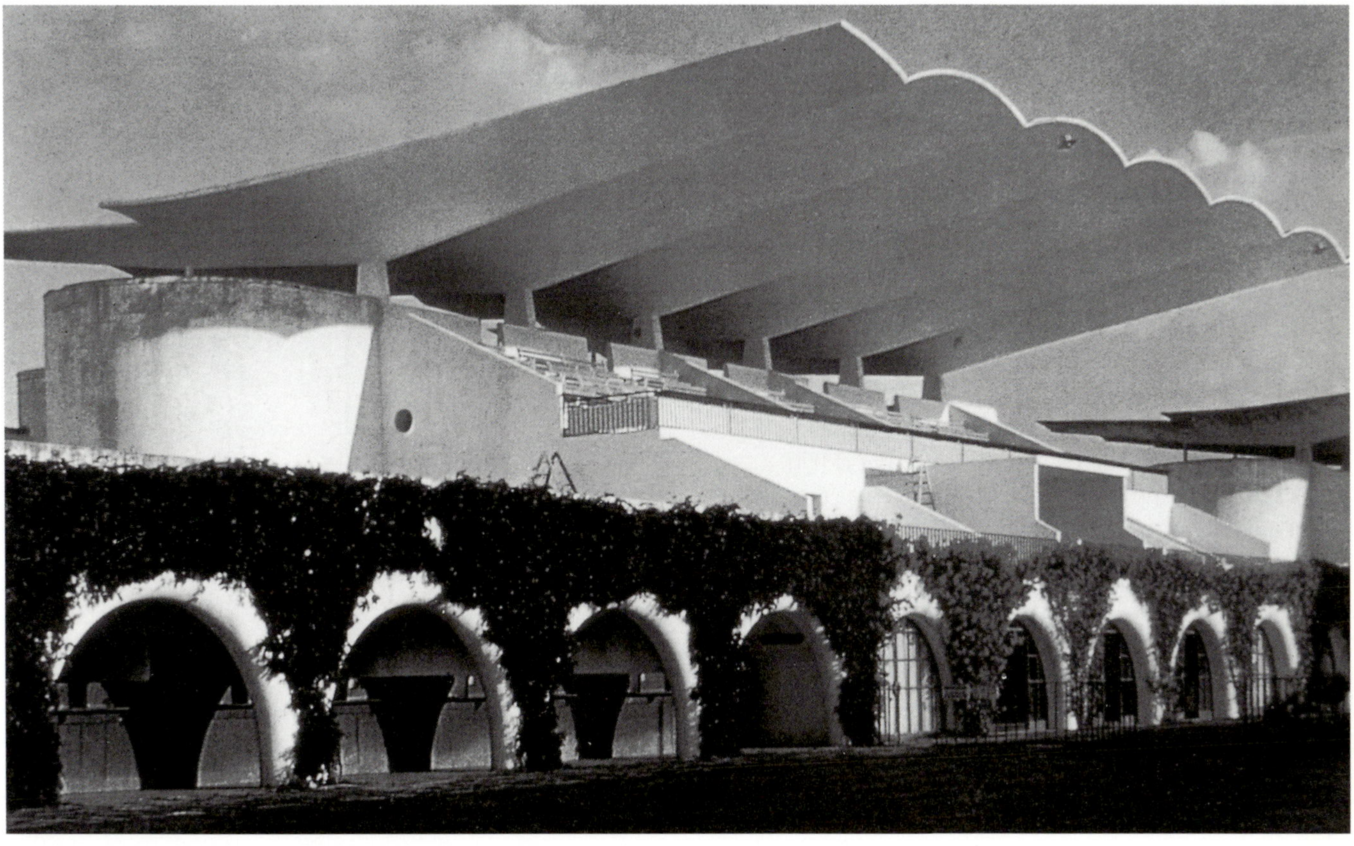

0.10 Eduardo Torroja, Grandstand, Zarzuela Race Track, Madrid, 1935.

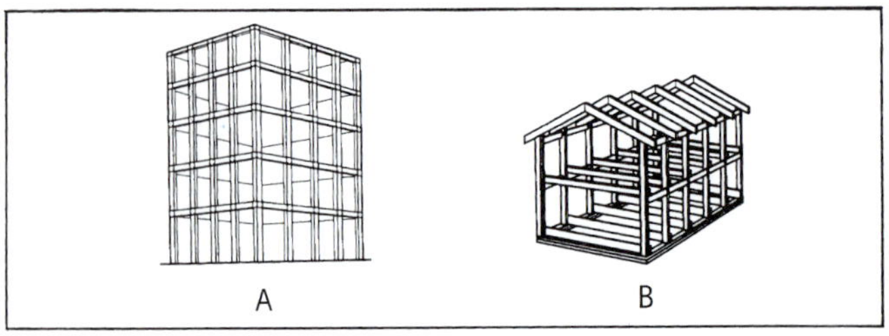

0.11 Skeleton frame structures: A. Steel-Cage Construction; B. Balloon Construction.

The system of *bearing wall* has had ancient and modern applications. In it, the wall supports itself, the floors, and the roof, and both log cabins and solid masonry buildings are examples in which the wall is the structure. When the wall material is continuous (not joined or pieced together) it is called **monolithic.**

Finally, *skeleton frame* structure uses a framework to support the building. The walls are attached to the frame, thus forming an exterior skin. When skeleton framing makes use of wood, as in house construction, the technique is called *balloon construction.* When metal forms the frame, as in skyscrapers, the technique is known as steel-cage construction (Fig. **0.11**).

Music

Genres

Listening to music often begins with genre identification, simply because it helps us to know exactly what kind of

TECHNIQUES

MUSICAL NOTATION

Musical notation is a system of writing music so the composer can communicate clearly to the performer the pitches and rhythms (among other things) of the piece. A brief familiarity with this method of communication is important because later in the text we will illustrate characteristics of musical compositions with written notation.

The pitches of music are indicated with symbols, called *notes,* placed on a *staff*—five parallel lines on which each line and space represent a pitch (Fig. **0.12A**). The higher a note's placement on the staff, the higher the pitch. Seven of the twelve pitches of an octave in Western music are named after the first seven letters of the alphabet: A, B, C, D, E, F, G. The remaining five tones are indicated by the use of two signs, the *sharp* sign (♯) and the *flat* sign (♭) (Fig. **0.12B**). A *clef* (in French, "key") is placed at the beginning of the staff to show the pitch of each line and space (Figs. **0.12C** and **D**). Music is written in different *keys*—each associated with the presence of a central note, scale, and chord—which are indicated by a *key signature* (Figs. **0.12E** and **F**). *Rhythms* are indicated with notes indicating time values relative to each other (Fig. **0.12G**). The duration of silences in a musical piece is indicated by a symbol called a *rest* (Fig. **0.12H**).

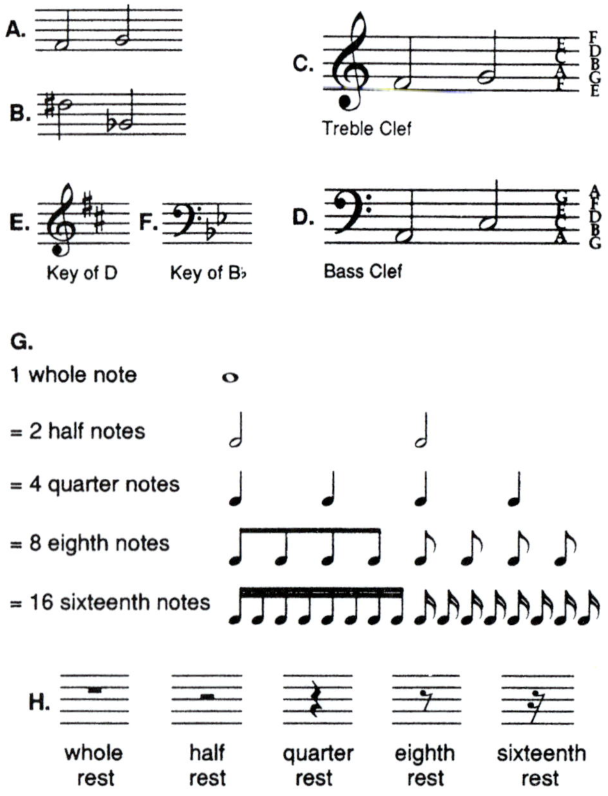

0.12 Musical notation.

composition we are hearing. Being aware that we are listening to a **symphony**—a large musical composition for orchestra, typically consisting of four separate sections called "movements"—provides us with clues that are different from a **mass**—a choral setting of the Roman Catholic service, the Mass. A **concerto** (kahn-CHAIR-toh), a composition for solo instrument with accompaniment, gives us different experiences from an **opera** or **oratorio**, a large-scale choral work such as Handel's *Messiah* performed in concert form.

Melody and Form

Whatever the generic category, all music employs the same technical elements, of which **melody** and form are perhaps the two most obvious. We will introduce others at appropriate points in the text.

Melody is a succession of sounds with rhythmic and tonal organization. Any combination of musical tones constitutes a melody, but melody usually has particular qualities beyond being a mere succession of sounds. Musical ideas, for example, come to us in melodies called **themes**; shorter versions, brief melodic or rhythmic ideas, are called **motives** or **motifs** (moh-TEEF).

Form, like the principles of composition in visual art, gives musical compositions shape and organization. Composers use form to arrange musical elements and relationships into successive events or sections. Basically, we can listen for two types of form: *closed* and *open*. Closed forms direct our attention back into the composition by restating at the end of a thematic section the element that formed the beginning. This pattern of development often is described as ABA or AABA. The letters stand for specific thematic sections. Open form, on the other hand, uses repetition of thematic material as a departure point for further development, and the composition ends without repeating the opening section.

Theatre

The word "theatre" comes from the Greek word *theatron* (THAY-uh-trahn): the area of the Greek theatre building where the audience sat. Its literal meaning is "a place for seeing." Like the other **performing arts**, theatre is an interpretive discipline, because between the playwright and the audience stand the director, the designers, and the actors.

Genres

As in music, our enjoyment of theatre can be enhanced by understanding the genre—that is, the type of play—from which the performance evolves. We are probably most familiar with the genres of **tragedy** and **comedy**, but there are others.

We commonly describe a tragedy as a play with an unhappy ending, and typically, tragic heroes make free choices that cause suffering and defeat or sometimes triumph out of defeat. Often, the hero—the *protagonist*—undergoes a struggle that ends disastrously. In many respects, comedy is much more complex than tragedy and even harder to define. Comedy embraces a wide range of theatrical approaches, and when it is defined in its broadest terms, comedy may not even involve laughter. Although we can say, probably with some accuracy, that humor forms the root of all comedy, many comedies employ satire, and comedies often treat serious themes while remaining basically lighthearted in spirit.

These and the other genres of theatre guide our expectations as we witness a production. If we know the genre in advance, our responses move according to those expectations. If we do not know the genre, we have to work it out as the production unfolds.

Plot, Character, Thought, and Visual Elements

Technically, theatrical productions are shaped to a large degree by *plot*—that is, the structure of the play—the skeleton that gives it shape. The plot determines how a play works—how it moves from one moment to another, how conflicts are structured, and, ultimately, how the play comes to an end.

Plays also turn on *character*: the motivating psychological makeup of the people in the play. Although many plays focus on visual elements such as settings, lighting, and costumes, we find theatre engrossing because of the way plays reflect human behavior and conflict in human decisions and actions. Thus, when we attend a performance of a play, our primary attention focuses on how dialogue reveals character and how actors portray actions. Most plays hinge on the actions and decisions of one major character, called the *protagonist*, and when we follow his or her development and the consequences of his or her actions, we are led to an understanding of the play's meaning.

The meaning of the play—sometimes called its *thought*—like the meaning of any work of art, reveals what artists are trying to communicate to us about our universe.

The visual elements of a play comprise a number of factors including the relationship of the audience to the acting area—for example, the arena form in which the audience surrounds the stage area. Visual elements also include scenery, costumes, lighting, and actor movement.

Literature

Literature operates through a system of language in which the words themselves trigger our understanding.

Genres

Like many of the other arts, we approach literature first through the formal door of its genres. These are fiction, poetry, biography, and essay.

Fiction is a work created from the author's imagination rather than from fact. Normally, it takes one of two approaches to its subject matter: realistic—the appearance of observable, true-to-life details—or nonrealistic—fantasy. Other literary forms, such as narrative poetry, however, can also be fiction, and fictional elements can be introduced into forms such as biography and epic poetry. Traditionally, fiction is divided into novels and short stories.

Poetry, on the other hand, is a type of work designed to convey a vivid and imaginative sense of experience. It uses concentrated language, selected for its sound, suggestive power, and meaning, and employs specific technical devices such as meter, rhyme, and metaphor. Poetry can be divided into three major types: *narrative*, which tells a story, *dramatic*, which utilizes dramatic form or technique, and **lyric**, which consists of brief, subjective treatments employing strong imagination, melody, and feeling to create a single, unified, and intense impression of the personal emotion of the poet.

Over the centuries, *biography*, a written account of a person's life, has taken many forms, including literary narratives, simple catalogues of achievement, and psychological portraits. Biographies of saints and other religious figures are called hagiographies.

Traditionally, the *essay* is a short literary composition on a single subject, usually presenting the personal views of the author. Essays include many subforms and a variety of styles, but they uniformly present a personal point of view with a conscious attempt to achieve grace of expression. Characteristically, the best essays are marked by clarity, good humor, wit, urbanity, and tolerance.

Point of View, Character, and Plot

In writing fiction, authors usually employ one of four *points of view*: (1) first person; (2) epistolary (the use of letters written by the characters); (3) third person; or (4) stream of consciousness (wherein a flow of thoughts and feelings comes from a specific character's psyche).

As in theatre, *character* also represents an important focus. The people in the work and their struggles with some important human problem give literature much of its appeal.

Plot in a work of literature may be a major or subordinate focus. Like theatrical plots, literary plots unfold the structure of the work and may come to a climax and resolution or leave the characters in a convenient place, allowing us to imagine their future lives continuing as their characters dictate.

Theme and Language

Most good stories have a dominant idea or *theme* by which the other elements are shaped. Although some critics argue that the quality of a theme is less important than what the author does with it, the best artworks are often those in which the author has taken a meaningful theme and developed it exceptionally.

In poetry, *language* that includes imagery—figures, which take words beyond their literal meaning, and **metaphors**, which give new implication to words—also provides an important focus.

Film

A product of modern technology, film brings us into a world that, apart from a lack of three-dimensionality, is often mistaken for reality. We are most familiar with the *narrative* film—that is, one that tells a story, such as the films directed by Alfred Hitchcock (Fig. **0.13**). Two other types of film also exist—documentary film and absolute film. *Documentary* film is an attempt to record actuality, using either a sociological or a journalistic approach, and it

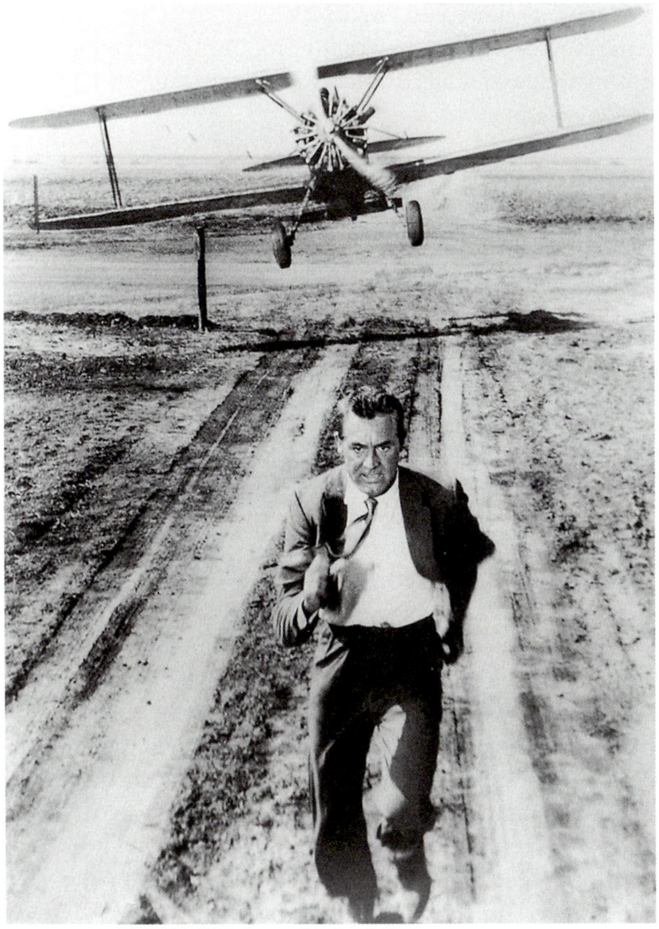

0.13 Alfred Hitchcock (director), *North by Northwest*, 1959. 136 minutes, MGM Studios, USA.

is normally not reenacted by professional actors but shot as the event occurs. *Absolute* film is film that exists for its own sake, for its record of movement or form. It does not use narrative techniques—although documentary techniques can be used in some instances. Created neither in the camera nor on location, absolute film is built carefully, piece by piece, on the editing table or through special effects and multiple-printing techniques.

Dance

Dance deals with the human form in time and space. In general, it follows one of three traditions: ballet, modern dance, and folk dance. *Ballet* comprises what can be called classical or formal dance; it is rich in tradition and rests heavily on a set of prescribed movements and actions. In general, ballet is a highly theatrical dance presentation consisting of solo dancers, duets, and choruses, or *corps de ballet* (kohr duh ba-LAY). According to the *Dance Encyclopedia*, ballet's basic principle is "the reduction of human gesture to bare essentials, heightened and developed into meaningful patterns."

Modern dance is a label given to a broad variety of highly individualized dance works limited to the twentieth and twenty-first centuries, essentially American in derivation, and antiballetic in philosophy. The basic principle of modern dance probably could be stated as an emphasis on natural and spontaneous or uninhibited movement in strong contrast with the conventionalized and specified movement of the ballet. Although narrative elements often exist in modern dance, the form emphasizes them less than does traditional ballet. Modern dance also differs significantly from ballet in its use of the human body and interaction with the dance floor.

Folk dance, somewhat like folk music, comprises a body of group dances performed to traditional music. As in folk music, the creator (in this case, the *choreographer*) remains unknown. Folk dance began as a necessary or formative part of various cultures with characteristics identifiable with a given culture. Folk dances developed over a period of years, passing from one generation to another. Each folk dance has its prescribed movements, rhythms, music, and costumes. At its core, folk dancing establishes an individual sense of participation in a society, tribe, or mass movement, and strengthens individuals' sense of belonging through collective dancing. On the other hand, however, folk dance often takes on the characteristics of concert dance—as many tourists can relate.

Line, Form, and Repetition

The compositional elements of line, form, and repetition apply to the human body in dance in exactly the same manner as they apply to painting and sculpture. As in all artworks occupying space, dance can create meaning by using horizontal line to suggest placidity, vertical line to suggest grandeur, and diagonal line to suggest movement. Dancers' bodies become like sculptures in motion as they move from one pose to another, and, because dancers move through time, the element of repetition serves a vital part of how choreographers put dances together and how we respond to them. Patterns of shapes and movement occur, and through them, like themes and variations in music, we find structure and meaning in dance works.

Features

Pronunciation

Throughout the text, whenever a name or term (whose pronunciation may be problematical) appears for the first time, a pronunciation guide follows immediately in parentheses. The stressed syllable appears in capital letters. The vowel and consonant selections to guide you in pronouncing the word are straightforward. The only usage that may be questionable is the use of the letter Y to suggest a long I sound—for example, the first person pronoun "I" would appear "Y," and the word "aisle" would appear "YL."

Profiles

Profile boxes appear throughout the text in order to draw our attention to the biography of a prominent person in the chapter. Profile boxes give us a chance to get to know these people a little better, spending more time with them than regular treatment in the text might allow.

Technology

Throughout history, humans have made discoveries and then turned those discoveries into tools or other useful devices that enhance the quality of life. As the text suggests, being a human being isn't much different today from what it was thousands of years ago. On the other hand, the nature of our world, as the result of our technological advancement, is considerably different. Thus, in each chapter we have a feature box to highlight some important technology that developed during the time covered in that chapter.

Masterwork

In a text such as this, which discusses nearly a thousand works of art in painting, sculpture, architecture, theatre, literature, dance, music, and film, we need occasionally to rest, to draw away from the flow of the material, and focus on a single, significant work of art. That is the purpose of the Masterwork boxes in each chapter. The presence of one particular work of art singled out as a Masterwork does not necessarily mean it is any better than the other works which have not been so designated. The works selected are "masterworks" by whatever criteria we wish to define that term, but the selection is not intended as a hierarchical ranking system.

Focal Point

At the conclusion of each chapter a "Focal Point" section appears. Here we take the time to isolate a group of works, a special time, a combination of artists, or a locale that represents some important facet of the preceding chapter. In a way, the Focal Point section serves as a summary, because the material has a representative quality. Nonetheless, it is complete in itself, and we might even think that it belongs in the body of the chapter itself.

A Dynamic World

The boxes in each chapter labeled "A Dynamic World" are intended to give us a taste of what was happening in the arts in a non-Western culture at the same time as the topics in the chapter occurred in the West. Although these boxes are brief, and to some may appear tokenistic, they remind us that there is a world beyond the Western one, and they give us another chance to apply our skills of perception and analysis. The artworks in the box may be similar to or quite different from the style of their Western counterparts. How they are similar or different is a question we should attempt to answer—using only the evidence of the art itself and the descriptive terminology we studied earlier in this section. The works of art in the Dynamic World boxes do have a relationship to the art of the chapter, and we should take the time to understand that relationship.

Maps and Timelines

Maps and timelines appear, mostly, at the beginning of each chapter. They contain information to help locate and correlate the art, history, philosophy, geography, etc. covered in the chapter. They also can be used to relate one chapter to another in time and place.

Chapter Opener

The opening pages of each chapter prepare you for what lies ahead. Firstly, an outline of the chapter is given, followed by key terms and definitions that will help you to understand the material covered. A short essay connects ideas and issues in the chapter with today's problems and circumstances.

How Art Works

At the beginning of each chapter, a feature page occurs, entitled "How Art Works," that discusses and illustrates a basic concept about art in general. Taken in total, these features present considerable, and important, information that helps us to understand what we can find in works of art. The result is that we possess fundamentals to increase our understanding about art and our confidence in approaching, analyzing, understanding, and relating to it.

Chapter Review

At the end of each chapter a Chapter Review box helps you connect the information you have just studied. The Critical Thought section stimulates your critical thinking about material in the chapter, again tying it to today's themes and concerns. The Summary prompts your comprehension with statements concerning what you should be able to do, having studied the chapter. Each box ends with a directive for you to practice your use of terminology and understanding of concepts by comparing works of art.

Cybersources and Examples

Throughout the text and at the end of each chapter are web addresses for additional examples and further study. With regard to URLs for connecting to the World Wide Web, however, a warning is necessary. First, things change. A website active when this book went to press may no longer exist. (Wherever possible, works from major museums have been chosen, and those websites should remain active or should be accessible by finding the museum's home page through a standard search engine. Then, using the "collection" option will lead to an index from which the artist and work can be accessed.) Second, an initial attempt to link to a site may prove unsuccessful: "Unable to connect to remote host." A rule of thumb is to try to connect to the site three successive times before trying another URL. Be careful to type the URL exactly. Any incorrect character will cause the connection to fail (capital letters matter).

In addition to the specific web addresses listed in the text, some general sites can provide a wealth of additional information. An easy and vast reference for visual art and architecture is the Artcyclopedia at http://www.artcyclopedia.com/index.html. Here, individual artists can be referenced along with their artworks, as can searching by style, medium, subject, and nationality. A good architectural archive is "Mary Ann Sullivan's Digital Imaging Project" at http://www.bluffton.edu/~sullivanm/index/index2html#P although this site is among the redirects located in the Artcyclopedia just mentioned. "Art History Resources on the Net," http://libweb.sdsu.edu/sub_libs/cfields/art.html provides many useful hyperlinks.

Understanding and Evaluating the Arts

PUTTING THE ARTS IN CONTEXT

For centuries, scholars, philosophers, and aestheticians have debated without general resolution a definition of "art." The challenging range of arguments encompasses, among other considerations, opposing points of view that insist on one hand that "art" must meet a criterion of functionality—that is, be of some societal use—and, on the other hand, that "art" exists for its own sake. Our purpose in this text is to survey rather than dispute. Thus, in these pages, we will not solve the dilemma of art's definition, despite the energizing effect that such a discussion might engender. We can, however, examine some characteristics of the arts that will enhance our understanding.

Art has and has had profound effect on the quality of human life, as the pages of this text will assist us to understand, and its study requires seriousness of purpose. Having said that, however, we must be careful not to confuse seriousness of purpose in the study of art with a sweeping sanctification of works of art. Some art is serious, some art is profound, and some art is highly sacred. On the other hand, some art is light; some humorous; and some downright silly, superficial, and self-serving for its artists. Which is which may be debatable, but eventually we will desire to make judgments, and once again this text will help sort out the details.

The remainder of this section—that is, "Putting The Arts In Context"—treats four general subjects: (1) *The Arts and Ways of Knowing*, (2) *What Concerns Art?* (3) *The Functions of Art*, and (4) *Evaluating Works of Art*.

THE ARTS AND WAYS OF KNOWING

Humans are a creative species. Whether in science, politics, business, technology, or the arts, we depend on our creativity almost as much as anything else to meet the demands of daily life. Any book about the arts is a story about us: our perceptions of the world as we have come to see and respond to it and the ways we have communicated our understandings to each other since the Ice Age, more than 35,000 years ago (see Fig. **1.7**, Cave chamber at Lascaux).

Our study in this text will focus on vocabulary and perception, as well as on history. First, however, we need to have an overview of where the arts fall within the general scope of human endeavor.

As we begin this text, learning more about our humanness through art, let us start where we are. That means two things. First, it means relying on the perceptive capabilities we already have. Applying our current abilities to perceive will develop confidence in approaching works of art. Second, starting where we are means learning how art fits into the general scheme of the way people examine, communicate, and respond to the world around them. A course in the arts, designed to fulfill a requirement for a specified curriculum, means that the arts fit into an academic context that separates the way people acquire knowledge. Consequently, our first step in this exploration of the arts will be to place them in some kind of relationship with other categories of knowledge. Visual art, architecture, music, theatre, dance, and film belong in a broad category of pursuit called the "humanities," and that is where we begin.

The humanities, as opposed, for example, to the sciences, can very broadly be defined as those aspects of culture that look into what it means to be human. The sciences seek essentially to describe reality whereas the humanities seek to express humankind's subjective experiences of reality, to interpret reality, to transform our interior experience into tangible forms, and to comment upon reality, to judge and evaluate. But despite our desire to categorize, there really are few clear boundaries between the humanities and the sciences. The basic difference lies in the approach that separates investigation of the natural universe, technology, and social science from the search for truth about the universe undertaken by artists.

Within the educational system, the humanities traditionally have included the fine arts (painting, sculpture, architecture, music, theatre, dance, and cinema), literature, philosophy, and, sometimes, history. These subjects are all oriented toward exploring what it is to be human, what human beings think and feel, what motivates their actions and shapes their thoughts.

In addition, change in the arts differs from change in the sciences, for example, in one significant way: new scientific discovery and technology usually displaces the old; but new art does not invalidate earlier human expression. Obviously, not all artistic approaches survive, but the art of Picasso cannot make the art of Rembrandt a curiosity of history the way that the theories of Einstein did the views of William Paley. Nonetheless, much about art has changed over the centuries. Using a spectrum developed by Susan Lacy in *Mapping the Terrain: New Genre Public Art* (1995), we learn that at one time an artist may be an *experiencer*; at another, a *reporter*; at another, an *analyst*; and at still another time, an *activist*. Further, the nature of how art historians see art has changed over the centuries—for example, today we do not credit an artist's biography with all of the motivations for his or her work; and we now include works of art from previously marginalized groups such as women and minorities. These shifts in the disciplines of arts history itself are important considerations as we begin to understand the nature of art.

WHAT CONCERNS ART?

Among other concerns, art has typically concerned creativity, aesthetic communication, symbols, and the fine arts and crafts. Let's look briefly at each of these.

Creativity

Art has always evidenced a concern for creativity—that is, bringing forth new forces and forms that cause change. How this functions is subject for further debate. Nonetheless, something happens in which humankind takes chaos, formlessness, vagueness, and/or the unknown and crystallizes them into forms, designs, inventions, and ideas. Creativity underlies our existence. For example, creativity allows scientists to intuit that there is a possible path to a cure for cancer, for example, or to invent a computer. The same process allows artists to find new ways to express ideas through processes in which creative action, thought, material, and technique combine to create something new, and that "new thing," without words, triggers human experience—that is, our response to the artwork. Creativity lets Peter Paul Rubens find a way to express sacred ideas in complex forms, lines, and colors (Figs **13.11** and **13.12**), different from his Renaissance predecessors like Michelangelo (Chapter 11).

In the midst of this creative process is the art medium. Although most people can readily acknowledge the traditional media—for example, painting, traditional sculpture, and printmaking—sometimes an artwork does not conform to expectations or experiences—for example, a gigantic installation in two parts, of blue and yellow umbrellas (Fig. **18.24**).

Aesthetic Communication

Art usually involves communication. A common factor in art is a humanizing experience. Arguably, artists need other people with whom they can share their perceptions. When artworks and humans interact, many possibilities exist. Interaction may be casual and fleeting, as in the first meeting of two people, when one or both are not at all interested in each other. Similarly, an artist may not have much to say, or may not say it very well. For example, a poorly conceived and executed painting probably will not excite a viewer. Similarly, if a viewer is self-absorbed, distracted, unaware, has rigid preconceptions not met by the painting, or is so preoccupied by what may have occurred outside the museum that he or she finds it impossible to perceive what the artwork offers, then at least that part of the artistic experience fizzles. On the other hand, all conditions may be optimum, and a profoundly exciting and meaningful experience may occur: the painting may treat a significant subject in a unique manner, the painter's skill in manipulating the medium may be excellent, and the viewer may be receptive. Or the interaction may fall somewhere between these two extremes. In any case, the experience is a human one, and that is fundamental to art.

Throughout history, artistic communication has involved *aesthetics*. Aesthetics is the study of the nature of beauty and of art and comprises one of the five classical fields of philosophical inquiry—along with epistemology (the nature and origin of knowledge), ethics (the general nature of morals and of the specific moral choices to be made by the individual in relationship with others), logic (the principles of reasoning), and metaphysics (the nature of first principles and problems of ultimate reality). The term "aesthetics" (from the Greek for "sense perception") was coined by German philosopher Alexander Baumgarten in the mid-eighteenth century, but interest in what constitutes the beautiful and in the relationship between art and nature goes back at least to Plato and Aristotle, who saw art as *imitation* and beauty as the expression of a universal quality. In the late eighteenth century, the philosopher Immanuel Kant revolutionized aesthetics in his *Critique of Judgment* (1790) by viewing aesthetic appreciation not simply as the perception of intrinsic beauty, but as involving a judgment—subjective, but informed. Since Kant, the primary focus of aesthetics has shifted from the consideration of beauty *per se* to the nature of the artist, the role of art, and the relationship between the viewer and the work of art.

Symbols

Art is also concerned with symbols. Symbols are things that represent something else. They often use a material object to suggest something less tangible or less obvious: a wedding ring, for example. Symbols differ from signs, which suggest a fact or condition. Signs are what they denote. Symbols carry deeper, wider, and richer meanings. Look at Fig **0.14**. Some people might identify this figure as a sign, which looks like a plus sign in arithmetic. But the figure might also be seen as a Greek cross, in which case it becomes a symbol because it suggests many images, meanings, and implications. Artworks use a variety of symbols in order to convey meaning. By using symbols, artworks can relay meanings that go well beyond the surface of the work and offer glimpses of the human condition that cannot be sufficiently described in any other manner. Symbols make artworks into doorways leading to enriched meaning. (See the discussion of symbolism in the "How Art Works" feature beginning Chapter 5, p. 142.)

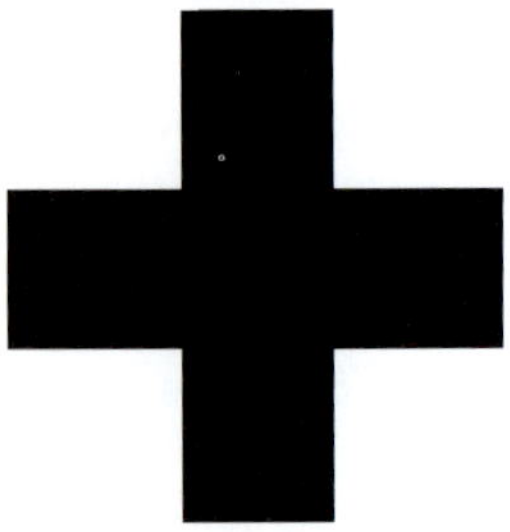

0.14 Greek cross?

Fine and Applied Art

One last consideration in our movement toward understanding what art concerns involves the difference between the terms "fine art" and "applied art." The "fine arts"—generally meaning painting, sculpture, and architecture—are prized for their purely aesthetic qualities. The terms "applied art" and "decorative arts" are used to describe art forms that have a primarily decorative rather than expressive or emotional purpose. The applied arts may include architecture. The decorative arts include handicrafts by skilled artisans, for example ornamental work in metal, stone, wood, and glass as well as textiles, pottery, and bookbinding. The term may also encompass aspects of interior design. In addition, personal objects such as jewelry, weaponry, tools, and costumes are considered to be part of the decorative arts. The term may extend, as well, to mechanical appliances and other products of industrial design. The term "decorative art" first appeared in 1791. Many decorative arts, such as weaving, basketry, or pottery, are also commonly considered to be "crafts," but the definitions of the terms are somewhat arbitrary and without sharp distinction.

THE FUNCTIONS OF ART

Art can function in many different ways: as *entertainment*, as *political or social weapon*, as *therapy*, and as *artifact*. One function is no more important than the others. Nor are they mutually exclusive: a single artwork can pursue any or all of them. Nor are these the only functions of art. Rather, they serve as indicators of how art has functioned in the past, and how it can function in the present. Like the types and styles of art we will examine later in the book, these four functions are options for artists and depend on what artists wish to do with their artworks.

Entertainment

Plays, paintings, concerts, and so on can provide escape from everyday cares, treat us to a pleasant time, and engage us in social occasions; they entertain us. They also give us insights into our hopes and dreams, likes and dislikes, as well as other cultures; and we can find healing therapy in entertainment.

The function of any one artwork depends on us. An artwork in which one person finds only entertainment may function as a social and personal comment for someone else. A Mozart (pronounced MOHT-sahrt) symphony, for example, can relax us, but it may also comment on the life of the composer and/or the conditions of eighteenth-century Austria.

Political and Social Commentary

When art seeks to bring about political change or to modify the behavior of large groups of people, it has political or social functions. In ancient Rome, for example, the authorities used music and theatre to keep masses of people occupied in order to quell urban unrest. On the other hand, Roman playwrights used their plays to attack incompetent or corrupt officials. The Greek playwright Aristophanes used comedy in such plays as *The Birds* to attack the political ideas of the leaders of fourth-century B.C.E.

Athenian society. In *Lysistrata* he attacked war by creating a story in which all the women of Athens go on a sex strike until Athens is rid of war and warmongers.

In late nineteenth-century Norway, Henrik Ibsen (IB-suhn) used his play *An Enemy of the People* (1882) as a platform for airing the issue of whether a government should ignore pollution in order to protect jobs or industry. In the United States at the turn of the twenty-first century, many artworks advance social and political causes and sensitize viewers, listeners, or readers to particular cultural situations.

Therapy

As therapy, art can help treat a variety of illnesses, both physical and mental. Role-playing, for example, frequently acts as a counseling tool in treating dysfunctional family situations. In this context, often called psychodrama, mentally ill patients act out their personal circumstances in order to find and cure the cause of their illness. The focus of this use of art as therapy is the individual. However, art in a much broader context acts as a healing agent for society's general illnesses as well. Artworks can illustrate society's failings and excesses in hopes of saving us from disaster. The laughter caused by comedy releases endorphins, chemicals produced by the brain, which strengthen the immune system.

Artifact

Art also functions as an artifact: a product that represents the ideas and technology of time and place. Artifacts, such as plays, paintings, poems, and buildings, connect us to our past. In this text, the function of art as artifact—as an example of a particular culture—takes on a central role.

When we examine art in the context of cultural artifact, one of the issues we face is the use of artworks in religious ritual. We could consider ritual as a separate function of art. Although we may not think of religious ritual as "art," in the broad context we have adopted for this text ritual often meets our definition of human communication using an artistic medium. Music, for example, when part of a religious ceremony, meets the definition, and theatre—if seen as an occasion planned and intended for presentation—would include religious rituals as well as events that take place in playhouses. Often, it is difficult to discern when ritual stops and secular production starts—for example, ancient Greek tragedy seems clearly to have evolved from ritual. When ritual, planned and intended for presentation, uses traditionally artistic media like music, dance, and theatre, we can study it as "art" and artifact of its particular culture.

EVALUATING WORKS OF ART

One of the questions everyone seems to ask about an artwork is, "Is it any good?" Whether it is rock music, a film, a play, a painting, or a classical symphony, judgments about the quality of a work often vary from one extreme to the other, ranging from "I liked it" and "It was interesting," to specific reasons why the artwork is thought to be effective or ineffective.

Criticism should be a detailed process of analysis to gain understanding and appreciation. Identifying the formal elements of an artwork—learning what to look for—is the first step. We describe an artwork by examining its many facets and then try to understand how they work together to create meaning or experience. We then try to state what that meaning or experience is. Only when that process is complete should we attempt judgment.

Value judgments are intensely personal, and some opinions are more informed than others, thus representing more authoritative judgments. However, disagreements about quality can actually enhance, rather than confuse, the experience of a work of art if they result in an examination about why the differences might exist. In this way, we develop a deeper understanding of the artwork. Nonetheless, criticism may be exercised without involving any value judgment whatsoever—and this is the point. We can thoroughly analyze and dissect any work of art and describe what it comprises without making value judgments. For example, we can describe and analyze line, color, mass, balance, texture, composition, and/or message. We can observe how all these factors affect people and their responses. We can spend significant amounts of time and write at considerable length in such a process and never pass a value judgment at all.

Does this discussion mean all artworks are equal in value? Not at all. It means that in order to understand what criticism involves, we must separate descriptive analysis, which can be satisfying in and of itself, from the act of passing value judgments. We may not like the work we have analyzed, but we may have understood something we did not understand before. Passing judgment may play no role whatsoever in our understanding of an artwork. But we are still involved in criticism.

As an exercise in understanding, criticism is necessary. We must investigate and describe. We must experience the need to know enough about the process, product, and experience of art if we are to have perceptions that mean anything worthwhile to ourselves and if we are to have perceptions to share with others.

Types of Criticism

There are a number of ways to "criticize" or analyze works of art. Some are fairly straightforward, and some are relatively complex and theoretically involved. Let's begin with two *basic* types of criticism. These are *formal* criticism and *contextual* criticism. Once we have these concepts in hand, we can branch out a little to examine the theoretically involved and opposing critical theories of *structuralism* and *deconstruction.*

Formal Criticism

Formal criticism is an analysis applying no external conditions or information. The artwork is analyzed according to style, composition—elements of line, form, color, balance—technique, melody, harmony, and so forth. Formal criticism approaches the artwork solely as an entity within itself and explains how the artist has taken these basic qualities and used them to build the work—how the employment of elements reveals style and makes the work affect the respondent. In so doing, we would develop a rather lengthy formal analysis of this artwork. In doing this, however, we would remain in our description and analysis strictly within the frame, so to speak. In other words, all of the conclusions we would reach about the work would come solely from evidence that exists in the work. In this formal approach, external information—about the artist, the times, the story behind the work, and so on—is irrelevant. Consequently, the formal approach helps us analyze how an artwork operates and helps us decide why the artwork produces the response it does. Formal criticism is exemplified by the work of the "New Critics" such as Allen Tate (1899–1979), who insisted on the intrinsic value of a work of art and focused attention on the work alone as an independent unit of meaning. As an example, we will do a brief analysis of Molière's (mohl-YAIR) comedy *Tartuffe* (tahr-TOOF; 1664):

Orgon, a rich bourgeois, has allowed a religious conman, Tartuffe, to gain complete hold over him. Tartuffe has moved into Orgon's house and tries to seduce Orgon's wife at the same time that he is planning to marry Orgon's daughter. Tartuffe is unmasked, and Orgon orders him out. Tartuffe seeks his revenge by claiming title to Orgon's house and blackmailing him with some secret papers. At the very last instant, Tartuffe's plans are foiled by the intervention of the king, and the play ends happily.

We have just described a story. Were we to go one step further and analyze the plot, we would look, among other things, for points at which *crises* occur and cause the characters to make important decisions; we would also want to know how those decisions moved the play from one point to the next. In addition, we would try to locate the extreme crisis—the *climax*. Meanwhile, we would discover auxiliary parts of the plot such as reversals: for example, when Tartuffe is discovered and the characters become aware of the true situation. Depending on how detailed our criticism were to become, we could work our way through each and every aspect of the plot. We might then devote some time to describing and analyzing the driving force—the character—of each person in the play and how the characters relate to each other. Has Molière created fully developed characters? Are they types, or do they seem to behave more or less like real individuals? In examining meaning, we would no doubt conclude that the play deals with religious hypocrisy, and that Molière had a particular point of view on that subject. In this approach, information about the playwright, previous performances, historic relationships, and so on is irrelevant.

Contextual Criticism

On the other hand, contextual criticism seeks meaning by examining related information "outside" the artwork, such as the artist's life, his or her culture, social, and political conditions and philosophies, public and critical reactions to the work, and so on. These can all be researched and applied to the work in order to enhance perception and understanding. This approach tends to view the artwork as an artifact generated from particular contextual needs, conditions, and/or attitudes. If we carry our criticism of *Tartuffe* in this direction, we would note that certain historical events help to clarify the play. For example, the object of Molière's attention probably was the Company of the Holy Sacrament, a secret, conspiratorial, and influential society in France at the time. Like many fanatical religious sects—including those of our own time—the society sought to enforce its own view of morality by spying on the lives of others and seeking out heresies, in this case, in the Roman Catholic Church. Its followers were religious fanatics, and they had a considerable effect on the lives of the citizenry at large. If we were to follow this path of criticism, any and all such contextual matters that might illuminate or clarify what happens in the play would be pursued.

Structuralism

Structuralism applies to the artwork a broader significance, insisting that individual phenomena—in this case artworks—can be understood *only* within the context of the overall structures of which they are a part. These structures represent universal sets of relationships that derive meaning from their contrasts and interactions within a specific context. Structuralist criticism, associated with Roland Barthes (BAHR-tuh; 1915–1980), derives by analogy from structural linguistics, which sees a "text" as a system of signs whose meaning is derived from the pattern of their interactions rather than from any external reference. This approach opposes critical positions that seek to determine an artist's intent, for example. Thus, the meaning of a work of art lies not in what the artist may have had in mind, but in the patterns of contextual relationships that work within the artwork. Finally, structuralism also opposes approaches, such as *deconstruction*, which deny the existence of uniform patterns and definite meanings.

Deconstruction

Deconstruction, associated with the French philosopher Jacques Derrida (dare-ee-DAH; b. 1930), was also originally associated with literary criticism, but has been applied to other disciplines. Derrida used the term "text," for example, to include any subject to which critical analysis can be applied. Deconstructing something means "taking it apart." The process of deconstruction implies drawing out all the threads of a work to identify its multitude of possible meanings, and, on the other hand, undoing the "constructs" of ideology or convention that have imposed meaning on the work. All of which leads to the conclusion that there is no such thing as a single meaning in a work of art, nor can it claim any absolute truth. Inasmuch as a work can outlast its author, its meanings transcend any original intentions. In other words, the viewer brings as much to the work as the artist, and, thus, there are no facts, only interpretations. The details of an artwork become only a sidebar to the interpretation that we, as viewers, bring to it based on our own experiences and circumstances.

Making Judgments

Now that we have defined criticism and noted two approaches we might take in pursuing it, we can move on to the final step—making value judgments.

There are several approaches to the act of judgment. Two characteristics, however, apply to all artworks: they are *crafted*, and they *communicate* something to us about our experiences as humans. Making a judgment about the quality of an artwork should address each of these.

Artisanship

Judging a work's artisanship means judging how it is crafted or made. Generally, such judgments require knowledge about the medium of the artwork. It is, for example, difficult to judge how a musical symphony is crafted without having some knowledge of musical composition. The same may be said of judging how well a painting, sculpture, building, or play is made. Nonetheless, some criteria exist that allow general judgment of works of art. These criteria include *clarity* and *interest*.

Applying the standard of clarity means deciding if the work has coherence. Even the most complex works of art need some handle that allows us to approach them and begin to understand how they work. This standard of judgment has stood the test of time. Artworks have been compared to onions in that the well made ones allow respondents to peel away translucent layers, with each layer taking us closer to the core. Some people are able to peel away all the layers, and some people are able to peel away only one or two, but a masterfully crafted work of art will have a coherence that allows a grasp on even the very surface layer.

Applying the standard of interest is similar to applying the standard of clarity in that there are layers of devices or qualities that artists use to capture and hold our interest. Masterfully crafted works of art employ such devices and qualities. Three such qualities are (1) universality (the artist's ability to touch a common experience or feeling within us), (2) carefully developed structures or focal points that lead us where the artist intends us to go, and (3) freshness of approach that makes us curious to investigate further. When we watch a tired and trite mystery, we know what is going to happen, the characters are stale clichés, and we lose interest almost immediately. A masterfully crafted work will hold us—even if we know the story. Such is the case with plays like Sophocles' *Oedipus the King* or Shakespeare's *Hamlet*.

If a work of art does not appear clear or interesting, we may wish to examine whether the fault lies in the work or in ourselves before rendering judgment.

Communication

Evaluating what an artwork is trying to say offers more immediate opportunity for judgment and less need for expertise. Johann Wolfgang von Goethe (GUR-te), the nineteenth-century poet, novelist, and playwright, set out a basic, commonsense approach to communication. Because it provides an organized means for discovering an artwork's communication by progressing from analytical to judgmental functions, Goethe's approach is a helpful way in which to end our discussion on criticism. Goethe posed three questions: What is the artist trying to say? Does he or she succeed? Was the artwork worth the effort? These questions focus on the artist's communication by making us identify, first, what was being attempted and, second, the artist's success in that attempt. Whether or not the project was worth the effort asks us to decide if the communication was important. Was it worthwhile?

1 The Ancient World

OUTLINE

HOW ART WORKS:
The Purposes of Art I

CONTEXTS AND CONCEPTS
- The Stone Age
- The Development of Civilization
  - TECHNOLOGY: The Invention of the Wheel
  - Religion
  - Writing

THE ARTS OF THE ANCIENT WORLD
- Cave Painting
- Sculpture
  - MASTERWORK: The Tell Asmar Statues
  - A DYNAMIC WORLD: Ancient China
- Architecture
- Music

FOCAL POINT:
Akhenaton and Monotheism—The Tell el Amarna Period
PROFILE: Akhenaton and Nefertiti

VIEW

ART: THE CREATIVE IMPULSE

This chapter takes us from the beginnings of humankind through the great civilization of ancient Egypt. What it shows us, among other things, is the interrelationship of humankind in its desire to create art—something that began when our ancestors still lived in caves. More than that, however, we will see that these three cultures—Ice Age humans, Mesopotamians, and ancient Egyptians—made choices about the ways in which they represented the figures of humans and animals. As a result, we can identify their representations and differentiate them from each other and from the representations of other cultures and times we will study in subsequent chapters. In addition, we will see relationships in the manners in which these cultures viewed death and the afterlife. Finally, we will note how, as early as ancient Mesopotamia and Egypt, literacy meant power.

KEY TERMS

Some of the basic terms and concepts we will encounter in this chapter include the following:

Paleolithic
The first stage of human culture, in which humans discovered fire, clothing, basic techniques for hunting and gathering, and simple social organization.

Pantheon
A word meaning "all the gods."

Cuneiform
Sumerian writing involving two types of sign—one for syllables and one for words—and consisting of wedge marks and combinations of wedge marks pressed into damp clay.

Pyramid
An Egyptian burial tomb of great size and scale containing hidden chambers.

1.1 Black bull, detail, c. 16,000–14,000 B.C.E. Paint on limestone, 13 ft (3.96 m) long. Lascaux, France.

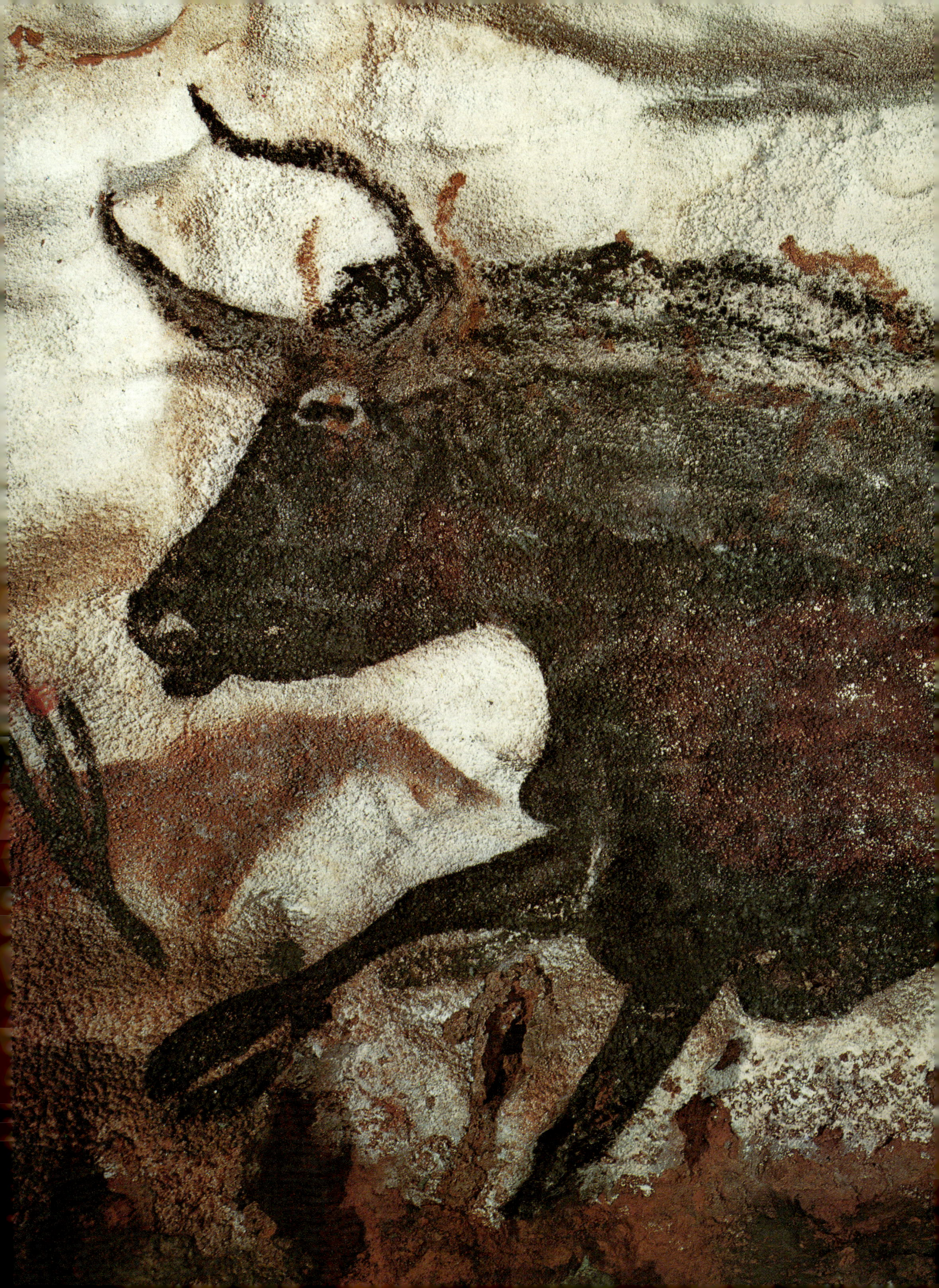

■ The Mask of Tutankhamun

One of the most popular artifacts from ancient Egypt is an exquisite funerary mask from the tomb of Akhenaton's son Tutankhamun, discovered in the Valley of Kings near Thebes. The mask is of solid beaten gold inlaid with semiprecious stone and colored glass (Fig. **1.3**). Designed to cover the face of the king's mummy and record his likeness, it reveals the royal *nemes* headdress with two flaps hanging down at the sides and a ribbon holding his braid at the back. The hood formed by the headdress reveals two symbolic creatures—divinities who protected Egypt.

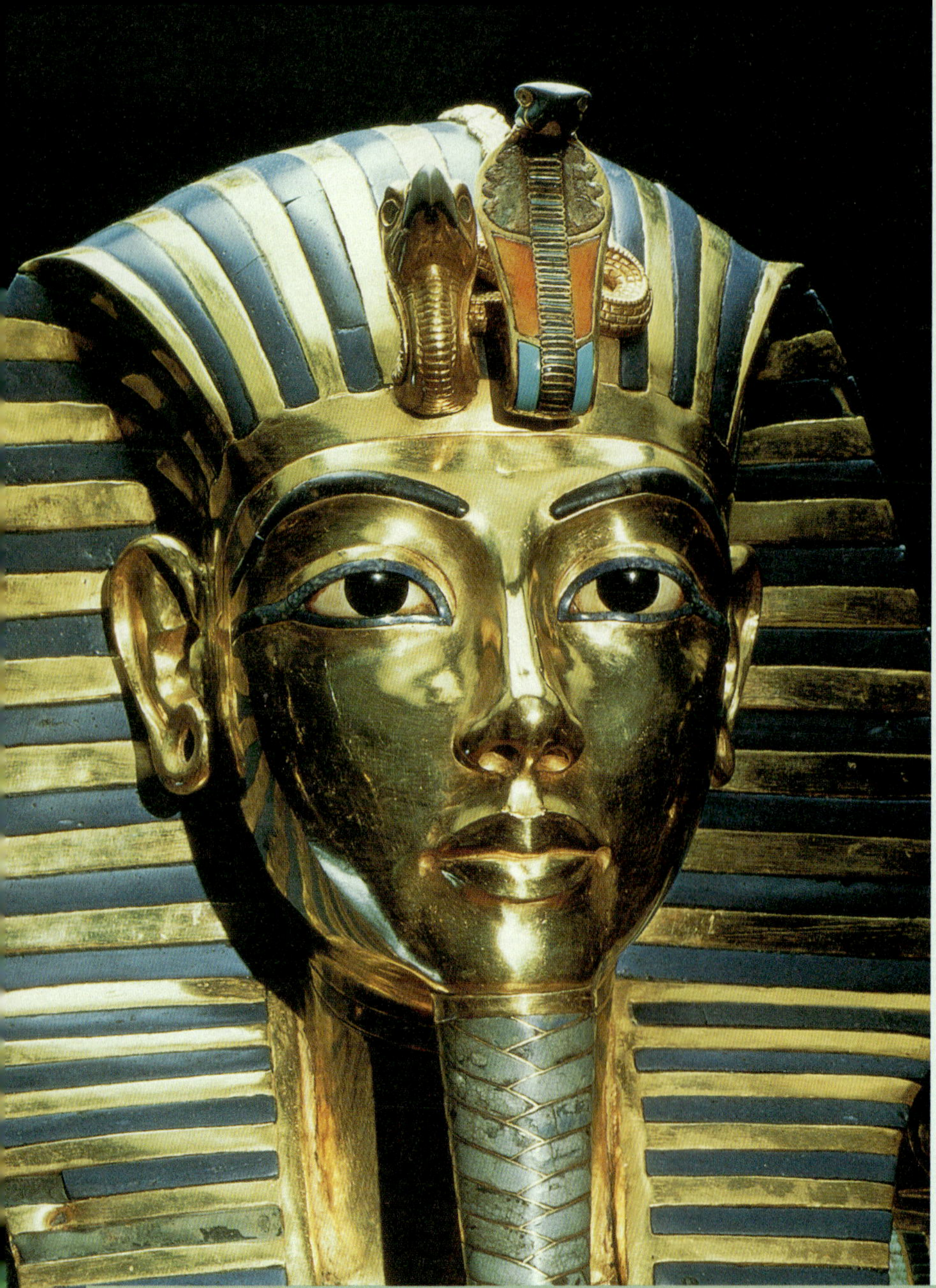

HOW ART WORKS

THE PURPOSES OF ART I:
Providing a Record

Throughout history, art has attempted to do a number of things. We will discuss some of these in this space in chapters to come, but one of the fundamental purposes of art, at least until the nineteenth century, was providing a record.

Until the invention of the camera, one of art's principle purposes was to enact a record of the world. Although we cannot know for sure, very likely the cave art we examine momentarily did this. The Egyptians, ancient Greeks, Romans, and so on, all undertook to record their times in pictorial form, whether in a funereal mask like that of Tutankhamun (Fig. **1.3**), a vase or, as in the case of the eighteenth-century Italian painter, Canaletto (kah-nah-LAY-toh), in highly naturalistic vedute (vay-DOO-tay; Italian for "views"; Fig. **1.2**) that he sold to travelers doing the grand tour of Europe.

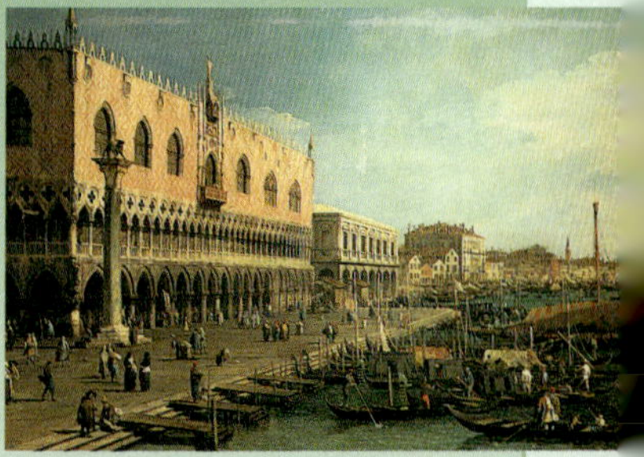

1.2 Antonio Canaletto, *Piazzetta of St. Marks, Rome,* 1735. Oil on canvas, 43½ × 73 ins (110.5 × 185.5 cm). Galleria Nazionale d'Arte Antica, Rome.

1.3 Funerary mask of Tutankhamun, c. 1337 B.C.E. Gold, semiprecious stones, glass, 21¼ × 15½ ins (54 × 39.5 cm). Egyptian Museum, Cairo.

CONTEXTS AND CONCEPTS

The Stone Age

The human journey began long before the chronicles of history. Several million years may have passed as humankind journeyed from prehistory to city life, civilization, and history. As humans evolved culturally, they adapted to a changing environment with creative discoveries and ingenious applications of those discoveries in technology and social inventions. They migrated across the globe.

The first stage of human culture was the Paleolithic (pay-lee-oh-LITH-ik) or Old Stone Age, reaching back beyond one million years B.C.E. Here, humans were hunters and gatherers. But in the Paleolithic period, humans discovered fire, clothing, basic techniques for hunting and gathering food, and simple social organization. Toward the end of the period, our ancestors probably began to think in artistic and religious terms (Map **1.1**).

The second stage of human culture was the Neolithic period or New Stone Age. Between approximately 8000 B.C.E. and 3000 B.C.E., people began to settle down and to raise crops rather than to hunt and gather. This

GENERAL EVENTS

- *Homo sapiens*, c. 50,000 B.C.E.
- Last glaciers in Europe, c. 8000 B.C.E.
- Agricultural settlements, c. 8000 B.C.E.
- Pottery, c. 8000 B.C.E.
- Sumerian civilization, 6000 B.C.E.
- Invention of the wheel, c. 3000 B.C.E.
- Bronze casting, 3000 B.C.E.
- Old Kingdom of Egypt, 2686–2181 B.C.E.
- Sargon I, 2400–2350 B.C.E.
- Middle Kingdom of Egypt, 1991–1633 B.C.E.
- Hammurabi, c. 1792–1750 B.C.E.
- Shang dynasty in China, 1600–1027 B.C.E.
- New Kingdom of Egypt, 1567–1085 B.C.E.
- Akhenaton and Nefertiti, 1385–1358 B.C.E.
- Tutankhamen, 1361–1352 B.C.E.
- Assyrian Empire, c. 850–612 B.C.E.
- Sargon II, 721–705 B.C.E.

	50,000 B.C.E. – 10,000 B.C.E.	10,000 B.C.E. – 5000 B.C.E.	5000 B.C.E. – 1000 B.C.E.	1000 B.C.E. – 500 B.C.E.
PAINTING & SCULPTURE	Cave at Lascaux (**1.1, 1.7**)		He-goat from Ur (**1.9**), Shang dynasty ceremonial vessel (**1.10**), Rahotep and Nofret (**1.11**), Tell el Amarna (**1.16–1.18**)	
ARCHITECTURE			Tell Asmar temple and statues (**1.8**), Giza pyramid complex (**1.12–1.14**)	
MUSIC & DANCE		Religious and secular music	Egyptian musical instruments	Funeral dances
LITERATURE & PHILOSOPHY	Human symbols		Egyptian hieroglyphics, Cuneiform writing	*Gilgamesh* epic

Timeline 1.1 The ancient world.

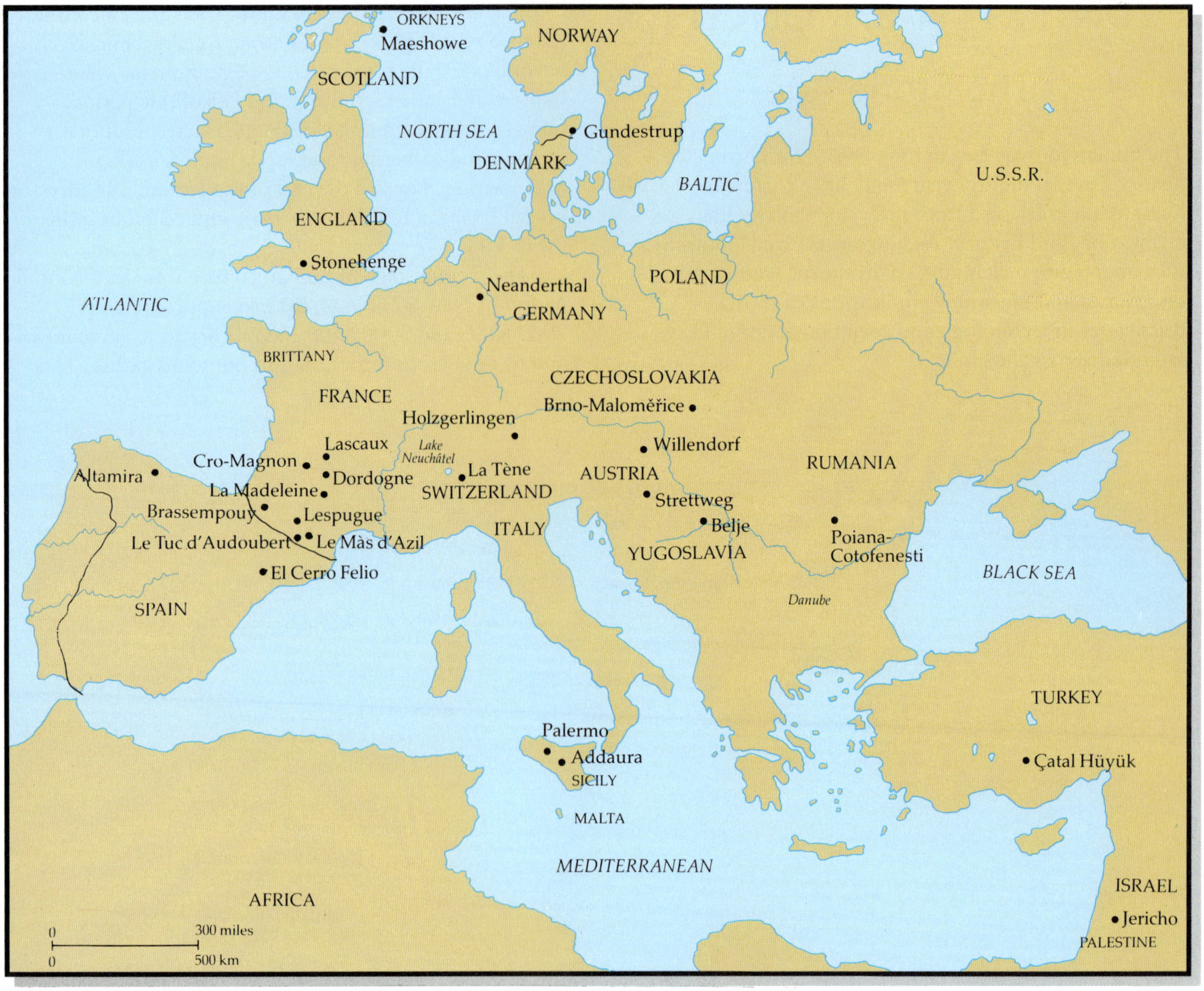

Map 1.1 Sites of prehistoric importance in Europe.

was the agricultural phase. Stone tools improved dramatically, and humans learned to make pottery and textiles. Social structure changed as well, as humans learned how to live together in small villages.

Some 50,000 years ago, humankind began to grasp the notions of selfhood and individuality. They began to make symbols as part of a strategy for comprehending reality and for telling each other what they discovered. They learned to make art in order to express more fully what they believed was their unique essence. They became aware of death and buried their dead with care and reverence. They realized that they had a complex relationship with the world into which they were born in mystery, in which they lived in mystery, and from which they departed in mystery. Progress since that early time in technological and socioeconomic sophistication has been immense, but we are no more human now than they were then.

If we have any tendency to think of our prehistoric predecessors as somehow less human than ourselves, we have only to consider the profundity of their art to set our thinking straight. However, because we are dealing with prehistory—that is, before recorded history—we can make only the broadest of conjectures, based on the slimmest of evidence. Studies of prehistoric societies and art leave us without a consensus on which to build, but even if we cannot accurately grasp all the whys or wherefores of the artifacts (see Introduction) that remain for us to study, we can appreciate the power of the human spirit that they express.

We cannot reconstruct what life was like during the latter half of the Old Stone Age, when the artistic achievements we are about to examine occurred. There is some evidence that perhaps as early as 100,000 B.C.E. these people had some sort of religion. Some historians have suggested that they put up the skulls of cave bears as though to worship these rivals for the spaces in which they lived. By 50,000 B.C.E., Neanderthal people are known to have buried their dead with ceremony and care, behavior suggesting a belief in the hereafter, for ancient corpses were painted with red ochre, positioned with their knees raised, and provided with weapons. There is no proof for such conjecture, but the evidence does suggest that religion was among the earliest examples of human capacity to think in the abstract. As we have seen, there can be little doubt that art was another example.

In the New Stone Age—that is, the period from around 8000 B.C.E. to around 3000 B.C.E.—humans began domesticating some of the animals they had been accustomed to chase and kill. At first these animals were only used for meat, but around 4000 B.C.E., some communities in and around the Middle East had devised new ways to use their flocks and herds—for example, for milk, an important new food source. Here the final link was forged from our earliest, unknown ancestors to our earliest known ancestors, who emerged from the darkness of prehistory into the light of history and civilization. That link leads us from Europe to a place in the Middle East called Mesopotamia.

The Development of Civilization

When villages evolved into cities, another stage of cultural development occurred, called **civilization**. From that time on, humans have engaged in complex cultures evolving around urban centers and empire building. They learned how to work with metals, to build monumental architecture, to write, to organize centralized bureaucracies, and to stratify social classes to ensure the survival of the group, for protection, and for control of the environment.

In myth, the Tower of Babel (BAY-buhl) rose to connect heaven and earth. In much the same way, the arts of the Mesopotamians symbolized the people's relationship to their kings and, through them, to their gods. Bridging prehistory and history, the cities and empires of the Fertile Crescent, the land "between the rivers"—the Tigris and the Euphrates—were our **prototype** civilizations (Maps **1.2** and **1.3**), and the earliest recognizable culture to emerge in this area around 6000 B.C.E. was that of Sumer.

TECHNOLOGY

The Invention of the Wheel

Insofar as Sumerians were capable of discerning scientific knowledge, they were also capable of applying that knowledge as technology. Sumerian mathematics employed a system of counting based on 60, and that system was used to measure time (we still have 60 minutes in 1 hour) and circles, divided into 360 degrees. The invention of number positioning—for example, 6 as a component of 6 or 60—made Sumerian mathematics unusually sophisticated. Mathematical calculation formed the basis for architectural endeavor, which, in turn, gave rise to higher levels of brick-making technology. Pottery was mass-produced and made the first known use of the potter's wheel. The wheel itself appeared as a transportation device in Sumer as early as 3000 B.C.E. By the same time, Sumerian technology had accomplished the casting of bronze and the invention of glass.

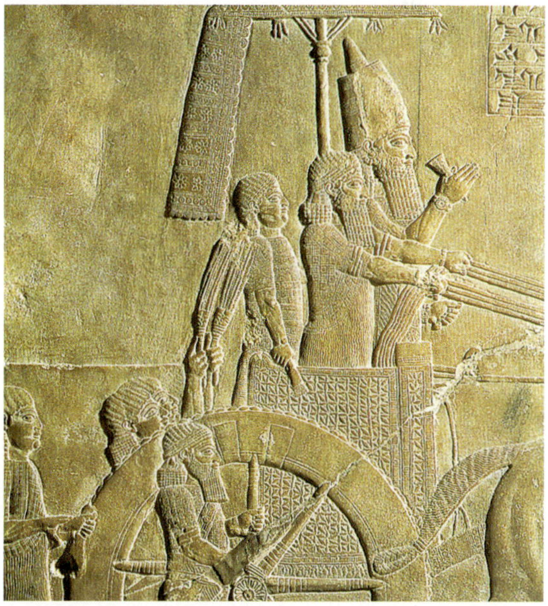

1.4 Ashurnasirpal II killing lions, from the Palace of Ashurnasirpal II, Nimrud (Calah), Iraq, c. 850 B.C.E. Limestone, 3 ft 3 ins × 8 ft 4 ins (99 × 254 cm). British Museum, London.

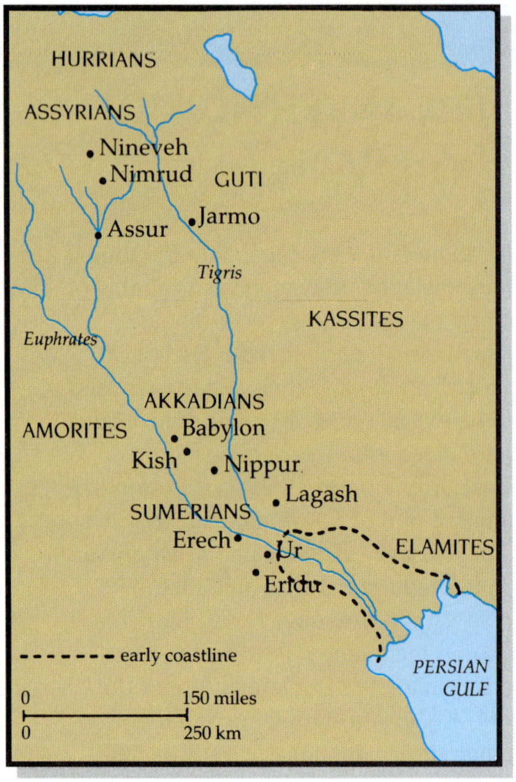

Map 1.2 Mesopotamia.

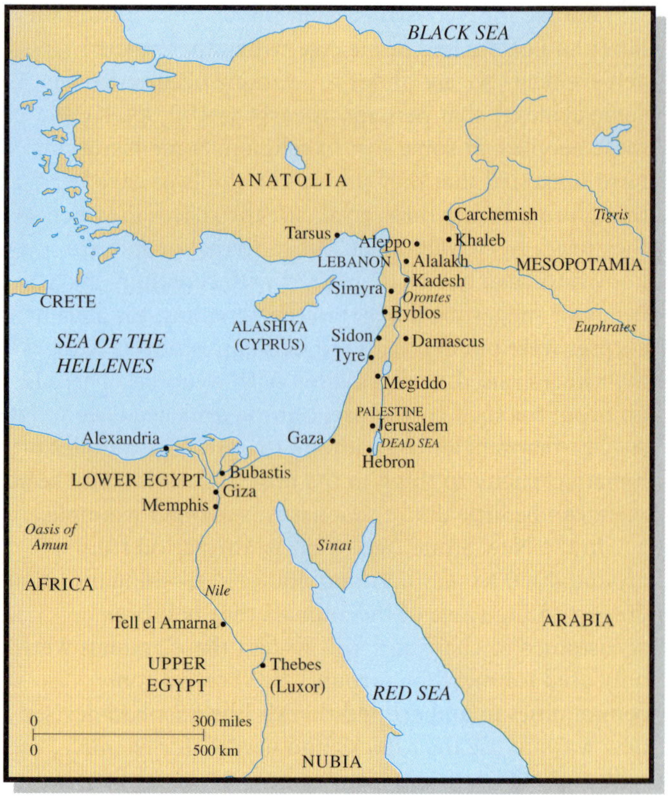

Map 1.3 Ancient Egypt and the Middle East.

The Sumerians (soo-MEER-ee-uhns) had a way of life similar to that of the other peoples in the region. They lived in villages and organized themselves around several important religious centers, which grew rapidly into cities.

As Sumerian civilization coalesced, the region remained in flux until the next great ruler emerged in the early 1700s B.C.E. This ruler was Hammurabi (hah-moo-RAH-bee). His capital was Babylon, and Babylon became the hub of the world—at least for a while. The first Babylonian empire encompassed the lands from Sumer and the Persian Gulf to Assyria. It included the cities of Nineveh (NIHN-uh-vuh) and Nimrud (nim-ROOD) on the Tigris and Mari on the Euphrates, and extended up the Euphrates to presentday Aleppo (see Map **1.3**). This empire, of approximately 70,000 square miles (181,300 square kilometers), rested on an elaborate, centralized, administrative system. It maintained its order through a wideranging judicial code, which we have come to call the Code of Hammurabi. These laws consist of 282 articles, which address the legal questions of the time.

Foremost in importance among the articles was the precept of "an eye for an eye." Before Hammurabi's time, damages for bodily injury were assessed on a monetary basis—for example, a lost eye would be assessed at 60 shekels. Under Hammurabi, the monetary system was retained only for an injury inflicted by a free man on one of lower status. If, however, the parties were of equal status, exact retribution was called for: "An eye for an eye, a tooth for a tooth," and so forth. We do not know what retribution was exacted for injury inflicted on a person of higher degree, but the penalty in such a case was undoubtedly even more severe. Hammurabi's code was pragmatic and clearly based on a rigid class system. Only the rich were allowed to escape retributive mutilation by monetary payment. A sliding scale, based on ability to pay, determined compensation for medical expenses and legal fees.

The rights and place of women, likewise, were specifically spelled out. The purpose of a wife was to provide her husband with legitimate sons and heirs. The penalty for adultery (by a wife) was drowning for both wife and paramour. Men were allowed "secondary" or "temporary" wives as well as slave concubines. On the other hand, beyond the area of procreation, women were largely independent. They could own property, run businesses, and lend and borrow money. A widow could remarry, which allowed greater population growth than was possible in cultures where the wife had to throw herself on her husband's funeral pyre.

In essence, the Code of Hammurabi dealt with wages, divorce, fees for medical services, family matters, commerce, and land and property, which included slaves. Hammurabi, like the rulers who preceded him, took his authority and also his law from the gods. Thus the concept of law as derived from extraordinary and supernatural powers continued unchallenged.

In approximately the same time frame, another civilization developed, and that was ancient Egypt, protected by deserts and confined to a narrow river valley (see Map **1.3**). It was a civilization unique in its dependence upon the regular annual flooding of a single river, for each year, as the Nile overflowed its banks to deposit a rich and fertile silt on the surrounding fields, it bore witness to the rhythm of a beneficent natural order that would continue beyond the grave. Death—or, rather, everlasting life in the hereafter—was the focus of the life and the arts of the Egyptians. Created mostly in the service of the cult of a god, or to glorify the power and wealth of a pharaoh, art and architecture centered on the provision of an eternal dwelling place for the dead. Life was celebrated and recreated in images intended to provide an eternal substitute for the mortal body.

Religion

Religion and government shared a close relationship in Sumer. Religion permeated the social, political, and economic, as well as the spiritual and ethical life of society. A long **epic** poem, the *Gilgamesh* (GIL-guh-mesh) *Epic*, gives us an insight into this religion, around which Sumerian society was organized. The list of gods is a long one. By about 2250 B.C.E., the Sumerians worshipped a well-developed and generally accepted **pantheon** (PAN-thee-ahn) of gods. Temples were erected throughout Sumer for the sacrifices that were thought necessary to ensure good harvests. It appears that each individual city had its own "supreme" god, and the local gods had their places in a larger **hierarchy** (HY-er-ahrk-ee). Like the Greeks later (see Chapter 2), the Sumerians gave human/animal attributes to their gods. The gods also had individual responsibilities. Ishtar was the goddess of love and procreation, for example. There was a god of the air, one of the water, one of the plow, and so on. Three male gods at the top of the hierarchy demanded sacrifice and obedience. To those who obeyed the gods came the promise of prosperity and longevity. Elaborate and intricate rituals focused on cycles involving marriage and rebirth: a drama of creation witnessed in the changing seasons.

Sumerian religion was concerned with life, and it seems to have perceived the afterworld as a rather dismal place. Nonetheless, there is evidence to suggest not only the practice of ritual suicide but also the belief that kings and queens would need a full complement of earthly possessions when they entered the next world.

Sumerian religion had important political ramifications as well. It ascribed ownership of all lands to the gods. The king was a king–priest, responsible to the gods alone. Below him, an elaborate class of priests enjoyed worldly power, privilege, and comfort, and to this class fell the responsibility for education and the writing of texts. And it is writing that undoubtedly represents the Sumerians' greatest contribution to the advancement of general civilization.

From the beginning of Egyptian civilization, the king was always identified with a god. At the time when Upper and Lower Egypt were united (c. 3000 B.C.E.), the king was considered to be the earthly manifestation of the god Horus, deity of the sky. The king was also considered to be the "Son of Ra," and thus represented a direct link between the royal line and the creator sun god.

Egyptian religion was a complex combination of local and national gods, and in a cumulative process new beliefs and gods were added over the thousands of years of Egyptian history. Two gods could be amalgamated and yet retain their separate entities. The same god could appear in various manifestations.

Religion played a central role in an Egyptian's personal and social life, as well as in civil organization. Death was believed to be a doorway to an afterlife, in which the departed could cultivate his or her own portion of the elysian fields with water apportioned by the gods. Life continued for the dead as long as the corpse, or some material image of it, continued to exist. Careful burial in dry sand, which preserved the corpse, was therefore essential, as was skillful mummification. The art of embalming had reached a proficient level as early as 3000 B.C.E. Great pains were taken to ensure a long existence for the corpse, and mortuary buildings became the most important architectural features of the culture, reflecting their role as eternal homes. These tombs and burial places, rich in funereal imagery and narrative, have provided most of what we know of Egyptian history. Religious practice dictated that only good things be said of the departed, however. Thus the picture of a country populated by young, handsome, well-fed men and women, and ruled by beneficent pharaohs who inspired reverence, optimism, and productivity, even among the lowest slaves, may need careful adjustment.

The pharaoh (FAIR-oh) acted as a link between mortals and the eternal. Priests, or servants of the god, were delegates of the pharaoh. The common people relied on their ruler for their access to the afterlife: the offerings that would secure the pharaoh's existence in the afterlife

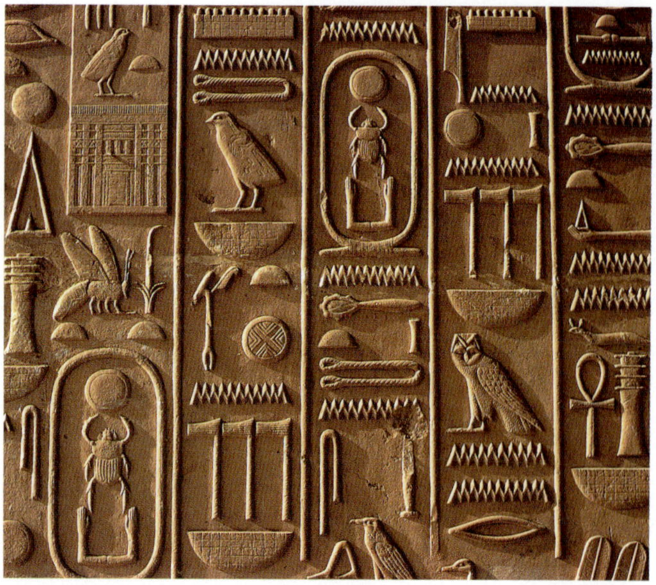

1.5 Egyptian hieroglyphics with dedicatory inscription to the god of Fertility, Amon-Min, c. 1950 B.C.E. Sandstone. "White Chapel" Sesostris I, Karnak, Egypt.

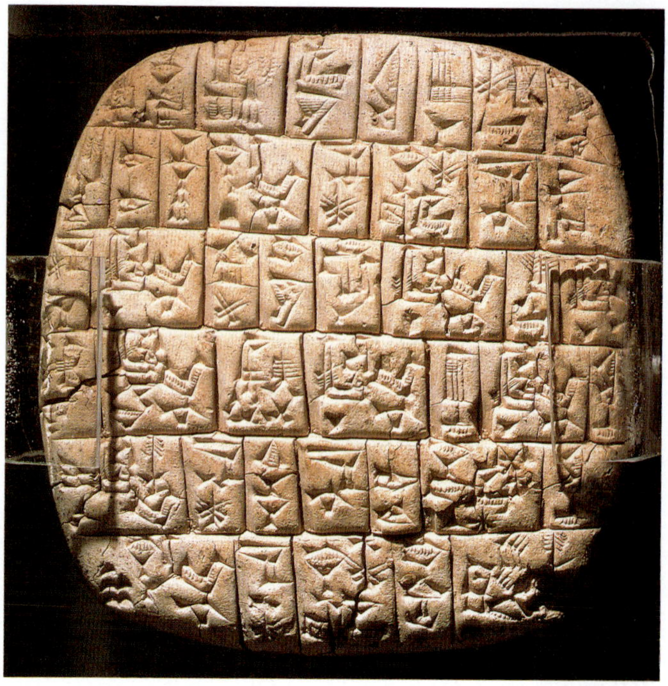

1.6 Clay tablet with cuneiform writing from Palace G, Elba, c. 2400 B.C.E. National Museum of Aleppo, Syria.

were the people's only key to the eternal. It was, therefore, in every Egyptian's interest to be sure that the pharaoh's tomb could sustain and maintain him. Images and inscriptions in the tombs included the lowliest servants, ensuring that they, too, would participate forever in the pharaoh's immortality. Magic charms for the revivification of the deceased king, which were at one time spoken by priests, came to be inscribed on the walls of the tomb so that, if necessary, the deceased could read them. Eventually the nobility began to usurp these magic formulas, and by the end of the twenty-first century B.C.E., they were copied regularly, and almost everyone could share the once unique privileges of the pharaoh.

The pharaoh joined the gods in the nether world after death. As befitting a ruler whose entourage also existed in the afterlife, he came to be associated with Osiris, king of the dead.

Writing

Various primitive peoples had used picture writing to convey messages. Sumerian writing, however, initiated the use of pictorial symbols that were qualitatively different: the Sumerians (and later the Egyptians) used pictures to indicate the syllabic sounds that occurred in different words rather than simply to represent the objects themselves. Egyptian picture writing is called hieroglyphic (HY-roh-GLIH-fik; Fig. **1.5**). Sumerian language consisted of monosyllables used in combination, and so Sumerian writing came to consist of two types of sign, one for syllables and one for words. Writing materials were an unbaked clay tablet and a reed stylus, which, when pressed into the soft clay, produced a wedge-shaped mark. The wedges and combinations of wedges that made up Sumerian writing are called "cuneiform," from the Latin *cuneus* (KYOO-nee-uhs), meaning "wedge" (Fig. **1.6**).

Written language can cause many things to happen in a society, and it also reveals many things about that society. As well as opening up new possibilities for communication, it has a stabilizing effect on society, because it fixes the past by turning it into a documentable chronicle. In Sumer, records of irrigation patterns and practices, tax collections, and harvest and storage details were among the first things written down. Writing was also a tool of control and power. In the earliest times, the government and the priestly class of Sumer held a monopoly on literacy, and literacy served to strengthen their government.

But literacy also led to literature, and the oldest known story in the world comes to us from earliest Sumer. The *Gilgamesh* epic, an episodic tale of a hero's adventures, is from this era, although its most complete version dates from as late as the seventh century B.C.E. Gilgamesh probably was a real person, a ruler at Uruk (OO-ruk) who lived during the first half of the third millennium B.C.E., although there is no historical evidence actually to document that. One fascinating part of this epic describes a flood, which parallels that in the story of Noah's ark in the Bible. It is a hero's quest against nature, man, and the gods. Other epics too, and even love songs, have survived from the literature of ancient Sumer. Access the flood story from the Gilgamesh epic at http://www.piney.com/Gilgamesh.html.

THE ARTS OF THE ANCIENT WORLD

Each of the ancient cultures we have noted produced its own forms of art. Very briefly we will sample it, beginning with the cave painting of Stone Age humans followed by some scultpure from Sumer and Egypt, pyramid architecture from Egypt, and, finally, music from Sumer and Egypt.

Cave Painting

The Cave of Lascaux (lahs-KOH) in France lies slightly over a mile (about 2 kilometers) from the little town of Montignac, in the valley of the Vézère (vay-ZAIR) River. The cave itself was discovered in 1940 by a group of children who, while investigating a tree uprooted by a storm, scrambled down a fissure into a world undisturbed for thousands of years. The cave was sealed in 1963 to protect it from atmospheric damage, and visitors now see Lascaux II, an exact replica, which is sited in a quarry 600 feet (180 meters) away.

Perhaps a sanctuary for the performance of sacred rites and ceremonies, the Main Hall, or Hall of the Bulls (Fig. **1.7**), elicits a sense of power and grandeur. The thundering herd moves below a sky formed by the rolling contours of the stone ceiling of the cave, sweeping our eyes forward as we travel into the cave itself. At the entrance of the main hall, the 8-foot (2.4-meter) "unicorn" begins a larger-than-lifesize montage of bulls, horses, and deer, which are up to 12 feet (3.7 meters) tall. Their shapes intermingle with one another, and their colors radiate warmth and power. These magnificent creatures remind us that their creators were capable technicians who, with artistic skills at least equal to

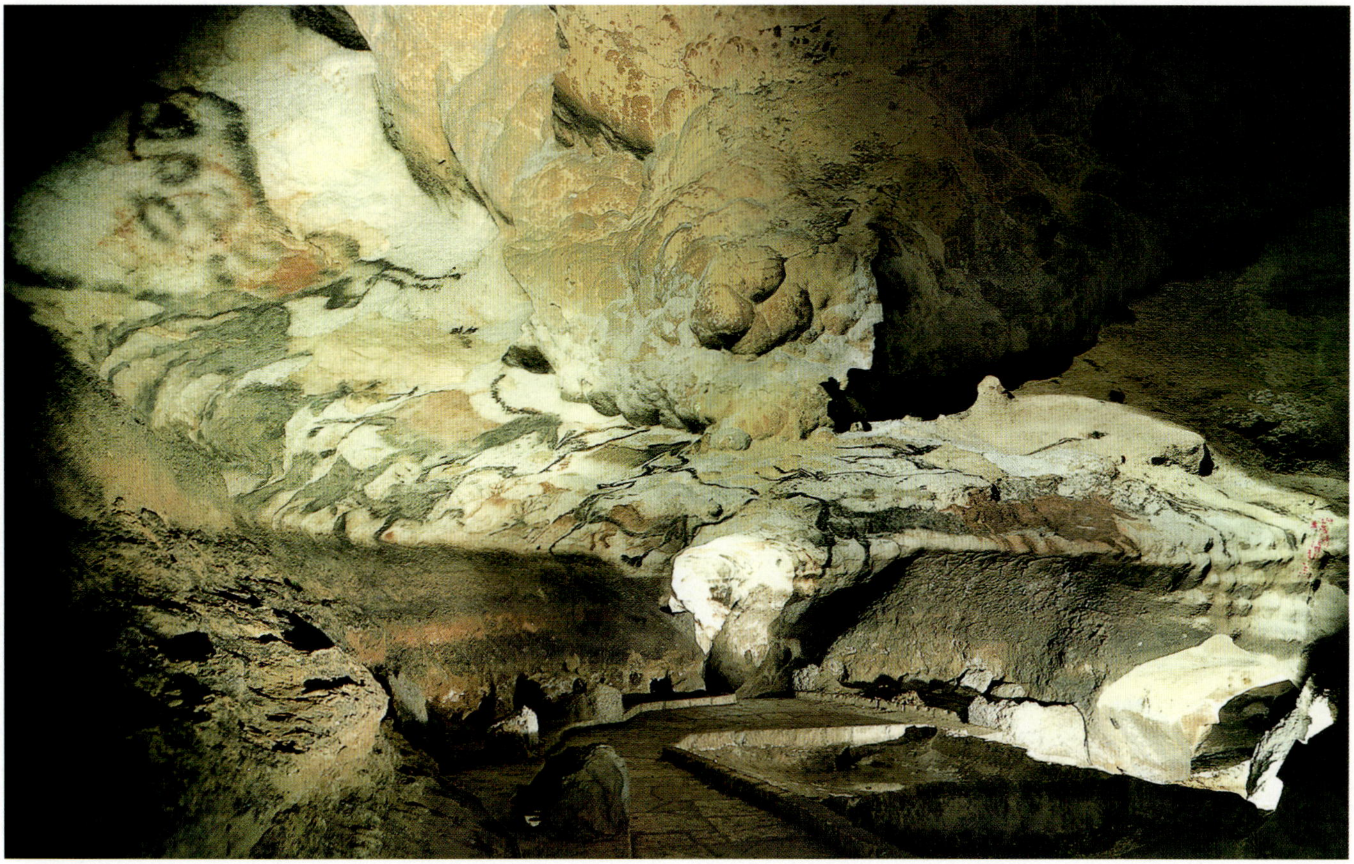

1.7 Main Hall, or Hall of the Bulls, Lascaux, France.

MASTERWORK

The Tell Asmar Statues

Undoubtedly the most striking features of these figures are their enormous, staring eyes, with their dramatic exaggeration. Representing the quasi-divine king Abu (AH-boo) (the large figure), a figure assumed to be his spouse, and a crowd of worshippers, the statues occupied places around the inner walls of an early temple, in prayer, awaiting the divine presence. The figures have great dignity, despite the stylization and somewhat crude execution. In addition to the staring eyes, our attention is drawn to the distinctive carving of the arms, which are separate from the body. The composition is closed and self-contained, reflecting prayer.

Certain geometric and expressive qualities characterize these statues. In typical Sumerian style, each form is based on a cone or cylinder, and the arms and legs are stylized and pipelike, rather than being lifelike depictions of the subtle curves of human limbs.

The god Abu and the mother goddess may be distinguished from the rest by their size and by the large diameter of their eyes. The meaning in these statues clearly bears out what we know of Mesopotamian religious thought. The gods were believed to be present in their images. The statues of the worshippers were substitutes for the real worshippers, even though no attempt appears to have been made to make the statues look like any particular individual: every detail is simplified, focusing attention on the remarkable eyes, which are constructed from shell, lapis lazuli, and black limestone. The figures are made of gypsum, a very fragile material.

Large and expressive eyes appear to be a basic convention of Sumerian art—although it is a convention found in other ancient art as well. Its basis is unknown, but the idea of the eye as a source of power permeates ancient folk-wisdom. The eye could act as a hypnotizing, controlling force, for good or for evil—hence the term "evil eye," which is still used today. Symbolic references to the eye range from "windows of the soul" to the "all-seeing" vigilance of the gods.

The Sumerians used art, like language, to communicate through conventions. Just as cuneiform script condensed wider experiences and simplified pictures into signs, so Sumerian art took lifelikeness, as it was perceived by the artist, and reduced it to a few conventional forms, which, to those who understood the conventions, communicated larger truths about the world. These works establish social hierarchy and are clear examples of conventionalism in the arts.

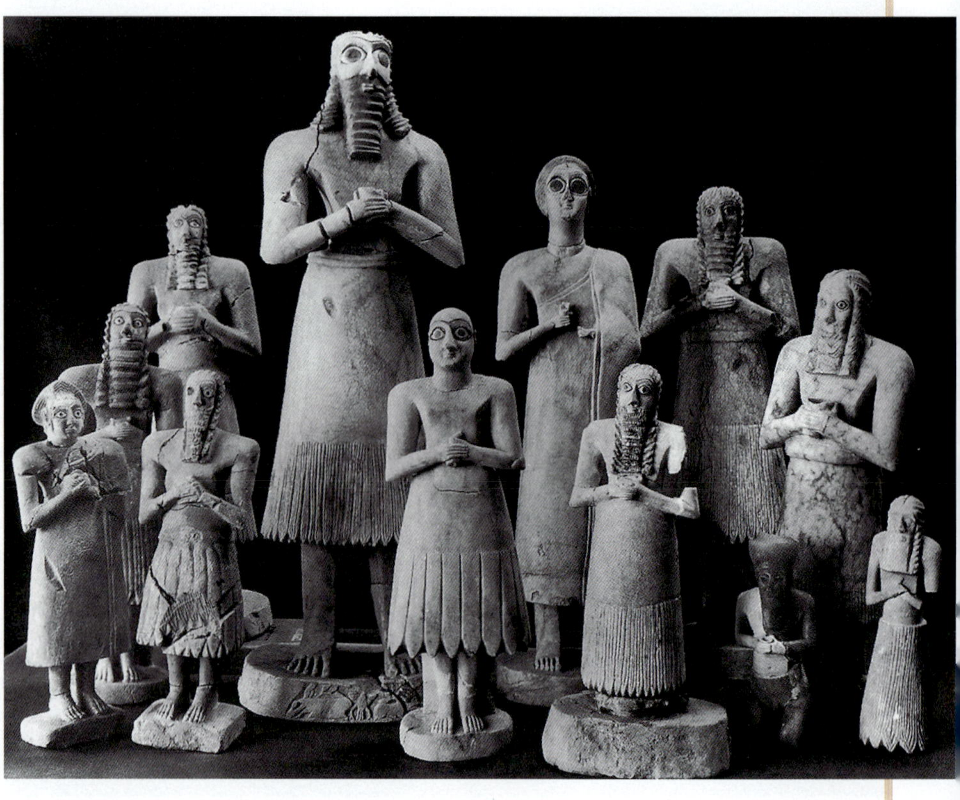

1.8 Statues of worshippers and deities from the Square Temple at Tell Asmar, Iraq, c. 2750 B.C.E. Gypsum, tallest figure 30 ins (76 cm) high. Iraq Museum, Baghdad, and Oriental Institute, University of Chicago.

our own, were able to capture the essence beneath the visible surface of their world. The paintings in the Main Hall were created over a long period of time and by a succession of artists, yet their cumulative effect in this 30- by 100-foot (9 by 30 meters) domed gallery is that of a single work, carefully composed for maximum dramatic and communicative impact. We must remember, however, that we see the work, illuminated by electric floodlighting, very differently from the people by and for whom it was created, who could only ever see small areas at a time, lit by flickering stone lamps of oil or animal fat.

Sculpture

Sumerian art progressed from stereotypical and anonymous portrayals to depictions of actual individuals, usually kings, who were portrayed in devotional acts rather than as warlords. The famous statues from Tell Asmar (as-MAR) and the Temple of Abu illustrate this well (see Fig. **1.8**).

But if crudity marks the depiction of the human figure in these votive statues, grace and delicacy are evident in works from the golden splendor of the Sumerian court. Inlaid in gold, the he-goat symbolizes the royal leadership of ancient Sumer and masculine fertility (Fig. **1.9**). Here,

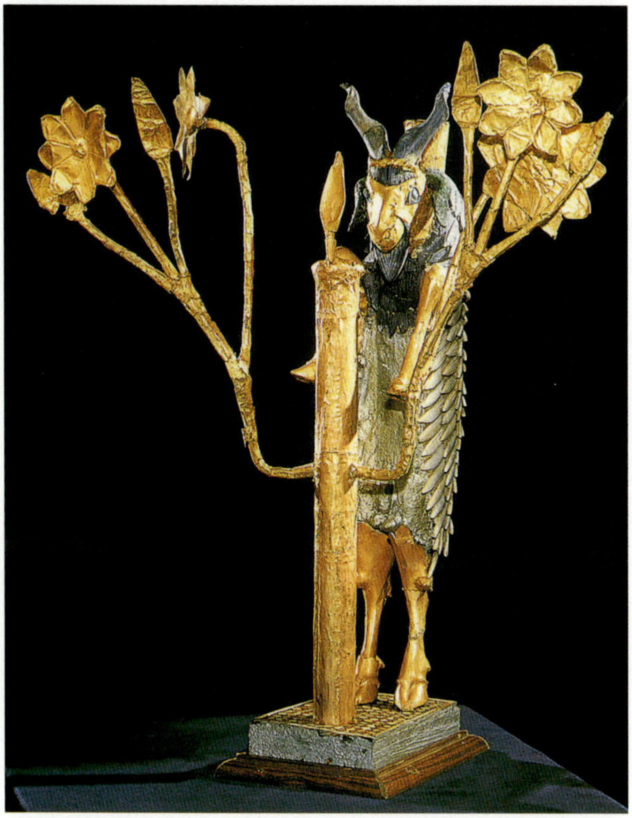

1.9 He-goat from Ur, c. 2600 B.C.E. Wood with gold and lapis lazuli overlay, 20 ins (50.8 cm) high. University Museum, University of Pennsylvania.

A DYNAMIC WORLD

Ancient China

One thousand years after Sumerian artists created the magnificent golden goat (see Fig. **1.9**), and the Hebrews were enslaved in Egypt (see p. 145), the ancient Chinese had mastered bronze casting. The ceremonial vessel shown here comes from the Shang Dynasty, c. 1400 B.C.E., and exhibits craftsmanship of magnificent quality. Each line has perfectly perpendicular sides and a flat bottom, meeting at a precise 90-degree angle, in contrast, for example, with incising, which forms a groove. The animal representation reveals a vision unlike that of Western culture but similar to that of Pacific northwest Native American design, in which the animal appears as if it had been skinned and laid out with the pelt divided on either side of the nose. A rigid bilateral balance results. Deftly placed ridges and gaps play against graceful curves, and, although the designs are delicate, the overall impression exhibits solidity and stability.

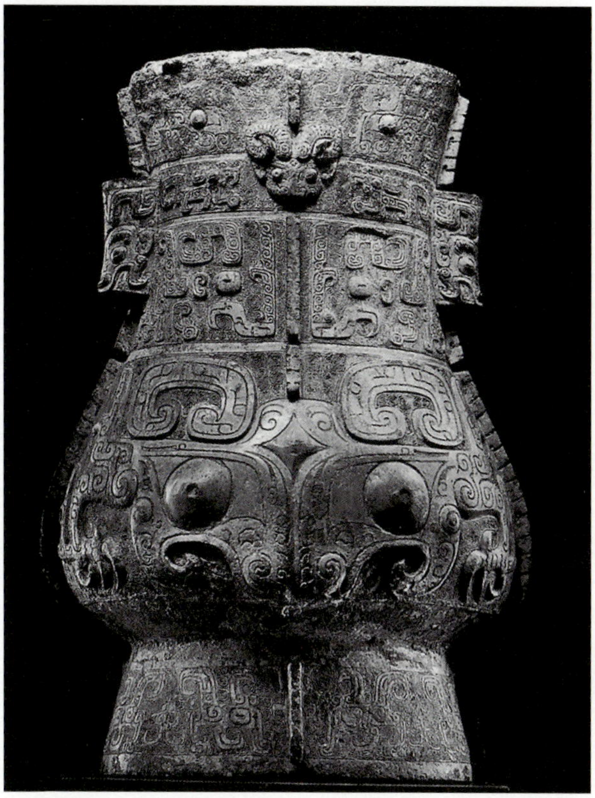

1.10 Shang Dynasty ritual wine vessel. Bronze, 16 × 11 ins (40.6 × 27.9 cm). The Nelson-Atkins Museum of Art, Kansas City, Missouri. (Purchase Nelson Trust.)

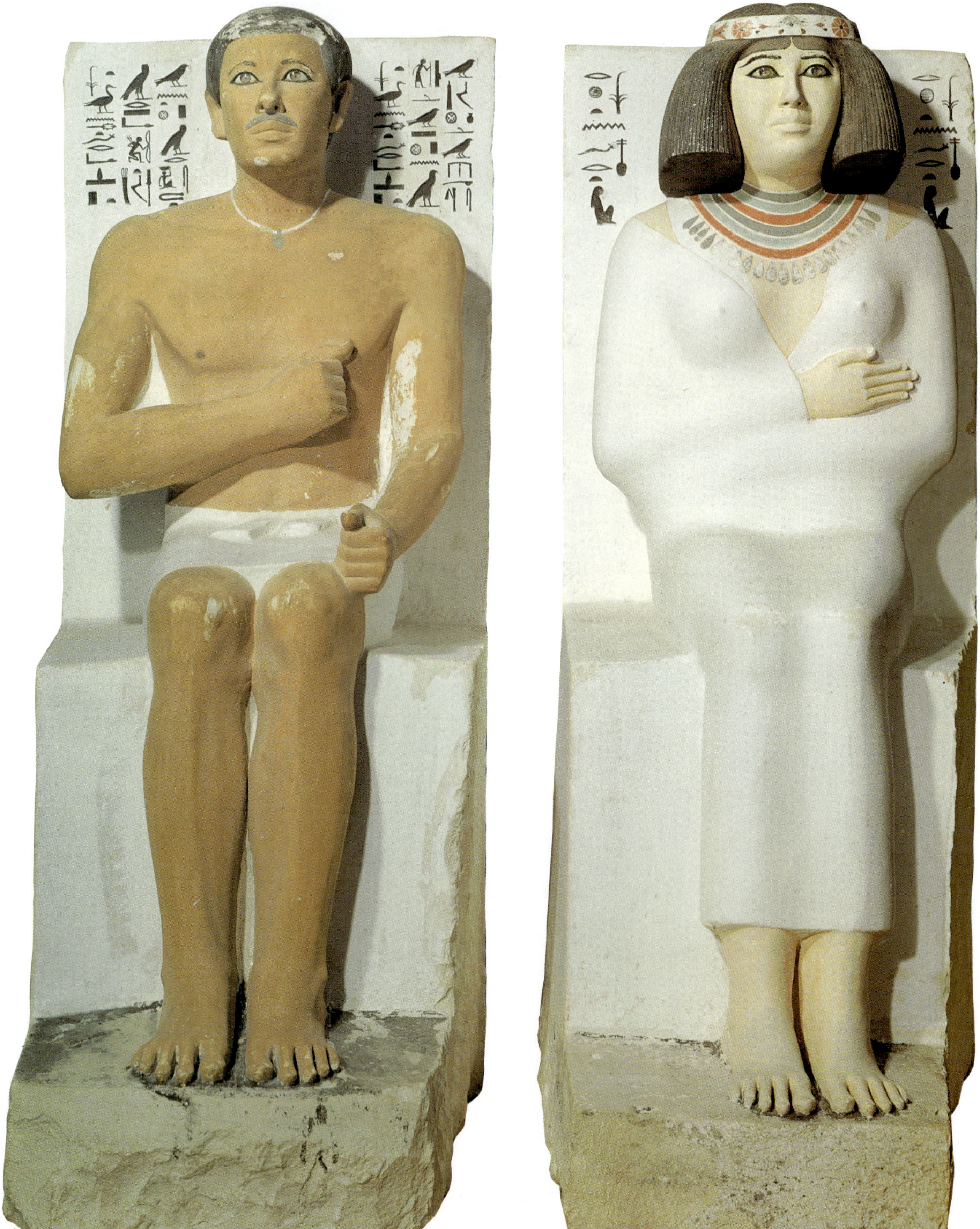

we glimpse an idea basic to Sumerian culture: the wisdom and perfection of divinity embodied in animal power. In this case, the goat is the earthly manifestation of the god Tammuz, and his superhuman character is crisply and elegantly conveyed. For additional examples, visit http://www.oi.uchicago.edu/OI/MUS/HIGH/OIM_A12332.html.

Sculpture was the major art form of the Egyptians. By 2700 B.C.E., sculptors had overcome many of the difficulties that plagued their predecessors. During those archaic times, religious tenets may have confounded sculptors, for many primitive peoples throughout history have regarded the lifelike portrayal of the human figure as dangerous. A close likeness of a person may have been thought capable of capturing the soul. There were also technical problems to be overcome. Early sculpture left detailing rough and simple. Sculptors seem to have relied on memory to portray the human form, rather than working from live models.

The sculpture of Prince Rahotep (RAH-hoh-tehp) and his wife Nofret (NOH-freht; Fig. **1.11**) has lifelike colors exemplifying the Egyptian tendency to use paint as a decorative surface for sculpture. The eyes of both figures consist of dull- and light-colored quartz. The eyelids are painted black. Both figures wear the costume of the time. As was customary, the skin tones of the woman are several shades lighter than those of the man. The kings of this time rose from peasant stock, an ancestry that is apparent in the sturdy, broad-shouldered, well-muscled physique of the prince. At the same time, his facial characteristics, particularly the eyes and expression, exhibit alertness, wisdom, strength, and capacity. The portrayal of Nofret expresses similar individuality.

The Egyptian admiration for the human body is clearly revealed in both statues. Precise modeling and attention to detail are evident in even the smallest items. Nofret's gown both covers and reveals the graceful contours of her body. Her facial features reveal an individual of less distinct character than her husband: she has a sensual and pampered face. She wears a wig shaped in the style of the day, but beneath the constricting headband we can see Nofret's much finer hair, parted in the center and swept back beneath the wig. The treatment of the hand held open against the body reveals not only the artist's skill and perceptiveness, but also the care and attention Nofret has bestowed on it. The hand is, indeed, delicate: small dimples decorate the fingers, and the nails exhibit extraordinary detail. The unpainted nails are correctly observed as being lighter than skin tone.

1.11 (*left*) Prince Rahotep and his wife Nofret from Maidum, c. 2580 B.C.E. Painted limestone, 3 ft 11½ ins (1.2 m) high. Egyptian Museum, Cairo.

Architecture

Pyramid building (c. 2700 B.C.E.) produced the most remarkable edifices of Egyptian civilization. Egypt's pyramids are the oldest existing buildings in the world. These ancient tombs are also among the world's largest structures. The largest stands taller than a forty-story building and covers an area greater than that of ten football fields. More than eighty pyramids still exist, and their once smooth limestone surfaces hide secret passageways and rooms. The pyramids of ancient Egypt served a vital purpose: to protect the pharaohs' bodies after death. Each pyramid originally held not only a pharaoh's preserved body but also all the goods he would need in his life after death.

Typical of Egyptian pyramids is a temple complex constructed a short distance from the pyramid and connected by a causeway. The most elaborate example of the temple complex is found at Giza, where the pyramids of Kings Khufu, Khafre, and Menkaura were built in close proximity to each other (Fig. **1.12**). Beginning in the tenth century C.E., the entire Giza complex served as a source of building materials for the construction of Cairo. The result was that all three pyramids were stripped of their original smooth outer facing of limestone.

The three pyramids at Giza have a carefully planned layout. Each is placed along the north–south meridian, with the faces of the pyramids pointing directly north, south, east, and west. The larger two are neatly placed along a southwest diagonal, with the third slightly offset and smaller. It is assumed that this peculiar layout was a deliberate choice made by the architects, but the reasons for such a choice (if one existed) remain mysterious. Perhaps they were part of a plan, not of individual pyramids, but a group symbolizing Orion's belt: a group of stars that the pyramids match precisely. The intensity of the stars is reflected directly in the size of the pyramids.

The largest pyramid, that of Khufu, or Cheops (KEE-ahps; Fig. **1.13**), measures approximately 750 feet square (70 meters square) and rises at an angle of approximately 51 degrees to a height of 481 feet (147 meters). The burial chamber of the king lay hidden in the middle of the pyramid (Fig. **1.14**). Construction consisted of irregularly placed, rough-hewn stone blocks covered by a carefully dressed limestone facing, approximately 17 feet (5 meters) thick. The pyramid of Cheops' son Chephren (Khafre) originally measured 707 feet square (65 meters

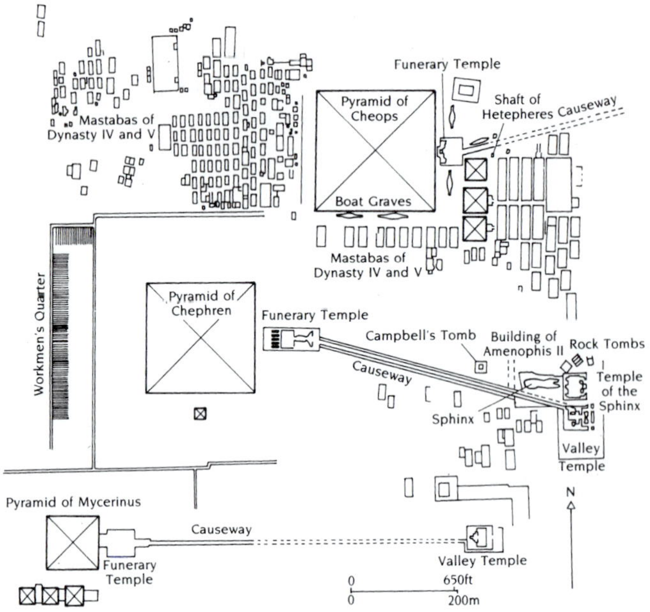

1.12 Plan of the Giza pyramid complex.

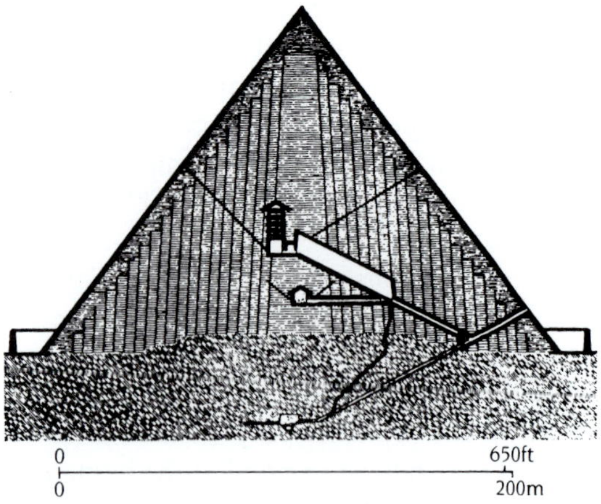

1.14 Longitudinal section, direction south–north, of the Great Pyramid of Cheops, Giza, Egypt, Dynasty IV (2680–2565 B.C.E.).

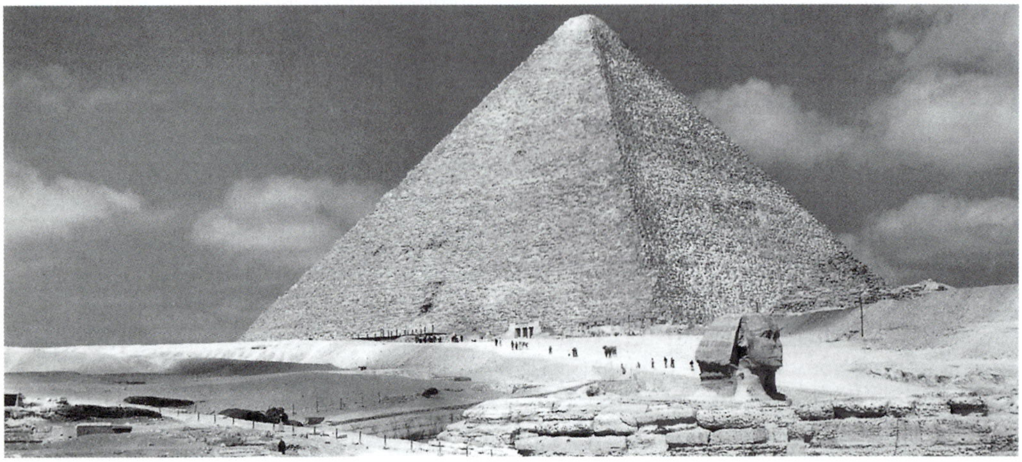

1.13 Great Pyramid of Cheops, Giza, Egypt, Dynasty IV (2680–2565 B.C.E.).

square), and rose, at an angle of 52 degrees, to a height of 471 feet (144 meters).

Music

The early Sumerians made music as an essential and lively part of their culture, and they had many musical instruments. Music fulfilled a variety of functions in Sumerian life. It seems to have been most popular as secular entertainment, but religious ceremonies also employed music. Solo performances, instrumental ensembles of single and mixed instruments, and solo and choral vocal music with instrumental accompaniment are all documented in surviving artifacts.

We can only speculate on what Sumerian music would have sounded like. Stringed instruments were predominant, while percussion and rhythm instruments seem to have been less popular, and the trumpet was mainly military in application. Thus, we may assume that Sumerian music favored lyrical, soft, restrained tones, rather than loud, brash ones.

The modern world is fairly well acquainted with Egyptian musical instruments: sculptures and paintings depict them, and fragments and even nearly complete instruments have been found. Harps, lyres, and numerous other stringed instruments, along with pipes, flutes, cymbals, and bells were all in the storechest of the Egyptian musician. As in Mesopotamia, the basic instrument in the Egyptian scheme was probably the harp. Harps varied tremendously in size, complexity, shape, and ornamentation (Fig. **1.15**). Harps are depicted with four, seven, and ten strings. Some are very plain, others ornate and brightly colored. How much of this variety is real and how much lies in the imagination of the painter, we do not know, but the frequent depiction of the harp does assure us of its popularity. Wall paintings also indicate that the larger harps, some of which appear to stand nearly six feet tall, were played essentially as modern harps are.

The tamboura (tuhm-BOO-ruh) of ancient Egypt had two basic shapes, one oval and the other with sides slightly incurved, like a modern violin or guitar. Illustrations show from two to four tuning pegs, and also indicate that the tamboura could be either with or without frets. Analysis of tambouras found with strings intact shows that the Egyptians used cat gut for stringing. Additional stringed instruments of innumerable shapes and sizes defy classification, but this variety certainly indicates that music held an important place among the arts of ancient Egypt.

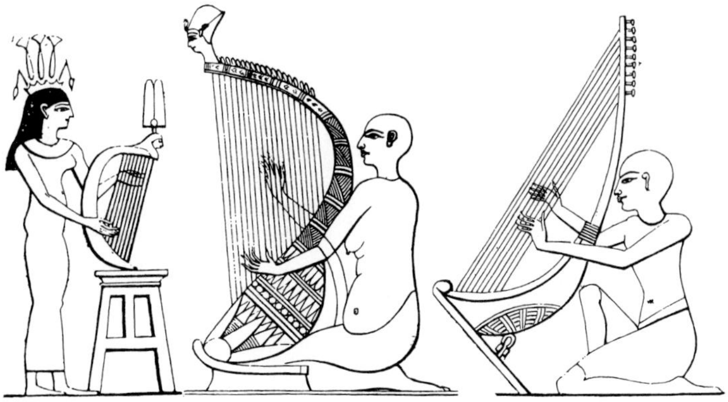

1.15 Egyptian harps.

Wind instruments were very varied in shape, size, and ornamentation. Small pipes made of reed with three, four, five, and more finger holes have been found in great quantity. Some of these appear to have been played by blowing directly across the opening at the end, and others seem to have required a reed, like the modern clarinet or oboe.

FOCAL POINT

Akhenaton and Monotheism: The Tell el Amarna Period

The reign of Akhenaton (ahk-ehn-AH-tuhn; c. 1385–1358 B.C.E.) marked a break in the continuity of artistic style. The stiff poses of earlier art disappeared, to be replaced temporarily by a more natural form of representation (Fig. **1.16**). The pharaoh, moreover, was depicted in intimate scenes of domestic life, rather than in the ritual or military acts that were traditional. He is no longer seen associating with the traditional gods of Egypt. Rather, he and his queen are depicted worshipping the disc of the sun (the sun god Aten), whose rays end in hands that bless the royal pair or hold to their nostrils the *ankh*, the symbol of life.

In the fifth or sixth year of his reign, Akhenaton moved his court to the city of Tell el Amarna (uhm-AHR-nuh), newly constructed in the sandy desert on the east bank of the Nile. It was a new city for a new king intent on establishing a new order based on a new religion. The new city, Akhetaten (today, Tell el Amarna), Akenaton believed was the birthplace of Aten and had not been corrupted by worship of other gods. Akhenaton failed, and Tell el Amarna, abandoned at his death, was never built over again because it lay away from cultivated land. It thus provides us with an unspoiled record of Akhenaton's social and cultural vision.

The town is dominated by the large estates of the wealthy. They chose the best sites and laid them out in the style of the Egyptian country house, with large gardens, numerous outbuildings, and a wall enclosing the entire establishment. Between these large estates lay the smaller dwellings of the less wealthy. The new city was

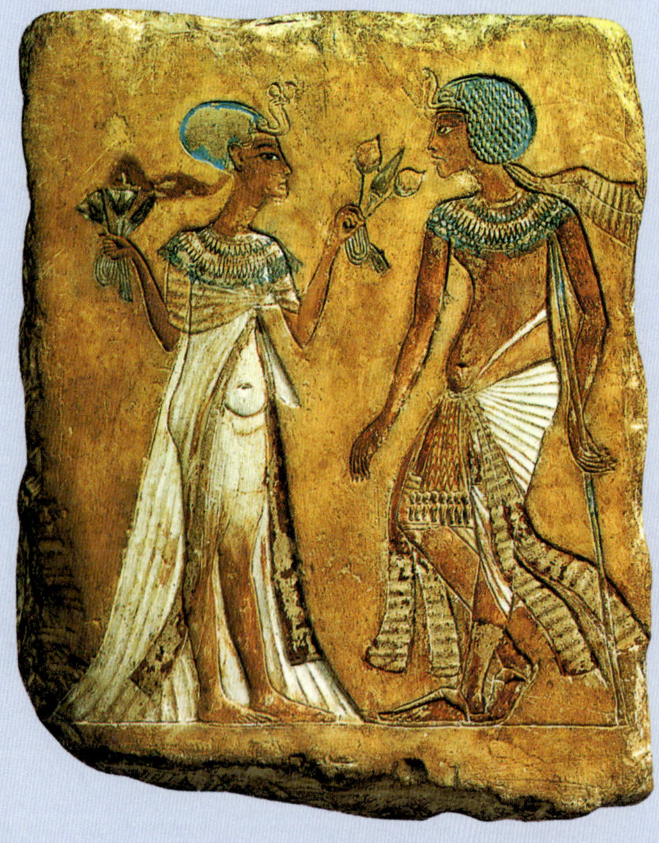

1.16 *King Smenkhkare and Meritaten*, Tell el Amarna, Egypt, c. 1360 B.C.E. Painted limestone relief, about 5 ft (1.53 m) high. Staatliche Museen, Berlin.

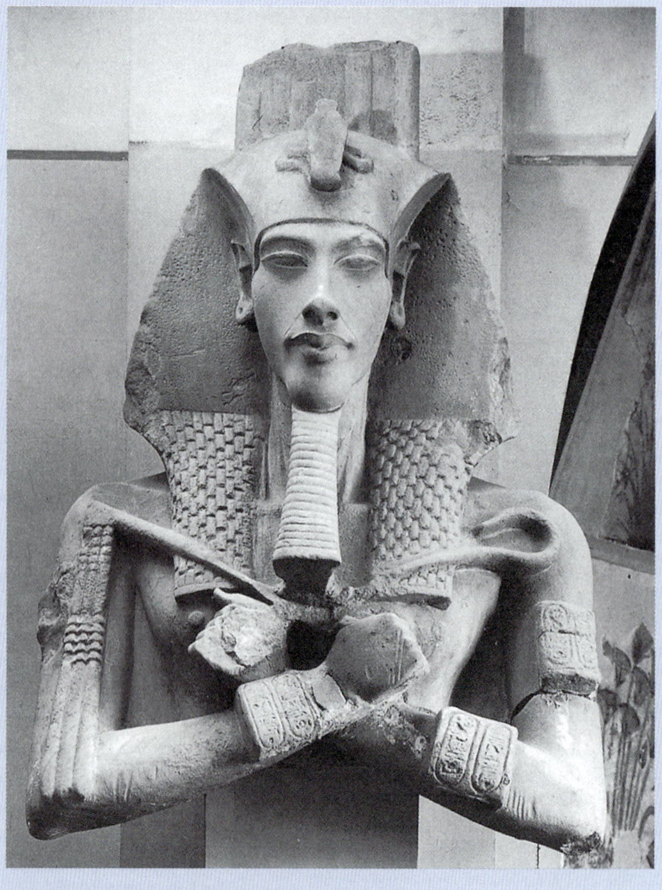

1.17 King Amenhotep IV, later Akhenaton, from a pillar statue in the temple of Aton near the temple of Amun at Karnak, 1364–1347 B.C.E. Sandstone, 13 ft (3.96 m) high, Egyptian Museum, Cairo.

PROFILE

Akhenaton and Nefertiti

Amenhotep IV, as Akhenaton was called before changing his name to reflect his god, was himself unusual. He possessed a "strange genius" for religious experience and its expression. He is shown as having a misshapen body, an elongated head, and a drooping jaw. Yet the eyes are deep and penetrating. The effect is one of brooding intensity.

In a hymn of praise to Aton, the sun god, thought to have been written by the king, Akhenaton exhibits a spirit of deep joy and devotion to the deity. In his lyrical description of the way the earth and humankind react to the rising and setting of the sun, we glimpse a man of sensitive character. His vision is universal: Aton is not merely a god of Egypt, but of all people, and Akhenaton himself is the sole mediator between the two.

Nefertiti (c. 1372–1350 B.C.E.; Fig. **1.18**) was Akhenaton's Great Royal Wife. Scholars debate whether she was a princess from another land or an Egyptian. Those believing her to be of Egyptian origin are themselves divided. One group claims she was the daughter of Aye and Tiy, and the other claims her as the oldest daughter of Amenhotep III and another wife besides Tiye, possibly Sitamun. Whatever her parentage, Nefertiti was married to Akhenaton and while living in Memphis gave birth to six daughters. It is possible that she also had sons, although no record has been found of this. It was a practice in Egyptian art not to portray the male heirs as children. Possibly, she may have been the mother of Tutankhamun, the boy pharaoh who succeeded to the throne at the age of eleven and died nine years later. Nefertiti achieved a prominence unknown to other Egyptian queens. Her name is enclosed in a royal *cartouche* (a frame for a hieroglyphic inscription formed by a rope design surrounding an oval space), and there are, in fact, more statues and drawings of her than of Akhenaton. Some have even claimed that it was Nefertiti, not Akhenaton, who instigated the monotheistic religion of Aton. Around year fifteen of Akhenaton's reign, Nefertiti mysteriously disappeared from view. Perhaps she died, but no indication of this can be found. Some scholars think that she was banished for some reason, and lived the rest of her years in the northern palace, raising Tutankhamun. Whatever may have happened, she was replaced by her oldest daughter, Meritaten, and disappeared from history.

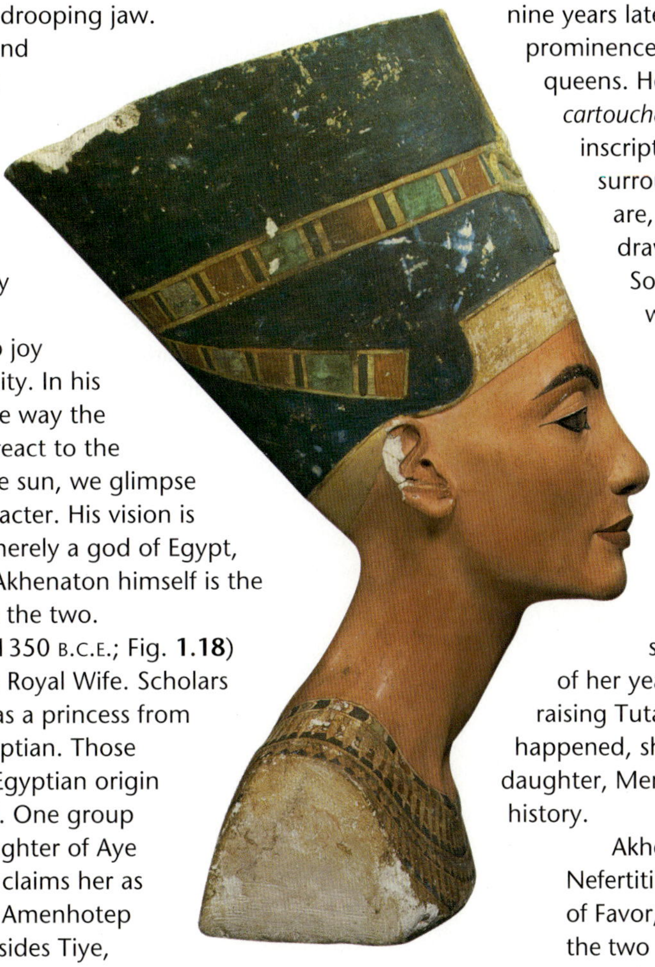

1.18 *Nefertiti*, from Akhetaten (modern Tell el Amarna), c. 1348–1336/5 B.C.E. Limestone, 20 ins (51 cm) high. Staatliche Museen, Berlin.

Akhenaton's own words describe Nefertiti: "The Hereditary Princess, Great of Favor, Mistress of Happiness, Gay with the two feathers, at hearing whose voice one rejoices, Soothing the heart of the king at home, pleased at all that is said, the Great and Beloved Wife of the King, Lady of the Two Lands, Neferu-aton Nefertiti, living forever."

complete, it seems, with a slum area outside the northern suburb. Near this area stood the grand North Palace.

In many ways, the architecture of Tell el Amarna reflects the common features of New Kingdom domestic architecture, although it is less sumptuous. Its lines and style seem relatively simple. Structures are open. At Amarna, numerous unroofed areas lead to the altar of the sun god, Aton, left open to provide access to his rays.

Sculpture at Tell el Amarna departs from tradition. It is more secular, with less apparent emphasis on statues and reliefs for tombs and temples. The Amarna sculptors seem to have sought to represent the uniqueness of human beings through their faces (see Fig. **1.18**). Amarna sculpture is highly lifelike, but it transcends the merely natural and enters the spiritual realm. The statue of Akhenaton shown in Figure **1.17** depicts the curious physical features of the king, and yet the stylization of the approach is also clear.

In the relief sculptures and wall paintings, the conventions of body proportions differ significantly from those of the other periods. In other periods, head and body proportions seem to be close to a ratio of 1:8. The total figure is thus nine head lengths from top to bottom. At Tell el Amarna, the total figure is seven to eight head lengths: in other words, the head is larger. Body proportions are also different. Arms are thinner and hands are larger. Abdominal and pelvic areas are emphasized in contrast to the focus on the shoulders and upper torso of earlier periods.

Many of the structural details of Amarna architecture are strikingly original. Plant motifs seem to have been favored, and palm-shaped columns are found in abundance. Also popular at Amarna were papyrus-bundle columns with **capitals** of clustered, open flowers, sometimes made of alabaster inlaid with blue paste. Most original are kiosk-like structures carved with convolvulus vines. The palace walls dazzled the eye with colored glazed tiles and painted stone reliefs. Indeed, the entire city must have shimmered in the sunlight of Akhenaton's single god.

Isolated from other periods by geographical and religious circumstance, the Tell el Amarna period encapsulates the artistic expressions of a single religious and philosophical concept. The religious reforms of Akhenaton were doomed to fail. Yet this Egyptian experiment in **monotheism** has left us with a vivid portrait of an integrated life-scheme.

CHAPTER REVIEW

❖ CRITICAL THOUGHT ❖

One of the critical challenges facing any culture is the manner in which it accommodates the viewpoints of those who dwell in it. By today's standards, the earliest "civilizations" were hardly more than counties on our political maps, but what distinguished them from other "civilizations" were what we might call their cultural ethos: that spirit of community that held them together as a people. Military conquest seems always to have been a major means of expanding that ethos beyond the immediate confines of the civilization, but once one people had conquered another, the question arose of how those who had been conquered were to be incorporated into the ethos of the ruling civilization. The question this raises, as we look back at the history of humankind's earliest civilization, is why do we find it so difficult to get along with people who are different from ourselves?

◆ SUMMARY ◆

Having read this chapter, you should be able to:

- Discuss the contention, and support your ideas with illustrations drawn from the art of the period, that earliest humans were "fully human," as we are.
- Identify the characteristics of Stone Age, Mesopotamian, and Egyptian art by recognizing defining artistic characteristics.
- Explain the linkages among politics, religion, and art in Mesopotamian and Egyptian societies.
- Analyze (describe) the works of art illustrated in this chapter using appropriate terms, such as line and form. For example, how does the statue of Queen Nofret employ line in comparison with the statues from Tell Asmar?

CYBERSOURCES

- **Mesopotamian art:** http://www.oi.uchicago.edu/OI/MUS/HIGH/OI_Museum_Mesopotamia.html
  http://www.louvre.fr/anglais/collec/ao/meso.htm
- **Egyptian Art:** http://www.powerup.com.au/~ancient/museum.htm
  http://www.louvre.fr/anglais/collec/ae/ae_oeuv.htm

2 ARCHAIC GREECE AND THE AEGEAN

OUTLINE

VIEW

RELIGION: TYING SOCIETY TOGETHER

In the previous chapter, as in the chapter to come (indeed in many of the chapters which follow), religion plays a central role in the cultures and arts we examine. It seems that in addition to creative impulses, we also find relationships among peoples in their search for communion with a power or powers higher than themselves. Greek culture was no exception and, in fact, much of its cultural ethos derived from its religion. Such an observation leads to one other, and that is the question, what does hold a society together? Can a society survive without some unifying characteristic with which most of its citizens can identify?

KEY TERMS

Some of the basic terms and concepts we will encounter in this chapter include the following:

POLIS
The basic Greek city-state, consisting of a collection of self-governing people.

ACROPOLIS
The "high city"—the elevated place in the center of the city occupied by the temples of the gods.

GEOMETRIC STYLE
A style of vase painting that made use of bold, simple, linear designs.

ARCHAIC STYLE
A style of two-dimensional and three-dimensional art. In two-dimensional art, it utilized a sense of three-dimensional space, whereas in sculpture, it consisted of figures that exhibit a stiff, frontal pose.

KOUROI
A term describing a freestanding statue of a nude male youth.

KORE
Describes a sculpture of a fully-dressed female—that is, the female counterpart of the kouroi.

DORIC ORDER
Refers to a style of architecture employing columns capped by heavy lintels and a pedimented roof.

2.1 Geometric amphora, c. 760 B.C.E. National Archeological Museum, Athens.

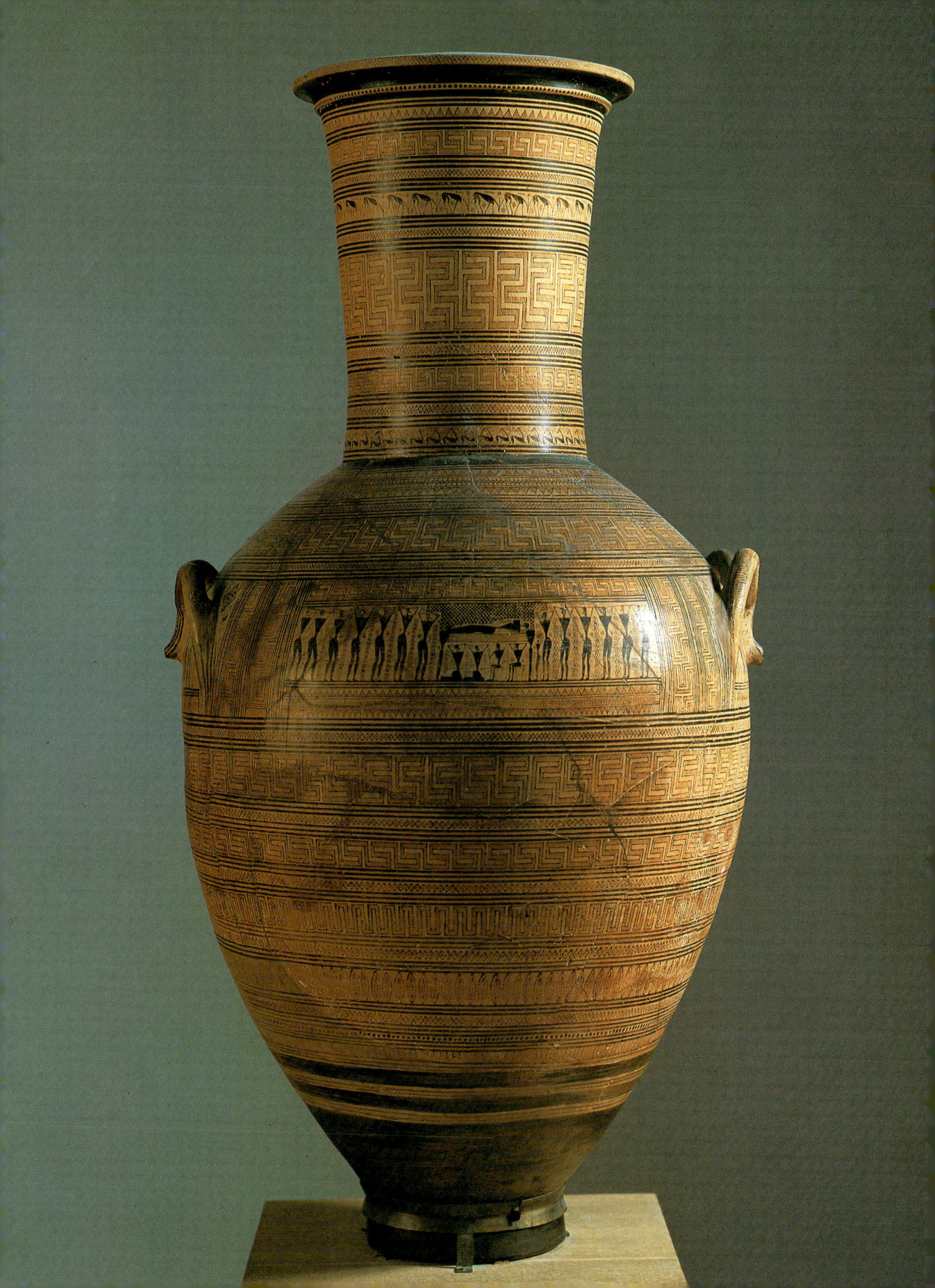

Helen of Troy

Few stories carry the emotion of that of Helen of Troy and the Trojan War. According to Greek legend, Helen (Helene) was the most beautiful woman in Greece and the indirect cause of the Trojan War. She was the daughter of Zeus (zoos), and wife of Menelaus (mehn-eh-LAY-uhs). During an absence of Menelaus, however, Helen fled to Troy with Paris, son of the Trojan king Priam. In vivid form, the vase painter Makron puts feeling into form as he depicts the story (Fig. **2.2**). When Paris was killed, Helen married his brother, whom she betrayed to Menelaus when Troy was subsequently captured. Menelaus and she then returned to Sparta, where they lived happily until their deaths.

According to one variant of the story, Helen, in widowhood, was driven out by her stepsons and fled to Rhodes, whose queen, Polyxo (pah-LIK-so), hanged her in revenge for the loss of her husband in the Trojan War. Another poetic version has Helen and Paris driven ashore on the coast of Egypt with Helen detained there by King Proteus. The Helen carried on to Troy was thus a phantom, and the real one was recovered by her husband from Egypt after the war. This version of the story was used by Euripides (yoo-RIH-pih-deez) in his play *Helen*.

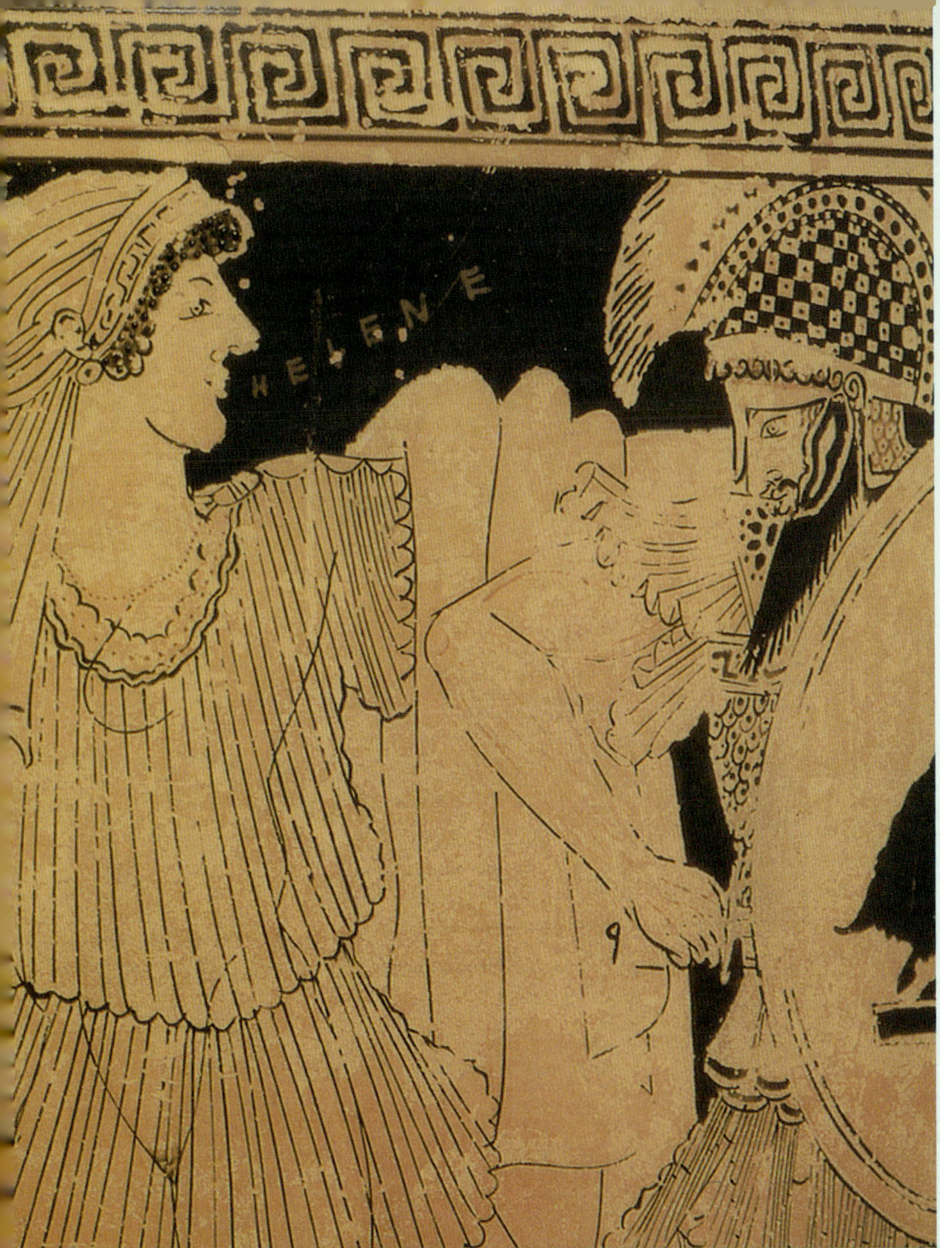

HOW ART WORKS

THE PURPOSES OF ART II:
Giving Form to Feeling

Throughout its history, another purpose of art (in addition to providing a record, as we noted in this space in Chapter 1) has been to give form to feelings. One, explicit, modern example of this purpose is the expressionist style of the early twentieth century (see p. 515), in which artists purposely strove to transmit their feelings and emotions about the content of their work to the viewer or listener. However, even when the attempt to transmit feelings may not be so primary, feelings are transmitted, and we often find ourselves discussing "how it makes us feel" when we hear a piece of music, watch a drama, or see a painting. Sometimes these feelings are deeply visceral. At other times they are more intellectual. Among the myriad choices artists have in putting together their works, is the choice of whether the form or the feeling is predominant or whether they balance each other. When form is so obvious, as in the geometric designs of the vases we study in this chapter, we might think that feeling is absent, but that is not so. Some feeling is always present in an artwork, however de-emphasized it may be.

2.2 Skyphos by Hieron, painted by Makron, showing the seduction of Helen, 500–480 B.C.E. (detail). 8½ ins (21.5 cm) high. Museum of Fine Arts, Boston (Francis Bartlett Donation).

CONTEXTS AND CONCEPTS

We leave the cradle of civilization in the Middle East and turn northeastward to the Aegean Sea (Map **2.1**). Here the roots of Western civilization took hold. Undoubtedly, Egypt and Mesopotamia had an effect on the emerging culture of the region—the Greeks of the classical period noted this, and the latest holders of Mesopotamian power, the Persians, conquered parts of the Grecian world, including Athens—but before there were "Greeks," there were others in the region.

Minoans and Mycenaeans

Around 3000 B.C.E., while sizable cities were being built in Mesopotamia, small towns on the island of Crete began to expand into large urban centers. The Minoan (mih-NOH-uhn) civilization, named after the legendary King Minos (MY-nuhs), emerged at this time, and by 1800 B.C.E. a great palace had arisen in the city of Knossos (NAHS-uhs) on Crete. Not much is known about the Minoans, but we can tell from the ruins of their palaces and their wall paintings that they were rich and adventurous. They depended on their naval power for defense, and their palaces, which were not fortified, were elaborate complexes, with the private homes of the aristocracy and religious leaders clustered around them. These palaces had running water and elaborate drainage systems, and, below ground, storage areas contained large earthenware pots of grains, oil, and wine. They also had systems for cooling during the summer and heating in winter. Through trading posts around the Aegean, Minoan Crete carried on a lively and rewarding commerce as far away as Egypt, exporting pottery, bronze, olive oil, and timber.

Many well-preserved archeological sites allow us to deduce a certain amount of information about the Minoan lifestyle and culture, even though their writing has yet to be fully deciphered. Wall paintings, executed in brilliant colors and displaying spontaneity and a deep love of nature, reveal portraits of royalty and scenes of nature. They reflect a flighty court life with high-born, bare-breasted ladies, bedecked in jewels, and strolling in lovely gardens. Sportive youths frolic and raise golden goblets of wine. Life was lavish in the labyrinthine palaces of Knossos, with their complex rooms and passageways. There were bureaucrats in abundance, but few soldiers, and Minoan civilization clearly had trade, not militarism or politics, at its center.

GENERAL EVENTS

- Minoan civilization, c. 3000–1500 B.C.E.
- Mycenaean traders in the Aegean, 1400–1200 B.C.E.
- Destruction of Troy, c. 1260 B.C.E.
- Greek "Middle Ages," 1200–800 B.C.E.
- Archaic period, 800–480 B.C.E.
- First Olympic games, 776 B.C.E.
- Persian Empire, 600–330 B.C.E.
- Persian War, 490–479 B.C.E.

	3000 B.C.E. – 1500 B.C.E.	1500 B.C.E. – 1250 B.C.E.	1250 B.C.E. – 750 B.C.E.	750 B.C.E. – 500 B.C.E.	500 B.C.E. – 350 B.C.E.
PAINTING & SCULPTURE			*Boar Hunt* (**2.4**), Lion Gate, Mycenae (**2.5**)	Dipylon Vase (**2.9**), Kouroi (**2.12, 2.13**), Korai (**2.14, 2.15**)	Macron, Skyphos (**2.2**), Wrestlers (**2.7**), The Pan Painter, red figure krater (**2.8**), Perseus bowl (**2.10**), *Kritios Boy* (**2.16**)
ARCHITECTURE		Palace of Minos, Knossos (**2.3**)		Doric Order (**2.18**), Temple at Paestum (**2.19**)	
MUSIC & DANCE				Choric dance festivals, First tragic competitions, Development of modes	
LITERATURE & PHILOSOPHY	Pictorial writing		Homer (*Iliad, Odyssey*), Hesiod (*Works and Days*)	Sappho of Lesbos, Pythagoras	

Timeline 2.1 Archaic Greece and the Aegean.

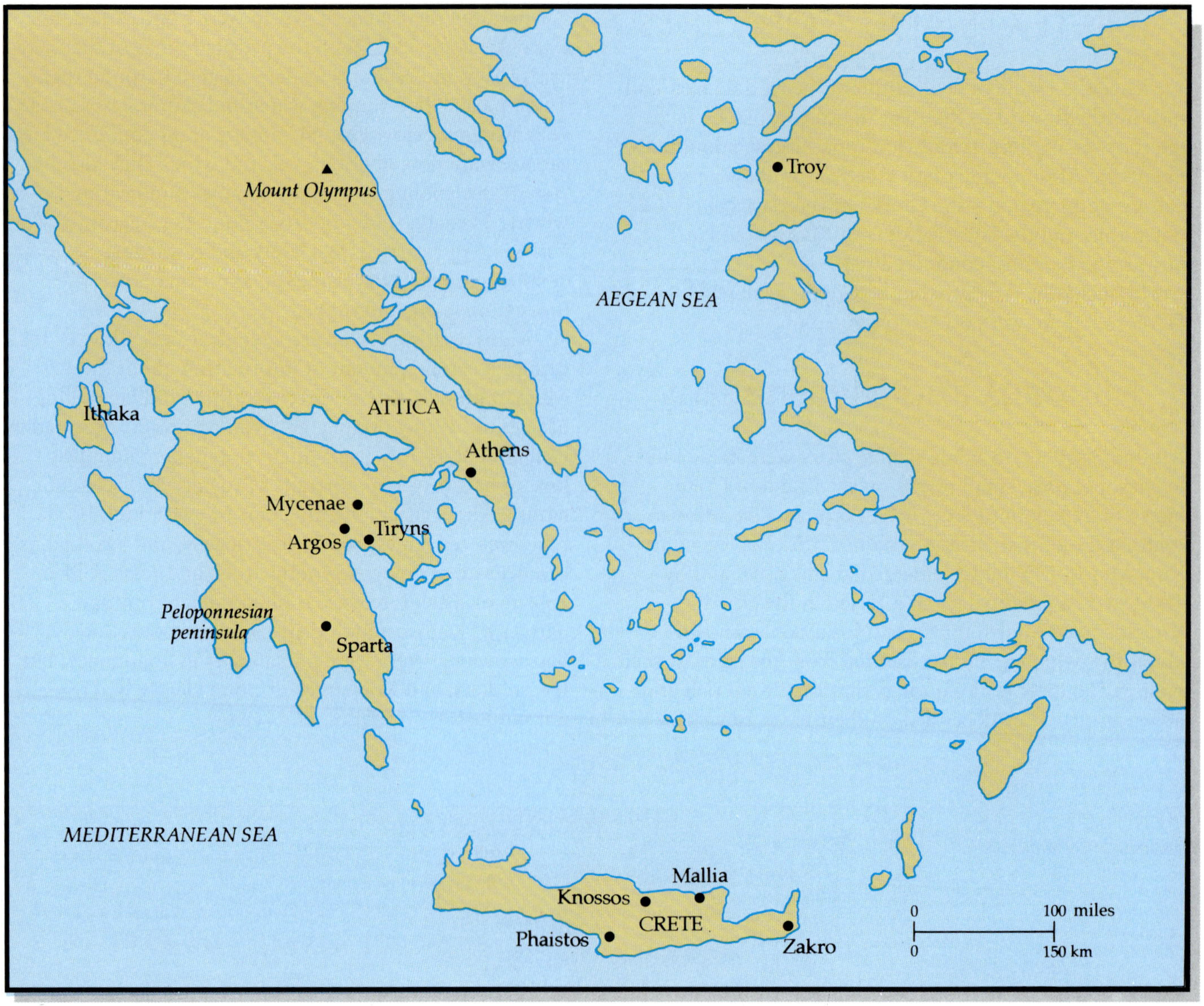

Map 2.1 The Aegean.

The Minoans were a wealthy, secure, and matriarchal civilization. If the so-called Palace of Minos (Fig. 2.3) is representative, they not only enjoyed comfort, but were also capable of sophisticated elegance in decor and design. The palace had so many rooms that it was remembered in Greek myth as the "labyrinth of the Minotaur (MIHN-oh-tohr)." The walls were built of masonry and decorated with murals and geometric motifs. Rectangular and circular **columns**, employed as supports, took the form of tapering wooden **shafts**, perhaps reflecting their origin as unworked treetrunks, with heavy, geometric capitals. The total impression is one of openness and lightness, combined with luxury and attention to detail.

The religion had a variety of gods, goddesses, and myths. Early versions of Athena—who later emerged as the patron goddess of Athens—first appeared here. The Minoans also had a cult of the sacred bull, which was celebrated by terrifying "bull dancing" or "bull leaping," a rite performed by naked young men and women on the backs and over the horns of the bulls. This was probably the origin of the Minotaur of Greek legend.

Minoan culture, however, experienced a short-lived glory. By 1500 B.C.E., the Minoans had been swept into darkness, perhaps by a series of earthquakes and volcanic eruptions or perhaps merely through conquest by their neighbors. However, their influence was felt on a later civilization that also emerged in the Aegean, that of the Mycenaeans (my-SEEN-ee-uhns).

The Mycenaeans were early, barbaric, Indo-European conquerors who settled the rugged southeastern coastline of mainland Greece and who, by the fourteenth century

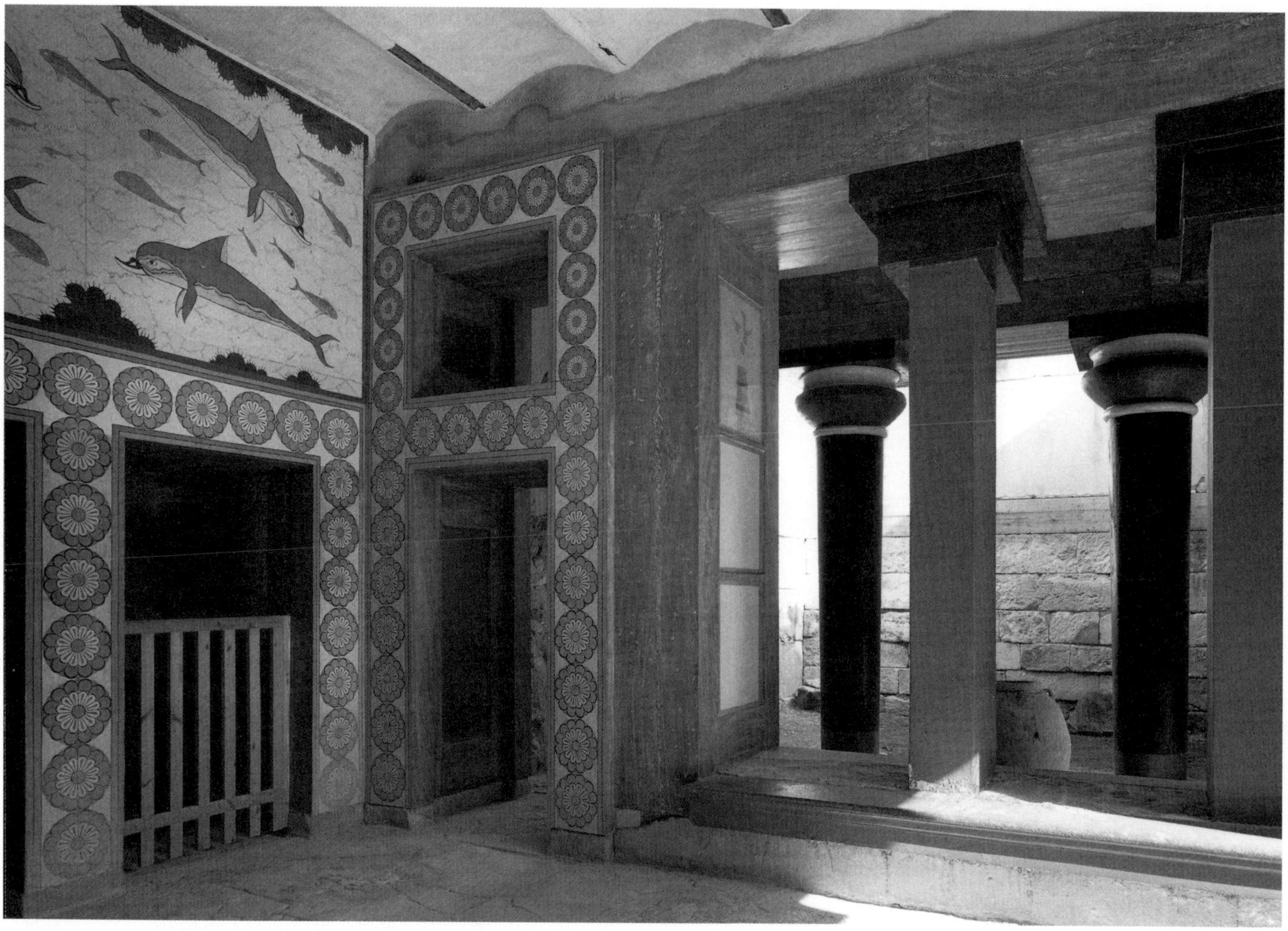

2.3 Queen's chamber, Palace of Minos at Knossos, Crete, c. 1500 B.C.E.

B.C.E., had supplanted the Minoans as rulers of Crete. Homer called them "tamers of horses," because they fought from chariots, and they left the lands they conquered in ruins. Unlike the Minoans, of whom the later Greeks were unaware, the Mycenaeans, through Homer, provided Greece with myths, legends, and heroes such as the mighty Achilles (uh-KIL-lees) in the *Iliad* (IHL-ee-uhd) and the wandering Odysseus (oh-DIHS-ee-uhs) in the *Odyssey* (AHD-ih-see). The Greeks also found in this people a source of ethics and moral order, and Homer's epics give a glimpse of a social organization in which the *oikos* (household domain) was the center of economic and social power.

Although conquest seems to have been their main occupation, the Mycenaeans did engage in some trade, their traders traveling throughout the Mediterranean between 1400 and 1200 B.C.E. Above all, however, they were warriors, and their rule was maintained by the strength of their military. It was their soldiers and armada of ships that reportedly conquered the legendary Troy and gave Homer the basis for his epic the *Iliad*.

A variety of local deities and household gods and goddesses, some of which appear also to have been predecessors of Greek deities, were worshipped in caves and at natural shrines. Religious practice included burying the dead with honor, and, like the Egyptians, the Mycenaeans mummified corpses and buried them with precious objects.

The walls of Mycenaean palaces bear decorative paintings, which also represent the activities of the time. The *Boar Hunt* (Fig. **2.4**) shows a group of dogs, hunting as a pack and attacking their prey. That the hounds are domesticated is evident from their collars, which appear to be tied around the neck. The hand and what looks like the lance of the hunter at the extreme right of the fragment indicate that the dogs have chased the boar into the vicinity of the hunters. This painting is clearly a testament not only to a successful hunt, but also to the dog breeder, whose well-trained dogs carry out their owner's commands.

The most powerful city of Mycenae boasted a great palace complex and great wealth. The palaces of the

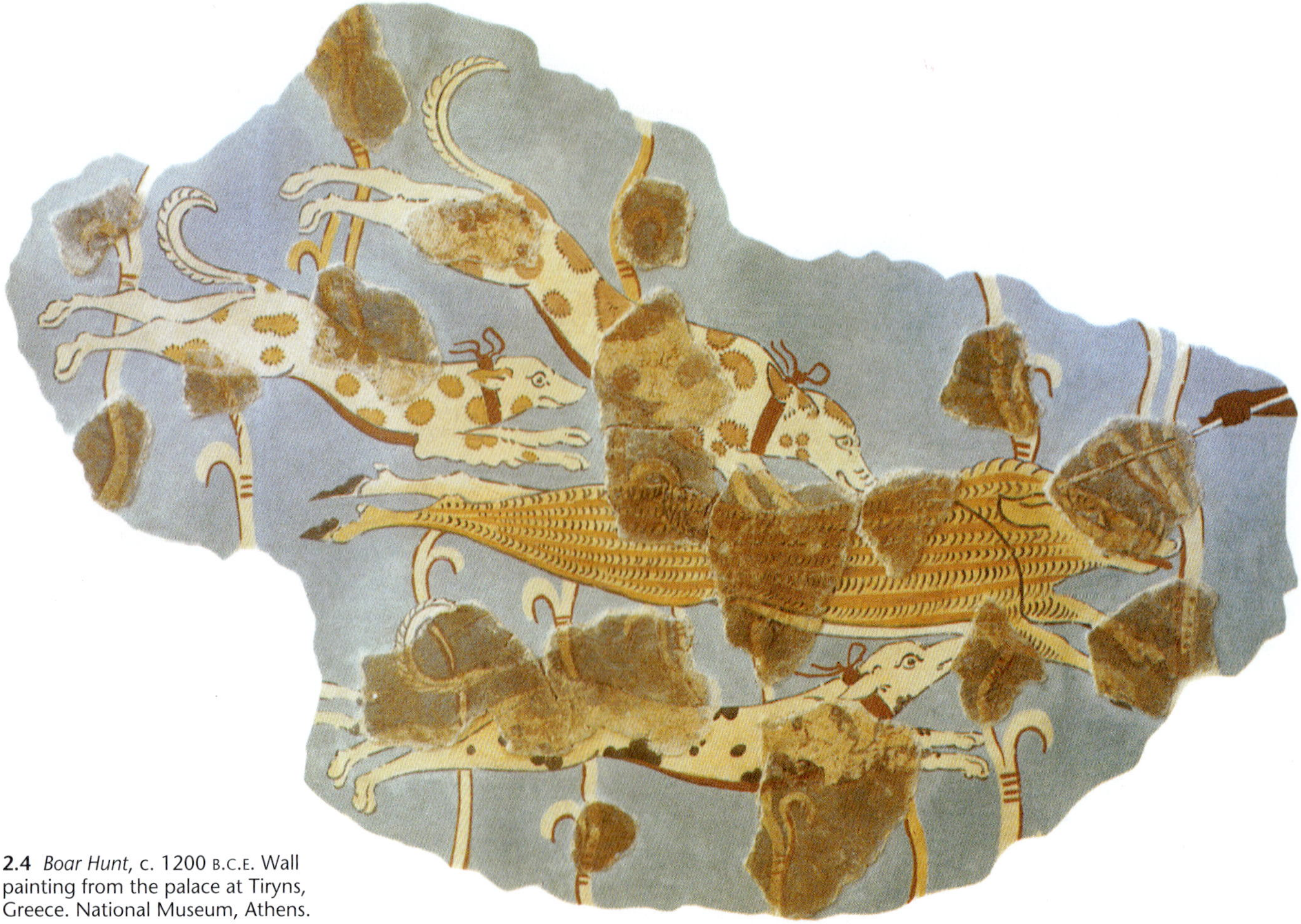

2.4 *Boar Hunt*, c. 1200 B.C.E. Wall painting from the palace at Tiryns, Greece. National Museum, Athens.

Mycenaeans were very different from those of the Minoans, for they were fortresses constructed of large, rough stone blocks placed at the center of a settlement on top of the highest hill. The individual boulders were so huge that the Greeks who viewed them centuries later called them "Cyclopean," believing that only cyclopses—mythological giants with one eye in the center of their foreheads—could have moved them.

The Lion Gate at the Palace of Mycenae (Fig. **2.5**) demonstrates the powerful effect of juxtaposing smoothly carved elements with the massive blocks of stone. In an alcove on top of the lintel, two lions, obviously intended as guardians, flank a tapering column similar to those found in Minoan palaces. The careful carving of the animals' musculature expresses strength, and it contrasts with the rough stone masonry, creating a slightly uncomfortable effect, which is reinforced by the cramped nature of the composition within the alcove. Yet, despite any crudity in the design, the execution is remarkably skillful, and the jointure of the stone is tight.

In spite of its great defenses and massively fortified palaces, the Mycenaean civilization collapsed shortly after 1200 B.C.E.

Between the time of the Mycenaean civilization, with its art and palaces, and that of the Greek city-states of the eighth century B.C.E., lies a historical vacuum of four centuries. Historians call this time the "Greek Middle Ages" or the "dark centuries," and it was during this period that wave upon wave of Indo-European peoples filtered into the area and spread throughout Asia Minor. The building of palaces ceased and what little artistic activity existed—for example, pottery—was crude. Although the Mycenaeans had writing, the skill seems to have vanished during this time. Life switched from fortified cities to isolated farming communities, and trade and commerce among communities isolated by the mountainous terrain was minimal if it had not ceased altogether.

Nonetheless, life was not static nor all dark. During this time, iron replaced bronze for tools and weapons, significant changes occurred in burial practices, the political hierarchy shifted from kings to powerful families, and new peoples drifted into the valleys, to neighboring islands, and to the shores of Asia Minor. Toward the end of the eighth century B.C.E., gatherings of Greeks listened rapturously to the epic poems of Homer

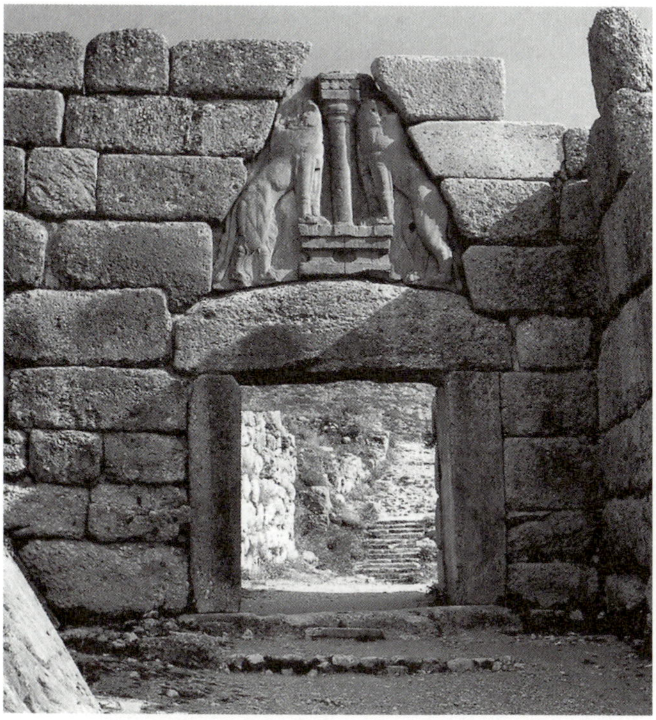

2.5 The Lion Gate, Mycenae, Greece, c. 1250 B.C.E.

and Hesiod, looking back on the heroes of Mycenae. And indeed, they did look backward, because it seemed that all glory lay in the past, with little to look forward to.

The Hellenes

There was a unifying spirit among the people of this region—they saw themselves as "Hellenes (heh-LEENZ)." All the different peoples of the area—for example, the Ionians, Dorians, and Aculians—had a common language, which, although old, had only recently developed a written form. The earliest surviving Greek written characters are found on a jug dating from 725 B.C.E. These characters appear to be adapted from Phoenician script, one example of the many outside influences, especially Middle Eastern, that helped to shape Greek culture.

The Hellenes used a common calendar, which dated from the first Olympic games in 776 B.C.E. These games embodied much more than a mere sporting event—they represented life's struggles ("athletics" is a Greek word, meaning contest or struggle), and they symbolized the joy that can be found in toil and cost. They were a time when Greeks could meet in a non-lethal context that recognized their larger cultural, linguistic, and religious identity. The contests were undertaken for the honor of competing, and victory was regarded as a sufficient prize. But although the victors gained nothing more than a simple wreath of wild olive leaves, the citizens of a victorious athlete's polis often complemented the simple prize with more lucrative ones, such as free meals for life. Only men and boys could compete in the five-day festival of the Olympic games, held every four years, at Olympia. They competed in the nude—married women were forbidden even to attend the games—and the principal event was a

TECHNOLOGY

The Olive Press

Often, one of the interesting things about the record of history is not its claims, but the fact that particular individuals are recorded as having invented particular pieces of technology, and the Greeks had a great regard for technological innovation. The status of the technician in Greece was raised high—much more so than in neighboring Asiatic countries—and an interest in technology was respectable, with inventors being regarded as benefactors.

As Greek civilization spread through the Aegean and Mediterranean during the archaic age, trade became increasingly important. One of the few products that Greece, with its mountainous terrain and poor soil, could produce in sufficient abundance to export was olive oil, which, together with wine and pottery, became their principal export. Manufacturing oil in quantity required technological advances in the presses by which olive oil is produced. Initially, the oil was extracted in a simple beam press illustrated in relief sculpture and vase paintings, but later, pulleys and screws worked the beam to press the oil (Fig. **2.6**).

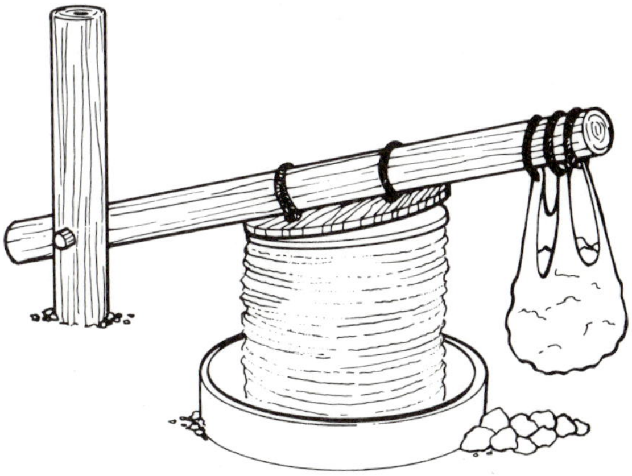

2.6 Reconstruction of an early beam press.

foot race to honor Zeus (ZOOS), king of the gods (see the discussion on religion on p. 61). Later, boxing, wrestling (Fig. **2.7**), other field sports, and chariot racing were added. The first day of the Olympic festival witnessed peripheral events, such as poetry readings and art exhibitions, and the third day was reserved for solemn religious sacrifices at the altar of Zeus.

The Polis

The Greek **city-states** that developed at the beginning of what is called the archaic period (800–480 B.C.E.) were already well established and functioning by the time recorded history began, but we do know, at least, that they did not all spring up simultaneously. Each city, or polis (POH-lis; plural poleis), consisted of a collection of self-governing people. The Greeks referred to cities by the collective name of their citizens—thus, for example, Athens was "the Athenians." Each polis was surrounded by a group of villages and a rural territory, and each was self-governing, functioning as an independent state. No central, unifying government drew these cities together, and each polis developed its own ethos—that is, a sense of self. Some, such as Athens, emerged as relatively peaceful, with a high esteem for the arts and philosophy. Others, such as Sparta, were militaristic and seemingly indifferent to high culture.

All the cities formed their social orders on distinct class structures: some people were free and others were slaves. Among free males there existed a clear demarcation between those who were citizens and those who were not: only citizens could participate in political decision-making, own land, or serve in wars. But access to citizenship could alter according to the city's circumstances at a given time.

Physically, the polis was formed of two cities: a lower city, in which the people lived, and a high city, or *acropolis* (uh-KRAHP-oh-lis), an elevated place in the center of the city occupied by the temples of the gods. (This practice was little different from the ways in which towns developed in the Middle Ages, when the cathedral was built on the highest elevation in the center of a city to symbolize the centrality and elevation of the Christian Church.) The citizens of the Greek polis owned the city, including the acropolis, and the pantheon of gods was more often a focus of civic pride than of reverence.

Originally, the typical polis had an organization similar to the tribal structure brought down from the north by the invaders, whose tribes were governed by an aristocracy or council of leading families. Typically, the leading landowners were part of such an aristocracy, and, occasionally, a polis might have a "king," like that of the ancient Minoans or Mycenaeans. Power in the polis actually belonged, however, to the landowners and tribal leaders, and the concept of a king gradually faded away, and was replaced by a group of elected magistrates. In the seventh and sixth centuries B.C.E., the aristocracy went into decline, giving rise to a new degree of freedom. The rise of trade and the increasing wealth of the merchant class siphoned power from the landowners.

As the polis developed, land, money, and military service became important qualifications for political power. Farmers, merchants, and craftsmen who could afford to buy weapons—each member of the army was self-armed—demanded inclusion in political decision-making. Often, *tyrants*—that is, spokesmen for the citizenry and quasi-rulers—arose from the ranks of the military. The word "tyrant" here does not have the negative connotations usually associated with it today.

By the end of the sixth century B.C.E., these unique Greek poleis were scattered throughout the Aegean and

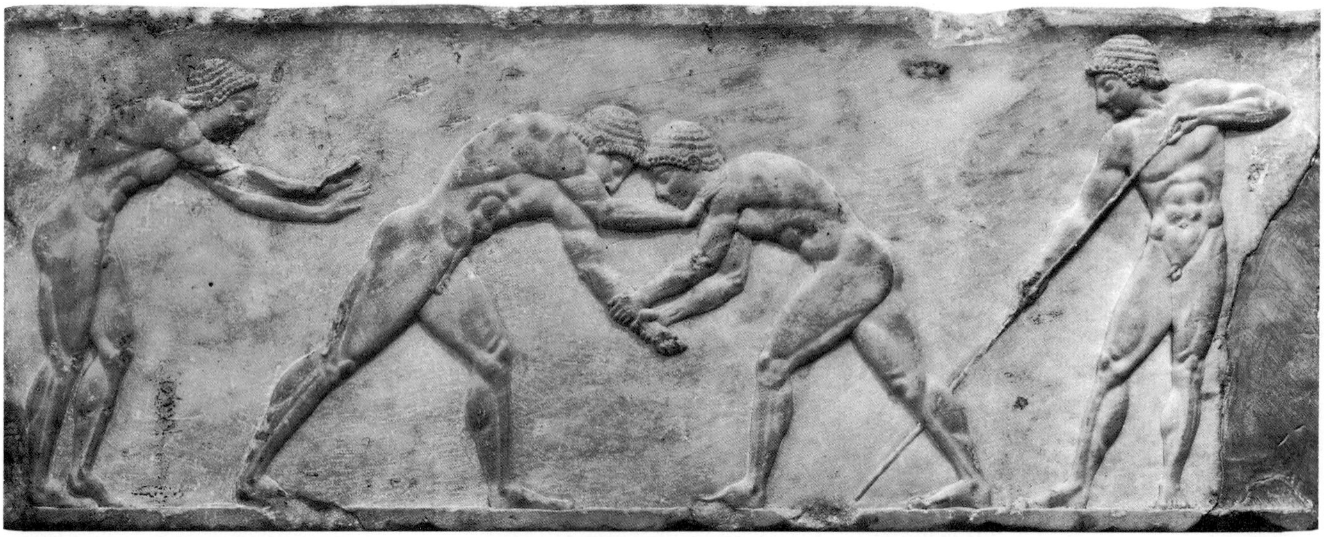

2.7 Wrestlers, from a statue base, c. 500 B.C.E. Marble, 12¼ ins (31.8 cm) high. National Archeological Museum, Athens.

Mediterranean area. Although they did not match the cities of Egypt, Mesopotamia, or even Crete or Mycenae in wealth and splendor, they contained thriving populations living in simple houses who, as a group, built impressive temples, theatres, and stadiums.

We look back on the Greek poleis and call them "democracies," seeing them as the forebears of our own "democratic" form of government. They were, of course, far from democratic in the modern sense of the word, for only native-born, free, adult males of a specific economic standing were citizens, and so had any voice in government. Nevertheless, the polis was a democracy in that the rule lay in the hands of the many and not in the hands of a few or, as in the monarchies of ancient Egypt and Mesopotamia, in the hands of a god king.

The Olympian Gods

The Greek mind was an earthy one, and Greek thought and religion centered on this life, rather than on the one to come. Ancient Greeks may often have looked for meaning in the order of the stars, but there, as on earth, the human mind was "the measure of all things."

At the core of Greek religion was a large family of superhuman gods. Their history in myth had been traced by the poet Homer in the *Iliad*. Greek religion had no holy books or scriptures. The stories of the gods were well known, however, through oral tradition and through writings such as Hesiod's *Theogony* (thee-AHG-oh-nee). These gods were called "Olympian" because they dwelt on the mythical (and also real) Mount Olympus. All were descended from a pair of older gods: Uranus (you-RAYN-uhs), representing the heavens, and Gaia (GAY-uh), representing the earth. But their genealogies were the subjects of so many varied myths that, although central to Greek religion, they are confusing, and, to some degree, confused. In addition to the central family of gods, the Greeks worshipped local deities who were thought to preside over certain human activities and to protect various specific geographical features such as streams and forests.

The Greeks represented their gods in human terms, sometimes superior to humans, sometimes worse than us. This is a radical departure from, for example, the gods of Assyria and Babylonia, and the implication is clear: if the gods can be like humans, humans can also be godlike. Thus, an intimacy existed between the gods and their human companions, and life on earth for the Greeks was similar to that of the gods.

Homer had elaborated many of the often bizarre relationships of the gods in the Olympic pantheon, and some of the gods took shape from earlier religions of the Minoans and Mycenaeans, which may account for what often are confusing traits and characteristics.

In the Greek pantheon, Zeus, the sky god, functioned as the king of the gods on Mount Olympus. He hurled thunderbolts and presided over councils of gods. Endowed with a rapacious sexual appetite, Zeus sired both gods and mortals. Hera (HIH-ruh), Zeus' wife—and also his sister—functioned as the patron of women, who appealed to her for help. In legend, she also spent a good deal of time trying to keep an eye on her philandering husband. Zeus' two brothers, Poseidon (poh-SY-duhn) and Hades (HAY-deez), ruled the rest of the universe: Poseidon ruled the seas, waters, and earthquakes; while Hades ruled the underworld and land of the dead. Zeus had twin children, Apollo and Artemis (ART-uhm-ihs), who symbolized the sun and the moon, respectively. Apollo represented the intellect and reason, while Artemis was patroness of childbirth and wild creatures (Fig. **2.8**).

Zeus' other children included Athena, goddess of wisdom and patron of the city of Athens. She sprang, fully developed, from the head of Zeus, and was worshipped as a virgin goddess. Ares was the god of war, who engaged in an incestuous and adulterous liaison with his half-sister Aphrodite, goddess of love and beauty, who was married to another of Zeus' sons, Hephaestus (hih-FEHS-tuhs), the god of craftsmen. According to legend, Hephaestus was both ugly and lame. Another son of Zeus, Hermes (HUHR-meez), served as the gods' messenger and patron of merchants and thieves. Zeus' sister Hestia (HEHS-tee-uh) protected the hearth in the Greek home.

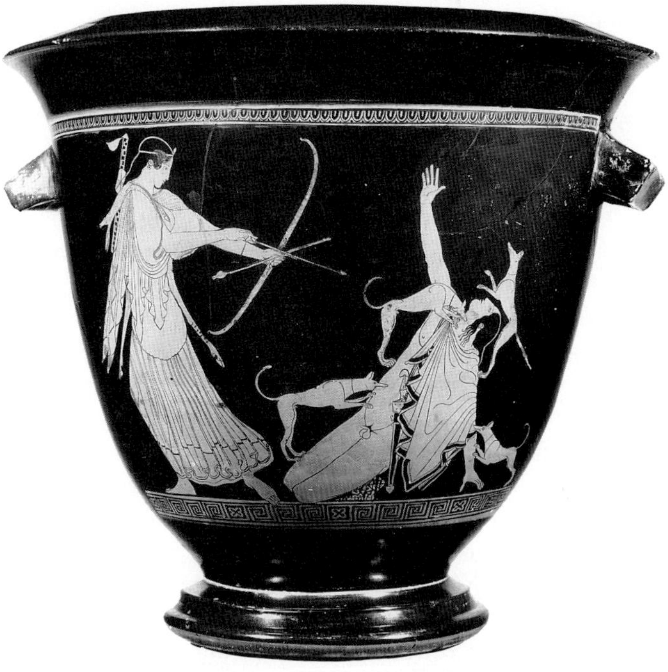

2.8 The Pan Painter, Attic red-figure krater showing Artemis shooting Actaeon, c. 470 B.C.E. 16¾ ins (42.5 cm) high. Museum of Fine Arts, Boston.

Two other important deities headed large cults. Demeter (dih-MEE-tuhr), sister of Zeus, was goddess of the harvest, whose power made the earth fertile and crops grow. Initiates from all over Greece traveled to Eleusis, a small village in Attica, to worship her in quiet dignity and to join her cult with its promise of immortality. In contrast, Dionysus (dih-ohn-EE-suhs) was the god of wine and reveling, and his devotees participated wildly in search of rejuvenation and rebirth. His annual ceremonies in Athens gave birth to the festivals of drama we will study in the next chapter.

The Love of Wisdom

The age of great Greek philosophers was yet to come, but during the archaic period the groundwork was laid for rationalism and intellectual acuity that would blossom in the fifth century B.C.E. The word philosophy means "love of wisdom," and its practice developed into searches for the meaning and significance of the human condition. In the archaic period, philosophy first turned away from its roots in religion and began to apply reason to the discovery of the origins of the universe and the place of human beings in it.

In deference to the great philosopher of the Greek classical age yet to come, succeeding generations have called the philosophers of the archaic period the *pre-Socratics*, a term that does not refer to any specific philosophic system, of which there were several during the archaic period. Undoubtedly, the best-known and, arguably, the most important was the system of philosophy developed by Pythagoras (pih-THAG-uh-ruhs) and called *Pythagoreanism*. In his search for truth, Pythagoras concluded that mathematical relationships were universal—that is, that there were universal constants that applied throughout life. For example, his deduction of what we call the Pythagorean theorem postulates that the square of the hypotenuse of a right-angled triangle equals the sum of the squares of the other two sides. We see this as a mathematical given, but Pythagoras rationalized that this mathematical truth revealed the larger, universal truth about the cosmos: that the universe has a single reality existing apart from substance. He called this the "harmony of spheres." He further believed that all living things were related. Beyond his philosophical contributions, his mathematical inquiries deduced the numerical relationships among musical harmonies, his research in this area forming the basis of contemporary musical practice that divides a musical scale into an **octave** or eight tones.

Another important school of pre-Socratic philosophy was that of the *atomists*. Led by Leucippus (loo-SIH-puhs) and Democritus (de-MAHK-rit-uhs; c. 460 B.C.E.), this system believed that the universe is an ultimate and unchangeable reality based on atoms—that is, small "indivisible" and invisible particles. A second quality of the universe was "the void" or nothingness. Of course, we recognize both the term and the definition of "atom" as a part of the twentieth-century physical science of quantum mechanics.

Other pre-Socratic schools included the *materialists*, headed by Thales (THAY-leez) of Miletus (c. 585 B.C.E.), who believed that water was the primary element underlying the changing world of nature. A century later, another materialist, Empedocles (ehm-PEHD-oh-klees) of Acragas (c. 495 B.C.E.) postulated that the elements of nature consisted of fire, earth, air, and water. Combined (love) and separated (war and strife), they accounted for the progress of creatures and of civilizations.

THE ARTS OF ARCHAIC GREECE

Vase Painting

Geometric Style

The term "vase" is somewhat misleading. Unlike modern fine-art ceramics, which are objects intended to convey beauty and comment on reality, the pots of Greece in this time were designed to serve exclusively utilitarian purposes. They were cups, jugs, and vessels for storing and carrying water, wine, and oil. Vase painting was thus, at best, a minor art form among the Greeks.

Nevertheless these vessels do provide some insights into their time. By the eighth century B.C.E., vase painting progressed to a **geometric** phase. Figures **2.1** and **2.9** show geometric **amphorae** in which the design utilizes linearity, using zigzags, diamonds, and the meander or maze pattern. The vessels themselves are more intricate in shape and larger in size. Some examples are nearly six feet (1.8 meters) high—so large, in fact, that they had to be constructed in sections.

Virtually every space on the vase is filled. The decoration is composed in horizontal bands called *registers*. When it appears, the human form is depicted in **silhouette**, with the head, legs, and feet in profile while the torso faces forward. In general, geometric vase design expresses absolute **symmetry**.

Archaic Style

Figure representation remained two-dimensional until the middle of the sixth century B.C.E. Depiction was restricted to full profile, or a full-frontal torso attached to legs in profile. The head, shown in profile, contained a full-frontal eye. Fabric was stiff and conventionalized. But by 500 B.C.E., artists were attempting to portray the body in a three-quarter position, between profile and full frontal.

MASTERWORK

THE DIPYLON VASE

The Dipylon (DIHP-ih-lahn) Vase (Fig. **2.9**), from the eighth century B.C.E., was found in the Dipylon Cemetery in Athens. This pot and others like it served as grave monuments. Holes in the bottom allowed liquid offerings to filter down into the grave.

The vase in Figure **2.9** shows the body of the deceased lying on a funeral bier, surrounded by mourners. Also depicted on the vase is a funeral procession with warriors on foot and in chariots drawn by horses. Every human and animal figure in this complex design suggests a geometric shape harmonizing with the other elements on the vase. Although recognizable and narrative in purpose, the figures appear as just another type of ornamentation within the larger context of the overall design. They follow the convention of portraying the torso frontally while the head and legs are in profile; turning the head to the rear would denote a figure in motion.

One of the amazing features of this vase is the amount and intricacy of detail that occupies every inch of its surface. Another important point is the organization of that detail into carefully balanced horizontal bands, each displaying a different geometric pattern. With only a few shapes, the artist has created a tremendously detailed painting with a subtle and sophisticated balance and focus. The dark, wide bands on the base and at the bottom of the bowl ground the design and help the viewer to focus on the story of the dead person. The patterns at the top and bottom of the vase are completely different, and yet they seem harmonious. Also notable is the balanced juxtaposition of straight lines and curves: the snake-like design and circles sit quite naturally alongside rectangles and triangles. Characteristic of its style, it fills every field with decoration and divides the surface into thirds with avoidance of overlapping.

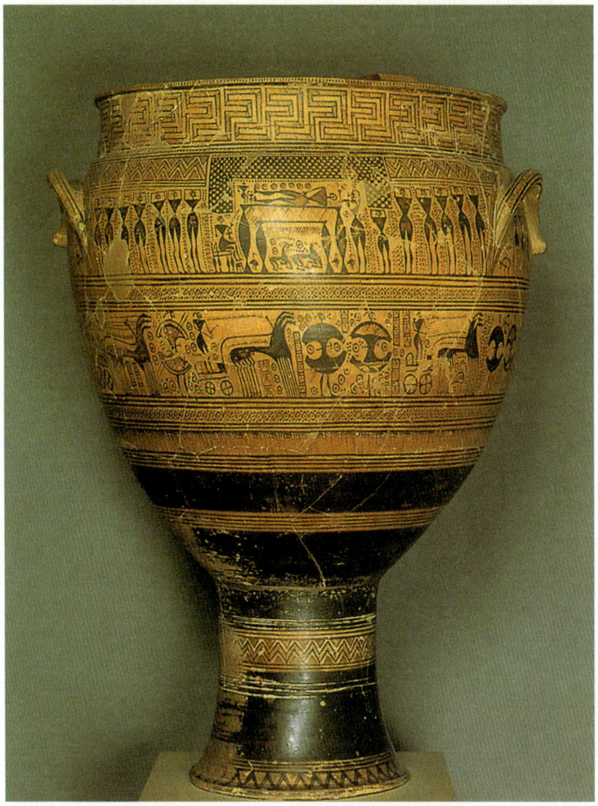

2.9 Dipylon Vase, Attic geometric amphora, eighth century B.C.E. 3 ft 6⅝ ins (1.08 m) high. Metropolitan Museum of Art, New York (Rogers Fund, 1914).

At the same time, a new feeling for three-dimensional space developed, and artists began to depict eyes more accurately. Fabric began to assume the drape and folds of real cloth. All these characteristics mark vase painting of the sixth century B.C.E., and they typify the various stages of the archaic style.

Individual vase painters' styles differed greatly from each other. We know some of these artists from their signatures. Others have been assigned names based on the subject or the location of their work. The Gorgon (GOHRG-uhn) Painter (Fig. **2.10**) was named after the Gorgons that decorate his work. In this example of the sixth-century style, the design is arranged in graduated registers, with an intricate and lovely geometric design as a focus on the middle band.

Red- and Black-Figure Pottery

Athenian pottery of this period can be divided into two types—black-figure and red-figure. In black-figure vases, the design appears in black against the light red clay background. Details are incised, and white and dark colors are added (http.//www.louvre.fr/img/photos/collec/ager/ grande/e0635.jpg). White tends to be used for women's flesh and for old men's beards. Red is used for hair, horses' manes, and for parts of garments (see Fig. **2.10**).

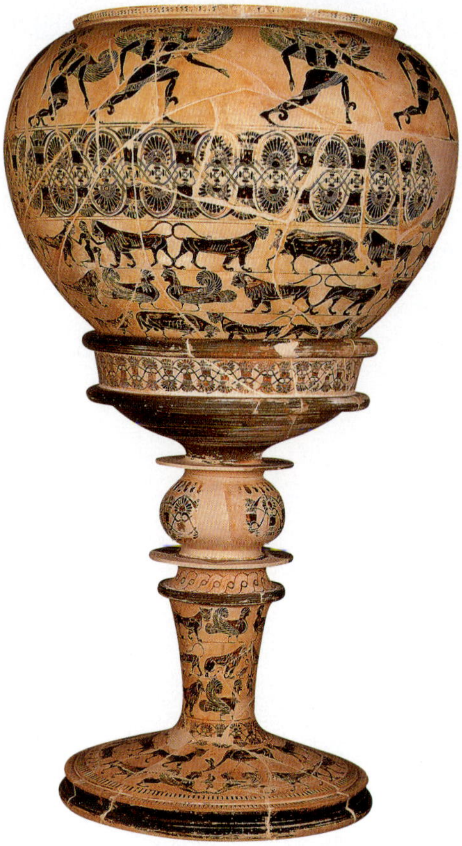

2.10 Attic bowl showing Perseus and the Gorgons, early sixth century B.C.E. 36½ ins (93 cm) high. Louvre, Paris. © Photo RHM (Hervé Lewandowski).

Red-figure work, which first appears around 530 B.C.E., reverses the basic scheme, with the figures appearing in the natural red clay against a glazed black background (see Fig. **2.2**). Contours and other internal lines appear in glaze and often stand out in slight relief (http://www.louvre.fr/img/photos/collec/ager/grande/g0103.jpg). In early red-figure work, incision is occasionally used for the contours of the hair, with touches of white and red. Other techniques that appeared in the fifth and fourth centuries B.C.E. include the use of **palmettes** and other motifs impressed in the clay and covered with black glaze. The firing process for both types was the same.

Painters discovered that figures were more lifelike when they appeared in the natural red color of the terracotta, with the background filled in in black. At first, the change from black-figure to red-figure was tentative. Some vases appeared with red-figure work on one side and black-figure on the other. Red-figure pottery continued through the classical and late classical periods (Chapter 3) and beyond.

Sculpture

Stone and metal are more durable than pottery, and sculpture often surpasses all other art forms in its survival of the centuries. However, Greek sculpture does not exist in great quantity, and it is unfortunately more than likely that some of the greatest examples have been lost to humanity forever.

Most of the freestanding statues in the archaic style are of nude youths, and are known as kouroi (KOO-roy). The term means, simply, "male youth," and the singular form is **kouros** (KOO-rohs). More than a hundred examples have survived. All exhibit a stiff, fully frontal pose. The head is raised, eyes are fixed to the front, and arms hang straight down at the sides, with the fists clenched. The emphasis of these statues is on physicality. The shoulders are broad, the pectoral muscles well developed, and the waist narrow. The legs show the musculature of a finely tuned athlete with solid buttocks and hardened calves. Nevertheless, these figures are clearly not lifelike. The sculptor seems overconscious of the block of stone from which the figures have been cut. Features are simplified, and the posture, despite the movement of one foot into the forward plane, is rigid. In spite of these limitations, however, these works represent a sculptural innovation. They are the first examples of truly freestanding stone sculpture. By freeing the statue of any support, the artist is able to represent the human form independently of any non-living matter. This accomplishment prepares the way for later, more successful representations of living beings.

Most of the kouroi were sculpted as funerary and temple art. Many of them were signed by the artist: "So-and-so made me." Whether the statues were intended to represent humans or gods—they are most definitely not portraits of individuals—is debatable. The fact that all are nudes is perhaps a celebration of the physical perfection of youth and of the marvelous nature of the human body. The kouroi may also represent, more directly, the naked athletes who took part in the games loved by the Greeks. The Greeks explained the practice of competing in the nude by telling the story of a runner who dropped his loincloth and, thus unimpeded, won the race. Other more symbolic explanations of the nudity of these statues have been offered, but no one view has prevailed (http://harpy.ucs.edu/greek/archaicsculpt.html).

Two significant characteristics are exemplified by the kouros from around 600 B.C.E. shown in Figure **2.12**. First is the fact that although there is an obvious attempt by the sculptor to depict the human figure in a fairly lifelike manner, the figure does not represent a particular person. Rather, it is a stereotype, or a symbol, and an idealization, perhaps of heroism. The sculpture, however, lacks

A DYNAMIC WORLD

NATIVE AMERICA

We recognize the approach to human figures illustrated in the Greek sculptures of this chapter. Native American artists, however, developed a different set of conventions as Figure **2.11** illustrates. Among the many tribes of Native Americans, there is no specific word equivalent for the term "art." In Native American culture, art is anything that is technically well done. The "artist" is simply someone who is better at a job than someone else. Only a few tribes had a group of professionals who earned a living producing what we would call art.

The earliest identifiable art in Mexico comes from the Olmec people—called the "rubber people"—and can be dated to the same period we are studying in this chapter, approximately 1000 B.C.E.

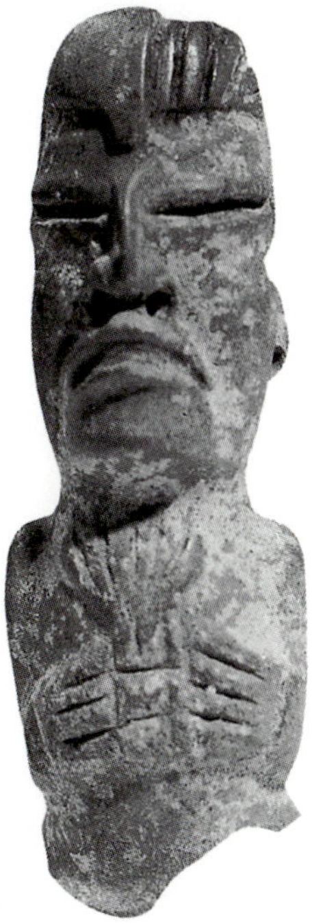

2.11 Fragment of carved stone figurine; Olmec-style head with trace of red paint inlay. Xochipala, Guerrero, Mexico, 1250–750 B.C.E. 3 × 1 ins (7.6 × 2.5 cm). National Museum of the American Indian, Smithsonian Institution.

These people carved a number of subjects—for example, the delicate, baby-faced figure shown in Figure **2.11**. This finely carved figurine has a noticeably turned-down mouth, a facial feature that is a common characteristic of Olmec sculpture of this period. Even though much of the body is missing, we can see that the carefully carved details on the green-gray stone effigy make a powerful statement.

refinement, and this is a characteristic that helps to differentiate the archaic from the classical style.

The second characteristic is the attempt to indicate movement. Even though the sculpture is firmly rooted, the left foot extends forward. This creates a greater sense of motion than if both feet were side by side in the same plane, yet the weight of the body remains equally divided between the two feet.

The striking similarity of form and style among the kouroi can be seen when we compare Figure **2.12** with the statue in Figure **2.13**. The same physical emphases, the same frontality and the same slight departure from the horizontal plane, with the left feet forward, occur. The stylized treatment of the hair is nearly identical. In both statues the kneecaps are curiously overarticulated. Nevertheless, the kouroi differ in proportion and in facial details.

The kouros had a female counterpart in the *kore* (KOH-ray, plural korai, meaning "maidens"). These figures are always fully dressed, and in other ways, too, the kourai show far more variety than the kouroi. Some of these differences may stem from variations in regional dress, but clearly the sculptor's interest lies in the treatment of that dress, in the technical mastery required for an accurate depiction of cloth in stone.

Figure **2.14** shows a typical kore. In this delicate and refined portrayal, the sculptor shows a lightness of touch and delicacy, not only in the anatomical features, but also in the precise folds of the robes, finely detailed jewelry, and stylized hair. These elements combine to give the statue a greater degree of lifelikeness than the kouroi we have examined.

In comparison with Figure **2.14**, the kore shown in Figure **2.15** lacks detail, but it thereby achieves cleaner, more graceful, lines. Although anatomical details are disguised by the heavy fabric, the body, with the waist emphasized, is convincingly present beneath the robes. The kore's smile exhibits more personality than the blank stare of many archaic statues, and the extension of the left arm forward into space indicates a new interest in movement outside the main block of the statue.

By the early fifth century B.C.E. the stiffness of the archaic style had begun to modify. The human form began to be portrayed with subtlety and to display movement. The transition began with the *Kritios Boy* (KRIHT-ee-ohs; Fig. **2.16**), named for its presumed sculptor. Here is a statue in which the body truly stands at rest while the head gently turns to one side rather than being fixed frontally. The artist has discovered the principle of weight shift—that is, the way in which the body parts position themselves around the flexible axis of the spine. The *Kritios Boy* is the first known portrayal of this important principle, and in it we can discern the beginnings of the classical style.

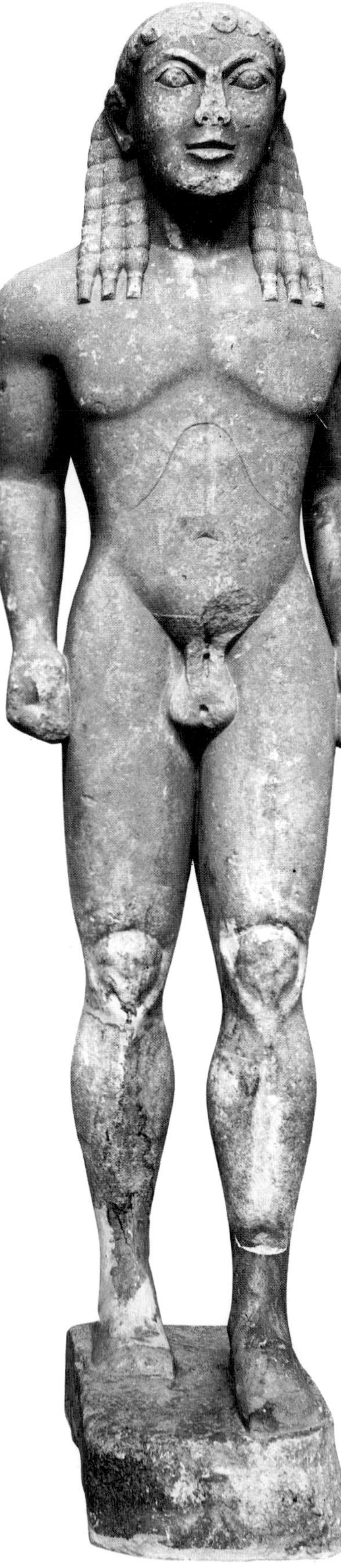

2.12 (*left*) Polymedes of Argos, Kouros, c. 600 B.C.E. Stone, 6 ft 5½ ins (1.97 cm) high. Archeological Museum, Delphi, Greece.

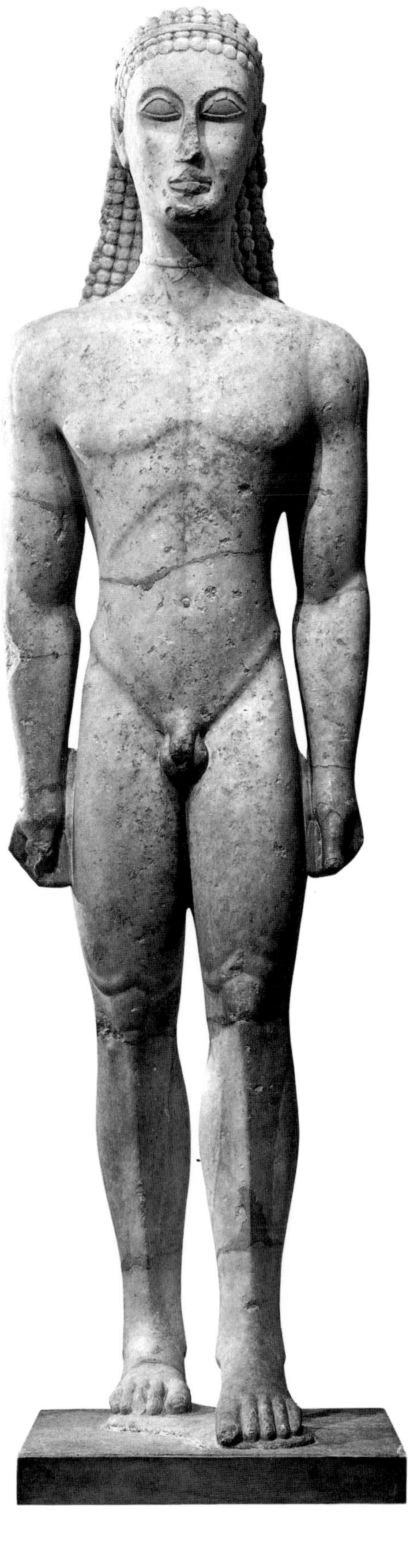

2.13 (*right*) Kouros, c. 615 B.C.E. Marble, 6 ft 4 ins (1.93 m) high. Metropolitan Museum of Art (Fletcher Fund, 1932).

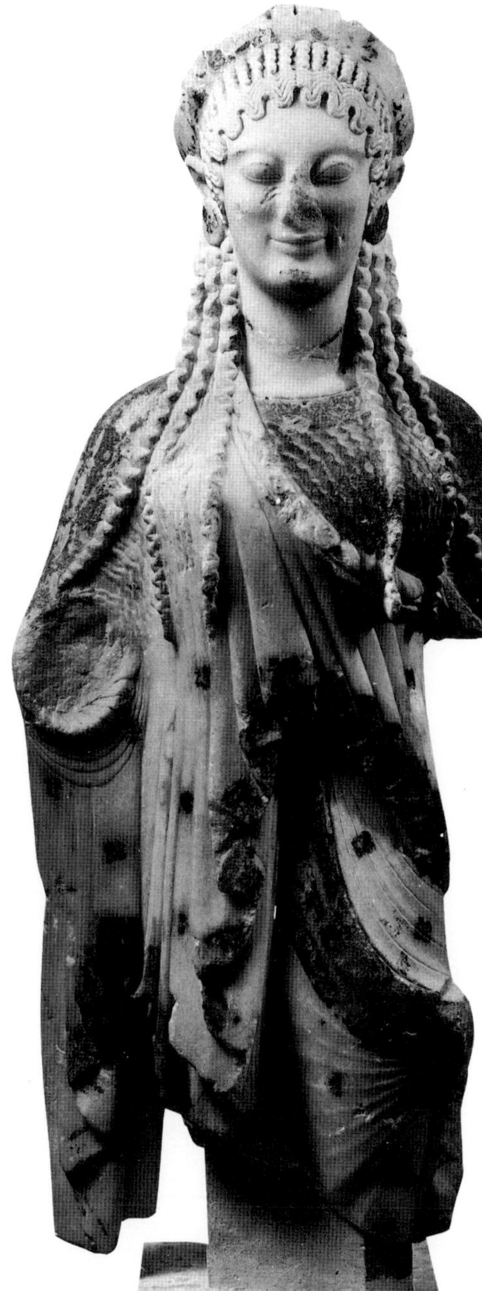

2.14 (*left*) Kore, c. 510 B.C.E. Marble, 21½ ins (54.6 cm) high. Acropolis Museum, Athens.

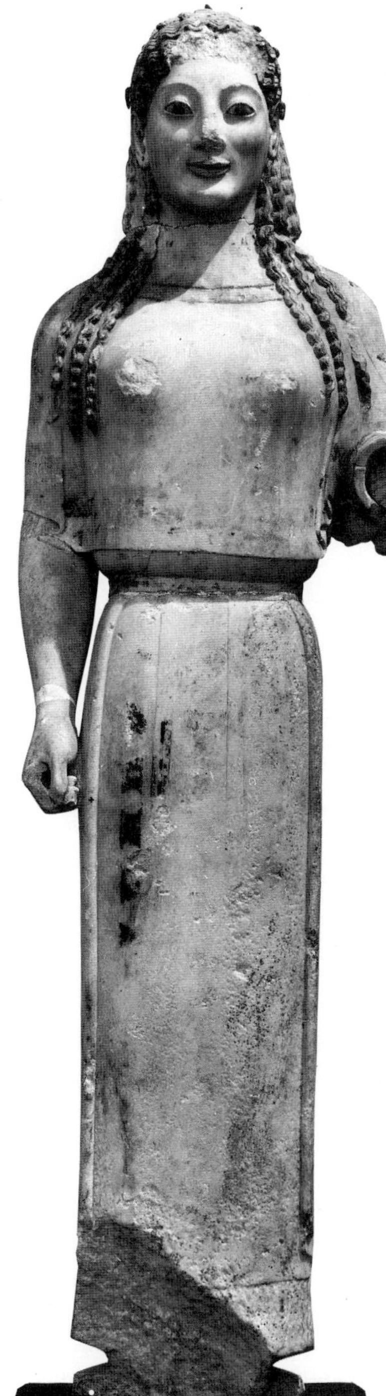

2.15 (*right*) Kore in Dorian peplos, c. 530 B.C.E. Marble, 4 ft (1.22 m) high. Acropolis Museum, Athens.

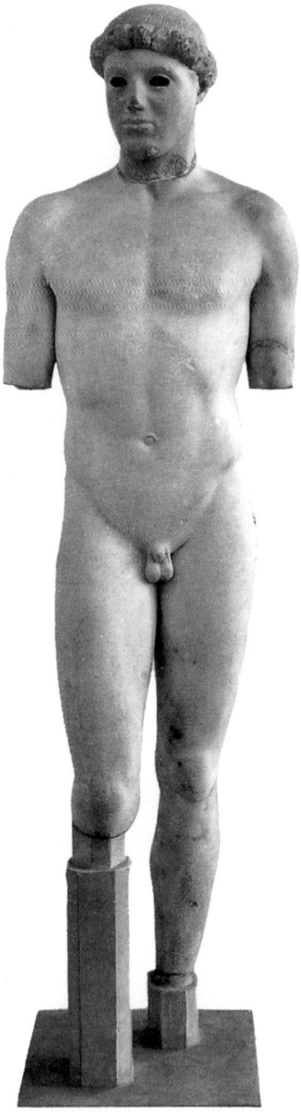

2.16 *Kritios Boy*, c. 480 B.C.E. Marble, about 34 ins (86 cm) high. Acropolis Museum, Athens.

Architecture

The archaic period witnessed the building of temples in a new adaptation of the **post-and-lintel** structure. The style employed imposing vertical posts or columns capped by heavy lintels and a **pedimented** roof, and it was probably drawn from elements of Egyptian, Mycenaean, and pre-archaic Greek structures—for example, the **fluted** or vertically grooved column was used in Egypt nearly two thousand years before its appearance in Greece. The style of some of these temples was called Doric after one of the Hellenic peoples, the Dorians, and it seems to have been well established by 600 B.C.E. Although the style itself changed over time, the early version had a cumbersome appearance, with thick columns and blocky, oversized capitals. Many of its characteristics came from earlier wooden buildings. We can sense the qualities and details of the order by examining a reconstruction drawing of the west front of the Temple of Artemis at Corfu (Fig. **2.17**). In this example, tapering columns sit directly on the **stylobate** (STYL-uh-bayt) or uppermost element of the foundation. The fluted **shaft**, the tubular main trunk of the column, tapers inward as it rises. The shaft leads to a flared **echinus** (ehk-IHN-uhs), a round collar-like cushion between the shaft and a square **abacus** (AB-uh-kuhs): the slab at the top of the column on which the **architrave** (AR-kih-trayv), or bottom portion of the lintel, rests (Fig. **2.18**). In the **entablature** we can see a **frieze** or band of relief elements known as triglyphs and metopes (MEHT-uh-peez). Above the frieze rest two **cornices.** One is horizontal and the other rises at an angle creating a triangular space called a **pediment**, which was often filled with relief sculptures (see Fig. **3.14** in the next chapter).

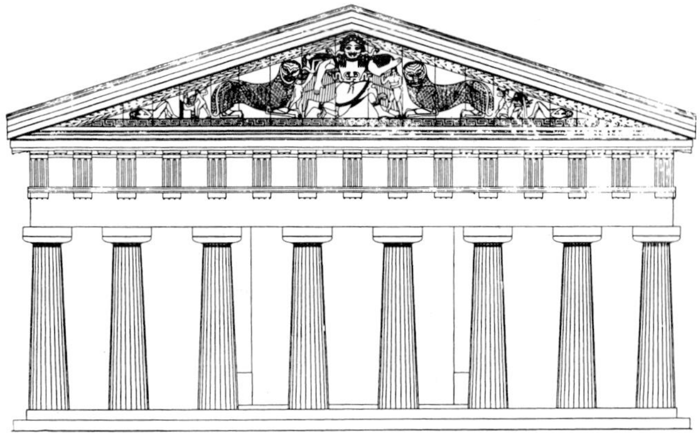

2.17 Reconstruction drawing of the west front of the Temple of Artemis, Corfu. [After Rodenwaldt.]

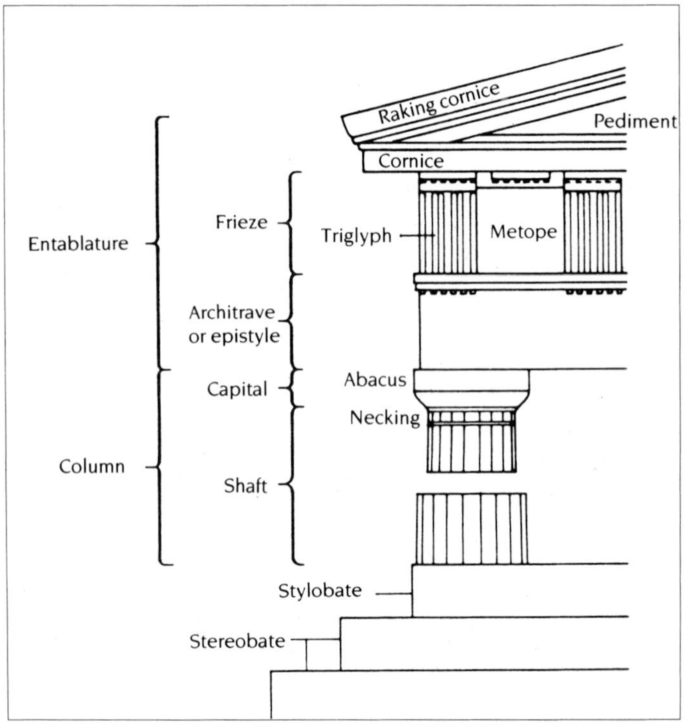

2.18 The Doric order.

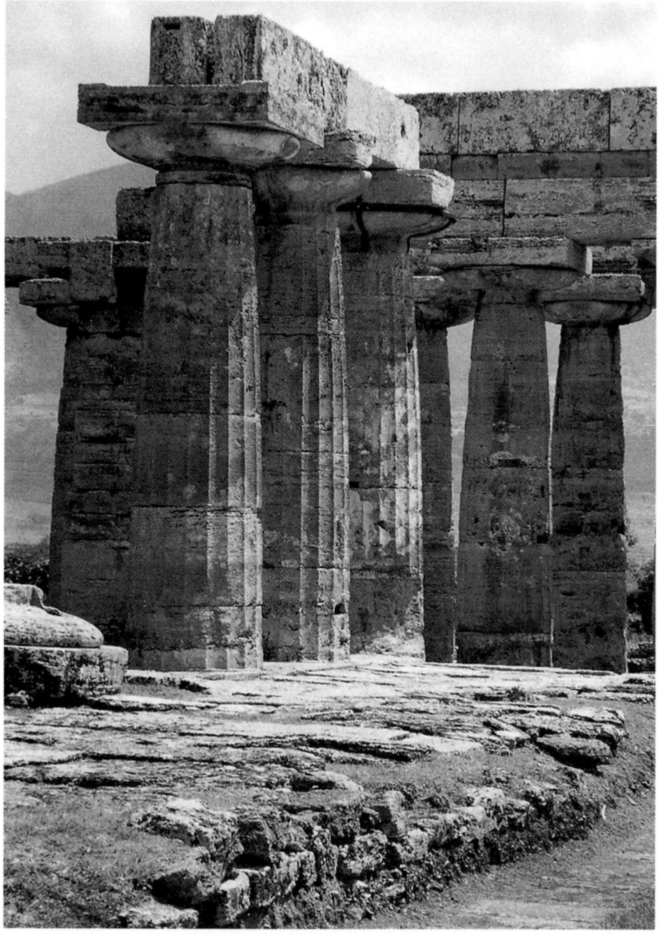

2.19 Corner of the temple at Paestum, Italy, c. 550 B.C.E.

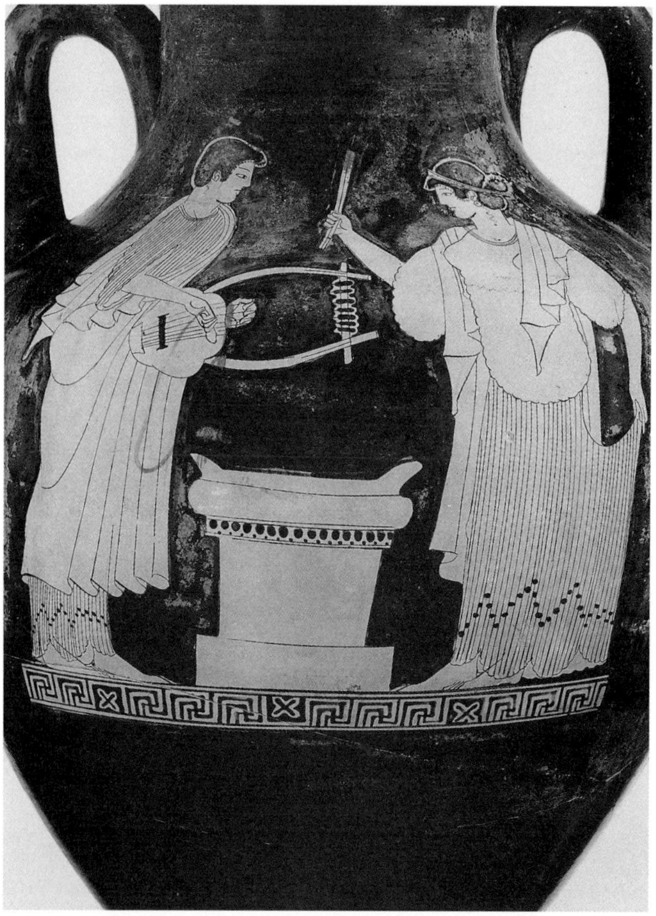

2.20 Attributed to the Eucharides painter, amphora showing Apollo playing a lyre and Artemis holding an aulos before an altar, c. 490 B.C.E. 18½ ins (47 cm) high. Metropolitan Museum of Art, New York (Rogers Fund, 1907).

The best-preserved temple from this period is at Paestum (PEEHS-tuhm; Fig. **2.19**), Italy. It was dedicated to the goddess Hera. Here, the flaring of the columns is exaggerated and the capitals seem unduly large, as if the architect were afraid that the lintels of the architrave would collapse if not supported along their length. The **proportion**, or relationship of the width of the columns to their height, gives the basilica a squat appearance with none of the grace of its classical successors.

Music

Although we cannot play any Greek music, because we simply do not know how to interpret the surviving records, we do know that music played a fundamental role in Greek life and education, and in Greek mythology, music had tremendous power to influence behavior. The gods themselves invented musical instruments, and the deities and heroes of Greek legend played them to remarkable effect. Apollo played the lyre (Fig. **2.20**), and Athena, the flute. Achilles, Homer's great hero of the *Iliad*, played proficiently.

Surviving records tell us that Greek music consisted of a series of **modes**, the equivalent of our **scales**. Each mode—for example, the Dorian and Phrygian—had a name and a particular characteristic sound, not unlike the difference between our major and minor scales, and the Greeks attributed certain behavioral outcomes to each mode. Just as we say that minor scales sound sad or exotic, the Greeks held that the Dorian mode exhibited strong, even warlike, feelings, while the Phrygian elicited more sensual emotions.

We have a fairly good picture of what Greek musical instruments looked like from vase paintings. Figure **2.20** illustrates the aulos, a double-reed instrument, and the lyre, a stringed instrument. The Greeks were particularly fond of vocal music, and instruments were used principally to accompany vocal music. The lyrics of songs have survived, and these include songs to celebrate acts by the various gods, from whom some mortal had gained special favor.

Literature

Homer, whose work we examine in more detail at the end of this chapter, is probably the best-known of the ancient

Greek poets, but he was by no means the only one. The growth of individualism in Greece produced a new literature: personal **lyric** poetry. Ancient lyrics, anonymous and often intended for use in rituals, had been concerned with experiences common to all. But by the end of the seventh century B.C.E., poets appeared along the Ionian coast who tell us their names, and sing of themselves, their travels, military adventures, political contests, homesickness, drinking parties, poverty, hates, and loves.

Sappho

The lyric poet Sappho (SAF-oh), who was born around 615 B.C.E., lived all her life on the island of Lesbos. She gathered around her a coterie of young women interested in poetry, and who may have been worshippers of the cult of Aphrodite. Many of Sappho's poems are written in honor of one or other of these young women.

Hesiod

Born at the end of the eighth century B.C.E., Hesiod (HEE-see-uhd) was the son of an emigrant farmer from Asia Minor. He depicts this hard life in his poem *Works and Days*. Hesiod's lesson is that men must work, and he sketches the work that occupies a peasant throughout the year, recounting how an industrious farmer toils and how work brings prosperity, in contrast to the ruin brought about by idleness. He captures the changing seasons and countryside with vivid word pictures. He also describes life at sea, and concludes with a catechism detailing how people should deal with each other. His style is similar to Homer's, but his subject matter is quite different, for rather than telling of heroes and gods, Hesiod dwells on the mundane and mortal.

Hesiod's most famous work, however, is the *Theogony*, in which he traces the mythological history of the Greek gods. He describes the rise of the earth out of chaos, the overthrow of the Titans by Zeus, and the emergence of each god and goddess (see p. 61). Scholars attempting to understand Greek art and religion have found this work invaluable as a source of information.

PROFILE

Sappho

One of the great Greek lyrists and few known female poets of the ancient world, Sappho was an aristocrat who married a prosperous merchant, and she had a daughter named Cleis. Her wealth afforded her the opportunity to live her life as she chose, and she chose to spend it studying the arts on the isle of Lesbos.

In the seventh century B.C.E., Lesbos was a cultural center. Sappho spent most her time on the island, though she also traveled widely throughout Greece. She was exiled for a time because of political activities in her family, and she spent this time in Sicily. By this time she was known as a poet, and the residents of Syracuse were so honored by her visit that they erected a statue to her. Sappho was much honored in ancient times. Coins of Lesbos were minted with her image during her own lifetime. Plato elevated her from the status of great lyric poet to one of the muses. Upon hearing one of her songs, Solon, himself an Athenian ruler, lawyer, and a poet, asked that he be taught the song "Because I want to learn it and die."

Although her work enjoyed great fame, it did not survive intact: only one of Sappho's poems is available in its entirety. All the rest exist solely as fragments. At one time, there were perhaps nine complete volumes of her poetry, but over the years neglect, natural disasters, and possibly some censorship took their toll. Late in the nineteenth century, however, manuscripts dating back to the eighth century C.E. were discovered in the Nile Valley, and some of these manuscripts contained pieces of her works. Many translations of these fragments have been made, and each offers a slightly different approach to her work. Translating Sappho's poetry is exceedingly challenging, in no small part because of the fragmented nature of the material.

Dance

The ancient Greeks believed that the gods invented dancing. They believed that the gods offered this gift to some select mortals only, who in turn taught dancing to the rest of humanity. The oldest Greek historical sources on dance come from Crete and the Minoan civilization, which cultivated music, song, and dance as part of their religious life and for their entertainment as well. The religious rituals of ancient Greece centered on dance. Beginning around 600 B.C.E., great festivals brought choruses of fifty dancers from each tribe together on special occasions for competitions. Most scholars agree that the Greek theatre developed directly from these dances. (The Greek tragic chorus had fifty members.)

Dance, music, and drama were inseparably entwined, and all played a fundamental part in early (and classical) Greek philosophy, religion, and life. The term "dance" had a broader definition for the Greeks than it does for us. In fact, it denoted almost any kind of rhythmic movement. Just as dance and music were inseparable, so were dance and poetry. A Greek could dance a poem, using rhythmic movements of his hands, arms, body, face, and head to interpret the verses recited or sung by himself or another person.

MASTERWORK

Sappho—"God's Wildering Daughter"

Sappho was called a *lyrist* because, as was the custom of the time, she wrote her poems to be performed with the accompaniment of a lyre. Sappho composed her own music and refined the prevailing lyric meter to a point that it is now known as *sapphic meter*. She innovated lyric poetry both in technique and style, becoming part of a new wave of Greek lyrists that moved from writing poetry from the point of view of gods and muses to the point of view of the individual. She was one of the first poets to write from the first person, describing love and loss as they affected her personally.

Her style was sensual and melodic; primarily songs of love, yearning, and reflection. Frequently the object of her affections was female—usually one of the women sent to her for education in the arts. She nurtured these women, wrote poems of love and adoration to them, and when they eventually left the island to be married, she composed their wedding songs. Sappho's tone is emotional and frank, her language simple and sensuous. One of her longer fragments, "He seems to be a God, that Man," was much admired and imitated by later poets. In it, Sappho gazes at a young bride sitting and laughing next to her bridegroom and is overcome with emotion. In "God's Wildering Daughter," Sappho entreats Aphrodite, the immortal child of the god Zeus.

God's Wildering Daughter
Sappho

God's wildering daughter deathless Aphrodite,
A whittled perplexity your bright abstruse chair,
With heartbreak, lady, and breathlessness
Tame not my heart.

But come down to me, as you came before,
For if ever I cried, and you heard and came,
Come now, of all times, leaving
Your father's golden house

In that chariot pulled by sparrows reined and bitted,
Swift in their flying, a quick blur aquiver,
Beautiful, high. They drew you across steep air
Down to the black earth:

Fast they came, and you behind them. O
Hilarious heart, your face all laughter.
Asking, What troubles you this time, why again
Do you call me down?

Asking, in your wild heart, who now
Must you have? Who is she that persuasion
Fetch her, enlist her, and put her into bounden love?
Sappho, who does you wrong?

If she balks, I promise, soon she'll chase,
If she's turned from gifts, now she'll give them.
And if she does not love you, she will love,
Helpless, she will love.

Come, then, loose me from cruelties.
Give my tethered heart its full desire.
Fulfill, and, come, lock your shield with mine
Throughout the siege.

FOCAL POINT

THE *ILIAD* AND *ODYSSEY* OF HOMER

Homer's *Iliad* and *Odyssey* created the mythical history that later Greeks accepted as their historic heritage. They took the dark and unknown past and created in a literary, originally oral, form a cultural foundation for an entire people. They told of heroes and described the gods. They depicted places and events, and they did so in a form that represented a supreme artistic achievement: epic poetry. Both poems deal with minor episodes in the story of the battle of Troy, which ended, with the destruction of the city, in about 1230 B.C.E.

Divided into twenty-four books, the *Odyssey* tells the story of Odysseus, king of Ithaca, as he travels home from the Trojan War to recover his house and kingdom.

The poem opens on the island of Orgygia (ohr-Gihj-uh), where, ten years after the end of the Trojan War, Odysseus has been detained for seven years by the nymph Calypso. After setting the scene, the poem shifts to Ithaca, where Odysseus' wife, Penelope (pehn-EL-oh-pee), and son, Telemachus (tuh-LEHM-uh-kuhs), struggle to retain their authority during Odysseus' long absence. In Book V, Zeus orders Calypso to release Odysseus, and Odysseus sets sail on a raft, which is destroyed by Poseidon, god of the sea, washing ashore on the land of the Phaeacians (FAY-uh-shuns). Odysseus recounts for the Phaeacians his adventures since leaving Troy: the land of the Lotus-Eaters; struggling with lotus-induced lethargy; blinding Polyphemus (pahl-ee-FEEM-uhs) the Cyclops, a son of Poseidon; losing eleven of his twelve ships; reaching the island of Circe (SUHR-see) the enchantress, who turned some of his companions into swine; visiting the Land of Departed Spirits and learning from the Theban seer Tiresias (teer-EE-see-uhs) how to calm Poseidon's wrath; encountering the Sirens, Scylla (SIHL-uh) and Charybdis (kuh-RIB-dis), and the Cattle of the Sun, which his companions, despite warnings, kill for food; finally, surviving, alone, the following storm and reaching Calypso's idyllic island.

The Phaeacians return Odysseus to Ithaca, where the goddess Athena (uh-THEEN-uh) disguises him as a beggar and he reveals his true identity to his son. Together they plot to rid their home of the suitors hounding Penelope. Still in disguise, Odysseus passes the clever test Penelope has devised to choose one of the suitors. After passing the test, Odysseus kills the suitors with the help of Telemachus and two faithful servants and is accepted by Penelope as her long-lost husband and as the king of Ithaca. Find a complete text of the *Odyssey* at http://www.perseus.tufts.edu/cgi-bin/ptext?doc=Perseus%3Aabo%3Atlg%2C0012%/2C002&query=1%3A1.

Set in twenty-four books, like the *Odyssey*, and exploring the *heroic ideal* with all its contradictions, the *Iliad* begins with an explanation of the quarrel between King Agamemnon (ag-uh-MEM-nahn), commander of the Greek army, and Achilles, the Greeks' greatest warrior. When the action opens, the Greeks have been besieging Troy for nine years, trying to rescue Helen, wife of Agamemnon's brother Menelaus (mehn-uh-LAY-uhs), from Paris, one of the sons of the Trojan King Priam (PRY-uhm). As a result of his quarrel with Agamemnon, Achilles leaves the Greek forces, taking his followers with him. Without Achilles, the Greeks suffer many losses. Unable to bear it when the Trojans set fire to the Greek fleet, one of Achilles' close friends asks permission to rejoin the fight. Achilles agrees and lends him his armor. When his friend is killed by the Trojan hero Hector, Achilles exacts revenge by killing Hector. Hector's father, King Priam, asks Achilles for his son's body so that it can be properly buried. Achilles agrees, and his anger is assuaged. The work ends with Hector's funeral.

Homer develops events on the battlefield and behind the lines of both adversaries. From his descriptions, an elaborate evocation emerges of the splendor and tragedy of war and the inconsistencies of mortals and gods. The heroes are types, not real people, and their characters were established in legend long before they were described in this epic poem. Here is a brief extract from Book XX:

> So these now, the Achaians, beside the curved ships were arming around you, son of Peleus, insatiate of battle, while on the other side at the break of the plain the Trojans armed. But Zeus, from the many-folded peak of Olympos, told Themis to summon all the gods into assembly. She went everywhere, and told them to make their way to Zeus' house. There was no river who was not there, except only Ocean, there was not any one of the nymphs who live in the lovely groves, and the springs of rivers and grass of the meadows, who came not.
> These all assembling into the house of Zeus cloud gathering
> took places among the smooth-stone cloister walks which Hephaestus

had built for Zeus the father by his craftsmanship and contrivance.
So they were assembled within Zeus' house; and the shaker
of the earth did not fail to hear the goddess, but came up among them
from the sea, and sat in the midst of them, and asked Zeus of his counsel:
"Why, lord of the shining bolt, have you called the gods to assembly
once more? Are you deliberating Achaians and
Trojans? For the onset of battle is almost broken to flame between them."
In turn Zeus who gathers the clouds spoke to him in answer:
"You have seen, shaker of the earth, the counsel within me,
and why I gathered you. I think of these men though they are dying.
Even so, I shall stay here upon the fold of Olympos
sitting still, watching, to pleasure my heart. Meanwhile all you others
go down, wherever you may go among the Achaians and Trojans
and give help to either side, as your own pleasure directs you,
for if we leave Achilles alone to fight with the Trojans
they will not even for a little hold off swift-footed Peleion.
For even before now they would tremble whenever they saw him,
and now, when his heart is grieved and angered for his companion's
death, I fear against destiny he may storm their fortress."
So spoke the son of Kronos and woke the incessant battle.

CHAPTER REVIEW

❖ CRITICAL THOUGHT ❖

We have now arrived at the birthing place of Western culture. Here, in archaic Greece, politics, art, architecture, literature, music, and dance reveal themselves as **prototypes**. We begin to see things we recognize—not from history books or even museums, but on the streets of our own towns. That is what prototypes are: the original ideas or forms on which later ideas and forms are based. Some of our public buildings emulate the Greek original, and certainly our form of government grew from concepts basic to the polis.

◆ SUMMARY ◆

After reading this chapter you should be able to:

- Identify and describe four pre-Socratic schools of philosophical thought.
- Characterize the Minoan, Mycenaean, and archaic Greek styles of architecture.
- Explain the differences among protogeometric, geometric, and archaic styles of pottery.
- Define the term polis and discuss its role as a fundamental concept in the Greek cultural ethos.
- Describe the characteristics of archaic Greek sculpture.
- Apply the elements and principles of composition to analyses and comparisons of archaic Greek, Egyptian, and Mesopotamian art and architecture.

CYBERSOURCES

http://witcombe.sbc.edu/ARTHancient.html#Aegean
http://harpy.uccs.edu/greek/archaicsculpt.html
http://www.mcad.edu/AICT/html/ancient/garchaic.html
http://atschool.eduweb.co.uk/allsouls/bm/room3.html

3 GREEK CLASSICISM AND HELLENISM

OUTLINE

VIEW

THE CLASSICAL IDEAL

The foundations of Western civilization rest firmly on the bedrock of classicism. The term classicism denotes the ideals and styles of ancient Greece and Rome as embodied primarily in their arts. Almost universally, these ideals and styles have been translated into notions of simplicity, harmony, restraint, proportion, and reason. We are related to the Greeks by these ideals, and, in fact, as we read subsequent chapters, we will see Greek classical ideas recur again and again. At times we will hear the classical/anti-classical struggle called the struggle between "form" and "feeling" or intellect versus emotion. That postulation means the struggle of artistic ideas in which appeal to rationality, simplicity, and restraint (form) comes up against ideals that appeal to emotion, complexity, and abandon (feeling). Classicism believes in the power of reason and searches for rational principles. Anti-classicism in its various styles promotes individualism and subjectivity.

KEY TERMS

Some of the basic terms and concepts we will encounter in this chapter include the following:

OLIGARCHY
Government by the few, especially by a small faction of persons or families—as opposed to a **democracy**.

AESTHETICS
A branch of philosophy dealing with the nature of beauty and art and their relation to human beings.

CLASSICISM
A style of art relying on the fundamentals of simplicity, clarity of structure, and appeal to the intellect.

IONIC ORDER
One of the Greek architectural decorative and elevational conventions and systems of proportion, characterized by columns with scroll-like capitals and circular bases.

CORINTHIAN ORDER
One of the Greek architectural decorative and elevational conventions and systems of proportion, characterized by columns employing an elaborate leaf motif in the capital.

HELLENISTIC STYLE
An approach to art characterized by individuality, virtuosity, and emotion.

3.1 The Parthenon, Athens, 447–438 B.C.E.

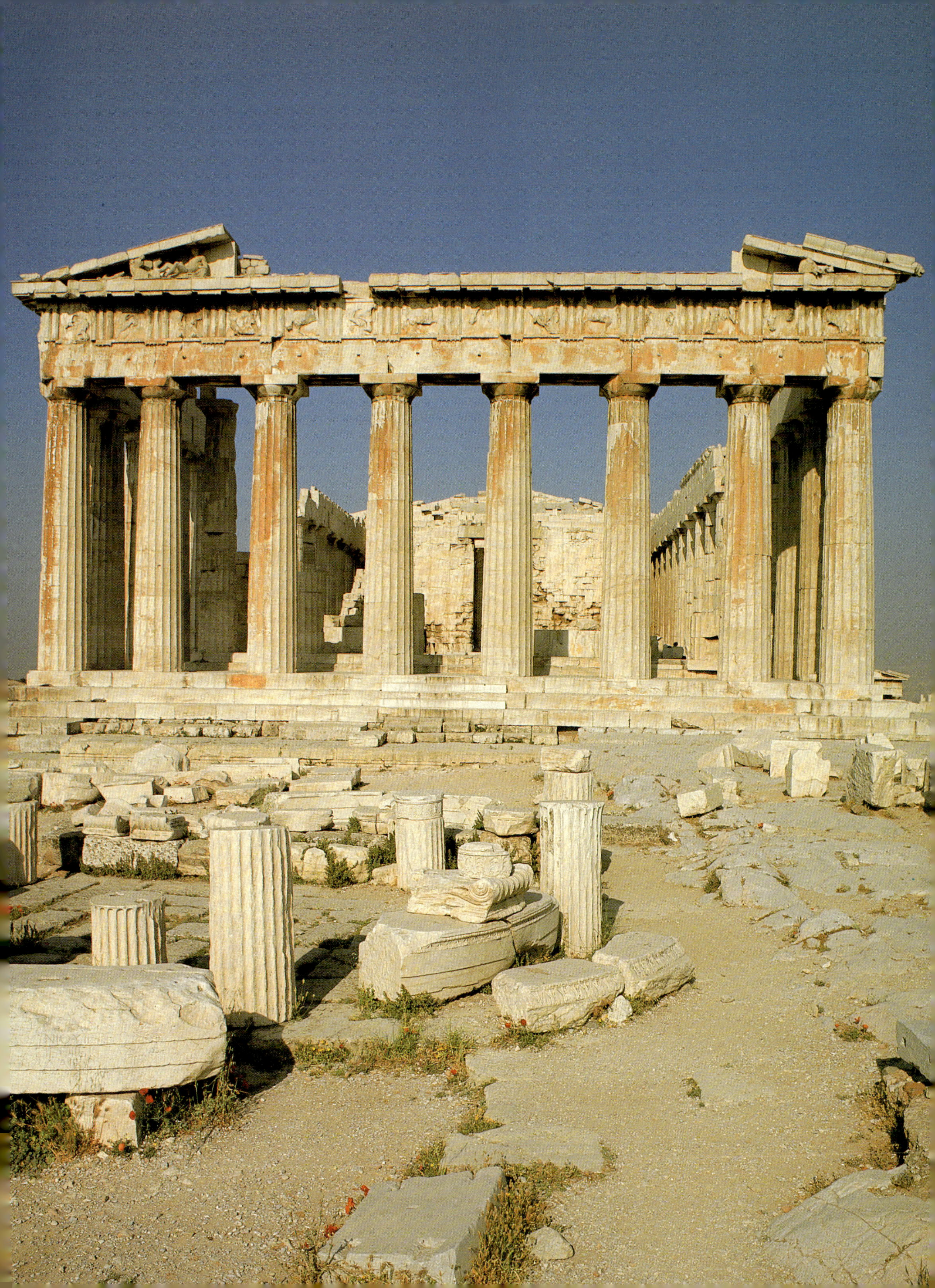

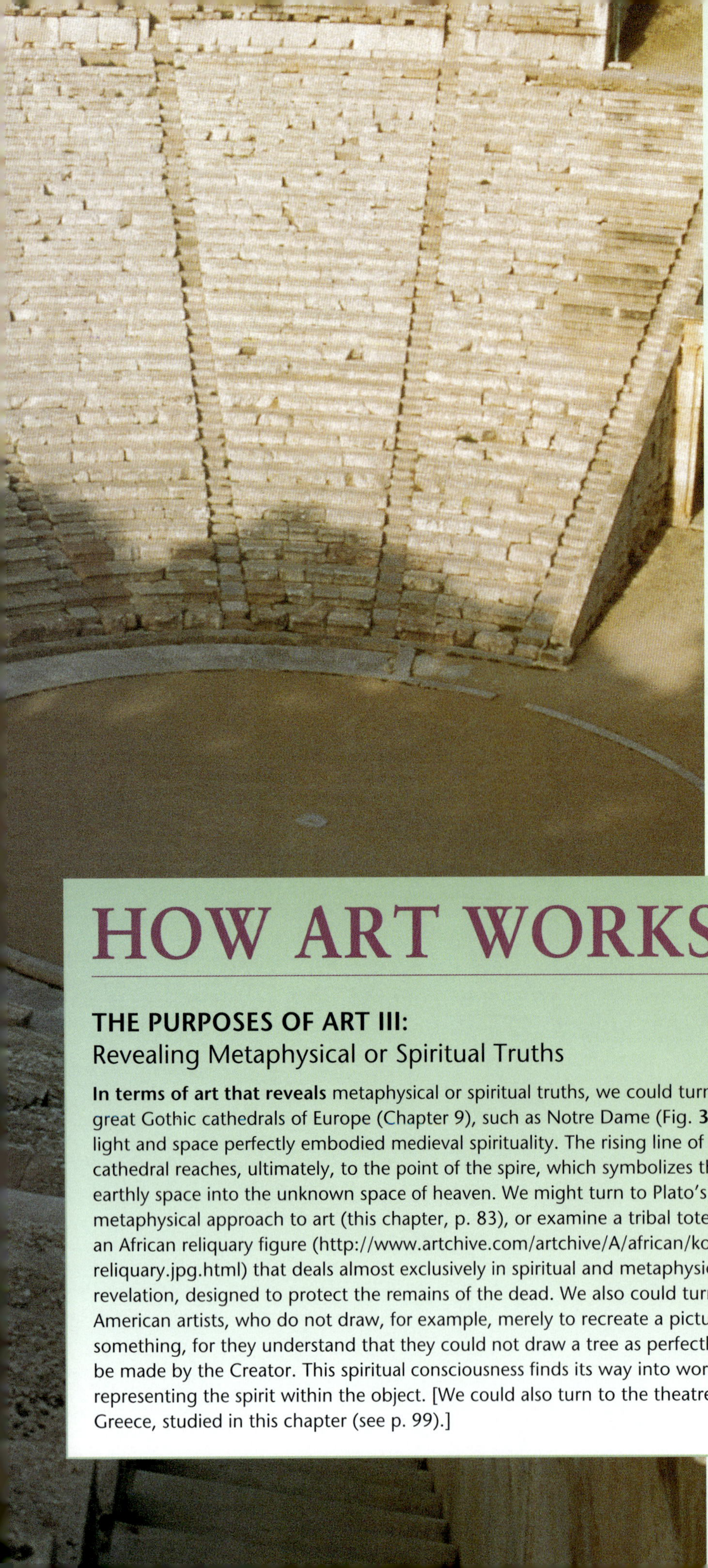

Greek Theatre as Spiritual Revelation

We think of theatre as entertainment—sometimes serious and profound—but entertainment, nonetheless. In ancient Greece the theatre was a vehicle for a communal expression of religious belief that employed music, dance, and drama (Fig. **3.3**). For the ancient Greek, the theatre implied a non-physical place—a special state of being for those who together watched the lives of the persons of the drama.

By the classical era—that is, the period we study in this chapter, the early Dytherambic (dihth-er-AM-bik) dance festivals that were religious celebrations dedicated to the god Dionysos (dy-oh-NY-suhs), had evolved into a carefully structured dramatic event. Nonetheless, although the original altar in the center of the *orchestra*, or playing area, had disappeared, a vestigial space, recognized as the space of the altar, remained. As we will come to learn, the **classical** spirit that dominated the age gave these religious celebrations a fairly rigid structure. Greek tragedy, the major dramatic form of the time, consisted of an introductory *prologos*, or prologue, a *parodos*, which marked the entrance of the chorus—a major feature of the drama (see p. 99)—several episodes constituting the main action of the play, and the *exodus*, or conclusion, that followed the last song of the chorus.

HOW ART WORKS

THE PURPOSES OF ART III:
Revealing Metaphysical or Spiritual Truths

In terms of art that reveals metaphysical or spiritual truths, we could turn to the great Gothic cathedrals of Europe (Chapter 9), such as Notre Dame (Fig. **3.2**), whose light and space perfectly embodied medieval spirituality. The rising line of the cathedral reaches, ultimately, to the point of the spire, which symbolizes the release of earthly space into the unknown space of heaven. We might turn to Plato's metaphysical approach to art (this chapter, p. 83), or examine a tribal totem, such as an African reliquary figure (http://www.artchive.com/artchive/A/african/kota_reliquary.jpg.html) that deals almost exclusively in spiritual and metaphysical revelation, designed to protect the remains of the dead. We also could turn to Native American artists, who do not draw, for example, merely to recreate a picture of something, for they understand that they could not draw a tree as perfectly as it could be made by the Creator. This spiritual consciousness finds its way into works of art by representing the spirit within the object. [We could also turn to the theatre of ancient Greece, studied in this chapter (see p. 99).]

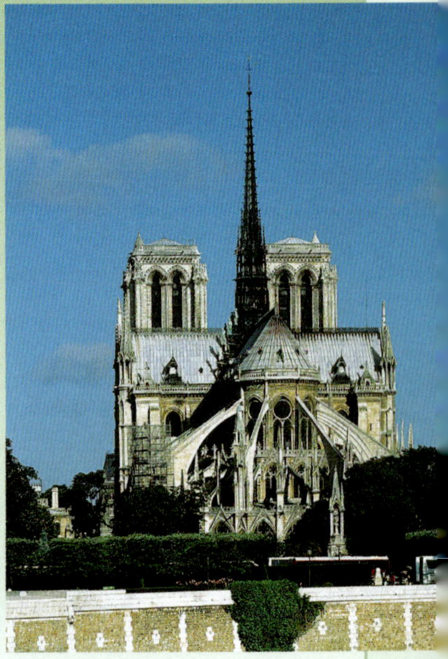

3.2 Notre Dame, Paris, 1163–1250. See also Fig. **8.17**.

3.3 Polyclitus the Younger, theatre at Epidaurus, Greece, c. 350 B.C.E. (detail). See also Figs **3.30** and **3.31**.

CONTEXTS AND CONCEPTS

The Persian War

The Persians, defeated by the Greeks at Marathon in 490 B.C.E., spent the next ten years regrouping under Xerxes I and preparing for another invasion of the Greek mainland. That invasion took place in 480, when an army of perhaps as many as 60,000 men proved unstoppable, completely overrunning northern Greece. It must have been a frightening spectacle: Medes and Persians clad in leather breeches and fishtail iron jerkins, with short, powerful bows; Assyrians in bronze helmets and carrying long lances; Arabs in flowing robes; and Ethiopians in leopard and lion skins. A coalition army headed by the Spartans battled valiantly, at a narrow northern pass named Thermopylae—the Hot Gates—which has gone down in history largely because a traitor revealed to the Persians how to take the defenders from the rear. As the Persian army moved steadily south, its

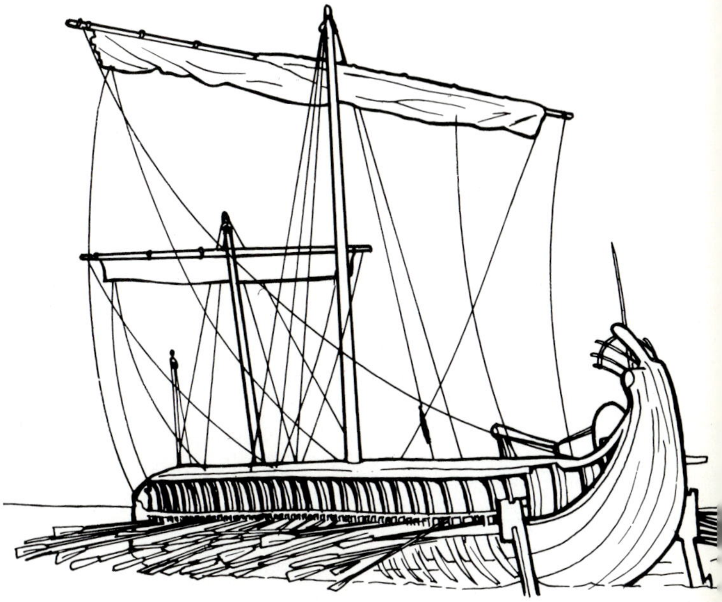

3.4 Reconstruction of a Greek trireme.

GENERAL EVENTS

- Battle of Marathon, 490 B.C.E.
- Persian invasion, 480 B.C.E.
- Delian League, 478 B.C.E.
- Pericles, 450–429 B.C.E.
- Peloponnesian War, 431–404 B.C.E.
- City-states defeated by Philip II, 338 B.C.E.
- Alexander the Great, 336–323 B.C.E.
- Invasion of Persia, 334 B.C.E.
- Library at Alexandria, 323 B.C.E.
- Ptolemy I, 323 B.C.E.

	500 B.C.E	450 B.C.E	400 B.C.E	300 B.C.E – 100 B.C.E
PAINTING & SCULPTURE	*Charioteer* (**3.10**)	Achilles painter (**3.9**), Polyclitis, *Lance Bearer* (**3.12**), Myron, *Discus Thrower* (**3.13**), *The Fates*, Parthenon (**3.14**), *Riace Warrior* (**3.15**), Parthenon frieze (**3.25**)	Praxiteles (**3.16, 3.17**), Lysippus, *Scraper* (**3.18**)	*Nike of Samothrace* (**3.19**), *Dying Gaul* (**3.21**), Altar of Zeus, Pergamon (**3.28**)
ARCHITECTURE		Parthenon (**3.1, 3.24, 3.25**), Temple of Athena Nike, Acropolis (**3.26**)	Theatre at Epidaurus (**3.3, 3.31**)	Temple of Olympian Zeus (**3.27**)
THEATRE	Aeschylus, Sophocles	Euripides, Aristophanes	Theatre at Epidaurus, Menander	
MUSIC & DANCE		Dionysiac cult revels		
LITERATURE & PHILOSOPHY		Herodotus, Protagoras, Socrates, Thucydides	Plato, Aristotle, Epicurus	Hippocrates, Zeno the Stoic, Theocritus

Timeline 3.1 Greek Classicism and Hellenism.

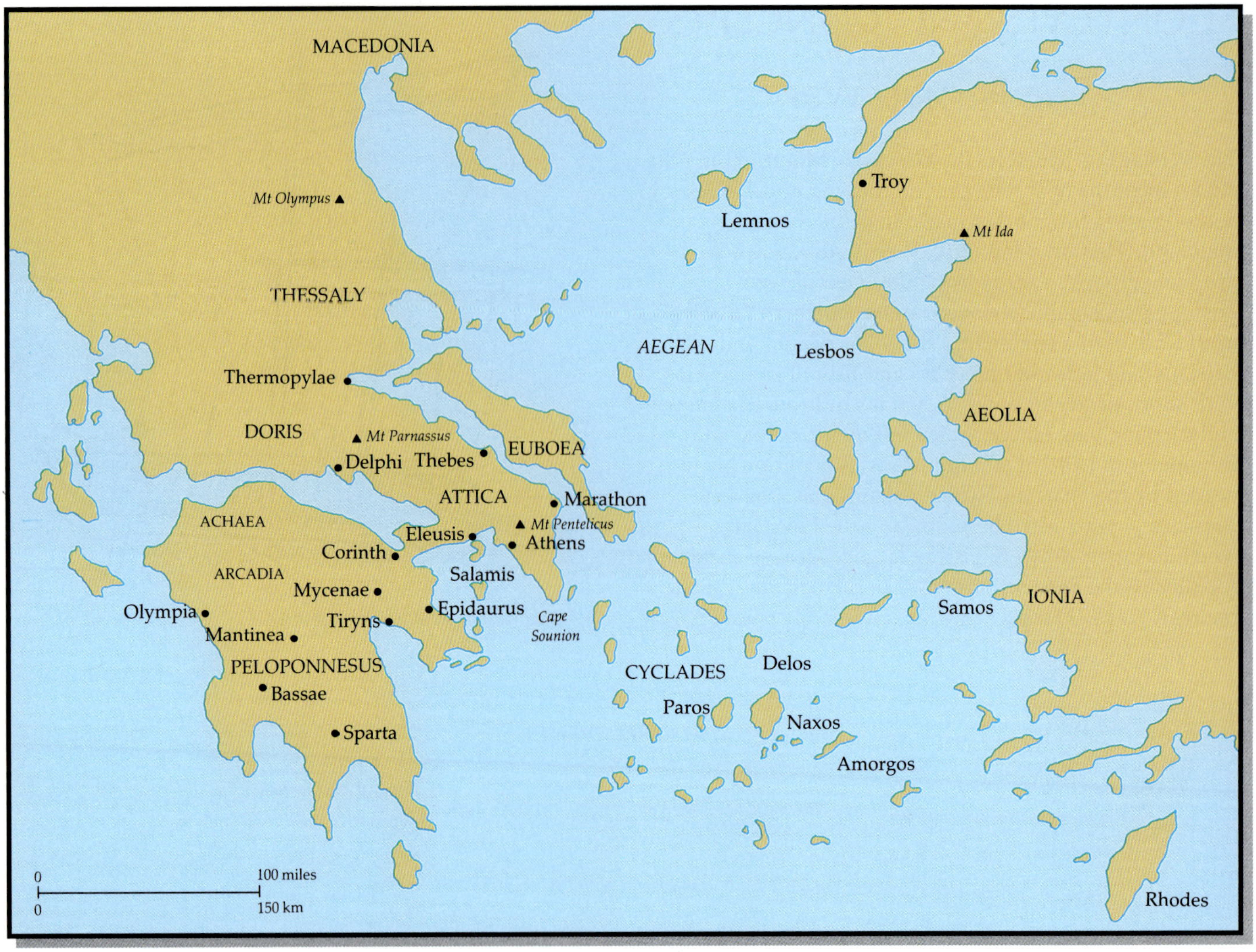

Map 3.1 Ancient Greece.

fleet sailed north against southern Attica. Athens was taken and destroyed, and ultimate victory for the Persians seemed a certainty.

The Greeks were, however, fighting on territory they knew well, they had brilliant leaders, and they were motivated by the desire to save their homeland. For years the Athenian Themistocles (thuh-MIS-tuh-kleez) had championed the Greek navy, and hundreds of new triremes (ships with three banks of oars; Fig. **3.4**) had been built. These long warships, manned by disciplined citizen–sailors, took to the sea against the Persian fleet. The critical battle came off the port of Athens, near the small island of Salamis, where the triremes (TRY-reemz) massed against the Persians, ramming them as Greek warriors swarmed aboard. The battle of Salamis was a Greek triumph, totally destroying the Persian fleet and leaving the Persian army unsupported.

The Persian army wintered in Thessaly, and in 479 B.C.E. it marched south again. Under Spartan command, the Greek army emerged victorious at the critical battle of Plataea. The beaten Persians withdrew, never again to set foot in Greece. The Persian War did not end for another thirty years, but after the battles of Salamis in 480 and Plataea in 479, the "war" consisted largely of annual raids by the Greeks on coastal lands of the Persian Empire.

The "Golden Age" of Pericles

Claiming to be the saviors of Greece, the Athenians set about liberating the rest of the country. Several city–states banded together with Athens to form the Delian (DEL-ee-uhn) League in 478 B.C.E. The league took its name from the Ionian island of Delos, where the group met and stored its money. The states made a contract, and the signatories agreed to follow a common foreign policy and to contribute ships and/or money, as Athens deemed necessary. Athens contributed the most money and commanded the fleet.

What followed was a systematic liberation of the Greek cities around the Aegean and the conquest of some islands populated by non-Greeks. The Delian League became, in fact, a highly prosperous Athenian empire.

The destruction of Athens, the victory over the Persians, and the formation of the Delian League helped to transform the young democracy of Athens, with its thriving commerce, unique religion, and inquisitive philosophies, into a culture of immense artistic achievement. The ruined city had to be rebuilt, and the spirit of victory and heroics prevailed. The Delian treasury, moved to Athens by Pericles, was used to help finance the immense costs of reconstruction.

Athens had witnessed a succession of rulers, and an interesting form of democracy had gradually emerged. Historians estimate that when Pericles came to power, in 461 B.C.E., the population of Athens was approximately 230,000 people. About 40,000 of these were free male citizens; 40,000 were Athenian women; 50,000 were foreign born; and 100,000 were slaves. Athenian democracy, however, allowed only free male citizens to vote. The long-believed view that in the golden age of Athens, women, although honored as wives and mothers, had little freedom, has been disputed by some recent historians who claim that, although women were denied the right to vote, they otherwise associated with men as equals. The tyrant, or ruler, wielded considerable power. This power emanated principally from ownership of land. Private estates provided not only for the tyrant's individual welfare, but also for the horses and arms necessary to make him a leader in warfare. The Greek tyrants seem in general to have been especially benevolent. They were not necessarily aristocrats, and their claims to leadership were often based on their popularity among the citizens.

By the fifth century B.C.E., Athens was the richest of the Greek city-states. Greek law had been reformed by the great Athenian lawmaker Solon, and after 508 B.C.E., constitutional changes created a complex of institutions that became the foundations of an almost pure form of democracy. All political decisions were made, in principle at least, by a majority vote of the citizens. Conditions were now right for an age of high cultural achievement. By historical standards, the golden age of Athens was very brief—indeed, it lasted less than half a century—but that middle third of the fifth century B.C.E. was one of the most significant periods in Western civilization.

The tyrant Pericles (PER-i-kleez; Fig. 3.5) dominated Athenian politics between 450 and 429 B.C.E. A descendant of the old aristocracy, he flourished under the new democracy. The Athenian historian Thucydides (thoo-SID-ih-deez) wrote that Pericles was enormously popular and known for his financial integrity. He clearly had a vision of Athenian greatness that he was able to bring to fruition.

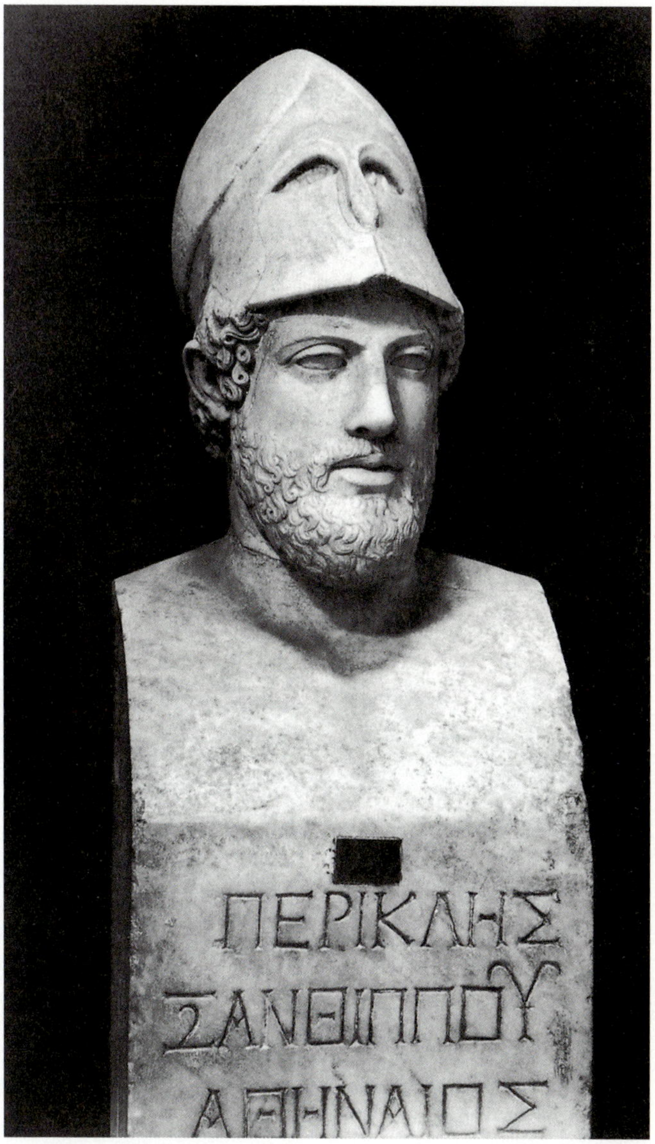

3.5 Kresilas, *Pericles*, Roman copy after original of c. 440 B.C.E. Marble, Vatican Museum, Rome.

The Peloponnesian War

Although they had joined forces to defeat the external threat of the Persians, the Greeks, with their independent city-states, never really coexisted peacefully, and toward the end of the fifth century B.C.E., that contentiousness led to a series of wars of attrition between Athens and Sparta called the Peloponnesian (pel-oh-pah-NEEZ-ee-uhn) War, that effectively brought to a close the golden age of Athens.

If Athens was a cultured society, democratic, and artistic, Sparta represented the old ways of warriors, courage, militarism, and **oligarchy** (AH-lih-gar-kee). Sparta was ruled by a council of elders, and its males were required to live in barracks, as soldiers, until they were thirty years old. In reality, every citizen had to be a soldier, because Sparta's agriculture depended on the labor of subject peoples, who far outnumbered the Spartans. In order to keep the population subdued, Sparta's men had to remain militarily expert. Spartans were, in consequence, the best soldiers in all of Greece.

In 404 B.C.E., the Spartans were victorious. Athens and the Athenians were humiliated, losing their navy and being forced to watch their empire collapse. Sparta made Athens tear down the defenses that guarded and connected Athens to its port, and also put Athens under the control of a council of conspirators called the Thirty Tyrants.

Although Sparta achieved political dominance, it did not assume any kind of cultural leadership nor much longlasting influence. Athens regained its freedom almost immediately, and although it was politically weakened and its role as a political power was diminished, its intellectual and aesthetic dominance continued to flourish.

The Hellenistic Age

Peace finally came to the Greek peninsula after the Macedonian conquest of the powerful King Philip II, who had seized the throne of Macedon in the middle of the fourth century. He assembled and trained a powerful army, conquered his neighbors, and became involved in the tangled alliances of the Greeks. In 338 B.C.E., at the battle of Chaeronea, Philip and his army routed the combined army of Athens and Thebes.

Two years later, Philip was assassinated by his own men, and his son, Alexander, ascended the throne as king and commander. A pupil of Aristotle, Alexander proved to be not only an able king and general, but also a man of sophisticated vision. Unlike his father, he was more interested in a world order than in mere conquest and pillage. His rule began with a twelve-year expedition in

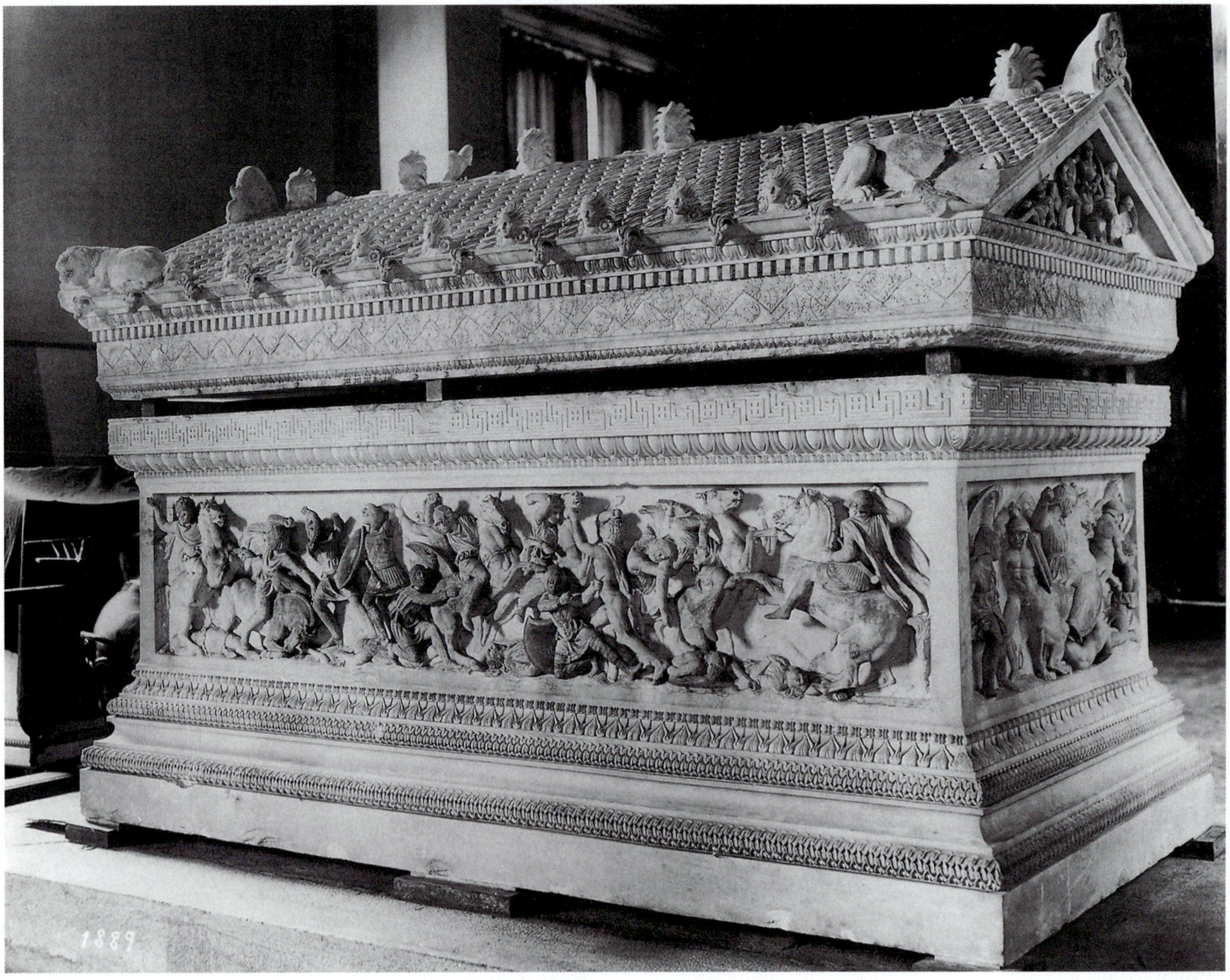

3.6 *Alexander Sarcophagus*, c. 310 B.C.E. Marble, 6ft 4½ ins (1.94 m) high. Archeological Museum, Istanbul, Turkey.

which he led an army, one quarter of which was Greek, into Asia. The brilliant twenty-two-year-old carried Greek—that is, Athenian—culture further afield than ever before. Alexander then defeated the Persian king, Darius III, at the battle of Issus. From there, Alexander led his forces against the city of Tyre in Syria, and pressed on to Egypt where, in the delta of the Nile, he founded Alexandria, one of the most influential and important cities in the Hellenistic world. A second defeat of Darius and the subsequent sacking of his capital, Persepolis, resulted in Alexander's installation as successor to the Persian throne. After pushing as far as the River Indus in India, Alexander's army balked, and so, after following the Indus south to the Indian Ocean, Alexander returned across the great desert and ended his odyssey in Babylon. According to legend, when Alexander the Great could find no more worlds to conquer, he sat down and wept. In any case, his destiny fulfilled, Alexander died of a sudden fever in Babylon at the age of thirty-three (Fig. **3.6**). He had married a Persian princess, declared himself a king and a god, and founded twenty-five Greek city-states. Along the way, Alexander's soldiers married native women and established Greek customs, trade, administration, and artistry throughout half of Asia.

The success of Alexander's conquests depended to a great extent on his forceful personality. On his death, the empire began to crumble as regional fragmentation and struggles for power marked the post-Alexandrian Hellenistic world. Nevertheless, the creation of so vast an empire fostered an internationalism of culture that persisted into, and was strengthened under, the Roman Empire. An important aspect of the Hellenistic period, which lasted into the Roman Empire, was *syncretism* (SIN-cruh-IZ-um)—that is, the fusion of diverse religious beliefs and practices. Commerce flourished, and international communication carried Greek thought and artistic influence to all parts of the known world. Intercultural relationships also blossomed: Buddhist sculpture in India, for example, shows signs of Greek influence, and the European pantheon of gods began to reflect Eastern emotionalism. Athens thus remained an important center for ideas and cultural accomplishments, in spite of the weakness of its commercial and military power.

The source of **Hellenistic** culture was Alexandria, which was, at this time, the greatest city in the world and was endowed with phenomenal wealth. Legally it was a Greek city "by" not "in" Egypt. Brilliant writers and new literary forms emerged, and the Ptolemies (TAH-loh-meez) patronized science and scholarship. Royal funds paid for many splendid buildings, including an enormous library, which became the focal point of the Hellenistic intellectual world.

History and Science

The Greek intellect probed the mysteries of this world as well as the more ethereal realms that were the domain of the philosophers. Before the fifth century B.C.E., accounts of the past were part of an oral tradition, more myth than fact, but at this time, history—the word derives from *historia*, meaning inquiry—became a written form, put together from careful research. The first to view history as a specialized discipline was Herodotus (huh-RAHD-uh-tuhs; c. 484–430 B.C.E.). A believer in the superiority of Greek civilization, he wrote nine great volumes of a work called *History of the Persian Wars*. The change from telling the narrative story in the form of epic or lyric poetry to relating it in a new descriptive form earned Herodotus the title "Father of History."

Although he was not an historian in our sense of the word—his writing tends to be filtered through the personalities of the people involved and he often invented inspiring speeches for kings and generals—he retained a neutrality and freedom from patriotic bias. He described the wars in colorful detail, seeking to show how human beings, in this case Greeks and Persians, settled their differences by resorting to arms, and he made full use of his tremendous powers of observation and recorded as much information as he could unearth, including conflicting points of view. He also examined the reliability of his sources and presented them so that his readers could draw their own conclusions about their veracity. However, he did not shy away from drawing his own conclusions about the causes of events. He believed that the present had its causes in the past, and his analysis of the Persian War concluded that the Greeks defeated the Persians because the Greeks were morally right and the Persians were morally wrong. The moral fault in the Persians lay in their **hubris** (HYOO-bris), or excessive pride and ambition. There was also a religious undertone to Herodotus' judgment, for he believed that the gods supported justice and truth and would ensure their victory.

Thucydides (thoo-SID-i-deez; d. c. 401 B.C.E.), who wrote a history of the Peloponnesian War, took history in a more subtle and thoughtful direction. He shared Herodotus' passion for the truth, and, although he had been an Athenian commander in the war, he dispassionately lists the foibles, follies, and errors made by the Athenians. Although it should be borne in mind that Thucydides was exiled from Athens for his failure as a naval commander early in the contest, his writing does not include self-justification. Rather, it is an unbiased compilation that strives to reveal human motives in ordinary events in order to draw a larger picture of history. His object was to instruct his readers so that they would be armed with knowledge when events of the past recurred—not in simplistic but in similar ways—in the future.

TECHNOLOGY

Hero's Steam Turbine

After the death of Alexander the Great, Ptolemy I became ruler of Egypt, proclaimed himself king, and gave himself the name Soter, or Savior. Despite a somewhat exaggerated view of his own importance, Ptolemy established what was essentially a research institute by founding the museum at Alexandria, the library of which was to become the most famous in the world. The museum attracted scholars from around the Hellenistic world to teach and to learn. One of these was Hero, whose tutor, Strato, had been a contemporary of Aristotle at the Lyceum in Athens. Hero compiled a textbook of engineering and invented a number of useful pieces of equipment, including a water clock. From his written account, it is clear that he gave a great deal of thought to maintaining an even flow of water into the mechanism so that it would keep accurate time. His steam turbine (Fig. **3.7**), which depended on the expansion of air and the vaporization of water when heated, could probably have been developed further to provide a useful source of power, but the machine appears to have been regarded merely as an entertaining toy.

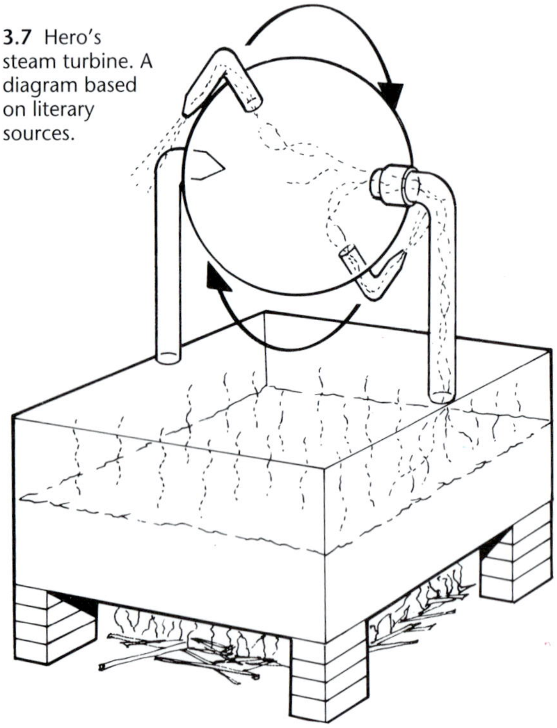

3.7 Hero's steam turbine. A diagram based on literary sources.

Greek intellects also turned to science and the natural world. Although they often erred in their observations, they also gave us many of our basic theories. Euclid's elements of geometry, for example, remained a standard text well into the twentieth century, and physicians still begin their careers by reciting the "oath" of the Greek physician Hippocrates (hip-AH-kruh-teez). Greek astronomers recognized that the earth was a sphere, and they even calculated its size and distance from the sun and moon through mathematics and trigonometry.

Philosophy and Religion

Sophistry

Humankind: "The measure of all things"

The middle of the fifth century B.C.E. was the end of a cycle of constructive activity and the beginning of a period of criticism and skepticism. The attention was now turning toward humanity and ethics in a practical way. The rise of Sophistic philosophy demonstrated the contemporary concern of humankind, thinking in a relativistic way, challenging the existence of truth. All established beliefs and standards, whether religious, moral, or scientific, came under fire. Reason, it was argued, had led only to deception.

Skepticism emerged in an Athens torn by disputes and ruled by a form of democracy that depended on persuasion and practicality. Debating skills were thus an absolute necessity, and these conditions produced teachers of rhetoric. Those who championed this new utilitarian art of persuasion were called Sophists, or "wise ones." They were well versed in rhetoric, grammar, diction, and logical argument, as well as in behind-the-scenes intrigue. They set up schools and charged high fees for their services—a most unethical act, according to traditional Greek thinking.

The outstanding Sophist, Protagoras (pro-TAG-uh-ruhs; c. 485–410 B.C.E.), reduced the entire mental life of the individual to perceptions, as expressed in his contention "Man is the measure of all things." According to Protagoras, knowledge, truth, and reality possess only a subjective existence—that is, they are only opinions in each person's mind. There are no objective facts or real truths applying to all people. What seems true for one individual is true for that individual alone. Inasmuch as objectivity cannot be achieved, people must be content with subjective knowledge or mere opinion.

Protagoras based his conclusion that truth was relative on the observation that human knowledge of the *phenomenal* world (the world we sense) is imperfect because human senses are imperfect. Further, Protagoras maintained, even if human sense equipment were perfect, it would still be inadequate for accurately perceiving real objects. Therefore, humans can obtain only a partial knowledge based on partial experience, which is different for every human.

In his treatise *On the Gods*, Protagoras indicates that one "cannot feel sure that they [the gods] are, or that they are not, nor what they are like in figure, for there are many things that hinder sure knowledge, the obscurity of the subject and the shortness of human life." He then amplifies this religious doubt into a denial of any absolute truths at all. The individual person is "the measure of all things, of things that are that they are, and of things that are not that they are not." Truth is therefore relative and subjective. What appears true to any given person at any given moment is true, and what appears as real is real so far as any one person is concerned. But one such truth cannot be measured against another. Read Plato's dialogue, *Protagoras* at http://classics.mit.edu/Plato/protagoras.html.

Socrates, Plato, and Aristotle

Socrates

Socrates (c. 470–399 B.C.E.), the father of ethics and initiator of the Socratic method, called himself the "gadfly" of Athens. He did not hesitate to condemn the Sophists for their lack of belief in a universal moral and intellectual order, but he also opposed many of the traditional values of Athens. He called on Athenians to examine their own lives and to think seriously about the real meaning of life. Sitting in the agora, or marketplace, he questioned everyone who passed by about subjects ranging from justice to art. He had no qualms about cornering a judge and asking him to explain justice, or in forcing an artist to define art, and was passionate in his defense of the right of individuals—including himself—to speak freely. He gathered around him young people, challenging them to examine their lives, and discussing with them how society should be organized and how life should be lived. For Socrates, the unexamined life was not worth living.

At the center of Socrates' thinking lay the *psyche*: the mind or soul. This, he believed, was immortal and much more important than the body, which perished. It was the responsibility of every individual to raise his or her psyche to its highest potential—that is, to fill it with knowledge acquired through rigorous debate and contemplation of abstract virtues and moral values. He believed that knowledge created virtuous behavior, and that those who did evil did so because they did not have knowledge—evil-doing was clear evidence of lack of knowledge.

As Plato reveals in his *dialogues*, Socrates' method was to question his students, and an inability to answer revealed the deficiency of their learning. His rigor was particularly upsetting to the elders of Athens who, in the years following the Peloponnesian War, believed Socrates to be a disruptive element in society, and many found evidence of blasphemy and even treason in his public arguments. In 399 B.C.E., Socrates was arrested for impiety and corrupting youth. He was tried by a jury, found guilty, and sentenced to death by drinking a cup of poisonous hemlock.

One of his mourners, a young man named Plato, was so moved by the apparent injustice of Socrates' death that he dedicated his life to immortalizing his teacher and explaining his philosophy.

Plato

Plato was born in Athens in 427 B.C.E., two years after the death of Pericles, and he grew up during the years of the Peloponnesian War, which brought an end to the Athenian Empire. His family belonged to the old Athenian aristocracy, but it escaped the financial ruin that befell many Athenian aristocrats, and managed to give him a good education. He emerged a thoroughly well-rounded individual, a good athlete, and with experience of painting, poetry, music, literature, and drama. He received military training and fought in the wars. Although well suited and well connected enough for a career in politics, Plato turned instead to philosophy and fell more and more under the influence of the teacher Socrates.

Plato's masterwork, *The Republic*, a series of dialogues involving Socrates, lays out Plato's concept of an ideal political state ruled one day by *philosopher kings*. His Theory of Forms, or Ideas, held that the material reality we humans perceive is only a shoddy copy of an unconditionally perfect reality that mere mortals can never know through sensory experience.

After Socrates' execution for "corrupting Athenian youth," Plato concentrated entirely on philosophy. Anti-Socratic feeling ran high in Athens, and for ten years Plato found it expedient to live outside the city, writing many of the early dialogues during this period. Much of his aesthetic theory can be found in these dialogues, which follow Socrates' customary question-and-answer format.

Plato invented **aesthetics** as a branch of philosophy, and Western thought has been profoundly influenced by his metaphysical approach to the philosophy of art. We find in Plato's dialogues a clear, though not very systematic, theory of art and beauty.

For Plato, art derived primarily from the skill of knowing and making, or *techne* (TEK-nay). Techne was the ability of an artist to be in command of a medium, to know what the end result would be, and to know how to execute the artwork to achieve that result. The fundamental principles of techne were measurement and proportion. Standards of taste—what is good and what is beautiful—could not be considered unless the work was correct in proportion and measure.

Plato's theory of beauty and the creation of beauty, or art, rests on his concept of imitation. According to Plato, the artist imitates the Ideal that exists beyond the universe. Indeed, the universe itself is only an imitation of ideas, or unchanging forms. This point is crucial to all Platonic thought, yet it is a difficult one. To simplify a complex notion, Ideas, or Forms, are reality. Everything on earth is an imitation of reality. Ideals are thus not thoughts conceived by an individual human mind (or a divine one). Forms are rather the objects of thought. They exist independently, no matter whether, or what, we think of them.

The arts are practiced to create imitations of Forms. Plato mistrusted the arts, and especially drama, however, because the individual artist may fail to understand the ultimate reality, and may instead present merely an "appearance of perceivable nature." Therefore, art must be judged by the statesman, who "envisages the human community according to the Ideas of justice, the good, courage, temperance, and the beautiful."[1] In the end, what is proper as art depends upon the "moral ends of the polis."

In addition to possessing technical ability and the ability to know and imitate Ideas, the artist must have a third quality, artistic inspiration. No one can ascend to the highest levels of artistry without divine inspiration and assistance. Plato calls artistry a form of "divine madness."

Aristotle

Born in 384 B.C.E., Aristotle (Fig. **3.8**) did not have Plato's advantages of birth. His family was middle-class, and his father was court physician to Amyntas of Macedon, grandfather of Alexander the Great. Aristotle was orphaned when he was quite young, and gained a home and his education through the generosity of a family friend. When he was eighteen years old he became a student at Plato's **academy,** where his affectations and self-absorption caused some trouble with the school's authorities. After Plato's death, Aristotle left the Academy and married. Around 343 B.C.E., he gained a favorable position as tutor to Alexander the Great. Aristotle sought to teach Alexander to revere all things Greek and despise anything barbarian—that is, non-Greek.

When Alexander acceded to the throne in 336 B.C.E., Aristotle returned to Athens to set up his own school, the Lyceum (ly-SEE-uhm). Over the next twelve years he produced a prolific outpouring of writings as well as research in physics, astronomy, biology, physiology, anatomy, natural history, psychology, politics, ethics, logic, rhetoric, art, theology, and metaphysics. Aristotle's "is probably the only human intellect that has ever compassed at first hand and assimilated the whole body of existing knowledge on all subjects, and brought it within a single focus."[2]

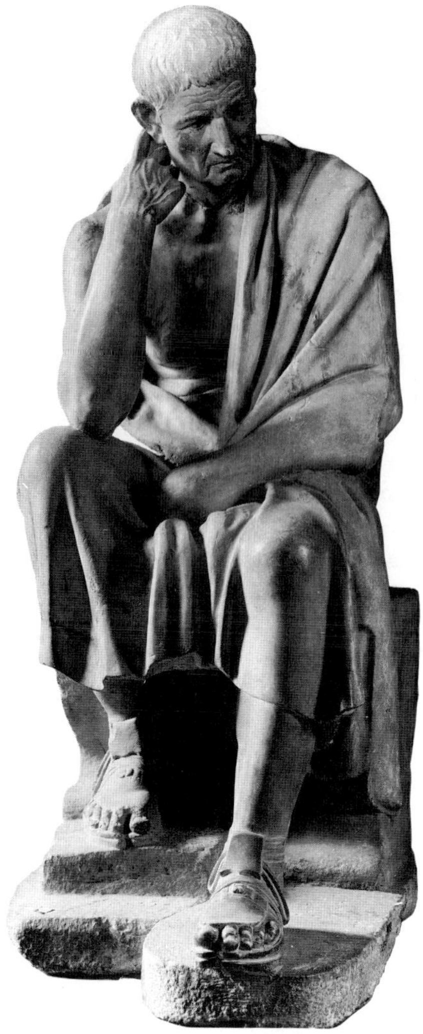

3.8 Aristotle.

Aristotle's writings on nature make him the world's first real scientist, although many of his conclusions have been superseded. In contrast to Plato, Aristotle believed that the material world is real and not a creation of eternal Forms. He taught that individual things combine form and matter in ways that determine how they grow and change. He was also the founder of formal logic.

Aristotle's major work on the philosophy of art is the *Poetics.* There he maintains that all the arts imitate nature, and that imitative character is rooted in human psychology. For Aristotle, the end of artistic creation determines the appropriate means for its realization. In order to assess the excellence of a work, we must determine whether the work has a perfection of form and a soundness of method that make it a satisfactory whole. The elements of composition must display symmetry, harmony, and definition.

Aristotle's theory differs considerably from Plato's. Plato insists that artistic imitation, especially tragedy, fuels the passions and misleads the seeker of truth.

Aristotle, by contrast, believes that the arts repair deficiencies in nature and that tragic drama in particular makes a moral contribution. Therefore the arts are valuable and justifiable. Aristotle rejects Plato's notion of the centrality of beauty and erotic love, as well as his metaphysical idealism. He sees beauty as a property of an artwork rather than its purpose, whereas for Plato the search for beauty is the proper end of art. He does agree with Plato "that art is a kind of *techne*, and that the most important human arts, such as music, painting, sculpture, and literature are imitative of human souls, bodies, and actions."[3]

The purpose of art, however, is not edification, nor the teaching of a moral lesson. The purpose of art is to give pleasure, and to the degree that it does that, it is good art. The pleasure Aristotle refers to comes when art excites our emotions and passions. These are then purged in response to the art and our souls lighten, delighted and healed. High art makes us think, of course, but the highest art must produce this **catharsis** (kuh-THAR-sis), or purging effect.

Art can also provide entertainment for the lower classes, who, he maintains, are incapable of appreciating high art properly. It is better that they enjoy some kind of art than none at all, and they are entitled to this pleasure. Thus, Aristotle's aesthetics encompassed both the higher and the lower arts.

Cynicism and Skepticism

Four schools of thought vied for philosophical supremacy in the Hellenistic period. These were Cynicism, Skepticism, Stoicism, and Epicureanism (ehp-i-kyoo-REE-uhn-izm). Led by Diogenes (dy-AH-jen-eez; c. 412–323 B.C.E.), the Cynics taught that humans are animals and that the good life lay simply in satisfying their animal needs. Since those needs can be troublesome, however, a wise person will have as few needs as possible but will disregard any social conventions that stand in the way of his own satisfaction. In other words, if a person wanted nothing, then he could lack nothing. The Cynics had little use for society as an organizing principle, believing that it stood in the way of individual freedom and independence, and they therefore isolated themselves as much as possible from society. Needless to say, Cynicism had little appeal either to the masses or the aristocracy.

Followers of Pyrrho (PEER-oh) of Elis, the Skeptics, asserted that nothing was certain and that the senses were completely unreliable as sources of knowledge. Ultimately, the only certainty was that truth was unachievable. They questioned everything and admitted the truth of nothing. For the Skeptic, everything was relative. Universal doubt ruled their world. Less popular, even, than Cynicism, Skepticism did make inroads in later times, particularly during the Roman era.

Stoicism and Epicureanism

Stoicism, founded by Zeno (ZEEN-oh, c. 495–430 B.C.E.), held that humans were the incarnation of reason or *logos* (LOH-gohs), which produces and directs the world and gave a spark to the individual soul in the form of rationality. The good life was defined as that which follows reason, wisdom, and virtue, but the only way to achieve these goals lay through renunciation and asceticism. The Stoic tended to leave everything to God and to accept whatever came his way. Once this state of mind was achieved, it was possible to disregard public opinion, misfortune, and even death—that is, one approached life with apathy. Stoicism maintained that happiness was the ultimate goal of the individual. It also stressed the importance of the senses in perceiving underlying moral law and the divine plan for the world. In the end, the Stoics perceived an ideal state, guided by *logos* and law, that included all humanity regardless of race, sex, nationality, or social standing. Stoicism proved a popular philosophy, especially among intellectuals and political leaders. Essentially Stoicism was an optimistic viewpoint that stood in strong contrast to the pessimism of the other philosophies of the time.

Epicurus (c. 342–270 B.C.E.) led Epicureans to a life of strict quietude. They concluded that human beings consisted of a temporary arrangement of atoms that dissolved at death. Because everything was temporary, the good life was simply an untroubled one. Wisdom dictated that one should avoid entanglements, maintain good health, tolerate pain, and accept death without fear. Epicurus founded a school in Athens, and his pupils, including women and slaves, gathered to discuss ideas. Epicureans believed that the senses could be relied upon to give an accurate picture of reality and that the mind functioned as a storehouse for those observations. Free will allowed humans to reach moral conclusions based on ethical constructs.

Mystery Cults

Hellenistic times were uncertain times, and human confidence in the ability to control anything waned. At such times, people tend to develop a belief that fate will do whatever fate will do and to adopt pietistic religious beliefs—that is, beliefs in which emotionalism takes the place of intellectualism or rationalism. In the Hellenistic world, a variety of mystery cults emerged from the East and from Egypt. The cult of Dionysus, god of revelry and wine, was particularly appealing in Greece proper. To unite Egyptians and Greeks, Ptolemy I, founder of the Alexandrian Museum, invented a new god, Serapis (suh-RAY-pis), who became popular throughout the Hellenistic world. Another powerful mystery cult that spread throughout the Mediterranean world and, later, became one of the most antagonistic forces met by the early Christians, was the cult of Isis. Originating in Egypt in the eighteenth century B.C.E., Isis was a nature goddess, who became the prototype for all goddesses. In Egyptian mythology she was the faithful wife and sister of Osiris and mother of Horus. After Osiris was slain by their brother, Set, and his body scattered in pieces, Isis gathered the pieces together; Osiris was then restored and became ruler of the dead. The legend symbolized the sun (Osiris) overwhelmed by night (Set), followed by the birth of the sun of a new day (Horus) from the eastern sky (Isis). Thus, it was a religion that emphasized resurrection after death: one of the characteristics that later put it into direct conflict with Christianity. Isis was universal mother and mistress of all magic, and her cult prevailed until the middle of the sixth century C.E. Probably, the appeal of the mystery cults lay in their mystery—that is, in secret initiation rites that gave the member a special status and, thus, satisfied a universal need to belong.

THE ARTS OF THE CLASSICAL AND HELLENISTIC AGES

Classicism and Hellenism

In a definitional sense, classicism is an artistic **style** and cultural perspective based on principles associated with the art and thought of ancient Greece and Rome. Specifically, this means a striving for harmony, order, reason, intellect, objectivity, and formal discipline. It contrasts with, for example, Romanticism (see Chapter 15) and other "anti-classical" styles and directions—for example the Baroque and Rococo (see Chapter 13) that emphasize bravura technique, imagination, emotion, and free expression. Artworks in the classical style represent idealized perfection rather than real life—for example, Myron's *Discus Thrower* (see Fig. **3.13**). As we will see, this is an embodiment of an ideal of beauty, sculpted according to the aesthetic principles of proportion, balance, and unity of form. Classicism is also an ideological viewpoint that reflects the idea of ancient Greece as the fount of civilization, later to be expanded to view Western European culture as its ultimate fulfillment.

Hellenism, which arguably could be defined as "anti-classical," moves away from classical principles toward reflections of emotion and naturalistic depiction. We will find this especially true of sculpture of the Hellenistic period.

Vase Painting

Fifth-century Athenian vase painting reflects some characteristics of earlier work, including the principally geometric nature of design. What distinguishes the classical style in vase painting (our only visual evidence of Greek two-dimensional art of this period) from earlier styles such as the archaic, is a new sense of **idealization** in figure depiction, which reflects a technical advance as well as a change in attitude. Many of the problems of foreshortening (the contracting of lines to produce an illusion of projection in space) had been solved. As a result, figures have a new sense of depth. The illusion could be strengthened in some cases by the use of light and shadow. Records imply that mural painters of this period were extremely skilled in representation, but we have no surviving examples to study. Vase painting does demonstrate, however, artists' concern for formal **design**—that is, logic and balance in the organization of space.

In the fifth century B.C.E., many of the most talented artists were engaged in sculpture, mural painting, and architecture. Nonetheless, vase painters such as the Achilles painter continued to express the idealism and dignity of the classical style. In Figure **3.9** the portrayal of the feet in the frontal position is significant, reflecting the new skill of foreshortening.

By the end of the fifth century B.C.E., vase painters had begun to break with the convention of putting all the figures along the base line: spatial depth was sometimes suggested by placing some figures higher than others. But it was not until the end of the next century that this convention was completely abandoned.

In general, we can identify four characteristics that define the classical style in vase painting. These are: (1) the figures are portrayed in simple line drawings; (2) the **palette** or color scheme is monochromatic—for example, red on black or black on red; (3) the palette depends on earthen tones—for example, red; and (4) the subject matter is heroic and idealized. For further examples go to http://atschool.eduweb.co.uk/allsouls/bm/room5.html.

Sculpture

Styles do not start on a given date and end on another, even in Athens during the rule of Pericles. Although much of what we can surmise about Greek classical sculpture is actually based on copies made at a later time, we know that the Greek classical style, especially in sculpture, was continually in a state of change. One artist's works differ from another's even though, in general, they reflect the basic characteristics of classicism. In classical sculpture, the tenets of Greek philosophy are reflected in the idealized, vigorous, youthful bodies that exhibit rational self-control and physical perfection.

From early in the fifth century B.C.E., we find an example of bronze sculpture representative of the new, developing classical style. The *Charioteer* from Delphi

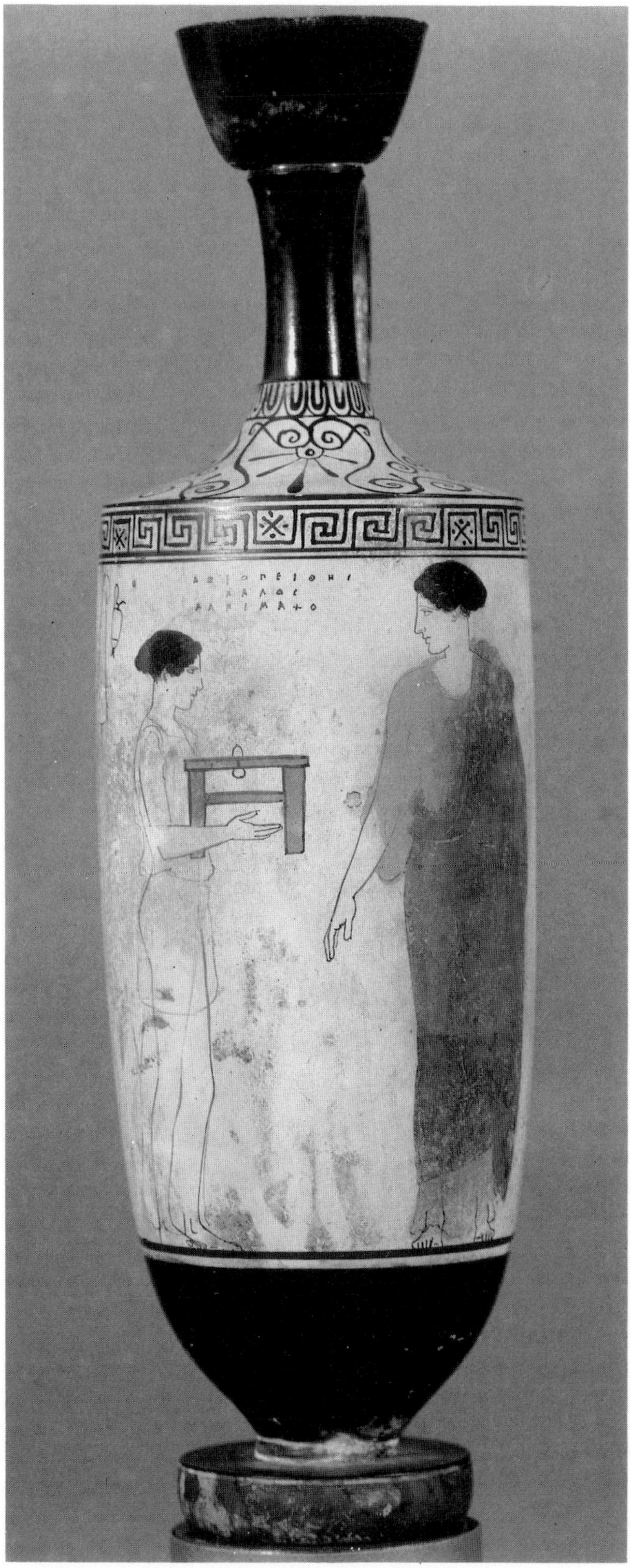

3.9 The Achilles painter, white ground lekythos from Gela(?), showing a woman and her maid, 440 B.C.E. 15 ins (38.4 cm) high. Museum of Fine Arts, Boston (Francis Bartlett Fund).

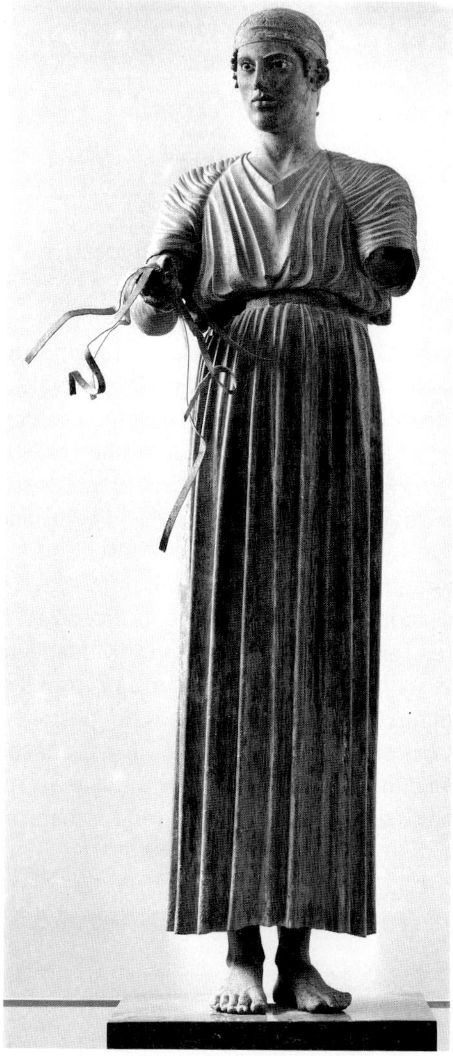

3.10 *Charioteer*, from the Sanctuary of Apollo, Delphi, c. 478 or 474 B.C.E. Bronze, lifesize. Archeological Museum, Delphi, Greece.

(Fig. **3.10**) records a victory in the games of 478 or 474 B.C.E. The figure is elegantly idealized, with subtle variation in the sleeves and drapery folds. The balance departs from absolute symmetry: the weight is slightly shifted to one leg, and the head turns gently away from the center line. The excellent preservation of this statue allows full appreciation of the relaxed control of the sculptor. This figure once stood atop an altar. He has a stern look on his face, as do typical images of Greek classicism, as an expression of rational self-control.

However, the age of Greek classical style properly began with the sculptors Myron (MY-ruhn) and Polyclitus (pah-luh-KLY-tuhs) in the middle of the fifth century B.C.E. Both contributed to the development of cast metal sculpture. (The example in Figure **3.12** is a marble copy of a bronze original, as is also Figure **3.13**.) In his *Lance Bearer* (*Doryphorus*; Fig. **3.12**), Polyclitus sought the ideal proportions for a male athlete: the *Lance Bearer*

A DYNAMIC WORLD

THE NOK STYLE OF AFRICA

For thousands of years, African artists and craftsmen have created objects of sophisticated vision and masterful technique. While the Greeks produced classical sculpture, on the Jos plateau of northern Nigeria, the Noks, a nonliterate culture of farmers, entered the Iron Age and developed their own accomplished artistic style. Working in terracotta, these artists produced boldly designed sculptures (Fig. **3.11**). Although they are stylized—with flattened noses and segmented lower eyelids, for example—each work reveals individualized character. Curiously, the unusual combination of human individuality and artistic stylization makes the works powerfully appealing. Probably, these heads are portraits of ancestors of the ruling class, because the technique and medium of execution seem to have been chosen to ensure permanence and for magical rather than artistic reasons.

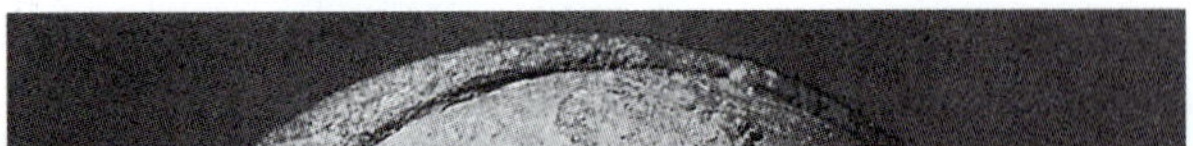

3.11 Head from Jemaa, c. 400 B.C.E. Terracotta, 10 ins (25 cm) high. National Museum, Lagos, Nigeria.

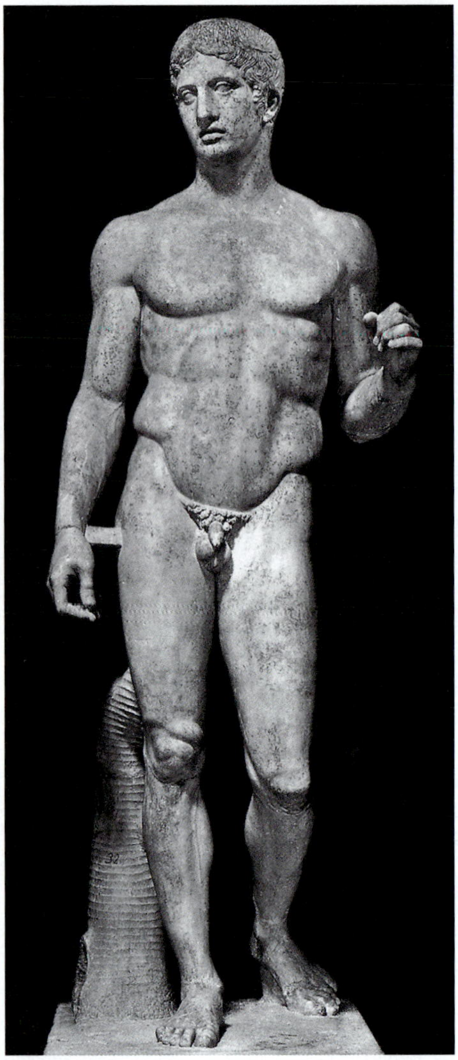

3.12 Polyclitus, *Lance Bearer (Doryphorus)*. Roman copy after a bronze original of c. 450–440 B.C.E. Marble, 6 ft 6 ins (1.98 m) high. Museo Archeologico Nazionale, Naples, Italy.

thus represents *the* male athlete, not *a* male athlete. The body's weight is thrown onto one leg in the *contrapposto* (cahn-truh-POHS-toh) stance. The resulting sense of relaxation, controlled motion, and subtle play of curves stands in contrast to the rigidity of the archaic style we witnessed in Chapter 2.

Polyclitus developed a set of rules for constructing the ideal human figure that he laid out in his treatise *The Canon* (*kanon* is the Greek word for "rule" or "law"). Probably, it was based on the ratios between some basic unit and the length of some body part or parts. Myron's best-known work is the *Discus Thrower* (see the Masterwork box).

The east pediment of the Parthenon once contained marvelous sculptural elements (Fig. **3.14**). The group of *Three Goddesses*, or *Fates*, is now on display in the British Museum in London. (This group of sculptures is known as the "Elgin Marbles" [EL-ghin] after Lord Elgin, who removed them from the Parthenon between 1801

MASTERWORK

MYRON—*DISCUS THROWER*

Myron's *Discus Thrower* (or *Discobolus;* Fig. **3.13**), exemplifies the classical concern for restraint in its subdued vitality and subtle suggestion of movement coupled with balance. But it also expresses the sculptor's interest in the flesh of the idealized human form. This example of the *Discus Thrower* is, unfortunately, a much later marble copy. Myron's original was in bronze, a medium that allowed more flexibility of pose than marble. A statue, as opposed to a relief sculpture, must stand on its own, and supporting the weight of the marble on a small area, such as one ankle, poses a significant structural problem. Metal has greater **tensile strength** (the ability to withstand twisting and bending), and thus this problem does not arise.

In *Discovery of the Mind: The Greek Origins of European Thought*, Bruno Snell writes: "If we want to describe the statues of the fifth century in the words of their age, we should say that they represent beautiful or perfect men, or, to use a phrase employed in the early lyrics for purposes of eulogy: 'god-like' men. Even for Plato the norm of judgment still rests with the gods, and not with men."[4] Even though Greek statuary may take the form of portraiture, the features are idealized. Human beings may be the measure of all things, but in art the individual is raised above human reality to the state of perfection found only in the gods.

Myron's representation of this young athlete contributes a sense of dynamism to Greek sculpture. Here Myron tackles a vexing problem for the sculptor: how to condense a series of movements into a single pose without making the sculpture appear static or frozen. His solution dramatically intersects two opposing arcs: one created by the downward sweep of the arms and shoulders, the other by the forward thrust of the thighs, torso, and head.

As is typical of Greek freestanding statues, the *Discus Thrower* is designed to be seen from one direction only. It is thus a sort of freestanding, three-dimensional "super-relief." The beginnings of classical style represented by celebration of the powerful nude male figure are an outgrowth of what is known as the "severe style." Myron was trained in this style, and the suggestions of moral idealism, dignity, and self-control in the statue are all qualities inherent in classicism. However, the *Discus Thrower* marks a step forward, in the increasing vitality of figure movement, a process we can trace from the frozen pose of the archaic kouros (see Fig. **2.12**), through the counterpoised balance of the *Kritios Boy* (see Fig. **2.16**), to Myron. Warm, full, and dynamic, Myron's human form achieves a new level of expressiveness and power. It is fully controlled and free of the unbridled emotion of later sculpture. For Myron, balanced composition remains the focus of the work, and form takes precedence over feeling.

3.13 Myron, *Discus Thrower* (*Discobolus*), c. 450 B.C.E. Roman marble copy after a bronze original, lifesize. Museo Nazionale Romano, Rome.

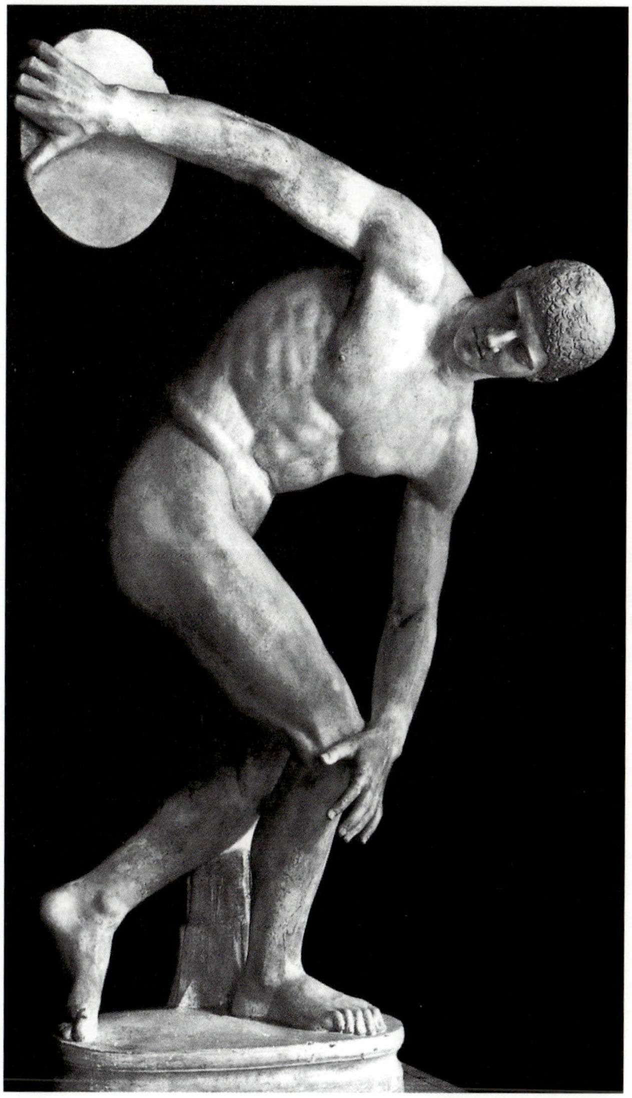

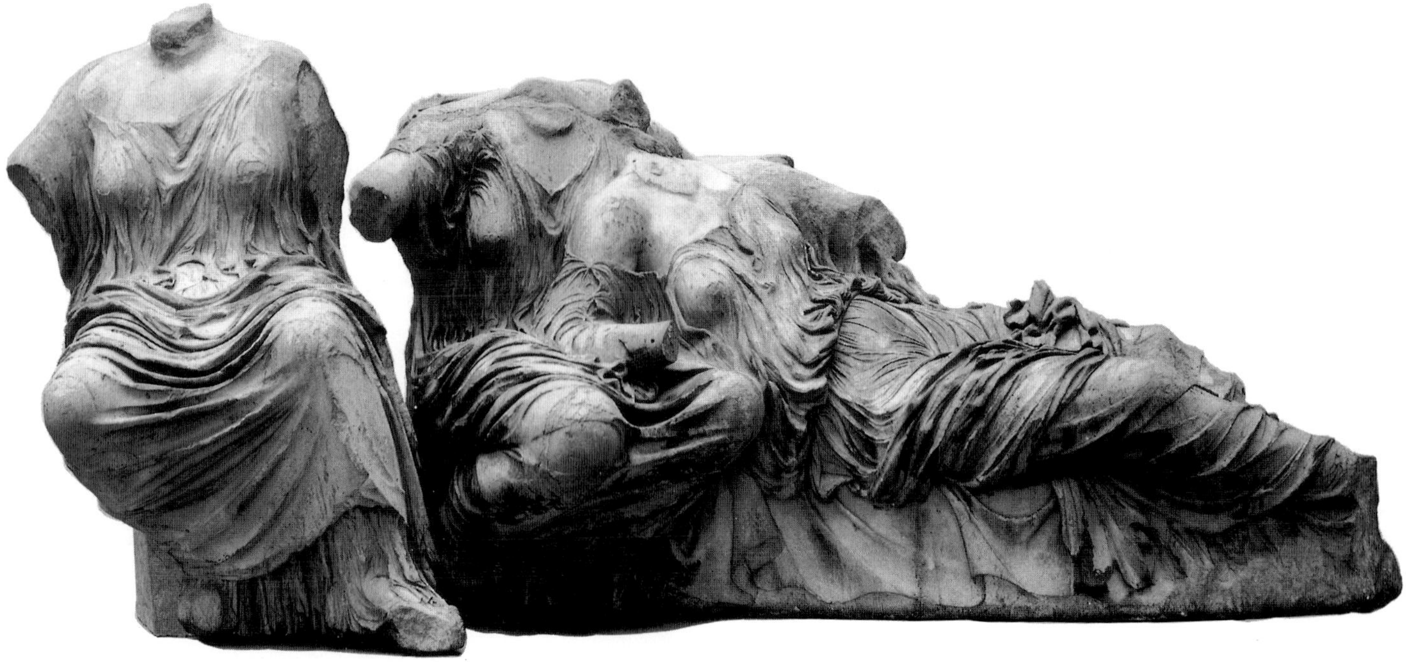

3.14 The *Fates*, from the east pediment of the Parthenon, c. 438–432 B.C.E. Marble, over lifesize. British Museum, London.

and 1803 and took them to London. British possession of these treasures is a continuing controversy between Britain and Greece.) Originally, this group formed part of the architectural decoration high on the Parthenon. There, its diagonal **curvilinearity** would have offset the straight lines, and strong verticals and horizontals, of the temple. The scene depicted on this pediment was an illustration of the myth of the birth of Athena, patron goddess of Athens, from her father Zeus' head.

We can learn much from these battered but superb figures. What strikes us first is the brilliant arrangement of the figures within the geometric confines of the pediment. This triangular design encloses curving lines that flow rhythmically through the reclining figures, leading the eyes naturally from one part to the next. The treatment of the draperies of the female figures is highly sophisticated, for not only do the drape and flow of the stone fabric reinforce the simple lines of the whole, but they also reveal the perfected human female form beneath. These, and the Dionysus, are forms raised beyond the merely specific and human, to the level of **symbols**, as is appropriate to their intended position on a temple.

Perhaps the most impressive sculptural finds of recent years are the two statues discovered in 1972 in the seabed off the coast of Riace, in southern Italy. Figure **3.15** shows one of these masterpieces, which are known as the *Riace* (ree-AH-chay) *Warriors*. The statue has been restored, but it shows the bone and glass eyes, silver teeth, and copper lips and nipples that would have adorned many ancient Greek bronzes. The simplicity with which the imposing musculature is portrayed, and the confident handling of the **contrapposto,** mark the work of a great sculptor of the mid-fifth century B.C.E. Some scholars even claim that the statues can be identified as part of a set of thirteen sculpted by Phidias (FID-ee-uhs), dedicated to the Athenian victory at Marathon in 490 B.C.E. They were probably shipwrecked around the first century B.C.E., on their way to Rome, having been plundered from Greece.

Late Classical Style

Sculpture of the fourth century B.C.E. changes toward greater emphasis on emotion. Praxiteles (prak-SIT-uh-leez) is famous for the individuality, delicacy, elegance, and grace in his treatment of subjects, such as the *Cnidian Aphrodite* (NY-dee-uhn af-roh-DY-tee; Fig. **3.16**). (Note that this is again a copy; the original has never been found.) His work looks inward in a way that differs from the formal detachment of earlier sculptors. Originally, Aphrodite rested her weight on one foot: her body sways to the left in the famous Praxitelean S-curve. Strain on the ankle of the sculpture was minimized by the attachment of the arm to drapery and a vase.

The elegance of the work of Praxiteles and his followers can also be seen in the *Hermes and the Infant Dionysus* (Fig. **3.17**). Although this marble statue is probably a copy, it nonetheless exhibits fine subtlety of modeling and detailed individuality. Here there is sensous beauty. The image is non-heroic, and the form, feminine.

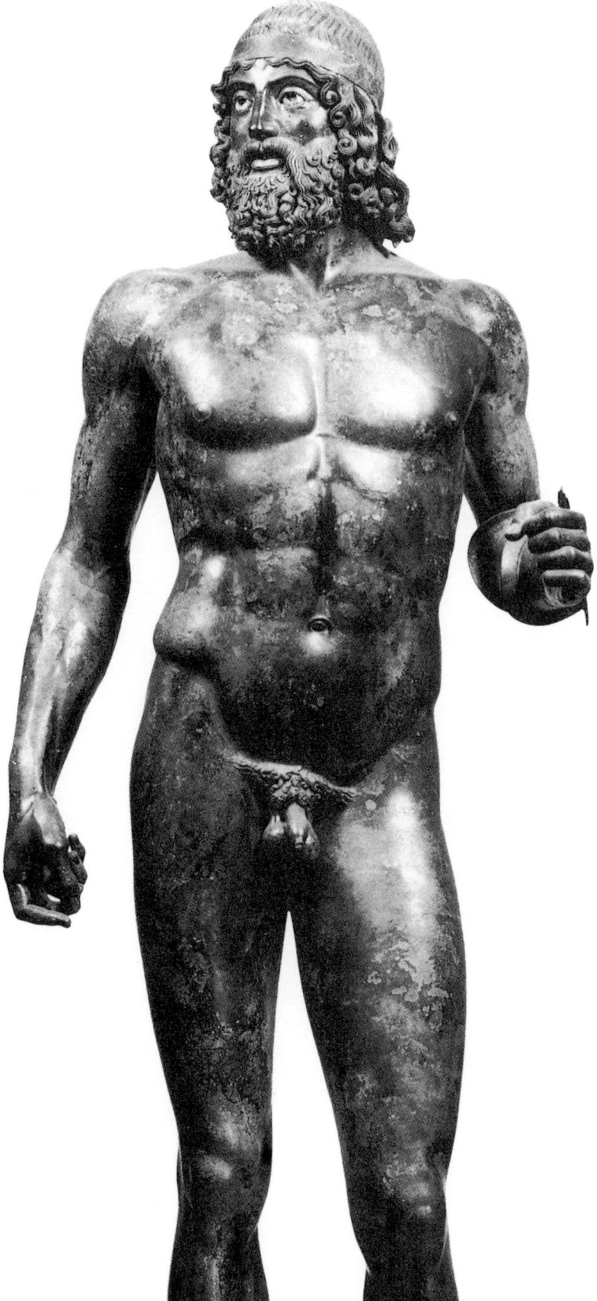

3.15 Phidias(?), *Riace Warrior*, fifth century B.C.E. Bronze with bone, glass-paste, silver, and copper inlaid. 6 ft 6⅘ ins (2 m) high. Museo Nazionale, Reggio Calabria, Italy.

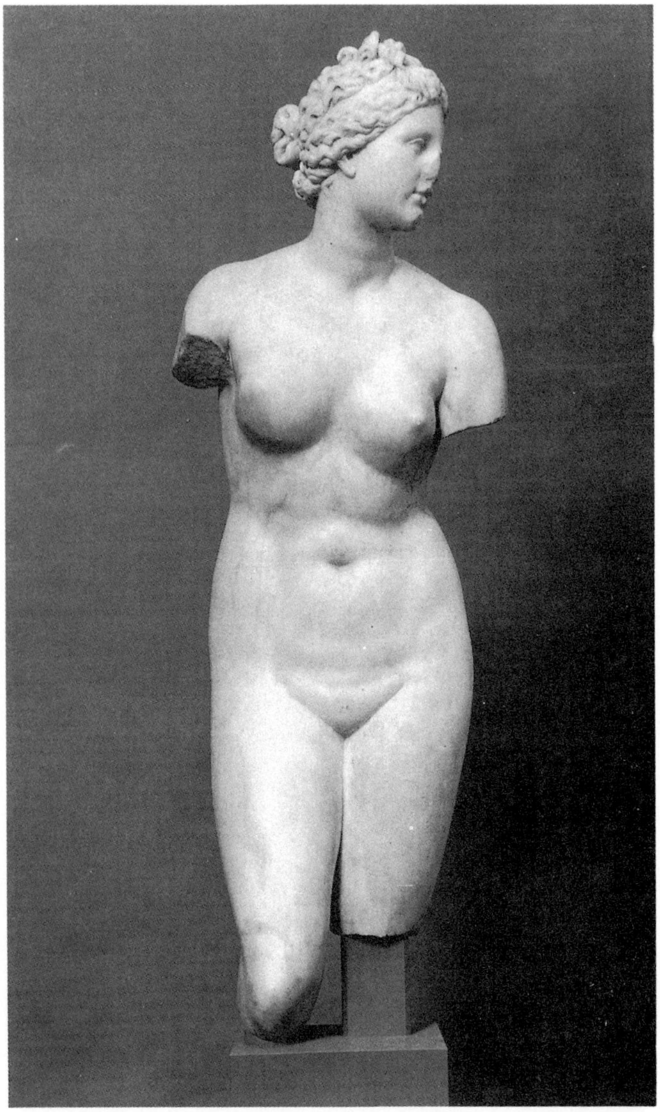

3.16 Praxiteles, *Cnidian Aphrodite*, probably Hellenistic copy of fourth-century B.C.E. original. Marble, 5 ft ½ in (1.54 m) high. Metropolitan Museum of Art, New York (Fletcher Fund, 1952).

From the late fourth century B.C.E., the sculpture of Lysippus (ly-SIP-uhs), a favorite of Alexander the Great, displays a dignified naturalness and a new concept of space. His *Scraper* (Fig. **3.18**) illustrates an attempt to depict the figure in motion, in contrast to many of the poses we have seen previously. The subject of the *Scraper* is mundane—an athlete scraping dirt and oil from his body. The proportions of the figure are even more naturalistic than those of Polyclitus (see Fig. **3.12**), but the naturalism is still far from complete.

Hellenistic style

In actuality a diversity of approaches, the Hellenistic style in sculpture continued to dominate the Mediterranean world until the first century B.C.E. As time progressed, it began to reflect an increasing interest in the differences

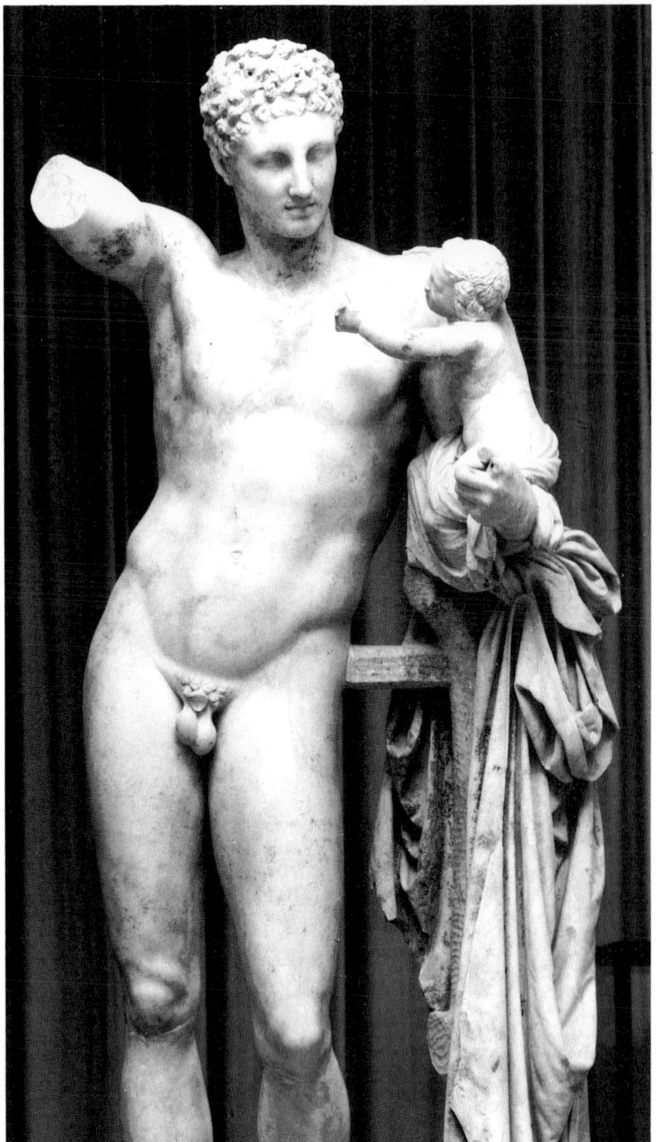

3.17 Followers of Praxiteles, *Hermes and the Infant Dionysus*, probably a Roman copy after an original of c. 300–250 B.C.E. Marble with remnants of red paint on the lips and hair, 7 ft 1 in. (2.16 m) high. Archeological Museum, Olympia. Discovered in the rubble of the ruined Temple of Hera at Olympia in 1875, this statue is now widely accepted as a very good Roman copy.

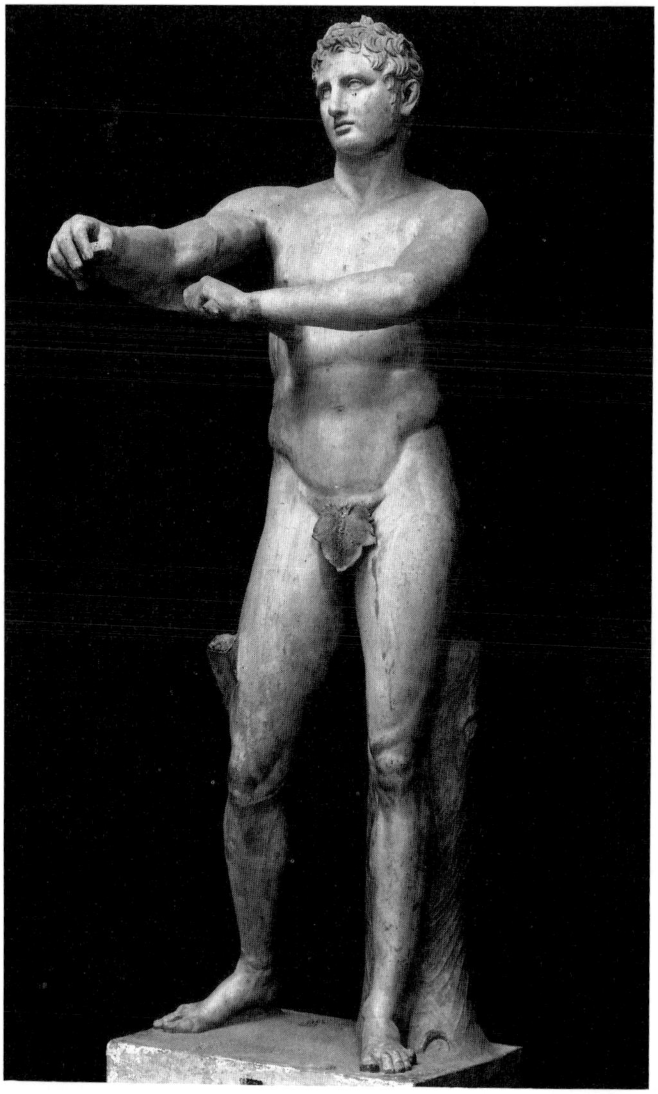

3.18 Lysippus, *Scraper* (*Apoxyomenos*), Roman copy, probably after a bronze original of c. 330 B.C.E. Marble, 6 ft 9 ins (2.06 m) high. Vatican Museum, Rome.

between individual humans. Hellenistic sculptors turned away from idealization, often toward **pathos**, trivia, even banality, or flights of technical virtuosity. These characteristics appear in Figures **3.19**, **3.20** and **3.21**. The *Dying Gaul* (Fig. **3.21**) is a powerful expression of emotion and pathos. This Roman copy of a statue from Pergamon places the figure on a stage, as if acting out a drama. The noble warrior, a Gallic casualty in the war between Pergamon and barbarian invaders, is slowly bleeding to death from a chest wound.

The *Nike of Samothrace* (NYK-ee; sam-oh-THRAYS), or *Winged Victory* (Fig. **3.19**), displays a dramatic virtuosity of technique. As the symbol of the victory of one of Alexander's successors, she is strong, heavy, and yet amazingly agile and graceful. The unsupported wings and flying garments represent an

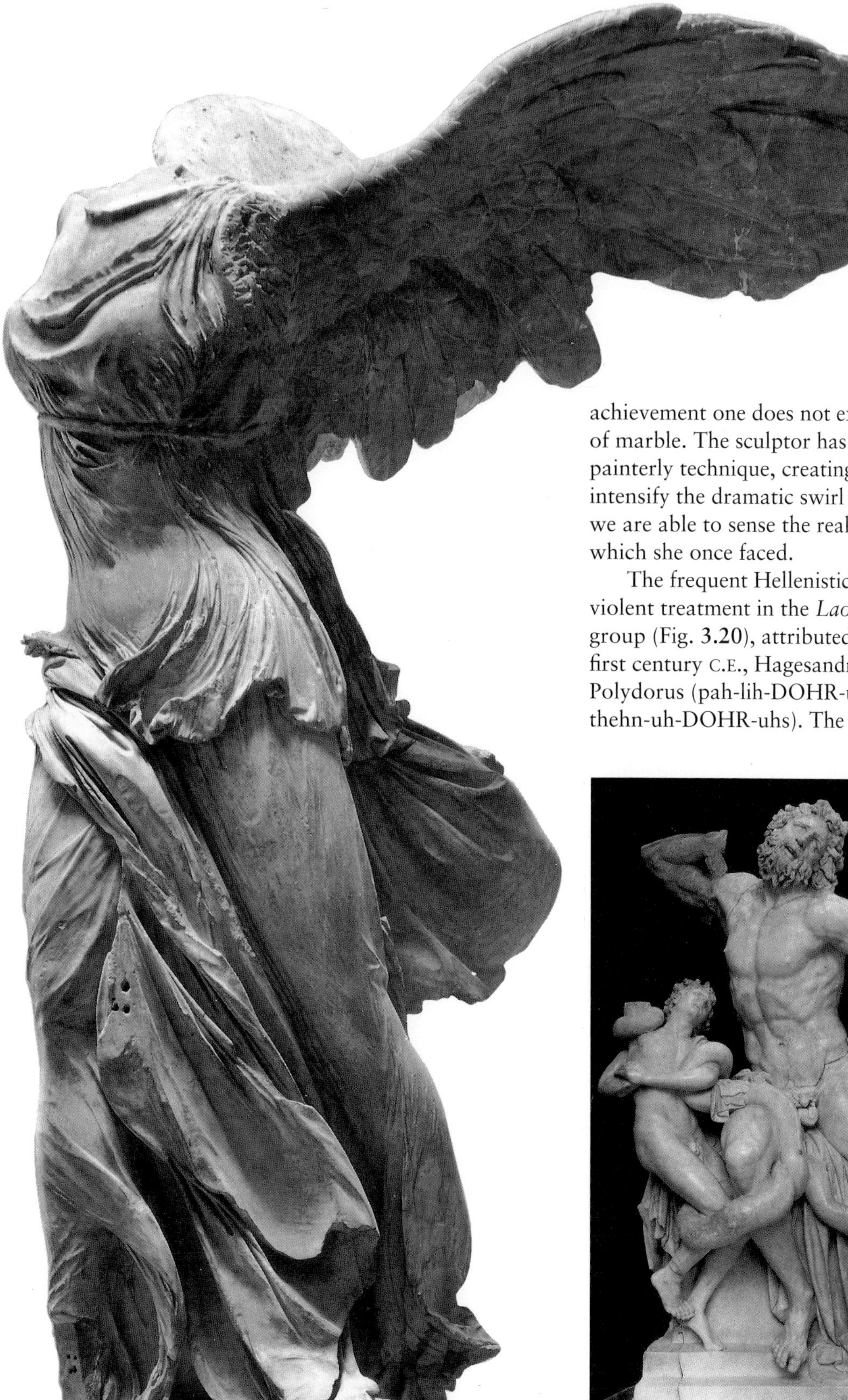

3.19 *Nike of Samothrace (Winged Victory)*, c. 190 B.C.E. Marble, 8 ft (2.44 m) high. Louvre, Paris.

achievement one does not expect to find in a carved work of marble. The sculptor has treated stone with an almost painterly technique, creating highlights and shadows that intensify the dramatic swirl of the draperies. As a result, we are able to sense the reality of the wind and sea into which she once faced.

The frequent Hellenistic theme of suffering receives violent treatment in the *Laocoön* (lay-AH-koh-ahn) group (Fig. **3.20**), attributed to three sculptors from the first century C.E., Hagesandrus (hag-uh-SAN-druhs), Polydorus (pah-lih-DOHR-uhs), and Athenodorus (ah-thehn-uh-DOHR-uhs). The Trojan priest Laocoön and

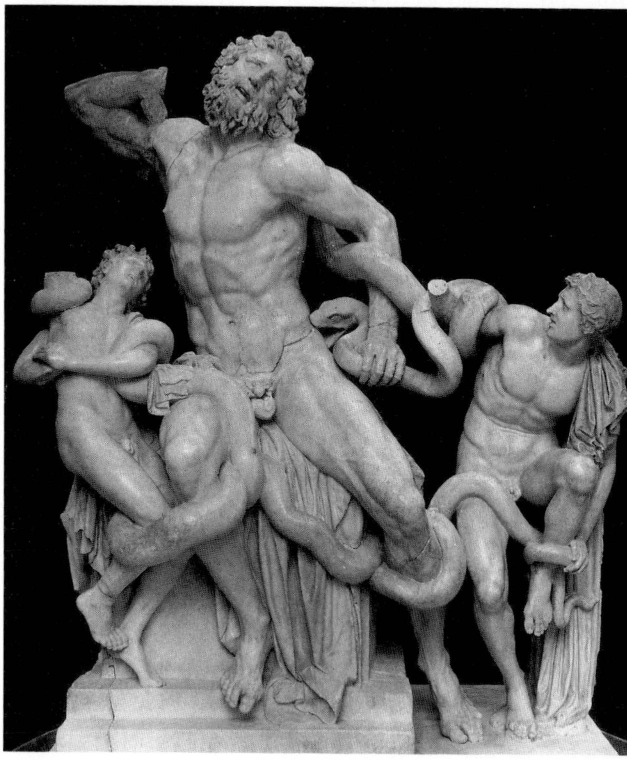

3.20 Hagesandrus, Polydorus, and Athenodorus, *Laocoön and his Two Sons*, first century C.E. Marble, 8 ft (2.44 m) high. Vatican Museum, Rome.

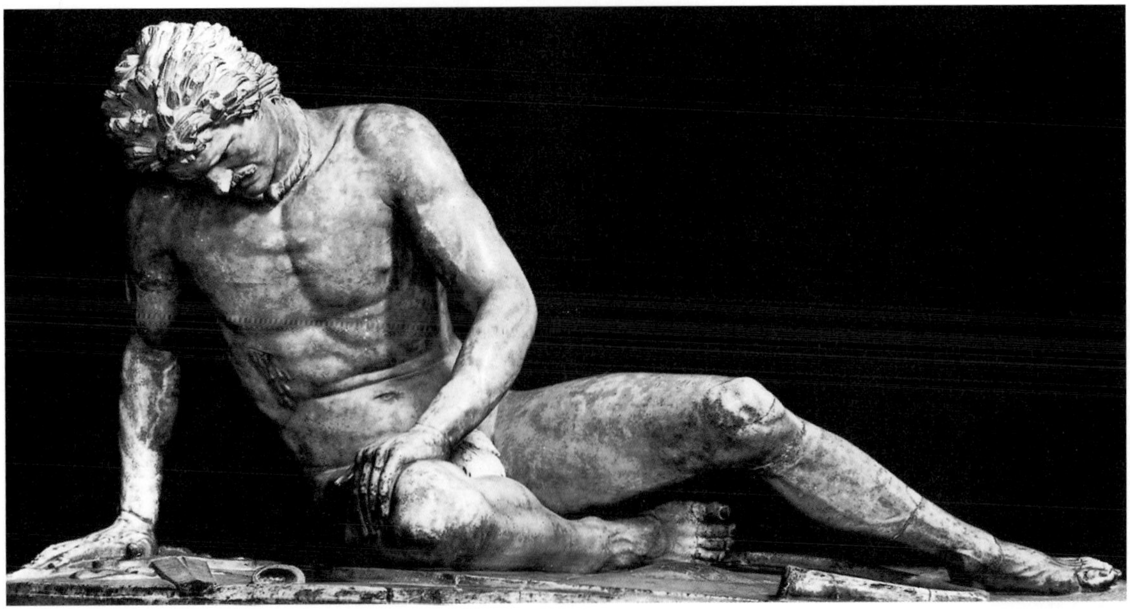

3.21 *Dying Gaul*, Roman copy of a bronze original of c. 230–220 B.C.E. Marble, lifesize. Museo Capitolino, Rome.

his sons are being strangled by sea serpents. According to Greek myth, this was Laocoön's punishment for defying Poseidon, god of the sea, by warning the Trojans of the Greek trick of the Trojan horse, in which soldiers were concealed. The expression of emotion is almost unrestrained. The figures writhe before our eyes, their straining muscles and bulging veins indicating mortal agony. For further examples visit http://www.mcad.edu/AICT/html/ancient/gcl_hell.html.

Architecture

Existing examples of Greek architecture offer a clear and consistent picture of the basic classical style, and nothing brings that picture so clearly to mind as the Greek temple. H.W. Janson makes an interesting point in *A Basic History of Art* when he suggests that the crystallization of the characteristics of a Greek temple is so complete that when we think of one Greek temple, we think of all Greek temples. Even so familiar a structure as a Gothic cathedral does not quite do this, because, despite the consistent form of the Gothic arch, it is used in such diverse ways that no one work can typify the many.

The classical Greek temple has a structure consisting of horizontal blocks of stone laid across vertical columns. This is called "post-and-lintel" structure. It is not unique to Greece, but the Greeks refined it to its highest aesthetic level. Structures of this type have some very basic problems. Stone has no great tensile strength, although it is high in **compressive strength** (the ability to withstand crushing). Downward thrust works against the tensile qualities of horizontal slabs (lintels) but for the compressive qualities of the vertical columns (posts). As a result, columns can be relatively delicate, whereas lintels must be massive.

This structural system allows for only limited open interior space. This was no great problem for the Greeks, because their temples were built to be seen and used from the outside. The Greek climate does not drive worshippers inside a building. Thus, exterior structure and aesthetics were the primary concern.

Greek temples used three orders, **Doric**, **Ionic**, and **Corinthian**. These are not just decorative and elevational conventions, but systems of proportion. The first, as we noted in the last chapter, is archaic in origin, although it was modified and used in classical style. The second is classical; the third, though of classical derivation, is of the later, Hellenistic style that we will examine further on in this chapter. As Figure **3.22** shows, simplicity was important to the Greek classical style, and the Doric and Ionic orders maintain clean lines even in their **capitals**. The Corinthian order has more ornate capitals. Taken in the context of an entire building, this detail may not seem significant. But columns, and particularly their capitals, are convenient ways of identifying the order of a Greek temple. Differences are also apparent in column bases and the configuration of the lintels, but the capitals tell the story at a glance. The earlier of the two classical orders, the Doric (see Fig. **2.18**), has a massive appearance compared with the Ionic. The Ionic column, with its round base, is raised above the baseline of the building. The flutings of the Ionic order, usually twenty-two per column, are deeper and more widely separated than those of the Doric, giving it a more delicate appearance. Ionic capitals consist of paired spiral shaped forms, known as

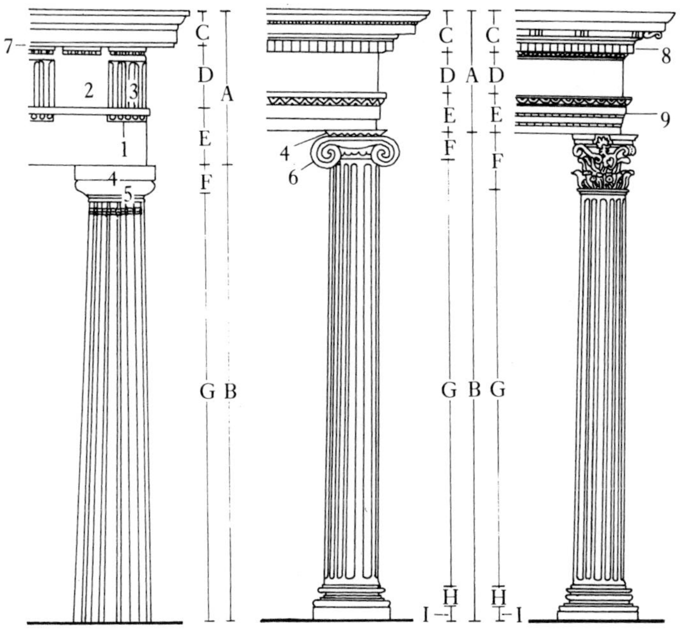

Greek Doric | Ionic | Corinthian

A Entablature
B Column
C Cornice
D Frieze
E Architrave
F Capital
G Shaft
H Base
I Plinth

1 Guttae
2 Metope
3 Triglyph
4 Abacus
5 Echinus
6 Volute
7 Fluting
8 Dentils
9 Fascia

3.22 The orders of Greek architecture. See also Fig. **2.18**.

volutes (vuh-LOOTS). The Ionic architrave, or lintel, is divided into three horizontal bands, which diminish in size downward, creating a sense of lightness, unlike the massive Doric architrave.

A final example of classical architecture takes us slightly beyond the classical period of the late fifth century B.C.E. Although no inscriptional information or other evidence provides a certain date for the Temple of Athena Nike (Fig. **3.26**), this small Ionic temple probably dates from the last quarter of the century. The pediments contained sculptures, but none of these has survived. What remain are sculptures from the frieze. The battle of Marathon of 490 B.C.E., the Athenians' greatest victory over the Persians, is the subject matter for the frieze on the south side of the temple. It is "the only known example in temple sculpture of a conflict from near-contemporary rather than legendary history."[5] The battle had apparently assumed a legendary status even by 420 B.C.E.

The Temple of Olympian Zeus (Fig. **3.27**) illustrates the Hellenistic modifications of classical style in architecture. The scale and complexity of the building are considerably different from the Parthenon. Order, balance, moderation, and harmony are still present, but these huge ruins reveal a change in proportions, with the use of slender and ornate Corinthian columns: temple architecture in this style was designed to produce an overpowering emotional experience. It is the product of an empire rather than a reflection of the aspirations of a free people in a city-state. Begun by the architect Cossutius (koh-SOO-shuhs) for King Antiochus (an-TY-oh-kuhs) IV of Syria, this is the first major Corinthian temple. Its elaborate detail pushed its completion date into the second century C.E. under the Roman emperor Hadrian. The ruins can only vaguely suggest the size and richness of the original building, which was surrounded by an immense walled precinct.

One center of Hellenistic power in Asia Minor was the city of Pergamon. Here, we find an example of Hellenistic style that ranks as one of the major accomplishments of the time. It was, in fact, considered to be one of the wonders of the then known world. The Altar of Zeus from the temple at Pergamon (Fig. **3.28**) was excavated in pieces beginning in 1873 and reassembled in a painstaking process that took more than fifty years. The altar was built by King Eumenes (YOO-min-eez) II as a means to glorify the king and to impress the Greek world with Eumenes' contribution to the spread of Hellenism by his victories over the barbarians. The great frieze of the altar stands more than seven feet (2.1 meters) tall and runs for more than 450 feet (137 meters) around the entire perimeter of the building. The frieze represents a radical departure from the design concept of the classical Greek temple. For example, in the Parthenon the **colonnade** serves as a part of the structure, supporting the entablature, which, in turn, elevates the frieze into a position of ethereal space and sustains the pediment and roof. In the Altar of Zeus, the frieze stands independently on a podium consisting of five steps. The colonnade retains no structural reason for being and becomes, rather, a unifying design device to give a boundary to the frieze.

The sculptures of the frieze narrate a typical battle between gods and giants, but the gods—now less potent in religious thought—symbolize qualities of good; the giants represent malevolent natural forces such as earthquakes and floods, and the portrayal symbolizes the struggle between the forces of light and the forces of darkness. An entire pantheon of gods is depicted, including Zeus, Helios the sun god, Hemera the winged goddess of the day, Artemis, and Heracles. Below the frieze we find the names of the sculptors who executed this magnificent work.

The technical details of the frieze are nearly as interesting as the power of its scale and the intricacies of its proportion. Throughout, great care was given to surface texture. Cloth, saddles, belt buckles, and flesh have been patiently finished to create textures of the real

MASTERWORK

The Parthenon

On the summit of the Acropolis at Athens (Figs **3.1** and **3.23**) stands the Parthenon, the greatest temple built by the Greeks and the prototype for all classical buildings thereafter. When the Persians sacked Athens in 480 B.C.E., they destroyed the existing temple and its sculpture. And when Pericles rebuilt the Acropolis later in the fifth century B.C.E. Athens was at its zenith, and the Parthenon was its crowning glory. The Parthenon (Figs **3.24** and **3.25**) exemplifies Greek classical architecture. Balance is achieved through geometric symmetry, and the clean, simple lines represent a perfect balance of forces holding the composition together. For the Greeks, deities were only slightly superior to mortals, and in the Greek temple, deity and humanity met in an earthly rendezvous. This human-centered philosophy is reflected by the scale of the temple.

In plan, the Parthenon has short sides slightly less than half the length of the long sides. Its interior, or *naos*, which is divided into two parts, housed a 40-foot (12-meter) high ivory and gold statue of Athena. The temple is peripteral—that is, it is surrounded by a single row of columns. The number of columns across the front and along the sides of the temple is determined by a specific convention. The internal harmony of the design rests in the regular repetition of virtually unvaried forms. All the columns appear alike and to be spaced equidistantly. But at the corners the spacing is adjusted to give a sense of grace and perfect balance, while preventing the monotony of unvaried repetition.

All the elements are carefully adjusted. A great deal has been written about the "refinements" of the Parthenon—those features that seem to be intentional departures from strict geometric regularity. According to some, the slight bulge of the horizontal elements compensates for the eye's tendency to see a downward sagging when all elements are straight and parallel. Each column swells toward the middle by about 7 inches (18 centimeters), to compensate for the tendency of parallel vertical lines to appear to curve inward. This swelling is known as ENTASIS. The columns also tilt inward slightly at the top, in order to appear perpendicular. The stylobate is raised toward the center so as not to appear to sag under the immense weight of the stone columns and roof. Even the white marble, which in other circumstances might appear stark, may have been chosen to reflect the intense Athenian sunlight. Parts of the temple were brightly painted.

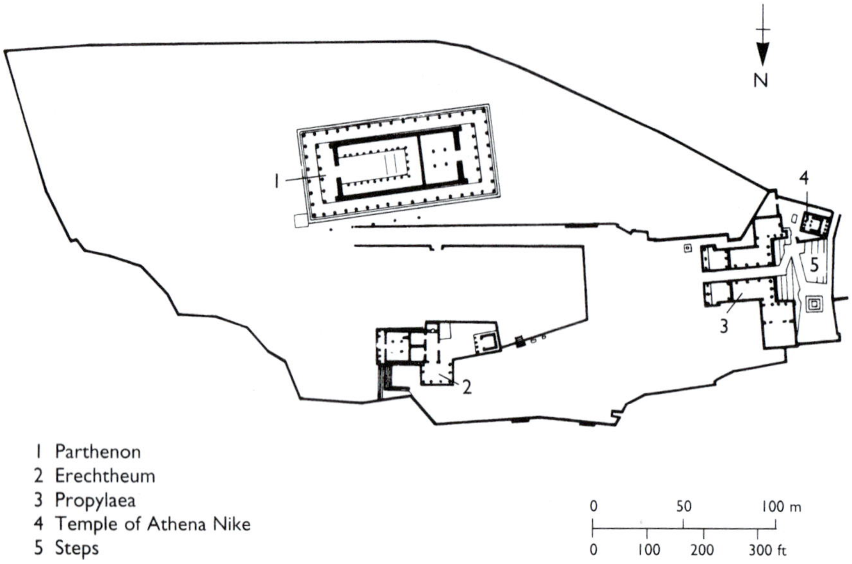

3.23 Plan of the Acropolis, Athens.

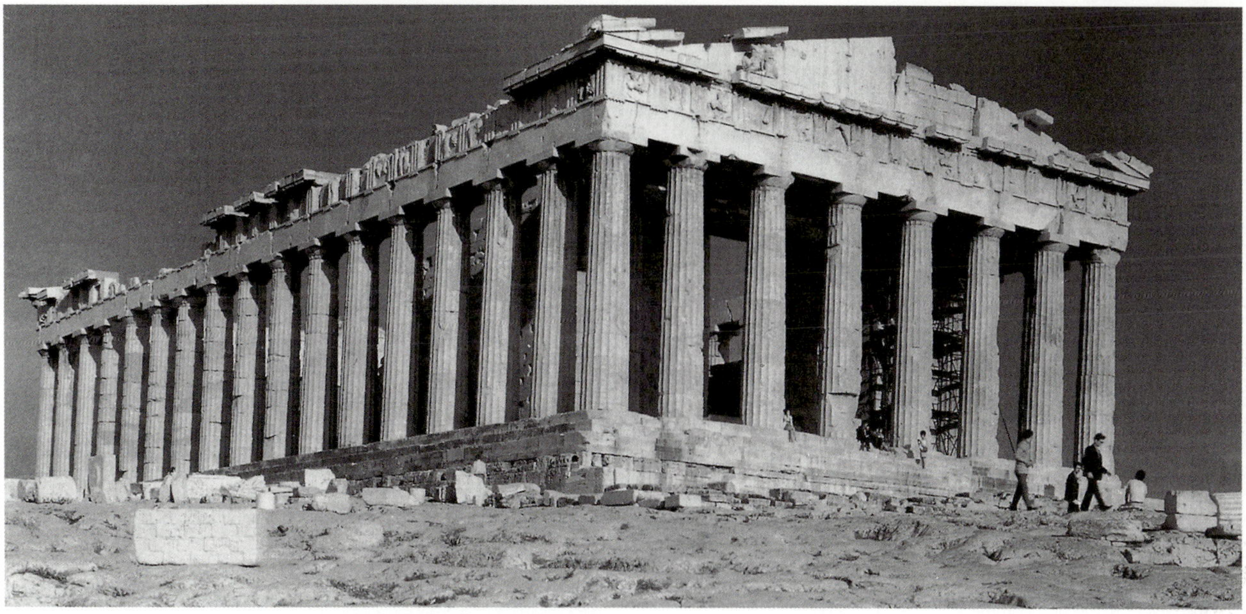

3.24 Ictinos and Callicrates, the Parthenon, Acropolis, Athens, from the northwest, 447–438 B.C.E. Marble.

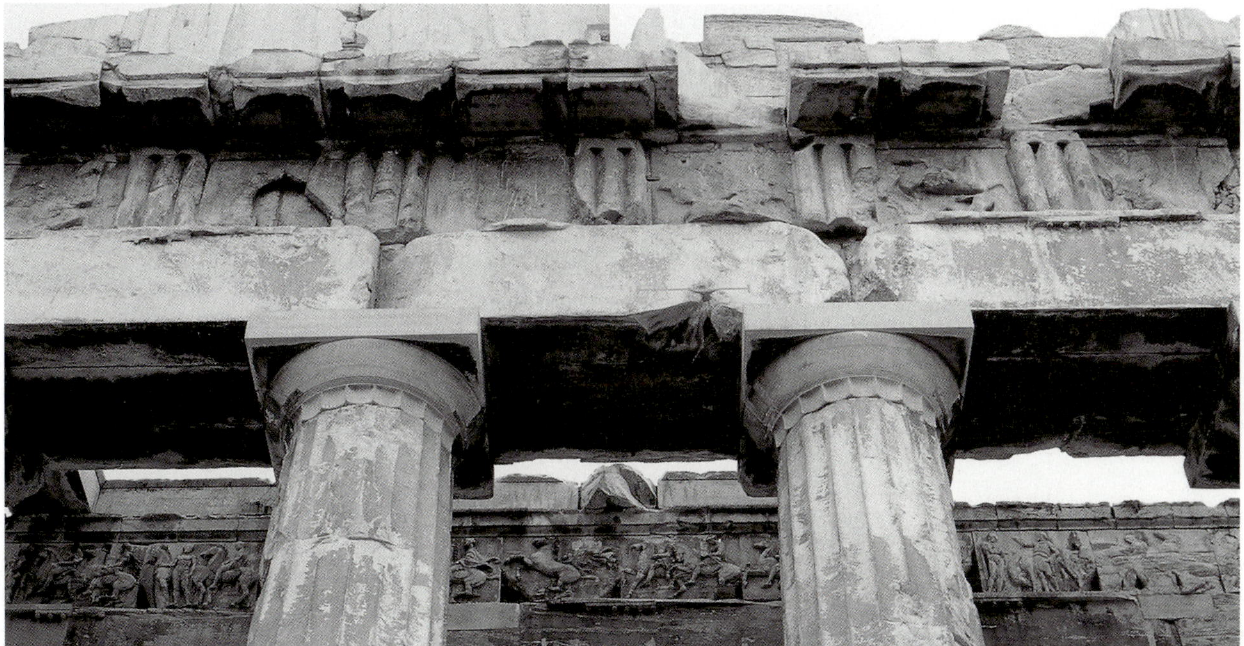

3.25 The Parthenon, frieze on the west cella, c. 440 B.C.E.

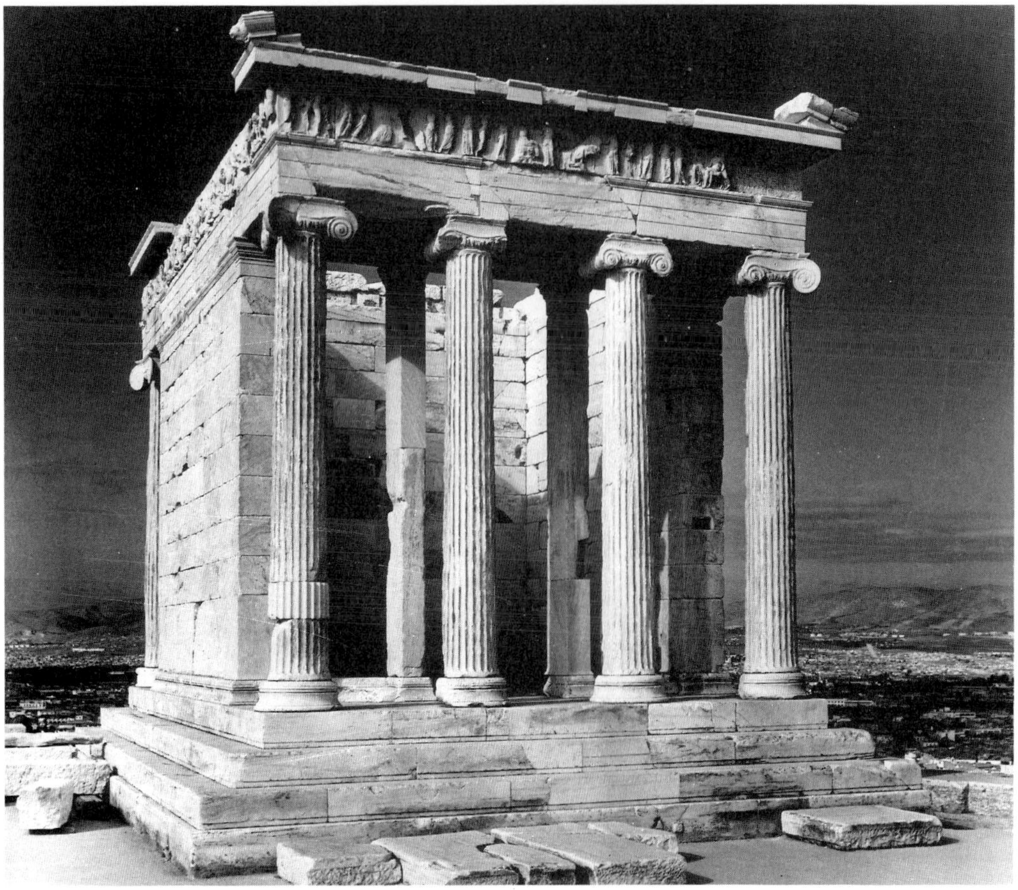

3.26 Temple of Athena Nike, Acropolis, Athens, (?)427–424 B.C.E.

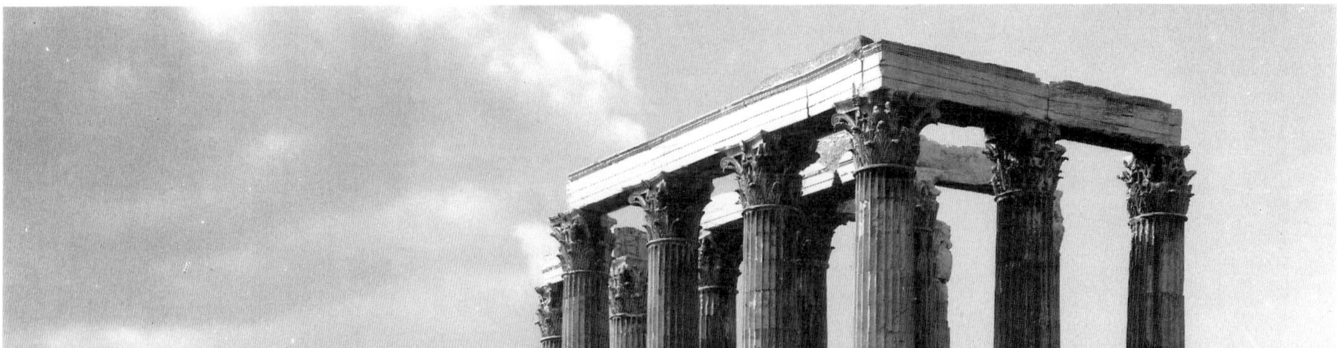

3.27 The Temple of Olympian Zeus, Athens, 174 B.C.E.–130 C.E.

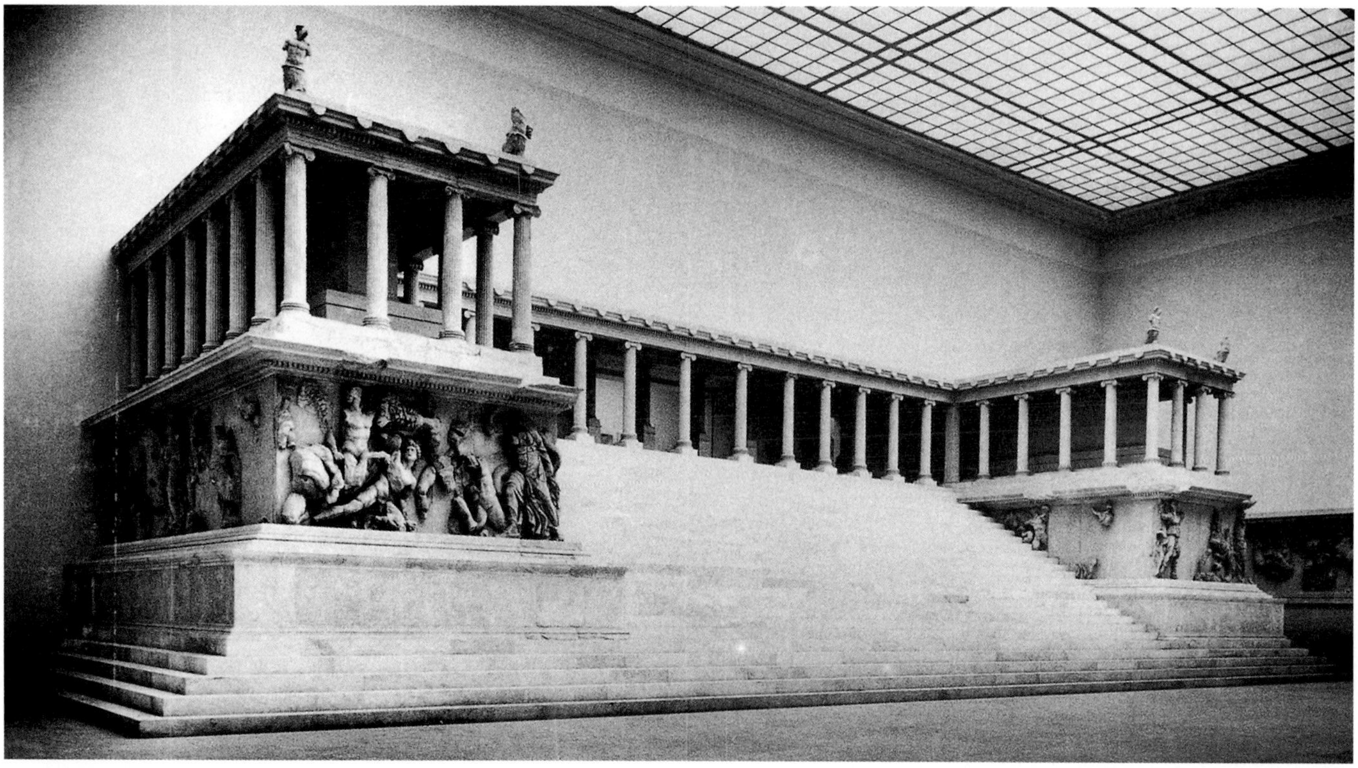

3.28 The west front of the Altar of Zeus, from the temple at Pergamon (restored), 197–159 B.C.E. Pergamonmuseum, Staatliche Museen, Berlin.

objects. Also of note is the depth of the relief. For additional examples visit http://gradweb.gradsch.uga.edu/archive/architecture.html.

Theatre

In contrast to sculpture and painting, which used more-or-less lifelike images to portray the ideal, Greek classical theatre pursued the same ends through quite different means. The theatre of Periclean Athens was theatre of convention, in which neither scenery nor costumes employs representational details. The audience accepts descriptions in poetic dialogue, without demanding to see the objects described. Imagination is the key to this kind of theatre.

Theatre productions in ancient Greece were part of three annual religious festivals: the City Dionysia (dy-uh-NY-see-uh), the Rustic Dionysia, and the Lenaea (leh-NAY-uh). The first of these was a festival of tragic, and the last, of comic plays. The City Dionysia took place at the Theatre of Dionysus in Athens. Contests held at these festivals were begun in 534 B.C.E., before the classical era. Although we do not have most of the plays themselves, we do know the titles and the names of the authors who won the contests, from the earliest to the last. From inscriptions we know that three playwrights figured prominently and repeatedly as winners. They were Aeschylus (EHS-kih-luhs), Sophocles (SAHF-oh-kleez), and Euripides (yoo-RIP-i-deez). All the complete tragedies we have were written by these playwrights—seven by Aeschylus, seven by Sophocles, and eighteen by Euripides.

Playwrights entering the contests for tragedy or comedy were required to submit their plays to a panel of presiding officers, who selected three winners for production. The early classical plays had only one actor, plus a chorus. At the time of selection, the playwright was assigned the chief actor and the patron who paid all the expenses for the production. The author was also director, **choreographer**, and musical composer, and often played the leading role as well.

Aeschylus

At the time the *Kritios Boy* (see Fig. **2.16**) was created, Aeschylus, the most famous poet of Ancient Greece, began to write for the theatre. He wrote magnificent tragedies of high poetry and on lofty moral themes. For example, in *Agamemnon*, the first play in the *Oresteia*

PROFILE

AESCHYLUS (C. 525–456 B.C.E.)

Aeschylus was the first and perhaps the greatest classical Greek tragedian. Together with Sophocles and Euripides, he is one of only three ancient Greek playwrights whose works have survived, and although he wrote fewer plays and won fewer contests than Sophocles, his contributions to the development of theatre are enormous. His contributions to dramaturgy and production make him, if not the greatest writer, then certainly the most important person in Western theatre history. He was instrumental in establishing tragedy as a genre, and some have referred to him as "the creator of tragedy." According to Aristotle, Aeschylus was responsible for adding the second actor to tragic performance.

Born into an aristocratic family, he fought in the important battles of Marathon and Salamis (between the Greeks and the Persians), and his firsthand knowledge of battle infuses his works, which illumine the miseries—not the glories—of war. Apart from a few documented travels to as far as Sicily, little else is known of the life of this major figure in Western literature and theatre. It is known that he won his first contest in 484 B.C.E., and won at least thirteen first prizes at the major festivals. His victory total increased to twenty-eight after his death because he was granted the singular honor of being allowed to compete through posthumous revivals. He may have written as many as ninety tragedies and satyr plays, although only eighty titles are known and only seven tragedies have survived.

The characters in Aeschylus' tragedies are "types" in the classically idealized mold. He treats history loosely and seeks to describe a broad religious view underwritten by patriotic exultation. He always remains within the controlled formality of the classic viewpoint, with its focus on intellect (form) as opposed to emotion (feeling), and he writes in an exalted style, using vocabulary that is clearly linked to the epic and lyric traditions of Homer (see p. 72). He handles the problems of evil and divine justice grandly and powerfully, and although his style may seem foreign to us, his questions and insights do not.

(or-es-TEE-uh) trilogy, Aeschylus' chorus warns that success and wealth are insufficient without goodness.

> Justice shines in sooty dwellings
> Loving the righteous way of life,
> But passes by with averted eyes
> The house whose lord has hands unclean,
> Be it built throughout of gold,
> Caring naught for the weight of praise
> Heaped upon wealth by the vain, but turning
> All alike to its proper end.[6]

Aeschylus poses questions that we still ask, such as: How responsible are we for our own actions? How subject are we to uncontrollable forces? His characters are larger than life, to be read as types rather than individuals, in accordance with the contemporary emphasis on the ideal. Yet in their strivings, as in their flaws, they are also undeniably human. Aeschylus' casts for his early plays consist of one actor and a chorus of fifty, conforming to the convention of the time. He is credited with the addition of a second actor, and, by the end of his long career, a third actor had been introduced and the chorus had been reduced to twelve. Read Aeschylus's *Agamemnon* at http://www.perseus.tufts.educ/cgi-bin/ptext?doc=Perseus%3Atext%3A1999.01.0004%3Aline%3D1&.submit=Change+now.

Sophocles

Sophocles' career overlapped with that of Aeschylus. With *Oedipus* (EH-dih-puhs or EE-dih-puhs) *the King*, his personal career reached its peak at the zenith of the Greek classical style. Sophocles' plots and characterizations illustrate a trend toward increasing **realism** similar to that in classical sculpture. The move toward realism did not involve any illusion of reality onstage, however, and even Euripides' plays, the least idealistic of the Greek tragedies, are not realistic as we understand the word.

Sophocles was certainly a less formal poet than Aeschylus, however. His themes are more human, and his characters more subtle, although he explores the themes of human responsibility, dignity, and fate with the same intensity and high seriousness that we see in Aeschylus. His plots show increasing complexity, but within the formal restraints of the classical spirit.

Sophocles lived and wrote after the death of Pericles in 429 B.C.E., and he experienced the shame of Athenian defeat. Even so, his later plays did not shift toward emotionalism and interest in action. Classical Greek theatre consisted mostly of discussion and narration. The stories often dealt with bloodshed, but, though the play might lead up to the violence, and action was resumed when it was over, it is important to note that blood was never seen to be shed on stage. Read Sophocles's *Oedipus*

MASTERWORK

SOPHOCLES—*OEDIPUS THE KING*

The story of Oedipus is one of the great legends of Western culture. When Sophocles used the legend in *Oedipus the King*, the story was familiar to all Athenians. In fact, it had also formed the basis for plays by Aeschylus and Euripides.

At the beginning of the play, Oedipus is the beloved ruler of the city of Thebes, whose citizens have been stricken by a plague. Consulting the Delphic oracle, Oedipus is told that the plague will cease only when the murderer of Queen Jocasta's (joh-CAS-tuh) first husband, King Laius (LAY-uhs), has been found and punished for his deed. Oedipus resolves to find Laius' killer, only to discover that the old man he himself killed when he first approached Thebes as a youth, was none other than Laius. Finally, Oedipus learns the truth about himself and his past. Laius was Oedipus' father, and Jocasta, now Oedipus' wife and mother of his children, is, in fact, his mother. At the end, Jocasta hangs herself, and guilt-stricken Oedipus blinds himself with Jocasta's brooch pin.

The action moves from one moment of dramatic tension to another, rising to a climax. The protagonist, or central character, Oedipus, starts with no knowledge of his true identity. Slowly he discovers the truth about himself and the terrible deeds he has unknowingly committed: the murder of his father and marriage to his mother. However, his tragedy lies in the discovery of his guilt, rather than in the heinous acts themselves.

In *Oedipus*, Sophocles explores the reality of the dual nature we all share. He poses the eternal question, can we control our destinies or are we the pawns of fate? In exploring this question, he vividly portrays the circumstances in which one's strengths become one's weaknesses. Oedipus' **hamartia** (huh-MAR-shuh), or tragic flaw, is the excessive pride, or *hubris* (HYOO-brihs), which drives him to pursue the truth, as a king—or a man—should, only to find the awful answer in himself.

Although the play is a tragedy, the message is one of uplift and positive resolution. (This type of structure is more fully described in the section below on Aristotle's theory of tragedy.) When Oedipus recognizes his own helplessness in the face of the full horror of his past, he performs an act of contrition: he blinds himself, and then exiles himself. As grotesque as this may seem, it nevertheless releases Oedipus onto a higher plane of understanding. The chorus chants, "I was blind," while seeing with normal eyes, and Oedipus moans, "I now have nothing beautiful left to see in this world." Yet, being blind, Oedipus is now able to "see" the nobler, truer reality of his self-knowledge.

the King at http://etext.lib.virginia.edu/cgibin/browse-mixed?id=SopOedi&tag=public&images=images/modeng&data=/1v1/Archive/eng-parsed.

Euripides

Euripides was younger than Sophocles, although both died in 406 B.C.E. They did, however, compete with each other, despite the fact that their works have quite different styles. Euripides' plays carry realism further than any other Greek tragedies and deal more with psychological probings and individual emotions than with great events. His language, though still basically poetic, has greater verisimilitude and much less formality than that of his predecessors. Euripides also experiments with, or ignores, many of the conventions of his theatre, relying less heavily on the chorus. He also explores the mechanical potential of scenery shifting and questions the religion of the day in his plays. They are more **tragicomedies** than pure tragedies, and some critics have described many of them as **melodramas**.

Plays such as *The Bacchae* (BAHK-ee) reflect the changing Athenian spirit and dissatisfaction with contemporary events. Euripides was not particularly popular in his time, perhaps because of his less idealistic, less formal, and less conventional treatment of dramatic themes and characters. Was he perhaps too close to the reality of his age? His plays were received with enthusiasm in later years, however, and they are unquestionably the most popular of the Greek tragedies today. Read Euripides's *The Bacchae* at http://www.perseus.tufts.edu/cgi-bin/ptext?doc=Perseus%3Aabo%3Atlg%2C0006%2C017&query=1.

Aristotle's Theory of Tragedy

We cannot leave the discussion of Greek classical theatre without noting Aristotle's analysis of tragedy. His ideas are still basic to dramatic theory and criticism, despite the fact that they have often been misunderstood and misapplied over the past 2,400 years. Drawing principally on Sophocles as a model, Aristotle laid out in the *Poetics* the six elements of tragedy. In order of importance they are: (1) *plot,* the basic structure of the play, which includes such things as decision-points for the characters and a climax, or high point of action; (2) *character*, the people of the play and their motivating psychological characteristics; (3) *thought*, what we would call the ideas explored by the play; (4) *diction*, the words of the play and their style, e.g. prose or poetry; (5) *music*, or what we would call the sounds of the production—for example, the manner in which the actors speak their lines, etc.; and (6) *spectacle*, all of the visual elements of the production, including scenery and costumes.

Plot, in tragedy, is far more than the simple storyline. For Aristotle, plot creates the basic structure of the play, just as form is the cornerstone of classical design. The parts of plot give shape to the play with a beginning (exposition), a middle (complication), and an end (**dénouement**), ensuring that the audience understands the progress of the drama. Additional points in the plot include *discoveries*, in which characters learn about themselves and others; *foreshadowing*, in which the playwright alerts the audience to future action; *reversals*, in which fortunes change; and *crises*, in which tension is created and characters grow.

For Aristotle, tragedy is a form of drama in which a protagonist goes through a significant struggle which ends in disaster. However, the protagonist is always a **heroic** character, who gains a moral victory even in physical defeat. Tragedy therefore asserts the dignity of humanity, as well as the existence of larger moral forces. In the end, tragedy is a positive experience, which evokes a catharsis, or purging, of pity and fear in the audience.

Costume

If the plays of the Greek classical tragedy treated lofty themes with theatrical, poetic language, the style of the productions displayed no less formality, idealism, and convention. The larger-than-life characters were portrayed by actors, always men, in larger-than-life, conventionalized costumes. Actors and chorus wore bright robes, whose colors conveyed specific information to the audience. The robes were padded to increase the actor's size; height was increased by thick-soled boots called *kothurnoi* (koh-THUHR-noy), and large masks whose fixed, conventionalized expressions were readily identified by the sophisticated and knowledgeable audience (Fig. **3.29**). Height was further increased by an *onkos* (AHN-kohs), a wiglike protrusion on top of the mask.

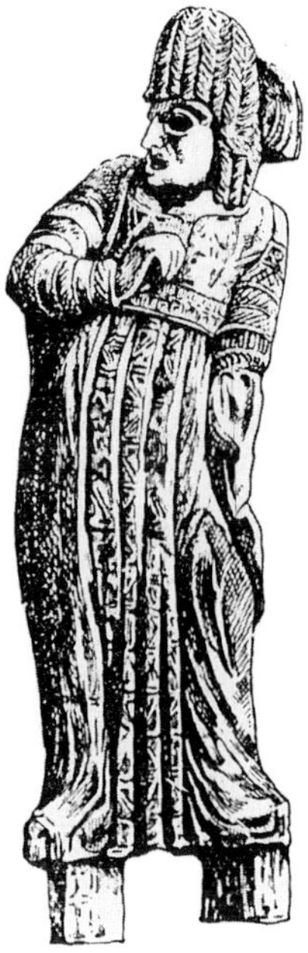

3.29 Greek statuette of a tragic actor, wearing a mask and a rich costume.

Aristophanes

Tragedies were not the only works produced in the theatre of the classical era in Athens. The Athenians were extremely fond of comedy, although no examples survive from the Periclean period. Aristophanes (eh-ris-TAH-fuh-neez; c. 450–380 B.C.E.), of whose plays we have eleven, was the most gifted of the comic poets. His comedies of the post-classical period, such as *Lysistrata* (lis-is-TRAH-tuh), are highly satirical, topical, sophisticated, and often obscene. Productions of his comedies are still staged, in translation, but as the personal and political targets of his invective are unknown to us, these modern productions are mere shadows of what took the stage at the turn of the fourth century B.C.E.

Theatre Design

Scholars do not agree about the exact layout of the classical Greek theatre building and the precise nature of the acting area and scenery. But we can summarize some of the architectural and archeological speculation, bearing in mind that it is only speculation.

The form of the Greek theatre owes much to its origins in the choral dances associated with the worship of Dionysus. In 534 B.C.E., Thespis is reported to have introduced a single actor to these dances. In 472 Aeschylus added a second actor, and in 458 Sophocles added a third. Throughout its history the Greek theatre was composed of a large circular **orchestra**—the acting and dancing area—with the vestige of an altar at its center, and a semicircular *theatron* (THAY-uh-trahn)—auditorium or viewing place—usually cut into or occupying the slope of a hill. Since the actors played more

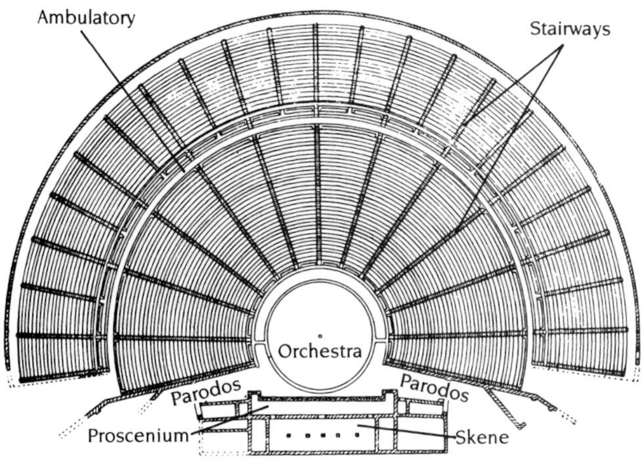

3.30 Plan of the theatre at Epidaurus, Greece, c. 350 B.C.E.

3.31 Polyclitus the Younger, theatre at Epidaurus, Greece, c. 350 B.C.E. Diameter 373 ft (114 m), orchestra 66 ft (20 m) across.

than one role, they needed somewhere to change costume, and so a **skene** (SKEEN-ay)—scene-building or retiring place—was added. The process by which the *skene* developed into a raised stage is somewhat obscure.

The earliest theatre still in existence is the Theatre of Dionysus on the south slope of the Acropolis. It dates from the fifth century B.C.E., and is where the plays of Aeschylus, Sophocles, Euripides, and Aristophanes were staged. Its current form dates from a period of reconstruction around 338–326 B.C.E. The theatre at Epidaurus (ehp-ih-DOHR-uhs; Figs **3.30** and **3.31**) is the best preserved. It was built by Polyclitus the Younger about 350 B.C.E. Its size demonstrates the monumental character the theatre had assumed by that time. The orchestra measures 66 feet (20 meters) in diameter, with an altar to Dionysus in the center. The auditorium, comprising slightly more than a semicircle, is divided by an **ambulatory** about two-thirds of the way up, and by radiating stairways. All the seats were of stone, and the first or lowest row consisted of seats for the dignitaries of Athens. These seats had backs and arm rests, some decorated with relief sculptures.

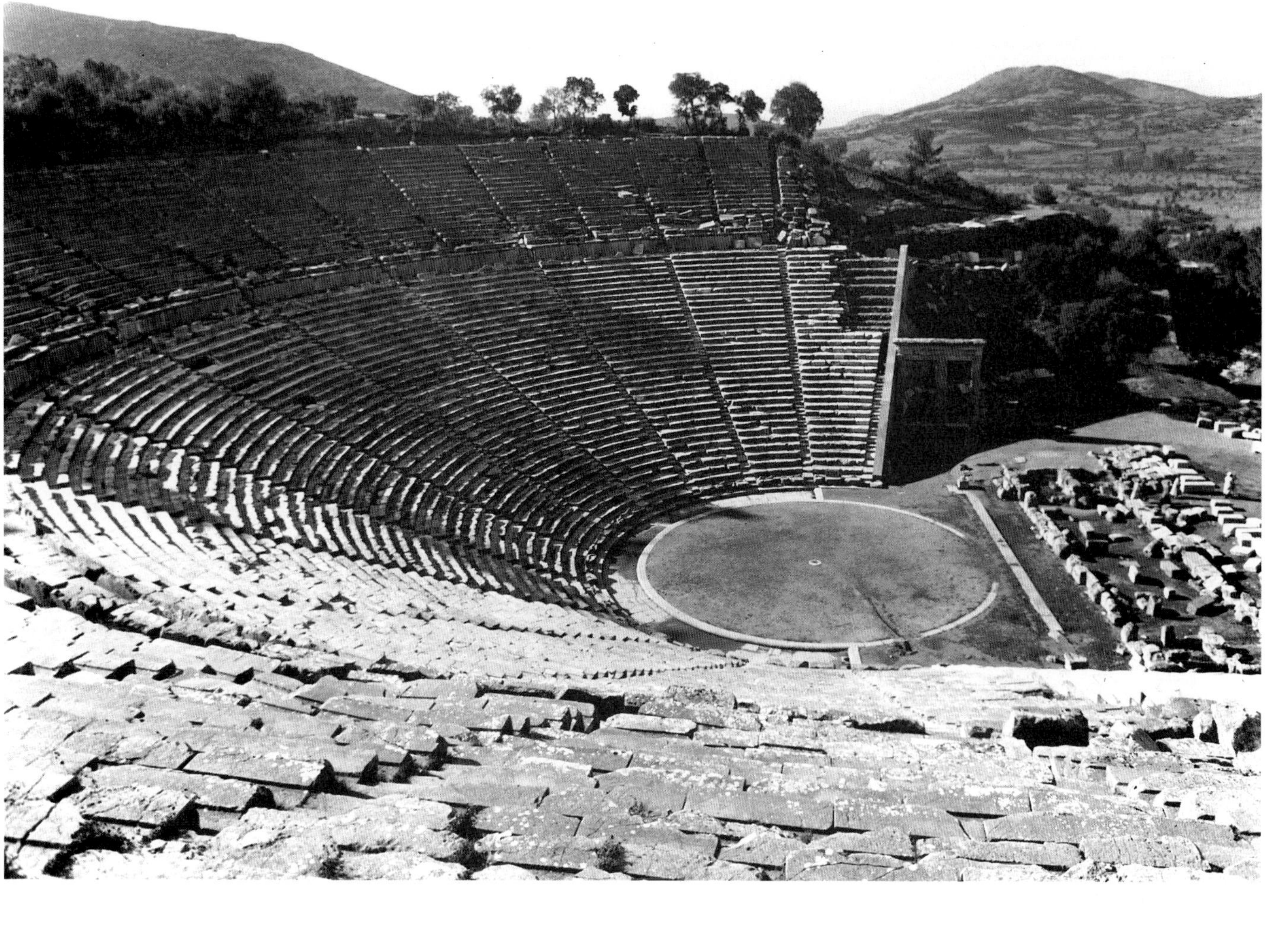

The design of theatres undoubtedly differed from place to place but time has removed most examples. The many theories about how Greek theatre productions worked, how scenery was used, and whether or not a raised stage was present, make fascinating reading, and the reader is encouraged to explore the area in detail elsewhere.

The Hellenistic period (roughly the fourth century B.C.E. to the Roman infiltration, about 250 B.C.E.), was a time of great expansion for the theatre in Greece. The general plan of the theatres did not change, but the *skene* frequently was two stories tall. After the chorus disappeared, in later Hellenistic times, a stage as high as twelve feet (3.6 meters) was not unusual.

In this period, comedy was the staple of the theatre. Only five, incomplete, plays by Menander (meh-NAN-duhr c. 343–291 B.C.E.) survive. The action is bawdy; the situations are pleasant and domestic, and for the most part superficial and without satire and the themes were similar to modern day sitcoms. Religion no longer played a central role in the theatre, and, as we have noted, the chorus disappeared entirely.

Music

Few examples of Ancient Greek music survive from any era—a handful of fragments with no clue as to how they were supposed to sound. The lyre and the aulos (see Fig. **2.20**) were the instruments basic to Greek music, and each had a significant role in pre-classical ritual. In the classical era the lyre and the aulos were used as solo instruments and as accompaniment.

The spirit of contest popular among the Greeks apparently extended to instrumental and vocal music. As with all the arts, music was regarded as essential to life, and almost everyone in Athens participated. Perhaps the word "dilettante," an amateur lover of the arts, would best describe the average Athenian. Professionalism and professional artists, however, were held in low esteem, and Aristotle urged that skill in music stop short of the professional. Practice should develop talent only to the point where one could "delight in noble melodies and rhythms," as he says in the *Poetics*. He also discouraged excessive complexity. We should not infer too much from such an observation: complexity for the ancient Greeks would no doubt still be simplicity by our musical standards. It appears reasonably clear, for instance, that all Greek music of this era was **monophonic**—that is without **harmony**. "Complexity" might therefore mean technical difficulty, and perhaps melodic ornamentation.

Aristotle said that music should lead to noble thought, but some music in the Greek repertoire certainly led the other way. Rituals in praise of the god Dionysus were emotional and frenetic, and music played an important role in these.

If Plato's *Republic* can be taken as an accurate guide, Greek music seems to have relied on convention. Most of the performances in Periclean Athens appear to have been improvised, which may seem at odds with formal order. However, "**improvisation**" should not be interpreted here as spontaneous or unrehearsed. The Greeks had formulas or rules concerning acceptable musical forms for nearly every occasion. So the musician, though free to seek the momentary inspiration of the Muses—the mythological sisters who presided over the arts—was constrained by all the rules applicable to the occasion.

Pythagoras taught that an understanding of numbers was the key to an understanding of the entire spiritual and physical universe. Those views, expressed in music, as well as the other arts, led to a system of sounds and rhythms ordered by numbers. The **intervals** of the musical scale were determined by measuring vibrating strings. As a result, sounds in Greek music were calculated on relationships of 2 to 1 (one note having exactly double the vibrations per second as another—we call it an octave: middle C compared to C^1, for example); 5 to 1 (what we call a fifth—for example, the relationship between C and the G above), or perhaps, 4 to 1 (what we call a fourth—for example, the relationship between C and the F above).

Dance

Dance in the age of Pericles reflected both classical and anti-classical styles. The dances of the Dionysiac cult revels, which may have decreased in popularity but certainly continued under Periclean rule, disregarded form, order, restraint, and idealization. They were characterized by emotional frenzy, not intellect. However, the philosophies of the era, the relationship of dance to music and drama, and the treatment of dance by Plato and Aristotle, indicate that those aspects of dance which were associated with the theatre, at least, must have reflected classical values.

Dance is an evanescent art form, however. Today, even with labanotation (lab-uh-noh-TAY-shun)—a system of writing down dance movements—we cannot know what a dance piece looks like if we do not see the event. So the literary treatises, the musical fragments, and the archeological evidence from which so many have tried to reconstruct the dances of the Greeks give us very little information. In fact, the conventional nature of Greek art is our most formidable obstacle. Some vase paintings and sculptures clearly depict dancers (Fig. **3.32**), but we do not know the conventions that apply to these poses, and so we are unable to reconstruct any actual dances.

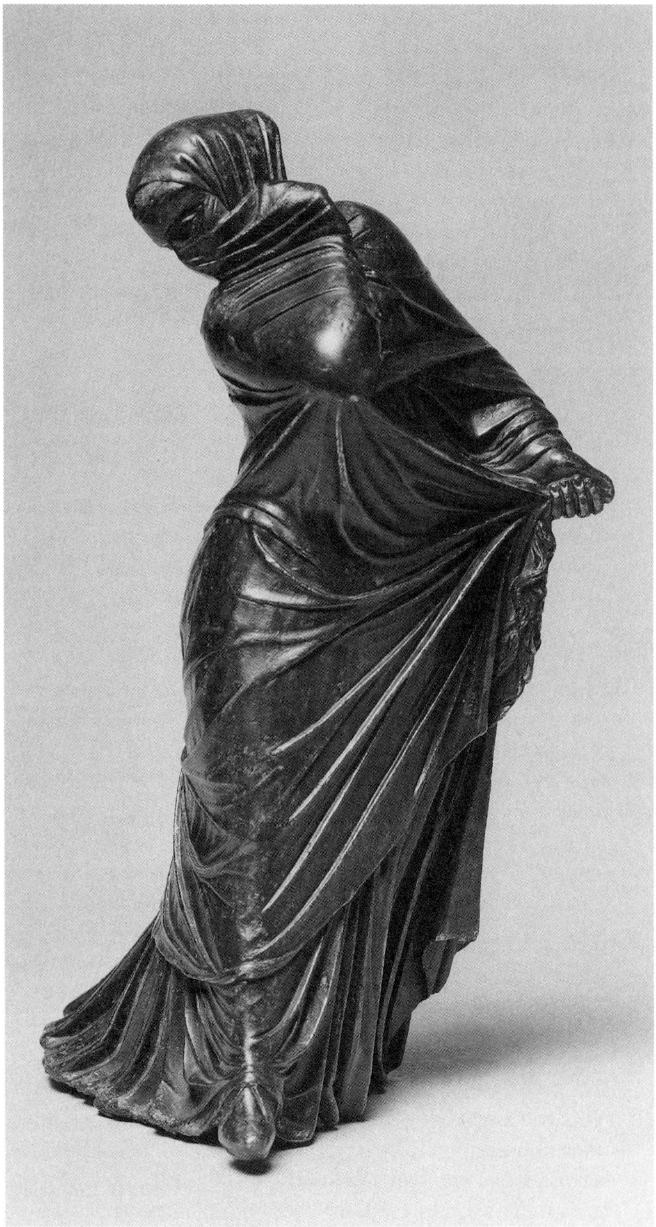

3.32 Statuette of a veiled dancer, c. 225–175 B.C.E. Bronze, 8⅛ ins (20.6 cm) high. Metropolitan Museum of Art, New York (Bequest of Walter C. Baker, 1972).

Literature

Earlier we examined Plato and his philosophy. Plato lived during the post-Golden Age. He had become disillusioned with the Atheneans' ability to govern themselves. The art and aesthetic that was contemporary with his age was Late Classical that, as discussed earlier, lacked the moralizing pretense of the Classical period. His ideas about education and politics were expounded in the *Republic* (see p. 83). Here he expresses his view that only a select few are able to ascend from the "cave" of ignorance and achieve true knowledge. Plato's ideal society is a meritocratic aristocracy—that is, a ruling class selected from the ablest people of all backgrounds and both sexes. After education, composed of physical regimen and study of philosophy, the most qualified would be groomed for power, which they would inherit automatically at the age of fifty. These would be "philosopher kings" who would live communally, sharing food, lodging, and spouses and owning no property. It followed to Plato that because the philosopher kings would be guided by true knowledge, they would govern for the benefit of all.

Soldiers would comprise a separate, intermediary class above the lower orders of merchants, farmers, and artisans, who would own property, but within strict limits. For example, there would be no slaves, and anyone whose wealth grew more than fourfold would be compelled to give the rest to the state. In Plato's ideal state, when everyone was doing the task to which he or she was best suited, society would achieve the four cardinal virtues of wisdom (the philosopher kings), courage (soldiers), temperance (commoners), and justice (the state itself). The arts, in this scheme, were at best peripheral and at worst, dangerous, because beauty (see p. 83) was but a pale reflection of the ideal—an imitation of an imitation.

The *Apology*, one of Plato's dialogues, gives his version of the speech Socrates gave in his own defense at his trial. Socrates was accused, and found guilty, of corrupting the youth of Athens and of believing in gods of his own devising rather than the gods of Athens.

Apology
Part I: Socrates' Defense Speech
(Section 2) The Old Accusers' Charges

And first, I have to reply to the older charges and to my first accusers, and then I will go on to the later ones. For of old I have had many accusers, who have accused me falsely to you during many years; and I am more afraid of them than of Anvtus and his associates, who are dangerous, too, in their own way. But far more dangerous are the others, who began when you were children, and took possession of your minds with their falsehoods, telling of one Socrates, a wise man, who speculated about the heaven above, and searched into the earth beneath and made the worse appear the better cause. The disseminators of this tale are the accusers whom I dread; for their hearers are apt to fancy that such inquirers do not believe in the existence of the gods. And they are many, and their charges against me are of ancient date, and they were made by them in the days when you were more impressible than you are now—in childhood, or it may have been in youth—and the cause when heard went by default, for there was none to answer. And hardest of all, I do not know and cannot tell the names of my accusers; unless in the chance case of a comic poet. All who from envy and malice have persuaded you—some of them having first convinced themselves—all this class of men are most difficult to deal with; for I cannot have them up here, and cross-examine them, and therefore I must simply fight with shadows in my own defense, and argue when there is no one who answers. I will ask you then to assume with me, as I was saying, that my opponents are of two kinds; one recent, the other ancient: and I hope that you will see the propriety of my answering the latter first, for these accusations you heard long before the others, and much oftener.

Well, then, I must make my defense, and endeavor to clear away in a short time, a slander which has lasted a long time. May I succeed, if to succeed be for my good and yours, or likely to avail me in my cause! The task is not an easy one: I quite understand the nature of it. And so leaving the event with God, in obedience to the law I will now make my defense.

I will begin at the beginning, and ask what is the accusation which has given rise to the slander of me, and in fact has encouraged Meletus to prefer this charge against me. Well, what do the slanderers say? They shall be my prosecutors, and I will sum up their words in an affidavit: "Socrates is an evildoer, and a curious person, who searches into things under the earth and in heaven, and he makes the worse appear the better cause; and he teaches the aforesaid doctrines to others." Such is the nature of the accusation: it is just what you have yourselves seen in the comedy of Aristophanes, who has introduced a man whom he calls Socrates, going about and saying that he walks in air, and talking a deal of nonsense concerning matters of which I do not pretend to know either much or little—not that I mean to speak disparagingly of any one who is a student of natural philosophy. I should be very sorry if Meletus could bring so grave a charge against me. But the simple truth is, O Athenians, that I have nothing to do with physical speculations. Very many of those here present are witnesses to the truth of this, and to them I appeal. Speak then, you who have heard me, and tell your neighbors whether any of you have ever known me hold forth in few words or in many upon such matters . . . You hear their answer. And from what they say of this part of the charge you will be able to judge of the truth of the rest.

As little foundation is there for the report that I am a teacher, and take money; this accusation has no more truth in it than the other. Although, if a man were really able to instruct mankind, to receive money for giving instruction would, in my opinion, be an honor to him. There is Gorgias of Leontium, and Prodicus of Ceos, and Hippias of Elis who go the round of the cities and are able to persuade the young men to leave their own citizens by whom they might be taught for nothing, and come to them whom they not only pay, but are thankful if they may be allowed to pay them. There is at this time a Parian philosopher residing in Athens, of whom I have heard; and I came to hear of him in this way:—I came across a man who has spent a world of money on the Sophists, Callias, the son of Hipponicus, and knowing that he had sons, I asked him: "Callias," I said, "if your two sons were foals or calves, there would be no difficulty in finding someone to put over them; we should hire a trainer of horses, or a farmer probably, who would improve and perfect them in their own proper virtue and excellence; but as they are human beings, whom are you thinking of placing over them? Is there any one who understands human and political virtue? You must have thought about the matter, for you have sons; is there any one?" "There is," he said. "Who is he?" said I; "and of what country? and what does he charge?" "Evenus the Parian," he replied, "he is the man, and his charge is five minae." Happy is Evenus, I said to myself, if he really has this wisdom, and teaches at such a moderate charge. Had I the same, I should have been very proud and conceited; but the truth is that I have no knowledge of the kind.

(Section 7) The Philosopher as Gadfly

And now, Athenians, I am not going to argue for my own sake, as you may think, but for yours, that you may not sin against the God by condemning me, who am his gift to you. For if you kill me you will not easily find a successor to me, who, if I may use such a ludicrous figure of speech, am a sort of gadfly, given to the state by God; and the state is a great and noble steed who is tardy in his motions owing to his very size, and requires to be stirred into life. I am that gadfly which God has attached to the state, and all day long and in all places am always fastening upon you, arousing and persuading and reproaching you. You will not easily find another like me, and therefore I would advise you to spare me. I dare say that you may feel out of temper (like the person who is suddenly awakened from sleep), and you think that you might easily strike me dead as Anytus advises, and then you sleep on for the remainder of your lives, unless God in his care of you sent you another gadfly. When I say that I am given to you by God, the proof of my mission is this:—if I had been like other men, I should not have neglected all my own concerns or patiently seen the neglect of them during all these years, and have been doing yours, coming to you individually like a father or elder brother, exhorting you to regard virtue; such conduct, I say, would be unlike human nature. If I had gained anything, or if my exhortations had been paid, there would have been some sense in my doing so; but now, as you will perceive, not even the impudence of my accusers dares to say that I have ever exacted or sought pay of any one; of that they have no witness. And I have a sufficient witness to the truth of what I say—my poverty.

FOCAL POINT

From Idealism to Realism—*Prometheus* and *Hecuba*

In this chapter, we have been able to compare the various art forms of classical and Hellenistic Greece, to isolate some shared themes, and to draw some general conclusions about them. Here we'll focus on the process of change in Greek culture. In particular, we can see how much change occurred over a brief time in a single discipline, the theatre. To do this, we will use two plays that bracket the classical period in Athens: Aeschylus' *Prometheus* (proh-MEE-thee-uhs) *Bound* and Euripides' *Hecuba* (HEHK-yoo-buh).

According to legend, Prometheus frustrated the plans of Zeus by giving fire to a race of mortals whom Zeus sought to destroy. Here is classical Greek idealism at work: through reason, application, and vision, human beings can defy the gods and win. They are capable of nobility and infinite improvement. As punishment for his presumption, however, Zeus has Prometheus chained to a rock. In Prometheus' justification of what he did, he suggests that humankind, through technology and reason, can have dominion over nature.

Prometheus is a play unusual even for Aeschylus in its heavy dependence on dialogue and character, and in its lack of action. The hero is motionless, chained to a rock. Nothing happens. There is only conversation between a parade of different people, through which the playwright reveals character and situation.

In this extract, the scene is set for an exchange between Force, Violence, and Hephaestus, the fire god. Violence does not speak, however, as there are only two actors. Force presents the situation:

> Far have we come to this far spot of earth,
> This narrow Scythian land, a desert all untrodden.
> God of the forge and fire, yours the task
> The Father laid upon you.
> To this high-piercing, headlong rock
> In adamantine chains that none can break
> Bind him—him here, who dared all things.
> Your flaming flower he stole to give to men,
> Fire, the master craftsman, through whose power
> All things are wrought, and for such error now
> He must repay the gods; be taught to yield
> To Zeus' lordship and to cease
> From his man-looking way.

Through speeches such as these, the characters are revealed—Force as a villain, and Hephaestus as a weak but kindly fool. After Force, Violence, and Hephaestus exit, Prometheus appears. He may have been revealed on a low wagon, called an *eccyclema* (ehk-i-KLAY-muh), which was rolled out from the central door of the *skene*. He speaks:

> O air of heaven and swift winged winds,
> O running river waters,
> O never numbered laughter of sea waves,
> Earth, mother of all, eye of the sun, all-seeing,
> On you I call.
> Behold what I, a god, endure for gods.
> See in what tortures I must struggle
> Through countless years of time.
> This shame, these bonds, are put upon me
> By the new ruler of the gods.
> Sorrow enough in what is here and what is still to
> come.

And so the myth unfolds itself in high poetry as Prometheus discourses with the chorus, a group of kindly sea-nymphs, with Hermes, with Ocean, a humorous old busybody, and with Io, an ephemeral creature. When the dialogue has run its course, Prometheus declaims:

> An end to words. Deeds now,
> The world is shaken,
> The deep and secret way of thunder
> Is rent apart.
> Fiery wreaths of lightning flash.
> Whirlwinds toss the swirling dust.
> The blasts of all the winds are battling in the air,
> And sky and sea are one.
> On me the tempest falls.
> It does not make me tremble.
> O holy Mother Earth, O air and sun,
> Behold me. I am wronged.[7]

Prometheus is an idealistic exploration of human capacity, achievement, and power, written as the height of the golden age of Athens approached.

Euripides' play *Hecuba*, on the other hand, is a bitter tragedy of the interrelationships between those who rule and those who obey. It was written at a time when failure of leadership had dragged Athens downward through a long war of attrition with Sparta. Here again the playwright deals with myth, in this case, the story of the sack of Troy.

Two separate events are related, giving the plot an episodic character. Hecuba is the wife of Priam, king of Troy, whose city has at last fallen to the Greeks. She endures first the slaughter of her daughter Polyxena (pahl-ee-ZEEN-uh) by the Greeks, then she discovers the body of her son, Polydorus, who has been murdered by Polymestor (pahl-ee-MEHS-tohr). Each of these events takes her one step further from grief and nearer to despair. She seeks the help of the Greek king, Agamemnon, in her quest for revenge on Polymestor, but receives only pity and the question, "What woman on this earth was ever cursed like this?" Hecuba replies in language less poetic and more realistic than that of Prometheus:

> There is none but goddess Suffering herself.
>
> But let me tell you why I kneel
> At your feet. And if my suffering seem just,
> Then I must be content. But if otherwise,
> Give me my revenge on that treacherous friend
> Who flouted every god in heaven and in hell
> To do this brutal murder.
>
> At our table
> He was our frequent guest; was counted first
> Among our friends, respected and honoured by me,
> Receiving every kindness that a man could meet—
> And then, in cold deliberation killed
> My son.
>
> Murder may have its reasons, its motives,
> But this—to refuse my son a grave, to throw him
> To the sea, unburied! . . .
>
> See me whole, observe
> My wretchedness—
>
> Once a queen, now
> A slave; blessed with children, happy once,
> Now old, childless, utterly alone,
> Homeless, lost, unhappiest of women
> On this earth . . .[8]

Step by step she moves inevitably toward her final acts of atrocity. The play focuses on how she is forced to yield, one at a time, her values, her self-respect, and "the faith which makes her human." Underlying the play is a stark condemnation of the logic of political necessity. When faced with power over which she has no control, she pleads the case of honor, decency, the gods, and moral law. All these appeals fail. As despair destroys her humanity, she passes beyond the reach of judgment. The chorus condemns the tragic waste of war and questions the necessity and logic of imperialism. Finally, Euripides attacks the gods themselves. Even if they exist, he implies, their justice is so far removed from humans that it has no relevance.

The transition from idealism, form, order, and restraint to greater realism and emotion represented by these two plays parallels the changes we have seen in painting, sculpture, and architecture. In all the arts, the idealization of classicism turned to the increasing realism of succeeding styles; restraint gave way to emotion, and form gave way to feeling.

Chapter Review

❖ Critical Thought ❖

Given the complete defeat of Athens by Sparta and their different ways of life and philosophy, but the continuing influence of Athenian culture, it is possible to conclude that artistic culture is more important than power and conquest. One can certainly speculate on the kinds of social conditions that are necessary for a culture to flourish, provide adequately for its citizenry, and have a lasting positive impact on the future.

It may well be that Socrates has as much to say about life today as he had about life in Athens 2,400 years ago. Is an unexamined life not worth living? Would you like to be one of his students, pummeled constantly by questions designed to illumine your weaknesses, or would you rather sit in a classroom letting a professor lecture to you and provide you with the answers?

We often classify some people as "rational" and others as "emotional," putting classical principles into our personal relationships. Sometimes, men are described as more logical or more mathematically inclined than women, who are then described as more intuitive and artistic. Is that an accurate way of assessing individuals? Perhaps we're more comfortable dealing with classicism in a less personal manner—for example, finding examples of classicism in the buildings of our campus and community or in the music we listen to. Obviously these are not Greek classical buildings or songs, because they were made long after the Greek classical period, but you will easily recognize some basic characteristics of classicism in them.

◆ Summary ◆

After reading this chapter you should be able to:

- Explain the factors that coalesced to make Athens the cradle of Western civilization.
- Define and compare the several philosophical systems of the classical and Hellenistic eras.
- Identify works and artists, and characterize the visual art and architecture of the classical and post-classical periods.
- Compare Plato's and Aristotle's theories about art.
- Discuss Aristotle's theory of tragedy and its relationship to the major playwrights and production circumstances of the classical and post-classical periods.
- Describe the music and dance of the classical period.
- Apply the elements and principles of composition to analyze and compare individual works of art illustrated in this chapter.

Cybersources

http://harpy.uccs.edu/greek/classsculpt.html
http://harpy.uccs.edu/greek/lateclasssculpt.html
http://harpy.uccs.edu/greek/hellsculpt.html
http://web.kyoto-inet.or.jp./org/orion/eng/hst/greek.html

4 The Roman Period

OUTLINE

HOW ART WORKS:
The Purposes of Art IV

CONTEXTS AND CONCEPTS
- The Roman Republic
  - Military Expansion
  - The Roman Civil War
- The Roman Empire
  - Augustus
  - Pax Romana
  - Roman Law
- Philosophy and Religion
  - Stoicism
  - Neo-Platonism
  - Divinities and Mystery Cults

THE ARTS OF ROME
- Painting
  - A DYNAMIC WORLD: Chinese Painting
- Sculpture
- Architecture
  - MASTERWORK: The Pantheon
  - TECHNOLOGY: Cement
- Theatre
- Music
- Dance
- Literature
  - PROFILE: Vergil

FOCAL POINT:
Augustus—Classical Visions

VIEW

DEMOCRACY AND LAW

Is it better to have a participatory government (democracy), than to have a monarchial or dictatorial government? For the second time in our study, we now watch as a relatively small and homogeneous citizenry cope with governing themselves. In ancient Rome, as life and population became more expansive, complicated, and diverse, the governmental form itself became problematical. Amazingly, the citizens of Rome willingly gave up their democracy in favor of a dictator. We wonder what might have transpired to bring about such an event and think of modern parallels such as Germany under Adolf Hitler and the Nazis. We also wonder, as we examine how democracy succeeded and failed in cultures such as those of ancient Greece and Rome, whether a country can become too large and too fragmented to sustain democracy. For example, could democracy ever work in a nation as large as modern China? Will the United States reach the point at which it is too diverse to continue as a representative democracy and still maintain any kind of social order?

Interestingly, however, as Rome grew and its emperors became all-powerful, it witnessed nearly two hundred years of peace and stability—the *Pax Romana*—and entered a period in which the rule of law flourished. So, is it governmental form or something else that gives a society a high quality of life?

KEY TERMS

Some of the basic terms and concepts we will encounter in this chapter include the following:

S.P.Q.R.
—*Senatus Populusque Romanus*—The Roman Senate and the People.

Pax Romana
"The Roman Peace" was a 200-year span of stability during the Roman Empire, beginning with the Emperor Augustus.

Trompe l'oeil
"Trick of the eye" or "fool the eye," a two-dimensional artwork designed to make the viewer believe it is in three dimensions.

Engaged columns
Columns, often decorative, that are part of, and project from, a wall surface.

Cella
The principal enclosed room of a Roman temple.

Sarcophagi (sahr-KAWF-uh-jy)
Stone coffins, a notable type of Roman sculpture.

Masonry
Stone or brickwork, a structural architectural feature at which the Romans excelled.

4.1 *Gemma Augustea* (detail of the crowning of Augustus), early first century C.E. Onyx cameo, whole cameo 7½ × 9 ins (19 × 23 cm). Kunsthistorisches Museum, Vienna.

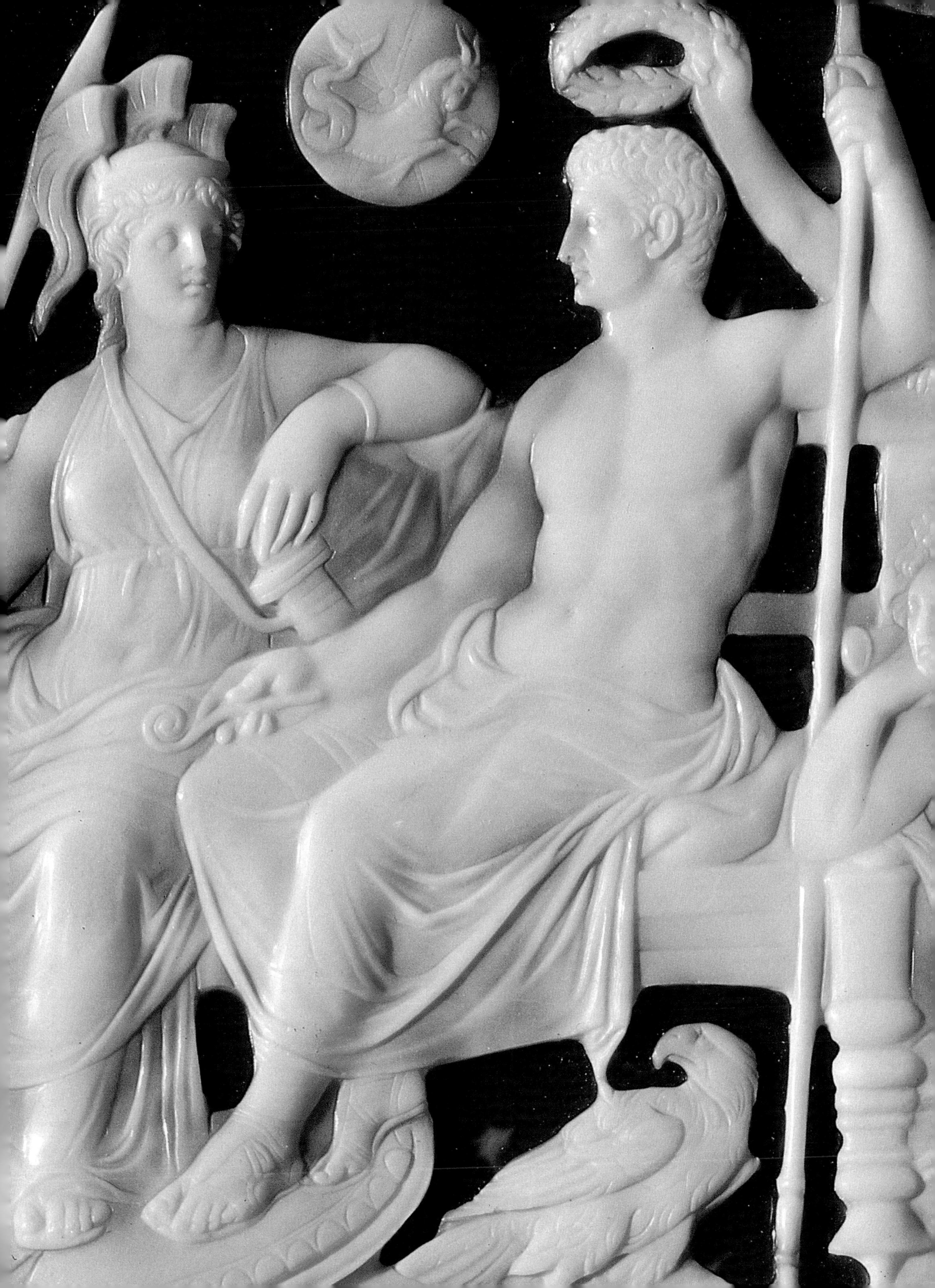

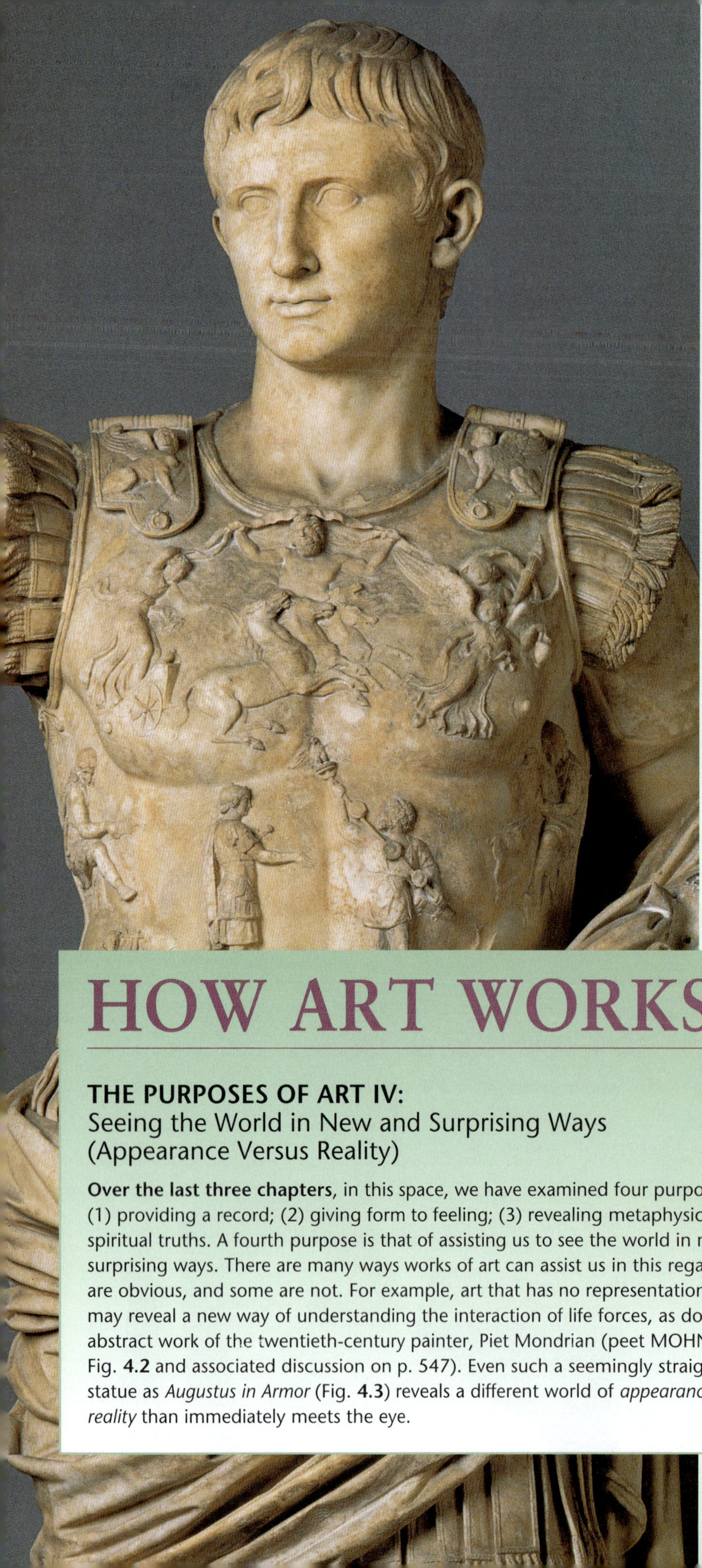

Appearance Versus Reality

When we realize that *Augustus in Armor* (Fig. **4.3**) is the head of the Emperor Augustus attached to an idealized body copied from a Greek classical sculpture, we recognize that this is not a reproduction of "reality." It is an appearance: someone's idealized portrayal (probably the emperor himself).

The idea that "things are not as they seem" is a common tenet of many philosophical and religious world-views. It is also fundamental to art. Creating the "essence" of something rather than reproducing its outward appearance alone can be traced through every chapter of this book in the works of art illustrated, regardless of style. Worthy of thought is the idea that under all of this "portrayal" lies the notion that the everyday world is not in fact the true world, but an illusion of some sort. An artwork seeking essences rather than illustration may, perhaps, provide the prism through which we may possibly glimpse the reality that surface appearance masks. This is what Plato had in mind (see Chapter 2) and what other philosophers like Kant (see p. 427) suggested. Others do not agree. Some people see the apparent or perceivable world as genuine and any other "world beyond" as a delusion. Whatever the case, when we view or hear a work of art, we need to pause to ask what world it is asking us to find in it.

HOW ART WORKS

THE PURPOSES OF ART IV:
Seeing the World in New and Surprising Ways (Appearance Versus Reality)

Over the last three chapters, in this space, we have examined four purposes of art: (1) providing a record; (2) giving form to feeling; (3) revealing metaphysical or spiritual truths. A fourth purpose is that of assisting us to see the world in new and surprising ways. There are many ways works of art can assist us in this regard. Some are obvious, and some are not. For example, art that has no representational content may reveal a new way of understanding the interaction of life forces, as does the abstract work of the twentieth-century painter, Piet Mondrian (peet MOHN-dree-ahn; Fig. **4.2** and associated discussion on p. 547). Even such a seemingly straightforward statue as *Augustus in Armor* (Fig. **4.3**) reveals a different world of *appearance versus reality* than immediately meets the eye.

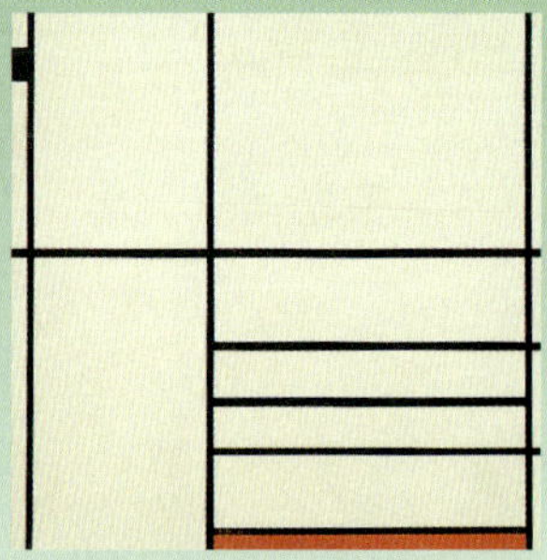

4.2 Piet Mondrian, *Composition in White, Black, and Red*, 1936. Oil on canvas, 3 ft 4¼ ins × 3 ft 5 ins (1.02 × 1.04 m). Museum of Modern Art, New York (Gift of the Advisory Committee). Photo: © 1998 Museum of Modern Art. © 2001 Mondrian/Holtzman Trust c/o Beeldrecht, Amsterdam and DACS, London.

4.3 *Augustus in Armor*, Villa of Livia, Prima Porta, c. 20 B.C.E. Marble, 6 ft × 8 ins (2.03 m) high. Vatican Museums, Rome.

CONTEXTS AND CONCEPTS

The civilization that would become the Roman one arose at the same time as that of ancient Greece. By the sixth century B.C.E., Etruscan invaders who had come out of Asia by way of Greece dominated the Italian peninsula. The Etruscans brought to their new land a militaristic and practical society, an **anthropomorphic** conception of the deities, and arts roughly equivalent to those of archaic Greece, whose style had influenced them (Fig. **4.4**). Roman legend held that Rome was founded in 753 B.C.E. by Romulus (RAHM-yoo-luhs), an orphan, who, with his twin brother, Remus (REEM-uhs), had been suckled by a wolf as the boys' foster-mother. One Etruscan religious cult revered wolves, and this legend is taken as further evidence that Roman civilization had Etruscan roots.

Toward the end of the sixth century B.C.E., Rome, an important location as a bridging point across the Tiber River, joined with other Latin cities in a revolt against Etruscan domination. In 509 B.C.E., according to Roman tradition, the last Etruscan king was expelled from Rome. This set the Romans on a 900-year course that would lead them to all corners of the then known world. Etruscan influence continued, however, and it was largely due to that influence and its inherited links with Greece that the Romans carried forward the classical ideas that still permeate the Western approach to life today.

The Roman Republic

Once free of Etruscan domination, the Romans developed a republican form of government that lasted until the first century B.C.E. This political stability provided important continuity for other Roman institutions. The motto "S.P.Q.R."—*Senatus Populusque Romanus* (the Roman Senate and People)—reflected the early Roman political and social order, and remained the watchword of Roman

GENERAL EVENTS

- Founding of Rome, 753 B.C.E.
- Roman Republic, 509 B.C.E.
- Roman conquest of Western Greece, 272 B.C.E.
- First Punic war, 264 B.C.E.
- Second Punic war, 218 B.C.E.
- Third Punic war, 149 B.C.E.
- Augustus, 63 B.C.E.–14 C.E.
- Expansion of Roman Empire, c. 60 B.C.E.
- Julius Caesar elected consul, 59 B.C.E.
- Julian calendar, 45 B.C.E.
- Battle of Actium, 31 B.C.E.
- Destruction of Temple, Jerusalem, 70 C.E.
- Vesuvius erupts, 79 C.E.
- Cult of Mithra, c. 100 C.E.

	800 B.C.E.	400 B.C.E.	200 B.C.E.	100 B.C.E.	0 – 200 C.E.
PAINTING & SCULPTURE				*Lady Playing the Cithara* (**4.9**), Villa at Boscoreale (**4.10**), *Portrait of an Unknown Roman* (**4.13**), *Ara Pacis* (**4.35**)	*Hercules and Telephos* (**4.11**)
ARCHITECTURE			Temple of Fortuna Virilis (**4.18**)		Trajan's Column (**4.16, 4.17**), Pantheon (**4.19, 4.21**), Colosseum (**4.25, 4.26**), Arch of Titus (**4.27**), Roman Aqueduct (**4.28**), Forum of Augustus (**4.33**)
THEATRE & CINEMA		Development of Roman comedy, Plautus	Terence, Blood sports, First stone theatres in Rome		
MUSIC & DANCE		*Hydraulos*, First brass instruments, Mime		Pantomime	
LITERATURE & PHILOSOPHY			Diogenes	Catullus, Panaetius, Posidonius, Horace, Vergil	Seneca, Plutarch, Livy, Epictetus, Juvenal, Marcus Aurelius

Timeline 4.1 The Roman period.

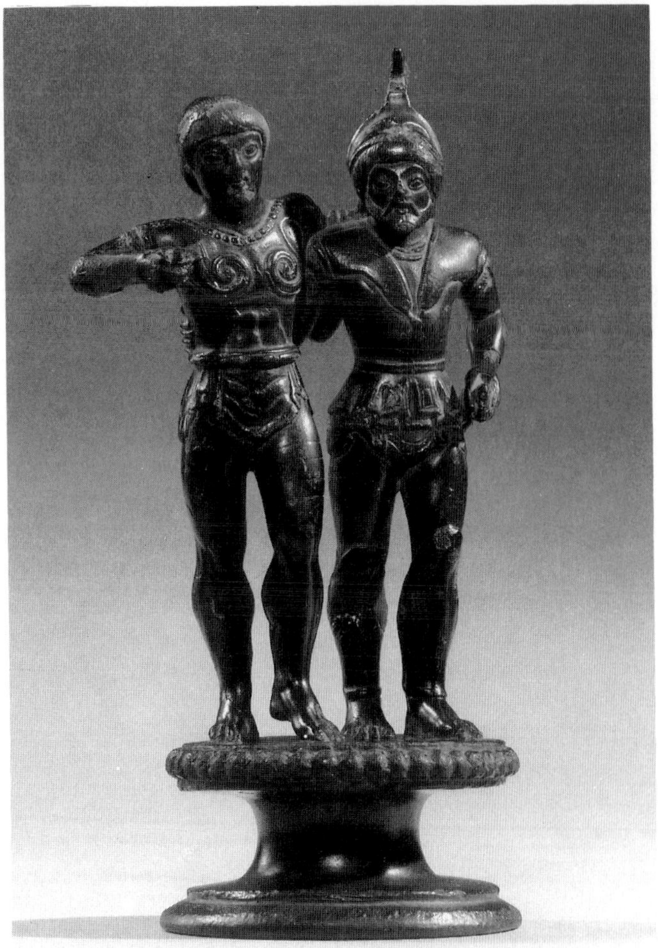

4.4 Etruscan warrior supporting a wounded comrade, early fifth century B.C.E. Bronze, 5¼ ins (13.4 cm) high (without base). Metropolitan Museum of Art, New York (Rogers Fund, 1947).

society until Imperial times. It meant that sovereignty rested in the people themselves, and not in any particular form of government. In many ways the Roman Republic functioned as a democracy. Decisions affecting society were made at assemblies, which all citizens attended to express their will. The Senate conducted the actual business of government, including the passage of legislation and the supervision of elected magistrates. Over the centuries, the greatest issues affecting Roman society were played out as dramas between the people and the Senate.

The Senate itself was an hereditary institution composed of an assembly of the heads, or *patres*, of old families and, later, of wealthy members of the citizenry, or *plebs*. The Senate's 300 members therefore represented old and new money, power, and social interest. It was a self-renewing **oligarchy**. The two most important officers who ruled the state were the *consuls*, who were elected by the representative assemblies for one-year terms, at the end of which they became members of the Senate.

In Rome, the rich ruled via the Senate and the general citizenry were little more than peasants. By the third century B.C.E., the division between aristocrat and peasant had widened appreciably, the former growing in riches and the latter sinking further and further into poverty. Yet as long as Rome remained reasonably small, the constitutional framework of the Republic held the social order together. It warded off revolution while permitting change and provided the body politic with reasonably well-trained leaders who knew how, above all else, to keep the Republic functioning and alive. It was, in fact, the internal stability of the Republic that made expansion possible, bringing about the next phase of Roman history.

Military Expansion

Roman expansion was based on military conquest. Through conquest Rome gained political dominance in the Hellenistic world during the third and second centuries B.C.E. (Map **4.1**) The internationalization of culture, evident in Hellenic times, grew under the Romans. Later, Rome would extend its control throughout Europe and eventually as far as the British Isles.

By 272 B.C.E., the Romans had conquered western Greece. Then they took on Carthage, the other major power of the period, in the first of the Punic wars. Over the next hundred years, in three great stages, Rome and Carthage battled each other for control of the whole Mediterranean world. It was during the second Punic war, which began in 218 B.C.E., that the Carthaginian general Hannibal marched his legions over the Alps into Italy. The end of the second Punic war in 202 B.C.E. left Rome in a position of advantage and at a watershed.

Rome had the choice either to consolidate order and security in the west by ridding itself of the Carthaginian threat or to expand toward the east. The Romans chose to move eastward, hoping to gain new riches from the conquered territories. The outcome, though unforeseen, was to leave Rome overlord of the entire Hellenistic world. But with the third Punic war, which began in 149 B.C.E., Rome also accomplished its other objective: within three years Carthage was destroyed.

The Roman Civil War

The continuous state of war on the borders of the Roman provinces, as well as the practical requirements for effective government, led to an increase of power in the hands of the Roman Senate and a decrease in the participation of ordinary citizens. Unlike Athens, Rome had very little commerce or industry, and the quality of life in Rome came to depend directly upon the wealth of conquered regions brought back to Rome as spoils.

The greatest danger to Rome did not lie in foreign wars, however, but in the threat of civil war. Conquests had made the Romans rich, and the *proconsuls* who

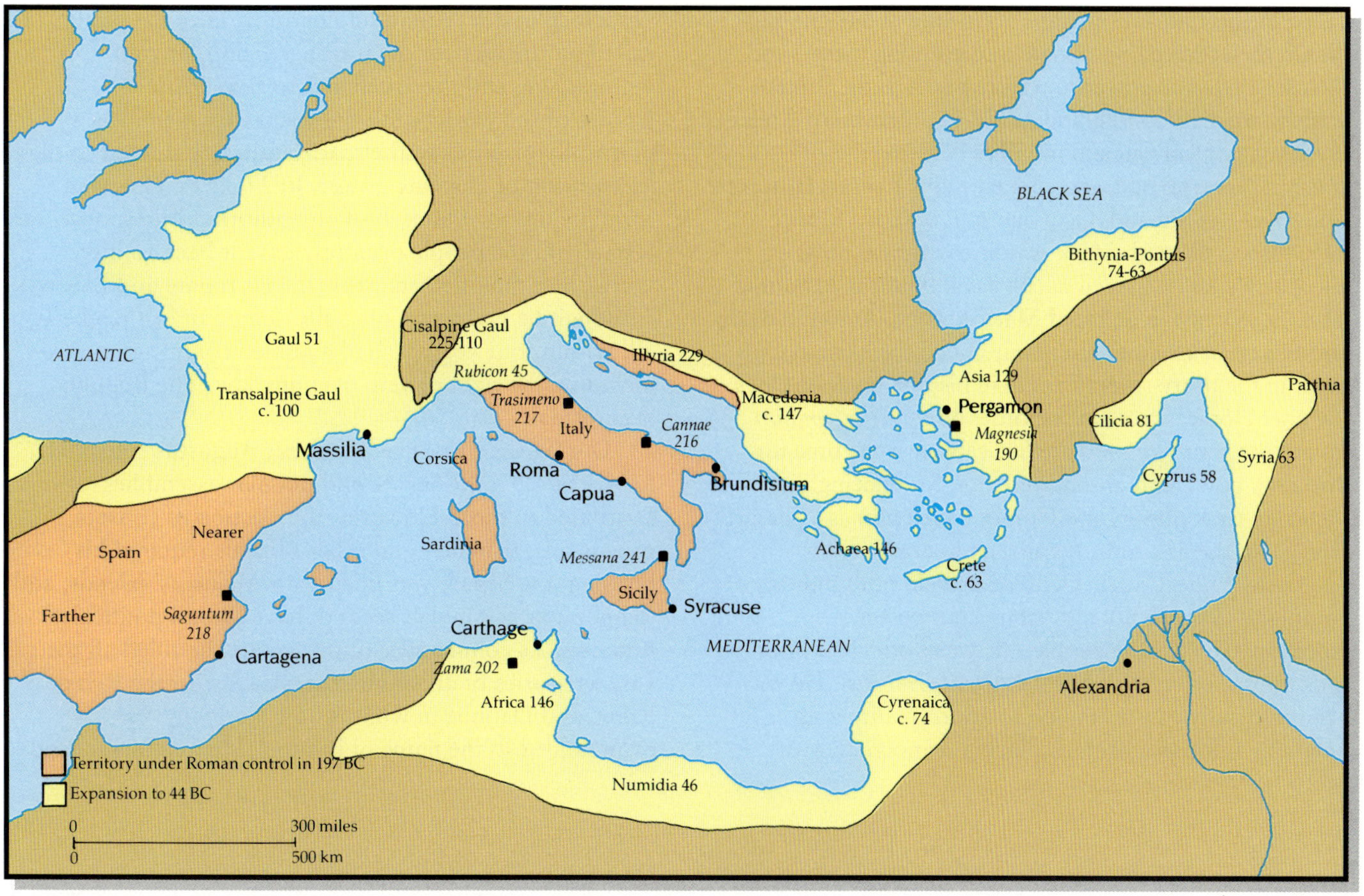

Map 4.1 The Roman Republic, showing important battles and dates (B.C.E.) that areas came under dominion.

governed the provinces took advantage of their positions, the availability of cheap land, slaves, and tribute money. Corruption was a temptation few could resist. They built vast estates and, in general, abused the poor, who became poorer. Rome itself became a Mecca for the rich and poor alike, and the widening gap between the two increased tension and bitterness among the masses. This was exacerbated by the violent excesses of generals who, having conquered the hinterlands, returned home with their armies intact. The result was a period of upheaval, which lasted from approximately 133 to 31 B.C.E. and which brought the Roman Republic to a close.

During this time a succession of men attempted leadership. Marius (MAR-ee-uhs) was the first of these. Then came a power struggle in the late first century B.C.E. from which the dictator Sulla emerged, to be followed by Pompey (PAHM-pee).

In 59 B.C.E., Marius' nephew Julius Caesar (Caesar was the family name) was elected consul. During a five-year campaign against the Gauls, he kept a close watch on Roman politics. Corruption, intrigue, and murder were disfiguring public life and discrediting the Senate. Having returned to Italy in 49 B.C.E., he declared war on Pompey by crossing the Rubicon River, which marked the limit of his province. By 44 B.C.E., he had returned to Rome in triumph, to be voted dictator for life. His life was cut short only days later, however, on 15 March 44 B.C.E., at the hands of assassins in the Senate.

One of Caesar's most lasting achievements was the invention of the Julian calendar, in which the year has 365 days, with an additional day every four years. The new calendar was used from 1 January 45 B.C.E.

The Roman Empire

Augustus

If anyone had hoped that the assassination of Julius Caesar would bring about the return of Republican rule, they must surely have been disappointed, for the political turbulence simply continued. Caesar's assassins and his old commanders battled for control, while orators like Cicero labored to save the old Republic. In the end, Julius Caesar's great nephew and adopted son Octavian—known to history as Augustus Caesar—outmaneuvered and outfought everyone.

The year after his uncle's death, Octavian and his allies of the Caesarian faction joined forces in an alliance called the Second Triumvirate. By means of intrigue and threat, they coerced the Senate into granting them—and their legions—the power to restore peace to the Roman state. In the battle of Philippi (fil-IP-y), in northern Greece in 42 B.C.E., Octavian and his allies defeated the conspirators who had assassinated Julius Caesar. However, peace was not at hand. Octavian split with his former allies, especially with Mark Antony, who was now Cleopatra's lover. In a climactic naval battle at Actium in 31 B.C.E., Octavian defeated Mark Antony. Antony's death and Octavian's victory effectively ended the Roman Civil War. In the thirty-seventh poem in his first book of *Odes*, the poet Horace wrote in response: *Nunc est bibendum nunc pede libero pulsanda tellus!* ("Now is the time for drinking, now, with unshackled foot, for dancing!"). Octavian took power, and Horace hailed him as "Caesar," which, for the first time, became an honorific title.

Gaius Julius Caesar Octavianus held both military command (*imperium*) and tribunician power (spokesperson for the people); he was both chief priest (*pontifex maximus*) and first citizen (*princeps*). He was also politically astute enough to adorn reality with palatable outward forms, replacing democracy with autocracy in a way that did not antagonize the public. He called on the services of culture, religion, literature, architecture, and the visual arts to help create a new picture of the world, with the result that there was a politically inspired aesthetic revolution, which led to the legalization of absolute power. In 27 B.C.E., Octavian formally divested himself of all authority. In response, the Senate and the people promptly gave it back to him, voting him the title Augustus (the Fortunate and Blessed). Although he was never officially "emperor" of Rome at all, within four years he had assumed complete power—including the right of veto over any law. The Republic was formally dead.

During the forty-five years that Augustus ruled (31 B.C.E.–14 C.E.), the Senate and popular assemblies continued to meet. However, the election of consuls, proconsuls, tribunes, and other officials required his blessing, the Senate was filled with Augustus' friends, and the popular assemblies seem to have lost all political function. As commander of the armies, he ruled all the vast territories of an empire that reached to the Rivers Rhine and Danube in what is now Germany. He commanded in the name of his uncle, Julius Caesar, and

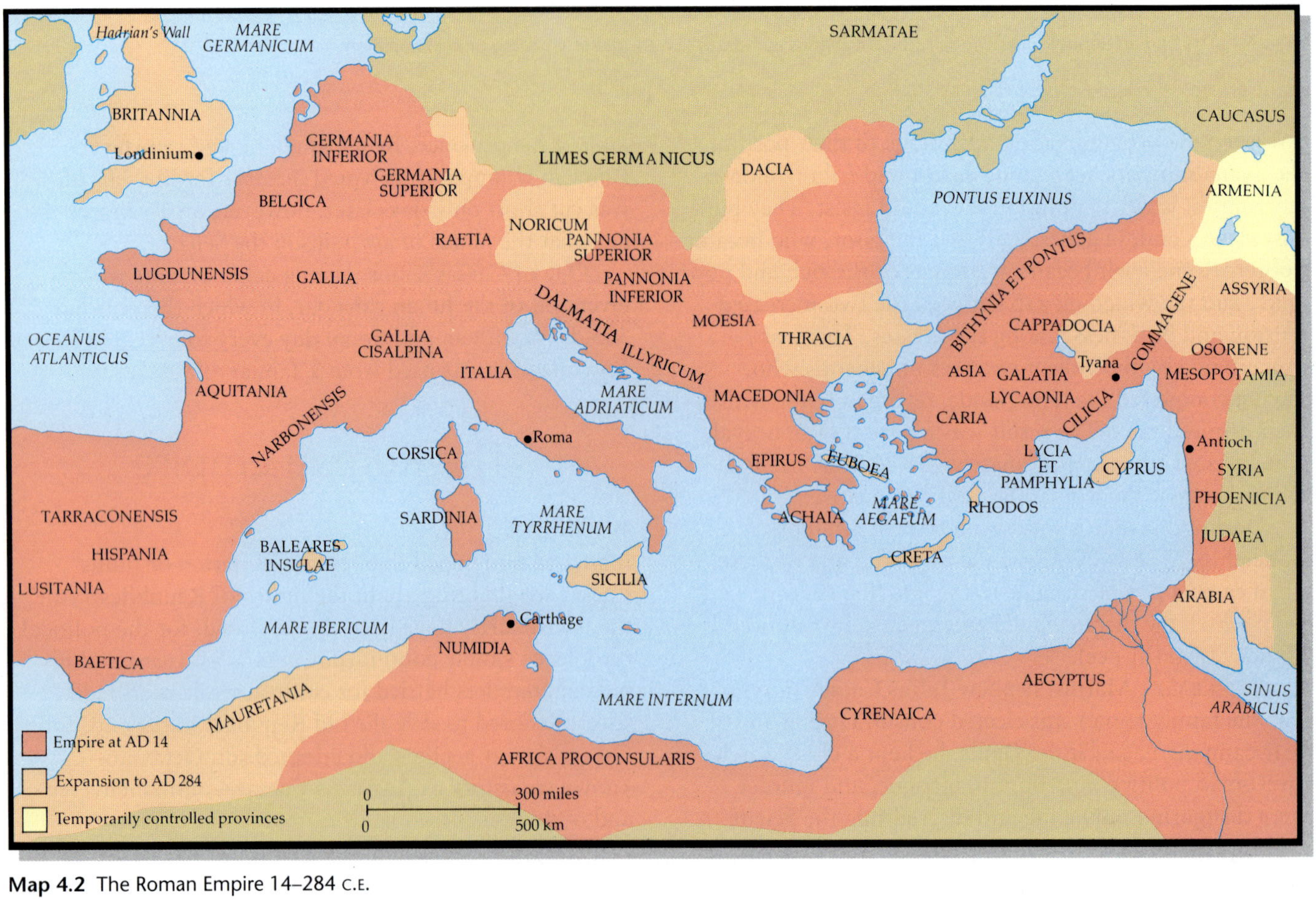

Map 4.2 The Roman Empire 14–284 C.E.

on the basis of his own military victories, claiming that he brought peace and order after a century of civil wars. He rebuilt temples to the Olympian gods, the "divine" Julius Caesar, and to "Rome and Augustus." He built roads, bridges, and aqueducts, established a sound currency, created the first full-time police force and firefighters, nurtured honest government, and maintained peace, which lasted nearly two hundred years.

Pax Romana

"The Roman Peace" (*Pax Romana*) brought under a single government a huge geographical area (Map **4.2**). The Augustan heritage was carried forward during the first and second centuries by a number of excellent emperors—for example, Claudius, Trajan, Hadrian, and Marcus Aurelius. The city of Rome spread out across its "seven hills" (Fig. **4.5**) and Roman citizenship was granted to the peoples of Italy and the far-flung provinces, which meant that they were equal to their conquerors and could serve in the army, the bureaucracy, and higher levels of government. Roman administration and Roman law kept order, prosperity, and peace intact. The Roman administrative system developed a closely supervised hierarchy of professional officials, who made the machinery of day-to-day living work for the people. At its height, the Roman Empire covered more than 3 million square miles (7.78 million square kilometers): just slightly less than the size of the United States of today. The population was approximately 80 million. The entire empire was linked by a system of roads reaching out from a central hub at Rome. Wherever the Romans went, they took their culture. Roman theatres, for example, were built in Orange, France, and Sabratha in North Africa.

The age was not entirely free of calamities and tyrants—in the modern sense of the word. Along with good emperors came the insane Caligula (kuh-LIG-yoo-luh) and Nero, who crucified Christians and drove Gaul to revolt. It was a time in which anyone who took up arms against Rome had their right hand severed as punishment. Overall, however, it was a time of peace and prosperity (Fig. **4.6**).

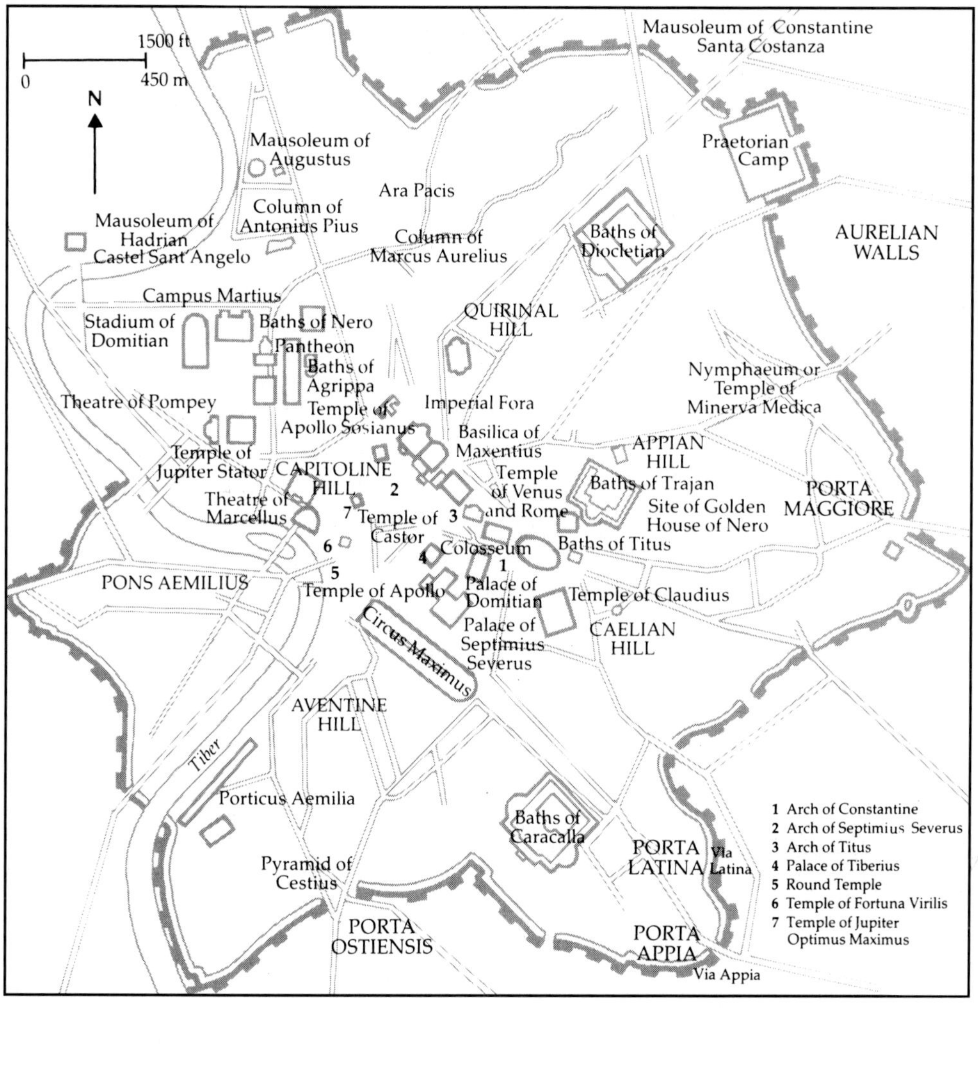

4.5 Imperial Rome.

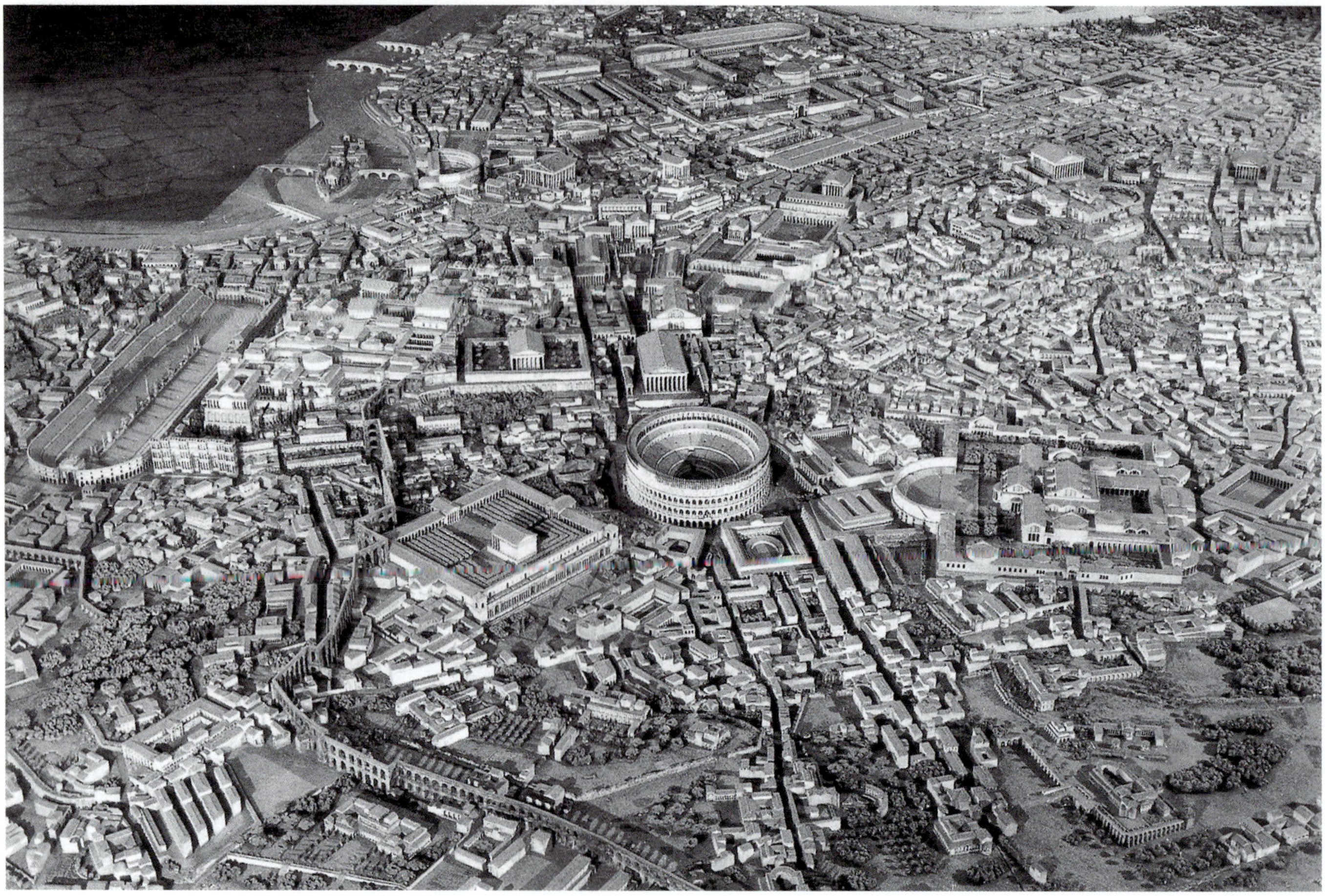

4.6 Scale model of ancient Rome. Museo della Civiltà Romana, Rome.

The best of times ended at the end of the reign of Marcus Aurelius (MAHR-kuhs oh-REEL-ee-uhs; 121–80 C.E.; r. 161–80 C.E.), called the Stoic emperor (see p. 119). In 180 C.E. the army seized power and, to all intents and purposes, central authority in Rome collapsed. Emperors came and went, largely at the whim of the army. Standards of living declined precipitously as the population moved from the countryside to cities that became bloated by the poor living on public charity. Taxes rose and the middle class shrank. New pressures along the borders further destabilized the empire. Although, as we shall see in the next chapter, the empire survived for another century, with a brief resurgence under Diocletian and Constantine, Rome was in its death throes as an empire.

Roman Law

Probably the most influential concept developed by the Romans in any field was the technique for deciding how general laws could be applied to specific cases (jurisprudence). This question was dealt with by legal experts—jurisconsults—who were not part of the state machinery, but who had special knowledge of the meanings of laws. Judges were able to choose only from opinions they submitted; the jurisconsults, in effect, became the lawmakers.

Thus a knowledge of the law and a body of expert opinion on its interpretation was established and handed down. Legal knowledge replaced family and position as a requisite for the practice of law.

Roman law was transformed from a set of isolated instances into a legal system by applying philosophical methods to legal cases: drawing out similarities and differences between them. General principles could thus be laid down. These showed how laws should be applied consistently, thereby making the law predictable and the same for all.

Philosophy and Religion

Stoicism

Roman culture was particularly receptive to Stoicism. For the Stoic, reason, or *logos*, governed the world, and the Great Intelligence was god. The main tenets of Stoicism were acceptance of fate and duty, and the kinship of all people. The latter idea gave to Roman law the goal of providing justice for everyone, and this was one of Rome's great contributions to subsequent Western culture. Essentially, however, Stoicism was deterministic. The Great Intelligence controlled all things, and a person could do nothing but submit to this greater will.

On its way to Rome, Stoicism passed into the hands of Diogenes of Babylon in the second century B.C.E., a period known as the Middle Stoa. Diogenes (dy-AH-jen-eez) brought Stoicism to Rome in 156–155 B.C.E., and he lectured on his philosophy, favorably impressing the Romans. In the early first century B.C.E., Stoicism finally lost much of its cynicism, became more cultured and universal, and more attuned to the Roman spirit. It adopted Aristotle's definition of virtue as a "golden mean," and espoused the belief that material goods might not only be a means to right living, but could also be pursued as an end in themselves. An emphasis on temperance, propriety in daily life, and the performance of daily duty made Stoicism even more attractive to the Roman way of thinking.

As a result, Rome became the home of Stoic philosophy. The worldliness and common sense of the Romans made it into a mellow, urbane, and tolerant set of beliefs, and freed it from intellectual and moral dogmatism.

The changes wrought on Stoicism by the Romans and the general nature of the times are illustrated by the writings of the Roman philosopher, dramatist, and statesman, Seneca (SEN-uh-kuh; 8 B.C.E.–65 C.E.). "Austere and somewhat sanctimonious by nature, he was given to deploring human weakness and to bewailing the vanity and wickedness of the world, from which he professed himself to await impatiently release in a happier home beyond the grave."[1] He was not, however, averse to success in his own life. His business sense was shrewd, and he was tireless in his attempts to increase the considerable fortune he had inherited. While the Epicureans deprecated wealth, Seneca staunchly defended the "righteousness of great wealth" in his philosophical sermons. He believed that reason was bankrupt, and late Stoicism saw sentimental and moral needs as sufficient grounds for religious convictions.

By the time of Augustus Caesar (63 B.C.E.–14 C.E.), Stoicism had gained popularity among the masses as well as the upper classes, by accepting popular religion as an allegory of the truth. But by the time of Nero (37–68 C.E.), who sought to suppress all freedom of thought, Stoicism, which propounded free inquiry and discussion, had fallen on hard times. It was seen as a threat to the state, and many of its leaders were executed or exiled.

Stoicism reemerged as a central doctrine under the Stoic Emperor Marcus Aurelius (121–80 C.E.), who, along with the slave Epictetus (eh-pik-TEE-tuhs), gave final definition to the revived philosophy. The *Discourses* and the *Manual* of Epictetus and the *Meditations* of Marcus Aurelius show us a somewhat old-fashioned Stoicism, leaning toward austerity and concerned mainly with moral and religious rules of behavior. Stoicism now appealed to the moral sense rather than to the intellect, and it turned people to the "way that led to happiness and peace." Salvation lay in cultivating independence from external circumstances, enriching oneself by religious sentiment, and having faith in "an assurance that all is for the best." Central to the thinking of both Marcus Aurelius and Epictetus was the idea that all people are the "children of one Father." Thus, everyone, regardless of age or status, should be loved uncritically, as one loves one's family.

Above all, the world was seen as rationally ordered. Everything was an expression of a divine reason. Death was the end of the individual, merging each of us with that from which we sprang, and reuniting our reason with the *logos* of which it was a part. Death was therefore to be neither feared nor desired: it was merely to be accepted. After Marcus Aurelius' death, however, Stoicism lost ground to the emerging Christianity.

Neo-Platonism

Plotinus (ploh-TY-nuhs; c. 205–70) was an Egyptian-born philosopher and the greatest exponent of the neo-Platonist school: that is, a partial return to Platonic doctrines with additions from Stoic and Epicurean teachings.

According to Plotinus, beauty in art and nature reflect a unified universe—individual beauty is a reflection of harmony in the universe and a higher "reality" on which all experiences of beauty depend. As a result, artists' products are valuable because they are symbols of a higher order of existence. Plotinus was the first philosopher to treat art in a comprehensive manner. In the *Ennead*, Plotinus uses dance as a symbol of how nature has harmony and exists as a "living whole." He also reasons that a universal "Good" is the source of all "Beauty"; artworks—that is, man-made objects of beauty—thus imitate the universal "Beauty" and, in so doing, imitate the "Good." In addition, the arts are able to perfect the incomplete beauty of natural objects. As a result, for Plotinus, artworks occupy a special place in human experience because they form a bridge between incomplete natural objects and the universal concept of beauty, and, therefore, good: art raises the mind to a higher moral plane. An artwork can thus be seen as symbolic in two senses: it symbolizes the natural world, but perfected; and it symbolizes ultimate reality in the only way comprehensible to human minds.

Divinities and Mystery Cults

Rome assimilated much of its philosophical thought from the Greeks and the Hellenistic world. The earliest divinities of Rome were nature-spirits who dwelt in trees, in springs, and on hilltops. In addition to Jupiter, the sky-spirit, Saturnus, a spirit of agriculture, and Mars, a spirit of agriculture and of war, there were gods of the home—for example, Janus, god of the doorway, and Vesta, goddess of the hearth-fire. No shrine was regarded with greater veneration than that of Vesta, where the sacred fire was kept burning. The round base of the shrine can still be seen in the Roman Forum.

As Rome's influence spread outward and interreacted with other cultures, other divinities took their place in the Roman pantheon, in some cases displacing and in other cases merging with earlier Roman gods and goddesses. In time, the gods of Rome were identified with the gods of Olympus and assumed their functions while retaining their Roman names. In 500 B.C.E., a great temple was dedicated to the triad Jupiter, Juno, and Minerva, the equivalents of the Greek gods Zeus, Hera, and Athena. In general, Roman religion meant the precise observance of established rites on behalf of the entire community. Prosperity, health, harvests, and victory in battle could be achieved only through the strict performance of rituals designed to cultivate the favor of the gods. Piety, thus, was not a matter of individual religious experience, as modern Americans might understand it, but, rather, the faithful observance of ritual duties.

By the end of the first century C.E., the most formidable religious cult in the empire was the Persian mystery-cult of Mithra (MITH-ruh), which took root in Rome and was carried by the Roman legions to the far corners of the empire. Roman monuments to Mithra can be found at the borders of Scotland, the shores of the Black Sea, and the frontiers of the Sahara Desert in Africa. Mithraism particularly appealed to soldiers, for it encouraged military virtues, imposed severe self-discipline, abstinence, and control of the passions, and imparted a sense of brotherhood. Mithra was not the supreme god in Mithraism; rather, he was the mediator between an unknowable and unreachable god who dwelt in eternal spheres and a suffering and struggling human race.

Mithra is pictured as constantly engaged in a struggle against the powers of evil (Fig. **4.7**). He had been compelled to catch a bull and, after a struggle, to slay him. From the body of the slaughtered bull came all plants and useful animals. Dogs, scorpions, and other creatures were considered malevolent, and it was with these creatures that Mithra did battle. Mithra also presided over the judgment of souls after death and guided them to their celestial homes, where he received them like children returning from a long voyage. Although Mithra was the god of light, his worship was carried on in underground temples. Those who sought membership of the cult were required to endure a long, painful course of preparation, after which the initiate took an oath called *sacramentum*. The initiate was eventually allowed to participate in a sacred rite in which a loaf of bread and a cup of wine and water were placed before the priest, who pronounced a sacred formula over it. By partaking of the mystical food, the new convert gained power to combat evil spirits and to gain immortality.

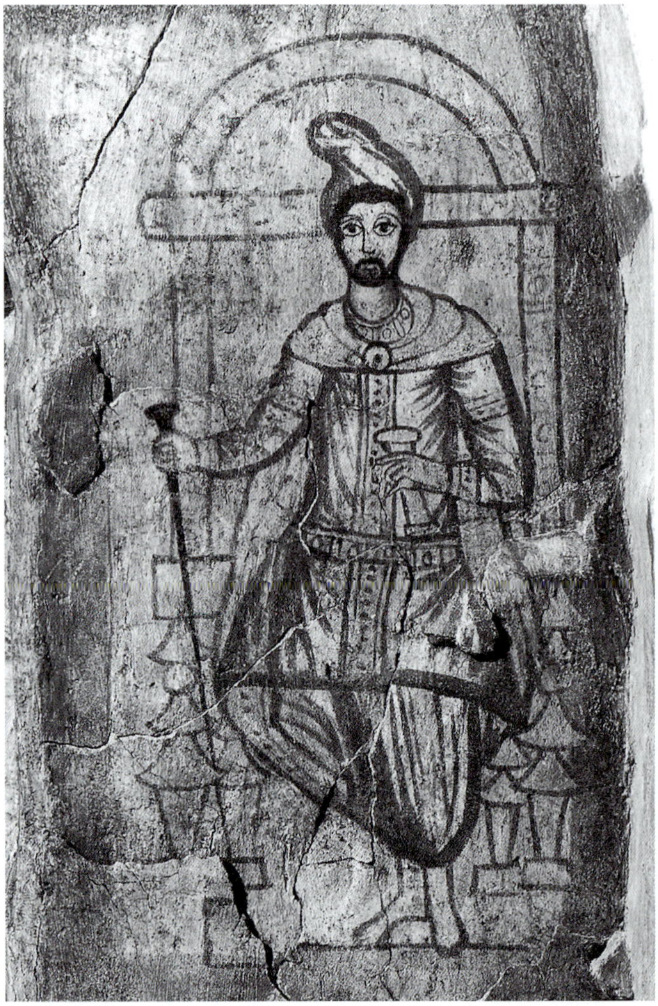

4.7 The prophet Mithra, from Dura-Europos, c. 245 C.E. National Archeological Museum, Damascus, Syria.

THE ARTS OF ROME

Painting

Very little Roman painting has survived. Most of what survives appears to have been done in bright colors, in **fresco**—that is, painting on wet plaster that becomes a permanent part of the wall surface—and much of that art seems inspired by Greek classical and Hellenistic work.

A Dynamic World

Chinese Painting

At almost the same time as the Roman Empire, the Han dynasty gave China a great empire in the East. The two empires had much in common—both covered vast areas and contained tremendous populations, and in each power was concentrated in the hands of an emperor and an immense, centralized bureaucracy. Like Rome, China perceived itself as the only true civilization, surrounded by barbarians, and in both cases, a significant breakdown of authority occurred early in what we call the Christian era. Interestingly, the two great empires knew of, and, indirectly, traded with, each other.

The Han dynasty produced remarkable scholarship and artistry. Three styles of painting existed during the period of the Han dynasty that spanned the first century C.E. The first style was a rather formal and stiff style, very geometric and **hieratic**, in which the figures were flat and outlined. In contrast, the second style depicted lively action and deep space. The third was midway between the two previous styles, being more painterly and exhibiting movement and lively depictions of, for example, mythic beings, dragons, and rabbits. As can be seen in Figure **4.8**, a tile taken from the lintel and pediment of a Han tomb, masterfully rendered figures are drawn with brushstrokes that suggest liveliness and movement. The figures appear in three-quarter poses, which gives the painting a sense of depth and action, and the active line, with its diagonal sweeps, adds to the sense of action. The poses of the people suggest character—that is, the psychology of the figure portrayed—but although the use of pose and direction reflects a sophisticated approach and technique, the figures remain on the same baseline, with no sense of placement in deeper space.

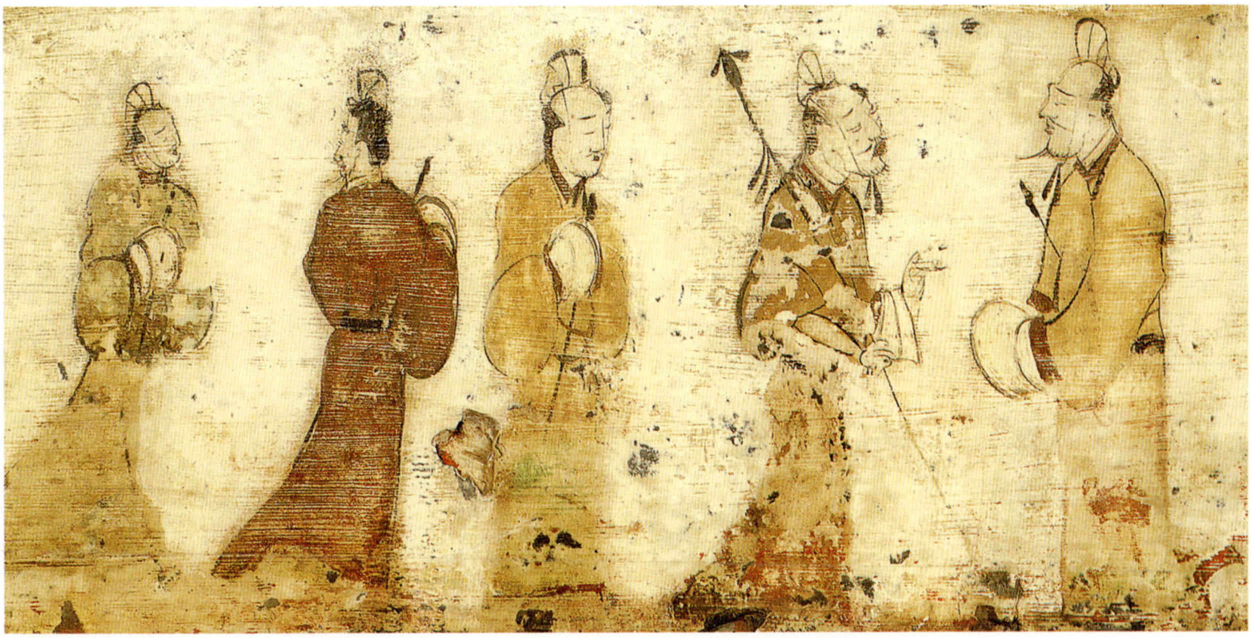

4.8 Lintel and pediment of tomb, Han dynasty, 50 B.C.E.–50 C.E. Earthenware, hollow tiles painted in ink and colors on a whitewashed ground, 29 × 80½ ins (73.8 × 204.7 cm). Museum of Fine Arts, Boston (Denman Waldo Ross Collection). (Gift of C.T. Loo.)

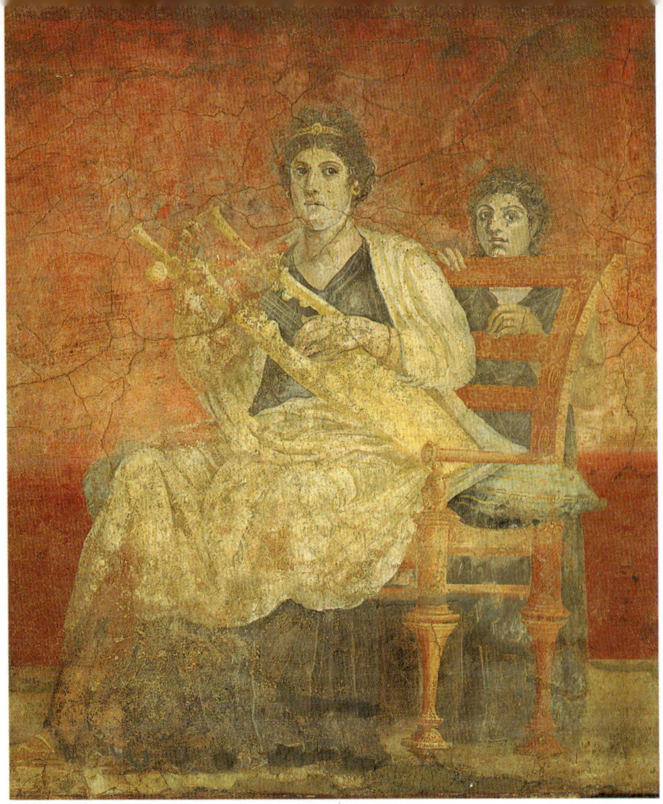

4.9 *Lady Playing the Cithara* c. 50 B.C.E. Wall painting, 6 ft 1½ ins (1.87 m) square. Metropolitan Museum of Art, New York (Rogers Fund, 1903).

Many Greek artists and craftspeople were brought to Rome, and it was they who produced most early Roman art, so it is not surprising that Roman painting reflected classical and Hellenistic themes and styles, although certain uniquely Roman qualities were added. The illustrations that appear in this chapter may not be typical of Roman painting. They are, however, typical of what survives.

In the painting of the *Lady Playing the Cithara* (Fig. 4.9), attentive detail merges with an everyday subject matter. From this illustration we get a taste of Roman clothing, hair style, accessories, and furniture. The ornately turned legs of the chair and the gold embossing indicate careful and skilled craftsmanship as well as opulence. Notice how carefully and naturalistically the folds of the fabric are rendered.

Roman wall painting may combine landscape representation with painted architectural detail (Fig. 4.10). Often, the outdoor view appears as a panoramic vista seen through a **trompe l'oeil** (trahmp-LOY) window.

4.10 Bedroom from villa of P. Fannius Synistor (detail no. 7) at Boscoreale, Italy, showing painted decorations, c. 50 B.C.E. Fresco on lime plaster, average height 8 ft (2.44 m). Metropolitan Museum of Art, New York, Rogers Fund, 1903. (03.14.13). Photo: © 1996 Metropolitan Museum of Art.

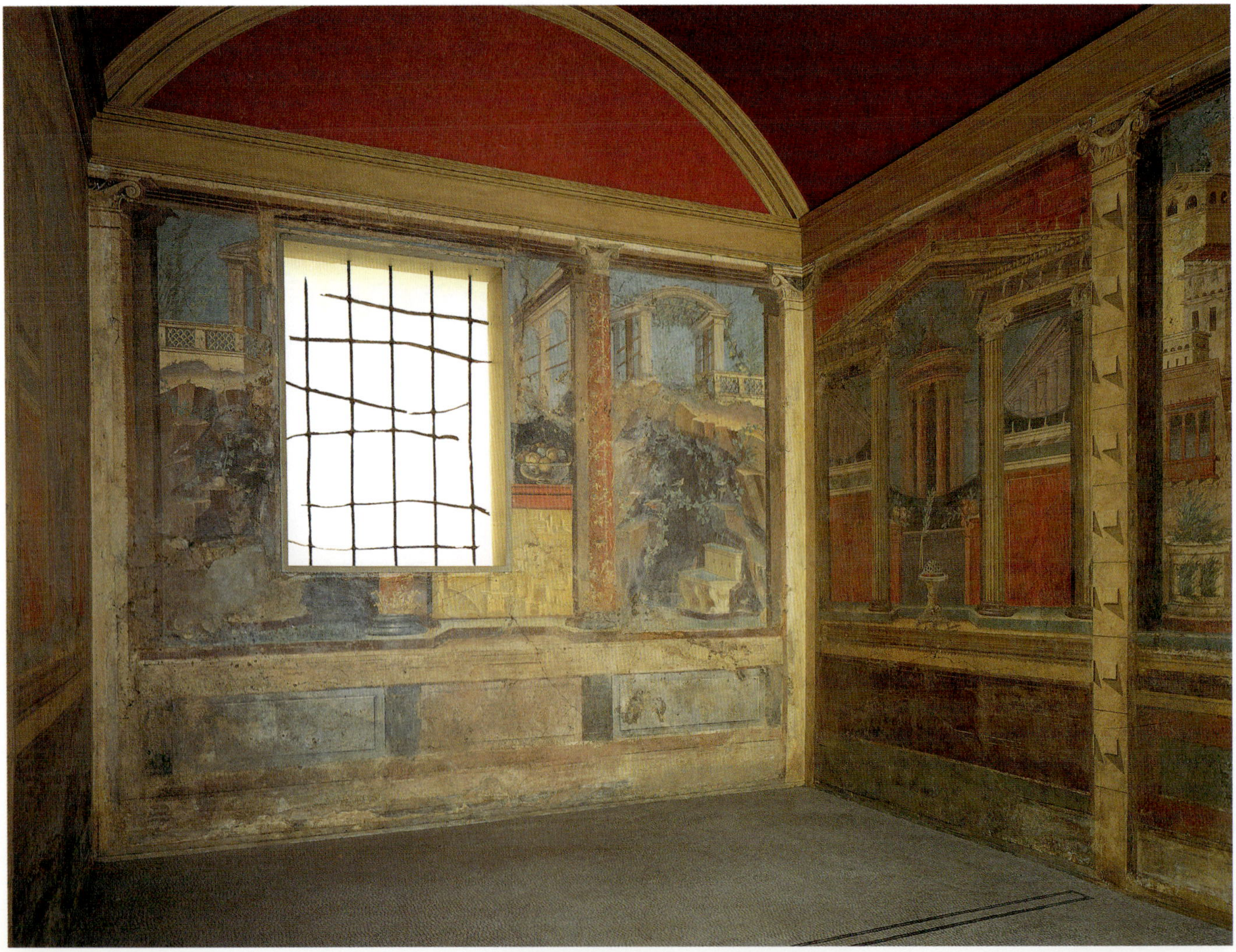

Rooms painted in this style reflect the tastes of late Republican aristocratic society. They took as their models the opulence and stylishness of the late Hellenistic princely courts, which were still influential around the Mediterranean.

Although it is less well known than Pompeii (pohm-PAY-ee), the city of Herculaneum (hur-kyoo-LAY-nee-uhm) provides us with excellent examples of wall painting from the Roman Empire period, which were preserved by the ash and lava of Mount Vesuvius' cataclysmic eruption in 79 C.E. In these works, as well as in works from Pompeii, we see that, as in wall painting from the Republican era, brightly colored frescoes were the order of the day. These works also share the naturalism of their predecessors. The wall painting *Hercules and Telephos* (TEL-eh-fohs; Fig. **4.11**) uses highlight and shadow to create marvelously rendered flesh and musculature as well as intricately detailed fabric in the Hellenistic style. Here the subject matter is mythical and heroic: Hercules' discovery of the infant Telephos in Arcadia. Hercules, the dynamic figure on the right, reveals warm flesh and sinewy musculature, full of life and warmth. In contrast, the personification of Arcadia, the semireclining figure, seems distant and remote—as cold as a piece of sculpture. The lion is rendered with quick, rough brushstrokes, which stand in stark contrast to the smooth, delicate treatment of the doe in the lower left. Above Arcadia, a playful Pan with his pipes shows an almost offhand treatment, as flippant as his smirk.

A second example from Herculaneum (Fig. **4.12**) exemplifies the Roman taste for forceful colors and the painted "architectural structuring" of large areas. Paintings are a permanent part of the wall and are

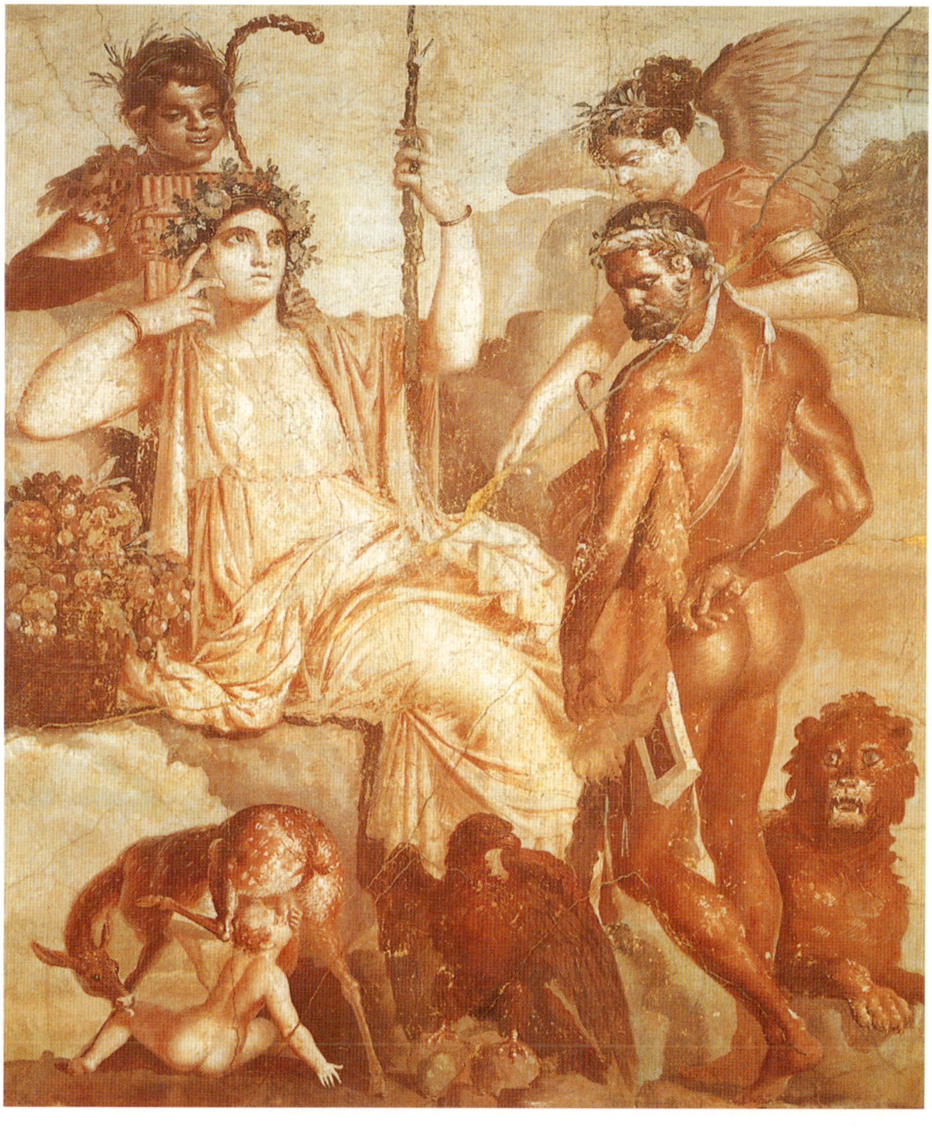

4.11 *Hercules and Telephos*, Roman copy of a Greek work of the second century B.C.E. Wall painting from Herculaneum, 5 ft 7½ ins (1.71 m) high. Museo Archeologico Nazionale, Naples, Italy.

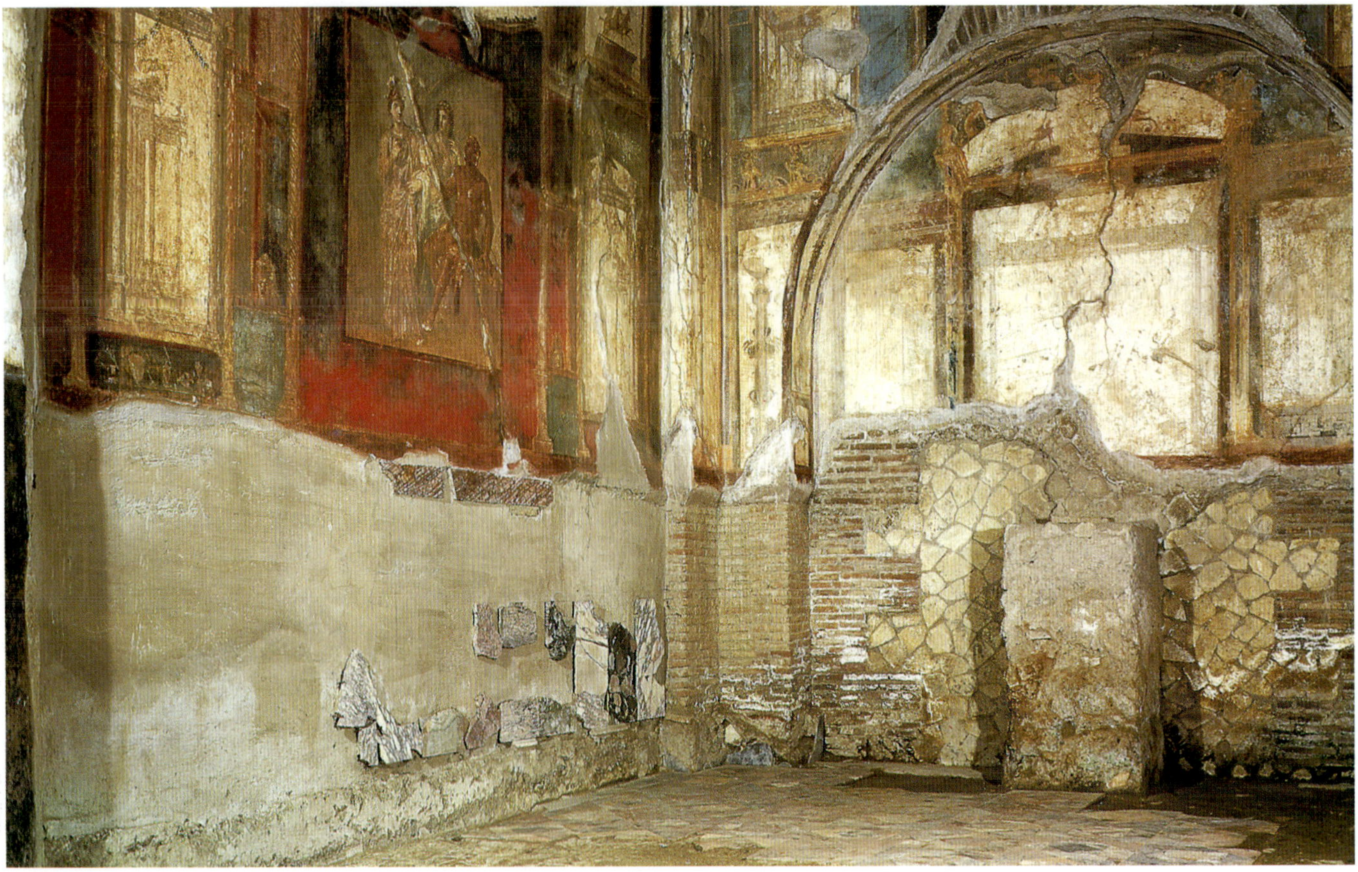

4.12 Wall decoration, c. 70–79 C.E. Wall painting, room dimensions 14 ft 2 ins × 13 ft 4 ins (4.32 × 4.06 m). Collegium of the Augustales, Herculaneum, Italy.

"framed" with painted architectural detail. This particular painting was a shrine devoted to the cult of the emperor, and the central panel, which depicts the introduction of Hercules into Olympus in the presence of Minerva and Juno, is a metaphor for the divinity of the emperor.

All the illustrations of Roman wall decoration in this chapter, whether of the earlier Republican or of the Imperial period, demonstrate the colorfulness of Roman interior design. The style of the painting is certainly theatrical, but it has a permanence, not only in that it forms an integral part of the wall, but also in that each panel contains an architecturally complete composition enclosed in a painted "frame." For examples of Roman mosaics visit http://www.artsednet.getty.edu/ArtsEdNet/Images/Trajan/gallery6.html.

Sculpture

Not all Roman art was an imitative reconstruction of Greek prototypes, although some Roman statues do fit this category. Some Roman sculpture, however, expresses a vigor that is uniquely Roman. Scholars do not always agree on what particular works of Roman sculpture mean or on why they were made. For example, the *Portrait of an Unknown Roman* (Fig. **4.13**) shows a "veristic" or highly lifelike representation. Etruscan–Roman religious practice undoubtedly had a strong influence. Portraits were an integral part of household and ancestor worship, and wax death masks were often made and kept by the family to remember a loved one. Wax is not a substance ideally suited for immortality, and it is possible that the bust in Figure **4.13** was made from a death mask. There may be more to this portrait, however, than mere accuracy. Some scholars point to an apparent emphasis on certain features which reinforces the ideas of ruggedness and character.

The straightforward naturalism of the Roman Republic was modified during the Augustan period. Although Hellenistic influence had become strong by the late first century B.C.E., Greek classical influence predominated in some quarters, but with a Roman—that is, a more practical and individual—flavor. By the time of the Empire, classical influence had gained precedence. Augustus (Fig. **4.14**) boasted that when he came to power, Rome was a city of sundried bricks, and that

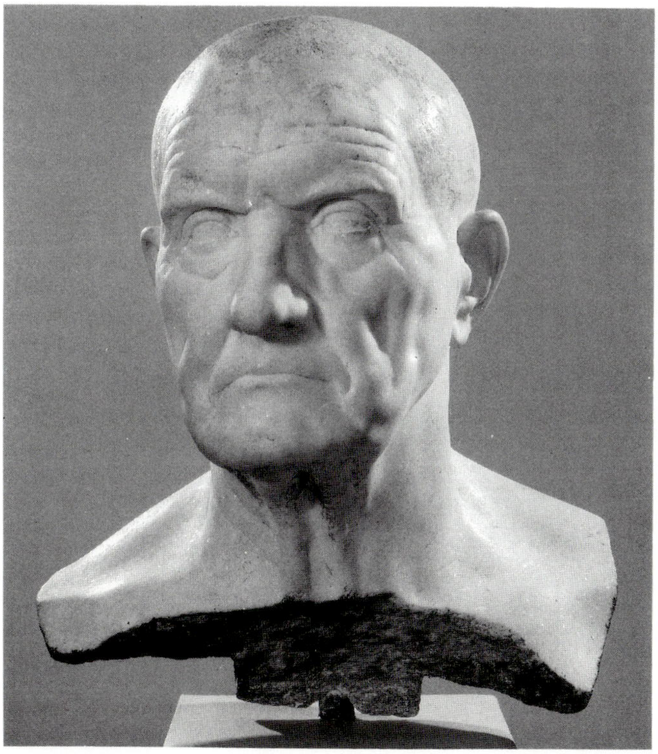

4.13 *Portrait of an Unknown Roman*, first century B.C.E. Marble, 14⅜ ins (36.5 cm) high. Metropolitan Museum of Art, New York (Rogers Fund, 1903).

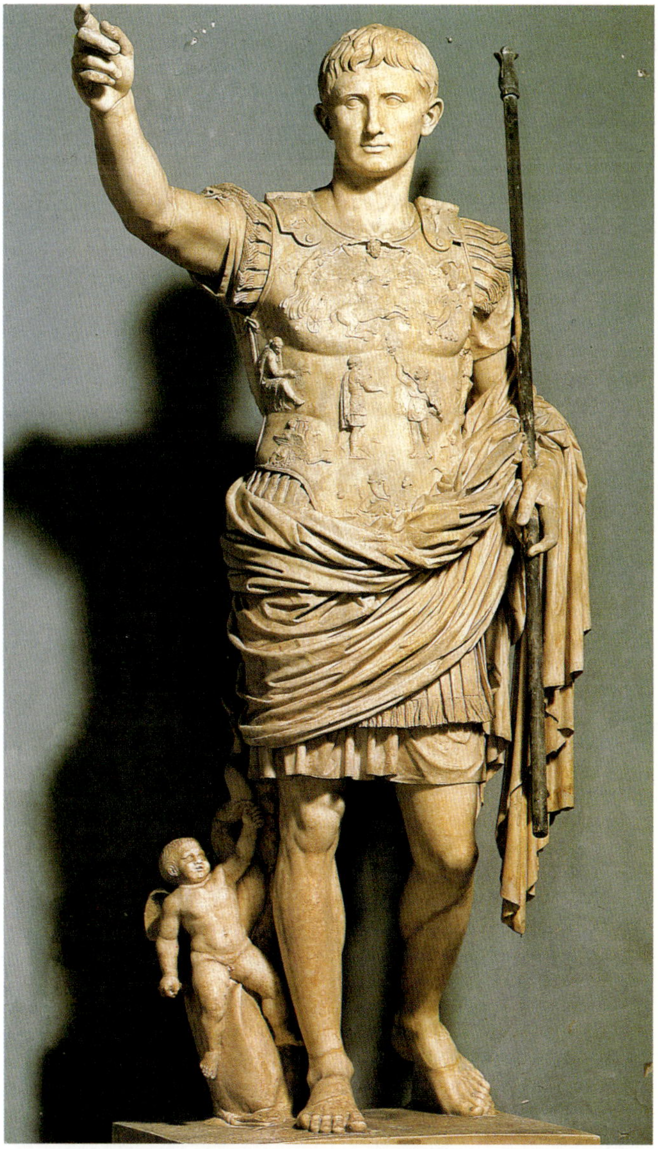

4.14 *Augustus in Armor*, Villa of Livia, Prima Porta, c. 20 B.C.E. Marble, 6 ft 8 ins (2.03 m) high. Vatican Museums, Rome.

when he left it, it had become a metropolis of marble. Greek classical form in sculpture was revived and translated into vital forms for the Romans. The Greek concept of the "perfect body" held sway. The aesthetics of sculptural depiction thus remained Greek. The pose, rhythm, and movement of the body originated in the past.

At this time much sculpture portrayed the emperor. Emperors had been raised to the status of gods, perhaps because in so far-flung an empire it was useful for people to revere their leaders as superhuman.

Other sculptures told the story of a leader's accomplishments. Trajan's (TRAY-juhn) Column, erected in the Emperor's Forum, rose 128 feet (39 meters) above the pavement on an 18-foot (5.5-meter) base. Atop the 97-foot (30-meter) column stood a more than twice lifesize statue of Trajan (Fig. **4.15**). (Trajan's statue was later replaced by a figure of St Peter.) Inside the column, a staircase winds upward to the top. The outside, from bottom to top, exhibits a spiral band of relief sculpture (Fig. **4.16**). Trajan himself appears ninety times in the narration, each appearance marking the start of a new episode.

The sculpture relies on symbolism and convention. Water is represented by a waving line; mountains, by jagged lines. Proportions are not lifelike, and perspective is irrational. For more detail, visit http://www.artsednet.getty.edu/ArtsEdNet/images/Trajan/gallery2.html. For more Roman sculpture, visit http://www.artsednet.getty.edu/ArtsEdNet/images/Trajan/gallery3.html.

We have touched already on the death mask as Roman funerary art. The intricate relief sculpture which decorated Roman **sarcophagi** (sahr-KAWF-uh-jy) shows the way that Roman art reflected private life. This type of sculpture emerged early in the second century C.E., when the practice of cremation fell out of favor. Marble sarcophagi were adorned with rich and varied relief decoration. There were three major centers of sarcophagus production—Athens, Asia Minor, and Rome—and sarcophagi were often exported before completion and finished at the site. Attic sarcophagi had decoration on all four sides, with scenes drawn from

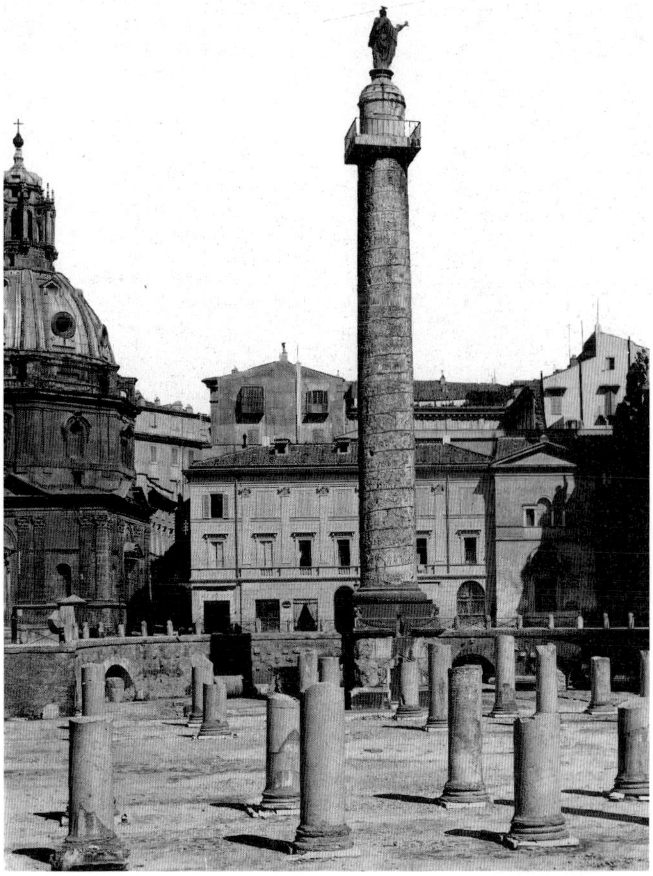

4.15 Apollodorus of Damascus, Trajan's Column and ruins of Basilica Ulpia, Rome. Trajan's Column, 106–13 C.E. Marble, base 18 ft (5.49 m) high, column 97 ft (29.57 m) high.

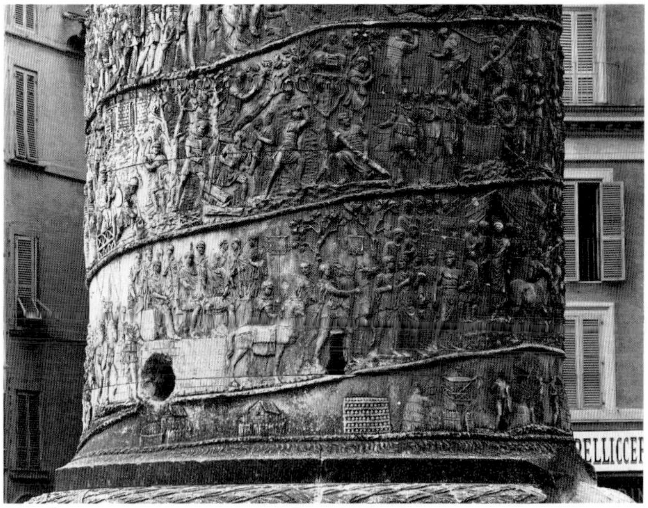

4.16 Trajan's Campaign against the Dacians, detail of Trajan's Column, 106–13 C.E. Marble, frieze band 4 ft 2 ins (1.27 m) high.

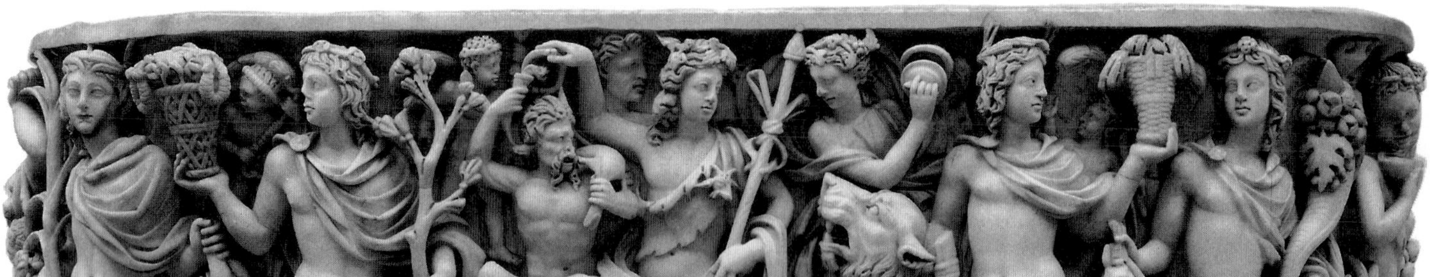

4.17 Roman sarcophagus, showing Dionysus, the Seasons, and other figures, c. 220–230 C.E. Marble, 7 ft 3¾ ins (2.23 m) long. Metropolitan Museum of Art, New York (Purchase, Joseph Pulitzer Bequest, 1995).

Greek mythology. They were typically carved in high relief, with a somber tone. Sarcophagi from Asia Minor had figures carved almost in the round, against a background of architectural detail. Roman sarcophagi were carved on three sides, with the fourth side designed to sit against a wall. The front typically showed a mythological scene, while the ends were carved with decorative motifs in low relief (Fig. **4.17**).

Architecture

Given the practicality of the Roman mind, it is not surprising to find that a distinctive Roman style is most evident in architecture. The clarity of form we found in the post-and-lintel structure of the classical Greek temple is also present in the Roman arch, but while in Greek architectural composition the part is subordinate to the whole, in Roman architecture each part often carries its own significance. The result is that we can usually surmise the appearance of a whole structure from one element.

Little survives of the architecture of the Republican period, but the use of Corinthian features and the graceful lines of what remains suggest a strong Hellenistic influence. There are notable differences, however. Hellenistic temples were built on an impressive scale (see Fig. **3.27**; Temple of the Olympian Zeus). Classical Greek temples were smaller, and Roman temples were smaller still, principally because Roman worship was mostly a private rather than a public matter.

Roman temple architecture employed **engaged columns**—that is, columns partly embedded in the wall—and as a result, Roman temples lacked the open colonnades of their Greek counterparts, and this gave them a closed, slightly mysterious atmosphere. The Temple of Fortuna Virilis (Fig. **4.18**), which dates from the second century B.C.E., is the earliest well-preserved example of its kind. Greek influence may be seen in the delicate Ionic columns and entablature, but Etruscan elements are also present in the deep porch and in the engaged columns that are necessitated by the wide **cella**, or main enclosed space. (The one-room cella departs from the Etruscan convention of three rooms.) The Romans used the cella for displaying trophies from military campaigns, as well as to house the image of the deity.

In the Augustan age at the beginning of the Imperial period, Roman architecture, like contemporary sculpture, was refashioned in Greek style. This accounts to a large extent for the dearth of surviving buildings from previous eras since old buildings were replaced with new ones, in the new style. Temples were built on Greek plans, but the proportions were significantly different from those of the classical Greek.

The first through the fourth centuries C.E. brought what is now typically identified as the "Roman style." The most significant characteristic of this style is the use of the arch as a structural element, in **arcades** and **tunnel** and **groin vaults** (Figs **4.23** and **4.24**; see also Fig. 0.8). The Colosseum (Figs **4.25** and **4.26**), the best-known of Roman buildings and one of the most stylistically typical, could seat 50,000 spectators. Combining an arcaded exterior with vaulted corridors, it was a marvel of engineering. The circular sweep of its plan and the curves of the arches are countered by the vertical lines of the engaged columns flanking each arch. The columns at each level are of different orders, and progress upward from heavy Doric columns, to Ionic ones, to lighter Corinthian ones at the top level.

Placed in the center of the city of Rome, the Colosseum was the site of gladiatorial games and other spectator sports. Emperors competed with their predecessors to produce the most lavish spectacles there. The Colosseum was a new type of building, called an **amphitheatre**, in which two semicircular theatres are combined, facing each other, to form an arena surrounding an oval interior space. Originally, a system of poles and ropes supported awnings to shade spectators. The space below the arena contained animal enclosures, barracks for gladiators, and machines for raising and lowering scenery.

Roman triumphal arches are also impressive architectural monuments. The Roman classical style survives in a memorial to Titus (TY-tuhs), which was raised by his younger brother, Domitian (doh-MIH-shun).

The Arch of Titus (Fig. **4.27**) was a political gesture of homage to the accomplishments of Titus and his father, Vespasian, during the conquest of Jerusalem. The reliefs on the arch illustrate historical and allegorical

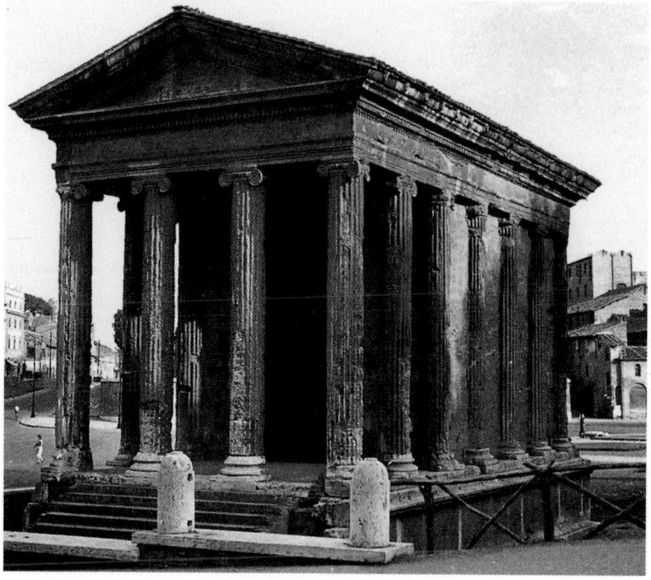

4.18 Temple of Fortuna Virilis, Rome, late second century B.C.E. Stone.

MASTERWORK

The Pantheon

As its name suggests, the Pantheon (PAN-thee-ahn; Figs **4.19**, **4.20**, and **4.21**) was designed and built, by Hadrian, to honor all the gods. The structure brought together Roman engineering, practicality, and style in a domed temple of unprecedented scale.

Until the mid-nineteenth century, only two buildings had equalled the span of its dome, and during the Middle Ages, it was suspected that demons might be holding up the roof of this pagan temple. Around the circular interior statues of the gods stood in **niches** (NIHCH-ehz) in the massive walls. Corinthian columns add grace and lightness to the lower level. Heavy horizontal moldings accentuate the feeling of open space under the huge dome. The dome itself is 143 feet (44 meters) in both diameter and height (from the floor to the **oculus**, or eye, the round opening at the top of the dome). The circular walls supporting the dome are 20 feet (6 meters) thick and 70 feet (21 meters) high. Square **coffers** on the underside of the dome give an added sense of lightness and reflect the framework into which concrete was poured. Originally the dome's interior was gilded to suggest "the golden dome of heaven."

In both plan and **cross-section** the Pantheon is designed on a perfect circle: the dome is a hemisphere (Fig. **4.20**). From the exterior, we see a simple, sparsely adorned cylinder capped by a gently curving dome. The entrance is via a porch in the Hellenistic style with graceful Corinthian columns. Originally the porch was approached by a series of steps and a rectangular forecourt, so what remains is only part of a larger, more complex original design.

Inside, both the scale and the detail are overwhelming, but the way in which practical problems have been solved is equally impressive. The drum and dome consist of solid monolithic concrete reinforced with bands of vitrified tile. The vertical gravity loads are collected and distributed to the drum by arches incorporated in the concrete. The wall of the 20-foot-thick drum has alternating rectangular and curved niches cut into it, thus forming a series of

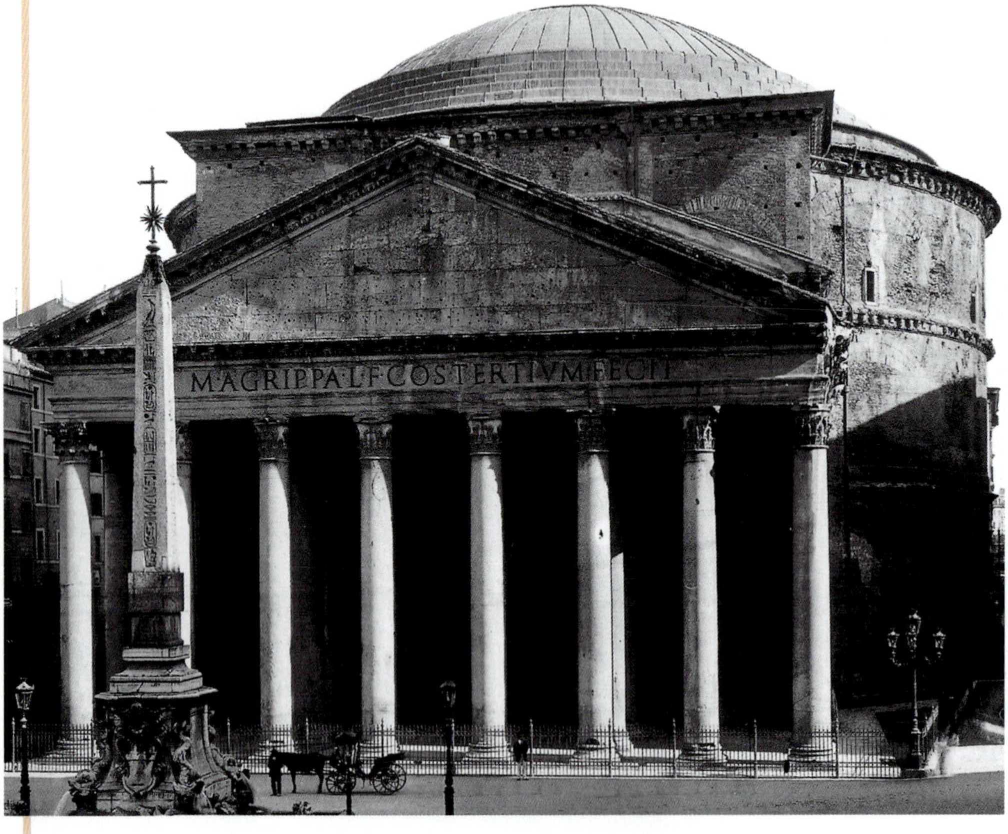

4.19 (*left*) Pantheon, Rome, c. 118–28 C.E. Marble, brick, and concrete.

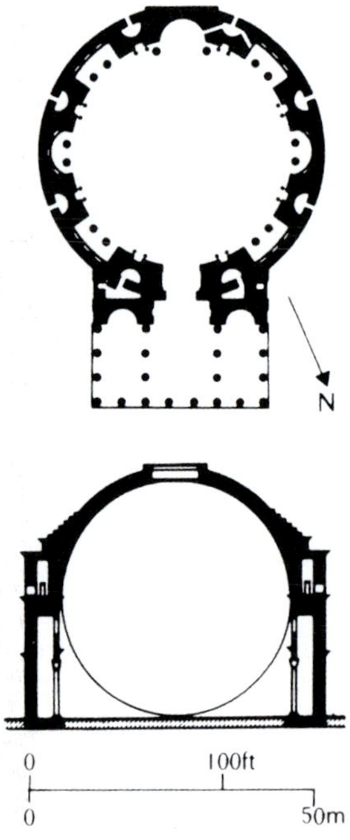

4.20 (*above*) Plan and cross-section of the Pantheon, Rome.

massive radial buttresses. Drains cut into the slightly concave floor of the building carry away any rain that falls through the oculus above.

What captures our immediate attention is the sense of space. In most Egyptian and Greek architecture, the focus is on mass—the solids of the buildings. Here, despite the scale and beauty of the solids, it is the vast openness of the interior that strikes us. This is Roman inventiveness and practicality at its best, yet the atmosphere of the building is not one of practical achievement but of sublimity.

How could the Romans build such a colossal structure? Some historians argue that the key lies in a new building technology made possible by concrete containing a specific kind of cement newly developed near Naples. The secret, however, may lie in the mysterious rings around the dome. As a study at Princeton University suggests, they probably "perform a function similar to the buttresses of a Gothic cathedral. . . . The extra weight of the rings . . . helps stabilize the lower portion of the dome. Rather than functioning like a conventional dome, the Pantheon behaves like a circular array of arches, with the weight of the rings holding the end of each arch in place."[3]

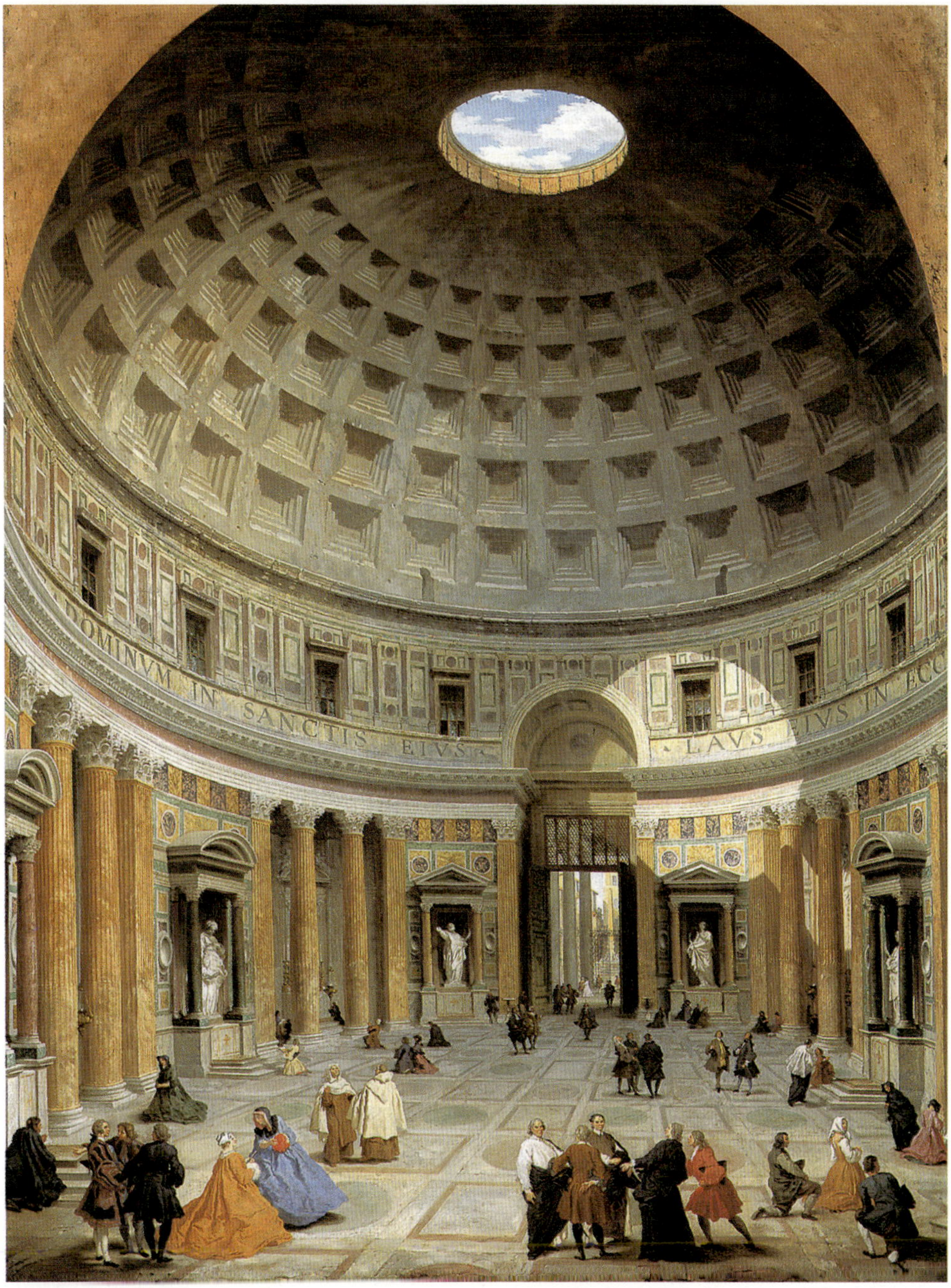

4.21 Giovanni Paolo Panini, *Interior of the Pantheon*, c. 1740. Oil on canvas, 4 ft 2 ins × 3 ft 3 ins (127 × 99 cm). National Gallery of Art, Washington D.C. (Samuel H. Kress Collection).

TECHNOLOGY

Cement

In their rapid conquests, the Romans learned quickly to appreciate and to copy other people's mechanical devices. The major contribution to technological development made by the Romans was probably their ability to absorb ideas and then to provide the administrative underpinnings to allow those ideas to be used to their fullest. Many technological practices are credited to Rome, but, in fairness, a large number of these had been invented and practiced elsewhere before the Romans acquired them. Even aqueducts, a much-vaunted Roman innovation, had seen predecessors in Greece, Assyria, Babylonia, Persia, and Egypt, and the same was true of drainage systems, which, as we noted, were part of the technology of Minoa. Roman roads were no better than those in Greece and Persia.

One of the truly original contributions of Rome to technology was the introduction of cement. In addition to its uses as a bonding material, the Romans discovered that it could be used in the making of concrete, which, when combined with a brick facing, allowed them to construct solid arches, thus eliminating the need for buttressing (Fig. **4.22**). This type of arch was seen most frequently in the construction of aqueducts, but the development of the brick-and-concrete arch may also be considered a major Roman contribution to technology. Essentially, this consisted of a brick arch reinforced with a heavy infill of concrete. Once the concrete set, the arch became a vast lintel that exerted little lateral pressure. Thus, the pillars that supported it required no supporting buttresses.

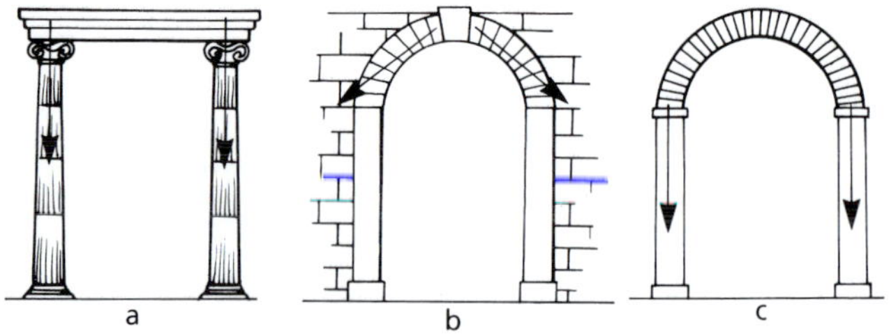

4.22 Diagram showing the stresses involved in (a) the Greek post and lintel; (b) a true arch; and (c) the Roman arch.

events. Titus appears as *triumphator*, along with figures such as the *genius Senatus*, or spirit of the Senate, and the *genius populi Romani*, or spirit of the people of Rome. The richly and delicately ornamented **façade** of this arch stands in marked contrast to its massive internal structure. This is an important characteristic of Roman architecture, which distinguishes it from Greek principles, in which the structure can always be seen.

Roman engineering not only made heating and cooling possible within homes, but it also created huge **masonry** structures for channeling water tremendous distances. Aqueducts such as that of the Pont du Garde at Nîmes in France (Fig. **4.28**) remind us of just how ingenious and practical the Romans were. For more Roman architecture visit http://harpy.ucs.edu/roman/html/repub.html.

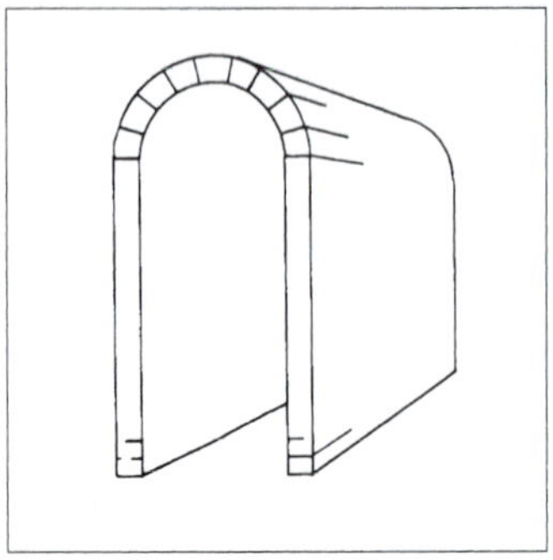

4.23 Arcade.

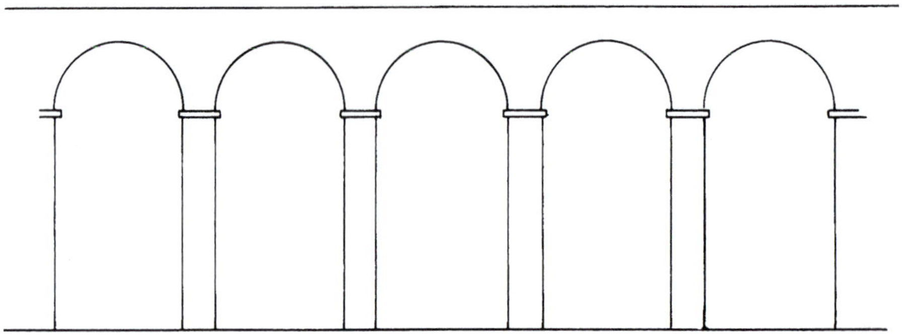

4.24 Tunnel vault.

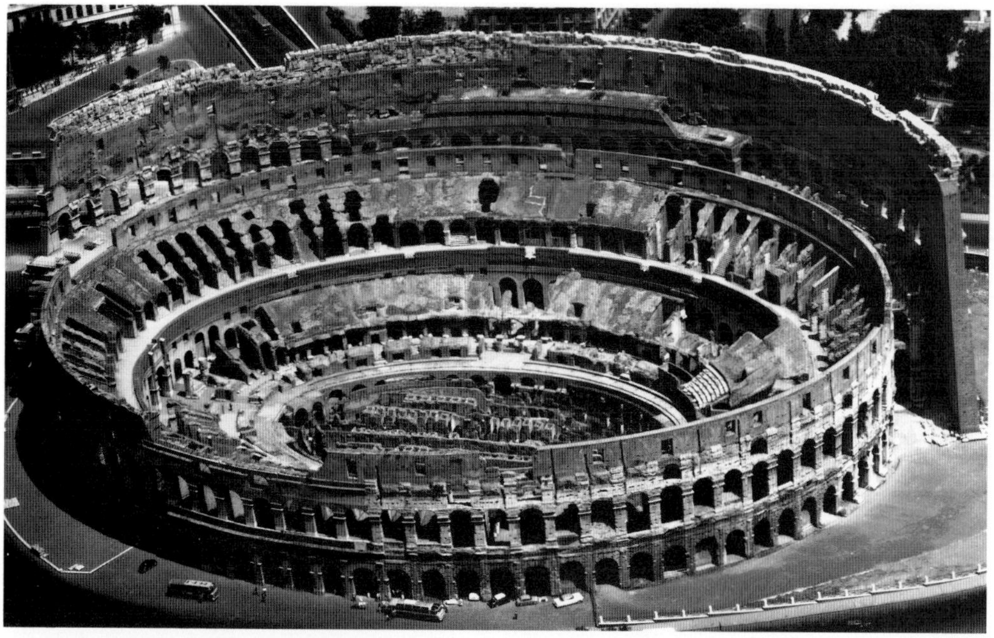

4.25 Colosseum, Rome, c. 70–82 C.E.. Stone and concrete, 159 ft (48.5 m) high.

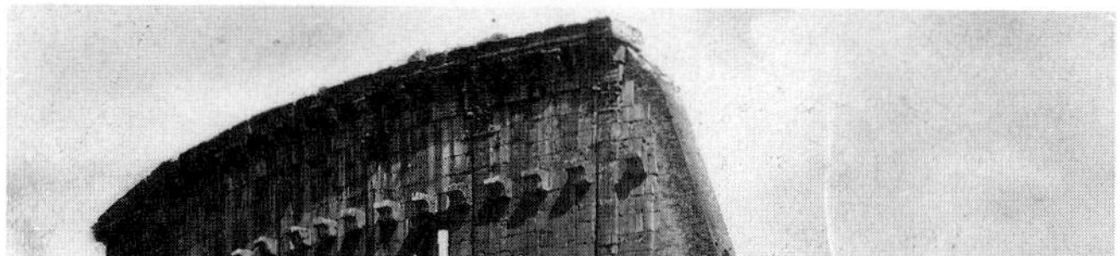

4.26 Colosseum, interior 616 ft 9 ins (188 m) long; 511 ft 10 ins (156 m) wide.

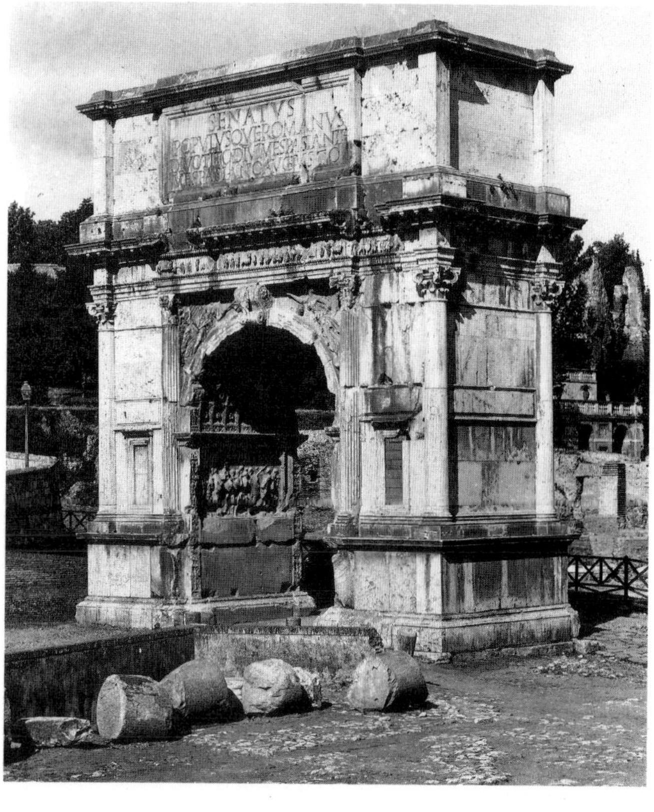

4.27 Arch of Titus, Roman Forum, Rome, c. 81 C.E. Marble, about 50 ft (15 m) high.

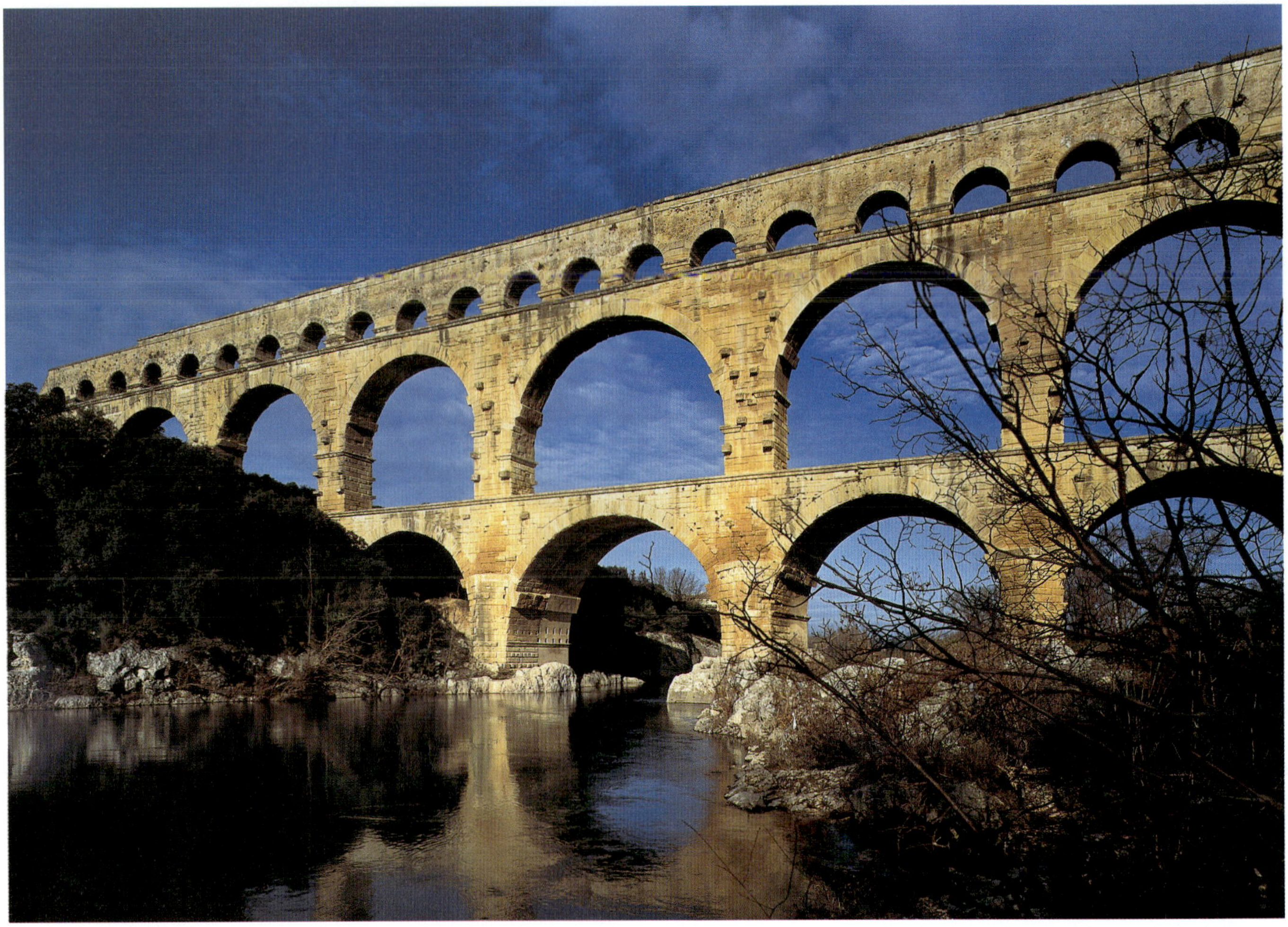

4.28 Roman aqueduct at the Pont du Garde, Nîmes, France. Photo: © Paul M.R. Maeyaert, Mont de l'Enclus (Orroir), Belgium.

Theatre

Comedy

The Romans loved entertainment. Roman comedy was wild, unrestrained, lewd, and highly realistic. Accounts of stage events suggest that very little was left to the audience's imagination. Actors wore various masks, and grotesquely padded costumes.

As Roman comedy developed in the third and second centuries B.C.E., it borrowed much from Hellenistic comedy, with its large theatres, high stages, and elaborate scene buildings (see Chapter 3). The Romans were receptive to comedy, and assimilated it quickly, and the importation of Greek comedy led to the rise of two of Rome's most important playwrights, Plautus (c. 254–184 B.C.E.) and Terence (c. 185–159 B.C.E.).

The twenty plays by Plautus (PLAW-tuhs) that survive provide a picture of a playwright who was principally a translator and adaptor. He copied Greek originals, changing the locations to Rome and inserting details of Roman domestic life. His characters were types, not individuals: the braggart soldier, the miser, the parasite, and the wily but mistreated slave. With their slapstick humor and "sight gags," Plautus' plays are full of farcical energy and appeal directly to the emotions, not to the intellect. They are not particularly well written, but they work well enough on stage.

Terence, who was better educated than Plautus and a more literary writer, enjoyed the support of a wealthy patron. In his six extant plays he appears to be a dramatist capable of drawing universal situations and characters. Like Plautus, he had a great influence on the theatre of later ages, but he was not particularly popular with Roman audiences, perhaps because he did not use banality and buffoonery.

Theatre fulfilled an important social function in keeping the minds of the masses off their problems. Yet it also served as a forum in which the general public could address grievances to the bureaucracy. When an official of the state had betrayed his trust, when a wrong had been suffered, or when an impropriety of state had become flagrant, the bite of Roman satire could be fierce, direct, and penetrating.

Blood Sport

Although we may not think of it in formal terms as theatre, blood sport had most of the trappings of theatre for the Romans and for other Mediterranean cultures that embraced it. A typical "performance" opened with the *pompa* or procession which featured the trainers, sponsors, and, of course, the gladiators. The acts included "lesser" animal fights, and, finally, the intermissions when public executions took place. These intermission–executions had nothing directly to do with blood sport. The gladiatorial fights were the featured performances and the majority of gladiators, by the late Republic, were not slaves but volunteers who willingly forfeited their rights and property, and pledged not only to suffer intensely but to die fighting.

Although gladiators may have been considered monsters outside the arena, they displayed, or "performed," what it meant to be Roman while they fought. The concept of *virtus* (honor above life), a specifically male trait to the Romans, was most often applied to the gladiator who fought well or continued to struggle even after defeat. If a gladiator displayed these honorable traits but was clearly at the end of a losing bout, a display of *virtus* would enable him or her to raise one finger—the plea for clemency or mercy. Because Romans were more interested in a good fight rather than bloodshed for its own sake, they could, and it seems usually did, grant *missio* or clemency for combatants so that the gladiator could fight another day.

Interestingly, this need for gladiators to display *virtus* in victory as well as in defeat (as in "baring one's neck") caused more conservative Romans to find it difficult to appreciate the Christian concept of martyrdom. Marcus Aurelius, when witnessing Christians making, in his mind, a show out of their deaths, complained that "Christians were shameless exhibitionists in their zeal for martyrdom." Marcus Aurelius expressed in Stoic fashion (see next section and p. 119) that Christians were essentially debasing the games.

The animal fights, however, provide evidence of the most elaborate theatrical performances. They included elaborate costumes and stage props, and a strong interest in illusions which would accompany the performing of debased Greek myths. For example, in one documented case, in Rome, the myth of Icarus was performed and involved the illusion of flight. The "fantasy" was abruptly shattered when the sorry individual came crashing back to earth—only to be met by a group of hungry lions.[2]

Music

Music was very popular among the Romans. Contemporary reports describe festivals, competitions, and virtuoso performances. Many Roman emperors were patrons of music, and Greek music teachers were popular and very well paid. Large choruses and orchestras performed regularly, and the *hydraulos* (hy-DRAWL-ohs), or water organ, was a popular attraction at the Colosseum (Fig. **4.29**). The *hydraulos* was apparently so loud that it could be heard a mile away, and the fact that it provided "background music" for the spectacles in which Christians were fed to lions meant that it was banned from Christian churches for centuries.

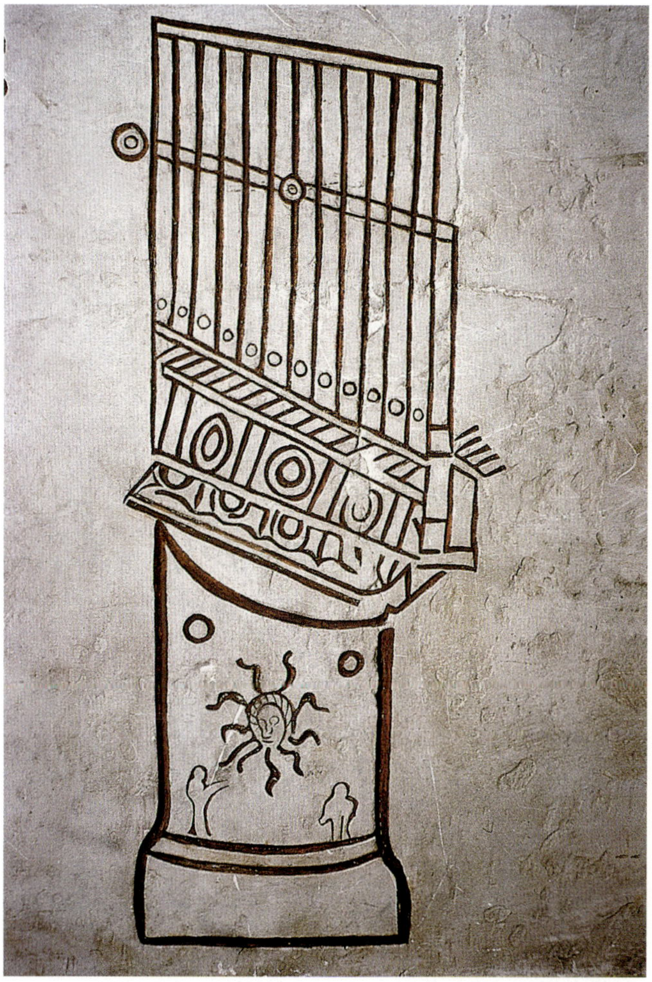

4.29 Roman *hydraulos*, copy of graffito in the church of St Paul, Rome, fourth century C.E. Photo: C.M. Dixon.

Aristotle had deplored professionalism in the pursuit of music. Music, he believed, existed for its own aesthetic qualities and as a moral force in character development. It was a measure of intelligence. The pragmatic Romans did not see it this way. Professional dexterity and *virtuosity* were social assets, and meaningless accomplishments, such as blowing the loudest tone or holding the longest note, were rewarded with great acclaim. Musical entertainment did fulfill an important social and political function for the Romans, however. As more and more people flocked to Rome from conquered territories, the numbers of the poor grew. The state began to provide entertainments to keep them occupied and under control. "Bread and circuses" became the answer to the dissatisfactions of the poor and the oppressed, and music also played an important role. As a result, music became less an individual pastime and more an exclusively professional activity.

The Romans seem to have contributed little to musical practice or theory. They took their music direct from Greece after it became a Roman province in 146 B.C.E., adopting Greek instruments and theory. But they did invent some new instruments, principally brass trumpets and horns for military use.

Dance

One of Rome's significant legacies was the unique dance form of **pantomime**. Pylades of Cilicia (PY-luh-deez; sil-IH-shuh) and Buthyllus (boo-THY-luhs) of Alexandria are credited with the invention of pantomime, around 22 B.C.E. They brought together a number of dance elements, some of which dated to prehistoric Greece. Although the words "mime" and "pantomime" are sometimes used interchangeably in our vocabulary, they were very different art forms. Pantomime was serious and interpretative. Some pictorial evidence suggests that a single dancer portrayed many roles by changing costumes and masks. Wind, brass, and string instruments played as the dancer leapt, twisted, and performed acrobatic feats. The interpretation of delicate emotions also played a part. Pantomimes often had tragic themes, apparently taken from Greek and Roman tragedies and mythology. But many pantomimes also had a distinctly sexual orientation that some sources call pornographic.

This dance form fell into disfavor as its lewdness increased. Treated comically, lewdness may have been tolerable, even endearing. The same subject matter treated seriously, however, may have become tedious or obnoxious, even to the pragmatic (and decadent) Romans. The more notorious emperors, such as Nero and Caligula, apparently loved pantomime, as did certain of the populace. Eventually, however, pantomimists were forced out of the major cities to the provinces. These itinerant entertainers may have helped to keep theatrical dance alive through the Middle Ages and into the Renaissance.

Literature

The practical early Romans did not produce any remarkable literature. When literature as an art form did become reasonably popular, it was Greek slaves who nurtured it. The first literary works were imitations of Greek works, and they were written in Greek. Latin was initially considered a peasant language, with few words capable of expressing abstract notions. A Latin prose style and vocabulary for the expression of philosophical ideas had to wait.

During the reign of Augustus, the poets Horace and Vergil were commanded to write verses glorifying the emperor, the origins of Rome, the simple honesty of rural Roman life, patriotism, and the glory of dying for one's country. Livy set about retelling Roman history in sweeping style. Vergil's *Aeneid*, an epic account of the journey of Aeneas from the ruins of Troy to the shores of Italy, far surpasses mere propaganda.

Vergil makes Aeneas the founder of Roman greatness by making him the founder of Lavinium, the parent town of Alba Longa and Rome. Aeneas had been told, as he left the burning ruins of Troy, that he was fated to found a new city with a glorious destiny in the west.

In Book I, Aeneas, traveling to his fated destination, runs into foul weather which forces him to land his fleet on the coast of Libya, where he is welcomed by the widowed Dido, queen of Carthage. In Books II and III, Aeneas tells Dido of the natural and supernatural events that led him to her shore. In Book IV, Dido confesses her love for Aeneas. Aeneas, however, regretting his fate, must set sail again—forced to do so by the gods. Dido prepares to kill herself. Book V finds the Trojans journeying to Sicily, where they engage in a series of contests to commemorate the death of Aeneas' father, Anchises. Then they cast off again. Book VI tells of Aeneas' journey to the underworld and Elysium, where he meets the ghosts of Dido and Anchises. Aeneas learns of the destiny of Rome. In Books VII through XII, the Trojans reach the Tiber River and are received by Latinus, the king of the region. Spurred by the gods, other Latins resent Aeneas and the Trojans' arrival and the proposed marriage of Aeneas to Lavinia, daughter of Latinus. War ensues, but the Trojans, with the help of the Etruscans, emerge victorious. Aeneas marries Lavinia and founds Lavinium.

PROFILE

Vergil (70–19 B.C.E.)

Rome's greatest poet, Publius Vergilius Maro, loved the rural countryside. He was born a peasant, and he focused the central force of his poetry on people. His writings also reveal his thorough education in Cremona, Milan, and Rome and the influence of the Epicureans and Stoics, who were central to the rhetoric and philosophy of his studies. Shy and retiring, he seems never to have participated in politics or the military; he was a poet first and foremost. Nevertheless, he kept in close contact with current events, and his works often reflect an overview of contemporary Roman life.

His first work, the *Eclogues* (EK-lawgs), brought him immediate recognition and access to the exclusive literary circles of Rome. The following years, 37–30 B.C.E., were spent writing the *Georgics*, and the remainder of his life was occupied by the *Aeneid* (i-NEE-id), which is to Rome what the *Iliad* and the *Odyssey* are to Greece (see p. 72).

The twelve books of the *Aeneid* tell the story of Rome, and in them Vergil sought to hold up to his readers the qualities of Roman character and Roman virtues that had made the city great. The first six books tell the story of Aeneas' wanderings—as Homer had told of Ulysses' travels in the *Odyssey*—and the final six books set the scenes of battle—as Homer did in the *Iliad*. Further internal similarities exist as well.

Vergil's influence on literature and Western thought is probably greater than any other classical poet. His poetry reflects consummate skill in the use of diction, rhythm, and word music. Above all, he captures a quality of the human condition, elevated to a grand scale, with which every human being can identify. At the time of his death, Vergil was highly troubled by the imperfections he found in the *Aeneid*, and he wanted to burn it. However, the Emperor Augustus refused to allow the work to be destroyed and had it published, with some minor revisions, two years after the poet's death.

Here is a brief excerpt from the beginning of Book I:

Arms and the man I sing, who first made way
Predestined exile, from the Trojan shore
To Italy, the blest Lavinian strand.
Smitten by storms he was on land and sea
By violence of Heaven, to satisfy
Stern Juno's sleepless wrath; and much in war.
He suffered, seeking at the last to found
The city, and bring o'er his fathers' gods
To safe abode in Latium; whence arose
The Latin race, old Alba's reverend lords,
And from her hills wide-walled, imperial Rome.[4]

The complete text of Vergil's *Aeneid* can be located at http://www.perseus.tufts.edu/cgi-bin/ptext?doc=Perseus%3Atext%3A1999.02.0054&layout=&query=toc&loc=1.

Horace (b. 65 B.C.E.) was an outstanding Latin lyric poet and satirist. The most frequent themes of his *Odes* and verse *Epistles* include love, friendship, philosophy, and the art of poetry. The son of a former slave, Horace was educated in Rome and traveled to Athens, where he attended lectures at the Academy. In the *Odes*, Horace represented himself as heir to earlier Greek lyric poets but displayed a sensitive, economical mastery all his own. The works of Horace can be found at http://www.perseus.tufts.edu/cgi-bin/ptext?doc=Perseus%3Atext%3A1999. 02.0063&query =card%3D%231&layout=&loc=1.1.5.

Little is known about Livy's life, and nothing about his family background. Probably he spent most of his life in Rome, and attracted the attention of Augustus while he was fairly young. Livy's lifework was the composition of his history of Rome, composed of 142 Books. Unfortunately, only Books 21–45 survive, along with summaries of the books after Book 45. Unique among Roman historians, Livy took no part in politics. Thus, his writing seeks no historical explanations in political terms. He saw history in terms of human personalities and representative individuals rather than partisan politics. Together with Cicero and Tacitus (TAS-ih-tuhs), Livy set a new standard for Roman literary style by writing in Latin rather than Greek.

On the other hand, Plutarch (PLOO-tahrk; c. 46–after 119 C.E.) wrote in Greek and strongly influenced the evolution of the essay, biography, and historical writing in Europe between the sixteenth and nineteenth centuries. Plutarch's literary output was immense, but his popularity rests on his *Parallel Lives*, a series of biographies of famous Greeks and Romans, an example of which follows. We can see a visual representation of the story in a painting by Poussin from the seventeenth century (see Fig. **13.13**).

Phocion
c. 402–317 B.C.E.
Translated by John Dryden

. . . Although he was most gentle and humane in his disposition, his aspect was stern and forbidding, so that he was seldom accosted alone by any who were not intimate with him. When Chares once made some remark on his frowning looks, the Athenians laughed at the jest. "My sullenness," said Phocion, "never yet made any of you sad, but these men's jollities have given you sorrow enough." In like manner Phocion's language, also, was full of instruction, abounding in happy maxims and wise thoughts, but admitted no embellishments to its austere and commanding brevity. Zeno said a philosopher should never speak till his words had been steeped in meaning; and such, it may be said, were Phocion's, crowding the greatest amount of significance into the smallest allowance of space. And to this probably, Polyeuctus, the Sphettian, referred, when he said that Demosthenes was, indeed, the best orator of his time, but Phocion the most powerful speaker.

His dead body was excluded from burial within the boundaries of the country, and none of the Athenians could light a funeral pile to burn the corpse; neither durst any of his friends venture to concern themselves about it. A certain Conopian, a man who used to do these offices for hire, took the body and carried it beyond Eleusis, and procuring fire from over the frontier of Megara, burned it. Phocion's wife, with her servant-maids, being present and assisting at the solemnity, raised there an empty tomb, and performed the customary libations, and gathering up the bones in her lap, and bringing them home by night, dug a place for them by the fireside in her house, saying, "Blessed hearth, to your custody I commit the remains of a good and brave man, and, I beseech you, protect and restore them to the sepulchre of his fathers, when the Athenians return to their right minds."

And, indeed, a very little time and their own sad experience soon informed them what an excellent governor, and how great an example and guardian of justice and of temperance they had bereft themselves of. And now they decreed him a statue of brass, and his bones to be buried honourably at the public charge.

Catullus (b. c. 84 B.C.E.) was a poet whose expressions of love and hatred are generally considered the finest lyric poetry of ancient Rome. The facts of Catullus' life are few, but the poet Ovid states that Catullus died young. His poetry reflects strong emotion and twenty-five of his poems portray an unhappy love affair with a woman named Clodia. Most of the poems are written in forms that served for inscriptions and dedications and as verse of light occasions, satirical comment, and elegant sentiment.

Here is one example:

—15—

If man can find rich consolation, remembering his
good deeds and all he has done,
if he remembers his loyalty to others, nor abuses his
religion by heartless betrayal
of friends to the anger of powerful gods,
then, my Catullus, the long years before you shall
not sink in darkness with all hope gone,
wandering, dismayed, through the ruins of love.
All the devotion that man gives to man, you have
given, Catullus,
your heart and your brain flowed into a love that
was desolate, wasted, nor can it return.
But why, why do you crucify love and yourself
through the years?
Take what the gods have to offer and standing
serene, rise forth as a rock against darkening
skies;
and yet you do nothing but grieve, sunken deep in
your sorrow, Catullus,
for it is hard, hard to throw aside years lived in
poisonous love that has tainted your brain
and must end.
If this seems impossible now, you must rise
to salvation. O gods of pity and mercy, descend and
witness my sorrow, if ever
you have looked upon man in his hour of death, see
me now in despair.
Tear this loathsome disease from my brain. Look, a
subtle corruption has entered my bones,
no longer shall happiness flow through my veins like
a river. No longer I pray
that she love me again, that her body be chaste, mine
forever.
Cleanse my soul of this sickness of love, give me
power to rise, resurrected, to thrust love aside.
I have given my heart to the gods. O hear me,
omnipotent heaven,
and ease me of love and its pain.

A moralizing Stoicism runs throughout the literature of the Augustan period. In poetry, this Stoicism was expressed through satire, which allowed writers to combine morality with popular appeal. Martial and Juvenal used satire to attack vice by describing it in graphic detail. Petronius produced satirical **picaresques** in verse and prose that were as readable as Martial's and Juvenal's work, but free of their moralizing.

Finally, Apuleius (ap-yuh-LEE-uhs) and Lucan (LOO-kuhn) followed in the same tradition. Apuleius' *Golden Ass* is one of the earliest precursors of the novel. The author creates a fictional biography that describes how the central character is tried and condemned to death for the murder of three wineskins. He is brought back to life by a sorceress, but as he tries to follow her in the form of a bird, he is changed instead into an ass. The only cure for this affliction appears to be the procurement of some rose leaves, and in his search for these, he has bizarre and fantastic adventures.

FOCAL POINT

Augustus—Classical Visions

The aesthetic revolution at the start of the Roman Empire saw a shift in the purpose of art toward propaganda. One of the artistic ramifications of Augustus' new political order was the emergence of the **neo-Attic** style.

Sculptural works, with their new emphasis on portraying the emperor, can be divided into three main types. These are differentiated by scholars primarily by hairstyle, while facial features remain recognizably the same. In the first type (Fig. **4.30**), before Octavian was made emperor, his hair is shown in disorder. The second type (Fig. **4.31**) depicts the same man (now called Augustus) as emperor, with a more refined, nobler face and the hair divided into two strands above the right eyebrow. In the third type (Fig. **4.32**), the forelock is gone, and the hair is combed to the side.

The essence of Roman neo-Attic sculpture, however, is to be found in the statue of Augustus shown in Figure **4.14**. The portrait head of the Emperor sits on an idealized, youthful body like that Polyclitus made for his *Lance Bearer* (see Fig. **3.12**). Unlike the lance bearer, however, Augustus reaches outside his cube of compositional space, and the final effect is much less introspective and more dignified than that of its prototype.

The Forum of Augustus in Rome (Figs **4.33** and **4.34**) exemplifies monumental Imperial art at its classical grandest. In both its conception and its dimensions, it speaks of greatness. Constructed from war booty, the Forum honors Mars the Avenger, to whom Octavian had made a vow during his wars against the assassins of Julius Caesar. The Forum's style reflects Augustus' view that in all the arts the Greeks had achieved perfection in the classical style. All this served to establish Augustus as the greatest among *summi viri*, or the greatest "among all the great men of Roman history."[5]

Vergil's *Aeneid* tells not only the story of the legendary founding of Rome by Aeneas of Troy, but, further, as a kind of dual birth, the Roman unification of the world by Augustus—both events viewed as extraordinary tasks, glorious achievements, and divinely ordained necessities.

Finally, we turn to a "jewel" of Augustan classicism, the *Ara Pacis*, or Altar of Peace (Fig. **4.35**). It is representative of a movement toward a saturating symbolism, in which every detail was intended to convey meaning. Here, even apparently decorative elements are symbolic: the garlands, or swags, strung from ox-skulls

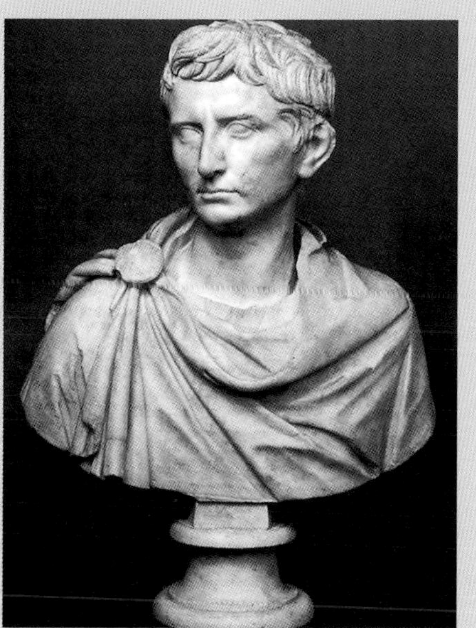

4.30 Octavian, copy of a type created in 31 B.C.E. Marble, 14⅝ ins (37.2 cm) high. Museo Capitolino, Rome.

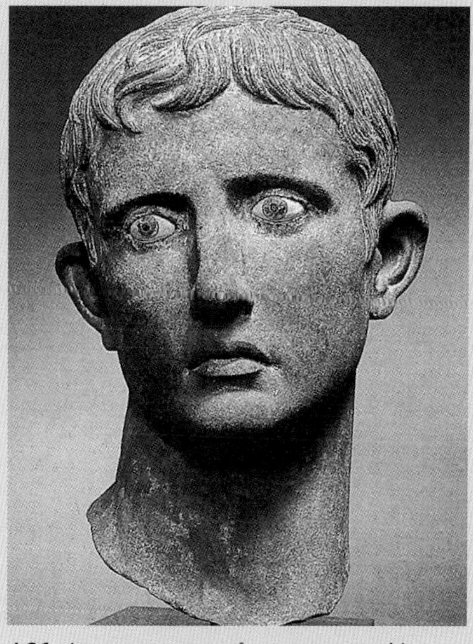

4.31 Augustus, copy of a type created in 27 B.C.E. Bronze, 16⅞ ins (42.9 cm) high. British Museum, London.

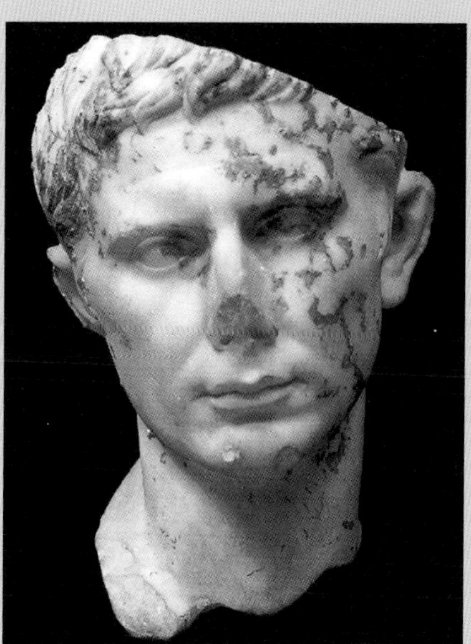

4.32 Augustus, final type before 12 B.C.E. Marble, 12 ins (30.5 cm) high. Museum of Fine Arts, Boston (Gift of Edward W. Forbes).

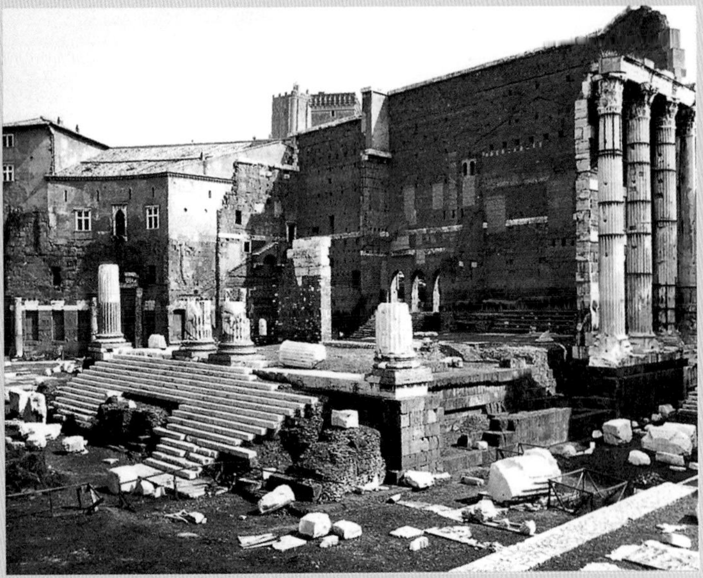

4.33 Temple of Mars the Avenger, Forum of Augustus, Rome, from the south, dedicated 2 B.C.E. Marble facing over stone and concrete.

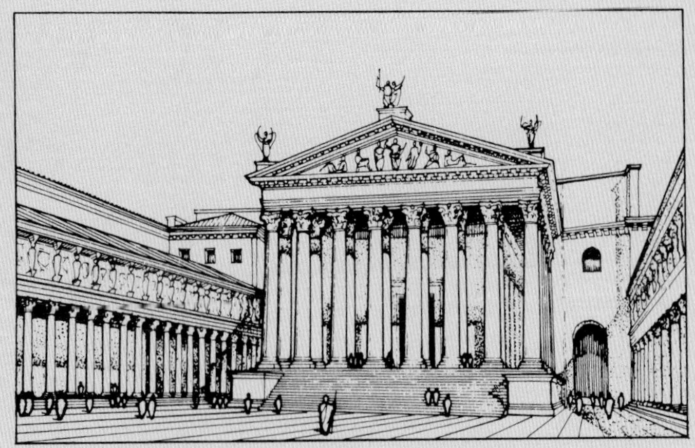

4.34 Temple of Mars the Avenger, Forum of Augustus, reconstruction view.

represent peace, while the fact that they are composed of varieties of fruit which do not ripen together symbolizes the unending nature of this peace. The figures themselves, though their poses are perfectly natural, exude royal dignity and nobility, characteristics that Augustus sought to emphasize in the popular conception of himself. The whole altar, dedicated to peace, thus serves as an image of the golden age of Augustus—that is, an era of peace and prosperity whose source was the emperor himself.

To contemporary Romans, the Golden Age of Greece was ancient and celebrated history. Monumentality, symbolism, practicality, and a resurrection of Greek classicism adapted to Roman tastes—these are the hallmarks of the Augustan age. Taken together, they describe what we have come to know as Roman classicism, and they reflect the quintessence of Roman life, as the Romans themselves saw it.

4.35 *Ara Pacis* (Altar of Peace), Rome, 13–9 B.C.E. Marble. Outer wall about 34 ft 5 ins × 38 × 23 ft (10.5 × 11.6 × 7 m).

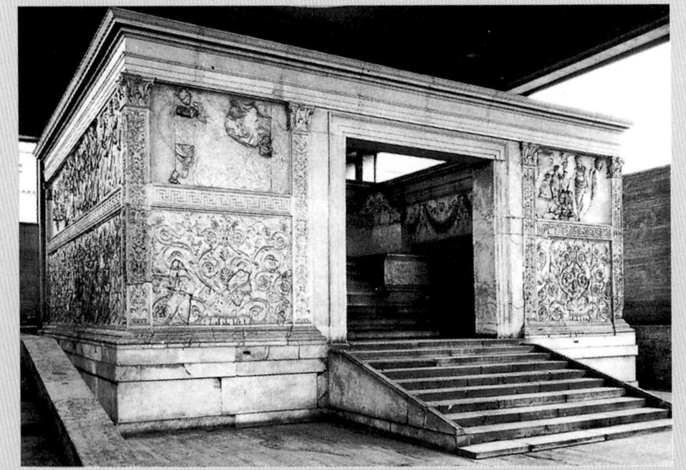

CHAPTER REVIEW

❖ CRITICAL THOUGHT ❖

Remarkably, the Roman genius for organization created a system that, although it certainly did not foster a cultural ethos like that of the Hellenes, nonetheless worked efficiently enough to ensure that, under a single government, the world knew relative peace and prosperity. Augustus Caesar was one of the cleverest politicians of all history. In addition to knowing how to manipulate public opinion in order to achieve his own ends, he knew the power of art and literature in shaping a public persona and public opinion, much as today's media consultants and "spin-doctors" do. Augustus used art and literature to invent not only his own aura but that of Rome itself.

If we walk the streets of Rome today, we see a curious amalgam of the old and the new. The Colosseum's tattered remains rise shakily above a heavily traveled thoroughfare, and across the street we walk through the Roman Forum, whose fragmented remains surround us like giant tombstones in a quiet cemetery. In other places, we can look down into the ruins of the Empire and marvel at how high the current street is above the ground of 2,000 years ago. Elsewhere, Imperial ruins have simply been incorporated into later construction to create a curious timewarp.

The ruins of Pompeii and Herculaneum, as well as Rome, tell us that life—at least for some—during the Roman Empire must have been fairly pleasant. In the mild Mediterranean climate, homes of marble, centered on an open courtyard and richly decorated with wall paintings, would be inviting and comfortable, even by modern standards. The solid proportions of classical Greece must have suggested to Romans a sense of order and stability that seemed eternal. Of course, it was not—but then, neither were they. Were they aware of the subtle changes taking place around the edges of their society? Were they able to compare it with what it once was? Were they able to grasp when the zenith had been reached?

◆ SUMMARY ◆

After reading this chapter you should be able to:

- Characterize Roman Republican art and architecture and compare them with those of the Roman Empire.
- Discuss Roman theatrical, musical, and dance forms.
- Explain the philosophies of Seneca, Marcus Aurelius, Epictetus, and Plotinus.
- Identify the various aspects of Roman religions and cults.
- Describe the main directions of Roman literature and its writers.
- Apply the elements and principles of composition to analyze and compare individual works of Roman art and architecture.

CYBERSOURCES

http//harpy.uccs.edu/roman/html/augustus.html
http//harpy.uccs.edu/roman/html/pompeiislides.html
http://www.bc.edu/bc_org/avp/cas/fnart/arch/roman_arch.html
http://www.chch.school.nz/mbc/patricia.htm

5 Judaism and Early Christianity

OUTLINE

HOW ART WORKS:
Symbols and Symbolism

CONTEXTS AND CONCEPTS
- Hebrews, Israelites, and Jews
  - The Patriarchs
  - The Ten Commandments
  - From Conquest to Exile
  - PROFILE: Solomon
  - The Hebrew Bible
- Christianity
  - Jesus Christ and His Teachings
  - The Apostolic Mission
  - The Early Christian Church
  - Early Christian Thought
- Christianity and the Late Roman Empire
  - Diocletian
  - TECHNOLOGY: Matches
  - Constantine

THE ARTS OF JUDAISM AND EARLY CHRISTIANITY
- Painting
- Sculpture
  - A DYNAMIC WORLD: Shinto Sculpture in Japan
- Architecture
  - MASTERWORK: The Temple of Jerusalem
- Music and Dance
- Literature

FOCAL POINT:
St Paul and the Westernization of Christianity

VIEW

THE JUDEO-CHRISTIAN HERITAGE

The chapters of this textbook unfold more or less chronologically. At this point in our journey, however, we must halt our forward momentum to backtrack, because during the Roman Imperial period a different heritage—the Judeo-Christian—made a new and significant impact on Rome and on Western civilization. Judaism was already an important religion and culture in the Mediterranean, but it was, essentially, an Eastern religion. Out of it came a new religion, Christianity, whose translation by the Apostle Paul into terms compatible with Greek thinking spread it throughout the Roman Empire, profoundly changing the course of Roman and European history. To pull these relationships together, we must return to the Middle East, some two thousand years before Augustus Caesar, and work our way forward again.

A relationship exists between Judaism and Christianity. As we will see, in the early years their worship forms were indistinguishable, and many Christians believed that becoming a Christian meant first converting to Judaism.

KEY TERMS

Some of the basic terms and concepts we will encounter in this chapter include the following:

Torah
"The Teaching," the Old Testament books of Genesis, Exodus, Leviticus, Numbers, and Deuteronomy, which include statements of Jewish doctrine, practice, religion, and morals.

Neoplatonism
A philosophy and religious system developed in the third century C.E., based on the doctrines of Plato and other Greek philosophers, and combined with elements of Oriental mysticism, and some Judaic and Christian concepts.

Affective
Related to feelings and emotions as opposed to facts.

Rebus
A riddle composed of symbols suggesting the sounds they represent.

Clerestory
A row of windows in the upper part of a wall.

Basilica
A term that in Roman times referred to building function, usually a law court; it was later used by Christians to refer to church buildings and to a specific form of church buildings.

5.1 The apse, S. Apollinare in Classe, c. 540–47 C.E. Ravenna, Italy.

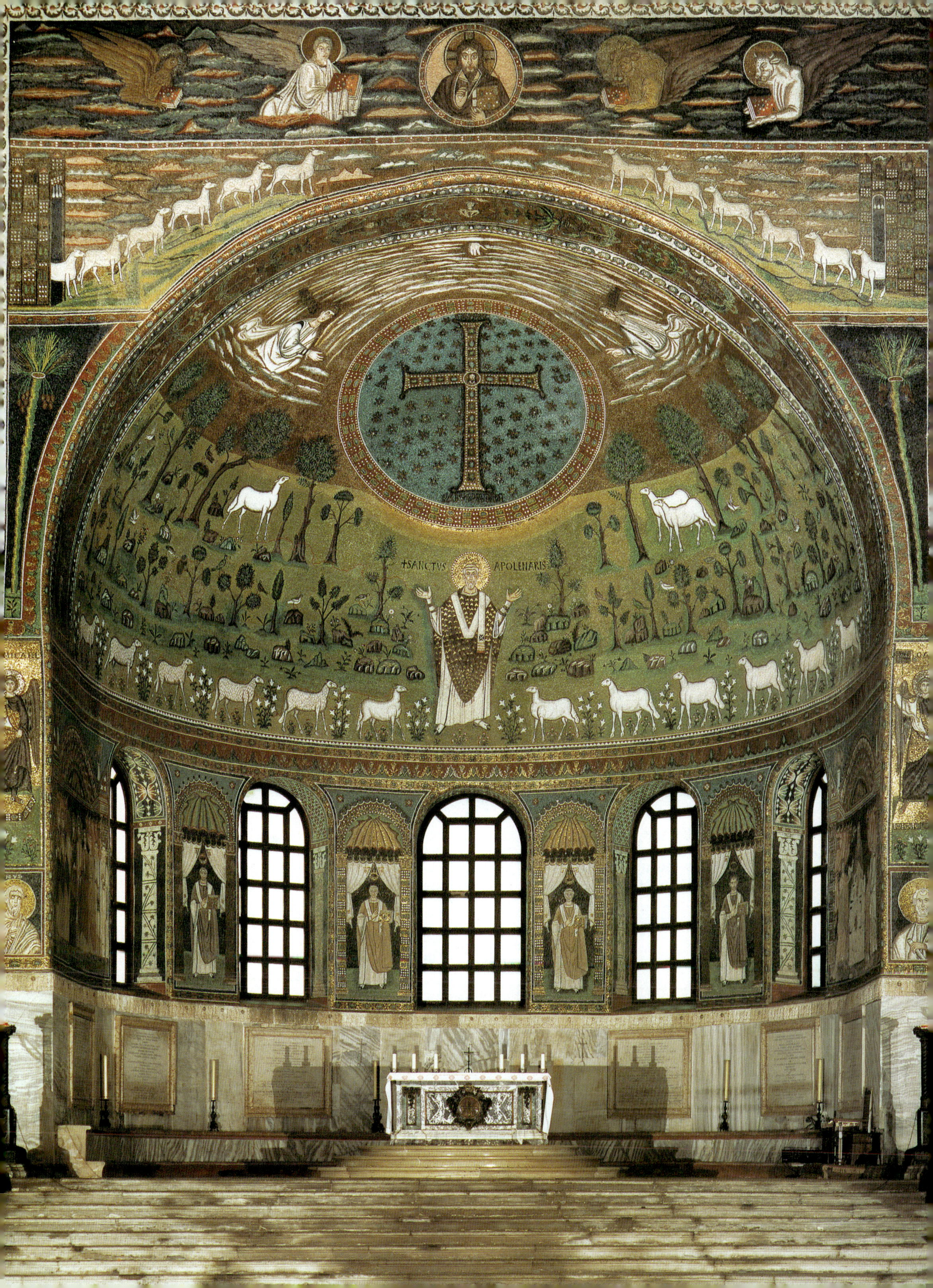
+SANCTVS
APOLENARIS

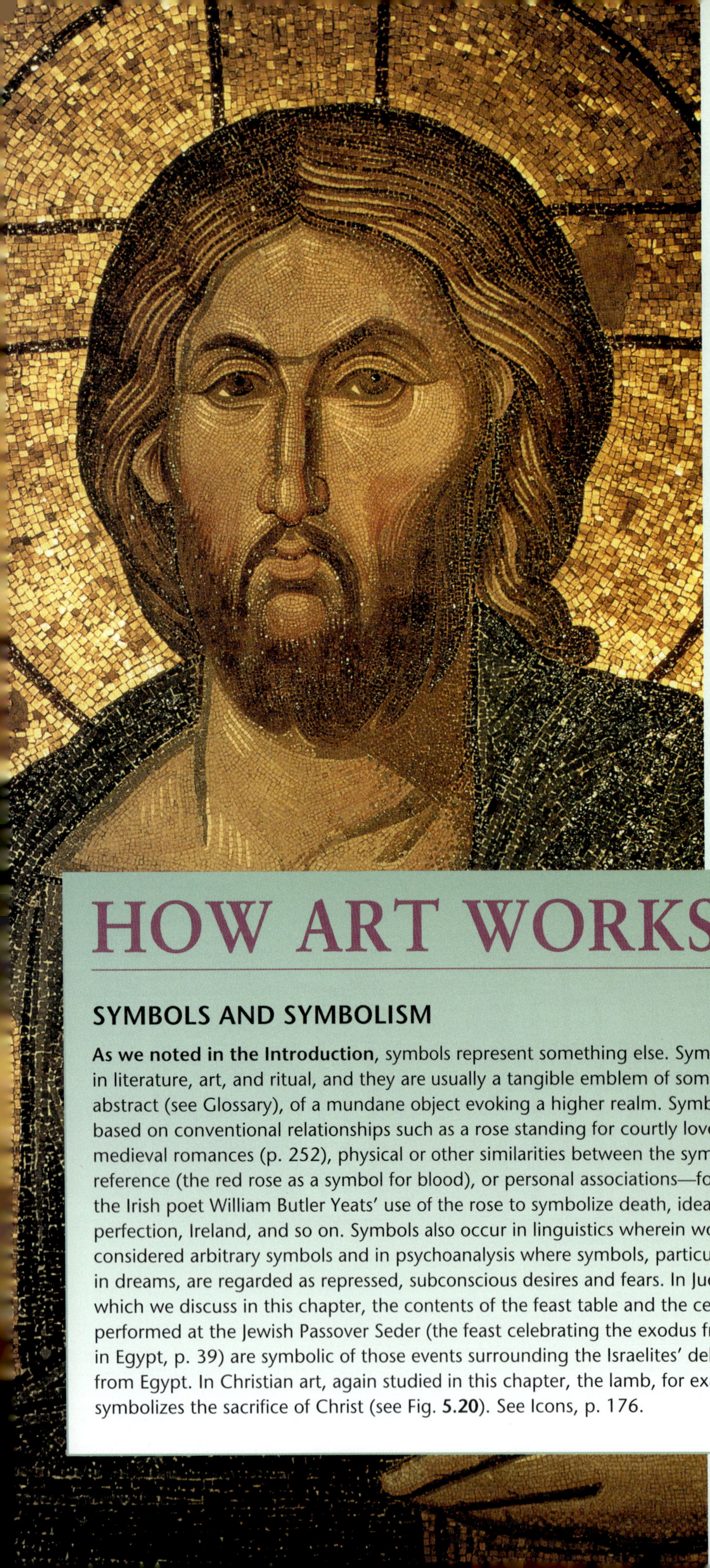

Symbolism

Symbolism is particularly noteworthy in this chapter in which two major religions are discussed, because symbols in religion are pervasive. In addition, "symbolism" is the name given to a European (mainly French) literary and artistic movement of the nineteenth and twentieth centuries, exemplified by Cézanne (Fig. **5.2**; see also p. 510), that rejected the representation of concrete reality in favor of the symbolic expression of ideas (we discuss this in Chapter 16 with regard to literature and theatre). Symbolism in the fine arts took two forms. Painters such as Gustave Moreau (1826–98) created dreamlike allegorical canvases on themes drawn largely from biblical and classical subjects. We can see this in *Oedipus and the Sphinx* (Metropolitan Museum, New York) at http://www.metmuseum.org/collections/view1.asp?dep=11&full=1&item=21%2E134%2E1. Others, for example Paul Gauguin and Vincent van Gogh (pp. 510–11), rejected, in their later works, the careful visual effects of the impressionists (pp. 505–9) in order to use pure color as a direct expression of emotion. That approach contributed to the rise of **abstract** art as depicted by Kasimir Malevich, for example (Fig. **5.3**; see also p. 547).

HOW ART WORKS

SYMBOLS AND SYMBOLISM

As we noted in the Introduction, symbols represent something else. Symbols occur in literature, art, and ritual, and they are usually a tangible emblem of something abstract (see Glossary), of a mundane object evoking a higher realm. Symbols can be based on conventional relationships such as a rose standing for courtly love in medieval romances (p. 252), physical or other similarities between the symbol and its reference (the red rose as a symbol for blood), or personal associations—for example, the Irish poet William Butler Yeats' use of the rose to symbolize death, ideal perfection, Ireland, and so on. Symbols also occur in linguistics wherein words are considered arbitrary symbols and in psychoanalysis where symbols, particularly images in dreams, are regarded as repressed, subconscious desires and fears. In Judaism, which we discuss in this chapter, the contents of the feast table and the ceremony performed at the Jewish Passover Seder (the feast celebrating the exodus from slavery in Egypt, p. 39) are symbolic of those events surrounding the Israelites' deliverance from Egypt. In Christian art, again studied in this chapter, the lamb, for example, symbolizes the sacrifice of Christ (see Fig. **5.20**). See Icons, p. 176.

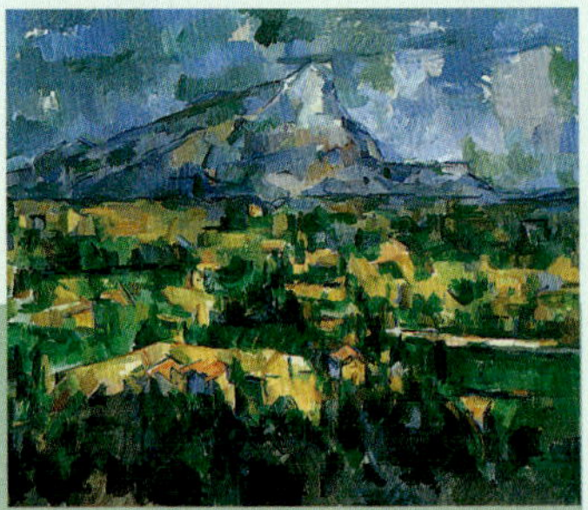

5.2 Paul Cézanne, *Mont Sainte-Victoire seen from Les Lauves*, 1902–04. Oil on canvas, 27½ × 35¼ ins (69.8 × 89.5 cm). Philadelphia Museum of Art (George W. Elkins Collection).

5.3 Kasimir Malevich, *Suprematist Composition: White on White*, c. 1918. Oil on canvas, 31¼ × 31¼ ins (79.4 × 79.4 cm). Museum of Modern Art, New York. Photo: © 2002 Museum of Modern Art, New York.

5.4 Christ as Pantocrator, early fourteenth century (detail). Mosaic. Kariye Church, Istanbul, Turkey. See also Fig. **5.10**.

CONTEXTS AND CONCEPTS

The timeframe of this chapter brackets that of Chapters 1–4 in that it begins back in Mesopotamia (Chapter 1) in the second millennium B.C.E. with Abraham, the "father of nations," and ends in the fourth century C.E. with the late Roman Empire. During this timeframe we will witness the rise of a people known variously as Hebrews, Israelites, and Jews, the rise of Christianity, and the end of the Roman Empire.

Hebrews, Israelites, and Jews

The people who wrote and collected the books of the Old Testament, the offspring of the Patriarchs, are known variously as Hebrews, Israelites, and Jews. They began as an identifiable group around 1200 B.C.E., and they described themselves as both a religious and a national entity. The word *Hebrew*, as we note momentarily, refers to Abraham's ethnic group. Eventually Abraham's descendants came to be called *Israel* (after Abraham's grandson). Around 922 B.C.E., the kingdom of Israel divided and the Northern Kingdom was destroyed. When Babylon destroyed the surviving Southern Kingdom, Judah (named for its major tribe), in 587 B.C.E., the people of the nation of Judah were taken into captivity in Babylon. Later, the expression of Israelite religion became known as Judaism, from which came the words *Jew* and *Jewish*, meaning followers of Judaism and/or members of the ethnic group from which Judaism originated.

	2000 B.C.E.	1500 B.C.E.	1000 B.C.E.	500 B.C.E.	0	500 C.E.
GENERAL EVENTS	Patriarchs in Canaan, c. 2000 B.C.E. Jacob's descendants in Egypt, c. 1600 B.C.E.	Moses, c. 1400 B.C.E. Exodus, c. 1300 B.C.E. Period of Judges, c. 1300–1260 B.C.E. United monarchy, c. 1200–800 B.C.E.	Divided Kingdom and Exile, c. 800–587 B.C.E. First exiles return, 538 B.C.E.	Maccabean rebellion, c. 165 B.C.E. Herod the Great, 73 B.C.E.– 4 C.E.	St Paul, ?–63 C.E. Domitian, 51–96 C.E. Roman capture of Jerusalem, 70 C.E. Diocletion, 245–306.C.E. Constantine, 274–337 C.E. Constantinople founded, 330 C.E. Jesus Christ, 4–30 C.E. Christianity recognized, c. 350 C.E. Fall of Rome, 410 C.E.	
PAINTING & SCULPTURE					Synagogue of Dura-Europos (**5.7, 5.13**), SS. Pietro e Marcellino (**5.11, 5.15**), Catacomb paintings (**5.14, 5.15**), *Chi-Ro* (**5.17**), *The Good Shepherd* (**5.21**), Sarcophagus of Bassus (**5.22**)	
ARCHITECTURE			Solomon's Temple (**5.24, 5.25**)		Baths of Diocletian (**5.23**), Herod's Temple (**5.27**), Basilica of Constantine (**5.29**), St Peter's Basilica (**5.31**), San Paolo Fuori le Mura (**5.32**)	
MUSIC & DANCE					Christian hymnody, Alleluia	
LITERATURE & PHILOSOPHY		Ten Commandments, First Bible			Synoptic Gospels, Tertullian, St Augustine	

Timeline 5.1 Judaism and early Christianity.

The Patriarchs

Abraham

The ancestors of Israel were seminomadic peoples from Mesopotamia. The Israelites traced their history back to a patriarch named Abram (later Abraham) who lived in "Ur of the Chaldees" in the second millennium B.C.E.

According to biblical tradition (Genesis/Exodus), Abram took his wife and household from the heathen environment of Haran and traveled to Canaan. Canaan held a particular spiritual appeal to Abram, because he believed that the land there was suitable for the fulfillment of a destiny to which he had been appointed by God. Canaan (KAY-nuhn) was a secluded hill country, which made it possible for Abram and his people to practice their religion in relative peace and isolation. On the other hand, Canaan lay quite close to important trade routes of the ancient world, and was thus in a good position for spreading the new religion (Map 5.1). Because they came from the other side of the Euphrates (yoo-FRAY-teez), Abram and his family were known as Hebrews, from a word meaning "the other side." Abram had a son, Isaac, through whose line of descent God's promises were seen to continue. As a boy, Isaac was nearly sacrificed by Abram at God's command (Genesis, chapter 22; Fig. 5.5).

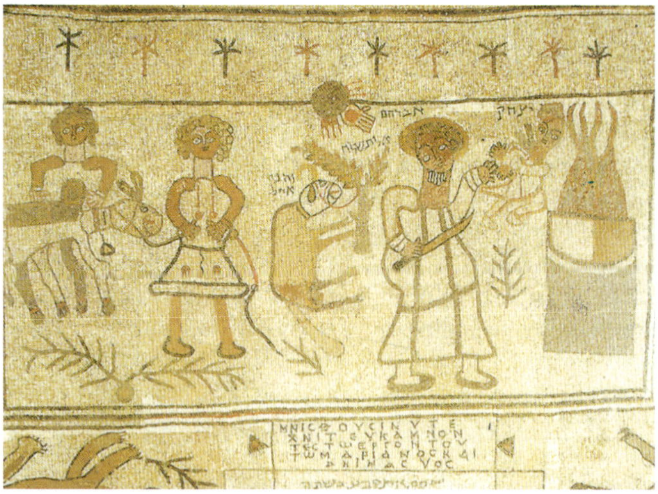

5.5 *The Sacrifice of Isaac.* Mosaic. Beth-Alpha Synagogue.

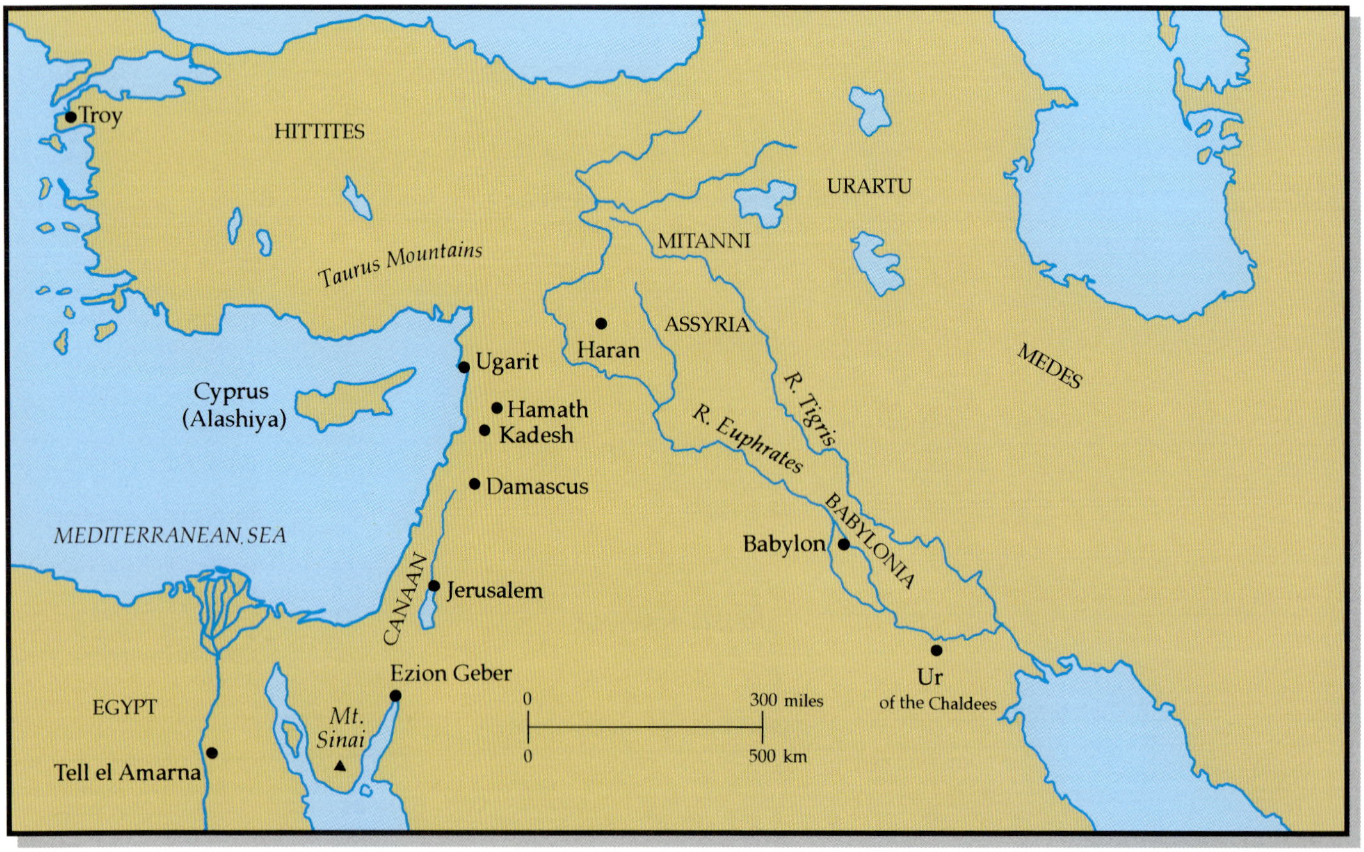

Map 5.1 Lands of the Bible.

Moses

In the late fourteenth century B.C.E. when the Hebrews were in slavery in Egypt, there arose a national liberator named Moses. During one particularly cruel oppression, the Pharaoh ordered the slaughter of all Hebrew children. To avoid this, the mother of the infant Moses made a basket of bulrushes and set the baby afloat in the Nile near where Pharaoh's sister bathed. The princess found the baby, adopted him, and brought him up in the royal court. However, when Moses killed an Egyptian who was abusing an Israelite, he was forced to flee the country to Midian, east of Egypt, where he became a shepherd.

One day, while he was tending his flocks in the Sinai wilderness, he came to Mount Horeb, and there heard the voice of God coming from a burning bush that was not consumed by the fire. God ordered him to return to Egypt to deliver his brethren from bondage and lead them to the land of promise. Moses returned to Egypt. The enslaved Hebrews soon recognized Moses' message as authentic, but convincing the ruling Pharaoh was another matter entirely. However, after a series of divine visitations, known as the ten plagues, Pharaoh's heart was softened and he allowed the people of Israel to depart from Egypt, by biblical reckoning, approximately 1300 B.C.E. (Fig. **5.6**).

Moses led his people from Egypt toward the Sinai wilderness by way of the Red Sea, which they crossed by a miraculous parting of the waters (Fig. **5.7**). Pharaoh had changed his mind, and the Egyptian army was in hot pursuit when they were swallowed up as the sea

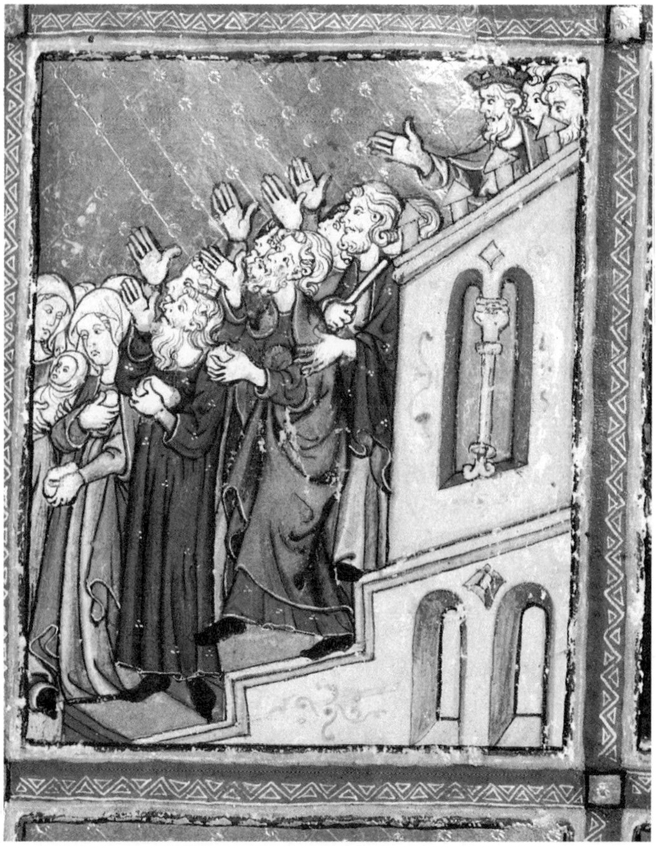

5.6 Miniature from the *Golden Haggadah* (Spanish), fourteenth century C.E. The Jews are portrayed leaving Egypt "with a high hand"—a Hebrew expression meaning "triumphantly," but here illustrated literally. British Museum, London.

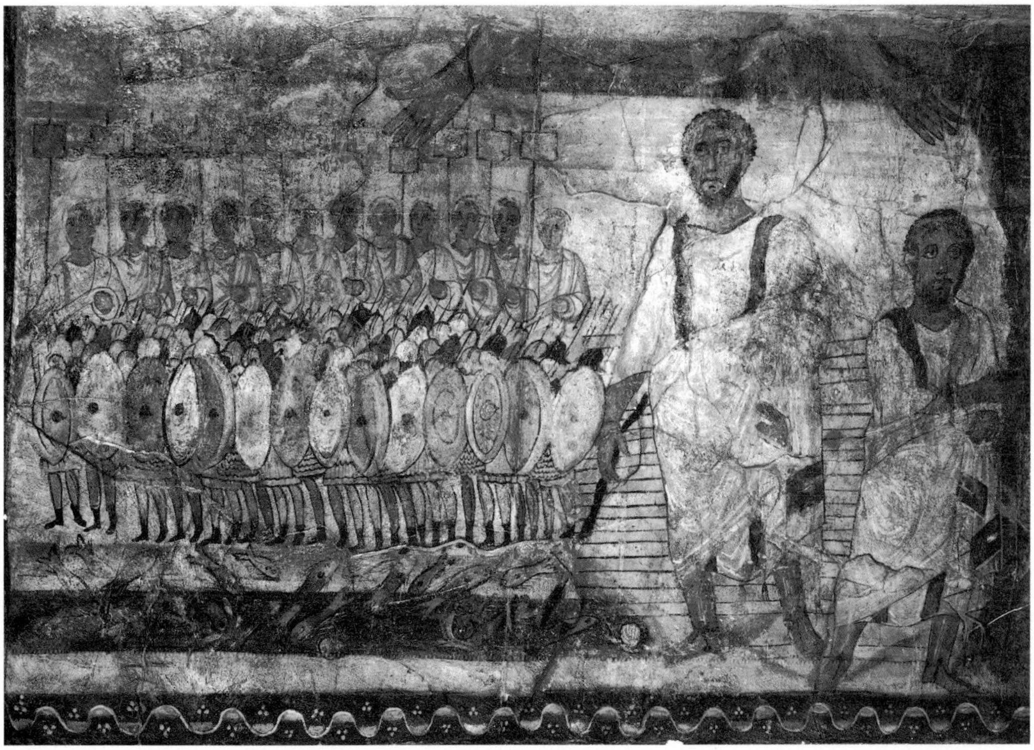

5.7 *Crossing the Red Sea*, c. 245 C.E. Fresco from the synagogue at Dura-Europos. National Archeological Museum, Damascus, Syria.

crashed in upon them. The result of the miracle gave Moses' people a greater sensitivity to divine promise and action and inspired their faith to new heights. The God of their fathers was seen as he who saved them from bondage and would spare them from the hands of their enemies.

The Selection of Israel

In the third month after their escape from Egypt, the Israelites arrived at Sinai, a burning desert with steep cliffs and volcanic mountains. Here, they made a covenant with their God (YHWH): He would be their God, and they would be his people. The Sinai covenant had its roots in Yahweh's covenant with Abraham, which, in turn, could be traced to the covenant with Noah, and, thereby, to a framework in which humanity, made in the image of God, must conform to the character of God. Because God is a creating God, humankind must also create and work with God in maintaining and developing the work God had committed, in the creation of the world, into human care. Obedience to God must express itself in obedience to his moral law—that is, *justice* and *righteousness*. Thus, the selection of Israel as a people formed an important moment of universal history in the eyes of the Judaic tradition.

Ratification of God's covenant with Abraham came in a covenant with Israel at Sinai, expressed in the giving of the Ten Commandments, or Decalogue.

The Ten Commandments

(Deuteronomy 5:6–21)

1. You shall have no other gods before me.
2. You shall not make for yourself a graven image, or any likeness of any thing that is in heaven above, or that is on the earth beneath, or that is in the water under the earth. . . .
3. You shall not take the name of the Lord your God in vain. . . .
4. Observe the sabbath day, to keep it holy, as the Lord your God commanded you. . . .
5. Honor your father and your mother. . . .
6. You shall not murder.
7. Neither shall you commit adultery.
8. Neither shall you steal.
9. Neither shall you bear false witness against your neighbor.
10. Neither shall you covet your neighbor's wife . . . or anything that is your neighbor's.

From Conquest to Exile

Judges

Immediately after the exodus from Egypt, neither Israel as a nation nor the nations that occupied the land of Canaan were ready for a Hebrew invasion and conquest. The Egyptian empire was still strong, and the land of Canaan contained several vassal kings of Egypt who were capable of banding together to resist such an invasion. As a people fresh from servitude, the Israelites had not yet progressed to a point of unification and cohesion, but were still an undisciplined, spiritually immature, and fractious group. They therefore wandered in the wilderness of Sinai for forty years, and although the route they took cannot be traced, it was circuitous and subjected them to the privation and hardship of the desert. That time of difficulty hardened Israel into a strong, disciplined nation, with well-inculcated spiritual values.

Under the leadership of Joshua, the people of Israel conquered Canaan and organized themselves into a relatively stable political and religious entity. A period of anarchy followed Joshua's death, and "every man did what was right in his own eyes" (Judges 17:6). Too weak to resist infiltration by bordering tribes, Israelites soon began intermarrying with outsiders and turning away from Yahweh to idolatrous religious practices. To counteract this defection from the covenant, a series of twelve "Judges" arose and set about liberating Israel from her enemies and recalling the nation to the worship of Yahweh. But the judges—for example, Deborah and Gideon—were more local tribal heroes than national leaders, and by the time of Samuel, who had emerged as a judge, a new threat had arisen: the Philistines. In a devastating defeat, the Philistines succeeded in capturing the Ark of the Covenant, Israel's most sacred object. The shock of this defeat provided Samuel with the impetus needed to bring about further reforms and to achieve some sense of centralization, which led, in turn, to a great clamor for the appointment of a king. After initial resistance by Samuel and the careful delineation of the powers of the king, Saul was chosen by common consent of the people, and became probably the first constitutional king in history.

The United Monarchy

Although he was unable to meet all the demands placed on him, Saul was able to free Israel from the Philistines and to unify the nation. It lay to David, however, to consolidate the monarchy. The prophet Samuel chose David as the instrument of God, and at first David was Saul's comforter and right arm, but he was also immensely popular with the people, which made Saul jealous and vengeful. In the ensuing struggle, David became king, and Israel's golden age began. He unified the tribes of Israel and extended the kingdom from Phoenicia in the west to the Arabian Desert in the east, and from the River Orontes in the north to the

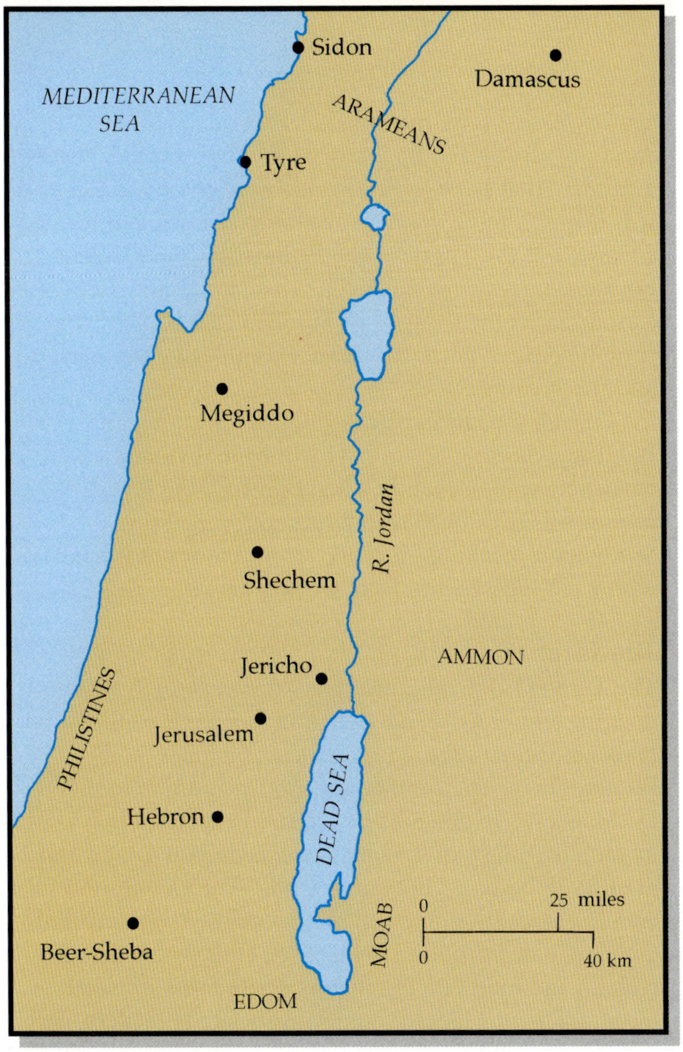

Map 5.2 Palestine.

Gulf of Aqaba in the south. He ultimately captured the Canaanite stronghold of Jerusalem, where he established a national and religious capital in which his son Solomon built the great Temple.

The Divided Kingdom and Exile

Following the death of Solomon, a dispute over succession split the nation into Northern and Southern Kingdoms, with Jerusalem remaining the capital of the Southern Kingdom. The division left the nation weakened, and in the eighth century B.C.E. the Northern Kingdom fell to the Assyrians. The period between Solomon and the Assyrian conquest of the Northern Kingdom, which was called Samaria, gave rise to the great prophet Isaiah. Subsequently, the exile and dispersion of the Northern peoples led to their being called the "Lost Tribes of Israel." In 587 B.C.E., the Babylonians conquered the Southern Kingdom, now called Judah, destroyed Solomon's Temple, and carried the people into the Babylonian Captivity.

The Post-Exilic Period and Beyond

At the end of the sixth century, Cyrus the Great led the Persian Empire to dominion in the Middle East. After conquering the Babylonians, Cyrus freed the Jews, as they were now called, and in 538 B.C.E. the first exiles were able to return from Babylon. In 515 the Temple was

PROFILE

Solomon (c. Tenth Century B.C.E.)

Solomon, son of David and Bathsheba, ruled Israel for forty years during the second third of the tenth century B.C.E. In Hebrew the name meant "Yahweh's beloved," as indicated in the biblical book of 2 Samuel, 12:25. While David still ruled, he affirmed his commitment to make Solomon his successor. The priest Zadok, with the assistance of the prophet Nathan, installed Solomon as co-regent until David's death, when Solomon's brother Adonijah sought Bathsheba's support in his request to marry Abishag, who had served David in his old age. Regarding this move as a threat, Solomon had Adonijah executed, and others, who were seen as accomplices, were expelled from Jerusalem.

Solomon effected a political consolidation of Israel and created administrative districts that cut across old tribal lines. He also expanded Israel's international affairs, and his empire included trade routes that linked Africa, Asia, Arabia, and Asia Minor. Solomon's political and commercial activities brought much wealth and a cosmopolitan sophistication to the kingdom, and his wisdom "surpassed the wisdom of all the people of the east, and all the wisdom of Egypt" (1 Kings 4:30, Hebrews 5:10). The Bible ascribes seven hundred wives to Solomon, including many whom he undoubtedly married as part of political alliances. Solomon's extensive building program included stone cities as well as fortifications, and in Jerusalem, he built an elaborate palace complex and a temple. His reign brought the promises made to the patriarchs of Israel to fruition. On the other hand, the influx of foreign practices marks the beginning of a religious decay that increased internal dissent and external enemies.

rebuilt, and the next hundred years witnessed the building projects and leadership of Nehemiah (nee-eh-MY-uh) and Ezra. It was a time of spiritual revival and the renewal of religious rites and practices for the Jews, who believed that their God had rescued them. As a result, they established a theocracy—that is, a government ruled by those who are believed to have special divine approval and direction. A group called the Pharisees (FAIR-i-seez), mistakenly confused with the Sadducees (SA-jyoo-seez) in the New Testament, were responsible for the preservation and codification of Jewish religious practice (the "Mishnah"), which had been centered, by law, around the Temple.

In 332 B.C.E., Alexander the Great conquered the region. After his death, the Hellenistic Empire was divided and Judah fell under a series of foreign rulers. At this time, Jewish visions of the apocalypse were popularized. Antiochus IV (an-TY-oh-kuhs), a descendant of the Seleucid (suh-LOO-sid) kings who ruled this part of the Hellenistic Empire after Alexander the Great's death, singled out and banned Jewish practice and culture in 168–167 B.C.E. As a result, a group of peasants, known as the Hasmoneans (haz-MOHN-ee-uhns), started a mini-rebellion. Two conflicting accounts of the period occur in Maccabees I and II. Initially regarded as saviors, the Hasmoneans soon became even more of a threat to Jewish religious practice than even Antiochus IV had been.

A brief uprising by the Maccabees under Judas Maccabeus (JOO-duhs mac-uh-BAY-uhs) brought a short period of independence around 165 B.C.E. Within a century, Israel fell under the rule of Rome. In 70 C.E., after an uprising in Jerusalem, the Romans sacked the city and destroyed the Temple. A small band of rebels held off the Romans for two years at a mountain fortress called Massada until it, too, fell in 73 C.E.

The Hebrew Bible

The word "bible" comes from the Greek word for book, and it refers to the town of Byblos, which exported the papyrus reed used in the ancient world for making books. The Jews compiled the history of their culture and religion into a collection of sacred writings later called scriptures. The compilation grew from the oral traditions of the Hebrew people and took shape over a period of years as it was assembled, transcribed, and verified by state officials and scholars. The Bible has been handed down in a variety of forms. The Hebrew Bible, often called the Masoretic Text (MT), is a collection of twenty-four books written in Hebrew, with a few passages in Aramaic.

The earliest written Bible probably dates to the United Monarchy in the tenth century B.C.E. It is composed of an assemblage of history, songs, stories, and prophecy. After the Babylonian Captivity, in the fifth century B.C.E., Jewish religious leaders and scholars carefully scrutinized the body of writings and established a canon—that is, an officially accepted compilation—that was believed to be divinely inspired. The first canon consisted of the Torah or the Pentateuch, the first five books of the current Bible. The current Hebrew Bible was canonized by the Council of Jamnia in 90 C.E. It contained three parts: The Law (Torah), the Prophets, and the Writings.

During the Hellenistic period major centers of Judaism existed in Syria, Asia Minor, Babylonia, and, particularly, in Alexandria, Egypt. Here, the Jewish Canon was translated into Greek and called the Septuagint, meaning "seventy" from the seventy scholars who were supposed to have worked on it.

The Torah

The Torah (TOH-ruh), meaning "the teaching," includes doctrine and practice, religion, and morals. It contains the books of Genesis, Exodus, Leviticus, Numbers, and Deuteronomy. The commandments, in addition to the Decalogue, were designed to prepare Israel for a holy mission that the nation would be called upon to undertake in order to become "holy unto God." The preparation entails a separation from all that is opposed to the will of God and a dedication to his service. Thus, holiness meant religion and morality. In religion, the holiness of Israel meant abhorring idolatry and its associated practices, such as human sacrifice, sacred prostitution, divination, and magic. It also meant adopting a cult and ritual that were ennobling and elevating. In morals, holiness meant resisting the urges of nature that were self-serving and adopting an ethic in which service to others lay at the center of life. Consequently, the Torah, as given to Israel, prescribes two sets of laws that connect religion and morality—that is, belief and practice. In their positive nature, they are intended to carry a dynamism that can transform individuals and, therefore, societies. Disregard of the law thus becomes not an individual but a social offense.

Fundamental to moral law in the Torah are the two principles, mentioned earlier, of justice and righteousness. These lie at the heart of humankind's creative cooperation with God. Justice meant the recognition of six fundamental rights: the right to live; the right of possession; the right to work; the right to clothing; the right to shelter; and the right of the person, which includes the right to leisure and liberty and the prohibition to hate, avenge, or bear a grudge. Righteousness manifested itself in the acceptance of duties—for example, concern for the poor, the weak, and the helpless, whether friend or foe—and although possession of earthly goods was a right, it was also a divine trust.

The Torah constitutes the uniqueness of the religion of Israel (Fig. 5.8). The distinct approach of the Torah to the conduct of human behavior is by way of the heart. It speaks to the mind concerning duties, but applies itself to the heart in terms of the perversities of vices and evil. Torah embraces all of life and, thus, becomes a means for strengthening the supremacy of holy will and bringing all life into relationship with serving God. In the Torah we find, for example, the stories of the Creation, Adam and Eve, Noah and the Flood, Joseph and the Coat of Many Colors, the Ten Commandments, and the law of "an eye for an eye."

The Prophets

The Prophets include the Former Prophets—that is, Joshua, Judges, Samuel, Kings—and the Latter Prophets—that is, Isaiah, Jeremiah, Ezekiel (y-ZAY-uh; Jair-uh-MY-uh; ih-ZEEK-ee-uhl), and the twelve minor prophets. These books record the history of Israel and Judah and further develop Hebrew concepts of God, his nature, and the Hebrews' relationship to him. They tell the story of the conquest of Canaan, the Judges, and the United Monarchy, and describe the development of the theocratic state in the post-Babylonian Captivity period. They also tell the stories of the battle of Jericho (JAIR-ih-koh), Samson and Delilah, Daniel and the lions' den, King Saul, David and Goliath, and King Solomon and the Temple of Jerusalem. They contain the well-known images from Isaiah of the "suffering servant" and the saying, "They shall beat their swords into plowshares." Of course, this is more than history. The prophets speak with the authority of God. We tend to think of a prophet as one who predicts the future, but such was not the case with the Hebrew prophets. The Prophets did speak of a coming time of peace and justice when the Messiah would come, but their principal message was one of reconciliation of the Hebrew people with their God. The prophets called upon the people of Israel to return to the ways of the covenant with God and pointed out exactly how they had fallen short of the expectations of that covenant. In a sense, the prophets were social critics. They admonished the people of Israel to remember the Law, which requires justice and decent treatment of the poor, and called on them to turn away from the self-indulgences of the current generation and to return to the compassionate behavior called for in the Torah.

Unlike the Levites (LEE-vyts)—that is, the priestly tribe—whose divine function came as a result of their birth into the tribe of Levi, prophets were individuals called directly by God to preach his word to the nation. The life of a prophet was not an easy one, and prophets like Isaiah often resisted their initial calling. Accepting God's prophetic ministry often meant a violent death—railing against contemporary practice has never been popular.

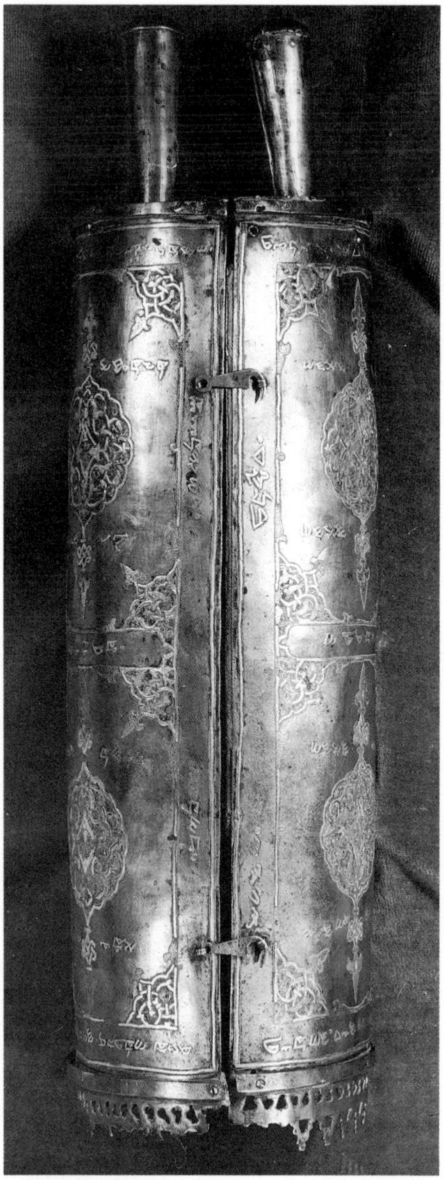

5.8 Joseph (maker, first name), Torah case from Damascus, Syria, 1565. Copper inlaid with silver, 32 ins (81.3 cm) high. Jewish Museum, New York.

The Writings

The writings, which contain a variety of literary forms, including poetry and apocalyptic visions, are made up of the biblical books of Psalms, Proverbs, Job, Song of Songs, Ruth, Lamentations, Ecclesiastes (ih-kleez-ee-AS-teez), Esther, Daniel, Ezra, Nehemiah, and Chronicles. The story of Job, for example, tells the story of a righteous man who is beset with calamity so that God can show Satan how a truly righteous man will respond to adversity. Satan maintains that a good man like Job is good only because he is blessed. Take away his comfort and he will curse God. The tale, like many, illustrates the qualities of righteous behavior more than it details the nature of God—although that is present as well. In the book of Ruth we learn of the qualities of love, devotion, and loyalty: "Where you go, I will go. And where you lodge, I will lodge. Your people shall be my people, and your God, my God; where you die, I will die, and there I will be buried. May the Lord do so to me and more also if even death parts me from you" (Ruth 1:16–17). Certain texts within the Writings purport to be from the time of Solomon, but are actually products of the Hellenistic age. These texts include, among others, Song of Songs and Ecclesiastes. These contain words and concepts which would have been completely foreign to Jews from Solomon's time—for example, philosophy, chance/luck, and wisdom ("hachmah").

Christianity

Rooted in Judaism's post-exilic Messianic hopes, Christianity arose in what its central personage and its later believers professed was God's intervention in human history to establish a new covenant to supplant the covenant established with Moses. Jesus of Nazareth was the Christ—Messiah. As Christianity spread through the Roman world after the death of Jesus, Christology became an important and divisive issue among Christians. Exactly what was the nature of Jesus Christ: Man or God or some combination? And what was the relationship of God, Christ, and the Holy Spirit, about whom Jesus preached? These and other fundamental concepts brought

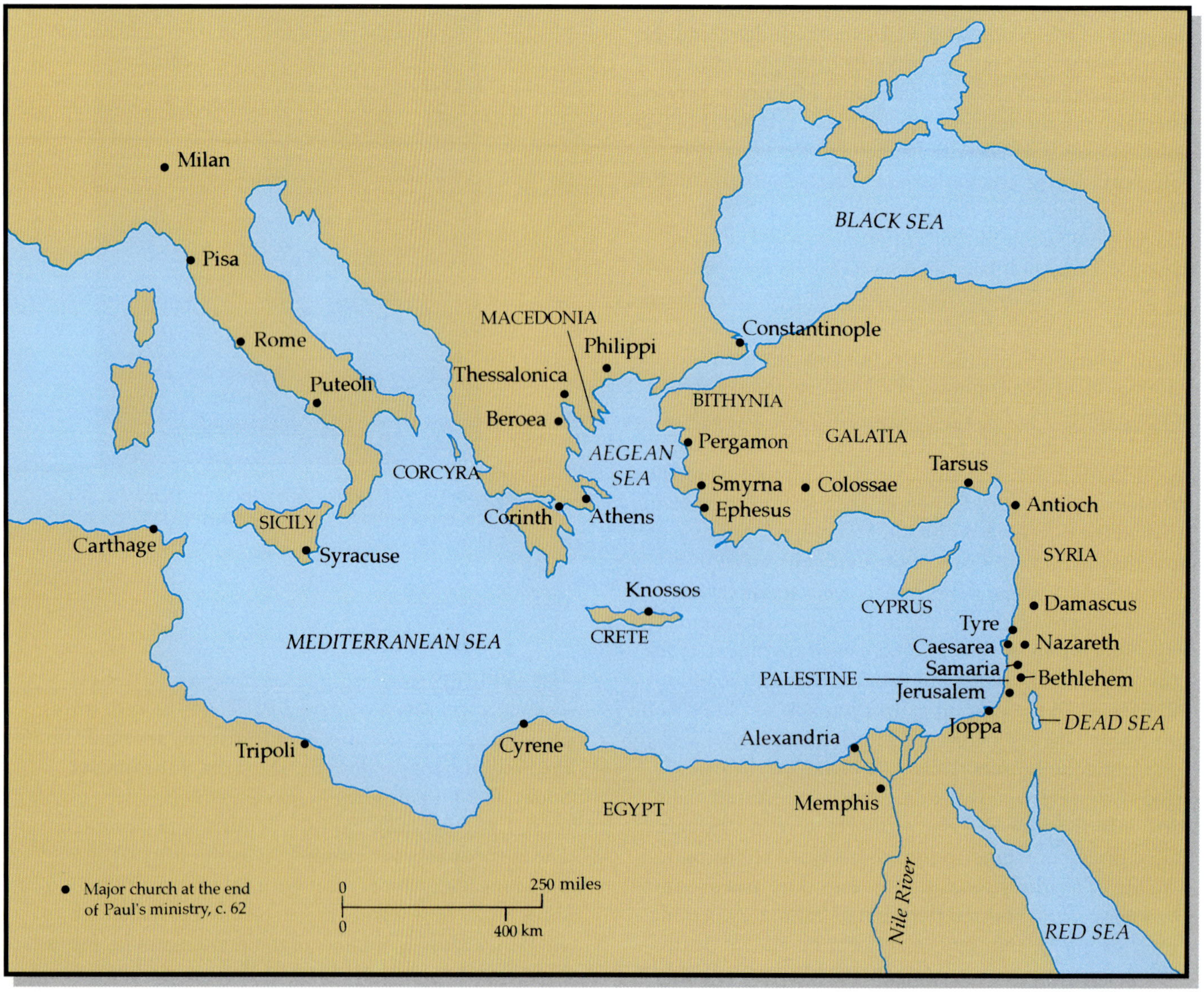

Map 5.3 The early Christian world.

Judaism, Rome, and the Western world together in a manner that has shaped humankind in the two thousand years since.

Jesus Christ and His Teachings

What we know of Jesus Christ comes from later writings called the gospels, the first four books of the New Testament of the Christian Bible. Jesus' early life remains unknown. The gospel of St Matthew includes a long genealogy tracing Jesus' ancestry to King David, and provides a number of stories about Jesus' birth, the Wise Men, the flight to Egypt, the slaughter of the innocents, the return to Israel, and the residence in Nazareth, but these provide few details of Jesus' life. In the gospel of St Luke (Fig. **5.9**) we find a poetic narration of the birth and connection between Jesus and John the Baptist through their mothers, Mary and her cousin Elizabeth, and we find historical figures such as King Herod, Caesar Augustus, Quirinius (kwir-IN-ee-uhs), governor of Syria, and a specific reference to Caesar's "first" enrollment. Correlating Herod's actual death in 4 B.C.E., Augustus' reign, and Jesus' birth story, and accommodating changes and corrections to the calendar that have occurred since, we get a birth date for Jesus at somewhere around 4 B.C.E.

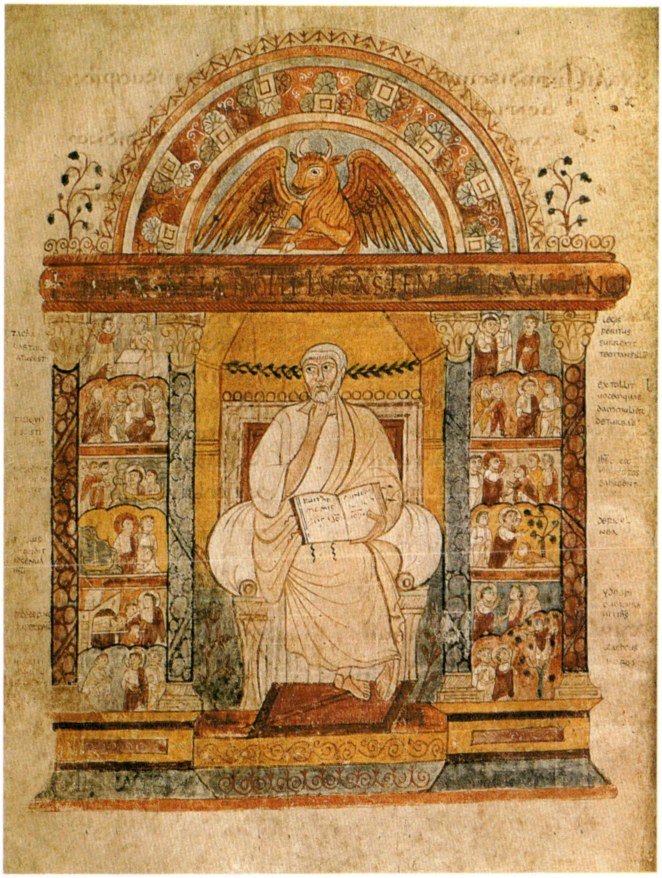

5.9 St Luke, from the presumed St Augustine Bible, sixth century. Corpus Christi College, Cambridge, England.

With the exception of the story of Jesus in the Temple as a youth, no further information is available about him until he began his public ministry when he was thirty years old. The gospel of St Mark is vague about whether Jesus was a carpenter—the reference could apply to Joseph, his father—and although he appears to have been a "teacher," no indication exists of his formal education. He had close associations with women, which would have been unusual for a Jewish teacher at that time, and we conclude that he must have had a relatively normal and typical home life in his formative years.

The actual beginnings of Jesus' ministry are also vague. He was baptized by John the Baptist, whom the gospels portray as a harbinger of Jesus, and he shared John's message that the people of Israel must "repent" and return to the ways of God. During his ministry, Jesus called twelve disciples to share his teaching and healing ministry. The symbolic link with the twelve tribes of Israel undoubtedly was intentional.

The core of Jesus' teaching was the Kingdom of God. Although the significance of the Kingdom with regard to human activity is strong, Jesus used the symbol as a means for revealing God himself. Through it, Jesus evokes God's active involvement in saving humankind and in establishing a reign of justice and peace. Above all, it reveals God's steadfast love and grace, which is offered to humankind without precondition. One of the most interesting aspects of this complex teaching is the step it takes away from conventional Jewish thought in regard to the judgment of God on the human race—the end of the world or the Time of Tribulation in Jewish theology—which it says has already begun. The central focus of Jesus' ethic is love, based on the Judaic commandment: "Thou shalt love the Lord thy God with all thy heart, soul, mind, and strength, and thy neighbor as thyself." The call for repentance, like that of the Old Testament prophets, presupposes that there is a tremendous distance between God and the daily life of his people. Hence, the need to repent, not just to polish up a few sinful acts, but to have a fundamental change of heart.

The gospels portray Jesus as a teacher, miracle worker, and friend of sinners (Fig. **5.10**). He goes out of his way to associate with the poor, the downtrodden, and the socially unacceptable. His ministry proclaims that such people, not the righteous, are the special objects of God's love and care.

Jesus' message was revolutionary. What he said and did—while not illegal by either Jewish or Roman standards—was cause for concern because it created unrest in the population. That, in first-century Palestine, was dangerous, and Jesus was put to death in the Roman custom—crucified with other criminals on a hill called

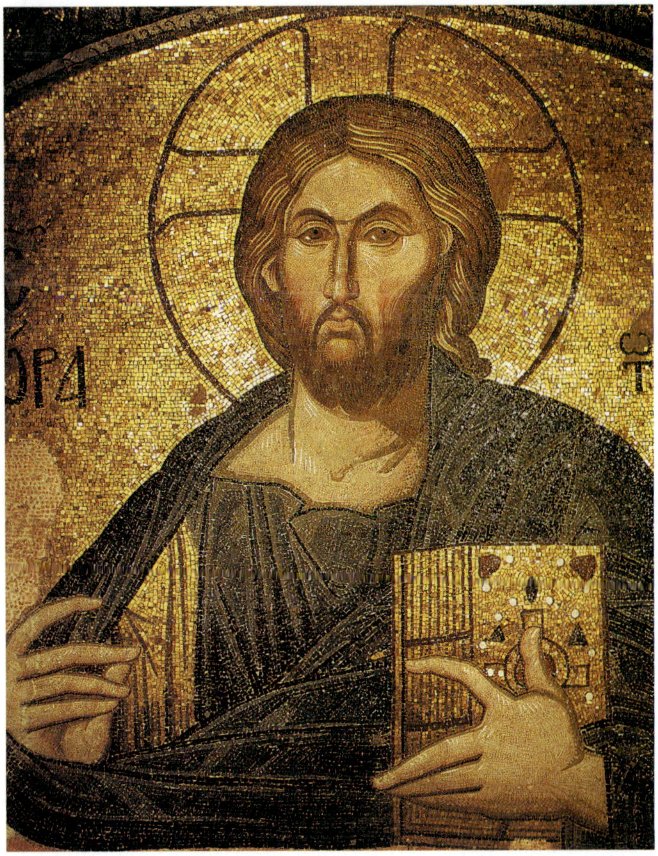

5.10 Christ as Pantocrator, early fourteenth century. Mosaic. Kariye Church, Istanbul, Turkey. Christ as Pantocrator (or Pantokrator) indicates Christ as judge of the world.

Golgotha (the place of the skull) outside the city of Jerusalem.

All four gospels maintain that on the third day after his death, Jesus rose from the dead and three of the Gospels maintain that Jesus, at various times, appeared to his disciples—not as a spirit, but in a solid body—before ascending into heaven. The Resurrection becomes for Christians not only a miracle, but also God's redeeming act in the salvation of the world.

The Apostolic Mission

Christianity spread principally because Jesus commanded his followers to carry on his commission from God. In the Synoptic Gospels—Matthew, Mark, and Luke—the charge is direct. After the Resurrection, Jesus appears to the disciples and tells them: "All authority in heaven and on earth has been given to me. Go therefore and make disciples of all nations, baptizing them in the name of the Father and of the Son and of the Holy Spirit, teaching them to observe all that I have commanded you" (Matthew 28:18a–20a). Implicit in this commission is the assumption that the Way, as the followers called themselves immediately after the Resurrection, would spread beyond the confines of Judaism and include the Gentile world as well. Within a generation, the new name, Christian, had appeared, and an organized movement with appointed leaders took shape. We should note that in the beginning Jews and Jewish Christians (so-called "Nazarenes") were indistinguishable in religious practice and places of worship. The Romans, in fact, made no distinction between the two groups. Pointedly, one of the early divisions among Christians concerned the issue of whether or not one could become a Christian without first converting to Judaism.

Critical to the spread of Christianity was its own written canon. Serious questions about exactly who Jesus was and what the faith entailed needed to be settled, and divisions within early Christianity were many. The Bible of the earliest Christians was the Old Testament—the Jewish canon—and this was supplemented in Christian worship by oral apostolic accounts of the words of Jesus, interpretations of his person and significance for the life of the Church. This was soon to change.

The books of the New Testament, which were later adopted as the Christian canon (KAN-uhn), were written within a period of less than one hundred years. They fall into four different literary forms. Four of them are "Gospels," so-called because they tell the "good news" of Jesus Christ. Early Church history occurs in the Acts of the Apostles, which is an account of the spread of the Christian faith during the first thirty years after the Resurrection. Twenty-one of the books are epistles, or letters, written to various churches and individuals by the early evangelists. The last book of the New Testament (the book of Revelation) is an apocalypse—that is, a revelation of God's will for the future.

The earliest of the four gospels was written by John Mark around the year 70 C.E. According to tradition, John Mark was a disciple of the Apostle Peter (Fig. **5.11**). The Gospels of Matthew and Luke use Mark as a source (each appeared ten to twenty years later than Mark), and because they have so much in common, they are called the Synoptic Gospels—from the Greek word *synopsis*, a seeing together. Unlike the Synoptics, which tell mainly of Jesus' public teaching and ministry, the Gospel according to John contains information concerning Jesus' early Judean ministry and extensive discussions with the disciples about the union of the Church with Christ. None of the parables of the Synoptics appear in John.

Much of basic Christian theology emerges from the letters section of the New Testament, much of which is attributed to St Paul. Probably the most important promulgator of Christian thought, Paul shaped the eastern tone of Judaic Christianity into the logical, intellectual patterns of the Greek-thinking world of the Roman Empire.

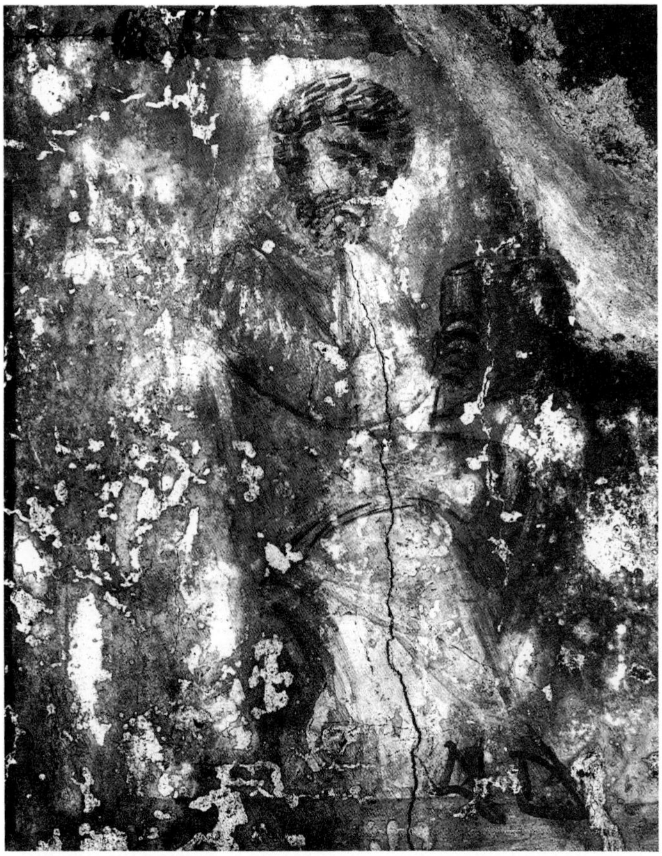

5.11 *St Peter,* third century C.E. Wall painting from a catacomb of SS. Pietro e Marcellino, Rome.

The book of Revelation, or Apocalypse, closes the Christian scriptures, and its last chapters portray the fulfillment toward which the entire biblical message of redemption is focused. It contains powerful poetic imagery that appeals to the imagination. It represents a vision of its author, whose name was John. Probably, parts of the book were written before the fall of Jerusalem in 70 C.E., but the book apparently achieved its final form on the rocky island of Patmos (PAT-mohs), to which the author had been exiled by the Emperor Domitian (81–96 C.E.). Over the centuries the Revelation to John has proved to be one of the most difficult and inspiring representations of God ever written.

The Early Christian Church

Like most emerging religions, Christianity felt an intense need to create institutions. Christianity was loosely organized and totally different in its theology from the religions around it. It needed a united front in order to grow and to make its way in a suspicious, pagan world. In the first centuries of its existence, Christians had shed each other's blood as various sects battled over questions of dogma, and this had to stop if the Church were to survive. In the thrust and counterthrust of all this, however, the emerging Church was a force coming together in a world that was mainly falling apart.

Why and how did Christianity survive? Its monotheism was an extension of the Jewish heritage. The historical immediacy of its founder and the doctrines he taught appealed to men and women of the late Roman and post-Roman periods. In its extreme simplicity on the one hand and its subtlety on the other, Christianity had a multi-faceted appeal that made it acceptable to the most lowly and illiterate people as well as those of sophistication and schooling.

Little is known about the spread of Christianity through the Roman Empire. Conversions among the aristocracy and upper classes enhanced its chances of survival substantially, and by the end of the third century, Christians were numerous enough to count as a political force. Every city of consequence had a Christian community presided over by a bishop who was assisted by priests and deacons. Regarded as successors of the original apostles, bishops were chosen by their communities, and theological disputes were decided in councils of bishops.

Christianity encountered varying degrees of tolerance from the Roman state. In general, the Imperial government treated all the various religious practices in its diverse empire with an even hand. Occasionally, however, Christians suffered fierce persecution, mainly because they refused to worship the emperor as a divine being. In addition, their secret meetings and rites troubled the authoritarian government. Christians also abhorred violence and refused to serve in the Roman army, which was very difficult for the besieged state to tolerate.

As we shall see, the last great persecution occurred under Diocletian (dy-uh-KLEE-shun) in 303. Shortly afterward, Constantine transformed Christianity into a favored religion in the Roman state. According to the bishop Eusebius (yoo-SEE-bee-uhs), Constantine reported that he had had a dream prior to the battle of Milvian Bridge against his co-ruler, the tetrarch Maxentius, in which he was told to send his soldiers into battle carrying standards marked with Christian symbols. Constantine did so, won the battle, and was converted to Christianity. He later claimed that he was "brought to the faith by God to be the means of the faith's triumph." Christianity soon became the official religion of the empire.

Numerous privileges came with this new status. The Church could receive legacies, its clergy were exempt from taxation, and bishops were permitted to settle disputes of law in all civil cases in which a Christian was a party. In addition, the Church obtained the rights of sanctuary for its buildings—that is, they became places where a criminal was safe from arrest or punishment.

After Constantine's conversion, the Church began to build up its own administration, adopting a structure similar to that of the civil bureaucracy. By the fourth century, each province was divided into bishoprics, with an archbishop at its head. There was, however, no centralized administration for the whole Church comparable to the Imperial government. The bishops of the four great cities of Rome, Jerusalem, Antioch, and Alexandria claimed special privilege because the Church in each of those cities was founded by the apostles. Rome, however, claimed supremacy both because it was founded by St Peter, to whom Jesus had entrusted the building of the Church, and because it was the capital of the empire.

Yet the opportunities presented by the conversion of emperors to Christianity were to some extent offset by problems that stemmed from the same source. In return for championing the faith, the emperor expected the bishops to act as loyal servants of the Imperial crown. When theological disputes arose, the emperor often insisted on deciding the matter himself.

The Popes

References to the primacy of Rome can be found as early as the letters of St Ignatius in 110 and St Irenaeus around 185. The claim of the medieval popes to exercise complete authority over all of Christendom was developed slowly, however. The bishops of Rome claimed supremacy because they were the heirs of St Peter and because their city was the capital. Other arguments included the sanctification of Rome by the blood of martyrs and its freedom from the contamination of the heresies that had touched other churches. Specific acknowledgement of Rome's supremacy by a Church council first came in 344 from the Council of Sardica. The Council of Constantinople placed the bishop of Constantinople second after the bishop of Rome "because Constantinople is the New Rome." A series of strong and able bishops of Rome consolidated the move toward Rome's supremacy during the next century.

The argument put forward by the bishops of Rome in support of their case came to be known as the "Petrine theory," and perhaps its clearest formulation came from Pope Leo I (r. 440–61), a man with considerable administrative ability who played a significant role in civil affairs as well as religious ones. Leo was twice called on by the emperor to negotiate with the leaders of the barbarian armies that invaded Italy in 453 and 455. He affirmed that because all other apostles were subordinate to Peter, all other bishops were subordinate to the bishop of Rome, who had succeeded to Peter's see at Rome. In fact, nearly all Western Christians came to acknowledge the pope of Rome as head of the whole Church. What remained unclear was the actual extent of his authority in temporal affairs and in affairs of Church governance.

Early Christian Thought

Tertullian and Legalism

The study of medieval thought of the first millennium is really the study of Christian thought. In order to understand the men and women of the early Middle Ages—how they might have seen the universe, and how that viewpoint was translated into art—it is important to examine some of early Christian thought. Two of its most important thinkers were Tertullian (tuhr-TUL ee uhn) and Augustine (aw-GUS-tuhn), and our examination focuses on them.

The main contribution of Tertullian (c. 160–230 C.E.) to Christian thought lies in two areas. He founded the language of the Western Church, and he enunciated those aspects of its theology that marked a break with the East. His writings were highly influential, and continued to be so even after his defection to Montanism destroyed his standing as a Catholic Father.

Probably the most important of Tertullian's writings is an elaborate analysis of the soul. His arguments lean heavily on Stoicism (see p. 119). He believed that the soul has length, breadth, and thickness, and although it is not identical with the body, it permeates all its parts, with its center lying in the heart. The soul controls the body, using the body as it wills. Yet, the soul remains spiritual, not material. For Tertullian, spirit and matter were two substances, different in nature but both equally real. Spirit, being indivisible, was therefore indestructible.

His notion of God and the Trinity was based on legal concepts. When Tertullian says that God has three parts, he means that God is "three persons in the legal sense, that is, three persons who share or own in common one substance or property."[1] God is a personal sovereign, to whom all people are subject. Independent and omnipotent, God created the world out of nothing. On the question of one's proper relationship to God, Tertullian was precise in defining God as an authority figure whom one approaches with humility and fear. "The fear of man is the honor of God. . . . Where there is no fear there is no amendment. . . . How are you going to love unless you are afraid not to love?" Virtue is thus obedience to divine law springing from fear of punishment if the law is broken. In this and many other areas, Tertullian's legal training is clear. He also formulated an elaborate list of sins, including the seven deadly sins of idolatry, blasphemy, murder, adultery, fornication, false witness, and fraud.

By the time of Tertullian, the Church had begun to see this life as a mere probation for the life to come. Earthly life was without value in itself and possessed meaning only in that it provided the opportunity to lay up rewards in the life beyond the grave. Tertullian believed the supreme virtues were humility and the spirit of otherworldliness, by which Christians could escape the perils of this life and be assured of enjoying the reward prepared for the saints in heaven. Read Tertullian's *The Soul's Testimony* at http://www.ccel.org/fathers2/ANF-03/anf03-20.htm.

St Augustine and Neo-Platonism

St Augustine (354–430) did not receive the sacrament of baptism until he was an adult. His mother, who was a Christian, believed that if he were baptized as a child, the healing virtue of accepting the faith would be destroyed b y the lusts of youth. Nonetheless, after a period of skepticism, and adherence to Manichaeism (MAN-ik-ee-iz-uhm)—a philosophy that combined Christianity with elements from other religions of the time—he was baptized into the Christian faith. He later became bishop of Hippo, in Asia Minor. A prolific writer, his works greatly influenced developing Christian thought. The *Confessions* and *City of God* are the best known of his works.

Apparently Augustine found great inspiration in the writings of Plotinus (see p. 119), and he was highly influenced by Platonic and neo-Platonic thought. He recoiled from Tertullian's emphasis on the senses and the body, but shared Tertullian's belief in intuition as the source of knowledge concerning God, although Augustine's concept of intuition had an intellectual cast. The senses, he believed, give us unreliable images of the truth. Instead, our intuition, our **affective** thinking, has a certainty which springs from "the fact that it is of the very nature of reason to know the truth."[2] Knowledge is an inner illumination of the soul by God. Whatever we find intelligible is, therefore, certain. Knowledge comes from intuition and "confirms and amplifies the certainty of faith."[3]

Augustine argued that to doubt the existence of the soul is in fact to confirm its existence: in order to doubt we must think, and if we think, we therefore must be thinking beings, and therefore souls. Unlike Tertullian, Augustine thought the soul immaterial, that is, a purely spiritual entity. This spiritual character, as well as its immortality, is demonstrated by our power to grasp eternal and immaterial essences.

His concept of original sin, as developed in *City of God*, held that all people are born to sin because of Adam's fall from grace when he disobeyed God in the Garden of Eden. Thus, we are "punished by being born to a state of sin and death, physical and spiritual, from which only Christ's passion and saving grace can redeem us." Augustine held that people were inherently bad and therefore did bad things.

Augustine attacked the question of predestination and divine foreknowledge—that is, whether God's omniscience robs humans of free will. His conclusion, that free will is not a certainty, influenced later contributors to the debate, which continues among Christian theologians today.

Augustine's philosophy of art represents a radical shift from that of Plato and Aristotle, especially in the principles of art evaluation. Plato and Aristotle approach art from political and metaphysical points of view. Augustine approaches the subject from a Christian point of view. Scripture, not philosophy, is his guide. Augustine considers the production and consumption of art to hold the interest for the Church that Plato felt they held for the polis. The Christian and the pagan face the same questions about the function and purpose of art. Augustine, however, finds the answers in a strictly Christian context, in the teachings of scripture and tradition. For him, the answers are found in an understanding of God's relationship with the world, and in the mission of the Church in dealing with art. Augustine untiringly attempted to satisfy the requisites of faith while doing justice to the natural pleasures that art can provide.

Even when the basic conflict is resolved, Augustine still has a problem in the immediate sensuous gratification of art. Although "divine order and harmony" are reflected in nature and to a degree in art, "perceptual objects tie the senses down to earthly things and prevent the mind from contemplating what is eternal and unchanging."[4] Art and beauty are thus guides for the soul. Those arts that depend least upon the senses best mirror the divine order.

The best teacher of all, however, is scripture. Properly interpreted, scripture provides the most direct knowledge of God's purpose and order, although the arts can contribute to our understanding as well. As long as art agrees with the tenets of faith and reflects the harmony of divine creation, it is justified. Read Saint Augustine's *Confessions* at http://www.library.adelaide.edu.au/etext/a/a92c/.

Christianity and the Late Roman Empire

Christianity spread to Rome early in the first century, brought there by nameless individuals who benefited from the freedom of travel that existed throughout the Empire during the *Pax Romana*.

Diocletian

The Roman Empire's crisis of the third century, which we discussed in Chapter 4, ended with the reforms brought about by two emperors, Diocletian and Constantine (KAHN-stuhn-teen), who also changed the fortunes of Christianity. Diocletian (r. 284–305) was born in the

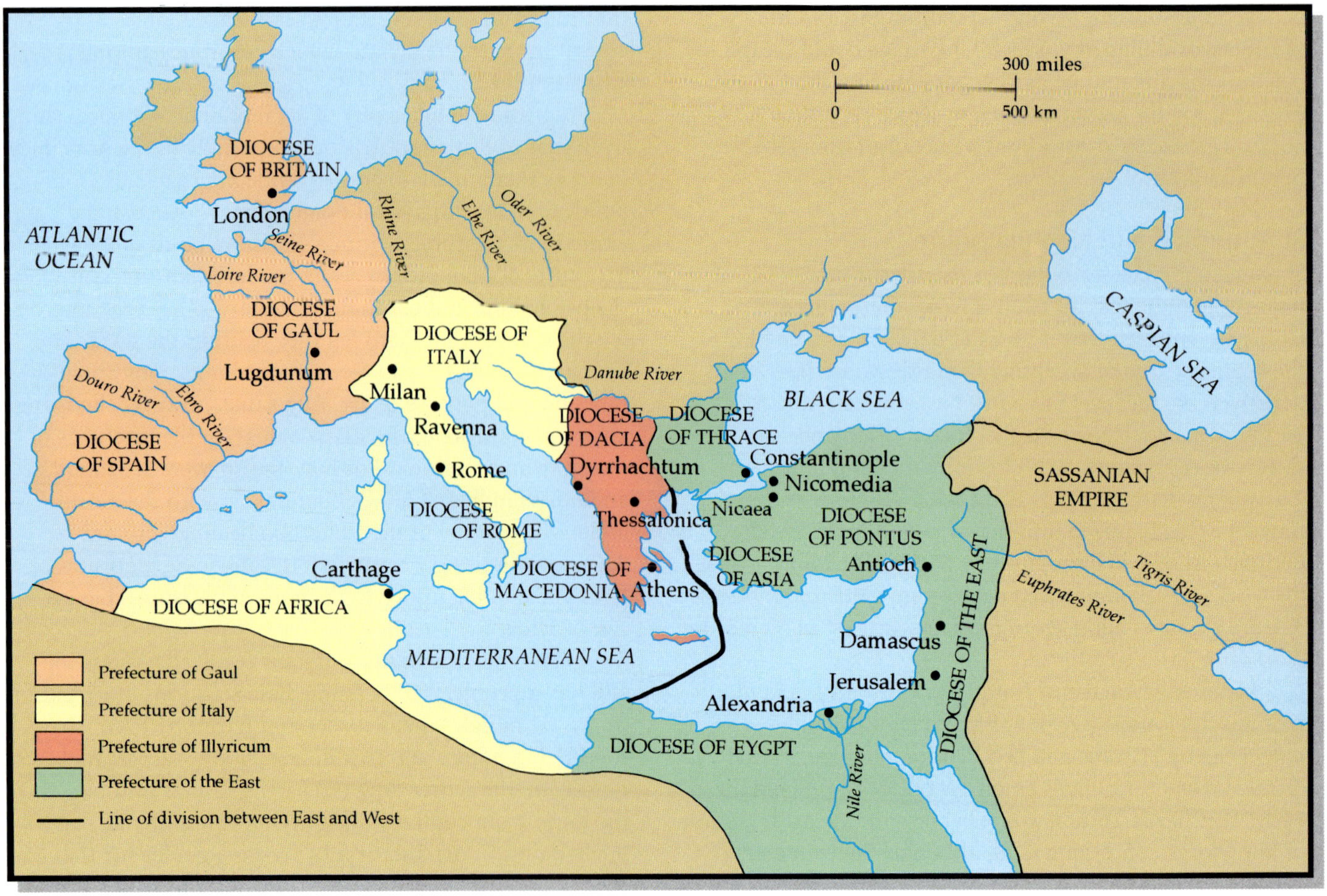

Map 5.4 The Roman Empire in the fourth century.

Balkans and rose to power through the ranks of the Roman army. He was strong-willed, insisting on divine status, and he took the image of emperor to grandiose heights—whenever he was in the presence of his subjects, for example, he separated himself from them by a wall of curtains. His self-image must have reflected the larger-than-life portrait that was necessary for him to cope with all the problems of the far-flung empire, in which anarchy was rampant, barbarians threatened every border, and the army turned rebellious.

Nonetheless, Diocletian attacked the problems with a creative and organized plan that, eventually—if only temporarily—brought some stability and reasonable prosperity. He restructured the empire by installing a Tetrarchy, wherein imperial power was shared among four rulers: two senior Augusti supported by two junior Caesars. Diocletian reformed and strengthened the imperial bureaucracy, reformed taxation to effect greater equality, and attempted to control wages and prices. His most ambitious undertaking was to split the empire into two halves, east and west, with each half administered by an Augustus and a Caesar. He also divided the provinces into dioceses. The cumulative effect of splitting the empire and restructuring the provinces was to centralize the state and to create an awkward and increasingly large class of bureaucrats.

In his last years Diocletian embarked on a major persecution of the Christian Church, whose expanding power he regarded as a threat to the hierarchy of the state. The persecution lasted for a period of eight years, extending beyond Diocletian's reign, which ended with his retirement in 305. The persecution, which was given official status by a series of edicts, was intended to eliminate Christianity altogether by forbidding Christians to worship, destroying their churches and books, and arresting their bishops. Anyone suspected of being a Christian was forced to make a sacrifice to the emperor, which amounted to a repudiation of their faith, and failure to do so was punishable by death. In 311 the persecution ceased. Its purpose had been to stamp out Christianity, but its effect, by creating martyrs, was just the opposite. Christianity won many new converts on the strength of the faith of those who died rather than renounce their beliefs.

TECHNOLOGY

MATCHES

The year 577 marked the invention of an item that today we take for granted—the match. In 950, in a book entitled *Records of the Unworldly and the Strange*, the Chinese author T'ao Ku writes: "An ingenious man devised the system of impregnating little sticks of pinewood with sulfur and storing them ready for use. At the slightest touch of fire, they burst into flame." Actually, T'ao Ku was wrong. Matches were a Chinese invention, but credit must go to some impoverished court ladies, who, during a military siege in the shortlived kingdom of the Northern Ch'i, were so short of tinder that they could not start fires for cooking and heating. They therefore devised a means of making it possible to start fires in a more opportune fashion. As T'ao Ku indicates, they devised a means of impregnating little sticks of pinewood with sulfur. The marvelous invention was initially called a "light-bringing slave," but it rapidly became an article of commerce, and its name was changed to "fire inch-stick."

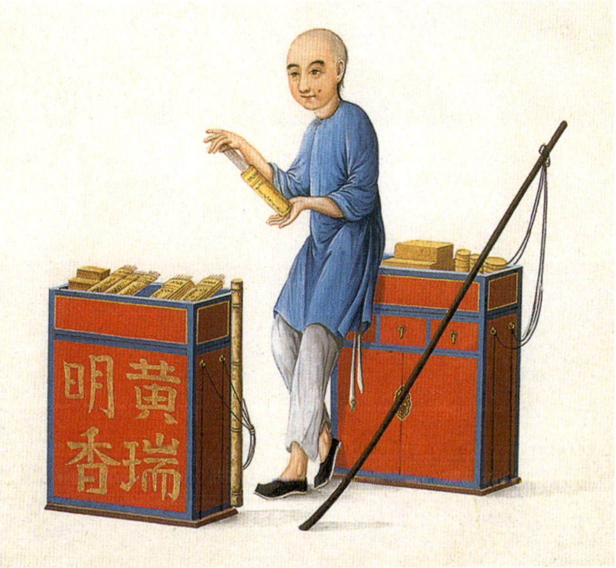

5.12 Pu Qua workshop, *A Boy Selling Pipe Lighters and Matches* (?), c. 1790. Watercolor on paper, $14\frac{1}{8} \times 17\frac{1}{4}$ ins (36 × 44 cm). Victoria & Albert Museum, London.

Constantine

The Tetrarchy (teh-TRARK-ee) collapsed after Diocletian, and a series of civil wars between the tetrarchs broke out. Eventually, Constantine (r. 306–37), son of one of the tetrarchs, fought his way to power as sole emperor of Rome, and carried Diocletian's reforms to even greater lengths. Constantine established two capitals—one in Rome, the other in Byzantium, later named Constantinople in his honor—thereby creating two Roman empires, one in the West and one in the East. The latter lasted for another thousand years, the former for barely a century.

Constantine arranged an elaborate administrative system, split into four huge imperial prefectures, a dozen dioceses, and 120 separate provinces, which stretched from Britain to Egypt. He separated the civil bureaucracy from the army, which he reformed to strengthen the frontiers, and in order to keep the empire afloat financially, he levied a series of taxes that had the net effect of reducing many to near-slave status. One group, however, loved Constantine—the Christians. As we noted, he legalized the Christian Church in Rome in 313, and it prospered under this new opportunity. Priests could be found in the army, and bishops at the imperial court. When Constantine moved his capital to Byzantium, he rebuilt the old city as a Christian center, renaming it Constantinople, and filling it with Christian churches and monuments. All the following emperors were Christian, and the faith had an unshakable hold on all levels of society, from peasant to aristocrat, the bureaucracy to the army.

The cumulative effects of the reforms introduced by Diocletian and Constantine enabled Rome to survive for a century, but the benefits of Roman rule had reached a point at which most people in the empire may well have welcomed the barbarian incursions that were to come.

The Roman Empire did not fall on a specific date, but by 406 Roman defenses had deteriorated considerably, and a mixed horde of Germanic peoples, mostly Vandals, surged into the empire and made their way through Gaul into Spain. Capitalizing on the situation, Alaric attacked Italy and succeeded in sacking Rome itself in 410.

THE ARTS OF JUDAISM AND EARLY CHRISTIANITY

Painting

Judaism

The biblical injunction against graven images means that there is little significant Jewish sculpture or painting.

Occasionally, however, the injunctions were relaxed sufficiently to allow decoration, and the assembly hall wall of the synagogue at Dura-Europos is one such example (Fig. **5.13**). Dating to approximately 250 C.E., this richly detailed account tells the history of the Chosen People and their covenant with the Lord, and is an attempt to put into pictures the traditions previously restricted to words. Unlike most paintings, there appears to be no unifying relationship among the details of this decoration. Animals, humans, buildings, and cult objects are all exquisitely portrayed, but we find nothing that would tell us how they relate to each other. It is as if the artist assumed that the viewer would understand how these objects coalesce. Nevertheless, if the meaning is hidden, the execution is explicit, and we can find pleasure in the luster of the execution and the sophisticated depiction of details. Although it is less naturalistic than the Roman wall decoration we have previously examined, these depictions reveal a concern with **plasticity**—that is, three-dimensional space. Human and animal forms are shaded and detailed in such a way as to give fullness to form and a sense of action and character. The figures are presentational and not intended for veneration or worship.

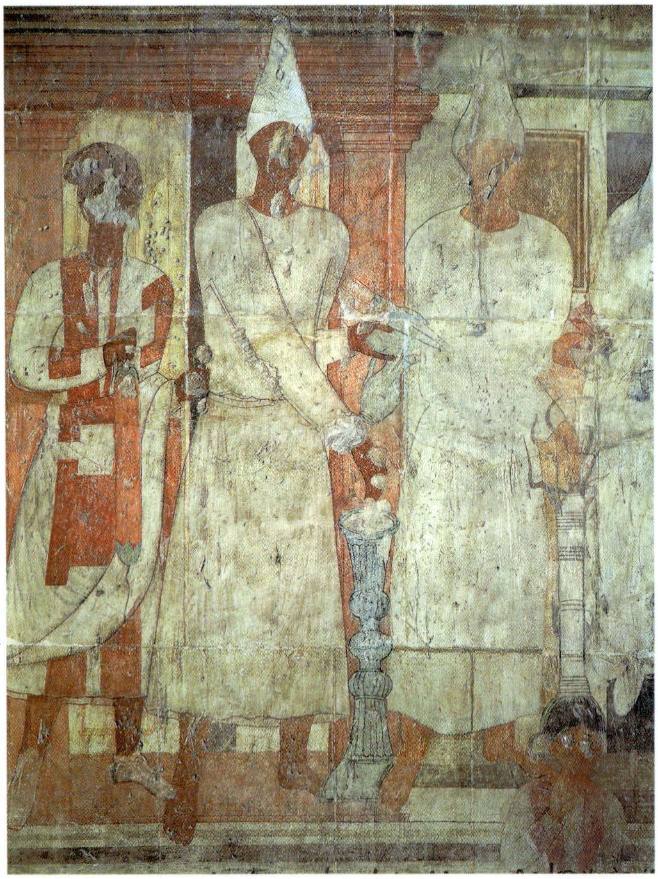

5.13 *The Sacrifice of Conon*, from the assembly hall of the synagogue at Dura-Europos, 245–56 C.E.. Mural. National Museum, Damascus,

Christianity

The earliest Christian painting is found in the catacombs of Rome. The catacombs served as underground cemeteries, for both Christians and Jews avoided public burial places that were dedicated to pagan deities. In addition, belief in the resurrection of the body meant that early Christians eschewed cremation, which was the norm for ordinary citizens in Rome. Wall paintings similar to that seen in Figure **5.14** often had multiple meanings. This work, which depicts men and women sitting at table with bread and wine, could represent the early Christian "love feast" (*agape*; AH-guh-pay), or it may represent Christ's first miracle—the wedding feast at Cana at which he turned water into wine. The obvious meaning was that of the sacrament of Holy Eucharist—that is, the reenactment of the Last Supper.

The catacombs reveal much about early Christian thought and communal spirit. An otherworldly outlook can be seen in the example shown in Figure **5.15**,

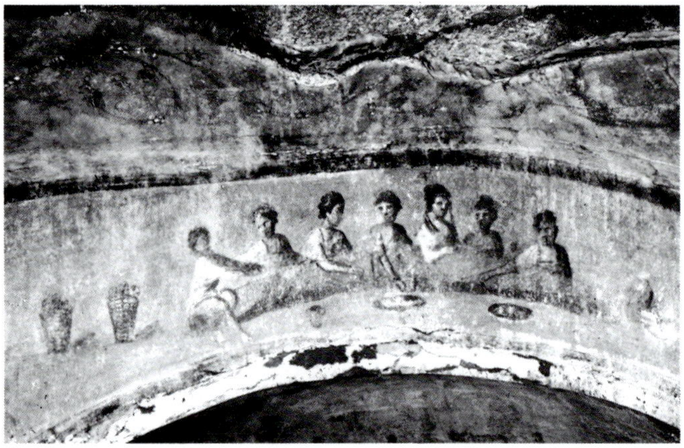

5.14 *The Breaking of Bread*, late second century. Wall painting in the catacomb of Priscilla, Rome.

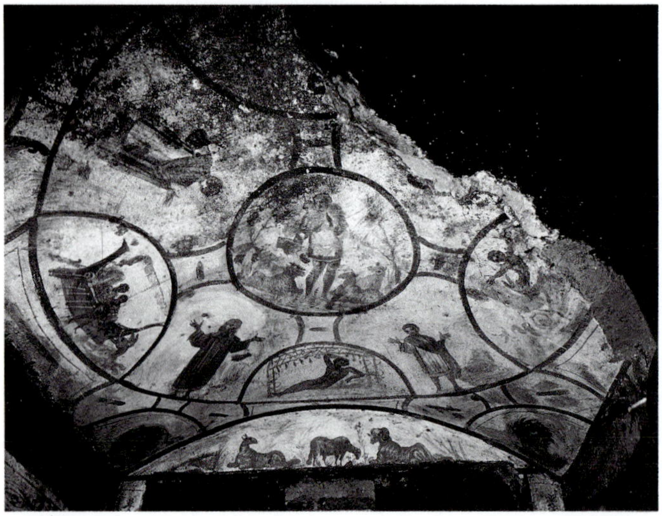

5.15 Painted ceiling, fourth century C.E. Catacombs of SS. Pietro e Marcellino, Rome.

although here, again, the art itself has pre-Christian influences. In this case, the ceiling is divided into compartments, as we witnessed in earlier Roman wall painting (see Fig. **4.10**). However, the artist, who was of only modest ability, translates old forms into new meanings: the great circle represents the dome of heaven inscribed with the cross; the symbol of the good shepherd with a sheep on his shoulders, similar to the statue in Figure **5.21**, adorns the central panel; and the semicircular panels tell the story of Jonah. The standing figures represent members of the Church, their hands raised in prayer for divine assistance. For more, go to http://ps.theatre.tulane.edu/lester/text/Early.Christian.Period/Early.Christian/Early.Christian2.html.

Sculpture

Late Roman

Roman visual art of the period continued the practice of Augustan times in the celebration of emperors. The exaggeration of anatomical form for symbolic effect may also be seen in a colossal bust of Emperor Constantine (Fig. **5.16**), a gigantic representation—the head is over 8 feet (2.4 meters) tall—exhibiting a stark and expressive realism that is countered by caricatured, ill-proportioned intensity. This likeness is not a portrait of Constantine—it is the artist's view both of Constantine's presentation of himself as emperor and of the office of emperor itself.

Early Christian

One of the major questions debated by Christians for nearly eight hundred years was whether or not to depict the figure of Christ. The first visual symbols of Christianity were symbolic rather than representational, and they stemmed from the fact that because they were members of a persecuted sect, Christians required some kind of arcane imagery that only they could identify. Perhaps the earliest Christian symbol was the *Chi-Rho* (ky-roh) monogram—that is, a combination of the first two letters of the word *Christos—XP*—in Greek. We see an artistic elaboration of the sign in Figure **5.17**, which is taken from a fourth-century **sarcophagus**. The *Chi-Rho* symbol stands at the center of a Roman triumphal wreath and above a cross. Doves, a symbol of the Holy Spirit and a reference to Jesus' baptism by John the Baptist, surround the monogram, which indicates the triumph of Christ over death, as two Roman soldiers, present at the crucifixion, sit below.

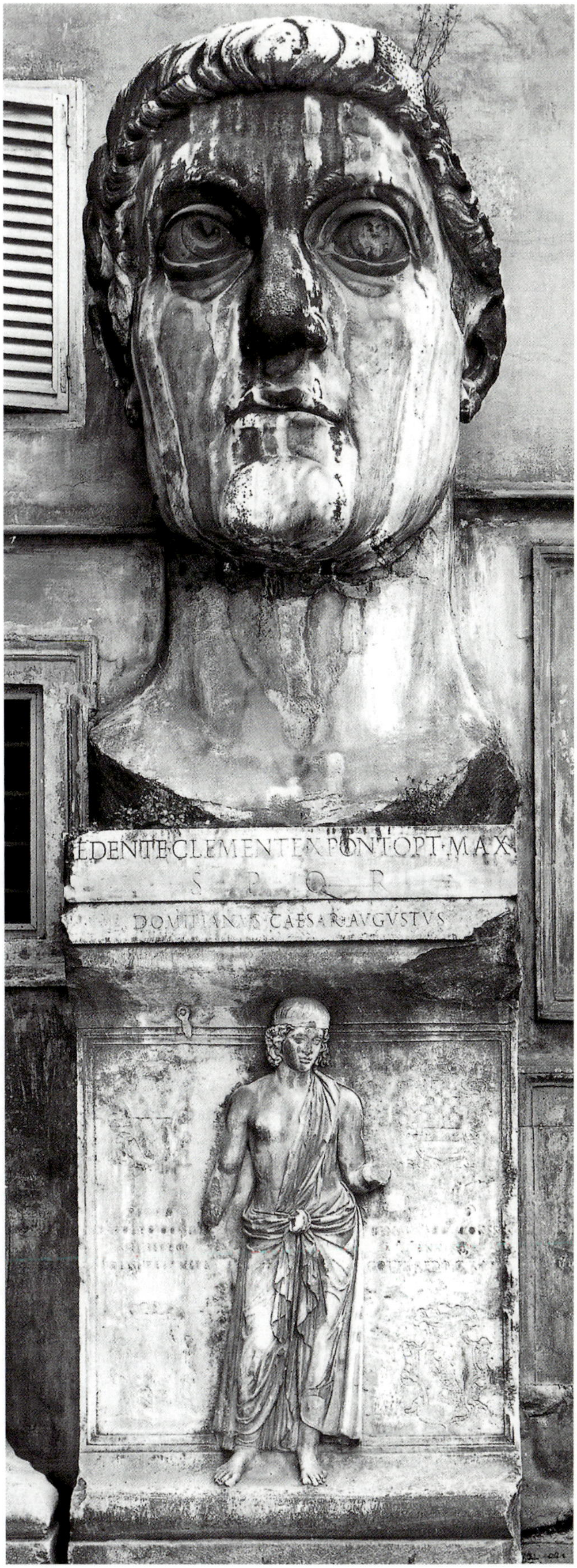

5.16 Head of Constantine the Great (originally part of a colossal seated statue), 313 C.E. Marble, 8 ft 6⅜ ins (2.61 m) high. Palazzo dei Conservatori, Rome.

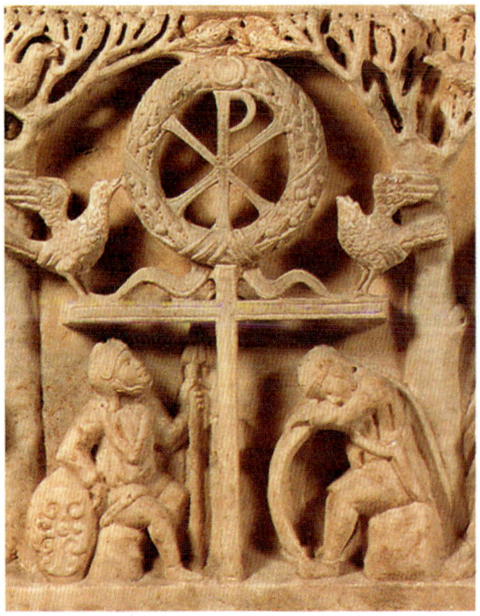

5.17 *Chi-Rho* monogram, detail of a sarcophagus, c. 340 C.E. Museo Pio Cristiano, Vatican Museums, Rome.

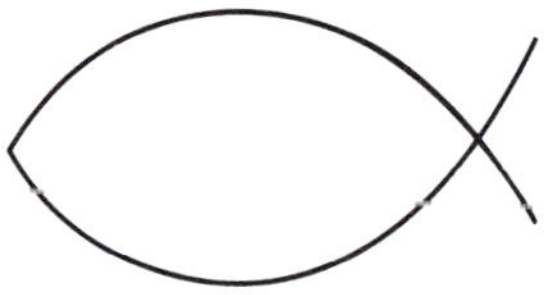

5.18 The "fish" rebus for "Jesus Christ Son of God, Savior." Early Christian symbol.

In addition to the *Chi-Rho*, Christians used a number of other visual symbols—for example, the fish and the lamb. The fish was a *rebus*—that is, a riddle composed of symbols suggesting the sound of the words they represent. The Greek word for fish, *icthus*, provided the initials for the formula "Jesus Christ Son of God, Saviour." The rebus of two curved, intersecting lines, created a means by which two Christians could secretly identify each other. One would trace a curve in the dirt. The other, if a Christian, would respond to create the sign of the fish (Fig. 5.18).

The lamb as a symbol referred to the metaphor used by John the Baptist, who described Christ as the "Lamb of God, which taketh away the sins of the world." Christ described himself as the "Good Shepherd" that "giveth his life for his sheep." The symbol of the lamb had been used in pagan art to represent benevolence or philanthropy, but it took a new meaning in Christianity and became one of the earliest artistic symbols in the faith (Fig. 5.20). In this early depiction of the Trinity, the diadem and *chlamys* (KLAH-mihs; a Greek mantle worn pinned at the shoulder) represent Christ the Son, the empty throne represents God the Father, and the dove

A DYNAMIC WORLD

Shinto Sculpture in Japan

Unlike the monotheism of Judaism, Shinto, or "Way of the Gods," Japan's indigenous religion, was a polytheistic nature cult without dogmas, scriptures, or images. At the same time as the late Roman Empire the graves of Japanese rulers were surrounded by moats and topped by huge burial mounds. One burial site near Osaka covers nearly 277 acres (112 hectares) in area and rises to a height of 110 feet (33.5 meters). Around the tombs, Shinto devotees erected terracotta tubes called *haniwa*. These stood 2 feet (61 centimeters) tall and were topped with human figures or heads or figures of animals. Tradition indicates that they were substitutes for real humans who at one time had been slaughtered at the chieftain's funeral. The figure shown in Figure **5.19** reveals high stylization. There is absolutely no attempt to portray anatomically correct details. The effect is one of exaggeration for visual effect. As in the pictograms of Japanese writing, the ebbing and flowing of curvilinear line is most important. Unlike the carefully detailed naturalism of Roman wall painting and sculpture, Shinto sculpture of the period shows a logical simplicity that draws attention to materials and overall form rather than on internal compositional particulars.

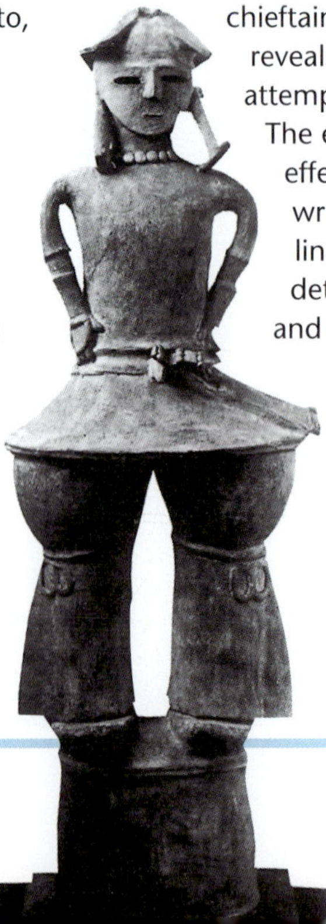

5.19 *Haniwa* figure, c. 300–600 C.E. Terracotta, about 2 ft (61 cm) high. Musée Guimet, Paris.

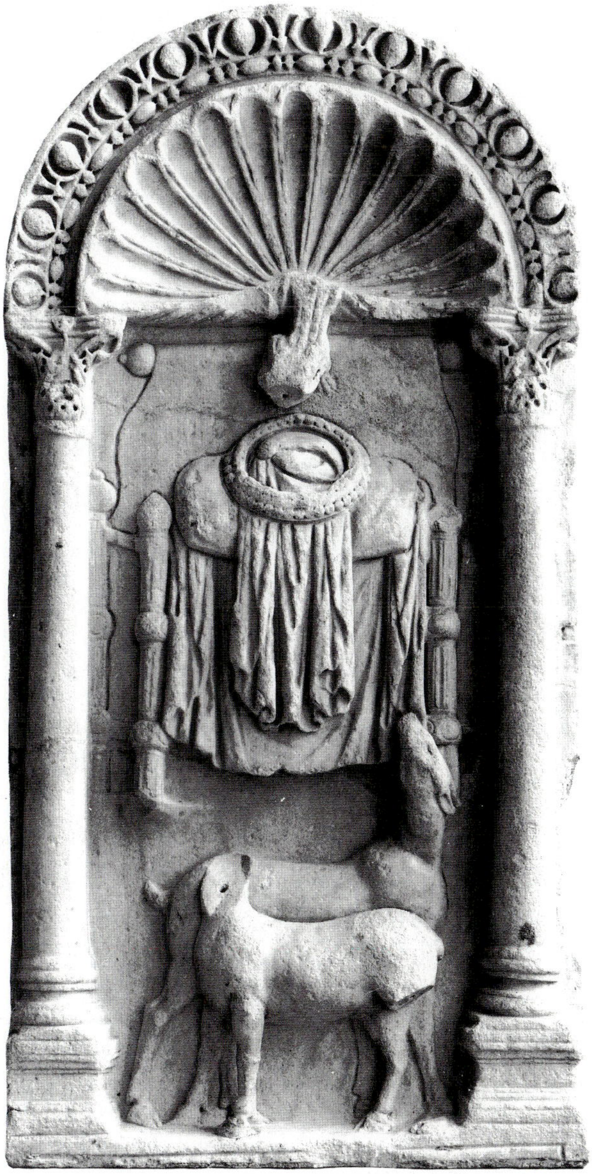

5.20 The Throne of God as a Trinitarian image, probably Constantinopolitan c. 400 C.E. Marble 65⅔ × 33 ins (167 × 84 cm). Stiftung Preussisches Kulturbesitz, Berlin-Dahlem, Germany.

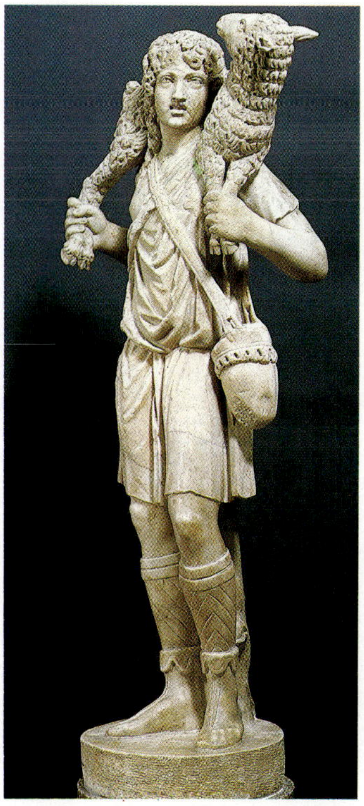

5.21 *The Good Shepherd*, c. 300 C.E. Marble, 36 ins (92 cm) high. Vatican Museums, Rome.

represents the Holy Spirit. It is probable that in this depiction, the lambs symbolize the classic virtue of beneficence rather than Christ.

The same is true of a beautifully detailed statue entitled *The Good Shepherd* (Fig. **5.21**). According to some scholars, depictions such as this, based on the injunctions we noted earlier, were not supposed to represent Christ but acquired Christian meaning only from their context in Christian tombs. In this particular case, the influence of classical Greek sculpture is clear. The detailing is skillful and naturalistic, with the clothing hanging like real fabric rather than decoration.

The spread of Christianity among the ruling classes in Rome gave rise to personal expressions in Christian art, as can be seen in the sarcophagus of Junius Bassus (Fig. **5.22**). Bassus was a prefect of the city of Rome, and his burial vault reflects a carefully designed creation. Two separate, elaborate arcades tell a variety of biblical stories, including those of the Hebrew children in the fiery furnace, the baptism of Christ, and the raising of Lazarus. The composition itself represents a sophisticated intricacy of high artistic quality. In the first place, the figures, although small, are carved with delicate attention to detail. They stand away from the background, creating a sense of deep space between the **colonnettes**, and this gives each scene an individual identity. The middle scenes create a central axis, which is balanced by symmetrical treatments on either side.

In addition, the scenes themselves balance thematically. For example, at either end of the lower register, we find an afflicted Job and St Paul being led to execution. These parallel treatments not only represent redemption through suffering but also refer to Christ's suffering for the redemption of humankind. Christ himself occupies the central focal points of both registers. On the bottom, he is shown in his triumphal entry into Jerusalem; on the top, he is enthroned between St Peter and St Paul. The enthronement signifies his regal triumph. Christ's feet rest on a canopy supported by the Roman sky god Coelus (CHAY-loos).

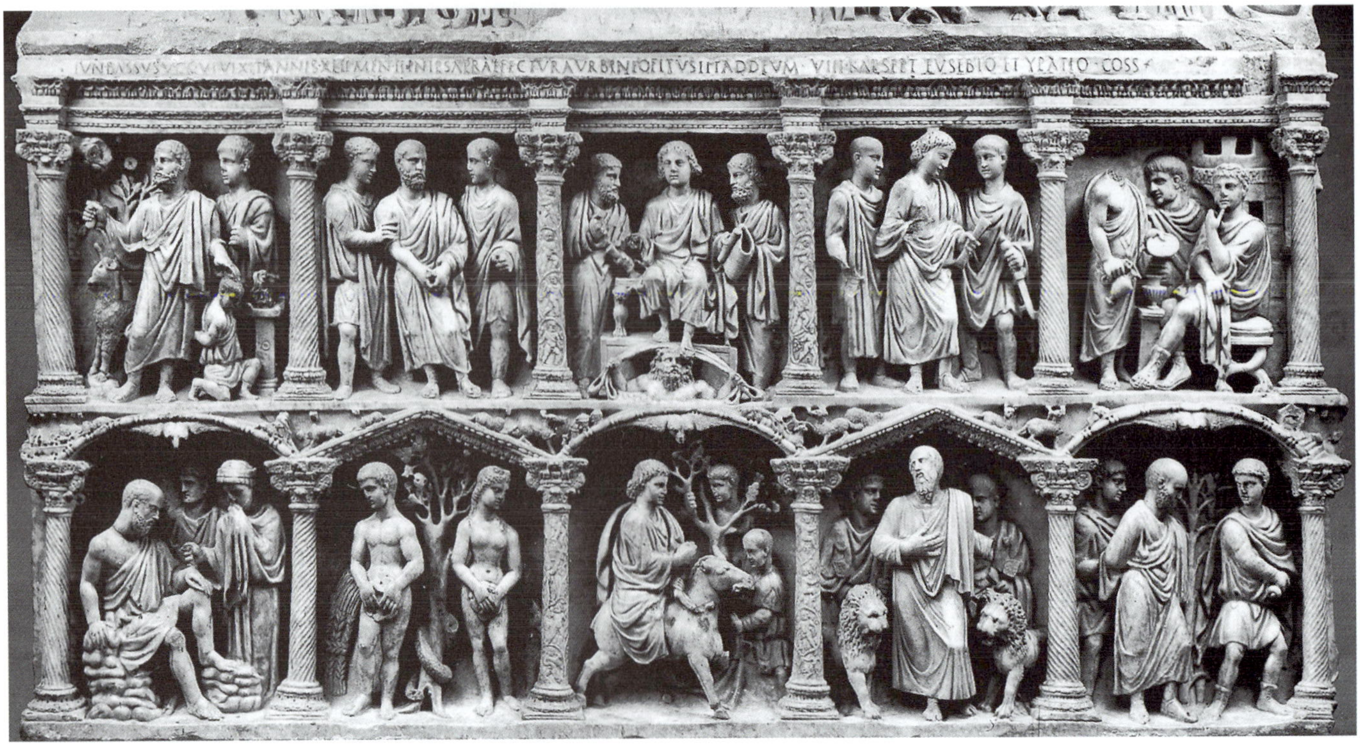

5.22 Sarcophagus of Junius Bassus, 359 C.E. Grottoes of St Peter, Vatican Museum, Rome.

Architecture

By the third century C.E., Rome may have been in decline, but the opposite may be said for the ornateness of its architecture. Opulent buildings with excessive decoration arose throughout the Roman Empire, especially in Egypt, Syria, and Asia Minor, where Hellenistic architectural principles were revised to reflect Roman ideals—for example, axial symmetry (equality of form around a central axis) and logical sequence.

Even though much of the political power of the empire was moving toward the East, Roman emperors still built their most lavish monuments in Rome. The best examples of Roman monumentality in architecture are the *thermae* or baths, and one of the most grandiose of these is the Baths of Diocletian (Fig. **5.23**). The interior proportions of the tepidarium or hall enclosed over 16,000 square feet (1,486 square meters). The space we see today has been diminished because of a later renovation that converted a section of the building to a church and raised the floor by 7 feet (2.1 meters). In its original form, the tepidarium contained huge openings that made it possible to see into adjacent spaces. The walls and ceilings were covered with mosaics and marble, which reflected light entering the space through high windows, but the renovation replaced the reflective surfaces with plaster and paint and closed in the openings. Nonetheless, we can appreciate the vastness of this work, which is supported by 50-foot-high (15-meter) columns of Egyptian granite, supported by eight huge concrete **piers**.

Another building based on the shape of the Roman baths, particularly that of Diocletian, is the Basilica of Constantine, whose height exceeded Diocletian's Baths. In its time, it probably was the largest roofed building in Rome (Figs **5.29** and **5.30**) but only the north aisle remains. The three groined vaults covering the **nave** and directing the thrust of force outward to four corners, made it possible to erect upper walls into which openings called **clerestory** (KLIR-stohr-ee) windows could be cut to allow light into the space. Thus, despite its tremendous size, the building must have had a light and airy atmosphere. This detail of design was used extensively from the Middle Ages onward.

When Christianity became a state religion in Rome, an explosion of building took place to accommodate the need for places to worship. Previously, small groups of the faithful had gathered as inconspicuously as possible wherever it was practical and prudent for them to do so. Even had it been safe to worship publicly, there was no need for a building of any size to house so few people. Respectability changed all that.

Early Christian architecture was, like painting, an adaptation of existing Roman style. For the most part, churches took the form of the Roman **basilica**. We tend to think of the word "basilica" as referring specifically to

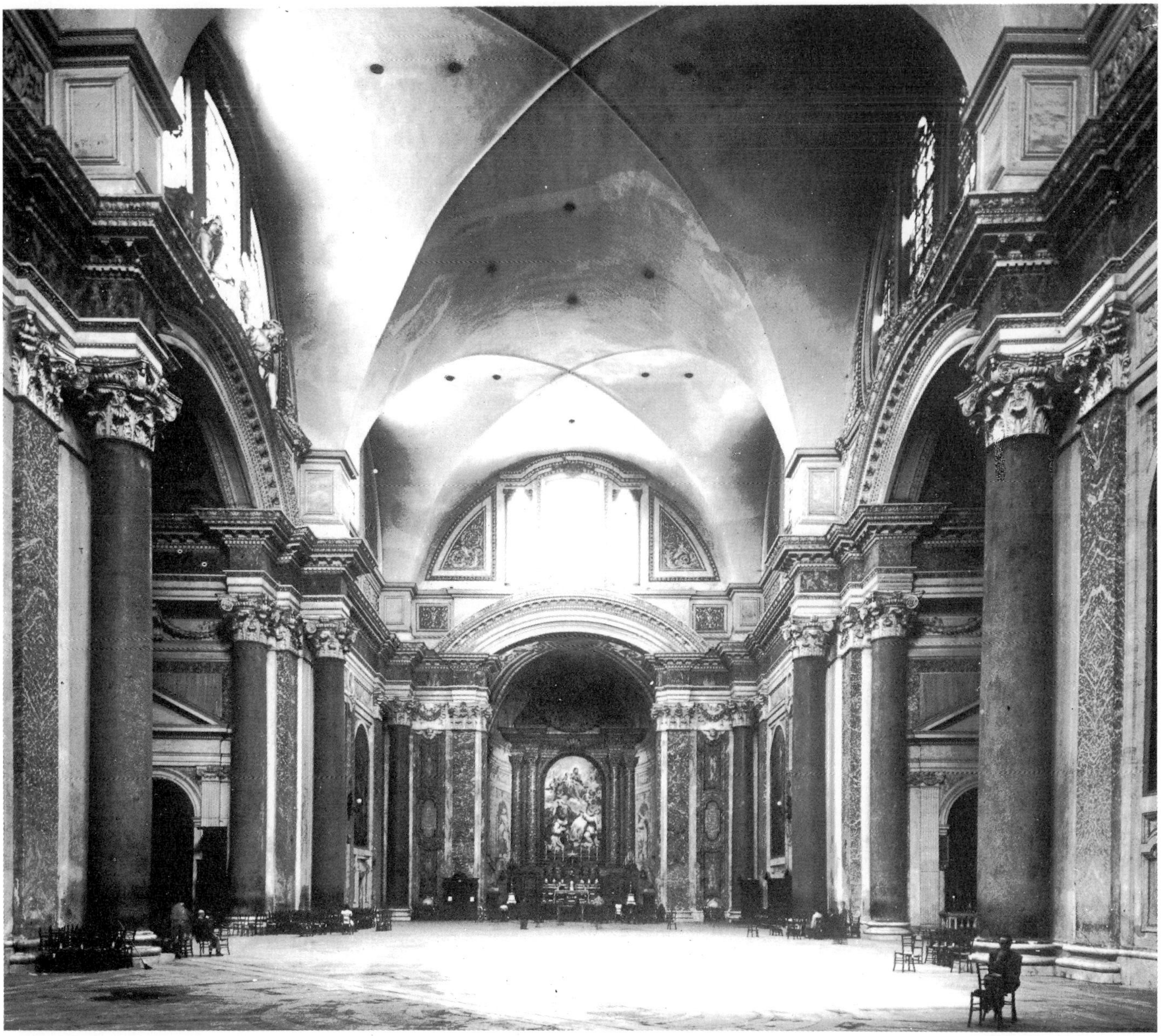

5.23 Tepidarium of the Baths of Diocletian, Rome, c. 298–305 C.E. (Converted by Michelangelo and others into the church of S. Maria degli Angeli.)

Christian structures, as in St Peter's Basilica in Rome. The term originally referred to Roman law courts, whose form the first large Christian churches took.

The original basilica had a specific architectural design, to which Christian architects made some simple alterations. Roman basilicas had many doors along the sides of the building to facilitate entrances and exits. Church ritual required the altar to be the focal point, and so the entrance to the Christian basilica was moved to the end of the building, usually at the western end, to focus attention down the long, relatively narrow nave to the altar at the far end. Often the altar was set off by a large archway reminiscent of a Roman triumphal arch (which became a symbol of Christ's triumph over death), and elevated to enhance sightlines from the congregation, who occupied a flat floor space.

The basic structure of a basilica (Figs **5.31** and **5.32**) has two or four long, parallel rows of columns, or piers, surrounded by an outer wall that is separated from the columns by an aisle. The central space, or nave, was heightened by a clerestory and a beam or simple truss roof describing an isosceles triangle of fairly low pitch. Low-pitched roofs covered the side aisles. The basilica was reasonably easy to build, yielding a nave width of 70

MASTERWORK

The Temple of Jerusalem

The Temple of Jerusalem was the symbol of Israel's faith as early as its third king, Solomon, son of David (c. 1000 B.C.E.). Described in 1 Kings 5–9, the Temple of Solomon was primarily the house of the Lord God—Yahweh—as opposed to a place to which common people came to worship. In fact, the general populace had access to only the Temple courts and not to the inside of the structure itself. Even the clergy did not have free access to the building. The inner sanctum remained off limits to everyone except the chief priest, and to him only on the Day of Atonement. Although the public did not have access to the Temple, it was very much a public building in all senses, including politically and economically. Ancient Israel, although a monarchy, remained a theocracy, and the Temple played an important role in the organization and administration of the national community.

Two major rebuilding projects took place between its construction under Solomon and its ultimate destruction by the Romans in 70 C.E. (Fig. **5.24**), and we often find reference to the First, Second, and Third Temples. The Temple of Solomon is the First Temple, and we know it primarily from the description in 1 Kings 6–8 and a parallel account in 2 Chronicles 2–4. No trace of the first Jerusalem Temple exists archeologically. The basic shape of the Jerusalem Temple (Figs **5.24** and **5.25**) was a rectangle subdivided laterally into three sections, each with the same interior width—20 cubits. The building was 60 cubits long and 30 cubits high. A cubit equals approximately 20.9 inches (53 centimeters), so the Temple was approximately 105 feet (32 meters) long, 35 feet (10.7 meters) wide, and 52 feet (15.8 meters) high. These are internal measurements given in 1 Kings, but the biblical book of Ezekiel gives a different set of dimensions—100 by 50 cubits. These, however, are probably external dimensions and include subsidiary rooms built around the Temple.

The Temple stood on a 6-cubit-high platform with a dominating entrance of huge wooden doors flanked by two bronze pillars, 18 cubits high, situated at the top of the ten stairs. The doors were decorated with carved palms, flowers, and cherubim—that is, guardian winged beasts sometimes shown with human or animal faces. To enter the Temple, one passed through the first of its three sections, variously referred to as a "vestibule," "porch," "portico," or "entrance hall." The second section of the Temple was its main or largest room, measuring 40 by 20 cubits and reaching a height of 30 cubits. The Hebrew word *hikhal* or *hekal* means that this room—the Temple's largest—was a "great house" or "holy place," and it signifies that the Temple was the "house of the Lord," an earthly dwelling place of the deity. A large, elaborate cypresswood doorway carved with cherubim and palm trees and overlaid with gold provided entry. Walls paneled with cedarwood exhibiting rich floral carvings had small rectangular windows at the top, through which light entered the space. In the room itself were various sacred furnishings—ten large golden lampstands, an inlaid table for priestly offerings, and a cedarwood altar covered with gold.

From a staircase behind the altar one entered the Holy of Holies, the most sacred part of the Temple. This was a windowless cubicle, 20 by 20 by 20 cubits,

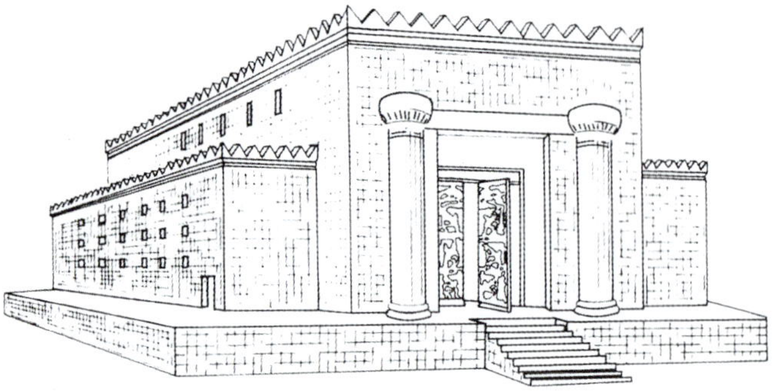

5.24 Reconstruction drawing of Solomon's Temple. The significance of the two bronze pillars is uncertain, but some scholars suggest that they may have represented the twin pillars of fire and smoke that guided the Israelites during their wanderings in the desert after the Exodus from Egypt.

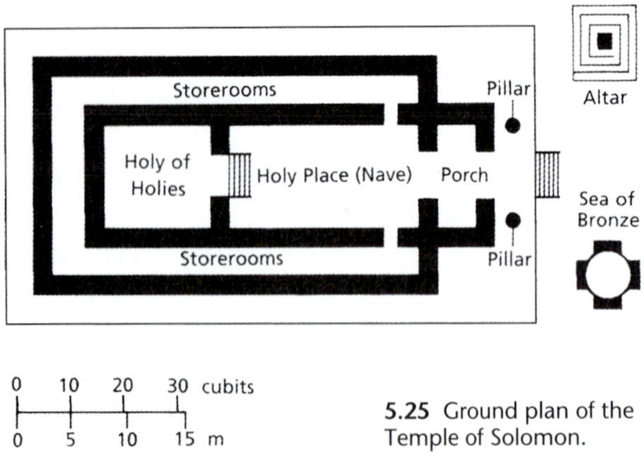

5.25 Ground plan of the Temple of Solomon.

which contained the Ark of the Covenant, the symbol of God's presence, which the Jews had carried with them from the wilderness. The Ark was flanked by two large cherubim.

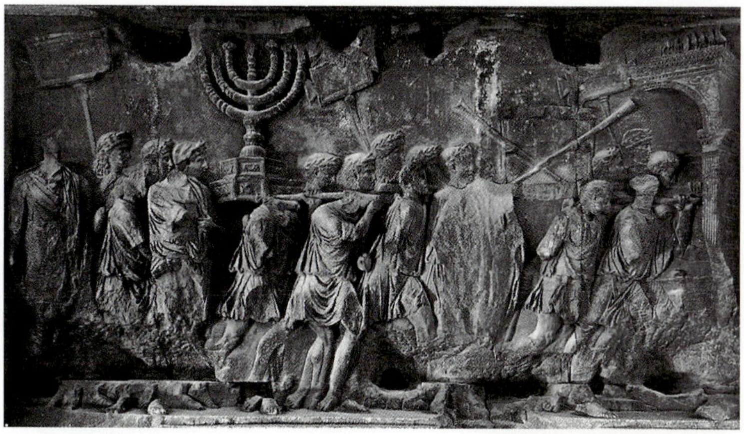

5.26 (*above*) Destruction of the Temple, a detail from the Arch of Titus, showing the menorah procession, 81 C.E. (A menorah is a ceremonial seven-branched candelabrum of the Jewish temple symbolizing the seven days of the creation.) Marble, arch 47 ft 4 ins (14.43 m) high. Rome.

The symbolic nature of the Temple as a residence for God went beyond providing assurance to the Israelites that God was with them. Construction of the Temple was anticipated by David, who brought the Ark of the Covenant to Jerusalem and began assembling materials. Solomon gave great priority to completing the Temple. He assembled an enormous workforce and completed the job in a remarkably short time: seven years.

Construction of the Temple coincided with the institution of the monarchy and the emergence of Israel, for the only time in its existence, as an independent and dominant political power in the region. Thus, the Temple symbolized not only the presence of the Lord God, but also Israel's very national identity.

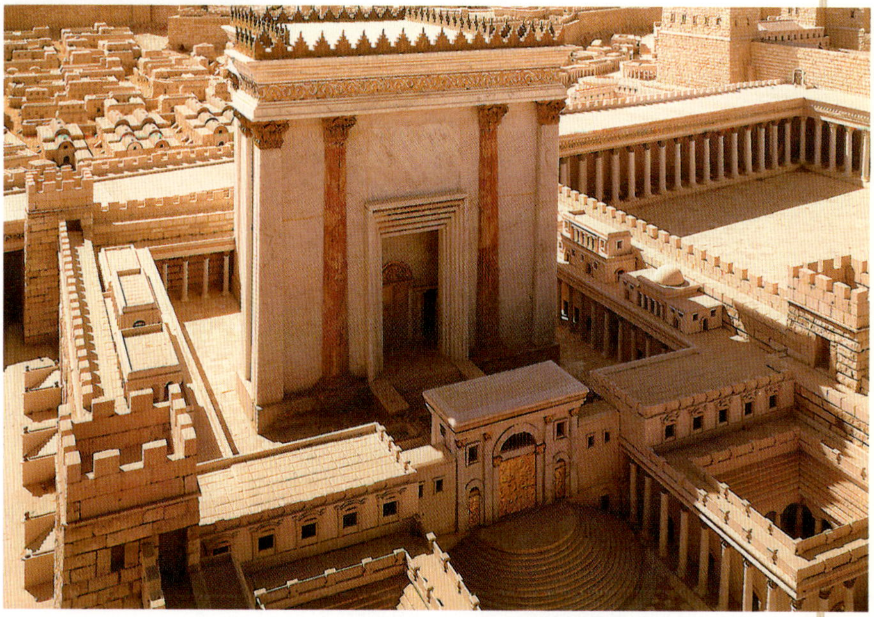

5.27 (*right*) The third (Herod's) Temple, 20 B.C.E. (reconstruction). Jerusalem, Israel.

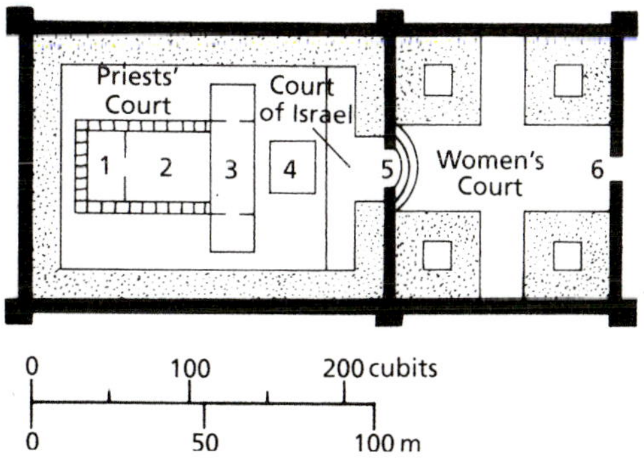

1 Holy of Holies
2 Holy Place (Nave)
3 Porch
4 Altar
5 Nicanor Gate
6 Beautiful Gate

The Temple was rebuilt extravagantly by Herod beginning c. 20 B.C.E. (Fig. **5.28**); a reconstruction can be seen in Jerusalem (Fig. **5.27**).

5.28 (*left*) Reconstruction of the third Temple.

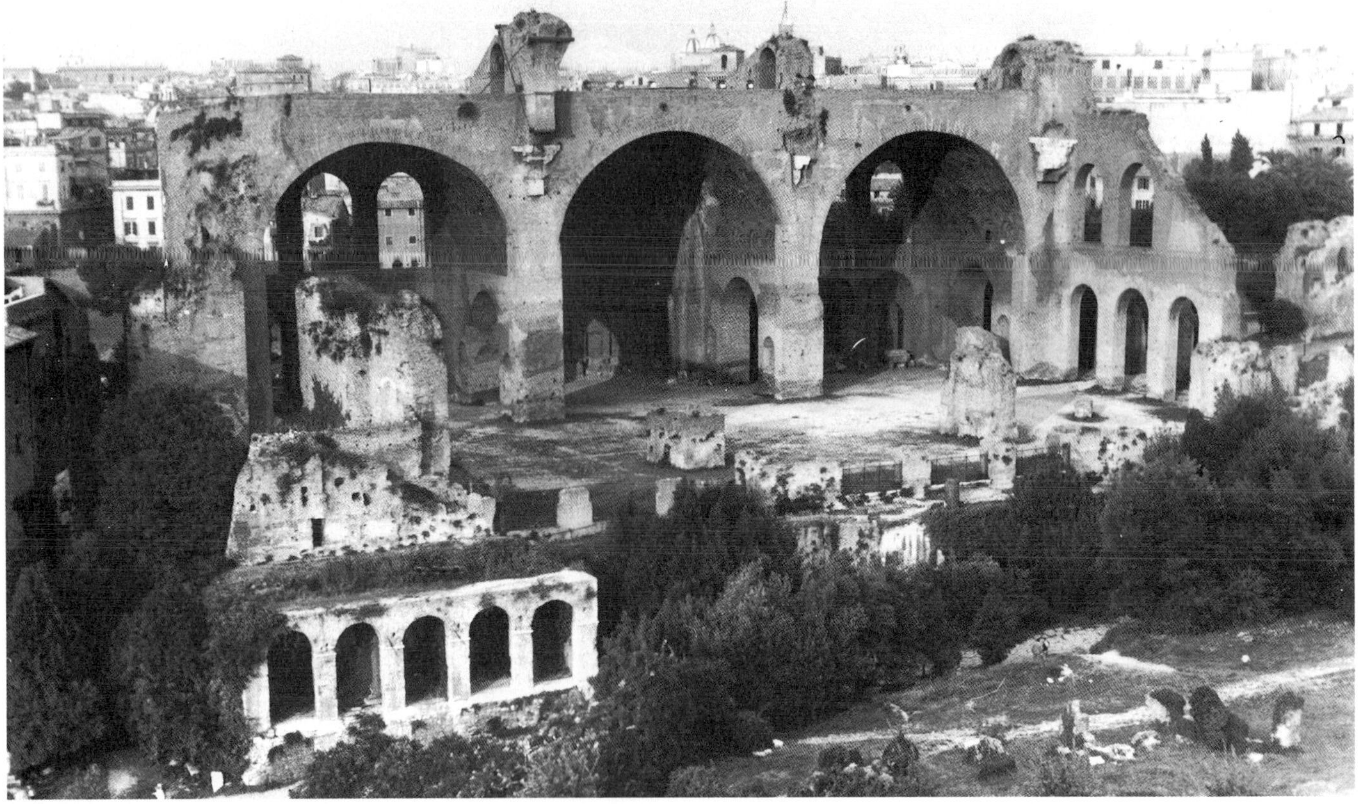

5.29 The Basilica of Constantine, Rome, c. 310–20 C.E.

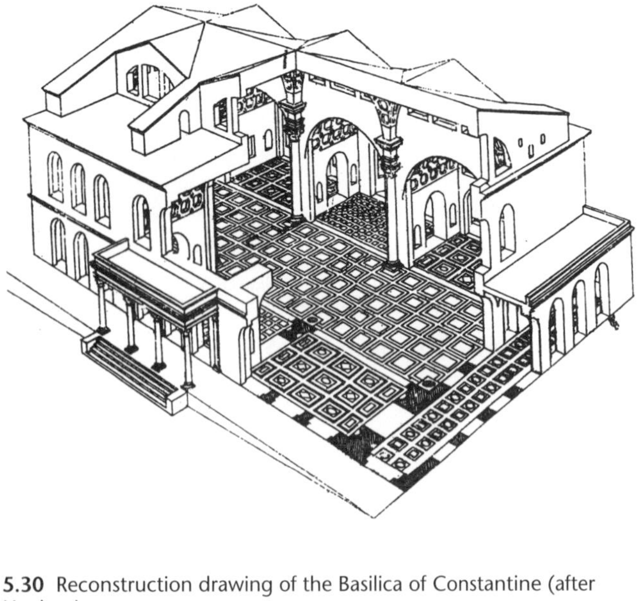

5.30 Reconstruction drawing of the Basilica of Constantine (after Huelsen).

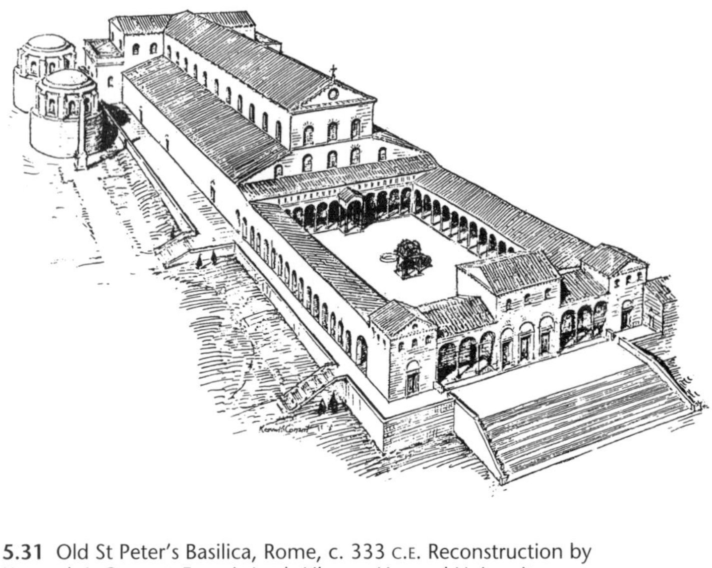

5.31 Old St Peter's Basilica, Rome, c. 333 C.E. Reconstruction by Kenneth J. Conant, Francis Loeb Library, Harvard University, Cambridge, MA.

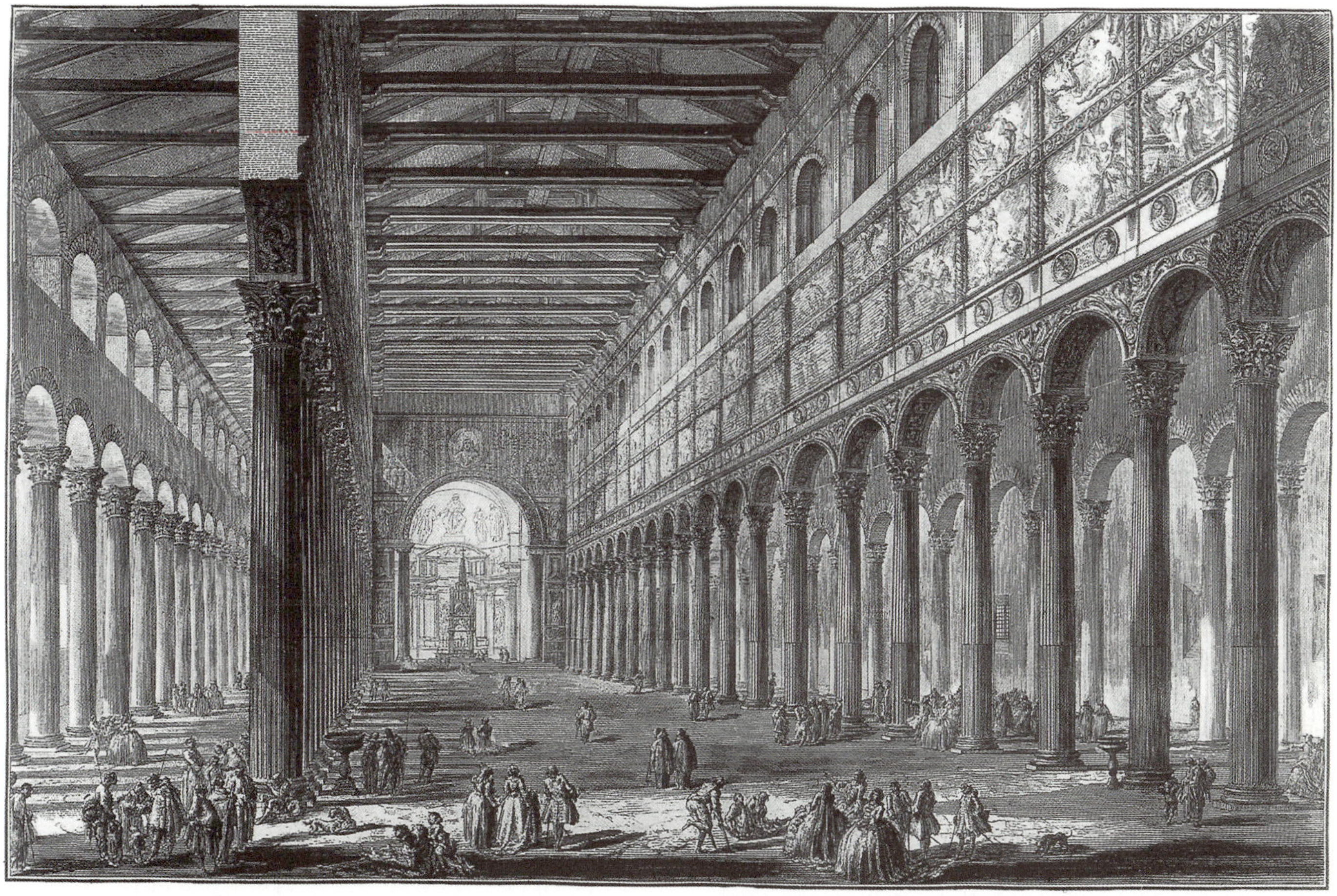

5.32 Interior of San Paolo Fuori le Mura, Rome, late fourth century. Engraving by Giovanni Battista Piranesi (1720–78).

or 80 feet (21 or 24 meters). In contrast to later church styles, the basilica was not monumental by virtue of its height, although its early association with the law courts gave it an air of social authority. Interior parts and spaces were clearly defined, and this form was stated in simple structural terms.

Another change occurred in the treatment of interior space as different from the exterior shell. In architectural design, there are two approaches to the interior–exterior problem. Either the exterior structure expresses and reveals the nature and quality of interior space and *vice versa*, or the exterior shell is just that—a shell—in many instances obscuring what lies inside. The basilica exemplified the latter style. Whether intentionally or not, it thus symbolizes the difference between the exterior world of the flesh and the interior world of the spirit. For more, go to http://ps.theatre.tulane.edu/lester/text/Early.Christian.Period/Early.Christian/Early.Christian1.html.

Music and Dance

References to music and dance occur frequently in the Jewish scriptures. Genesis 4:21 refers to those who play the "lyre and the pipe." In Exodus 15:20–21:

> Miriam the prophetess, the sister of Aaron, took a timbrel in her hand; and all the women went after her with timbrels and with dances.
>
> And Miriam answered them, Sing ye to the Lord, for he hath triumphed gloriously; the horse and his rider hath he thrown into the sea.

The musicianship of David is documented in 1 Samuel 16:23. When King Saul was tormented, "David took the lyre and played it with his hand; so Saul was refreshed, and was well, and the evil spirit departed from him."

As with almost everything else we have noted, music in the late Roman period reflected Roman decline and Christian ascension. Just as St Paul took the Judaic and Eastern mystical traditions of Christian thought and shaped them into the logical processes of the Greco-Roman world, so early Christian music began to combine the music of Jewish worship with forms from the classical heritage. Most of the music from the Greek, Hellenistic, and Roman traditions was rejected by the early Christian Church, while music that was cultivated simply for enjoyment together with any music or musical instrument associated with activities objectionable to the Church, was considered unsuitable. The *hydraulos* (see Fig. **4.29**), for example, was banned. On the whole, the music of the classical West was simpler than the more ornate elaborations of liturgical texts in the East, especially in congregations with a large Jewish contingent. The consequent intermingling of the two styles resulted in a rich pastiche of hymnody and liturgy that was both vocal and instrumental. There was, nevertheless, a deep suspicion of instrumental music in many quarters and an outright rejection of it in others, because it was reminiscent of pagan customs. Disapproval of Roman or Greek music did not reflect a negative attitude toward music itself as much as a need to break ties with pagan traditions.

There was also a reaction against the use of trained choruses, initially instituted to help lead congregations who were unfamiliar with the chanting of psalms. When trained choruses were used, the congregation tended to sing less and the chorus more. In turn, this led to more complex music, which church leaders eventually found undesirable. In 361 the Provincial Council of Laodicea (lay-oh-di-SEE-uh) ruled that each congregation could have only one paid cantor or performer. In responsorial **psalmody**, the leader sang a line of the psalm, and the congregation sang a second in response. The melody began with a single note for the first few words, changing for the final words to a **half cadence**. The congregation then sang the beginning of the response on the same note, concluding with a **cadence**. The early Church also used an **antiphonal** (an-TIF-oh-nuhl) psalmody, in which singing alternated between two choruses.

We know that from earliest times music played a role in Christian worship, and because Christian services were modeled on Jewish synagogue services, it is likely that any music in them was closely linked to liturgical function. In Rome, Christian liturgy (literally, "the work of the people") included only chants and unaccompanied singing. In Antioch, however, a new form, **hymnody**, emerged via the Jewish synagogue and its songs. The hymn, a song of praise to God, quickly spread throughout the Christian world as part of the liturgy that comprised the worship service, or Mass, in which the eucharist was the focus.

Hymns were introduced into the Western Church early in the fourth century. Some sources credit St Ambrose for this innovation, others credit Hilary, bishop of Poitiers. Early hymns had poetic texts consisting of several verses, all of which were sung to the same melody, which may have been taken from popular secular songs. The hymns were mostly syllabic (sil-A-bik)—that is, each syllable was sung on a single note—and they were intended to be sung by the congregations, not by a choir or a soloist. In style and content, early Church hymns tended to express personal, individual ideas, although other sections of the liturgy were more formal, objective, and impersonal.

Another type of Church music at this time was the *alleluia*, which presented an interesting contrast in style to the hymn. The *alleluia* was melismatic in style—that is, there were many notes for each syllable of text—and it was sung after the verse of a psalm. The last syllable of the word was drawn out "in gladness of heart." Eastern in influence and emotional in appeal, the *alleluia* came to the Christian service directly from Jewish liturgy.

Literature

The literature of the late Roman Empire reflected a dispirited decline, parallel to that of the Empire in which it existed. Compared with earlier times, little work of any quality was produced—there was no experimentation with new forms, nor a major production of old forms—and it seemed as if the only writers whose outlook was to the future and optimism were the Christians.

The Bible, which was not widely available until 313, emerged as the most significant literature of the period. By the mid-second century, Irenaeus, a bishop of Lyon, had put forward a **canon** of twenty-one of the present twenty-seven books—the inclusion of Revelation raised considerable disagreement—and some books not at present in the Bible were often included. Church councils in Hippo (393) and Carthage (397) recognized the twenty-seven-book canon.

Although the Bible speaks to Judaic and Christian religious needs, it also contains some of the most vibrant literature of all time. Certainly, its poetry is without peer, even though it comes to us in translation. Later, we will witness the epistolary form of Paul's letters, but one of the most beautiful hymns ever written is the Magnificat of Mary, which is found in the Gospel of St Luke. This is Mary's response to God's plan for her to bear his son, and it is an example of the kind of obedience deemed righteous by both Jews and Christians. The passage is steeped in the Old Testament, and is especially akin to Hannah's song of praise in 1 Samuel 2:1–10. Some commentators have seen the Magnificat as a revolutionary document because it speaks of three revolutions of God. First, it speaks of a moral revolution, because God will scatter the proud in the plans of their hearts. A basic tenet of Christianity is the death of pride, and seeing oneself in the light of Christ is a death blow to pride. Second, it speaks of a social revolution: "He casts down the mighty—he exalts the humble." Prestige and social labeling have no place in the new covenant. Third, it speaks of an economic revolution: "He has filled those who are hungry . . . he sends away empty those who are rich." There is no room here for an acquisitive society—that is, one in which people are out for as much as they can get. What the Magnificat argues for is a society in which no one dares to have too much while others have too little.[5]

Thus, within this poetry, there is a powerful upheaval—a revolution of thinking that is as applicable today as it was two thousand years ago. In Luke 1:46–56:

And Mary said, "My soul magnifies the Lord, and my spirit has exulted in God, my Saviour, because he looked graciously on the humble estate of his servant. For—look you—from now on all generations shall call me blessed, for the Mighty One has done great things for me and his name is holy. His mercy is from generation to generation to those who fear him. He demonstrates his power with his arm. He scatters the proud in the plans of their hearts. He casts down the mighty from their seats of power. He exalts the humble. He fills those who are hungry with good things and he sends away empty those who are rich. He has helped Israel, his son, in that he has remembered his mercy—as he said to our fathers that he would—to Abraham and to his descendants forever."

FOCAL POINT

ST PAUL AND THE WESTERNIZATION OF CHRISTIANITY

In this section we look at one of the most influential Christian figures, St Paul (Fig. 5.33). Although Constantine cleared the way for Christianity to proceed without overt persecution, it was undoubtedly St Paul who made it palatable to the more logical inclinations of the Roman Empire, whose heritage lay in Greek classical thought. Paul carried the Christian gospel into Greece, and his interpretation of the Christian message and the nature of Christ were singularly successful in adapting what, basically, was an Eastern, mystical religion into a Western, intellectual one. Because Paul represents the transition of Judeo-Christian culture successfully into the Greco-Roman culture, he provides us with a picture of how these two cultures coalesced, to the point that soon one would supplant the other.

The Apostle Paul was the most effective missionary of early Christianity and its first theologian. He is sometimes called the "second founder" of Christianity, having written more than one-fourth of the New Testament and having been responsible for translating Christianity into terms that could be accepted by the Greek-thinking people of the Roman Empire. His theology emerges from the many letters he wrote to the young churches throughout Asia Minor and Greece, but his Letter to the Romans probably stands as the greatest systemization of Christian theology ever produced. Although generally not a systematic theologian, Paul uses the Letter to the Romans as a means for establishing Christian dogma. While acknowledging his theological debt to Judaism, including his concept of righteousness, his cosmology—that is, his philosophy about the origin and shape of the universe—reflects that of the Hellenistic world. His belief that improper participation in the Lord's Supper causes sickness and death is not unlike ideas found in some of the Hellenistic cults. Above all, however, Paul is a biblical theologian, and his basic purpose was to interpret the revelation of the God of the Old Testament in the death and resurrection of Jesus Christ.

One of the central premises in Pauline theology is the concept of justification through faith. He presents this view in the Letters to the Romans and Corinthians, in which he argues that God moved first to save humankind and that nothing that humans can do—except believing in Jesus Christ as Lord—can earn them salvation. Also central to Paul's thinking is a kind of apocalyptic mysticism—that is, an emphasis on the coming of the end of history. In this view, Paul accepts and affirms the ultimate triumph of God over evil.

All of this rests, of course, on the assumption that Jesus is Lord and Messiah, and, because Messiah has come, the end is at hand. The decisive event has occurred in the crucifixion and resurrection of Christ, and the cross becomes a central force in Paul's Christology—that is, his definition of Christ. Through the crucifixion, God reveals his love for humankind and uses it as a propitiation for all sin. However, Paul's theology includes God's judgment. Humankind has failed to follow the word of God and lives enslaved by sin, which leads to death. The Law is insufficient for redemption. Only God's grace, with its consequent gift of righteousness, can lead to eternal life. In Christ, God reveals his mercy to those who respond in faith.

Paul's theology is far more complex than this brief description can encompass, but his systematic explanation of who Christ is and what God intended in Christ has underpinned Christian thought and belief for nearly two thousand years. Paul explained his theology in a series of occasional letters written to specific local churches undergoing specific local problems. They were intended to be read to the entire congregation and are structured according to the letter-writing standards of the day. They begin with an introductory salutation, followed by a statement of thanksgiving; then comes the main body of the letter, which addresses the major points of concern. Paul first treats questions of doctrine, then he uses persuasive exhortation in order to move the congregation to the action he desires of them, before ending the letter with a statement of his travel plans, a greeting, and benediction. The letters were arranged in their current form after their collection toward the end of the first century. They represent the heart of Christian doctrine as it was shaped into canon by the early Church, and it is through Paul's inspiration and interpretation that the Christian world has viewed the events described in the Gospels and chronicled in the Acts of the Apostles.

Paul's favorite form is the Hellenistic discourse known as the *diatribe*. In this argumentative structure, the correspondent raises a series of questions and then answers them. Because Paul dictated his letters, their style is often awkward and, occasionally, difficult to

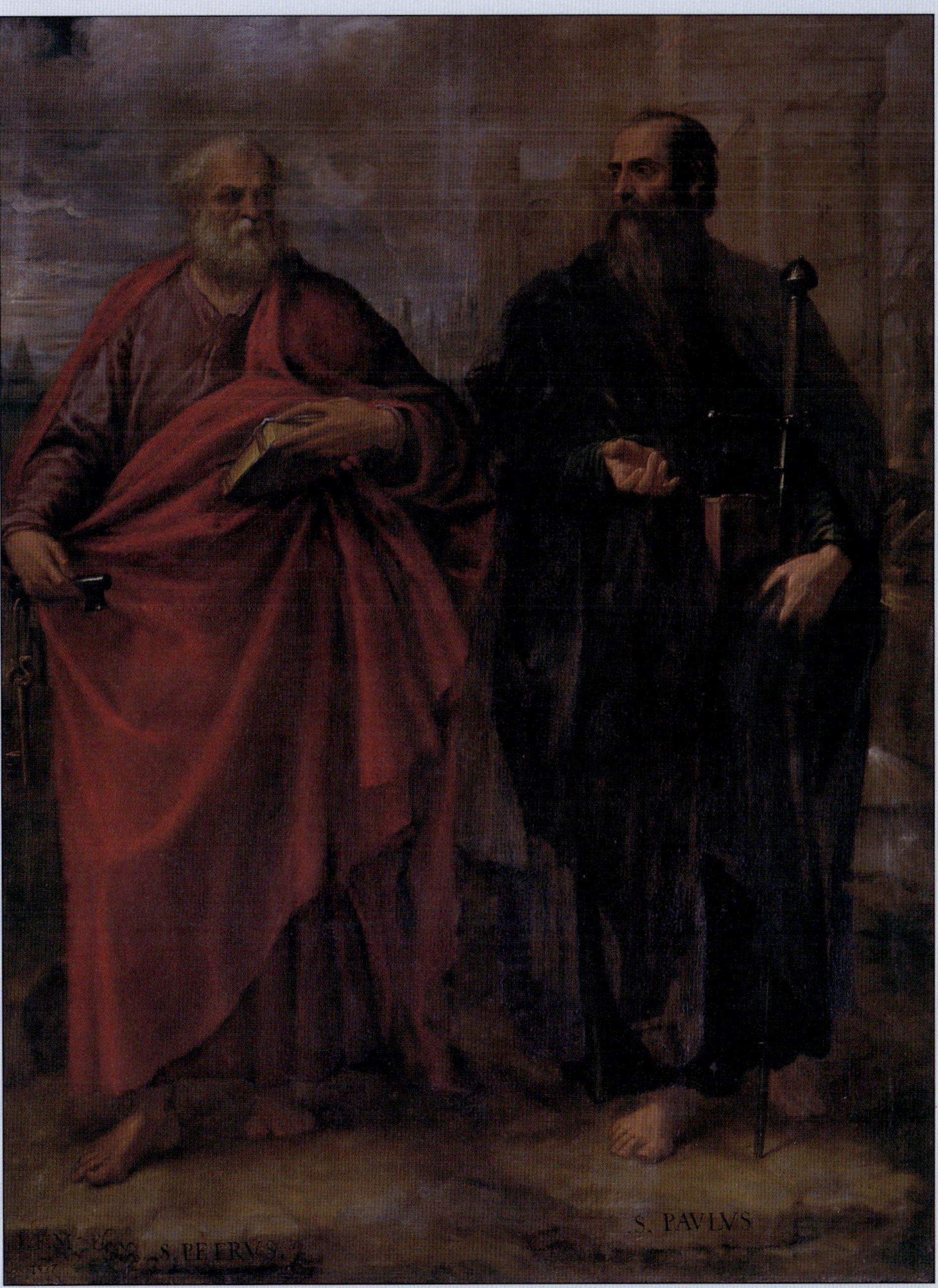

5.33 Juan Fernández de Navarrette, *St Peter and St Paul*, 1577. Oil on canvas, 7 ft 6½ ins × 6 ft (2.3 × 1.8 m), The Escorial.

comprehend. Complex sentences, which never seem to end, are not infrequent, and thoughts are often truncated or expressed in incomplete sentences. When they are placed in the framework of modern practice, his cultural assumptions sometimes cause problems—for example, his comments in the Letters to the Corinthians about restricting the role of women. Scholars and clerics have been dealing with these issues for two millennia, but it is important to remember that the letters were written to address specific circumstances in specific locations. It has, for example, been suggested that the comments about women in Corinthians were made in response to the fact that some women in Corinthian society were especially disruptive, and applying Paul's comments in general distorts their original intention.

Paul sees women in a role of equality: "Let the husband give to the wife all that is due to her; and in the same way let the wife give to the husband all that is due to him. A wife is not in absolute control of her own body, but her husband is. In the same way a husband is not in absolute control of his own, but his wife is. Do not deprive each other of each other's legitimate rights, unless it be by common agreement" (1 Corinthians 7:3–7).

The letters were arranged in their current form after their collection toward the end of the first century. They represent the heart of Christian doctrine as it was shaped into canon by the early Church, and it is through Paul's inspiration and interpretation that the Christian world has viewed the events described in the Gospels and chronicled in the Acts of the Apostles.

During his second missionary journey, Paul, accompanied by Silas and Timothy, went to Thessalonica, the capital of Macedonia, where, for three successive Sabbaths, he preached in the Jewish Synagogue, proclaiming Jesus as Messiah and using scripture to prove the necessity of Jesus' death and resurrection. Many Jews, including recent Hellenistic converts to Judaism, were converted to Christianity by Paul, and as a result the leaders of the synagogue accused him of sedition, making it necessary for Paul and Silas to be spirited out of town by their friends. Concerned for the young Christian community in Thessalonica, which had been deprived of its leadership, persecuted by the synagogue, and subjected to some scurrilous attacks on Paul's character, motives, and authority, Paul sent Timothy to strengthen and encourage the Thessalonican church. When Timothy returned with good news about the faith and loyalty of the Christians in Thessalonica, Paul wrote the first letter to that congregation. He expresses his gratitude and joy at their perseverance, exhorts them to Christian conduct, and answers two questions that concerned them: Is a Christian deprived of the blessings of the kingdom if he dies before the second coming of Christ? and When will Christ come in glory?

The earliest of Paul's correspondence, the letter was written from Corinth around 50 C.E.

Among Paul's admonitions and theology come some truly great poetic passages that have endured the test of time and endeared themselves to millions. Perhaps the best example is the "Hymn of Love" from 1 Corinthians 13:

> I may speak with the tongues of men and of angels, but if I have not love, I am become no more than echoing brass or a clanging cymbal. I may have the gift of prophecy, I may understand all sacred secrets and all knowledge, I may have faith enough to remove mountains, but if I have not love I am nothing. I may dole out all that I have, I may surrender my body that I may be burned, but if I have not love it is no good to me.
>
> Love is patient; love is kind; love knows no envy; love is no braggart; it is not inflated with its own importance; it does not behave gracelessly; it does not insist on its rights; it never flies into a temper; it does not store up the memory of any wrong it has received; it finds no pleasure in evil-doing; it rejoices with the truth; it can endure anything; it is completely trusting; it never ceases to hope; it bears everything with triumphant fortitude.
>
> Love never fails. Whatever prophecies there are, they will vanish away. Whatever tongues there are, they will cease. Whatever knowledge we have, it will pass away. It is only part of the truth that we know now and only part of the truth that we can foretell to others. But when that which is complete shall come, that which is incomplete will vanish away. When I was a child I used to speak like a child; I used to think like a child; I used to reason like a child. When I became a man I put an end to childish things. Now we see only reflections in a mirror which leaves us with nothing but riddles to solve, but then we shall see face to face. Now I know in part; but then I will know even as I am known. Now faith, hope, love remain—these three; but the greatest of these is love.

CHAPTER REVIEW

❖ CRITICAL THOUGHT ❖

Judaism followed a challenging course from the Patriarchs through the Judges to the Monarchy. The story is one of a people to whom God revealed himself, with whom he made a covenant, and whom he led to nationhood. It also is the story of a recurring cycle of disobedience, contrition, and forgiveness centering on the constant struggle of humankind to follow its own dictates rather than those of a divine being—even one who performed mighty acts to show his power and his steadfast love for his chosen people. There is much to find in the story of the Hebrews about theology and the emergence of monotheism, about the nature of revealed truth, about human obstinacy and self-will, and about the consequences of disobedience.

The theme of obedience moves from Judaism to Christianity in the first century, and we have seen it expressed beautifully in the Magnificat of Mary. The concept of obedience has proved difficult not only for devoted Christians; it is problematic in general, for it raises the question of the fundamental nature of the individual and of his or her "freedom" or "rights" to pursue individual happiness. Under what conditions should individuals submit to authority—religious or secular?

◆ SUMMARY ◆

After reading this chapter, you should be able to:

- Describe the history of the Jewish people, the rise of Christianity, and the impact of Judeo-Christian culture and religion on the Roman Empire.
- Discuss the major divisions of the Bible and relate them to the basic story and beliefs of Judaism and Christianity.
- Compare Augustine with Tertullian on the nature of the soul, and with Plato and Aristotle on the nature of art.
- Identify the reforms of Diocletian and Constantine and explain how these reforms rejuvenated the late Roman Empire and affected the spread of Christianity.
- Explain the relevance of the "Petrine Theory" to the development of the Western Christian Church.
- Identify and characterize Judaic, Christian, and late Roman art, architecture, and music.
- Apply the elements and principles of composition to describe, analyze, and compare individual works of art illustrated in the chapter.

CYBERSOURCES

http://harpy.uccs.edu/roman/html/archconslides.html
http://www.catacombe.roma.it/welcome.html
http://ps.theatre.tulane.edu/lester/text/Early.Christian.Period/Early.Christian/Early.Christian3.html

6 Byzantium and the Rise of Islam

OUTLINE

VIEW

CHURCH AND STATE

A number of critical issues will be explored in this chapter. These include major early factors that caused the split between the Eastern and Western Empires of Rome. Implicit in that split, although we sometimes barely acknowledge its importance, was the split of the Christian Church into Roman Catholicism and Eastern Orthodoxy. The split of the Roman Empire into East and West had profound implications for both the Christian religion and secular politics. Central to it all was Byzantium or Constantinople. Later, Byzantium would connect not only East and West but also Christianity and Islam—in a geographical sense, if not a theological one. Byzantium occupies a pivotal geographical location, as critical today as it was one thousand years ago. It is the place where Islam, Eastern Orthodoxy, and Roman Catholicism meet. The overlapping and conflicts among Orthodox Christianity, Roman Catholicism, and Islam are as old as Byzantium and as recent as today's newscast.

KEY TERMS

Some of the basic terms and concepts we will encounter in this chapter include the following:

Orthodoxy
The practice of adhering to the accepted, traditional, and established religious, in this case Christian, faith.

Humanism
A philosophy concerned with human beings, their achievements, and interests, as opposed to abstract beings and problems of theology.

Mosaic
A decorative work for walls, vaults, floors, or ceilings, composed of pieces of colored material set in plaster or cement.

Hieratic style
An artistic style of depicting sacred persons or offices: it means "holy" or "sacred" and its treatment of the proportions of the human body is elongated as opposed to naturalistic.

Apse
A large niche or niche-like space projecting from and expanding the interior space of a building.

Hajj
A Muslim's sacred pilgrimage to Mecca.

6.1 Empress Theodora and attendants, c. 547. Detail of wall mosaic. San Vitale, Ravenna, Italy.

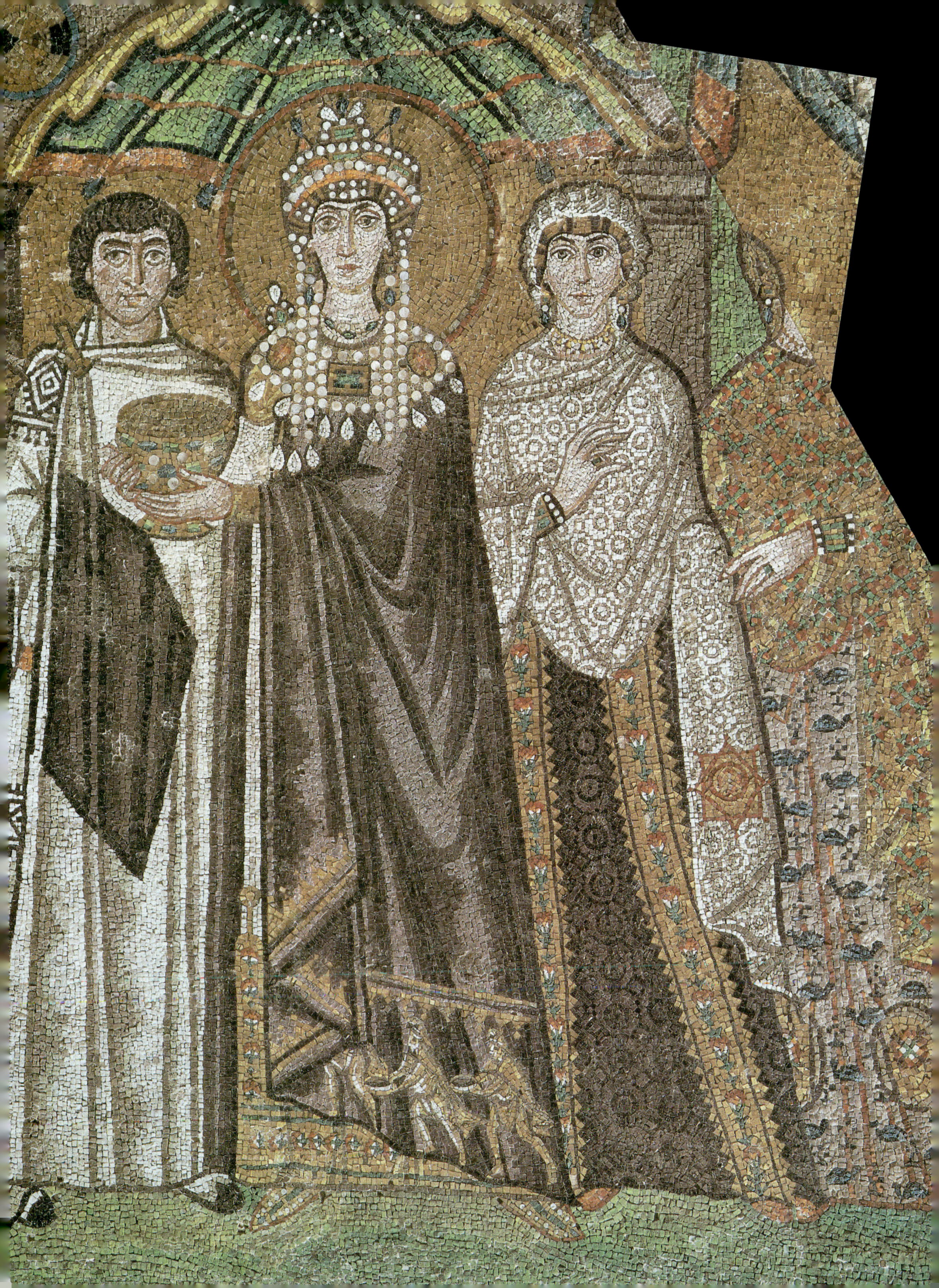

Religious Icons

The term **icon** is variously applied to the devotional panel paintings that were produced under the auspices of the Eastern Orthodox Church. The primary function of these pictures, as was the case with paintings and sculpture in the churches of Western Christianity that we will discuss in the next three chapters (7–9), was to convey the main points of the liturgy to a largely illiterate congregation. As the fourth-century theologian, St Gregory of Nyssa, explained, "The silent painting speaks on the walls and does much good." Unlike the church art of the West, however, icons in the Eastern Church were not straightforward illustrations of biblical events. Rather, they were venerated as sacred objects—spiritual tools—that allowed the faithful to commune directly with God. As a result, their format was strictly enforced by Church authorities. Not only were creativity and personal interpretation discouraged, there was a direct attempt to preserve the structure of earlier models. Consequently, some compositions survived unaltered for centuries.

In the actual composition of these objects, perspective and naturalism were displaced by symbolism, which, to the post-Renaissance (Chapters 9–11) eye, gives them an unfair characteristic of "primitiveness." The theory and tradition of holy icons rose from the belief that St Luke had made paintings of the Virgin holding the infant Jesus.

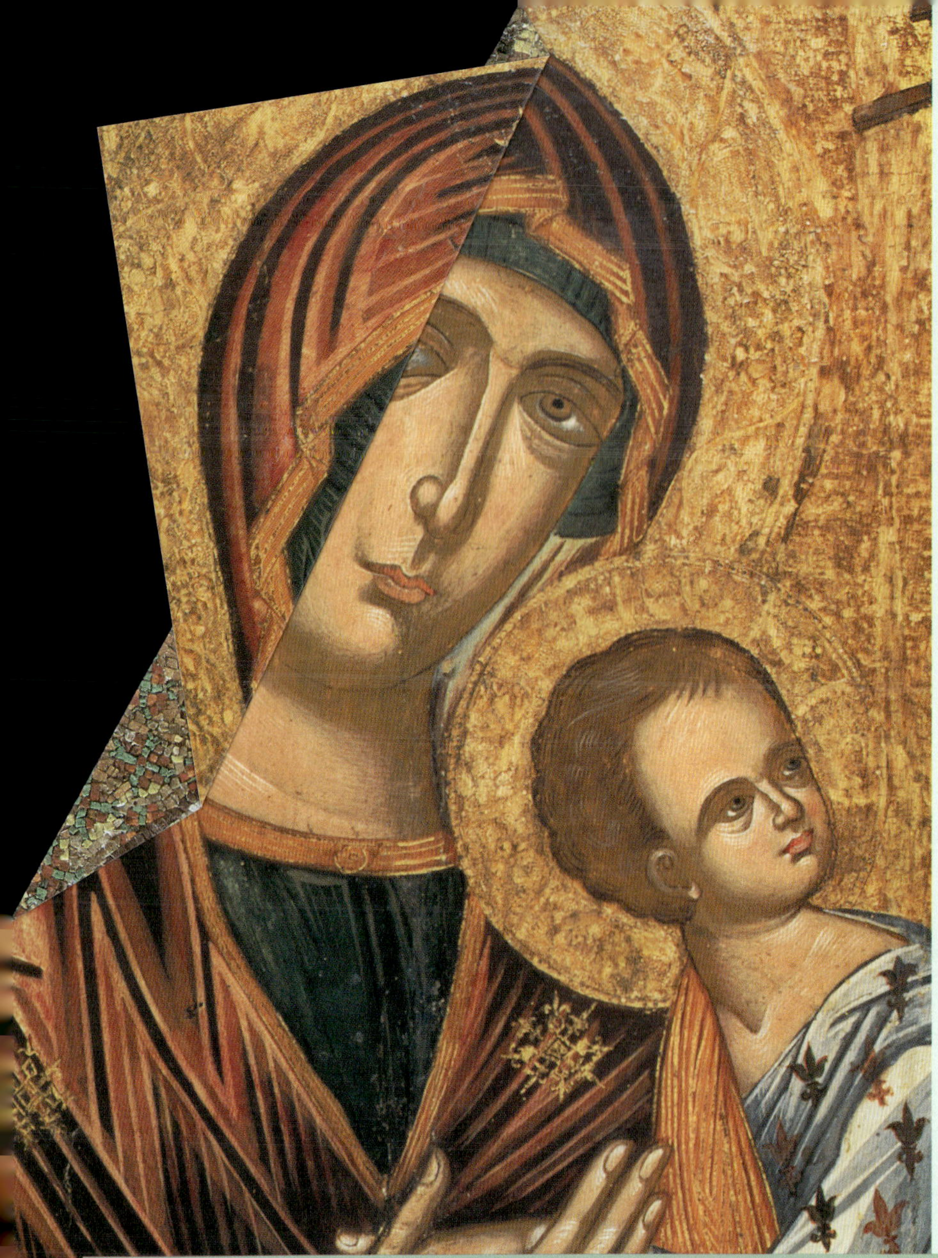

6.3 *Mother of God of the Passion*, early sixteenth century. Oil on wood. Crete.

HOW ART WORKS

ICONS

Doubtless, to most of us an icon is the graphic representation of a computer command. In a certain sense, that definition (minus the computer) is not unlike the icons that occur in art. The term "icon" (from the Greek word for likeness or image) has a number of applications. In a general sense, the word can be applied to any visual image that is designed to suggest another quality (like a symbol). For example, the fifteenth-century Flemish painter Jan van Eyck uses icons in *The Arnolfini Marriage* (Fig. **6.2**). Its assemblage of visual images such as the green dress was well understood by his contemporaries: Green, a traditional color for weddings, implied natural fertility. The dog, as today, represents faithfulness—in this case, marital fidelity. **Iconography** is the study or description of the use of visual symbols or symbol systems. [In a more restricted sense, as we discover in this chapter, icons have a specific religious connotation.]

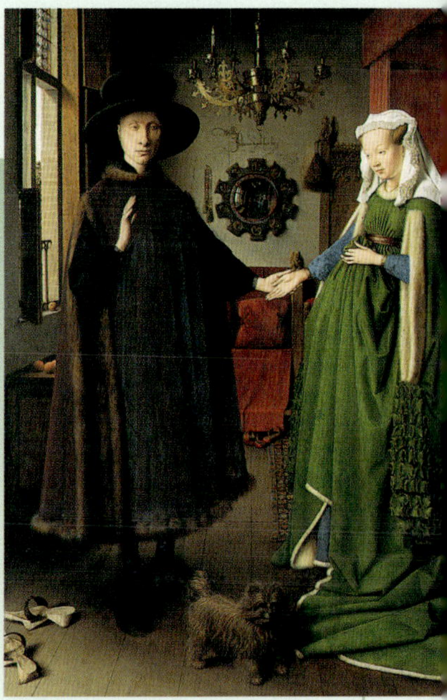

6.2 Jan van Eyck, *The Arnolfini Wedding Portrait*, 1434. Oil on wood, 32¼ × 23½ ins (81.9 × 59.7 cm). National Gallery, London.

CONTEXTS AND CONCEPTS

Byzantium

Astride the main land route from Europe to Asia and its riches, the city of Byzantium had great potential as a major metropolis. The city's defensible deep-water port, which controlled the passage between the Mediterranean and the Black Sea, and agriculturally fertile environs, made it into an ideal "New Rome." And this was precisely the objective of the Emperor Constantine when he dedicated his new capital in 330 C.E. and changed its name to Constantinople (it is now known as Istanbul). The city prospered, becoming the center of Christian Orthodoxy and the source of a unique and intense style in the visual arts and architecture. When Rome fell to the Goths in 476, it had long since handed the torch of its civilization to Constantinople, where the arts and learning of the classical world were preserved and nurtured, while Western Europe suffered the turmoil and destruction of wave upon wave of barbarian invasion.

Although the Eastern Empire of Byzantium is geographically considered part of the Eastern world, its relationship with and influence on Western thought and art were highly significant. Here we examine the history and culture of the capital city of the Eastern Roman Empire from the year 330 until its conquest by the Muslim Turks in 1453. Parallel developments in the West are covered in Chapters 7, 8, and 9.

The Byzantine Empire was founded on 11 May 330. On that day, Constantine made Byzantium the second capital of the Roman Empire, and renamed it Constantinople. The geographical location of the city, at the bridging point between Europe and Asia, made it an ideal center for trade, governance, and the development of the arts. The culture of the region at that time was based upon a mixture of Hellenistic tradition and Christian thought.

The separation of the Eastern Roman Empire from Rome and the Western Roman Empire became fact in the year 395. Emperor Theodosius the Great died in that year, and he divided his empire between his two sons, Arcadius and Honorus. While Eastern in many respects, Constantinople maintained its Roman traditions after the

	300–600	600–900	900–1200	1200–1600
GENERAL EVENTS	Constantinople founded, 330; Eastern and Western Empires split, 395; Fall of Rome, 410; Reign of Justinian, 527–65	Spread of Islam, from c. 600; Death of Muhammad, 632; Isaurian rulers, 717–867; Battle of Poitiers, 732	Comneni rulers, c. 1050–1185; Muslim conquest in west Africa, 1054	Fourth crusade, 1202; Constantinople falls to Ottomans, 1453
PAINTING & SCULPTURE	Mosaics (**6.1, 6.7, 6.8, 6.22, 6.24, 6.28**), Theodosian obelisk (**6.13**), *Barberini Ivory* (**6.15**)	*Vision of Ezekiel* (**6.9**), *Raising of Lazarus* (**6.10**)	*Harbaville Triptych* (**6.14**), *Virgin and Child* (**6.16**)	*Dormition of the Virgin* (**6.6**)
ARCHITECTURE	San Vitale, Ravenna (**6.26, 6.28, 6.31**), St Sophia (**6.29, 6.33, 6.35**)	Dome of the Rock (**6.21**), Great Mosque, Damascus (**6.23**)	St Theodosia (**6.18**), St Luke and the Virgin (**6.19**)	St Mary Pammakaristos (**6.20**)
THEATRE, MUSIC, & DANCE		*Kanones*		
LITERATURE & PHILOSOPHY	Early hagiography, Justinian legal code, Procopius of Caesarea, Anthemis of Tralles, Isidorus of Miletus		Revival of Platonism, Prodromic poems	*The Ascension of Mohammed*

Timeline 6.1 Byzantium and the rise of Islam.

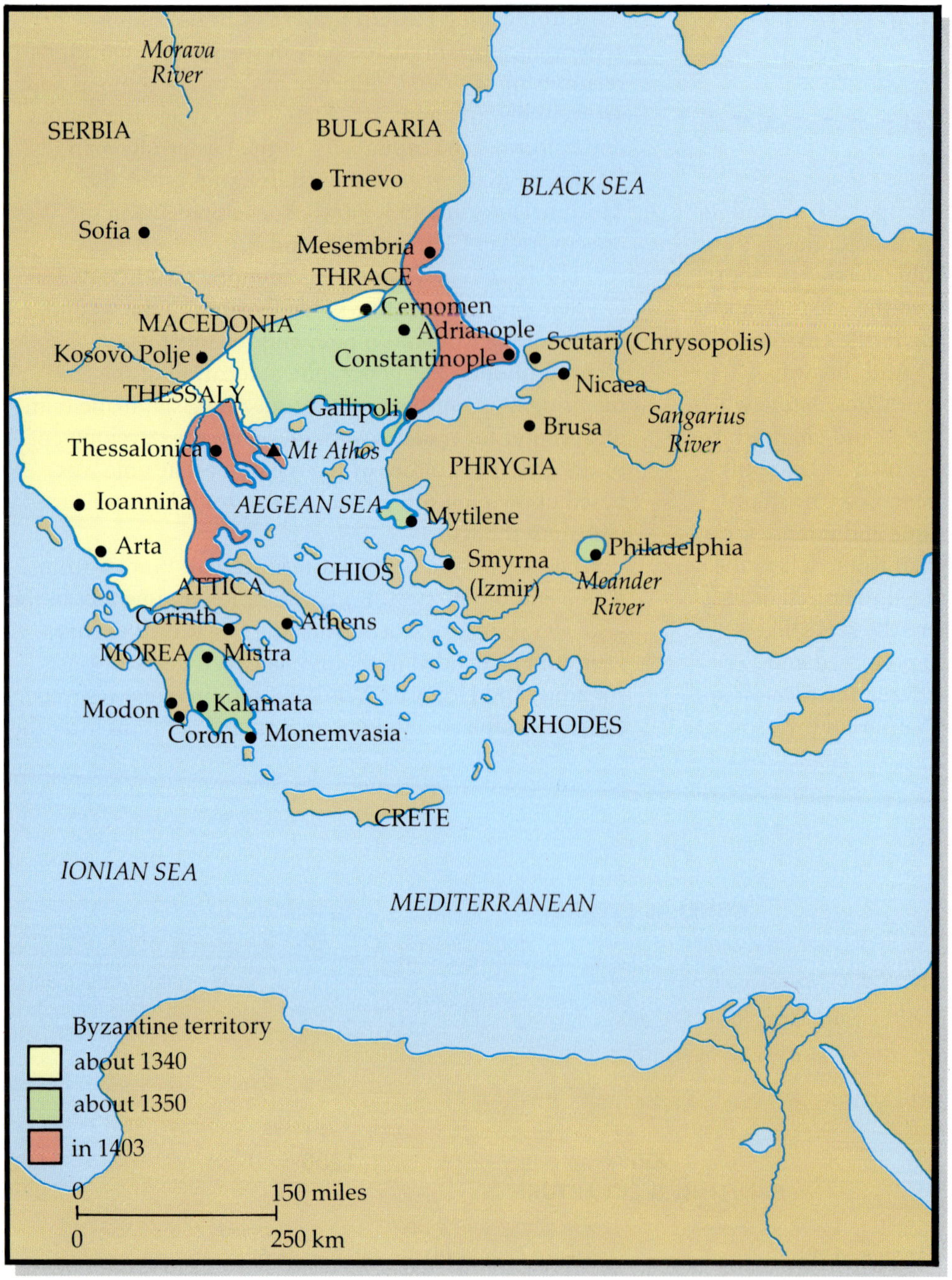

Map 6.1 The Byzantine Empire 1340–1403.

fall of the Roman Empire in 476 until the end of the sixth century. From then on, it followed its own independent course.

Two crises contributed to the distinctive character of the Eastern Empire. First, barbarians invaded Europe in the fifth century—the Visigoths, led by Alaric; the Huns, led by Attila; and the Ostrogoths, led by Theodoric. The barbarians were successful in carving up the Western Empire, yet they were unable to make more than superficial inroads into the East. This gave the New Rome political supremacy. The second crisis was religious. During the fourth and fifth centuries, the Eastern Empire was the seedbed of several "heresies" in the Christian Church. True to its Greek spirit, the Eastern Orthodox Church reveled in subtle theological metaphysics. This characteristic led to the development of ideas that conflicted with the official theology of the Church in Italy and eventually caused a schism between the Eastern and Roman Church establishments that persists to this day. Out of this schism emerged the important concept of a purely Eastern Empire. Its system of government was an absolute monarchy in the Eastern tradition. Its Church used the Greek language in its writings and rituals, and it was closely linked with the government that ruled it.

Justinian

The movement toward total separation from the Western Empire lost some momentum under the rule of the Emperor Justinian (juhs-TIN-ee-uhn; 527–65). He aspired to be Roman emperor as well as emperor in the East, and tried to promote both imperialism and Christianity. He claimed to be heir to the Caesars, and his great ambition was to re-establish Roman unity. This ambition was partly achieved as he reconquered Africa, Italy, Corsica, Sardinia, the Balearic Islands, and part of Spain (Map **6.2**). The Frankish kings of Gaul recognized his sovereignty, and as head of the Eastern Empire, he was also revered as Vicar of God on earth and champion of Orthodoxy.

In an attempt to hold his reconstructed empire together, Justinian sought a close alliance with the Roman papacy. As he concentrated on the West, however, he left the Eastern Empire vulnerable to hostile forces from the East, who tried to exploit this weakness over the following two centuries.

A major factor in Justinian's rule consisted of the role played by his wife, Empress Theodora (thee-oh-DOHR-ah; c. 500–548), whom some sources call "joint ruler." In his unreliable *Secret History*, Procopius of Caesarea (proh-COH-pee-uhs; seh-zuh-REE-uh) alleges that before her marriage to Justinian in 525 she had been an actress and prostitute. There is some credence in the former assertion, at least, as we will note later in the section on theatre. Her charms and personality undeniably exerted great influence over Justinian. During the Nika (NEE-kuh) Rebellion (532), her intervention prevented him from fleeing the capital and probably saved his crown, although there is scholarly dissension about her popularity and acceptance.

The Nika (the word means conquer) Rebellion was an uprising of thousands of citizens that occurred when two factions of soldiers, who were rival horseracing charioteers known as the blues and the greens, united to oppose Justinian's policies. It was Theodora who refused to yield, and at her instigation, a young general named

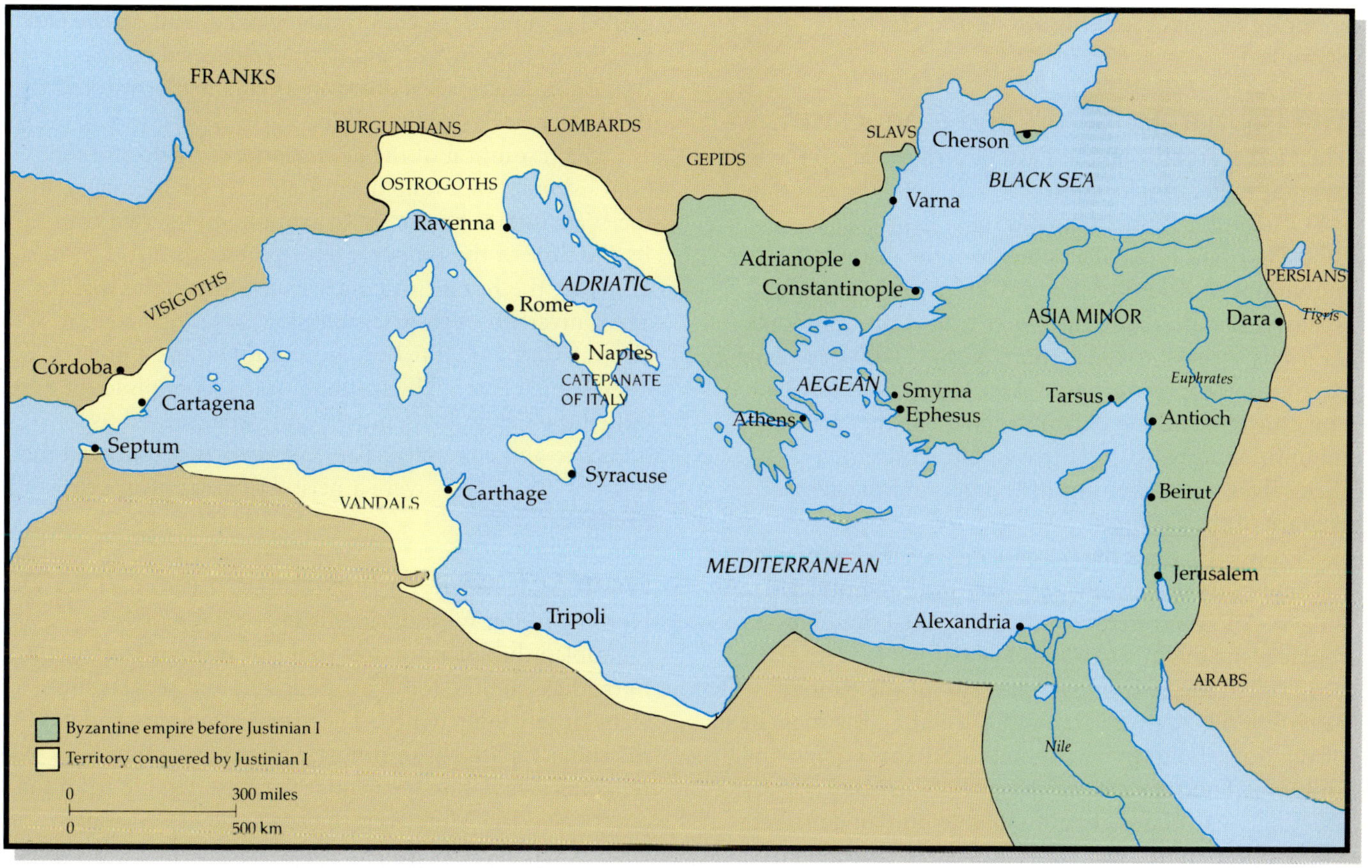

Map 6.2 The empire of Justinian I.

Belisarius led troops in a massacre of thousands in the Hippodrome. Although parts of the city were destroyed in this rebellion, Justinian's (or Theodora's) victory ushered in a new era of absolute imperial rule. Theodora was also decisive on other public policy issues. After Theodora's death, Justinian's rule lost intensity and purpose.

Justinian's greatest legacy lies not in his brief reconstruction of the Roman Empire, however, but in the enormous work of recodifying the outmoded and cumbersome apparatus of Roman law. The result was the *Corpus Juris Civilis* (KOR-puhs JOOR-is si-VIL-is), which reduced the reference books needed by a Roman lawyer from 106 volumes to six. This recodification of the law greatly influenced Justinian's own and succeeding centuries.

Because Justinian's power was concentrated, his abilities great, and his spending extravagant, his death left the Eastern Empire severely weakened, both economically and militarily. It was not until the advent of the Isaurian emperors in 717 that Byzantium recovered, but critical changes resulted. All political power was invested in the military leaders. Latin was replaced by Greek, and literary forms began to take on Eastern characteristics. Orthodox Christianity, with its emphasis on monastic retreat from worldly life, strengthened its hold on public affairs. In all areas of life, the breach with the Roman legacy widened. Out of all this arose a truly Eastern and enduring empire, militarily strong and efficiently organized.

The Isaurian Emperors and Iconoclasm

The task of stabilizing the Eastern Empire fell to the first oriental rulers to take control. These were the Isaurian (i-SOR-ee-uhn) emperors, who ruled from 717 to 867. They had originally come from the distant mountains of Anatolia. The first ruler of the Isaurian dynasty, Leo III, drove the Arabs from Constantinople in 717. His successor, Constantine V, re-established control over important territories in Asia Minor, and fortified and consolidated the Balkan frontier. As they tried to minimize internal strife, the Isaurians concerned themselves with administrative order and the general welfare of their subjects.

From 717–867, the bureaucracy of the Empire thus became more closely associated with the imperial palace. An even briefer legal code, called the *Ecloga*, replaced Justinian's *Corpus*. The *Ecloga* (ehk-LOHG-uh) limited the traditional authority of the Roman *paterfamilias* (pah-tair-fah-MEE-lee-ahz), the male head of the household, by increasing rights for women and children. This was a concept new to Christian society: marriage was no longer a dissoluble human contract, but, rather, an irrevocable sacrament. The oriental punishment of mutilation replaced the death penalty in criminal justice, reflecting at least some concern for rehabilitation.

This period also saw a violent conflict within the Christian Church known as the "iconoclastic controversy" and concerned with the use of **icons** in the Eastern Church. Icons, or images, depicting the saints, the blessed Virgin, and God himself, by now occupied a special place in Orthodox churches. From the sixth century onward, these paintings and mosaics had been extremely important in Orthodox worship and teaching, but in the eighth century, their use was questioned, and those who were opposed to them maintained that icons were idols—that is, they had become objects of worship in themselves, perverting the worship of God. They demanded the removal of icons, and on many occasions they used force to impose their will, hence the name "iconoclast," or "icon-destroyer."

In 730 the emperor issued a proclamation forbidding the use of images in public worship. One reason for the edict appears to have been the belief that the Arab invasions and volcanic eruptions at the time indicated God's displeasure with Orthodox practices. The iconoclast movement was formally approved by the council of bishops in 754. Over the next century, icons remained at the center of controversy, and their use ebbed and flowed, depending on the current emperor. Gradually, however, the "iconophiles," or "icon-lovers," gained ground. Persecution was relaxed, and on the first Sunday of Lent in 843, a day still celebrated as an Orthodox feast-day, icons were permanently restored to their place in Eastern worship.

The resolution of the iconoclastic struggle and the establishment of a united empire under Charlemagne in the West in 800 finally set Byzantium on its own course. By the time of the Emperor Theophilus (thee-AH-fil-uhs; 829–92), the Byzantine court rivaled any in the world. The University of Constantinople was reorganized, in about 850, by Caesar Bordas, and it became a great intellectual center. The triumph of the iconophiles in 843 united the Orthodox Church, and strengthened its influence and character. The 150 years that followed the reign of Theophilus were a period of great prosperity and brilliance.

From Splendor to Destruction (867–1453)

Nothing in the West during this period remotely resembled the splendor and sophistication of Byzantium. In the East, unlike the West, religious and secular life were closely intertwined. The visual arts flourished, and the subject matter was almost without exception religious. The Church calendar was inseparable from the court calendar. Moreover, the spectacle of court and Church ritual had a theatrical splendor, which reinforced the majesty of the empire and the place of the emperor as the vice-regent of God. Even the emperor's public appearances were staged. Seated behind a series of heavy curtains which were raised one by one, he was revealed only when the final curtain was lifted. Yet despite its strong economic and commercial base, and its military strength, Constantinople was unable to withstand the trials ahead.

A slide into chaos was checked for a time under the rule of the Comneni (kuhm-NEE-nee) emperors. The Comneni dynasty, which lasted until 1185, succeeded in ridding Greece of the Normans and defending the Empire against the Petchenegs, a group of southern Russian nomads. Venice had supplied naval assistance, however, and in return demanded important commercial concessions. Venetian influence and power increased immensely, while Byzantium could not recover its former strength, and internal struggles and conflicts proliferated.

In 1203 a crusade set out from the West for the Holy Land, but the Venetian contingent diverted it instead to Constantinople, whose wealth Venice was keen to plunder. In 1204 a riot provided the Crusaders with an excuse for sacking the city. This delivered the fatal blow to the Empire. The treasures of the city—books and works of art centuries old—were almost all destroyed or carried off. Central organization collapsed. Trying to preserve themselves, parts of the empire broke away. The Crusaders had stripped the empire of its strength, and it lay defenseless against the Ottoman Turks when they overran it in 1453.

The importance of the sack of Constantinople cannot be overemphasized. Two major results occurred: (1) the terrible slaughter of innocents stained the Crusades in the eyes of all Orthodox Christians—a further exacerbation of the rift between Eastern and Western Christianity; (2) the booty taken from Constantinople to Europe—especially to Venice—contained such value and quality that it formed the foundation for the Renaissance, providing models for artists across Europe—particularly in northern Italy.

Intellectualism

Nowhere in the medieval world was the classical tradition better preserved than in Constantinople. Although it was heir to the Roman Empire, the Eastern Empire was directly descended from classical Greece. The Greek cities of Athens, Antioch, and Alexandria all lay within its borders. Constantinople itself was to all intents and purposes a Greek city. Its native language was Greek—at a time when no nation of the Western Empire even spoke the language—and so its citizens were better versed in Greek classicism than anyone else. Eastern libraries overflowed with treasured classical texts. Greek literature formed the basis of Byzantine education. Homer, Hesiod, Aristophanes, Aeschylus, Plato, and Aristotle were widely read among the cultured classes. At the University of Constantinople, the "consuls of the philosophers" and the "masters of the rhetoricians" found inspiration in classical traditions. The same love of antiquity seems also to have been felt by private individuals. Even at its very lowest ebb, Constantinople never fell into a cultural dark age.

The study of history took pride of place in Byzantine thought. In the sixth century great historians arose, who were without equal in the Western world. They understood both politics and human psychology and their writings display superb composition and style. Although some, such as Anna Comnena, imitated the ancients so faithfully that their style became cramped and involved, she and others, such as Nicephorus Bryennius, were inspired to make the historian's task a true art, rather than a sterile recitation of events.

Theology held the second highest place among Eastern intellectual pursuits. The proliferation of theological literature was undoubtedly fueled by the seemingly endless heresies that troubled Byzantium and required defenses of Orthodoxy. Numerous works were devoted to scriptural commentary, and the development of monasticism produced a new genre: mystical literature. Classical rhetoric influenced religious speaking, which became very popular.

In the realm of philosophy, Platonic thought re-emerged in the University of Constantinople during the eleventh century. The intellectual accomplishments of the Eastern Empire influenced the West considerably. The Byzantine conception of imperial power, which derived from the Justinian Code, had a profound effect on emerging Western ideas of absolute monarchy. The law of Justinian was brought to Italy, and by the eleventh century, law schools in Rome, Ravenna, and Bologna were teaching its doctrines. Here Frederick Barbarossa (bahr-buh-ROH-suh) found strong arguments for establishing his imperial claims in the middle of the twelfth century. In the thirteenth century, scholars in Bologna provided the bases on which the Emperor Frederick II Hohenstaufen (HOH-en-shtow-fen) proclaimed himself "law incarnate upon earth," and justified "his right to order ecclesiastical affairs as freely as the secular interests of his empire."[1] In the same tradition, the king of France was later declared "above the law."

Theological accomplishment in the Eastern Orthodox Church was superior to that in the West, at least until the twelfth century. Its influence can be seen in the works of many Western theologians, among them Thomas Aquinas (uh-KWY-nuhs). French literature and legend also display strong links with Byzantine sources, and particularly its hagiography, or descriptions of lives of the saints.

Other Byzantine legacies included the promulgation of Aristotelian philosophy and a strong current of **humanism**, both of which figured prominently in the

Renaissance of the mid-fifteenth century in Western Europe, centered on Italy. Platonic doctrine had taken a place of honor in the University of Constantinople in the eleventh century, and it was from there that Platonic thought spread, first to Florence, in Italy, and then to the rest of Europe. The Greek scholars who left Constantinople after its sack and came to Italy brought Byzantine humanism with them. Humanism enjoyed great currency during the thirteenth and early fourteenth centuries in Europe. These scholars also brought many important Greek manuscripts, and rekindled an appreciation of Greek intellectual accomplishment in the West.

Byzantine Art and Culture

In summary, we can make the following observations about the relationship between Byzantine art and Byzantine culture. (1) The power and expressiveness of the figures in Byzantine art suggest the strength and vitality of Byzantine traditions. (2) Rich materials, such as gold, indicate a culture of great wealth. (3) The great variety in subject matter, media, and types of art reveal a culture of taste and sophistication as well as tremendous artistic skill among artists themselves. (4) The presence of classical themes and style proves the importance of the classical heritage to Byzantine culture. (5) The presence of Byzantine artistic style in cultures as far removed as Russia, Europe, and the Middle East indicates the vast expanse of Byzantine cultural influence.

ISLAM

Islamic Religion

The Islamic tradition springs from the religion of Islam, of which Muhammad (c. 570–632) was the prophet. The latest of the three great monotheistic religions, it drew upon both Judaism and Christianity. When Muhammad, the prophet of Islam, was called to preach, the conditions included great suffering among the poor—notably in the city of Mecca in southwestern Arabia. Most of the people worshipped a variety of gods and prayed to various idols and spirits. Muhammad taught that there was only one God and that this God requires people to make Islam—that is, submission—to him.

Muhammad began preaching in Mecca around 610 C.E., but, as noted in the Profile on p. 183 that follows, his teachings were not immediately accepted. However, by the time of his death in 632 he was acknowledged as Prophet. His companions preserved his revelations and combined them to form the holy book of the Muslims, the Koran. The word Koran (koh-RAN) means "recitation," and Muslims consider the Koran to contain the words of God himself, spoken to Muhammad by an angel. Parts of the Koran resemble the Hebrew Bible and contain many stories about the prophets who appear in the Old Testament. The Koran also has stories from the New Testament about Jesus, whom it calls the "Word of God." The strictures of the Koran prohibit usury, games of chance, and the consumption of pork and alcohol. Like the Bible, it forbids lying, stealing, adultery, and murder, but it does not require "an eye for an eye." Instead, the offender can pay "blood money" and is urged to seek forgiveness. Polygamy—up to four wives—is permitted under some conditions.

In the religion of Islam, there is one absolute and all-powerful God, known as Allah. He is the creator of the universe, and is just and merciful. God desires that people repent and purify themselves so that they can attain Paradise after death. God communicates with the human race through prophets, and the predecessors of Muhammad were the Old Testament prophets and Jesus. Muhammad was the last of the prophets. Muslims respect Muhammad, but they do not worship him.

Like Judaism and Christianity, the Islamic faith teaches that parents should be honored, orphans and widows protected, and charity given to the poor. It proclaims faith in God, kindness, honesty, industry, courage, and generosity. An Islamic wife has rights against her husband to protect her from abuse. Islam also teaches that life on earth is a period of testing in preparation for an afterlife. Angels keep a record of individual good and bad deeds, and God's justice determines a person's reward. Death is the gateway to eternal life, and at the last day, judgment will occur. The record book of each individual will be placed in the right hand of those who will go to heaven and in the left hand of the wicked who will go to hell. The descriptions of the agonies and tortures of hell are similar to those in the Bible, while heaven is a garden with flowing streams, delicious fruit, richly covered furniture, and beautiful maidens.

Five duties are prescribed for every Muslim, the last being that he must, if he can, once in his life make the pilgrimage, or Hajj (hahj), to Mecca (MEHK-uh). This last provision has made the pilgrimage the greatest in the world and a great unifying force in Islam. The other duties are profession of God and the prophethood of Muhammad, prayer, almsgiving, and fasting.

Muslims pray five times daily: at dawn, noon, in the afternoon, in the evening, and at nightfall. A crier or muezzin (myoo-EZ-in) announces prayer time from a tower, or minaret, in the mosque, the Muslim place of worship, meaning a place of kneeling. Noon prayer is expected to be performed in the mosque. Immediately before prayer, Muslims wash their face, hands, and feet. Friday is a day similar to the Jewish Sabbath and the Christian Sunday. During prayer, the leader faces Mecca, and the men stand in rows behind him, with women

PROFILE

MUHAMMAD (c. 570–632)

The name Muhammad means Praised One, and there are several common spellings of the name, including Mohammed and Mahomet. Muhammad was born in Mecca, but his father died before he was born, and his mother died shortly thereafter. Raised under the guardianship of his grandfather and, later, his uncle, Muhammad lived for a while with a desert tribe tending sheep and camels. Tradition maintains that he went with his uncle on caravans throughout Arabia and to Syria.

When he was twenty-five years old, Muhammad went to work for a wealthy widow who was fifteen years older than he was and whom he later married. They had two sons and four daughters, and although the sons died young, one of the daughters, Fatima (FAT-i-muh), married Ali, son of Abu Talib. Many Muslims trace their ancestry to Muhammad through his daughter in a genealogy called the Fatimid dynasty.

When Muhammad was thirty-five years old and living in Mecca, a flood damaged the most sacred shrine, the Kaaba (KAH-uh-buh). Because of his moral excellence, Muhammad was selected to put the sacred stone back into place. The angel Gabriel (Fig. **6.4**) later appeared to Muhammad in a vision and called him to serve as a prophet to proclaim God's message to his people. Although he was at first unsure of the vision, he was convinced of its validity by his wife, who became his first disciple. However, no further visions occurred, and Muhammad grew disheartened. Then, Gabriel appeared again and told him: "Arise and warn, magnify thy Lord . . . wait patiently for Him."

Muhammad began to preach periodically in public, and although, at first, most of the people who heard him ridiculed him, he gained a few followers. He continued preaching in Mecca until both his wife and son-in-law died, but the people of Mecca persecuted him for his claims and attacks on their way of life. In 622 C.E., therefore, he fled to Medina in the north. That emigration is called the *Hegira* (huh-JY-ruh), and Muslims date their calendar from this year. In Medina he found a welcome, and most of the population became his followers. He eventually became both head of a religion and a political leader—his religious message became law, and he made a variety of changes in the legal system and customs to conform to the precepts of Islam.

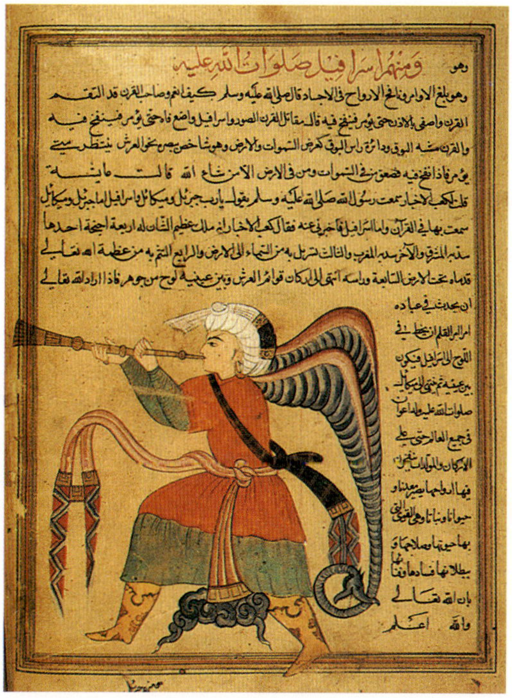

6.4 The Archangel Gabriel. British Library, London.

At first it seems as though Muhammad expected Christians and Jews to recognize him as a prophet. He was benevolent to them and decreed that Jerusalem was to be faced in prayer. However, a conspiracy among Jews in Medina and Muhammad's enemies in Mecca caused him to drive them from the city and to organize a strictly Muslim society. In order to recognize the independence of the religion, he decreed that from that time onward his followers face Mecca in prayer, a practice still observed.

In 630 Muhammad and his followers attacked Mecca and successfully destroyed all the idols in the Kaaba, turning it into a mosque. In a gesture of reconciliation, Muhammad offered to pardon the people of Mecca, who accepted Islam and acknowledged Muhammad as a prophet. The two cities of Medina and Mecca became the sacred cities of the religion. Muhammad died in Medina (muh-DEE-nuh) two years later, and his tomb is in the Prophet's Mosque there.

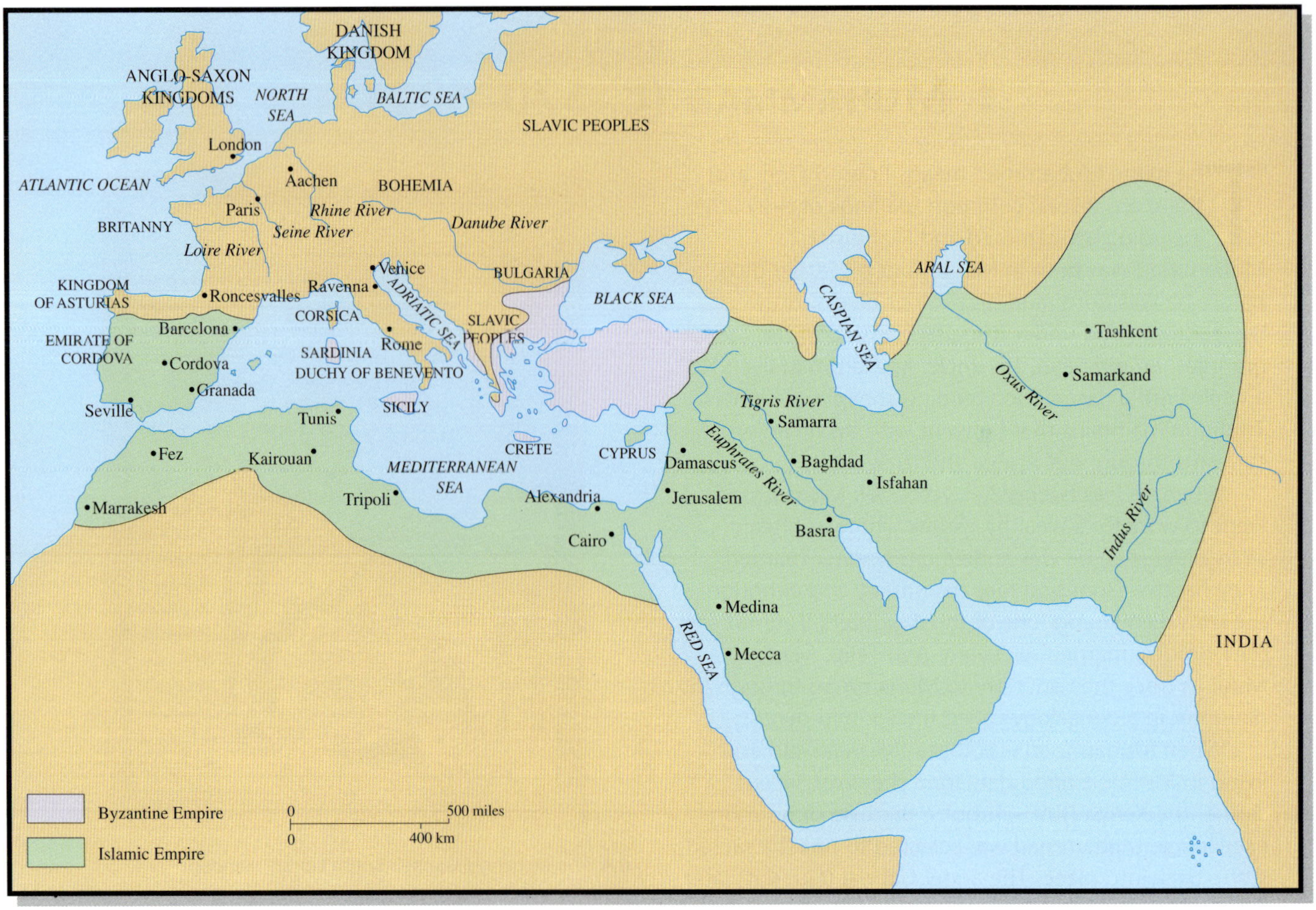

Map 6.3 The Byzantine and Islamic Empires, c. 814.

standing behind the men. Prayers include bowing from the hips and kneeling with one's face to the ground. Friday prayers include a sermon. Islam does not have an organized priesthood—any virtuous and able Muslim can lead prayers—but most mosques have an imam, or leader, who is the chief officer of the mosque and leads the people in prayer.

Early in its history, Islam split between the Sunnites (SOON-yts) and Shiites (SHEE-yts), and this split has persisted. The original split was over the caliphate, which was the crowning institution of the theocratic structure of Islam—that is, the placement of both religious and political leadership in the hands of a single ruler. The caliphs were the successors, or deputies, of Muhammad, and their claim to authority rested on their descent from the families of the Prophet or his early associates. Although secularism has modified the unity somewhat, in theory the civil law in Muslim countries is not separate from religious law; religion governs all aspects of life. There have developed some four different systems of interpretation of the law in Sunnite Islam, all regarded as orthodox. Islamic philosophy is in effect part theology; rationalism and mysticism both grew up in Islam, but were equally absorbed.

The Spread of Islam

Islam spread rapidly throughout the Middle East and North Africa in the seventh and eighth centuries, beginning with conquests launched from Mecca and Medina (Map 6.3). After Muhammad's death, the Caliph Abu Bakr (KAYL-if AHB-oo BAHK-uhr) and his successors encouraged jihad, or holy war, in order to expand the faith's sphere of influence. Within a century, an Islamic empire stretched from northern Spain to India, engulfing much of the Byzantine and Persian empires, and the Muslims threatened to overrun Europe until they were

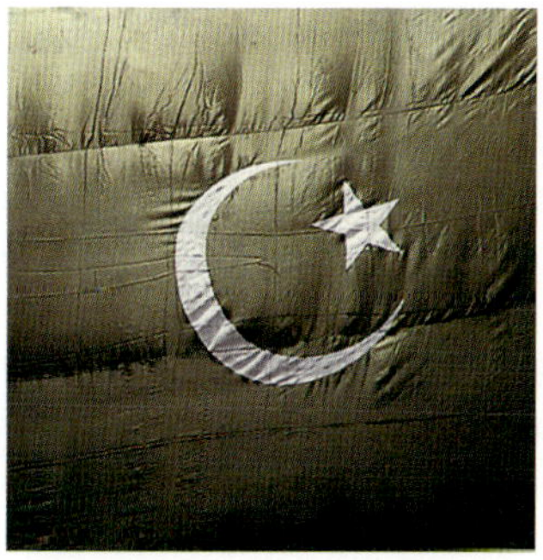

6.5 Symbol of Islam on Pakistan's national flag.

defeated by Charles Martel (mahr-TEL) at the battle of Poitiers (Tours) in 732.

A religion that was originally spread "by the sword," Islam's appeal lay in its openness to everyone. It stresses the brotherhood of the faithful before God, regardless of race or culture, although the Arab warriors who started out to conquer the world for Allah did not expect to make converts of conquered peoples—they expected the unbelievers to be obedient to them, the servants of the One True God. The Koran was not translated into any languages because it was dictated by God to Muhammad in Arabic. Converts were expected to become Arabs, and they had to submit to the social and legal precepts of the Muslim community (Fig. **6.5**). As a result, the conquering Arabs resisted the usual fate of conquerors—being absorbed into the culture of the conquered.

During the early Middle Ages in Europe, the Muslims were responsible for transmitting much of the classical knowledge of the ancient world. They were proficient mathematicians and scientists, as well as artists, writers, and architects.

THE ARTS OF BYZANTIUM AND ISLAM

Painting, Mosaics, and Manuscript Illumination

Byzantium

Fundamental to the visual art of the Eastern Empire is the idea that art can be used to interpret as well as to represent its subject matter. Byzantine art was conservative, and, for the most part, anonymous and impersonal. The artist was clearly subordinate to the work. Much of Byzantine art remains undated, and questions about how styles developed and where they came from are unresolved. We can, however, draw a few general conclusions with regard to Byzantine art (which, we must remember, encompasses nearly a thousand years of history and, thereby, several shifts in style). First, the **content** of Byzantine art focuses on human figures. Those figures reveal three main elements: (1) *holy figures*—Christ, the Virgin Mary, the saints, and the apostles with bishops and angels portrayed in their company; (2) *the emperor*—believed to be divinely sanctioned by God; (3) *the classical heritage*—images of cherubs, mythological heroes, gods and goddesses, and personifications of virtues. In addition, the **form** of Byzantine two-dimensional art increasingly reflected a consciously derived spirituality.

The ostentation of the Imperial court influenced artistic style, and Christ and the saints were depicted as frozen in immobile poses and garbed in regal purples. Lacy ornamentation ended what was left of classical purity in the sixth century.

The period of Justinian marks an apparently deliberate break with the past. What we describe as the distinctly "Byzantine style," with its characteristic abstraction and its focus on spirituality, began to take shape in the fifth and sixth centuries. Throughout the seventh century, classicism and decorative abstraction intermingled freely.

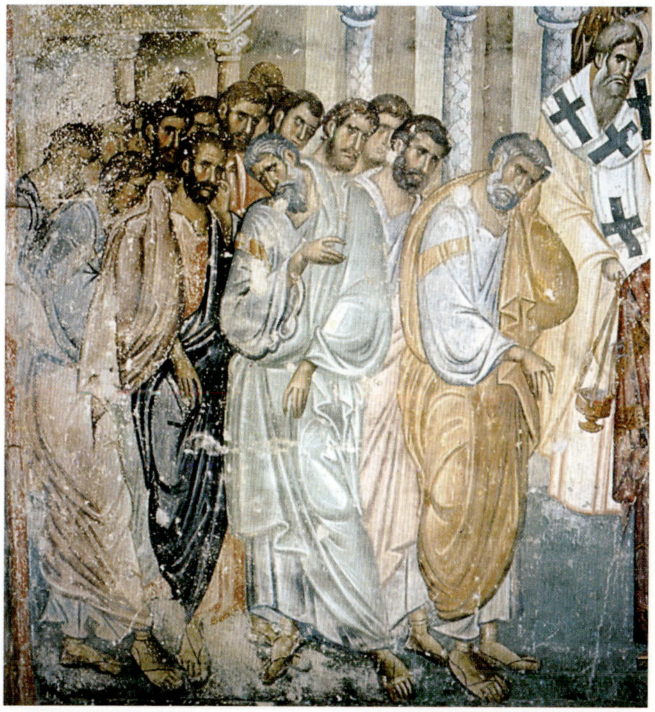

6.6 *Dormition of the Virgin* (detail), 1258–64. Fresco. Church of the Trinity, Sopoćani, Yugoslavia.

By the eleventh century, Byzantine wall painting and mosaics had developed a hierarchical (hy-er-ARK-i-kuhl) formula. There was reduced emphasis on narrative. The Church represented the kingdom of God, and as one moves up the hierarchy, one encounters figures ranging from human to the divine. Placement of figures in the composition depended upon religious, not spatial, relationships. Figures are strictly two-dimensional, but portrayal is elegant and decorative. In twelfth- and especially in thirteenth-century art, this approach intensifies, detailed with architectural backdrops, flowing garments, and elongated but dynamic figures (Fig. **6.6**). This fresco depicts the death and assumption into heaven of the Virgin Mary, a subject known as the Dormition (sleep) of the Virgin. The fourteenth century produced small-scale, crowded works that are highly narrative. Space is confused by irrational perspective, and figures are distorted, with small heads and feet. The effect is of intense spirituality.

Hieratic Style

In the middle centuries of the Empire, a style known as *hieratic* (hy-er-AT-ik), meaning here "holy" or "sacred," emerged, consisting of formal, almost rigid images. (Do not confuse this style with the hierarchical formula just discussed.) It was less intended to represent real life than to inspire reverence and meditation. The canon of proportion of the hieratic style ordained that a man should measure nine heads in height (seven heads gives a lifelike proportion). The hairline was one nose length above the forehead. In addition, "if the man is naked, four noses' lengths are needed for half his width."

By the thirteenth century, mosaics had returned to more naturalistic depictions, but they did not lose the clear sense of the spiritual that was apparent in the much earlier Ravenna mosaic of Emperor Justinian and his court (Fig. **6.7**). The hieratic style also occurs in other media, for example, in the *Harbaville Triptych* (TRIP-tik; see Fig. **6.14**) and *Virgin and Child* ivories (see Fig. **6.16**). In both, we see the formality, frontal poses, and slight elongation of forms that are typical of this style.

When the emperor was depicted in Byzantine art, we may note any of several characteristics. The emperor may be shown in the presence of Christ to validate his supreme powers. One or several exclusive attributes of the emperor may be present—for example: (1) red shoes

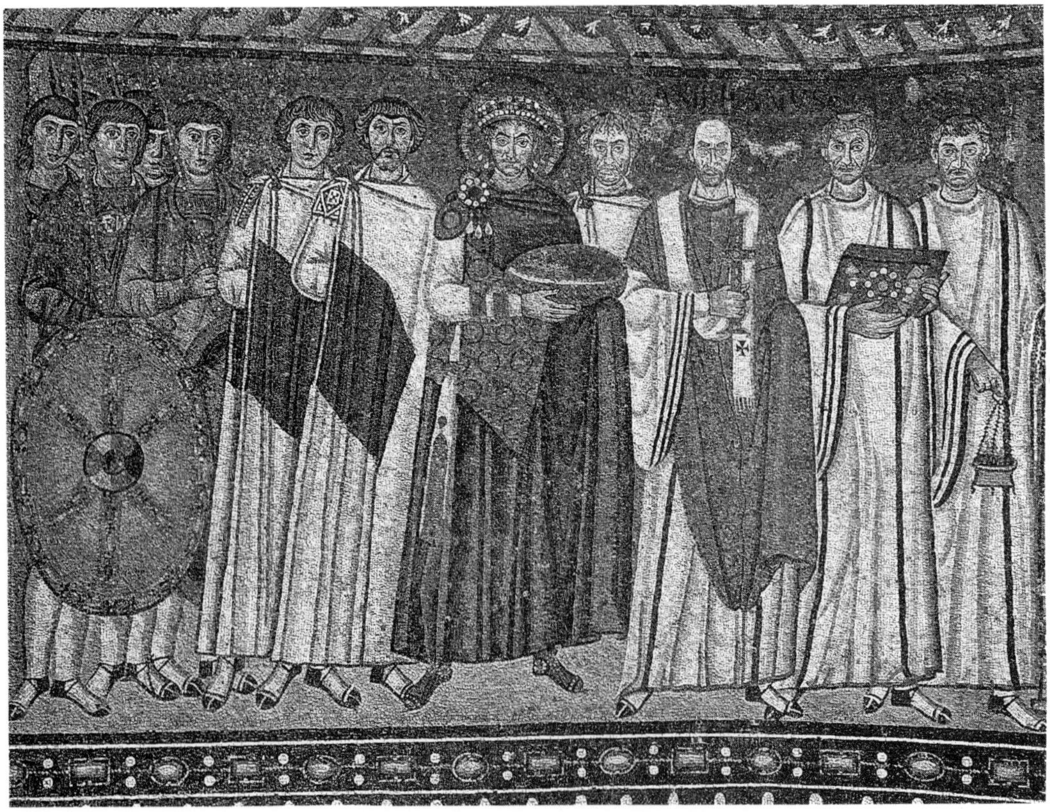

6.7 *Emperor Justinian and his Court*, c. 547. Wall mosaic, San Vitale, Ravenna, Italy.

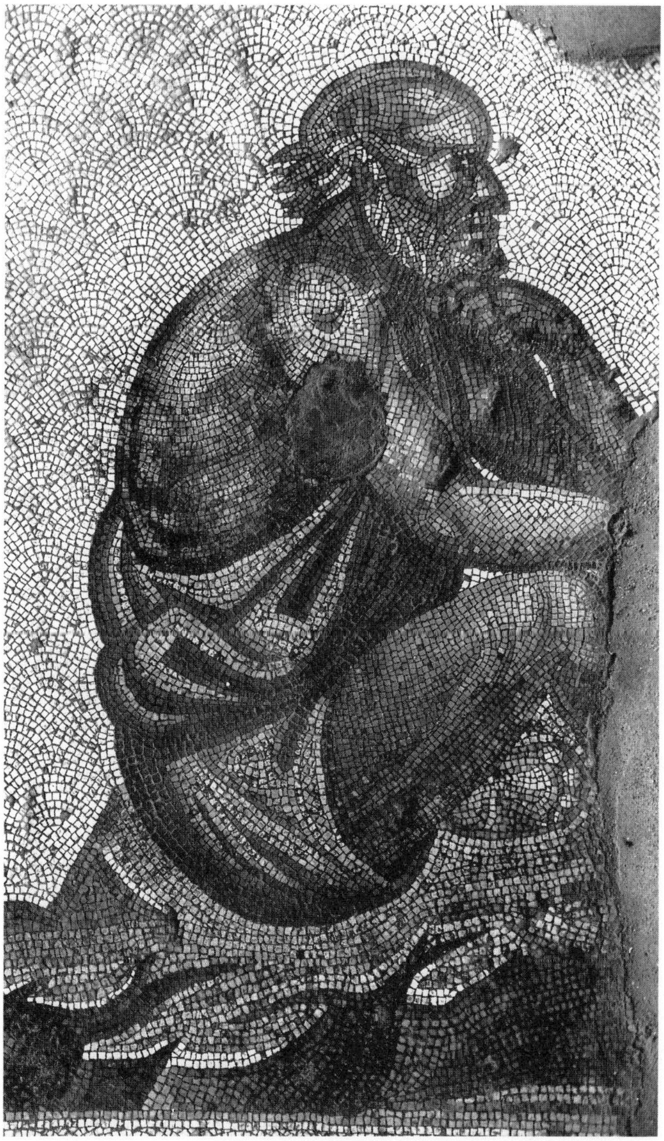

6.8 A seated "philosopher," early sixth century. Floor mosaic, Imperial Palace, Istanbul, Turkey.

decorated with jewels; (2) a long purple robe over which is worn a scarf covered with jeweled patterns; (3) a crown from which a strand of pearls is suspended on each side of the face (called a *pendulia*); (4) a scepter. More detail about Byzantine painting can be found at http://www.metmuseum.org/explore/Byzantium/byzim_37.html.

Mosaic

Covering a period of a thousand turbulent years, Byzantine art contains a complex repertoire of styles. When Constantine established his capital at Constantinople, a group of artists and craftsmen, trained in other centers, was already there. When these people set to work on Constantine's artistic projects, they naturally rendered their subjects in a manner quite different from the Roman style.

One of the earliest examples of two-dimensional art is a **mosaic** floor in the Imperial Palace of Constantinople. Mosaic was a characteristic Byzantine medium, and Figure **6.8** shows an example whose finely detailed execution allows for an essentially naturalistic style. The mosaics depict figures, buildings, and scenes, unconnected with each other, presented against a white background. The grandeur and elegance of these works reveal Greek classical influence. Although the figures are fairly naturalistic, the absence of background and shadow indicates that pictorial reality was neither intended nor important. Rather, each figure has a mystical, abstract feel that is clearly unclassical.

Manuscript Illumination

In addition to the mosaics that decorated palaces and the wealthier churches, manuscript **illumination** and wall painting were also important in Byzantine art. From the period immediately after the iconoclastic controversy come exquisite manuscript illuminations. The rich colors are handled with masterful control and delicacy, to give assured shading and elegant detail.

The scenes shown in Figures **6.9** and **6.10** tell stories. *The Vision of Ezekiel* treats the story from the Old Testament in four separate panels. Continuity is established by some part of each scene (except the last) breaking through its border into the neutral space between the panels. In the upper right corner, one picture actually breaks into the adjoining scene. Figure **6.10** unfolds its narrative in two registers, depicting the New Testament stories of Jesus raising Lazarus from the dead, and of his entry into Jerusalem shortly afterward. The technique is called "continuous narration," with the episodes laid out across the top, and then continuing in the bottom register. There is much in these works that is classically derived, and yet the treatment of space, with its crowded figures, its concentration on the surface plane, and lack of rational linear perspective, is entirely Byzantine.

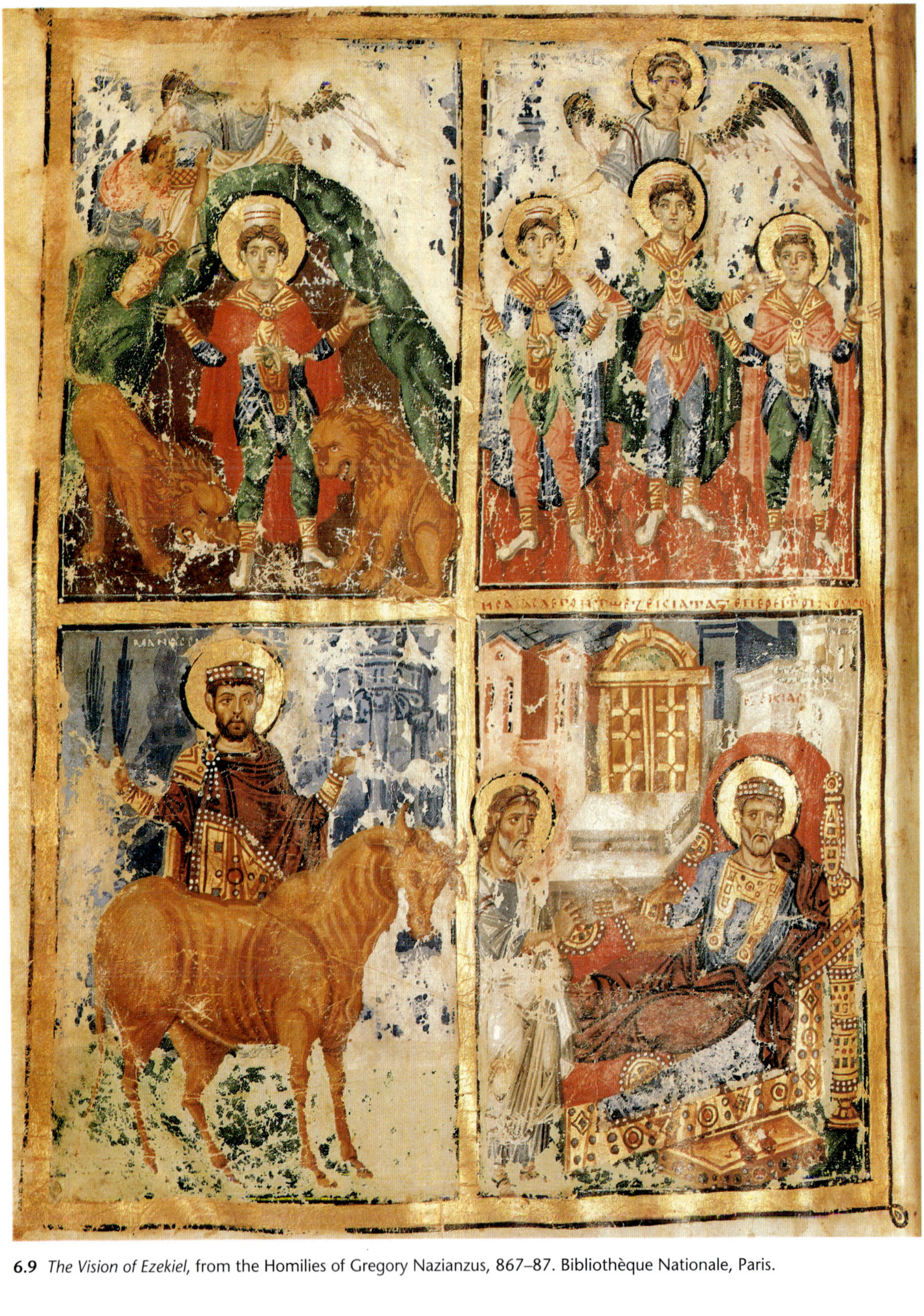

6.9 *The Vision of Ezekiel*, from the Homilies of Gregory Nazianzus, 867–87. Bibliothèque Nationale, Paris.

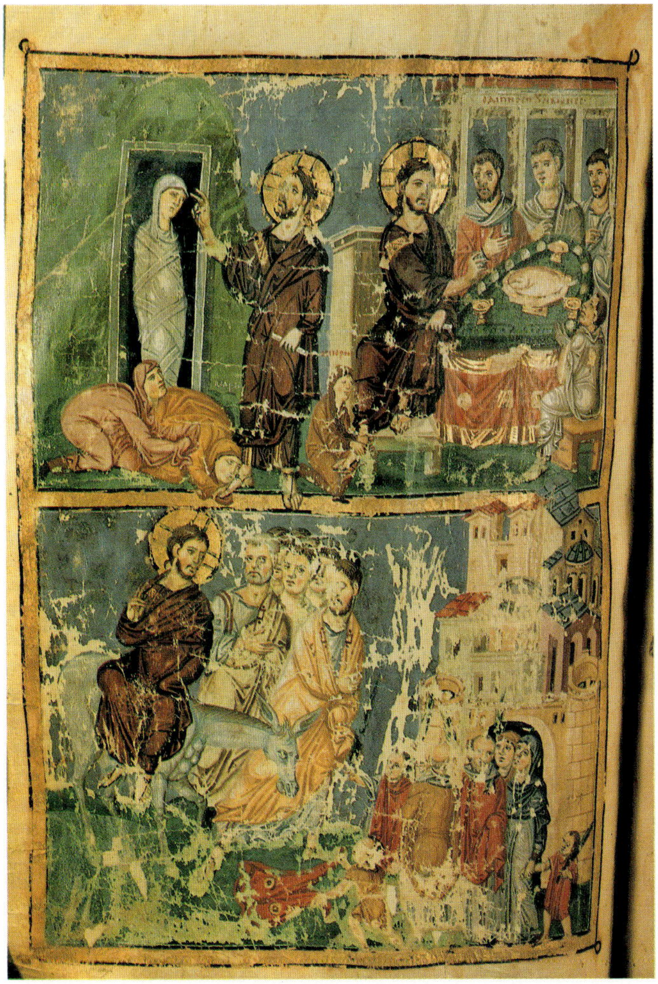

6.10 *The Raising of Lazarus and the Entry into Jerusalem*, from the Homilies of Gregory Nazianzus, 867–86. 16⅛ × 12 ins (41 × 30.5 cm). Bibliothèque Nationale, Paris.

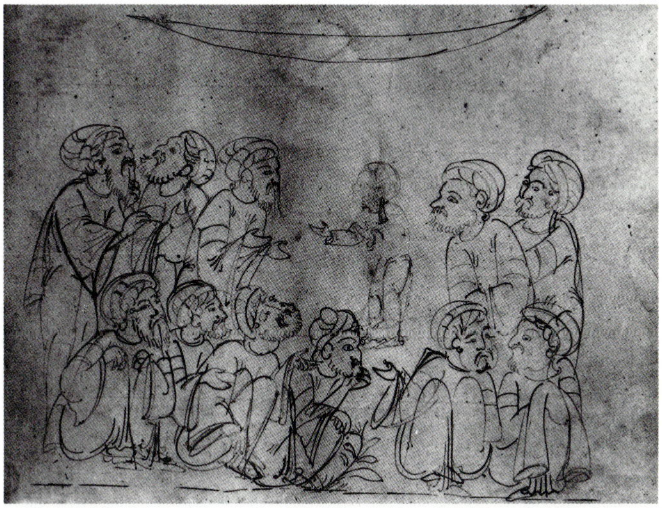

6.11 Al-Qasim ibn 'Ali al-Hariri, *Maqamat al-Hariri* (a book of stories), 1323. Mesopotamian manuscript, Oriental Collection, British Library, London.

Islam

Theoretically, all human and animal figures are prohibited from Islamic art, but in reality, images are widespread: the only prohibition seems to have been on those objects intended for public display. In the courts of the caliphs, for example, images of living things were commonplace. They were considered harmless if they did not cast a shadow, were small in scale, or appeared on everyday objects.

A continuity of visual art seems to have occurred during the early years of Islam through the illustration of scientific texts. The Arabs obtained manuscripts from Byzantium, and were tremendously interested in Greek science. The result was a plethora of texts translated into Arabic. Illustrations from original Greek works also were copied. Typical of the illustration drawn in Arab manuscripts is a pen-and-ink sketch, perhaps from a Mesopotamian manuscript of the fourteenth century (Fig. **6.11**). The drawing has a clear presentation, with many of the strokes seeming to act as accents. The lines flow freely in subtle curvilinear movements to establish a comfortable rhythm across the page. In very simple line, the artist is able to capture human character, thus showing a strong observational ability. The witty flavor of the drawing goes far beyond mere illustration.

Even before Islam, Arab traders had penetrated the Far East, and as a result Chinese influence can be seen throughout the Middle East. This is particularly true in the emergence of religious subjects for visual art. The Mongol rulers were very familiar with the Buddhist tradition in Chinese art, and brought that interest to Islamic art—ignoring their predecessors' reluctance to pictorialize Muhammad. Thus, in the fourteenth century painting that depicted narratives about Muhammad became quite common. Chinese influences are strongly at work in an Islamic manuscript illustration from sixteenth-century Persia. *The Ascension of Muhammad* (Fig. **6.12**) tells the story from the Koran, in which Muhammad ascends into Paradise after "a journey by night . . . to the remote place of worship." The reference in the Koran was later expanded upon: Muhammad ascended from Jerusalem under the guidance of the Angel Gabriel, rising through seven heavens and meeting Adam, Abraham, Moses, and Jesus before coming into the presence of God.

The images in the painting are fascinating. Muhammad rides a curiously oriental centaur—a mythological beast with a horse's body and the head of a man. The surrounding angels have oriental faces, and the composition seems to divide along the diagonal axis—also similar to some oriental works. The crescent-shaped

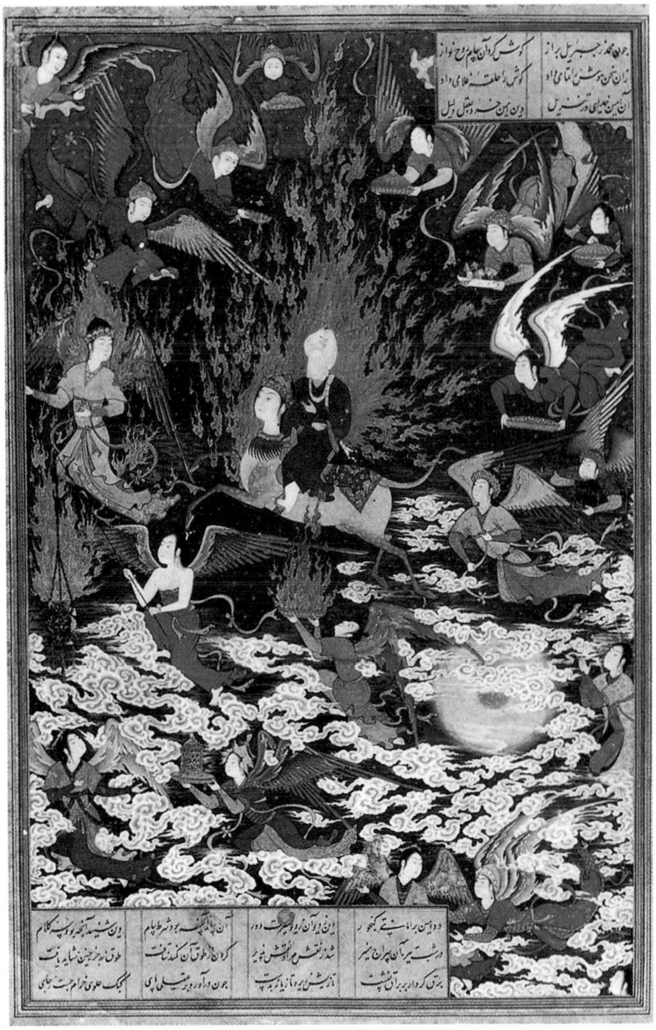

6.12 Unknown illustrator, *The Ascension of Muhammad*, 1539–43. Persian manuscript. Oriental Collection, British Library, London.

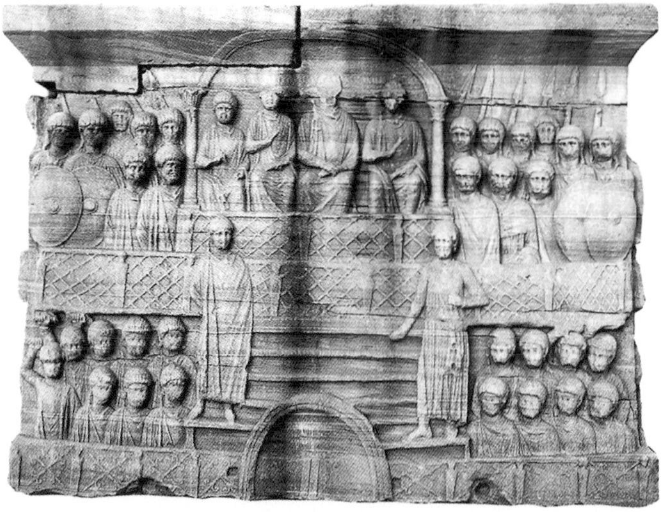

6.13 Base of the Theodosian obelisk, c. 395. Marble, about 13 ft 11 ins (4.2 m) high. Hippodrome, Istanbul, Turkey.

figures appear to swirl in an elliptical path around Muhammad, and the artist shows a sophisticated color composition by carrying the predominant colors of one section into another section—for example, the white of the clouds carries into the upper parts of the painting in small details of trim and in the lighter flesh tones; reds that provide an encircling motif in the upper portion are carried into the lower section, where they accent rather than dominate.

Sculpture

Sculpture developed in the same historical context as the two-dimensional arts. Early works include sculptural vignettes illustrating Old and New Testament themes of salvation and life after death. For two centuries or so, the old art of Roman portrait sculpture held sway. But by the end of the fourth century, styles had begun to change. In Figure **6.13**, the base of an **obelisk** set up by Theodosius I, the frontal poses of figures, the ranks in which they are grouped, and the large, accentuated heads reflect oriental influence. Oriental and classically inspired works existed alongside each other in this period. Large-scale sculpture virtually disappeared from Byzantine art after the fifth century. Small-scale reliefs in ivory and metal continued in abundance, however. The clear-cut, precise style of Greek carving later became an outstanding characteristic of Byzantine sculpture. As in painting, sculpture took a classical turn after the iconoclastic struggle, but with an added awareness of the spiritual side of human beauty.

Ivory, traditionally a precious material, was always very popular in Byzantium. The number of carved works in different styles provides evidence of the various influences and degrees of technical ability in the Eastern Empire. Many of the ivories are **diptychs** (DIP-tiks), that is, in two panels. The *Barberini Ivory* (bahr-bair-EE-nee; Fig. **6.15**) is a work of five separate pieces, one of which is missing. At the center, an emperor is depicted on horseback. To the side is a consul in military costume, and above is a bust of Christ with winged victories on either side. The long panel at the bottom depicts Gothic emissaries on the left side and emissaries from India on the right; interestingly, the latter are portrayed carrying elephant tusks—the source of the artist's material. The rounded features and brilliant high-relief technique are typical of the period. The portrait of the emperor is individualized and recognizable. Later ivories show a more delicate elegance and a highly finished style.

The only known Byzantine freestanding sculpture in ivory is the tenth-century *Virgin and Child* (Fig. **6.16**). The drapery falls exquisitely and the surface is highly

MASTERWORK

THE *HARBAVILLE TRIPTYCH*

The tenth and eleventh centuries have left us the greatest number of ivory objects, many decorated with small, elegant reliefs. In secular art, ivory caskets covered with minute carvings were the most popular form. Byzantine ivory carvers of the time showed remarkable ease and skill in imitating classical models. The same technique was used for small-scale reliefs of religious subjects. The *Harbaville Triptych* (Fig. **6.14**) is an exquisite example.

The **triptych** was probably intended as a portable altar or shrine. The two wings folded shut for traveling, across the center panel. In the top center Christ is enthroned and flanked by John the Baptist and the Virgin Mary, who plead for mercy on behalf of all humanity. Five of the apostles appear below. The two registers of the central panel are divided by an ornament repeated, with the addition of rosettes at the bottom border, and three heads in the top border. On either side of Christ's head appear medallions depicting angels holding symbols of the sun and moon. The figures have hieratic formality and solemnity, yet the depiction exhibits a certain softness that may result from a strong classical influence.

The figures stand on a plain, flat ground, ornamented only by the lettering of their names beside the heads. The side wings contain portraits of four soldier saints and four bishop saints. Between the levels are bust-length portraits of other saints. All the saints wear the dress of various civilian dignitaries. The triptych thus aligns the powers of Church and State, within the hierarchical formula of Byzantine art: each personage has his or her own place in the divine hierarchy, with Christ at the top.

This work and others from the same period belong to a class of works known as "Romanus," after a plaque in the Bibliothèque Nationale in Paris that shows Christ crowning the Emperor Romanus IV and his empress, Eudocia. The works of this Romanus school of ivory carvers are identifiable by style but they also have a particular **iconographic** peculiarity. The cross in Christ's **nimbus**, or halo, shows the usual rectangular outline, but a pearled border has been added to both cross and nimbus. Similarly fine workmanship is found in the mosaics and painting of the time; in fact, stylistic developments in the ivories were closely associated with those in painting.

6.14 The *Harbaville Triptych*, interior, late tenth century. Ivory, 9½ ins (24.2 cm) high, central panel 5⅝ ins (14.2 cm) wide. Louvre, Paris.

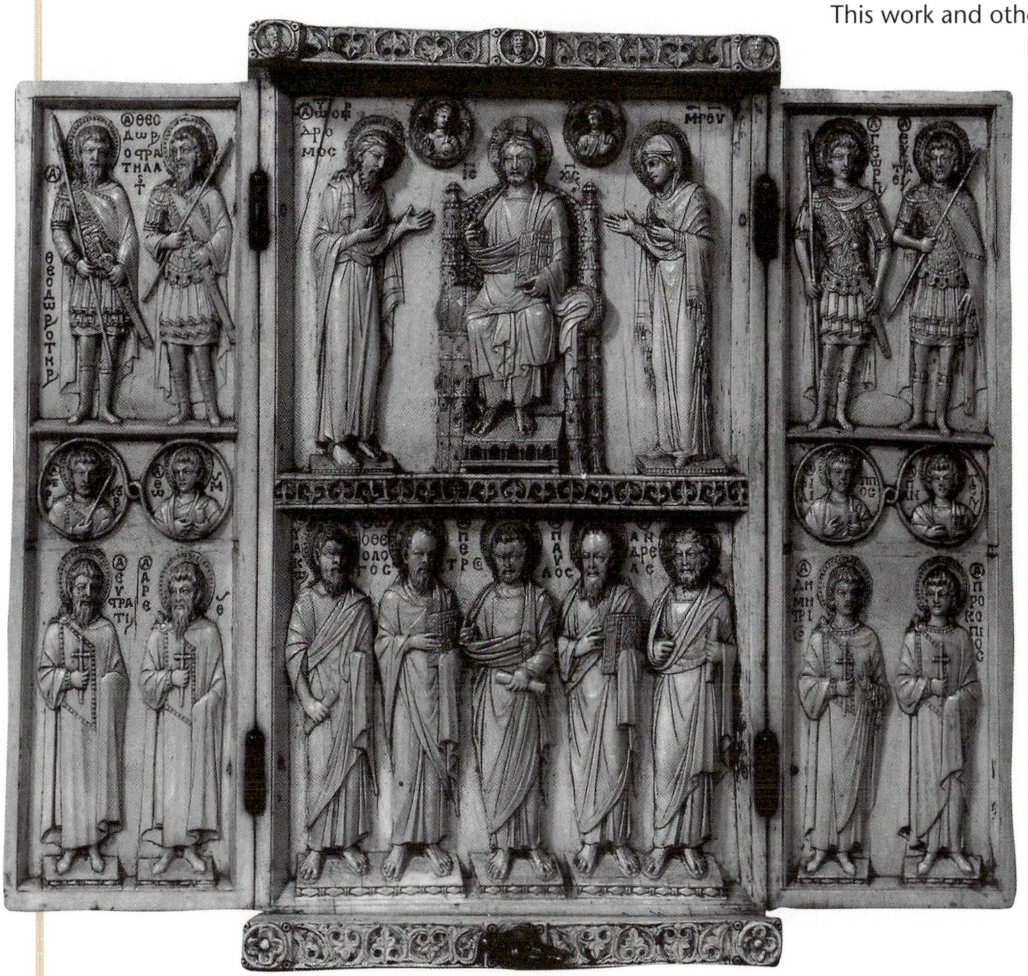

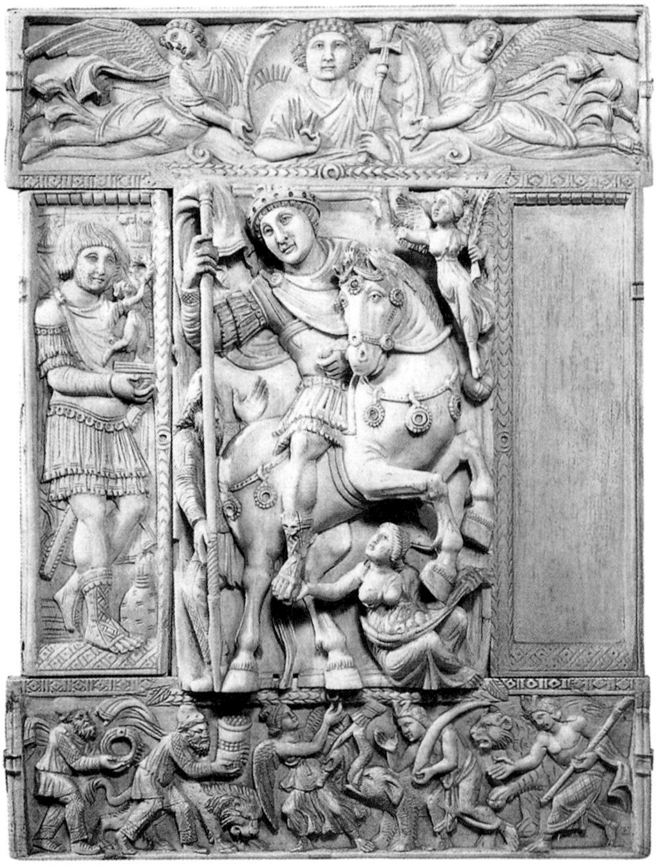

6.15 *Barberini Ivory,* showing a mounted emperor, c. 500. Ivory, 13½ × 10½ ins (34.1 × 26.6 cm). Louvre, Paris.

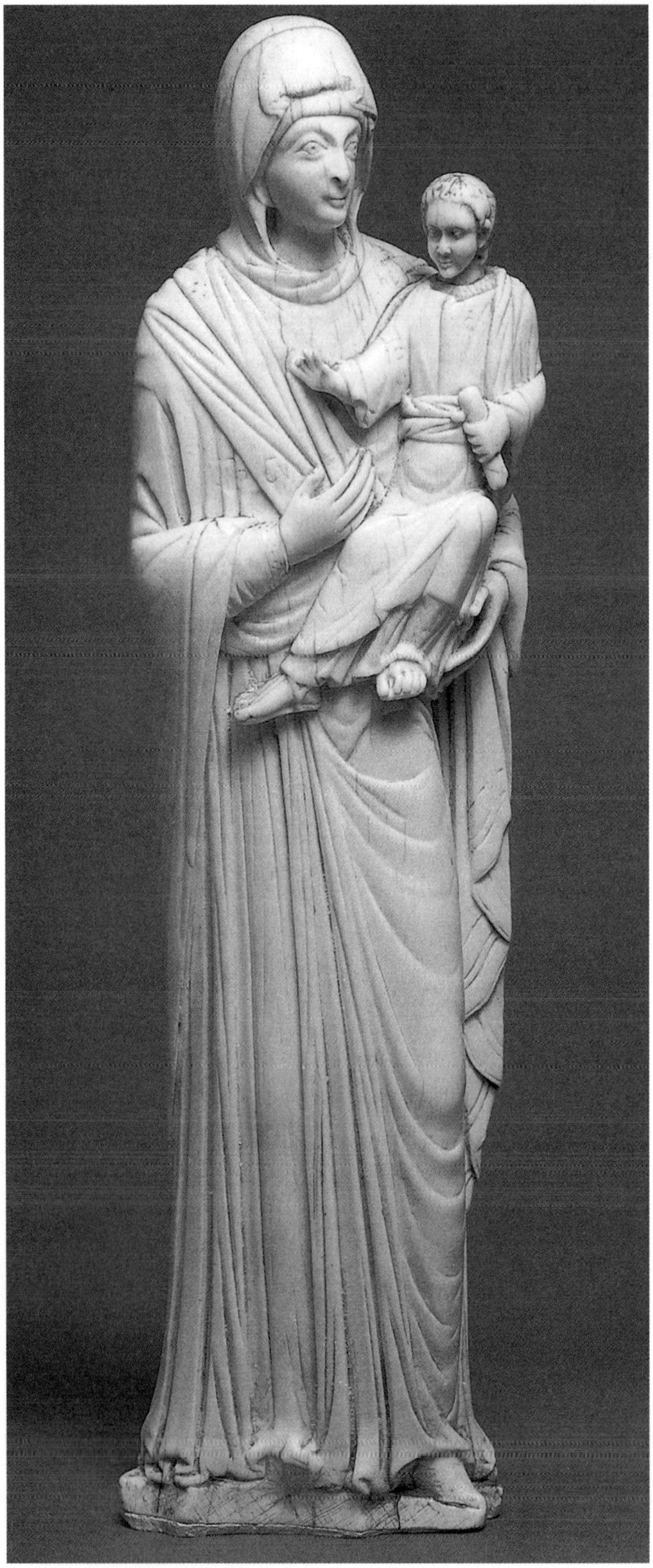

6.16 *Virgin and Child,* tenth century. Ivory, 12⅞ ins (32.5 cm) high. Victoria & Albert Museum, London.

finished. The facial features, hands, and torsos display characteristic hieratic elongation.

Architecture

Byzantium

The architecture of the early years of the Eastern Empire was dominated by the personality and objectives of the Emperor Justinian. It was an age in which royal patronage encouraged artistry, but the arts clearly reflected the source of that encouragement. Justinian's purpose was to glorify Justinian, and, in a remarkably creative way, the arts and architecture of the age succeeded in doing just that. The results of his efforts can be seen both in the West (see Figs **6.7** and **6.31**) and in the East (see Figs **6.29**, **6.32–6.35**).

After Justinian's death, the construction of public churches all but ceased. The palace was the only important building project. Yet the churches that were built at this time became models for later Byzantine architecture. The general form of these early churches, such as that of St Clement in Ankara, consists of a central dome and a group of three **apses** at the east end (Fig.

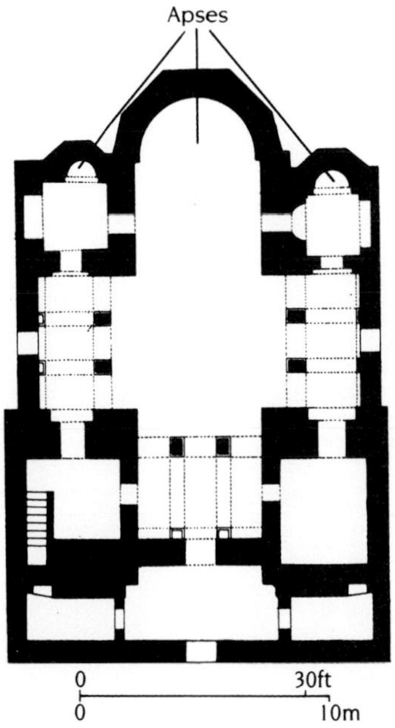

6.17 (*above*) Ground plan of the church of St Clement, Ankara.

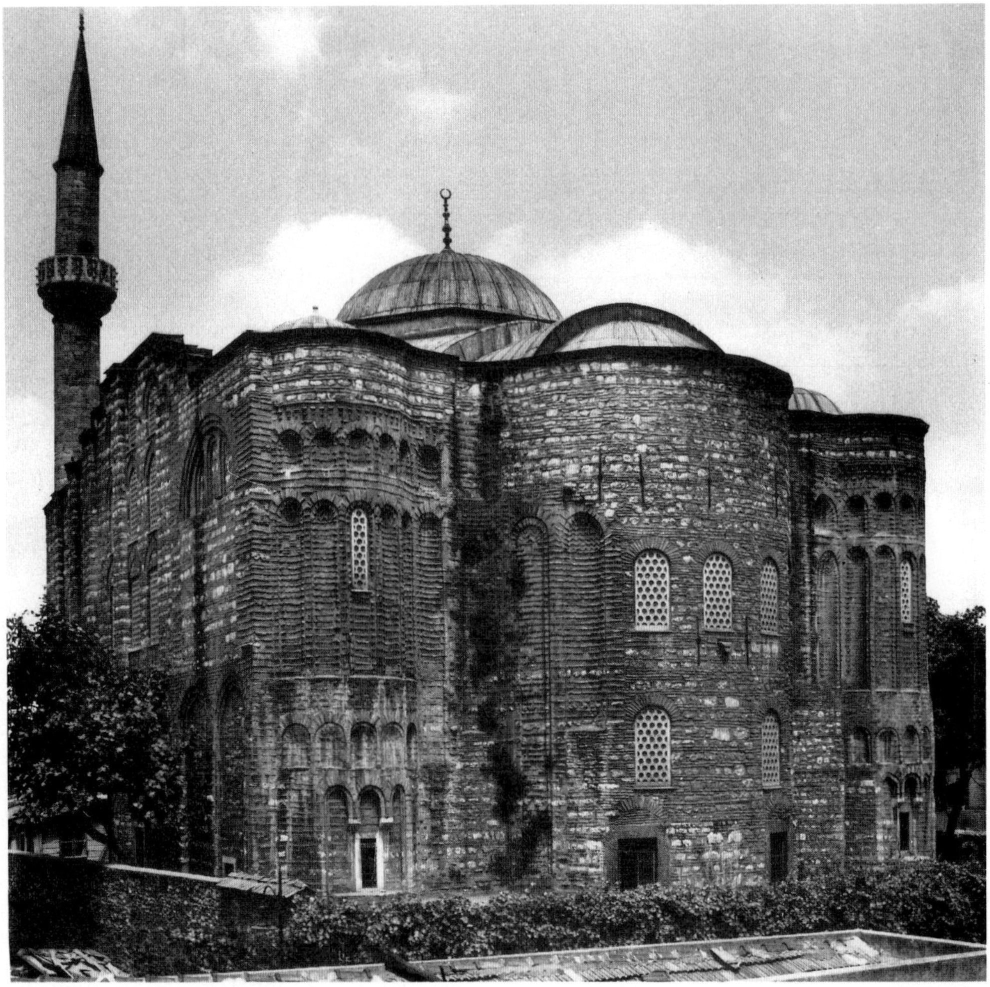

6.18 St Theodosia, Istanbul, Turkey, c. 1000.

6.17). The entire space describes a cross-in-square layout, which, again, can be seen in later churches. The cross-in-square is outlined on the ground plan: look outward from the center to the end of each of the transverse arms, the lower arm of the nave, and the upper arm just to the edge of the circular apse at top center.

The churches constructed in the two or three centuries after St Clement's employed the classical principles of harmony among their parts, and composition to express human aspirations (Fig. **6.18**). The three apses just described point toward the viewer, and the dome above the central pavilion is visible at the top. The church's vertical striving and precise symmetry give it an elegant solidity. Delicate, arched **niches** and grilled windows tend to counter the heaviness of the walls.

As Byzantine power waned, the vigor and scale of new church construction reduced. The ground plans became smaller, and in partial compensation, height was increased. Greater emphasis was also placed on the appearance of the exterior, with decorative surface treatment of the brickwork or masonry of the walls (Figs **6.19** and **6.20**). Another characteristic of later church building was the addition of churches or chapels to existing ones, creating very different forms from the organized massing of the single-domed church. The elaborate detail and frequent changes of plane that these additions created give us a fascinating surface with which to interreact, as the churches of St Luke and the Virgin illustrate (Fig. **6.19**). Here, verticality or upward striving line is much less apparent—the strength of horizontal elements and the shorter apses give the impression that the building is much more squat.

The interiors of these churches are elegant, jewel-like, sumptuous, glowing with color, and heavily decorated. They are reached through **narthexes**, and sometimes side porches, that create a spatial and visual transition from the outside world to the interior. The spaces of the church flow smoothly from one to another and are carefully designed to meet liturgical needs. A deep, vaulted sanctuary and apse house the altar. Chambers adjoin the apse on either side. Just beyond the eastern columns, a screen painted with icons stands across the sanctuary. The entire effect of the mosaic-covered vaults, elaborate ecclesiastical vestments, chants, ancient rites, and incense sought to create for the worshipper the spiritual and physical sense of another world.

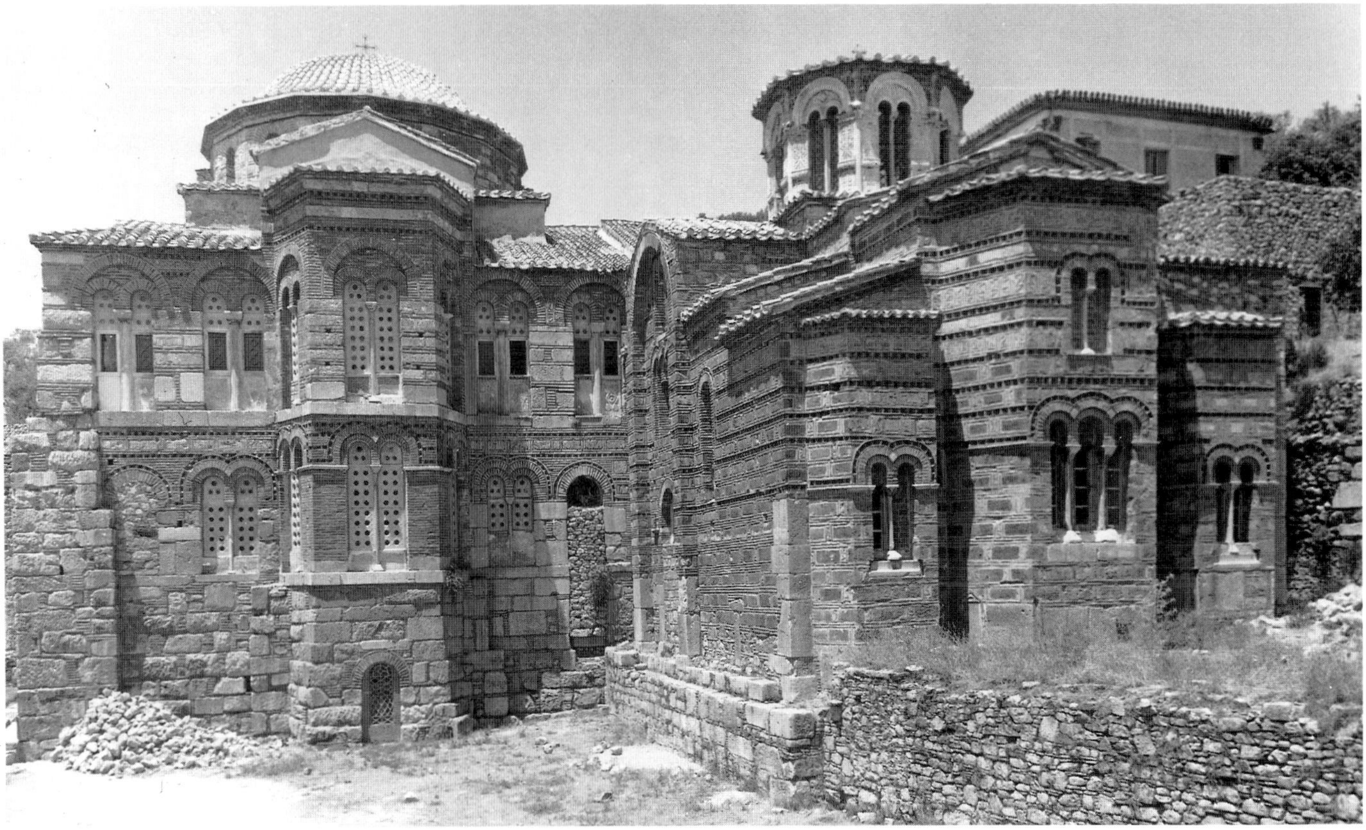

6.19 Churches of St Luke and the Virgin, Stiris, Turkey, eleventh century.

6.20 St Mary Pammakaristos, Istanbul, Turkey, thirteenth century.

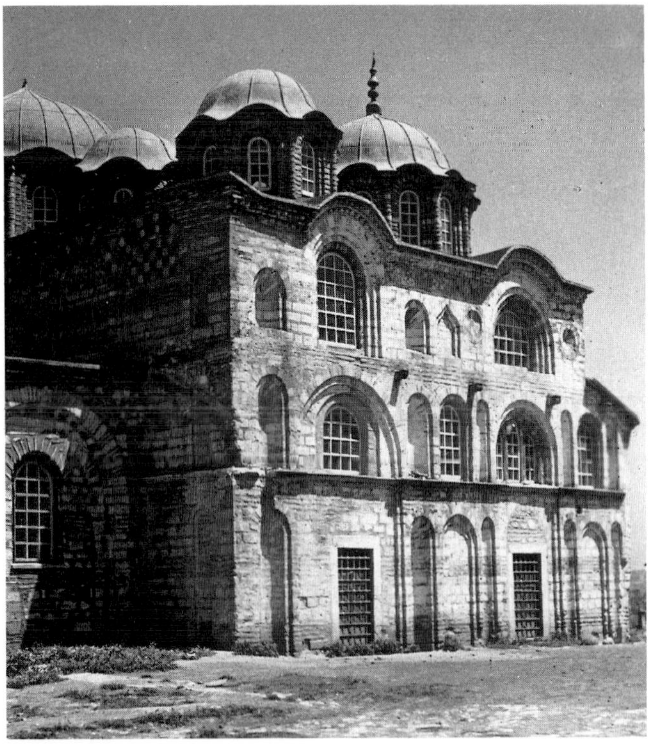

Islam

The first major example of Islamic architecture did not appear until 691 C.E., when work began on the Dome of the Rock in Jerusalem (Fig. **6.21**). Built near the site of the Temple of Solomon, it was begun by Islamic emperors who were direct descendants of the Prophet's companions. Shaped as an octagon, it was designed as a special holy place—not an ordinary mosque. Inside, it contains two concentric ambulatories, walkways, surrounding a central space capped by the dome. The mosque sits on a site revered by Jews as the tomb of Adam and the place where Abraham prepared to sacrifice Isaac. According to Muslim tradition, it is also the place from which Muhammad ascended into heaven. Written accounts suggest that it was built to overshadow a sacred temple of similar construction on the other side of Jerusalem—the Holy Sepulchre. Caliph Abd al-Malik (AHB-uhd al-mah-leek) wanted a monument that would outshine the Christian churches of the area, and, perhaps, the Kaaba in Mecca. The exterior was later decorated with the glazed blue tiles that give the façade its dazzling appearance; the inside glitters with gold, glass, and mother-of-pearl, in multicolored mosaics. A detail of the richly intricate mosaics of the Dome of the Rock in Jerusalem can be seen in Figure **6.22**. This symmetrical

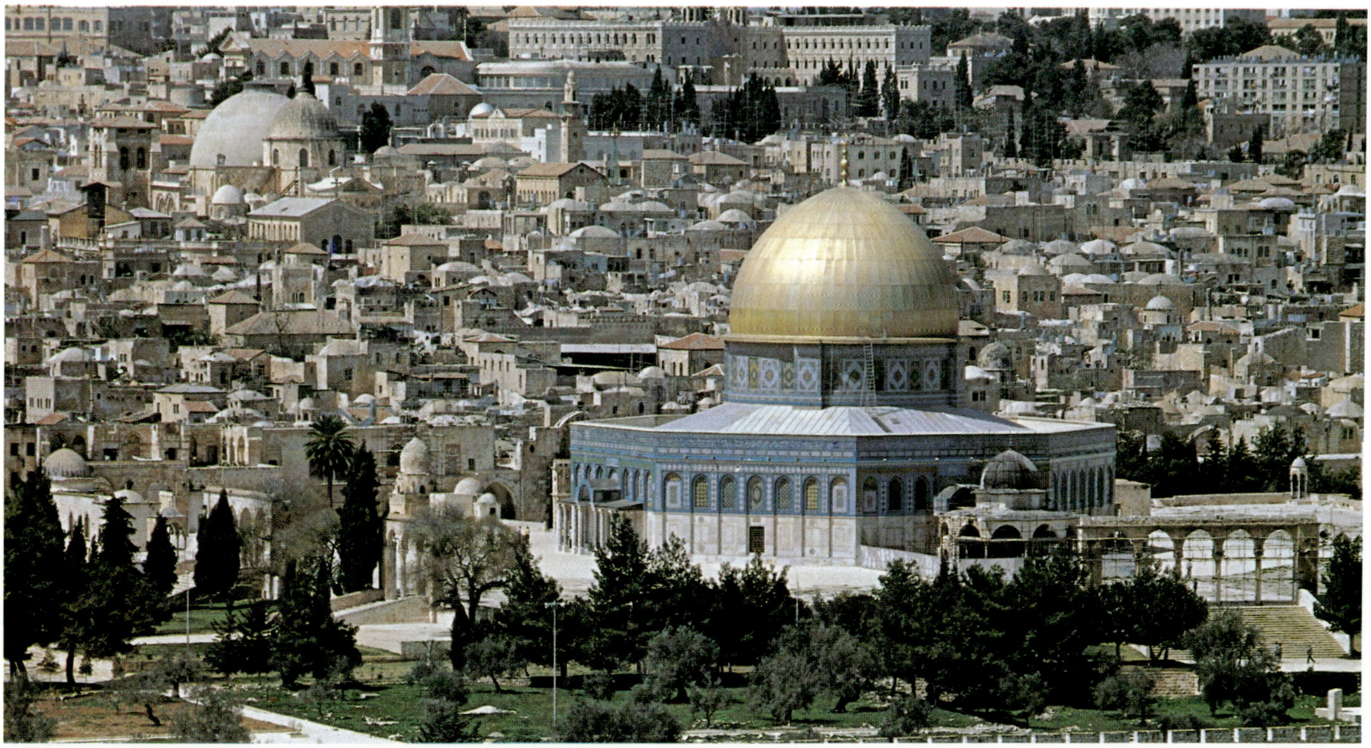

6.21 Dome of the Rock, Jerusalem, late seventh century.

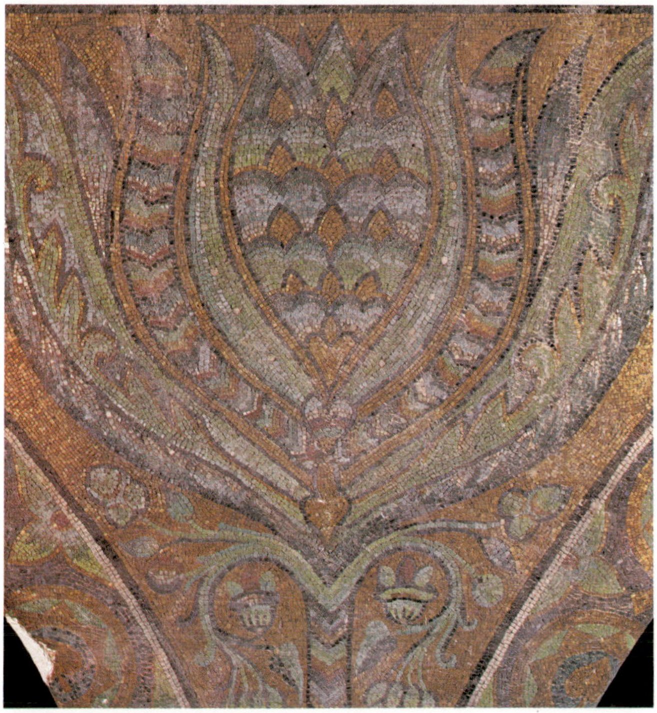

6.22 Details of mosaic decoration, Dome of the Rock, Jerusalem, Israel, 691–2.

pattern in deep red and gold, highlighted with accents of white and purple, illustrates the skill and delicacy that Muslim artists brought to this form. Undoubtedly, the Dome of the Rock was intended to speak to Christians as well as Muslims, distracting the former from the splendor of Christian churches. Inside the mosque is an inscription: "The Messiah Jesus Son of Mary is only an apostle of God, and His Word which he conveyed into Mary, and a Spirit proceeding from Him. Believe therefore in God and his apostles and say not 'Three.' It will be better for you. God is only one God. Far be it from his glory that He should have a son."

Another excellent example of Islamic architecture is the Great Mosque of Damascus (Fig. **6.23**). When the Muslims captured Damascus in 635, they adapted the precinct of a pagan temple, which had been converted into a Christian church, into an open-air mosque. Seventy years later, al-Walid demolished the church and set about building the largest mosque in Islam. The only feature of the original buildings left standing was the Roman wall, although the four original towers were metamorphosed into the first minarets, from which the faithful were called to prayer. Unfortunately, the centuries have not been kind to the Great Mosque. Sacked a number of times, much of the splendor of its lavish decorations has been lost. However, some of its grandeur can be seen in the arcaded courtyard, with fine, gold-inlaid detailing visible in the returns of the arches (Fig. **6.23**). Inside, colorful mosaics (Fig. **6.24**) express great subtlety of detail and texture. These works rank among the most accomplished of mosaics and were probably produced by Byzantine craftsmen.

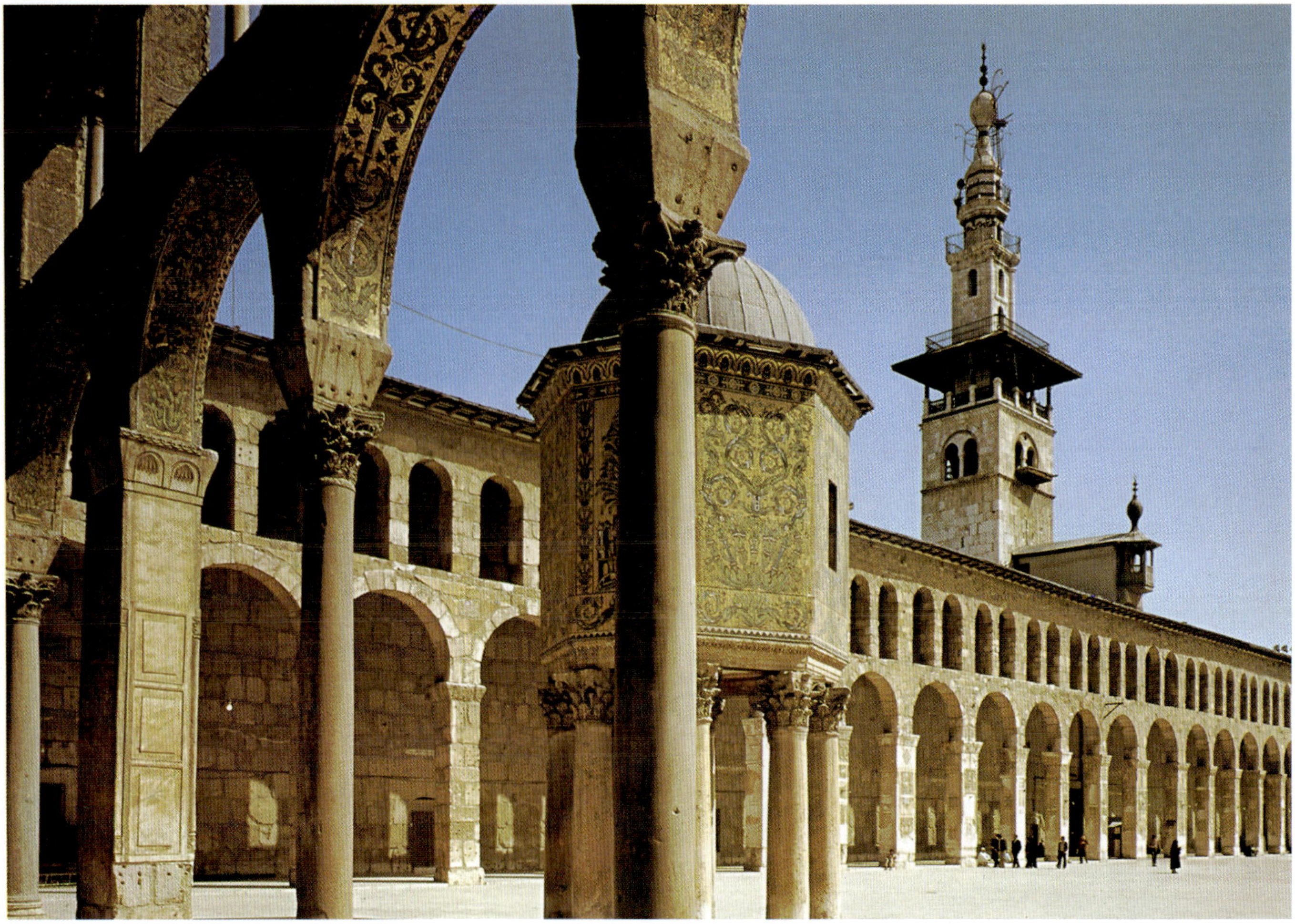

6.23 (*above*) Great Mosque, Damascus, Syria. Courtyard looking west, c. 715.

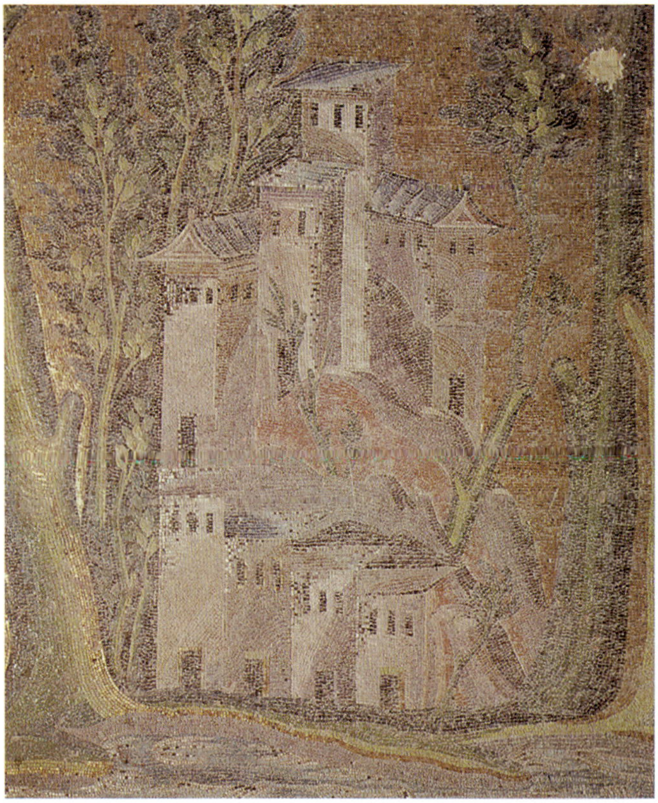

6.24 (*right*) Details of mosaic decoration, Great Mosque, Damascus, c. 715.

Theatre, Music, and Dance

The Byzantines were undoubtedly familiar with theatre. Ruins of Hellenistic theatres have been found throughout the Eastern Empire. Justinian's wife, Theodora, was an actress, and theatrical spectacles surrounded the life of the Imperial court. There are references to an exodus of actors and playwrights from Byzantium at the time of the Turkish conquest.

But what of theatre itself? The period between the fall of Rome and the late Middle Ages witnessed the virtual extinction of theatre in both East and West, except in its most rudimentary form. The Byzantine preference for artistic anonymity might account for the absence of dramas, and the literature of Byzantium certainly excluded drama from its priorities. In a society dominated by the Christian Church, the kind of debased spectacles popular in the late years of the Roman Empire were undoubtedly frowned upon. Such was the moral tone of

A DYNAMIC WORLD

CHINESE THEATRE

At the time that East was separating from West in Rome, Confucius put to death an entire troupe of actors who took part in a play that violated his teaching.

Chinese drama forbade women on stage. All female roles in Chinese theatre were played by men, who mimicked the teetering style of walking that resulted from the practice of footbinding among the upper classes, and utilized a device called *tsai jiao* (tsy-jow) to keep the actor "on point"—in the balletic sense—throughout the performance.

Costume and makeup played a significant and symbolic role in Chinese theatre. Color, especially, portrayed emotion and social standing. Chinese theatrical costume, like its scenery, did not attempt to depict historical accuracy. Styles and periods mixed freely so as to create dramatic effect and reinforce nuances. Like the American movie genre the Western, in which the "good guys" wore white hats, and the "bad guys" black ones, in Chinese theatre, the good guys wore square hats, and the bad guys, round ones.

6.25 Chinese theatre performance in progress.

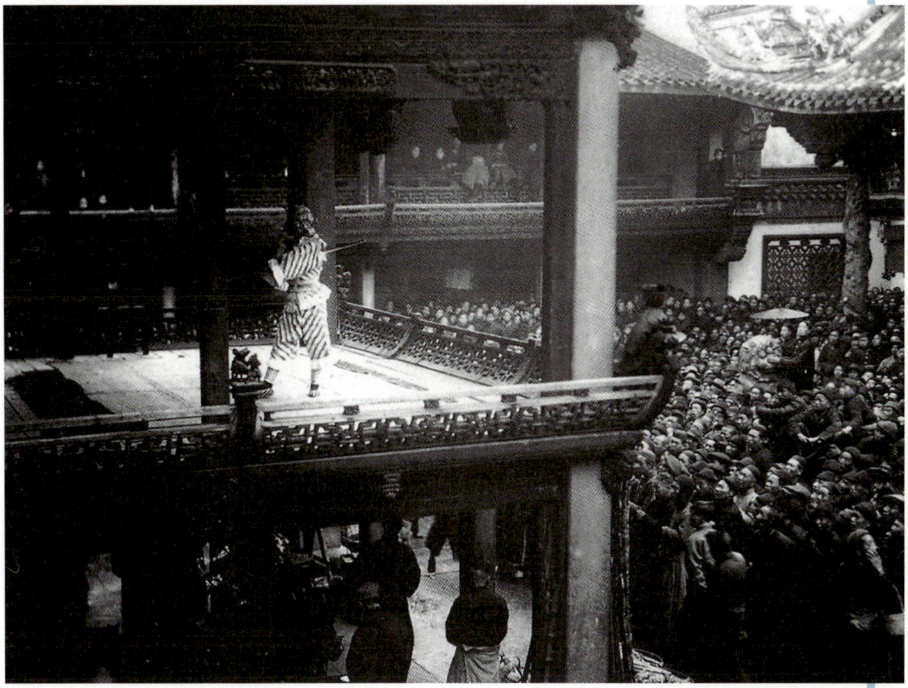

the time that senators were barred by law from marrying actresses: Justinian had to change this law in order to marry Theodora. We hear of professional actors in Byzantium as late as the seventh century, but after that formal theatre performances seem to have disappeared. As one commentator puts it, "In the East problems more serious soon set people thinking of things sterner than merry supper-parties with groups of dancing girls."[2]

Throughout the Middle Ages, critical remarks to the effect that it was "better to please God than the actors" suggest that some form of performance art continued, however, and it is not unlikely that this was also the case in Byzantium. Mime, and some form of pantomime, were probably the only forms of theatrical activity.

Before reaching Europe, the Christian Church spread throughout Asia Minor, accumulating musical elements on its way. Byzantium appears to have acquired much of its musical heritage from the monasteries and churches of Syria, where the development of antiphonal psalmody and the use of hymns originated. Clear evidence of hymn singing can be found in the New Testament, both in the Gospels and in the letters of Paul and James, and in the writings of Pliny the Younger in Bithynia and Asia Minor in the second century. Some early Christian hymns were probably sung to folk melodies. Thus there seem to have been both Eastern and Greek influences on early Christian music.

Although no music manuscripts survive from this period, the strong traditions of the Greek Orthodox, Russian, and other Eastern Churches still preserve what must be a flavor of the Byzantine chants that served as their models. Based on Syrian melodies and incorporating short responses between verses of the psalms, an independent hymnody gradually developed. Byzantine hymns had an elaborate structure, which stood in contrast to the simple hymns of the Western Church.

One type, developed in the eighth to tenth centuries, was based on sixth-century hymns and was called *kanones* (kuh-NAHN-ehs). Its texts were commentaries based on passages from the Bible. Its melodies, also not entirely original, were constructed on a principle common to Eastern music but were unfamiliar in the West. Rather than building a new melody from the tones in a scale, Eastern singers constructed melody out of a series of short given motifs, which they chose and combined. Some motifs were designed for beginnings, some for middles, some for endings, and some for links. There were also standard ornamental formulas, and originality in performance depended on the combination, variation, and ornamentation of the motifs. Byzantine music had eight forms, or *echoi* (EHK-oy). These *echoi* played a fundamental part in the development of Western music. Our knowledge of them is limited, however, by the fact that in the Byzantine Church music was passed on by oral tradition for centuries before being written down.

Undoubtedly Eastern music had a contemplative, even mystical, character and a degree of complexity that was quite in keeping with the character of Eastern thought.

References to dance occur from time to time throughout this period. Whether we should consider Byzantine dance as an artistic form is problematical, however. Two situations, at least, in which dance occurred are known. Some form of dancing apparently took place as part of religious services, but we do not know any details of its content or purpose. A second form of dancing provided entertainment. This was probably a vestige of the Roman pantomime (see p. 134), in which case it would have exhibited subtlety of movement and expression. Pantomime was mounted throughout the Byzantine Empire, either as solo performances at fairs and village festivals or using small traveling bands.

Literature

Byzantium

The literature of Byzantium is often thought of as Greek literature. That is true of the majority of Byzantine literary works, and certainly of the literature coming out of Constantinople. But the Eastern Empire of Byzantium was not confined to Constantinople. The literature of the Empire in fact includes works in Latin, Syriac, Coptic, Church Slavonic, Armenian, and Georgian.

Byzantine literature in Greek, however, does comprise a vast quantity of works. Much from the early period has unfortunately been lost, and much remains unpublished, in manuscript form. Most of Greek Byzantine literature is on religious subjects, and much of it is hagiographic—that is, covering the life stories of saints and other religious figures. In addition, there are sermons, liturgical books, poetry, theology, devotional works, scriptural commentaries, and so on. Of the thousands of volumes that have survived, only a few hundred are secular.

To understand Byzantine literature, we need to know something about Byzantine aesthetic taste, which was quite different from our own. Modern readers do not obtain much pleasure from Byzantine literature, because we expect to find quite different qualities in what we read: we like originality of thought and expression. Educated Byzantines did not wish to be surprised. They liked clichés. Where we value clarity and directness, they admired elaboration and verbiage.

The Greek language itself had gone through several stages: an epic stage (the language of Homer and Hesiod); a literary stage (the Attic of the fifth and fourth centuries B.C.E.), and a New Testament Greek stage, which Byzantine scholars considered decadent. Sensitive to the rhetorical excesses of the past, churchmen admired only humble Byzantine speech and rejected "the fine style of the Hellenes," which they compared "to the proverbial honey that drips from the mouth of a whore." They would have considered that using the epic meters of the past was "an insult to Christ and the apostles."[3] As a result, each generation of Byzantine authors resisted the influence of its predecessors, going directly to ancient models. Many Byzantine works, therefore, exist in a sort of stylistic vacuum, without an acknowledged author, without contemporary references, and without place.

Byzantine literature falls into three principal genres. The first is historiography. This is not the history we speak of when we refer to a chronicled record of events, which was a separate activity in Byzantium. Historiography is, rather, a specific literary genre, related to rhetoric. It is written in ancient Greek, in imitation of ancient models, and interprets events and their influence on each other. As Theophanes Continuatus wrote: "The body of history is indeed mute and empty if it is deprived of the cause of actions." Probably the best-known of the Byzantine historiographers was Procopius of Caesarea. His broad, sweeping narratives, which were known for their objectivity and accuracy, were modeled on the work of the Athenian historian Thucydides.

The bulk of Byzantine literature belongs to the second genre, hagiography. Many of these texts on the lives of the saints survive, most of them written in ecclesiastical Greek. They consist of anecdotes about the saints, as well as full life-histories, which had been preserved by Egyptian monks. The anecdotal accounts were first circulated by word of mouth, then collected in books. The stories told of supernatural deeds attributed to monks, and stressed the moral precepts they followed in their lives. Principally designed to praise the behavior of its subject, a "life" usually follows a specific rhetorical format. The writer first proclaims embarrassment at undertaking a task so great; then the birthplace (if it is worthy of note) or the nation in which the subject was born is described and praised; next comes a description of the family, but only if it is glorious; then the subject's birth and any miraculous signs accompanying it, real or invented, are noted; finally, in carefully organized subdivisions, physical appearance, education, upbringing, deeds, and so on, are described. This outline, or **schema**, made it easy to develop biographies of saints about whom little was known or who may never have existed. The "lives" are interesting and readable, if somewhat predictable, and they provided heroes and heroines for the medieval world. Written in simple language, they were intended for as wide an audience as possible.

The third genre was literature written in the vernacular, or language of the common people. The earliest works of this sort, the Prodromic poems, date to the first half of the twelfth century. They are attributed to the court poet Theodore Prodromos, although they may have been written by several authors.

These poems employ a popular verse-form based on fifteen syllables and are written as complaints directed to the Emperors John II and Manuel I and other members of the Comneni family. One of the poems tells the story of a hen-pecked husband; another, the story of the father of a large family who cannot make ends meet on his small salary. These works are largely humorous, with a tendency to monotony and repetition and the coinage of bizarre words. Romances of chivalric knights, maidens, witches, and dragons in the fashion of the Western Empire were also popular. Epic poems that told heroic tales of the eastern border between Byzantium and the Arabs in the ninth and tenth centuries also found favor.

Much of Byzantine literature, however, is solemn, even somber in mood. Its writers seem most at home with themes of calamity, death, and the precariousness of human existence.

Islam

Probably the most familiar Islamic literature, aside from the Koran, is a collection of tales called *The Arabian Nights* or *The Thousand and One Nights*. These tales accumulated during the Middle Ages, and as early as the tenth century they were part of the oral traditions of Islam in the Near East. Over the years more tales were added, including a unifying device called a **framing tale**, which placed all the separate stories within a larger framework. By around 1450, the work had assumed its final form.

The framing tale recounts the story of a jealous Sultan who, convinced that all women were unfaithful, married a new wife each evening and put her to death the following morning. A new bride, Shaharazad, or Scheherazade, gained a reprieve by beginning a story on her wedding night and artfully maintaining the Sultan's curiosity. She was able to gain a reprieve for one thousand and one nights—during which she produced three male heirs—after which the Sultan abandoned his original practice. The tales capture the spirit of Islamic life, its exotic setting, and sensuality. Although no particular moral purpose underlies the stories, there is a moral code within the fantasies. The tales cover a variety of subjects and range from fact to fiction. They include stories of camel trains, desert riders, and insistent calls to prayers. They are supernatural, aristocratic, romantic, bawdy, and satiric. Read *The Arabian Nights* at http://www.belinus.co.uk/fairytales/FaerypiecesArabianNights.htm.

FOCAL POINT

In Praise of the Emperor—the Mark of Justinian

Our Focal Point material for this chapter comes from the individual who tried to reunite the Eastern and Western Empires. Like Augustus Caesar, he saw art as a way of perpetuating his image as an emperor, although a Christian one. We draw the focus by examining two great edifices, the church of San Vitale (sahn vee-TAH-lay) in Ravenna and the monumental Hagia Sophia (HAH-juh soh-FEE-uh), Church of St Sophia, in Constantinople. We have to imagine the Church of St Sophia without its four minarets. These were added after the Muslims conquered Byzantium and converted the building to a mosque. Today St Sophia is a museum, and there is no picture that can prepare you for the breathtaking nature of its scale. After nearly fifteen hundred years, its dome still represents one of the greatest engineering feats of human history. Thus, these two edifices, one in the East and one in the West—reflecting the persona of the emperor who would reunite East and West and altered by Islamic minarets—give us a closing overview of Byzantium, the crossroads of Europe and Asia, Roman Catholicism, Eastern Orthodoxy, and Islam.

The portraits of Justinian that appear in mosaics—such as that in Figure **6.7**—reveal a man who does not look like an emperor. He was of average height and build, and had dark hair and a ruddy complexion. He was clean shaven, and every portrait shows a slight smile. However, despite his unexceptional appearance, he was a brilliant thinker who possessed enormous talents. He apparently liked the role of emperor and played it to the hilt, but he seems to have been likeable, in spite of his vigor and arrogance.

San Vitale in Ravenna (Figs **6.26** and **6.27**) is the major Justinian monument in the West. It was probably

PROFILE

Anthemius of Tralles (c. sixth century)

It may seem strange to include a profile about someone like Anthemius of Tralles (an-THEE-mee-us), about whom virtually nothing is known. However, the fact that we know his name at all is a testament to the vision and profound quality of his architectural work. During this period of history, individual artists—especially architects—did not gain fame. Their work was an expression, usually religious, that glorified God, the emperor, or the Church, and individualism, as we know it, in artistic work had ceased. However, we know of Anthemius. Although Anthemius was not an architect or master mason by training, he wrote a treatise on the geometry of conical sections, had a knowledge of projective geometry, and was familiar with the mechanical inventions of Archimedes (ark-ih-MEE-deez), a Greek mathematician, physicist, and inventor who lived in the third century B.C.E.

Anthemius' lasting fame, however, came as a result of his design for what was at the time, and still remains, one of the greatest architectural accomplishments of history—the church of St Sophia in Constantinople. Commissioned by the Emperor Justinian, Anthemius designed a building that, according to Justinian's court historian, Procopius, "through the harmony of its measurements . . . is distinguished by indescribable beauty." Inasmuch as Anthemius was a mathematician, it does not surprise us to discover that he and his partner, Isidorus of Miletus (also a mathematician), based the design for St Sophia on a sphere standing upon a circle. To Anthemius, architecture was the "application of geometry to solid matter," and his designs brought to Constantinople an entirely new approach to architecture by showing an inventive structure of form that stood entirely outside the Roman tradition. Such a departure reveals a profound intellect and great courage.

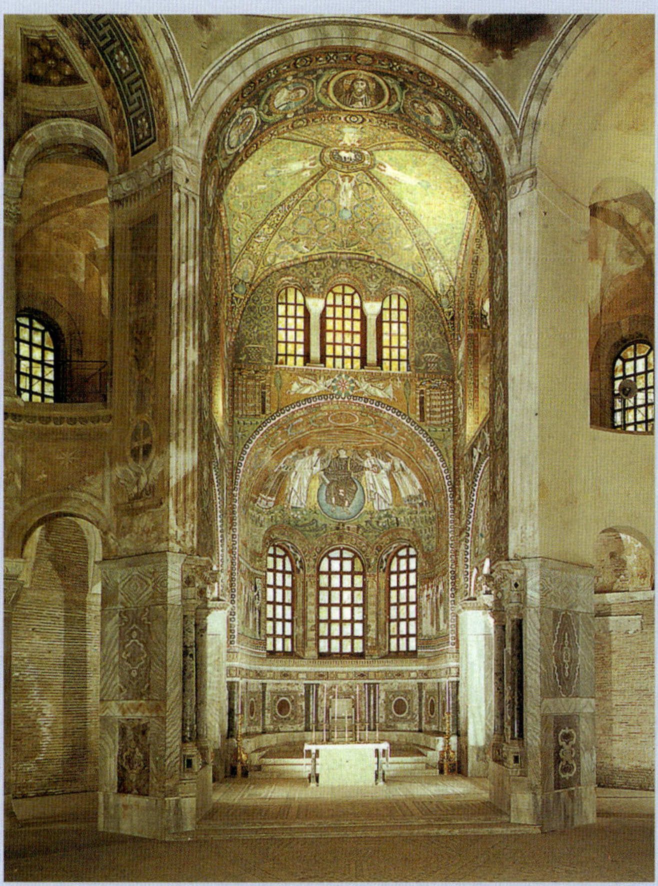

6.26 San Vitale, Ravenna, Italy, 526–47. Interior, looking east.

built as a testament to the power of Orthodoxy in the declining kingdom of the Ostrogoths.

The church consists of two concentric octagons (see Fig. 6.27). The hemispherical dome, 100 feet (30 meters) above the floor, rises from a drum above the inner octagon, which is pierced with windows that flood the interior with light. Below, eight large piers alternate with columned niches to define precisely the central space and to create an intricate, many-layered design. The narthex is placed at an odd angle. There are two possible explanations for this: the

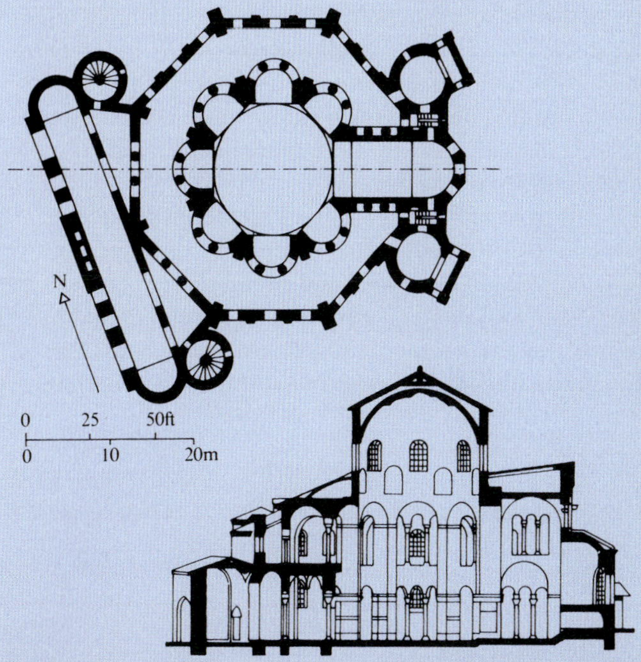

6.27 Plan and transverse section of San Vitale, Ravenna, Italy.

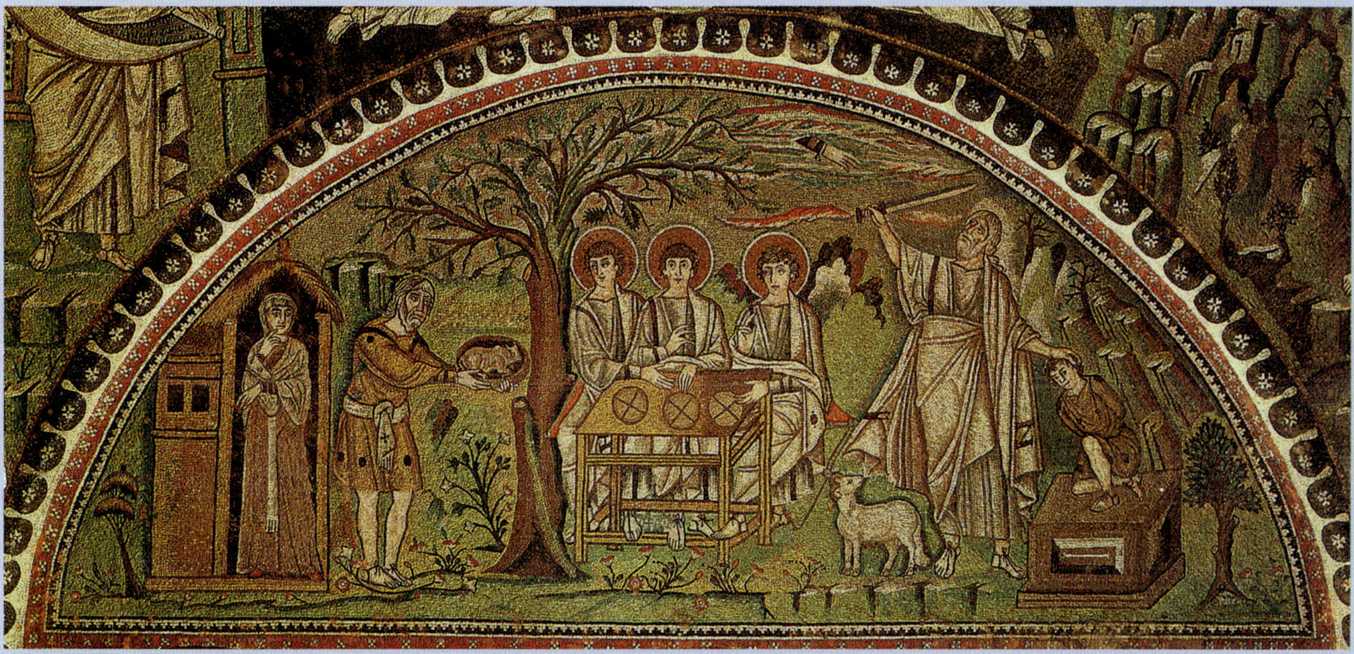

6.28 *Abraham's Hospitality and the Sacrifice of Isaac.* Wall mosaic, San Vitale, Ravenna, Italy.

practical one is that the narthex paralleled a then-existing street; a more spiritual one is that the narthex was so designed in order to force worshippers to reorient themselves on entering, thereby facilitating the transition from the outside world to the spiritual one.

On the second level of the ambulatory was a special gallery reserved for women—a standard feature of Byzantine churches.

The internal spatial design is intricate. The visitor experiences an ever-changing vista of arches within arches, linking flat walls and curved spaces. All the aisles and galleries contrast strikingly with the calm area under the dome. The clerestory light reflects off the mosaic tiles with great richness. In fact, new construction techniques in the vaulting allowed for windows on every level and opened the sanctuary to much more light than had previously been possible.

The sanctuary itself is alive with mosaics of the Imperial court and of sacred events. The difference in style between two mosaics in the same church is particularly fascinating. *Abraham's Hospitality and the Sacrifice of Isaac* (Fig. **6.28**) demonstrates what is, by Byzantine standards, a relaxed naturalism. The mosaic showing Justinian and his court (see Fig. **6.7**), on the other hand, demonstrates the orientalized style, more typically Byzantine, with the figures posed rigidly and facing forward. The mosaics clearly link the church to the Byzantine court, reflecting again the connection of the emperor to the Faith, of Christianity to the State, and, indeed, the concept of the "Divine Emperor." Justinian (see Fig. **6.7**) and Theodora (see Fig. **6.1**) are portrayed very much like Christ and the Virgin. The two mosaics face each other behind the high altar of San Vitale. In Figure **6.7** the emperor has a golden halo with a red border, he wears a regal purple robe, and he is shown presenting a golden bowl to Christ, who is pictured in the **semidome** above the mosaic (see Fig. **6.26**).

If San Vitale praises the emperor and Orthodoxy in the West, St Sophia is a crowning monument to his achievement in the East (Figs **6.29**, **6.32–6.35**). Its architect, Anthemius, was a natural scientist and geometer from Tralles in Asia Minor. St Sophia is characteristic of the Justinian Byzantine style in its use of well-rehearsed Roman vaulting techniques combined with Hellenistic principles of design and geometry. The result is a building in an orientalized, antique style.

6.29 Anthemius of Tralles and Isidorus of Miletus, St Sophia, Istanbul, Turkey, 532–7.

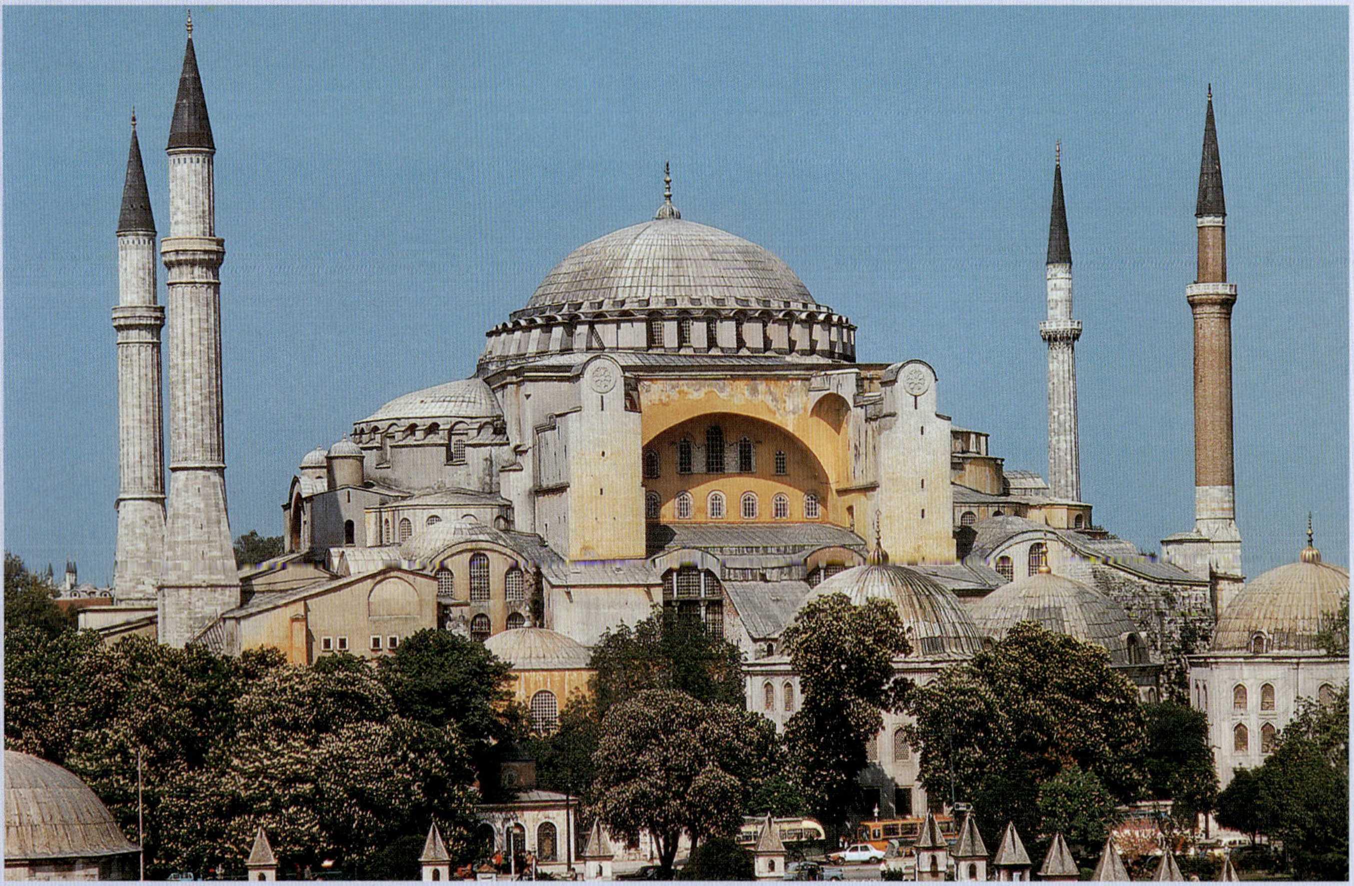

TECHNOLOGY

Spanning Space with Triangles and Pots

The ingenuity of human achievement is often revealed in the subtleties of invention that have allowed architects to create great open spaces under remarkably heavy materials such as stone and cement. We have seen this in the great dome of the Pantheon of Rome, and now we see it in what is still the largest dome ever created, St Sophia in Constantinople. It is a reminder that what was best in the West came from the uninterrupted Roman building tradition of that city. In 537, when Western Europe was at its most barbaric, Justinian's great brickwork cathedral was dedicated. What made it remarkable was the invention of a device to transfer the weight of a great dome downward—not on a cylindrical tub as in the Pantheon, but through a triangular device called a **pendentive** (pehn-DEHN-tihv; Fig. **6.30**)—to the corners of a square tower, 180 feet (55 meters) above the ground. Dedicated to the Divine Wisdom, St Sophia illustrates the sublime ingenuity of humankind.

In another of Justinian's marvels, as we have noted, Byzantine influence and technological creativity reflects itself in the church of San Vitale in Ravenna (Fig. **6.31**). Here, in order to compensate for the potentially crushing weight of a solid dome, the architect used hollow earthenware pots for construction. Thus, space was enclosed without utilizing a base so cumbersome as to ruin the aesthetic considerations of lightness and beauty. Whether in soaring domes or towers that reach 110 stories into the air, technological inventiveness has always lain at the heart of new dimensions in architecture. None has superseded the marvels of Byzantium, where, in addition to unsurpassed domes, stone was jointed with such precision that some buildings did not require mortar.

6.30 Dome with pendentives (P).

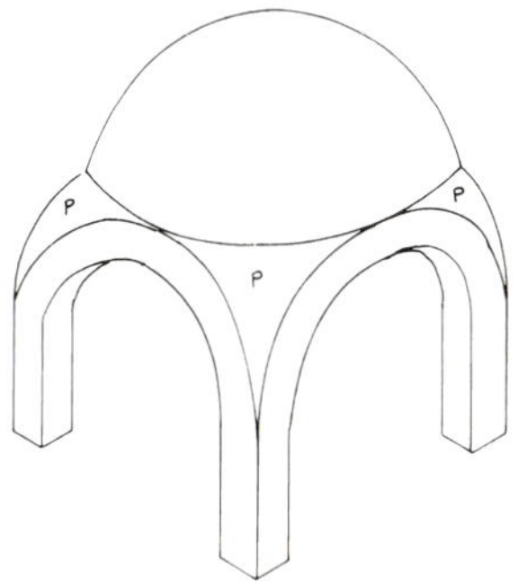

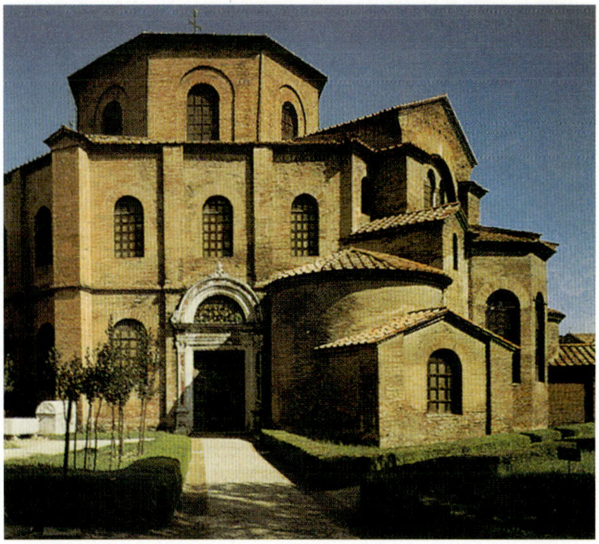

6.31 Façade of San Vitale, Ravenna, Italy.

Built to replace an earlier basilica, St Sophia was for a long time the largest church in the world. It was completed in only five years and ten months, between 532 and 537. The speed of the work, together with Byzantine masonry techniques, in which courses of brick alternate with courses of mortar as thick as, or thicker than, the bricks, caused great weight to be placed on insufficiently dry mortar. As a result, arches buckled, and **buttresses** had to be erected almost at once. The additional effects of two earthquakes caused the eastern arch and part of the dome itself to fall in 557.

The flatness of a dome so large—110 feet (33.5 meters) in diameter—remains unique, and the delicate proportioning of the vaults that support such great weight is also remarkable. Basic to the conception is the elevated central area, with its picture of heaven in the dome and its large, open, and functional spaces. The building could hold large numbers of worshippers in a transcendental environment, where thoughts at once rise to a spiritual sphere. "It seemed as if the vault of heaven were suspended above one," wrote Procopius.

The capitals of the columns in St Sophia (Fig. **6.35**) illustrate a style that is totally Byzantine. The deeply undercut ornament shows originality and technical

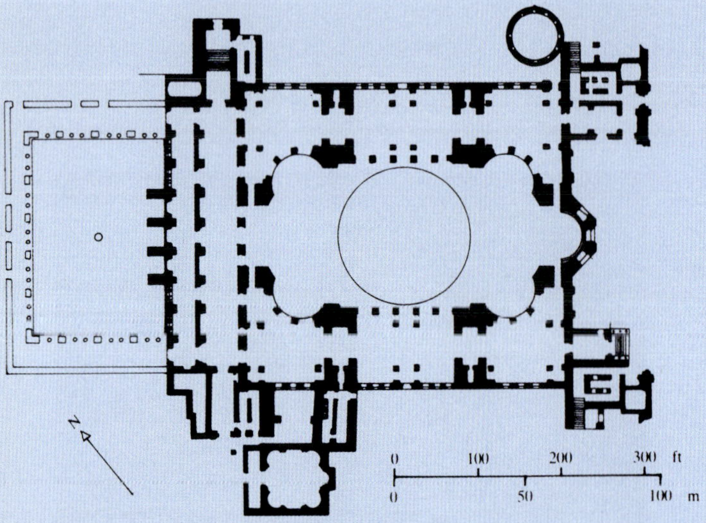

6.32 Plan of St Sophia, Istanbul, Turkey.

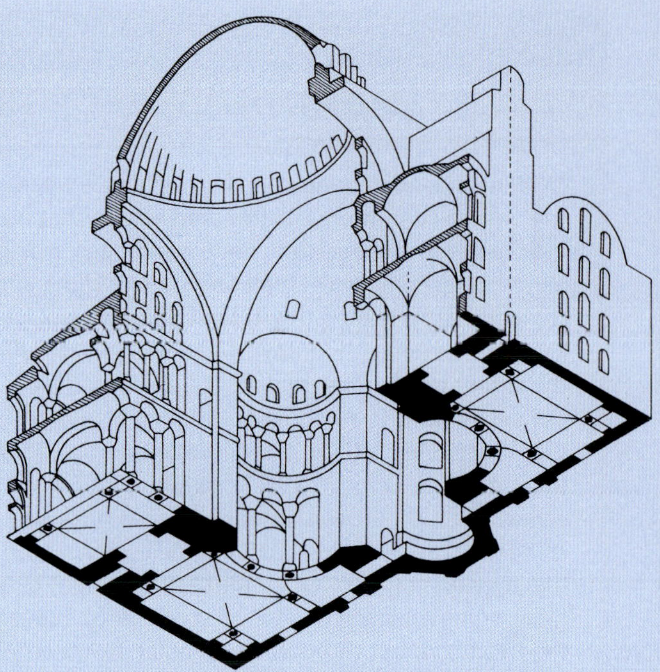

6.34 Axonometric section (perspective view) of St Sophia, Istanbul, Turkey.

6.33 St Sophia, Istanbul, interior.

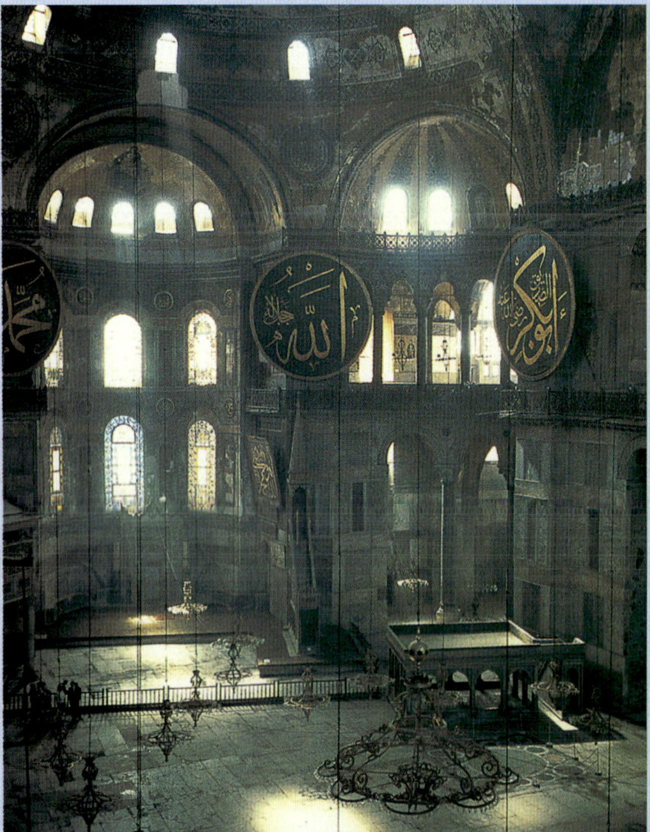

6.35 Capitals in St Sophia, Istanbul, Turkey.

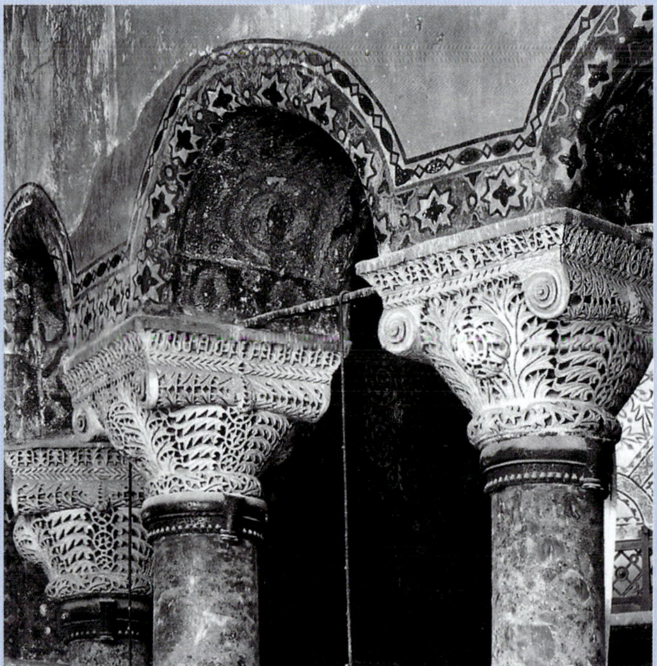

mastery. Classical elements, such as volutes and leaves like those on Corinthian capitals, are subsumed into the vigorous decoration. This is in no way a dilution of classicism, but the birth of a new style. Justinian's other buildings show work of the same type, but that in St Sophia represents the highest quality.

Justinian's reign inaugurated the style called "Byzantine," blending traces of previous styles, Eastern and Western, to form a new style. The hieratic art from the reign of Justinian expresses the relationship between God and the State. With the emperor governing by, and for, the will of God, all reality—political, philosophical, and artistic—became spiritualized. More detailed pictures of St Vitale and Hagia Sophia can be found at http://ps.theatre.tulane.edu/lester/text/Early.Christian.Period/Byzantine/Byzantine.html.

CHAPTER REVIEW

❖ CRITICAL THOUGHT ❖

Looking at a map of the region, we get a clear picture of Byzantium's pivotal location—it is the point where, today, Islam, Roman Catholicism, and Eastern Orthodoxy touch and where the Middle East, Europe, and Asia meet. Byzantium, because of that location, became a vital center for creative ingenuity and artistic vitality, producing, at the same time as it nurtured Greek and Roman classicism, a new and distinct approach to art—an approach whose uniqueness renders it easily recognizable and powerful a thousand years after the fact.

Byzantium also has been a flashpoint. Islam, Christianity, and Judaism trace their heritages to a common ancestor. Judaism is fundamental to Christianity, and Jesus plays a prominent role in the Islamic faith, especially its view of the end of the world. Islam, Christianity, and Judaism rest on the premise of "revealed truth"—a set of holy scriptures in which the single God of the universe is claimed to have revealed his nature and his will directly to an individual or individuals who have, then, passed that revealed truth on to others. Why is it that "revealed truth" appears to cause such discord among cultures that value so many basic principles, including peace, in common?

◆ SUMMARY ◆

After reading this chapter, you will be able to:

- Relate the history of Byzantium to Eastern Orthodoxy, Greek classicism, and intellectual development in the West.
- Identify and describe the basic characteristics of Byzantine art, architecture, literature, theatre, music, and dance.
- Explain the basic precepts and spread of Islam.
- Discuss Islamic art and architecture and relate them to the tenets of the faith.
- Define hieratic style and characterize its qualities in two- and three-dimensional art.
- Apply the elements and principles of composition to analyze and compare the works of art and architecture illustrated in this chapter.

CYBERSOURCES

http://www.artcyclopedia.com/history/byzantine.html
http://www.hp.uab.edu/image_archive/ebyzantine/index.html
http://www.geocities.com/Athens/Parthenon/8063/byzantine.html
http://www.metmuseum.org/collections/department.asp?dep=14

7 The Early Middle Ages

The Monastic and Feudal Romanesque Period

OUTLINE

VIEW

CARPE DIEM

Pope Gregory I, the Great, believed that the world would not last much longer. Thus he saw his decisions as affecting only the immediate future. What is the best timescale in which to view decisions? Some people say, "carpe diem," meaning "seize the day!"—that is, today may be the only day we have, so we should make the most of it. The critical phrase is, of course, "make the most," and our reaction hinges on how we define "most." One person's interpretation of carpe diem might be "eat, drink, and be merry, for tomorrow you may die," but to another, making the most of a day may mean doing as much good as we can for others.

In the early Middle Ages, people slaved for the lord of the manor in a system called feudalism. Although feudalism may have disappeared, feudal thinking has not. Many have world-views centered only on themselves and events immediate to them.

KEY TERMS

Some of the basic terms and concepts we will encounter in this chapter include the following:

Middle Ages
The time in Western European history that occurred between Antiquity (Chapters 1–5) and the Renaissance (Chapters 10–13), from approximately 476 C.E.

Feudalism
A political and economic system in Europe from the ninth to about the fifteenth century, based on the relation of lord to vassal.

Monasticism
(From the Greek *monos*, meaning "single" or "alone.") Usually refers to a way of life in which an ideal of perfection or a higher level of religious experience is pursued through living together in a community.

Romanesque style
A style that flourished throughout Western Europe from about 1050 to about 1200. The word Romanesque originally meant "in the Roman manner."

Gregorian Chant, Plainsong, or Plainchant
The name commonly given to the monodic (single melodic line) vocal liturgical music of the Christian Catholic churches.

7.1 Scenes from the life of St Paul, from the Bible of Charles the Bald, c. 875–7. San Paolo Fuori le Mura, Rome.

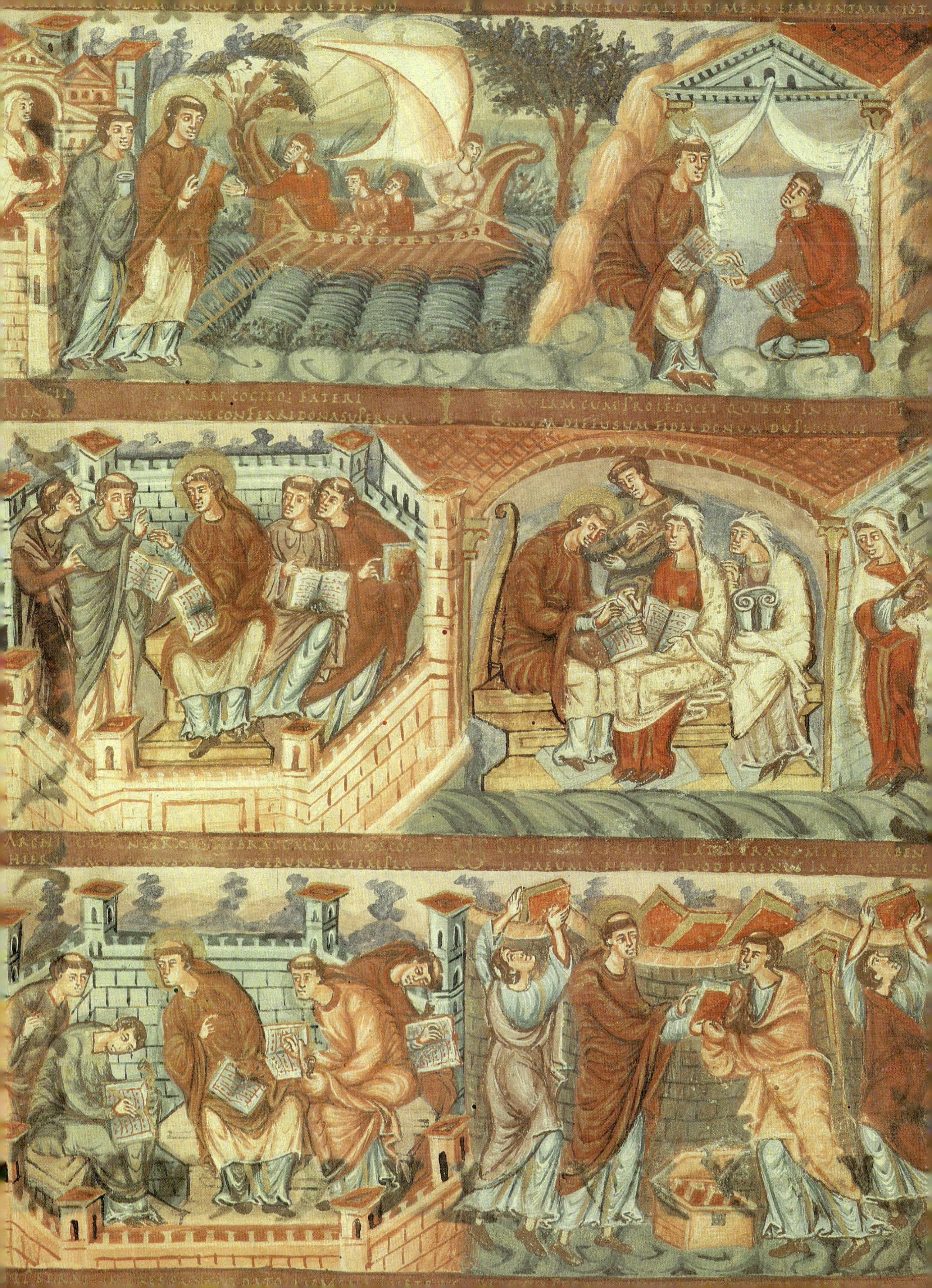

ERRORUM COGITO: FATERI
CONFERRI DONA SUPERNA
PAULAM CUM PROLE DOCET QUIBUS
DIFFUSUM FIDEI DONUM
EBURNEA TEMPLA

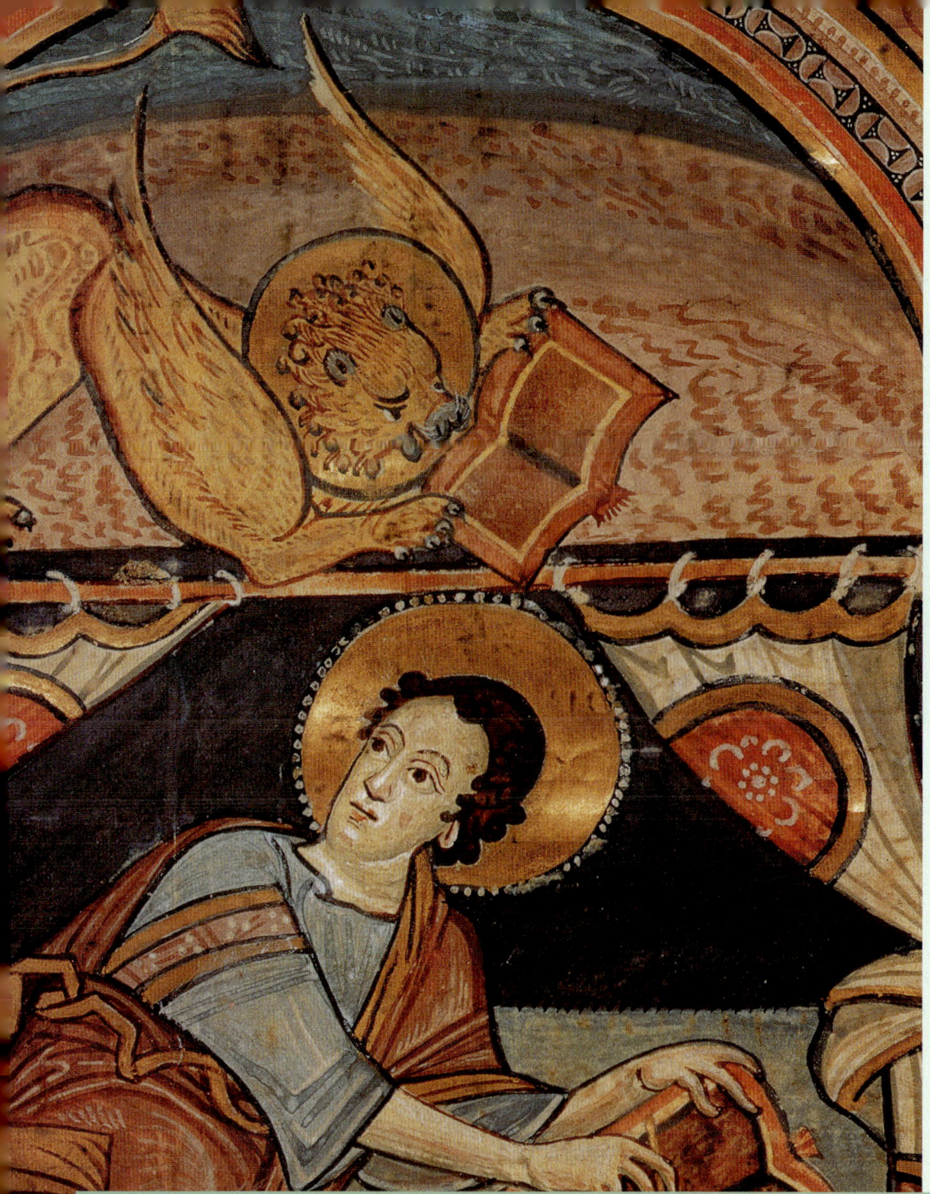

Emphasis—Confluence of Line, Encirclement, and Color

Emphasis or focal area in works of visual art occurs in a number of ways, three of which are *confluence of line*, *encirclement*, and *color*. These characteristics apply to all works in all periods and styles. To draw attention to a particular point in the picture, an artist may make all lines lead to that point. That is what High Renaissance (Chapter 11) painter Leonardo da Vinci did in *The Last Supper* (Fig. **7.2**). The expressed lines of the ceiling and the implied lines from the disciples' eyes all lead us to the face of Christ, the focus of the work. In a similar manner, the focal object may be placed in the center of a ring of objects. The medieval sculptor Giselbertus used the curved framework of the **tympanum** of a cathedral door, as well as the placement of subordinate figures, again, to emphasize the figure of Christ (see Fig. **7.14**). Finally, color acts as a focal point. In Max Beckmann's twentieth-century **expressionist** painting, *Christ and the Woman Taken in Adultery* (Fig. **7.3**), the red of the woman's scarf immediately draws us to her. She is the focus and the color tells us that, even though the Christ figure is larger.

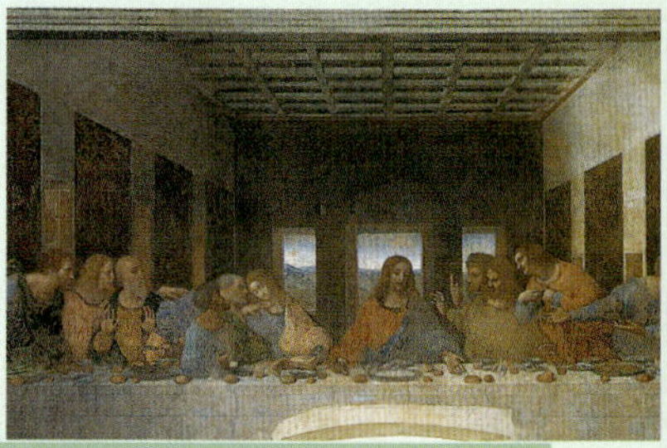

7.2 Leonardo da Vinci, *The Last Supper*, c. 1495–8. Mural painting, 15 ft $11\frac{1}{8}$ ins × 28 ft $10\frac{1}{2}$ ins (4.6 × 8.56 m). Santa Maria delle Grazie, Milan, Italy.

HOW ART WORKS

EMPHASIS

Although we may engage in disagreement about what, in works of art, artists may or may not intend us—the readers, listeners, or viewers—to find, interpret, and/or infer from the work, *emphases* or *focal areas* exist in every work. These are areas, passages, themes, and so on, which draw our attention. In theatre, for example, loud noise, rapid action, and even the position of actors on the stage itself cause us to focus. In the theatre, common wisdom argues that downstage center—the center of the stage closest to the audience—is the "strongest" position, all other things being equal. This is followed by downstage right—audience left—downstage left—audience right—upstage center, upstage right, and upstage left (upstage being the half of the stage furthest from the audience). In music, we attend to stresses, called accents, and to breaks in tempo or sudden changes in dynamics (louds and softs). Engaging works of art means paying attention to where our eye, ear, and mind travel. Whether the artist intended us to travel thus is sometimes indeterminable. But travel we do, and that tells us something about how the work works.

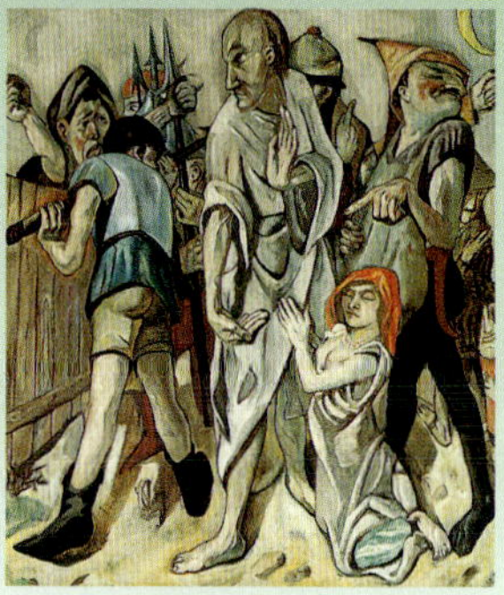

7.3 Max Beckmann, *Christ and the Woman Taken in Adultery*, 1917. Oil on canvas, 4 ft $10\frac{1}{4}$ ins × 4 ft $1\frac{1}{8}$ ins (1.49 × 1.27 m). Saint Louis Art Museum (Bequest of Curt Valentin). © DACS 2001.

7.4 St Mark, from the Gospel Book of Saint Médard of Soissons, early ninth century. Paint on vellum, $14\frac{3}{8}$ × $10\frac{1}{4}$ ins (36.5 × 26 cm). Bibliothèque Nationale, Paris.

CONTEXTS AND CONCEPTS

The Middle Ages

We have come to use the name the Middle Ages for the period that began with the fall of Rome and closed with the Renaissance in Italy. The years from around 200 C.E. to the middle of the sixth century are often called the *Early Christian* period. We have already looked at part of this period, and our examination continues in this chapter. The term *Dark Ages* is occasionally used to describe the years between 550 and 750. The *Carolingian and Ottonian* period occurred from 750 to 1000; the *Romanesque*, from 1000 to 1150; and the *High Gothic*, from 1150 to 1400. The *late Gothic* period from 1300 to 1500 overlaps High Gothic, and was a time of transition when the flower of the Renaissance began to bloom. This chapter will take us from approximately 500 to 1150, or from the Dark Ages through to the artistic style called Romanesque.

The thousand years between the fifth and the fifteenth centuries have been called the Middle Ages or medieval period on the theory that nothing—or worse than nothing—happened between the classical perfection of Greece and Rome and the revival of classical humanism in the fifteenth century.

Pessimism and disillusionment had increased in ancient Rome, and this mood, summed up in a well-known epitaph—"I was not; I was; I am not; I care not"—continued into the Middle Ages. Civic, secular government had all but ceased to exist. When Constantine I founded the second capital of the Roman Empire at Constantinople, he set in motion a division that became permanent in 395. In the West, the cloak of internationalism, which had loosely united the Mediterranean world since Alexander, fell apart. It became a case of "every locality and every people for themselves." Nations as we know them did not exist. Borders changed from day to day as one or another people wandered into the nebulously defined territory of its neighbors, bringing confusion and war.

The Medieval Church

Devils and Division

The devil, as a symbol of the powers of darkness and evil,

GENERAL EVENTS

- Gregory I sends St Augustine to England, 597
- Sutton Hoo burial ship, c. 624
- Charles Martel in France, 732
- Charlemagne, 768–814
- Viking expeditions, c. 790
- Earliest dated book printed in China, 868
- Sung dynasty, 960–1279
- Norman invasion of England, 1066

	400–700	700–900	900–1100	1100–1300
PAINTING & SCULPTURE	Medieval manuscript illumination (**7.11**)		*Gero crucifix* (**7.13**)	*Last Judgment* tympanum, Autun (**7.14**), *The Mission of the Apostles* tympanum, Ste-Madeleine (**7.15**)
ARCHITECTURE		Palatine Chapel, Aachen (**7.27**)	Hildesheim Cathedral (**7.17**), St Sernin (**7.18, 7.19**), Cluny III (**7.22**)	Autun Cathedral (**7.14**), Ste-Madeleine (**7.15**)
THEATRE			Hrosvitha, Tropes	
MUSIC & DANCE	Gregorian chants	Polyphony		Hildegard of Bingen
LITERATURE & PHILOSOPHY	First Latin Bible of St Jerome, St Benedict, *Book of Pastoral Care*, Lindisfarne Gospels	*Beowulf*, Gospel of Godescale, Dagulf Psalter, Lorsch Gospels, Carolingian Renaissance		*Nibelungenlied*, *Song of Roland*

Timeline 7.1 The early Middle Ages.

was a strong force in medieval thinking, and the Church manipulated those fears as it sought, often fanatically, to convert the pagan world of the early Middle Ages. The promise of heaven and the prospect of the fires of hell were constant themes of the times. Ever-present devils and demons fostered a certain fascination as well as fear—as we shall see in medieval theatre, for example, the devil often had the best part.

The Church was itself divided, however, and it did little to reduce the isolation and ignorance of its followers. Very early, the clergy separated into two groups, one consisting of the regular clergy, monks, and others who preferred to withdraw into a cloistered life—a lifestyle that greatly appealed to many intellectuals as well—and the other consisting of the secular clergy—that is, the Pope, bishops, and parish priests who served in society at large. The overall effect of this division was to confine learning and philosophy to monasteries, and to withhold intellectual activity from the broader world. Inquiry among both groups was rigidly restricted. Detailed and unquestioned dogma was deemed essential to the Church's mission of conversion—and, indeed, to its very survival—and as a result, the medieval world was one of barricades, physical, spiritual, and intellectual. Each man, woman, and institution retreated behind whatever barricade he, she, or it found safest.

The Roman Papacy

By the middle of the sixth century, it appeared likely that the Roman Church and its pope would simply become tools of Byzantine Imperial policy. Rome appeared to have been demoted to a peripheral status as a mere center of Catholic Christianity, with little actual power or influence. Rome was rescued from potential demise by one of the greatest pontiffs in the history of the Roman Church, Gregory I (the Great), who was pope between 590 and 604. Gregory showed great abilities as a ruler and teacher that significantly affected numerous aspects of the Church and society. His land reforms and his administration of estates that had been given to the Church revitalized Church income, relieved famine, and provided money for churches, hospitals, and schools. His influence spread from Rome to the rest of Italy and beyond. One of the most important tasks he undertook was the sponsorship of St Augustine in his mission to convert England in 597. The most significant of Gregory's written works was his *Book of Pastoral Care*, in which he spoke idealistically of the way a bishop should live and how he should care for his flock.

As a result of Gregory's efforts, Rome regained its position of primacy among the Western Christian Churches. Despite the long-term results of Gregory's actions, he did not himself consider that he was building

PROFILE

Pope Gregory I, the Great (540–604)

Nothing is known about Pope Gregory's early years and education. He rose to the position of prefect of the city of Rome, but left politics and founded the Monastery of St Andrew in Rome. Pope Pelagius II sent Gregory to Constantinople—then the seat of Roman Imperial government—as ambassador, and his experiences and the contacts he made over six years in that position proved invaluable. When Pelagius died in 590, Gregory was elected pope when he was fifty years old.

One of the major difficulties confronting the new pope lay in the conflict over the Roman ideology of emperor as divinity on earth. In such a scheme, the pope was merely another patriarch. While he had served as ambassador in Constantinople, Gregory had gained a realistic understanding of the political situations of the day, and he recognized the delicacy of the pope's relationship to the secular, Imperial government. Gregory wisely turned his attention to Western Europe, a domain that lay outside Imperial jurisdiction, where he could push the claim of the supremacy of the Church of Rome without any interference from Constantinople.

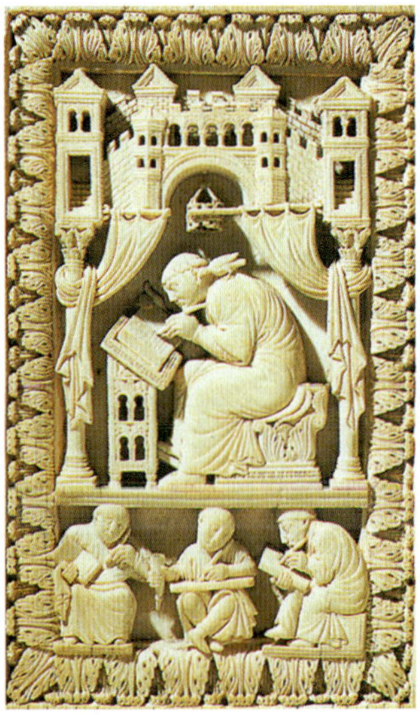

7.5 Pope Gregory I, the Great (540–604).

One of his major missionary achievements was the conversion of England, which began in 597 with the mission of St Augustine. Gregory also supported St Benedict, leading to the development of Benedictine monasticism. His extraordinary administrative abilities brought most of Europe and North Africa under Roman papal authority, and he provided the driving force in the unification of much of Church doctrine and practice, exercising in all these ways a tremendous influence throughout the Western world.

for the future. He believed that the Second Coming of Christ was near, and he merely did what he thought had to be done in what little time remained. Thus, unintentionally, he built a base for an enduring Church and a dominant papacy of wealth and prestige.

Monasticism

Seeking refuge from the temptations and tribulations of the medieval world, monks, nuns, some aristocrats, and others sought refuge behind the walls of perhaps the most typical example of medieval life—the monastery and the convent, which were outposts of order and charity. Often, too, they were well-organized and productive centers of agriculture. Monasteries and nunneries were established in the centers of non-Christian populations as means of converting pagans to Christianity. If monastery life offered an escape from some of the tribulations of the secular world, it did not permit an escape from rigor and hard work. Pious men and women of the monastic communities combined labor in the fields with religious thought, meditation, prayer, and other activities, such as copying sacred scripts and creating beautiful manuscript illuminations. Monks, who took vows of poverty, chastity, and obedience, renouncing all worldly goods, family life, and the pleasures of the senses, owned nothing—not even their own wills. They were subject to a strict discipline under the authority of the abbot and the will of God (Fig. **7.6**).

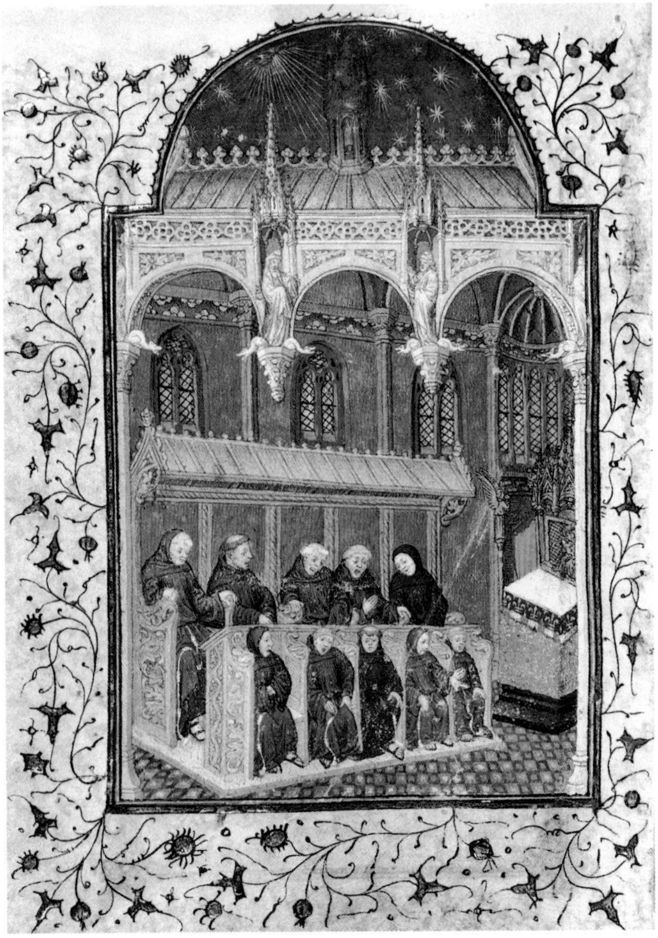

7.6 Monks in choir. Illustration from Cotton Domitian, A XVII, folio 122v. British Library, London.

Within the walls of the monastery, everything that was necessary for bodily and spiritual existence was provided, and the objective of the monastery was to be fully independent from all secular authority and life. In the monastery, a fine example being the great monastery at Cluny (see Figs **7.20**, **7.21**, and **7.22**), the ascetic world and the secular world often rubbed shoulders, however. In addition to clerics and contemplatives, Cluny, for example, often harbored criminals seeking refuge from secular authorities.

Life for the Cluniac monk exemplified life in the cloistered communities of Europe in general. Religious contemplation alternated with other religious duties, and the abbey church witnessed prayer and worship day and night. Prayers were held according to the appointed hours of liturgy, running from sunrise to sunset in a form similar to the following:

2:00 a.m. Rise
2:10–3:30 Nocturns (matins). The first office of prayer
3:30–5:00 Individual study and contemplation
5:00–5:45 Lauds (morning prayer)
5:45–8:15 Prime (an office of prayer); private reading; Mass; or breakfast, depending on the season
8:25–2:30 Work, separated by the offices of Tierce, Sext, and None (third, sixth, and ninth hours)
2:30–3:15 Dinner
3:15–4:15 Private reading and contemplation
4:15–4:45 Vespers; Compline (night prayers)
5:15–6:00 Retire for the night

The daily schedule, or *horarium* (hohr-AR-ee-uhm), changed somewhat for Feast Days and to allow for the longer days of the summer months.

Many monasteries were also centers for pilgrimages, and travelers as well as pious pilgrims came for veneration and overnight accommodation to those monasteries that contained sacred relics. A hospice, or guest house, provided lodging, especially for visitors during the pilgrimage season, and barns, stables, and places for blacksmithing were often among the components of a monastic community.

The way of the monk and nun was the way of *asceticism* (eh-SEHT-i-sihz-uhm)—that is, a life of austerity and self-discipline. Reflecting religious thought of the time, monks and nuns considered earthly life to be a mere preparation for the eternal life to come, and in order to develop the thoughts and actions required for the life to come, they renounced the distractions of the world, seeking instead a disciplined but rich inner life of the spirit that, they believed, could come only through poverty, chastity, and humility.

The earliest communal monasteries preceded the fall of the Western Roman Empire. St Martin founded Ligugé in 360. But the greatest influence of all was that of St Benedict of Nursia (c. 480–550), who formulated the most widely adopted of all monastic rules, the Benedictine.

Charlemagne's Empire

In 732, the threat of Islam and the Moorish conquest was repelled by Charles Martel at the battle of Poitiers (pwah-TYAY) in France. The succeeding Carolingian period, under his grandson Charlemagne—the name means "Charles the Great"—saw the first significant centralized political organization since the fall of Rome.

Charlemagne (SHAHR-luh-mayn; 768–814) was a giant of a man, standing well over 6 feet (1.8 meters) tall, and a mighty warrior, womanizer, drinker, and glutton (Fig. 7.7). He was semiliterate, and kept a slate beside his bed so that he could practice the letters of the alphabet. He spent most of his reign at war, in the process coalescing a large empire that ran from northern Spain to western Germany and northern Italy, with modern-day France as its center.

Grateful for his help against barbarian intruders and political enemies in Rome, in 800 C.E., Pope Leo III crowned Charlemagne Holy Roman Emperor and hailed him as "Pious Augustus, crowned by God." Charlemagne retained the office until his death, but he was hardly an heir to the Caesars. Nonetheless, his endless warfare

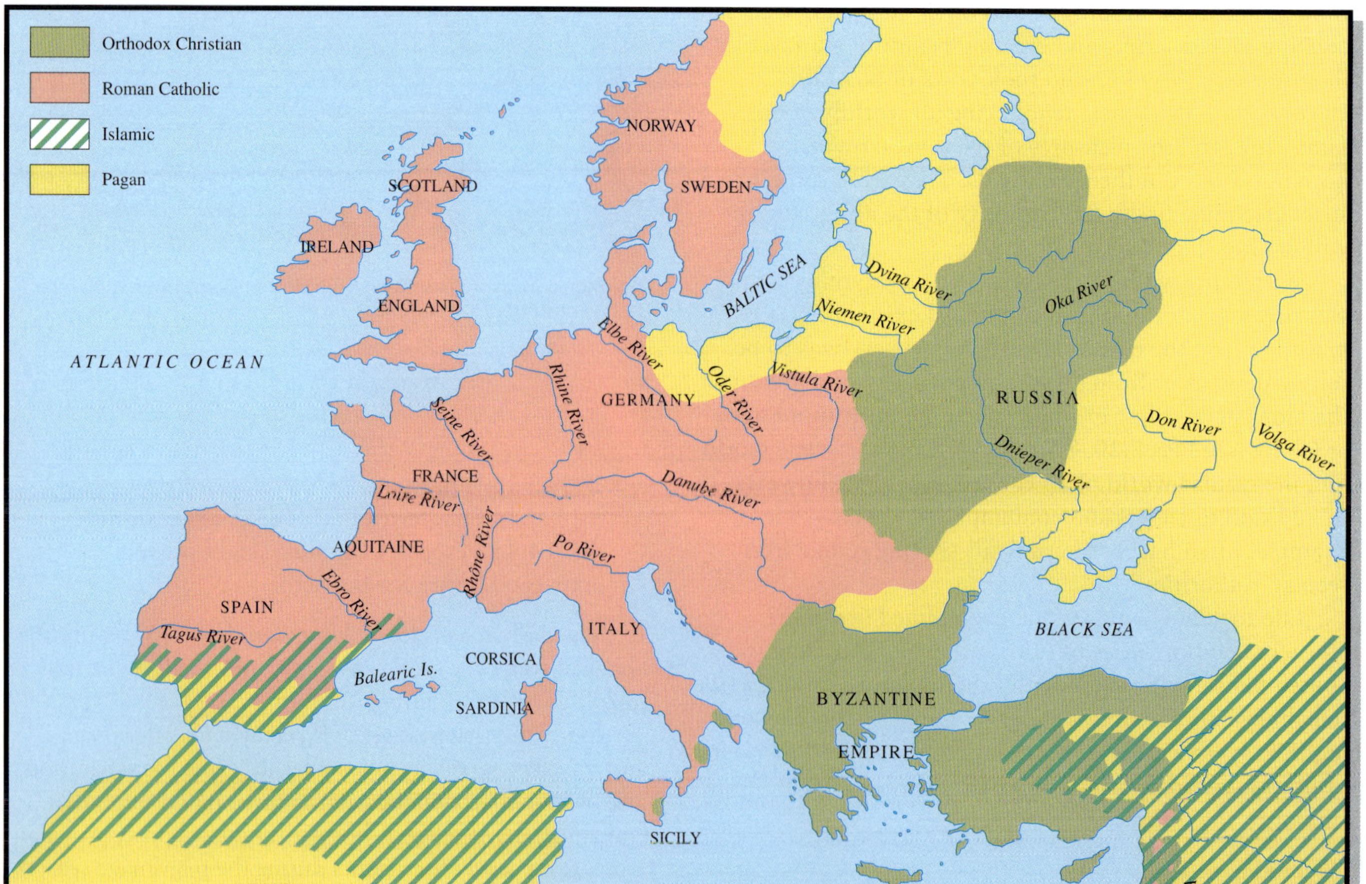

Map 7.1 Medieval Christianity and Islam.

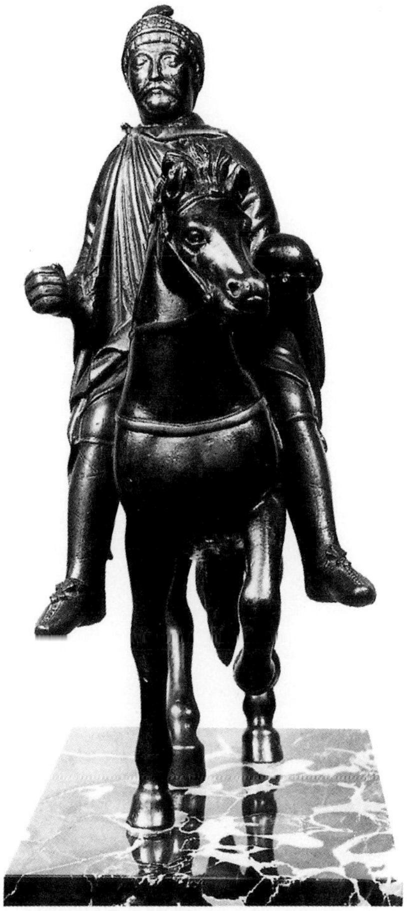

7.7 So-called *Statuette of Charlemagne*, c. 860–70. Bronze cast and gilt, 9¼ ins (23.5 cm) high. Louvre, Paris.

spread Christianity and Frankish rule across western Europe. Despite his own lack of learning, he briefly revived interest in art, antiquity, and learning, as we shall see in the Focal Point section at the end of this chapter.

Charlemagne's reign succeeded in slowing—perhaps halting—the long decline of Europe, and it illumined a pathway whereby peace and prosperity might be restored. However, the heir to the Carolingian throne did not have Charlemagne's physical strength or his strength of will. Less than thirty years after his death, his grandsons divided the kingdom into three.

Feudalism

Feudal Lords

Perhaps the main reason why centralized authority had difficulty taking hold in the Middle Ages was a societal system called *feudalism* (FYOO-duhl-iz-uhm). The real political powers in Europe in the Middle Ages were the dukes, counts, knights, and other warrior lords, who were linked together in a loose confederation of units, each one small enough to be governed by one man. Because no powerful authority ultimately controlled the individual parts, the system encouraged bloodshed and warfare as feudal lords continually raided each other to increase their wealth and property.

Feudalism was a system of military service and land ownership that created a pyramid of political and military power. Under this system, the less powerful knights sought protection and economic support from more powerful knights who, thus, became their feudal lords, or *seigneurs* (sehn-YUHR), and who required military service, money, and political support from their vassals. Although feudalism was based on a system of vassalage, by which barons were responsible to, or vassals of, kings, sufficient power to effect real control rarely existed at any level above the individual landholder.

The *oath of fealty* was performed at a solemn and symbolic ceremony. The vassal knelt, put his hands between those of his lord, and pledged allegiance to the lord, promising a certain number of days of military service each year and specific sums of money on occasions such as the knighting of the lord's son (Fig. **7.8**) or the marriage of the lord's daughter, or ransom for the lord himself if he were captured by his enemies. To complete the ceremony, the lord would present to the vassal a piece of earth or a sprig from a tree to symbolize the lord's grant of a fief—that is, a parcel of land including villages of serfs to work it.

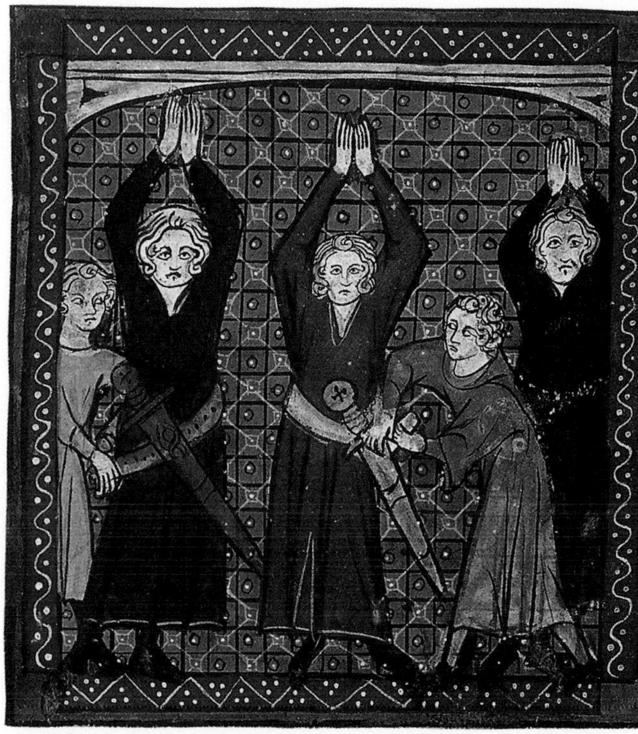

7.8 The girding-on of swords, part of an increasingly formalized ritual associated with the making of a knight. MS D XI fol 134 vi. British Library, London.

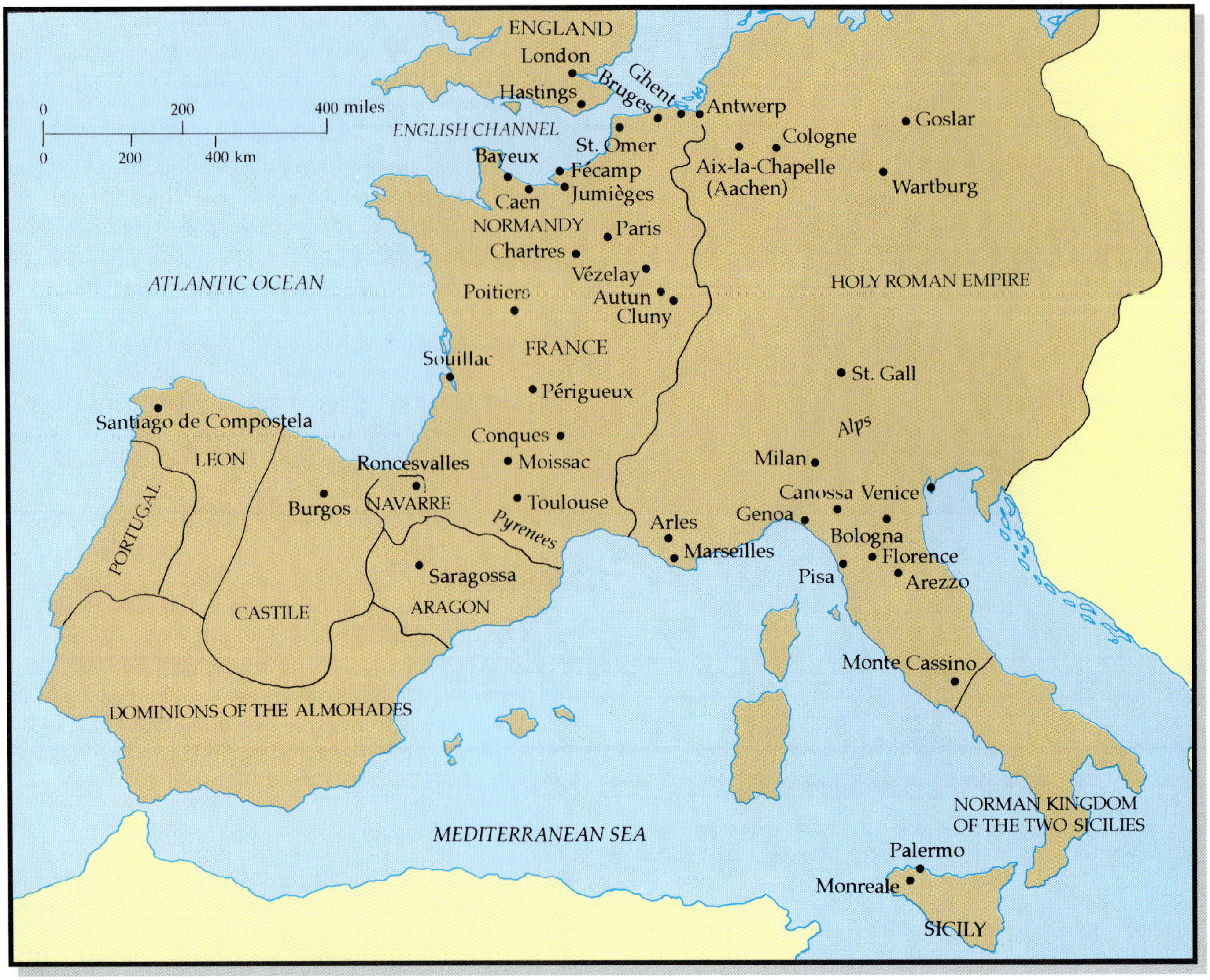

Map 7.2 Europe in the early twelfth century.

Serfs and Women

Feudal society comprised a thick network of contractual relationships that linked the highest to the lowest in the realm. The lowest in the realm was a serf, whose life was one of ignorance and destitution, and of subservience to the manor's lord. Serfs did the work of the manor, and in return paid the lord for the privilege. All law enforcement and punishment occurred within the manor, and no serf could marry without the lord's consent. In the strictest sense of the ancient world, serfs were not slaves, but they were bound to the land of the estate for life, and, bound to the land, they were bound to the lord of the manor for as long as the lord owned it. In return, the lord was obliged to provide guardianship for his serfs—that is, provide basic necessities and care for them in their old age, should they reach it.

Drudgery marked the daily life of the village. People lived in one-room, sparsely furnished huts with earthen floors. They shared the hut with members of the family, chickens, and whatever other animals may have been theirs, and at night the entire family slept huddled together on straw bedding. In the spring, life took a decided turn for the worse, for typically the fall's harvest barely lasted the winter, and it was too early in the growing season for new crops to mature. As a result, starvation in the springtime provided a constant threat, as did raids by other, equally hungry, people who formed raiding parties of barbarians or other local barons. Disease was a constant companion, and there were no doctors (Fig. **7.9**). All told, the medieval serf could only resign himself to his fate and trudge on from day to day, hopeful that death would release him into a better condition.

Women played a central role at every level of medieval society. In the manor house as well as the village

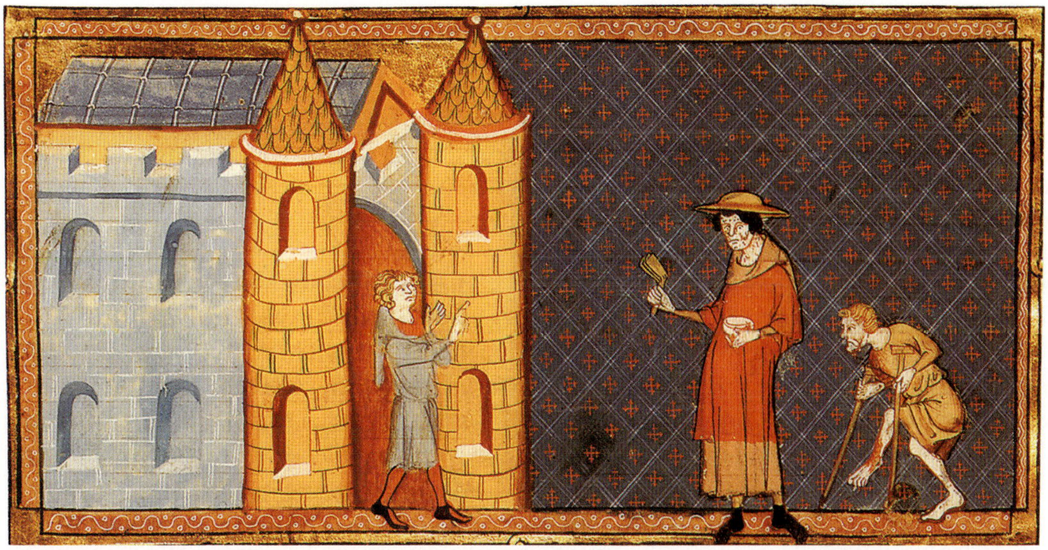

7.9 Leprosy, from the manuscript *Miroir historial de Vincent de Beauvais*, trans. by Jean de Vignay, 1330–50. Bibliothèque Nationale, Paris.

TECHNOLOGY

The Viking Ships

While feudal Europe struggled and while Charlemagne was emerging as Holy Roman Emperor, the Vikings of Scandinavia were sailing as far as the shores of North America, preceding Columbus to the New World by more than six hundred years. Their means of transport was the Viking ship (Fig. **7.10**), and its construction and use prove that these hearty and hardy peoples were as skillful in their technology as they were warlike and adventurous. The vessel had a true keel, a single steering-oar with a tiller handle, well-raked—that is, angled—stem- and stern-posts, sixteen rowing ports cut into each side, and a square-sail rigged on a single mast amidships. Light and buoyant, they were called long-ships because their length was such a striking feature, exceeding the beam by more than five to one. In time, the Viking ships grew until they had thirty and even sixty oars to a side. It was in these large vessels that the Vikings made their raids, conquests, and far-reaching explorations to Russia and America.

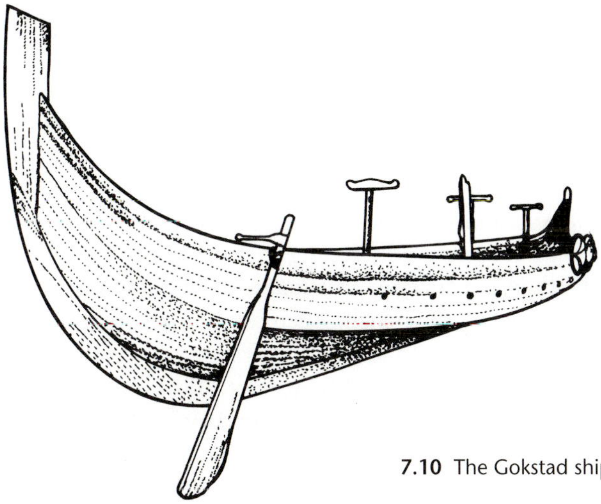

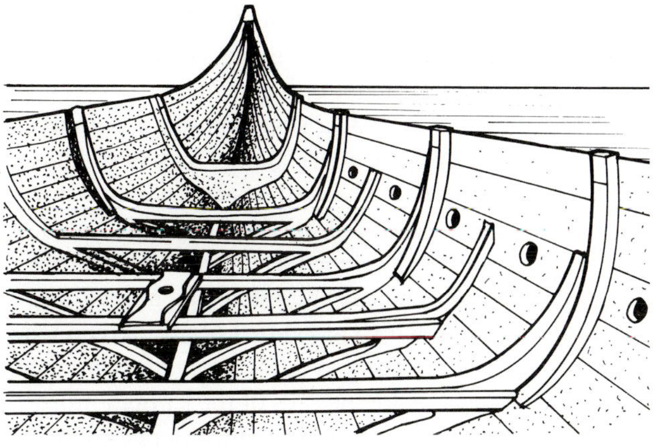

7.10 The Gokstad ship, c. 800, after restoration.

hut, the family was the core of the social order, and among serfs, it also provided the central production unit. Women shared the burdens of daily existence, caring for children and animals and working small vegetable plots near the hut. They prepared food, made clothing, and helped with the harvest. Their life expectancy was short.

On the other hand, women of the manor often shared ruling functions and responsibilities. The power structure, again, was based on the family, and one was born into the aristocracy. The system depended on inheritance and marriage, and because women could inherit, they often owned vast estates. As wives of feudal barons, women were often faced with the necessity of managing the manor in its entirety while the lord was away for long periods, fighting wars on behalf of his liege lord.

Women could also find individual identity and authority in the Church. If the burdens of secular life proved overpowering, women could "take the veil" by entering a convent. A wealthy woman could establish her own convent and become a mother superior or abbess, wielding absolute authority over her subservient nuns. A woman who so devoted her life to the Church and worked diligently on behalf of it and her fellow humans could dream of sainthood—an honor bestowed by the Church after death—which would place her at the right hand of God for eternity.

THE ARTS OF THE EARLY MIDDLE AGES

Painting

Early Christian painting adopted local styles. The tomb paintings in the catacombs of Rome were, for example, Roman in style but incorporated Christian symbolism. Roman Christians were converted Roman pagans, and their paintings had a frankly practical intent. In its earliest phases, before Constantine, Christian painting was a secret art in a secret place, and its function was simply to affirm the faith of the follower on his or her tomb.

One often finds in early Christian painting a primitive quality; it is probably more a reflection of lack of technical ability than anything else. The need to pictorialize the faith was foremost. Artistic skill was not important.

Christian painting developed in several stages. From the beginning, it reflected the absolute belief in another, superior, existence in which individual believers retained their identity. Painting was a tangible expression of faith. Later, it was used to make the rites of the Church more vivid. Its final role was that of depicting and recording Christian history and tradition. Inherent from the start was a code of symbolism whose meaning could be grasped only by a fellow Christian.

As the Roman world first split and then fell apart, plunging the West into chaos, painting became once again a private art, more an intellectual pursuit than an inspiration to the faithful. A new and exquisite form of two-dimensional art emerged, not on canvases or church walls, but on the beautifully illustrated pages of scholarly Church manuscripts. By the time Christianity had sufficient status to come into the open, a dramatic change had occurred in the format of written texts. Rolls of papyrus had been replaced by more convenient and durable parchment pages bound together between hard, protective covers, known as a *codex*. Although scrolls continued to be used for special occasions throughout the Middle Ages, they were now made of stitched parchment.

The only illustrated manuscript of the New Testament in Latin to survive from this early period is a copy of the Gospels that probably came to England in 597 with St Augustine, the first archbishop of Canterbury and a missionary from Pope Gregory the Great. (This Augustine (aw-GUHS-tuhn) is not to be confused with the earlier St Augustine of Hippo.) Only two full-page miniatures survive, one of which (see Fig. **5.9**) shows St Luke and twelve scenes from his Gospel. It is a full-page frontispiece. We see the saint seated in the foreground within an arched border. In the sides of the frame are little compartments portraying events, including the story of the washing of feet, with an unbearded Peter. The rich colors and detailing of this miniature rival those of the wall mosaics and decorations of Byzantium. The artistic quality of the St Augustine Gospels is not very high, however, in that the figure proportions are inaccurate, the medium is handled loosely, and details are carelessly executed. Perhaps it was not considered worthwhile to send a more valuable book to the still largely heathen England.

Nonetheless, this work is an interesting example of an early *picture cycle*, and it typifies certain stylistic qualities that became more marked in medieval painting and sculpture. Compositions are close and nervous: figures bump against each other amid an atmosphere of frenetic energy. We feel a certain discomfort emanating from these "walled-in" and crowded scenes, which perhaps mirror the closed-in world of the medieval illustrator.

An Irish contribution to medieval manuscript illumination appears in Figure **7.11**. Here the figures are flat and almost ornamental, though they are precisely and delicately rendered. Highlight and shadow give a sense of depth in the curtain, and space is suggested by the oblique treatment of the bench. Accurate linear **perspective** is unknown to these artists. Colors are few and subtle. Of note here is the frontal treatment of the angel's eye, in contrast to the head, which is in profile. The figures are also outlined. The picture is carefully composed, with both color and form controlled to achieve a pleasing balance.

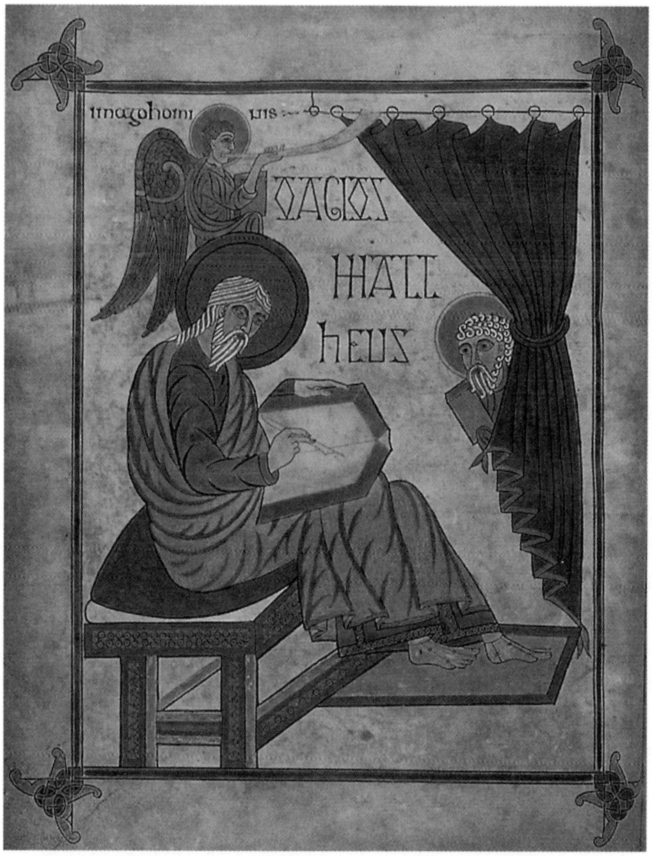

7.11 St Matthew, from the Lindisfarne Gospels, before 698. 13½ × 9¾ ins (34.3 × 24.8 cm). British Library, London.

From the fifth to the eleventh centuries, a tremendous wealth of artistic work emerged in several nontraditional areas. Life was generally in a state of flux throughout Europe in the early Middle Ages, and it was to ordinary and portable media that nonmonastic nomadic people turned much of their artistic energy. Clothing, jewelry, and ships, for example, all exhibited the artistry of the Germanic, Irish, and Scandinavian peoples (Fig **7.12**).

Emotionalism in art increased as the approach of the millennium sounded its trumpet of expected doom. The fact that the world did not end on 1 January 1001 reduced this feeling only slightly. Emotionalism was strengthened further by an influx of Eastern art when Otto II married a Byzantine princess. A combination of Roman, Carolingian, and Byzantine characteristics typifies Ottonian manuscript illustration. Despite the crowding and an inherent appeal to feeling, such work testifies to the increasingly outward-looking approach of the early years of the second millennium.

Sculpture

Sculpture played only a very minor role in the centuries between the collapse of the Roman Empire and the rise of the Romanesque style in the eleventh century. The fact that the Old Testament prohibited graven images may have been partly responsible for this. The association of statuary with pagan societies, notably Rome, was fresh in the memory of the Church. Thus, when Christian sculpture emerged, it was largely funerary and not monumental. The earliest examples are all sarcophagi.

Some of the most beautiful sculptural work of the Christian era after Constantine resembles manuscript illumination in its small-scale, **miniature**-like detail. Its restless, linear style is eloquent with emotion, and it is very precise in its detail.

Especially poignant is the *Gero* (GAIR-oh) *crucifix* (Fig. **7.13**). The realism of the crucified Christ, whose

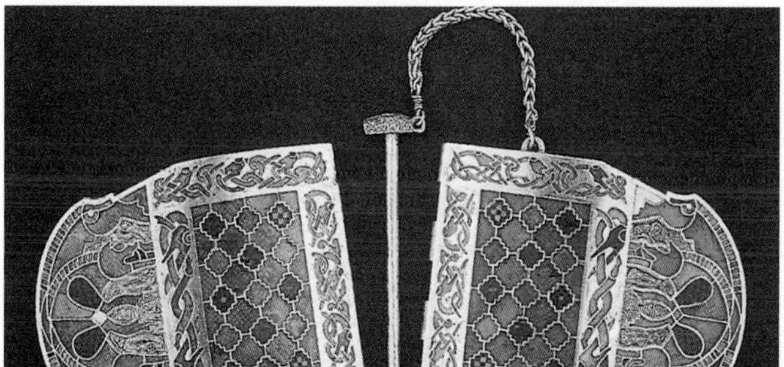

7.12 Hinged shoulder clasp from the ship burial at Sutton Hoo, England, Anglo-Saxon, c. 625–30 C.E. Gold decorated with garnets and millefiore glass. British Museum, London.

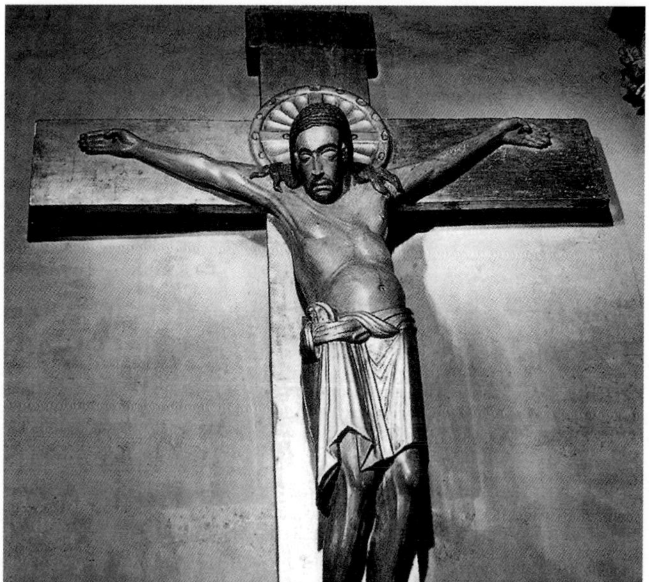

7.13 *Gero crucifix*, 969–76. Oak, 6 ft 1⅝ ins (1.87 m) high. Cologne Cathedral, Germany.

downward- and forward-sagging body pulls against the nails, and the emotion with which it is rendered, are very compelling. The muscle striations on the right arm and chest, the bulging belly, and the rendering of cloth are particularly expressive. This work has a hardness of surface. The form is human, but the flesh, hair, and cloth do not have the soft texture we might expect. The face is a mask of agony, but no less full of pathos for that. An intense spirituality reflects the mysticism prevalent in the early Middle Ages. The *Gero crucifix* depicts a suffering Christ whose agony parallels the spirit of the times. This portrayal contrasts markedly with the *Christus Rex* crucifixes that became popular later and are frequently seen today, in which Christ on the cross is a victorious, resurrected King.

Like the architecture of the period, sculpture of the eleventh and early twelfth centuries is also called Romanesque. In the case of sculpture, the label refers more to an era than to a style. Examples of sculpture are so diverse that we probably could not group them under a single label, were it not for the fact that most of them take the form of decorative elements attached to Romanesque architecture. We can, however, draw some general conclusions about Romanesque sculpture. First, it is associated with Romanesque architecture; second, it is stone; third, it is monumental. The last characteristic represents a distinct departure from previous sculptural style. **Monumental** stone sculpture had all but disappeared in the fifth century. Its reemergence across Europe at the end of the eleventh century over such a short period was remarkable. The emergence of sculptural decoration indicated at least the beginning of dissemination of knowledge from the cloistered world of the monastery to the general populace. Romanesque sculpture was applied to exteriors of buildings where the lay worshipper could see it and respond to it. The relationship of this artistic development to the increase in religious zeal among the laity was probably strong. In works such as the *Last Judgment* **tympanum** (TIM-puh-nuhm) of Autun (Fig. **7.14**), the illiterate masses could now read the message of the Church, an opportunity previously reserved for the clergy. The message of this carved scene is quite clear. In the center of the composition, framed by a Roman-style arch, is an awe-inspiring figure of Christ. Next to him, malproportioned figures writhe in various degrees of torment. The inscription of the artist, Gislebertus (jis-ul-BAIR-tuhs), tells us that their purpose was "to let this horror appal those bound by earthly sin." Evil was still central to medieval thought, and devils share the stage with Christ, attempting to tip the scales of judgment in their favor and gleefully pushing the damned into the flaming pit.

Another Romanesque tympanum comes from the central portal of the narthex of the abbey and pilgrim church of Sainte-Madeleine, Vézelay (vay-zeh-LAY), in

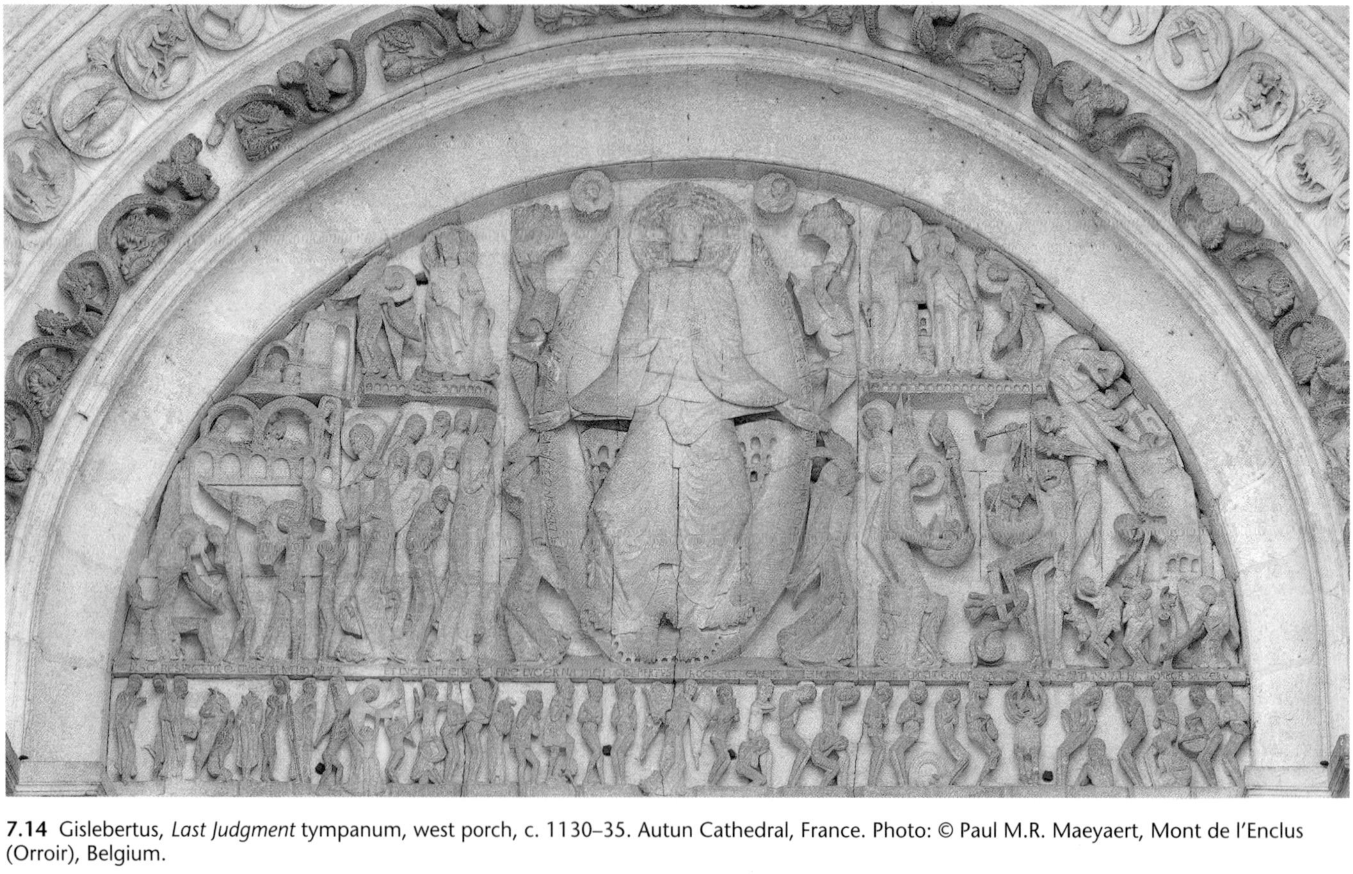

7.14 Gislebertus, *Last Judgment* tympanum, west porch, c. 1130–35. Autun Cathedral, France. Photo: © Paul M.R. Maeyaert, Mont de l'Enclus (Orroir), Belgium.

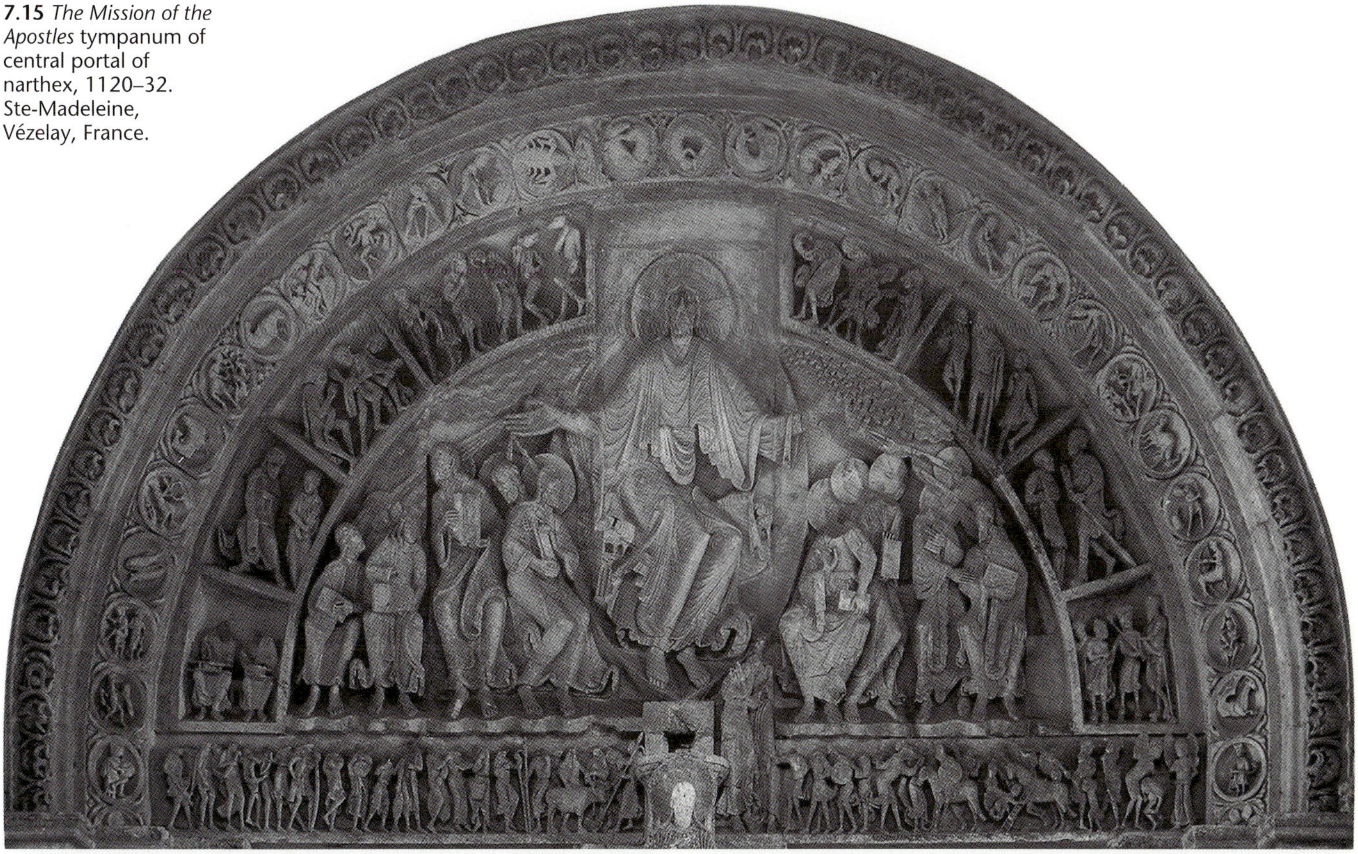

7.15 *The Mission of the Apostles* tympanum of central portal of narthex, 1120–32. Ste-Madeleine, Vézelay, France.

A DYNAMIC WORLD

IGBO-UKWU

During Europe's early Middle Ages, African artists and artisans not only used but mastered bronze, and a remarkable example of that mastery is in a ritual water-pot found in the village of Igbo-Ukwu in eastern Nigeria (Fig. **7.16**).

The level of skill achieved by ninth- and tenth-century Africans in this object is astounding. In the first place, it was cast using the same sophisticated *cire-perdue* (lost-wax) method employed in casting the bronze doors of Hildesheim Cathedral (see Fig. **7.17**). This method involves the making of a wax model around which a mold is placed. The mold is heated, the wax melts and runs out of the mold, and the void is then filled with the molten metal that forms the finished work. This leaded bronze artifact has amazing virtuosity. The ritual water-pot stands enclosed in a net of simulated rope. The knots and delicate striations are perfect, and the graceful design of its recurved lines and flaring base by themselves are exquisite. This is a design and execution of immense sophistication of both technique and vision.

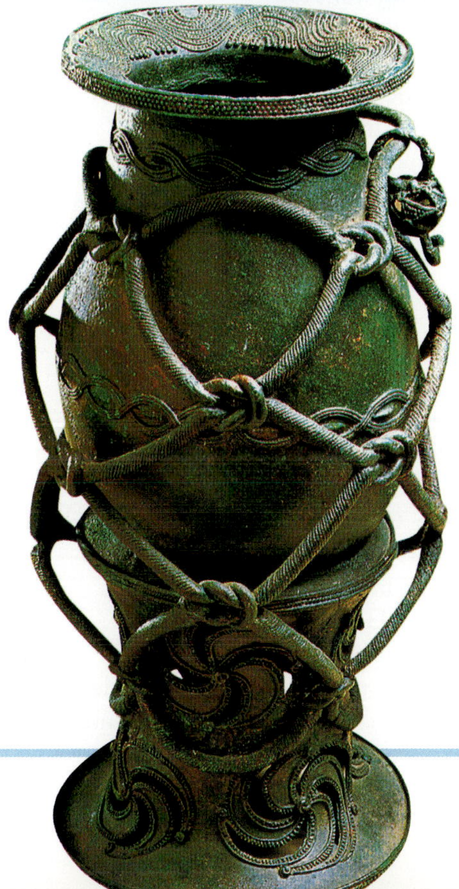

7.16 Roped pot on a stand, from Igbo-Ukwu, ninth to tenth centuries. Leaded bronze, 12½ ins (32 cm) high. National Museum, Lagos, Nigeria.

MASTERWORK

The Bronze Doors of Hildesheim Cathedral

During Bernward of Hildesheim's years as bishop (993–1022), the city of Hildesheim became a center for manuscript painting and other arts. Bernward's patronage, however, was largely confined to the area of metalwork, in particular, the bronze doors of the Hildesheim (hil-duh-SHYM) Cathedral (Fig. **7.17**). These doors were cast by the *cire-perdue* (sihr-pair-DOO), or **lost-wax**, process.

The building of the Abbey Church of St Michael at Hildesheim was part of Bishop Bernward's plan to make the town a center of learning. The doors for the south portal of St Michael's were completed in 1015 and they were probably installed before 1035. Apparently cast in one piece, Hildesheim's doors are the first in a succession of figured bronze doors throughout the Middle Ages and the Renaissance, a tradition that culminated in Ghiberti's *Gates of Paradise* for the Baptistery in Florence (see p. 305). The massive doors of Hildesheim also represent a return to larger scale sculpture that was to become typical of the Romanesque period.

The scenes portrayed on Bernward's doors tell biblical stories in a carefully arranged order. The number of scenes depicted—sixteen—is an example of medieval number symbolism. (Sixteen is the number of the Gospels multiplied by itself.) Reading from top to bottom, the scenes are paired, so that the left door unfolds the Old Testament story of the fall, and the right, the New Testament story of the redemption. For example, *The Temptation of Adam and Eve* (third from the top, left), which depicts the fall from grace, is purposely aligned with the *Crucifixion* (third from the top, right), which illustrates the redemption of humankind. The scenes are highly reminiscent of manuscript illustration, and they tell their stories with a simple directness. In the fourth panel from the top on the left, an angry God reproaches Adam and Eve. His angry glare is heightened by his accusatory, pointing finger, and Adam and Eve cower under his condemnation. As the sinners try to shield their nakedness, Adam points to Eve, passing to her the blame for his transgression; she, in turn, looks downward, and with her left hand points an accusing finger at the serpent.

What is striking about all the scenes is the strong sense of composition and physical movement. Every set of images, against a plain background of open space, speaks forcefully in dumb show. The doors tell their story in medieval fashion, as a vivid but silent drama, effectively communicating the message of the Christian faith to a largely illiterate public. Replace these simple scenes with a clergy-actor, and you have the beginnings of liturgical drama (see the theatre section below). Just as the mystics of the Middle Ages understood communication through the intuition and nonrational emotions, so the artists of the period understood the raw power and effectiveness of the simple nonverbal image.

7.17 Doors of Hildesheim Cathedral, 1015. Bronze, 16 ft 6 ins (5.03 m) high. Hildesheim, Germany.

Burgundy (Fig. **7.15**). The story depicts the mission of the apostles and became especially meaningful to medieval Christians at the time of the Crusades (see Chapter 8). Here the artist proclaimed the duty of every Christian to spread the gospel to the ends of the earth. At the center of the tympanum, a rather elongated figure of Christ spreads his arms, from which emanate the rays of the Holy Spirit, empowering the apostles, who carry the scriptures as tokens of their mission. Around the border is a plethora of representatives of the heathen world. The arch is framed by the signs of the zodiac and labors appropriate to the months of the year, stressing that the preaching of the faith is an ongoing, year-round responsibility without end. Examples of Italian Romanesque sculpture are featured at http://www.thais.it/scultura.romanica.htm.

Architecture

As Charlemagne's empire in the ninth century, and then the tenth century, passed, a new and radical style in architecture emerged. Unlike its counterparts in painting

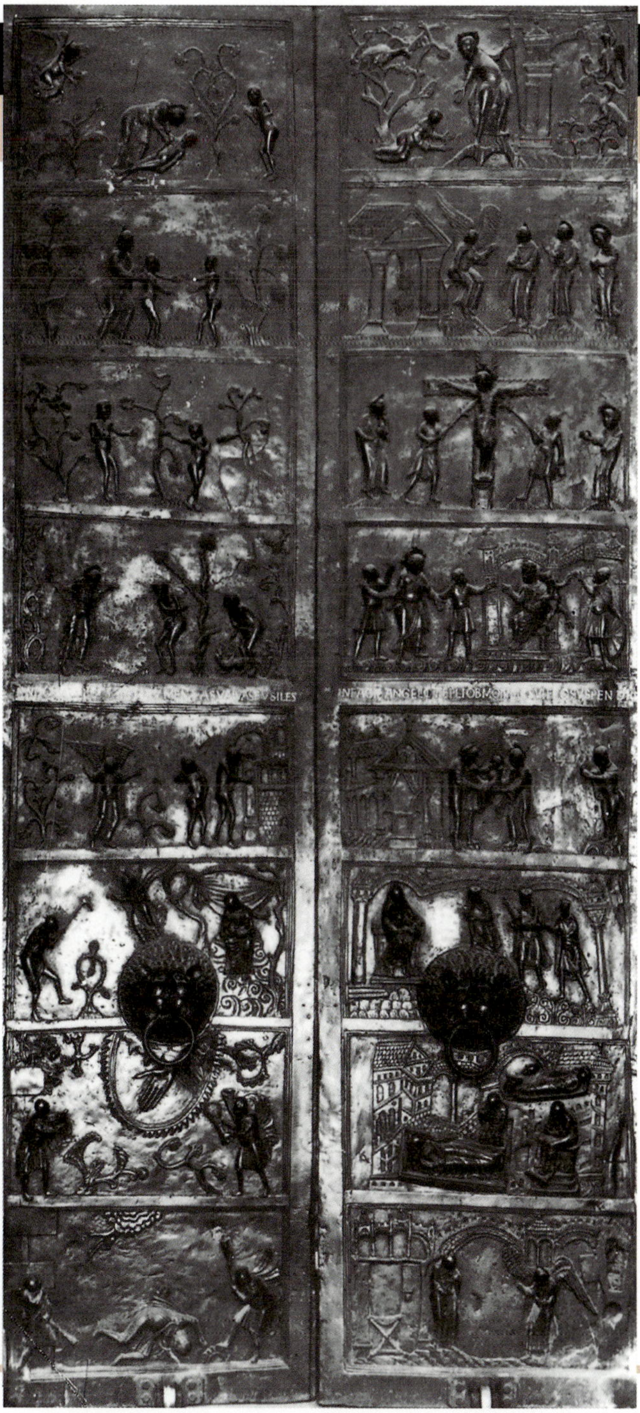

and sculpture, Romanesque architecture had a fairly identifiable style, despite its diversity. The Romanesque took hold throughout Europe in a relatively short period of time. When people of the Renaissance saw its curved arches over doorways and windows throughout Europe, they saw a style that was pre-Gothic and post-Roman—but like the Roman. Therefore, they called it "Romanesque." With its arched doorways and windows, this style was massive, static, and comparatively lightless, which seems further to reflect the barricaded mentality and lifestyle generally associated with the Middle Ages.

The Romanesque style nonetheless exemplified the power and wealth of the Church militant and triumphant. If the style mirrored the social and intellectual system that produced it, it also reflected a new religious fervor and a turning of the Church toward its growing flock. Romanesque churches were larger than earlier ones; we can see their scale in Figures **7.18** and **7.19**. St Sernin (san Sair-NAN) reflects a heavy elegance and complexity we have not previously seen. The **plan** of the church describes a Roman cross, that is, a cross with the lower staff longer than the arms. (Recall the cross-in-square, or Greek cross design, of Byzantine churches in Chapter 6.) The side aisles extend beyond the crossing to create an ambulatory, or walking space. This was so that pilgrims, most of whom were on their way to Spain, could walk around the altar without disturbing the service.

One additional change is worth noting. The roof of this church is made of stone, whereas earlier buildings had wooden roofs. As we view the magnificent vaulted interior, we wonder how successfully the architect reconciled the conflicts between engineering, material properties, and aesthetics. Given the properties of stone and the increased force of added height, did he try to push his skills to the edge, in order to create a breathtaking interior? Did he aim to reflect the glory of God or the ability of humanity?

Returning to the exterior view, we can see how some of the stress of the high vaulting was diffused. In a

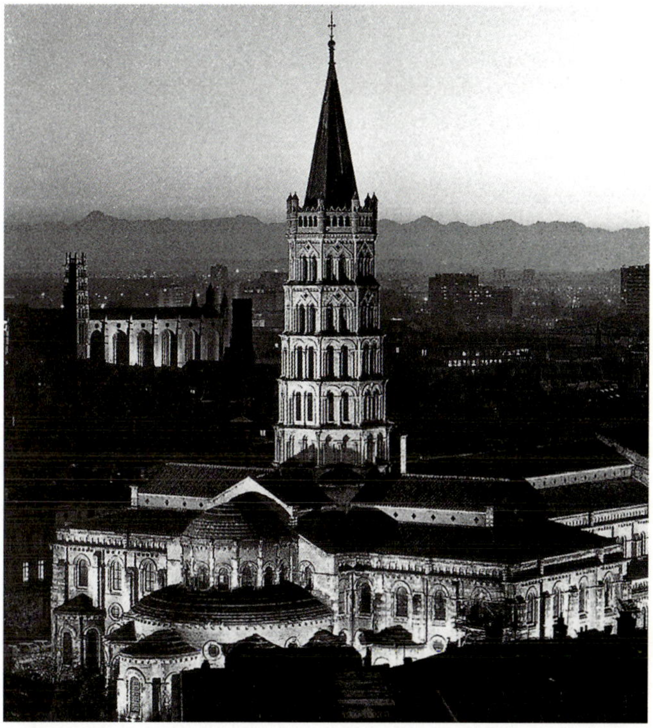

7.18 St Sernin, Toulouse, France, c. 1080–1120.

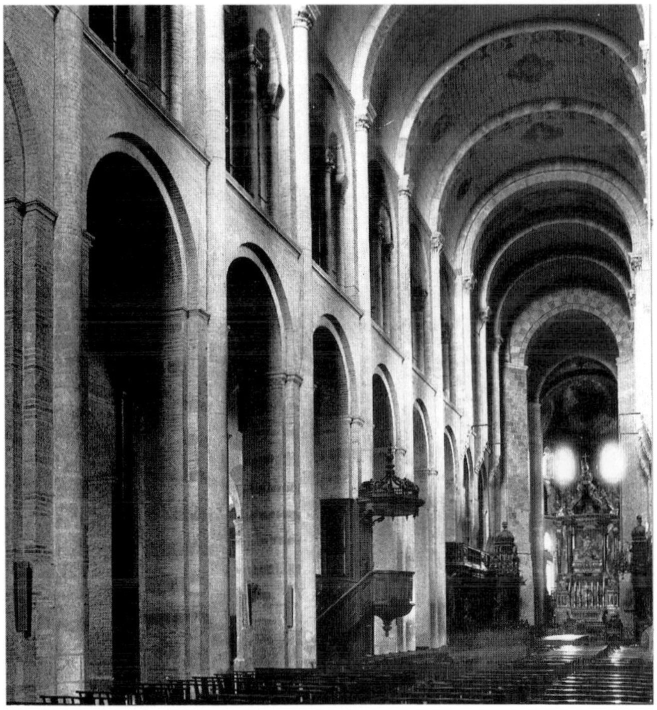

7.19 Interior of the nave at St Sernin, Toulouse, France, c. 1080–1120.

complex series of vaults, transverse arches, and bays, the tremendous weight and outward thrust of the central vault were transferred to the ground, leaving a high and unencumbered central space. If we compare this structural system with post-and-lintel structure and consider the compressive and tensile properties of stone, we can see why the arch is superior as a structural device for creating open space. Because of the weight and the distribution of stress in this style, only very small windows were possible. So, although the fortress-like,

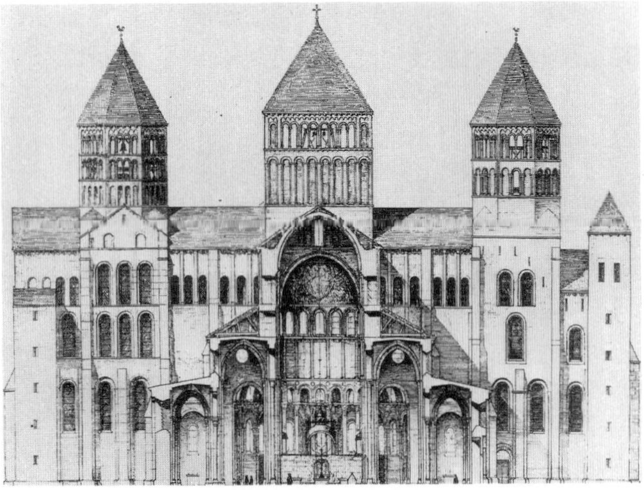

7.20 Transverse section of the nave, and west elevation of the great transept of the Abbey Church, Cluny III, France, 1088–1130.

lightless qualities of Romanesque architecture reflect the spirit of their time, they also had a practical explanation.

The tenth-century church of Cluny, known as Cluny II, inspired numerous buildings throughout the West in the eleventh century. When it became too small, a new church, Cluny III, was begun in 1088. It remained the largest church in Christendom until St Peter's in Rome was rebuilt in the sixteenth century. Although Cluny III (Figs **7.20**, **7.21**, and **7.22**), was badly damaged during the French Revolution, we know that the nave, which had

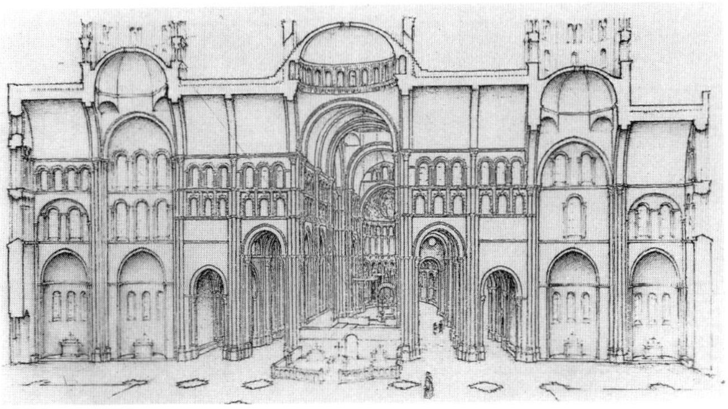

7.21 Transverse section of the transept. Drawing by Kenneth J. Conant. Frances Loeb Library, Harvard University, Cambridge, MA.

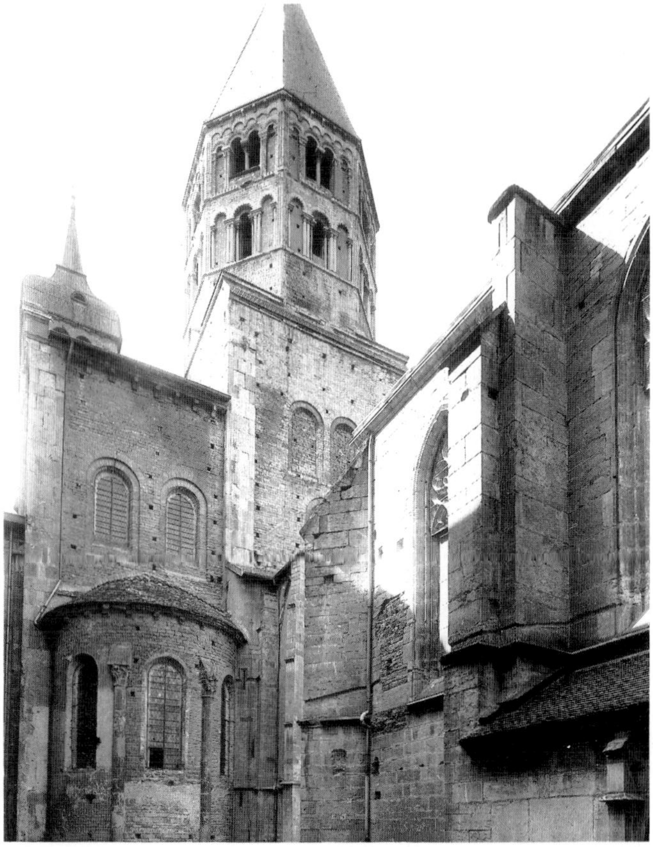

7.22 Exterior of southwest transept of Cluny III.

double aisles, the double **transepts**, and the choir with an ambulatory were all enormous in scale. The arcades of the nave had pointed arches, and the interior housed magnificent wall paintings. Protruding apses and numerous towers adorned the exterior. Another aspect of Romanesque architecture was English Norman architecture, whose excellent examples can be seen at http://www.geocities.com/Athens/Parthenon/8063/norman3.html.

Theatre

Scholars used to argue that theatre ceased to exist in the Western world for a period of several hundred years. However, two pieces of evidence certainly suggest that theatrical productions continued. One is the presence of wandering entertainers (see Chapter 8). In this tribe of entertainers were mimists, jugglers, bear baiters, acrobats, wrestlers, and storytellers. The propensity of human beings for acting out or mimicking actions and events is too compelling to deny its existence amid the entertainments we know existed in this era. We do not know, however, how such entertainments were presented during the early Middle Ages. They may have consisted simply of the acting out of a story silently or the reading of a play script, rather than the formal presentations we call "theatre."

Our second piece of evidence proves more conclusively that theatre existed. Writings from north Africa argue that mime continued there and it is probable that if it still existed in north Africa, it also existed in Europe. The king of Spain in the seventh century refers to the popularity of old Roman festival plays at marriages and feasts, adding that members of the clergy should leave when these were performed. In France in the ninth century, the Council of Tours and the Council of Aix-la-Chapelle (EKS-lah-shah-PEHL) ruled that the clergy should witness neither plays nor the obscenities of actors. These railings of the Church against the theatre certainly suggest that it existed. Charlemagne added his powerful backing in defense of the clergy by ruling that no actor could wear a priest's robe under penalty of corporal punishment or banishment. This edict has been taken by some as evidence of theatrical presentation and also, perhaps inaccurately, as evidence of the beginnings of liturgical drama. If this were the case, the prohibition would imply the use of actors other than the clergy in Church drama.

In the tenth century, the German nun Hrosvitha (hrohs-VEET-ah) is known to have written six plays based on comedies by Terence. We do not know if Hrosvitha's plays were performed, but if they were, the audience would have been restricted to the other nuns in the convent.

We are sure, however, that liturgical drama began as an elaboration of the Roman Catholic Mass, probably in France. These elaborations were called **tropes**, and they took place on ceremonial occasions, especially at Easter, the dramatic highlight of the Church year. Records at Winchester in southern England dating from the late tenth century tell of a trope in which priests acted out the discovery of Jesus' empty tomb by his followers on Easter morning.

The first dramatic trope was the "Quem Quaeritis" trope. This earliest Easter trope dates from 925, and the dialogue was:

> *Angels*: Whom seek ye in the tomb, O Christians?
> *The Three Marys*: Jesus of Nazareth, the crucified, O Heavenly Beings.
> *Angels*: He is not here, he is risen as he foretold. Go and announce that he is risen from the tomb.

So theatre, along with all the other arts, except dance, was adopted by the Church and became an instrument of God in an age of faith and demons.

Music

Sacred Music

Gregorian Chant

By around the year 500, a body of sacred—that is, religious—music called chant, *plainchant*, or **plainsong**, had been developed for use in Christian worship services. (The terms, along with **Gregorian chant**, are commonly used as synonyms, although detailed study reveals differences.) Chant was vocal and took the form of a single melodic line (*monophony;* muh-NAH-foh-nee) using notes relatively near each other on the musical scale. The haunting, undulating character of early chant possibly points to Near Eastern origins. Chants were sung in a flexible **tempo** with unmeasured rhythms following the natural **accents** of normal Latin speech. There were two types of chant settings. In one, called *syllabic*, each syllable of the chant was given one note. In the other, called **melismatic** (mehl-iz-MAT-ik), each syllable was spread over several notes. The selection "Kyrie: Hodie Christus Resurrexit" (CD track 4) lets us sense the flavor of the undulating and ethereal melody of the melismatic type. The Kyrie is one of the five parts of the *mass ordinary*—texts that remain the same from day to day throughout most of the Church year. The other parts of the Mass are the *Gloria* (Glory be to God on high), *Credo* (I believe . . .), *Sanctus* (Holy, holy, holy, Lord God of Hosts), and *Agnus Dei* (O Lamb of God that takest away the sins of the world). The Kyrie entreats, "Kyrie eleison" (Lord have mercy upon us), "Christe eleison" (Christ have mercy upon us), "Kyrie eleison" (Lord have mercy upon us). These sections, sung by the choir, are alternated with the affirmation, "Hodie Christus Resurrexit" (Today Christ is Risen), sung by a soloist, which gives the piece an ABABA structure.

Plainchant is often called Gregorian chant because Pope Gregory I (540–604) supervised the selection of melodies and texts he thought most appropriate and compiled them for Church services. Although Pope Gregory did not invent plainchant, his contributions of selection and codification were such that it acquired his name.

Polyphony: Organum

At some time between the eighth and tenth centuries, monks in monastery choirs began to add a second melodic line to the chant. At first, the additional line paralleled the original at the interval of a fourth or a fifth. Medieval music that consists of Gregorian chant and an additional melodic line (or lines) is called **organum** (OHR-guh-nuhm). Between the tenth and the thirteenth centuries, organum became truly **polyphonic**. As time progressed, the independent melodies became more and more independent of each other and differed rhythmically as well as melodically.

Secular Music

The Middle Ages also witnessed a growth in secular music—that is, not related to the Church. As might be expected, secular music used vernacular texts—that is, texts in the language of the common people, as opposed to the Latin of Church music. The subject matter mostly concerned love, but other topics were also popular. Medieval secular song was probably mostly **strophic** (STROHF-ik) (composed of several stanzas that were sung to the same melody).

Musical instruments of this era (Fig. 7.23) included

PROFILE

Hildegard of Bingen (1098–1179)

One of the significant musical and literary figures of the time, Hildegard of Bingen was educated at the Benedictine cloister of Disibodenberg and became prioress there in 1136. Having experienced visions since she was a child, at age forty-three she consulted her confessor, who in turn reported the matter to the archbishop of Mainz. A committee of theologians subsequently confirmed the authenticity of her visions, and a monk was appointed to help her record them in writing. The finished work, *Scivias* (1141–52), consisted of twenty-six visions, prophetic, symbolic, and apocalyptic in form. About 1147, she left Disibodenberg to found a new convent, where she continued to prophesy, to record her visions in writing, and perform her musical plays.

Hildegard is the first composer whose biography is known. She wrote music and texts to her songs, mostly liturgical plainchant honoring saints and the Virgin Mary. She believed that music was the means of recapturing the original joy and beauty of paradise and that music was invented and musical instruments made in order to worship God appropriately. She wrote in the plainchant tradition of a single vocal melodic line that we have just discussed. She wrote seventy-seven chants and the first musical drama in history, which she entitled "The Ritual of the Virtues."

Hildegard of Bingen's music was written for performance by the nuns of the convent she headed. She combined all her music into a cycle called "The Symphony of the Harmony of the Heavenly Revelations," from which the "Lauds of Saint Ursula" ("O Ecclesia" excerpt, CD track 5) is one example. This music is sung by three sopranos accompanied by an instrumental drone, which serves as a sustained bass above which the voices soar in the chantlike melody. It celebrates St Ursula who, according to legend, was martyred with eleven thousand virgins in Cologne.

Hildegard believed that many times a day, humans fall out of sorts and lose their way. Music was the sacred technology that could best redirect human hearts toward heaven. It could integrate mind, heart, and body and heal discord.

Hildegard's numerous other writings include a morality play, a book of saints' lives, two treatises on medicine and natural history, and extensive correspondence, in which are to be found further prophecies and allegorical treatises. Her lyrical poetry, gathered in "The Symphony of the Harmony of the Heavenly Revelations" (*Symphonia armonie celestium revelationum*), consists of seventy-seven poems (all with music), and together they form a liturgical cycle.

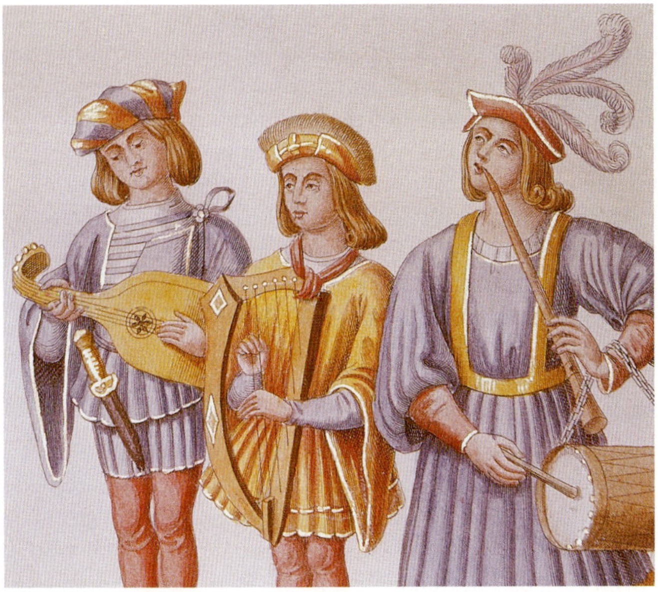

7.23 *Medieval Minstrels playing to Nobleman*, MS. Fr 13096 fol 16. Bibliothèque Nationale, Paris.

the lyre, the harp, and a bowed instrument called the vielle, or fiedel (the viol, or fiddle). The psaltery, which was similar to a zither, the lute, the flute, the shawm, which was a reed instrument like an oboe, trumpets, horns, drums, and bagpipes were all popular. Small, portable organs were also popular, despite the instrument's unpleasant associations with the Roman persecution of Christians, and the organ eventually found its way into the medieval church.

Dance

Dancing did not surrender to the dictates of Christianity in the early Middle Ages. Church writings continue to condemn dancing from Constantine's time to the eleventh century and beyond. St Augustine complained that it was better to dig ditches on the Sabbath than to dance a "Choric Reigen" (RY-gehn; a type of "round dance").

Bitter conflict understandably characterized a previously pagan world in an age of expanding Church influence. A religious philosophy in which all pleasures of the flesh were evil clashed with a pagan belief to which fertility rites, including wild dances and orgies, were central. History records many examples of masked pagan dancers attempting to invade churches. Even when Christianity gained a firm hold, it was impossible to eradicate ritualistic dancing completely. It appears that a certain unspoken compromise was reached. Dancing continued because people will continue to do what gives them pleasure, Church or not, the threat of damnation notwithstanding. But the pagan contexts of dance were put aside. The Christian Church made many such compromises with life as it found it.

Any dance in this period, however, was largely spontaneous and took no account of a performer/ audience relationship. Such dancing was a response to a chaotic and frightening world in which people were reduced to their baser selves. Later, demonic dances, dances of death, and animal mummeries would take on a more formal, presentational character—Death as a dancer was a frequent medieval image.

Theatrical dance remained alive, however, through successors to the Roman pantomimes. Dancers appeared at fairs and festivals, performing nearly always for the peasants—rarely for the nobility.

Literature

It seems clear that in the early Middle Ages—with the notable exception of the Carolingian court—the politically powerful cared little for culture, and for the most part could neither read nor write. Thanks to the efforts of the monastic community, and particularly the Benedictine monks, however, important books and manuscripts were preserved and copied. St Benedict (c. 480–550) was one of the few great scholars of the Dark Ages.

The Muslims had come into contact with Greek culture when they invaded Egypt, and they brought it with them to Spain, where literature flourished. The schools they set up in Cordoba studied Aristotle and Plato alongside the Koran. Toledo and Seville were also centers of learning. It was biblical literature, however, that became the central focus during the early Middle Ages.

St Jerome (c. 342–420) was a contemporary of St Augustine of Hippo, and his writings assumed a position of primary importance in the last years of the Roman Empire. St Jerome was familiar with the classical writers, and the style of the scriptures seemed somewhat crude to him. He had a dream, however, in which Christ reproached him and accused him of being more a Ciceronian than a Christian. As a result, Jerome resolved to spend the rest of his life in the study of the sacred books. He made a famous translation of the Bible into Latin, called the Vulgate Bible, and assisted by Jewish scholars, he also translated the Old Testament from the Hebrew.

Another major literary accomplishment of the early Middle Ages, one with a completely different subject matter, was the German *Nibelungenlied* (nee-beh-LUNG-en-leet; "Song of the People of the Mists," meaning the dead). These early hero-stories of northern peoples, which took their final shape in southeast Germany c. 1200, are a rich mixture of history, magic, and myth. There are ten complete and twenty incomplete manuscripts of the *Nibelungenlied*, folk tales of thirty-nine adventures, commencing with that of the hero Siegfried, son of Siegmund, king of the Netherworld.

The poem begins by introducing Kriemhild (KREEM-hilt), a Burgundian princess of Worms, and Siegfried (SEEG-freed), a prince from the lower Rhine who is determined to woo her. When he arrives in Worms, he is identified by Hagen (HAHG-ehn), a henchman of Kriemhild's brother King Gunther. Hagen then recounts Siegfried's earlier heroic deeds, including his acquisition of a treasure. When the Danes and Saxons declare war, Siegfried leads the Burgundians and distinguishes himself in battle. Upon his return, he meets Kriemhild, and their affections develop during his residence at court.

Hearing of the contest for Brunhild, a queen of outstanding strength and beauty who may be won only by a man capable of matching her athletic prowess, Gunther decides to woo her. He enlists the aid of Siegfried, to whom he promises the hand of Kriemhild if successful. By trickery the two men defeat Brunhild, and she accepts Gunther as her husband. Siegfried and Kriemhild are then married as promised, but Brunhild is suspicious. The two queens soon quarrel, and Kriemhild reveals how Brunhild was deceived. Hagen sides with Brunhild and kills Siegfried.

During these events, Brunhild drops almost unnoticed out of the story. Siegfried's funeral is conducted with great ceremony, and the griefstricken Kriemhild remains at Worms, though for a long time estranged from Gunther and Hagen. Siegfried's treasure is brought to Worms, but Hagen sinks the treasure in the Rhine.

The second part of the poem deals principally with the conflict between Hagen and Kriemhild and her vengeance against the Burgundians. Etzel (Attila), king of the Huns, asks the hand of Kriemhild, who accepts. After many years, she persuades Etzel to invite her brothers and Hagen to his court. Though Hagen is wary, they all go, and carnage ensues. Kriemhild has Gunther killed and then, with Siegfried's sword, she slays the bound and defenseless Hagen. Kriemhild herself is slain by a knight named Hildebrand.

The favorite Old English epic, *Beowulf* (BAY-oh-wuhlf; c. 725), is the earliest extant poem in a modern European language. Composed by an unknown author, it falls into separate episodes that incorporate old legends. The poem is written in unrhymed alliterative verse. Its three folk stories center on the hero, Beowulf, and his exploits against the monster Grendel (GREHN-duhl), Grendel's mother—a hideous water hag—and a fire-breathing dragon. In the poem, the "battle-brave" Beowulf crosses the sea from "Geatland" (possibly Sweden) to the land of the Danes and frees that country from a terrible ogre, Grendel. In revenge, the ogre's mother carries off a king's councillor. Beowulf follows her to her lair under the waters of a lake and slays her. Beowulf becomes king of the Geats and rules for half a century. He is fatally wounded when he battles a fire-breathing dragon. Mourned by his subjects, he is buried under a great barrow, or mound. Read *Beowulf* at http://www.ipl.org/cgi-bin/common/redirect?http://etext.lib.virginia.edu/cgibin/browse-mixed?id=AnoBeow&tag=public&images=modeng&data=/1v1/Archive/eng-parsed.

Another popular poem, the *Chanson de Roland* or "Song of Roland," tells of Charlemagne. The poem probably dates to around 1100. Its author was probably a Norman poet named Turold, whose name is mentioned in the last line of the poem. It is the story of the historical battle of Roncesvalles, which was fought in 778 between the armies of Charlemagne and the Saracens of Saragossa in the Pyrenees mountains between France and Spain. In reality, the battle was little more than a skirmish against the Basques, but the poet turns the event into a heroic encounter on the level of the Greek battle of Thermopylae, which we studied earlier.

In style, the poem is direct and sober. It focuses on the clash between the recklessly courageous Roland and his more cautious friend Oliver, a conflict that illustrates divergent views of feudal loyalty.

The poem begins as Charlemagne, having conquered all of Spain except Saragossa, receives overtures from the Saracen king. In response, Charlemagne sends the knight Ganelon to negotiate peace terms, but Ganelon, Roland's stepfather, is angry because Roland proposed him for the dangerous task, and he conspires with the Saracens to achieve Roland's death. On his return to Charlemagne's camp, Ganelon ensures that Roland will command the rear guard of the army as it withdraws from Spain. As the army crosses the Pyrenees, the rear guard is surrounded at the pass of Roncesvalles by an overwhelming Saracen force.

The headstrong Roland, preoccupied with valor, rejects his friend Oliver's advice to blow his horn and summon help from the rest of Charlemagne's army. The battle ensues, and the valiant French soldiers fight until only a handful remain alive. Finally, the horn is sounded, but it is too late to save Oliver or Roland, who is fatally wounded in error by a blow from a blinded Oliver. However, it is not too late for the arriving army to avenge the heroic vassals. Read *The Song of Roland* at http://sunsite/berkeley.edu/OMACL/Roland/.

When Charlemagne returns to France, he breaks the news to Aude, Roland's fiancée and Oliver's sister, who falls dead at the news. The poem ends with the trial and execution of Ganelon.

FOCAL POINT

The Carolingian Renaissance

On few occasions in history have individuals been able to put their individual temperament on so many aspects of society and art as did Charlemagne. His reign was so all-encompassing and his interest in all the aspects of life so wide that the word "renaissance" has been applied to the time of his rule. As we will see, the Carolingian renaissance had its limits, but, given its time and circumstances, it truly was remarkable.

When Pepin III died in 768, he was succeeded by his two sons, Charles and Carloman. Carloman died three years later, and Charles, denying the succession of Carloman's infant sons, acquired for himself the entire Frankish Empire. Carrying on the work of his father and grandfather, Charlemagne set about subduing the Frankish peoples and other tribes throughout Europe. He ruled over a vast empire of many nations, and became protector of Pope Leo III in Rome. On Christmas Day in the year 800, as Charlemagne knelt in prayer before the altar in the old church of St Peter, Pope Leo suddenly placed a crown on his head, and the people acclaimed him as emperor.

Perhaps his greatest contributions to European civilization lay in his support of education, reform of the Church, and cultivation of the liberal arts. Under the leadership of Alcuin (AL-kwin) of York, scholars were assembled from all parts of the West to reunite the scattered fragments of the classical heritage. The classical revival initiated by Charlemagne was part of his attempt to revive the Roman Empire.

Manuscript Illumination

Carolingian manuscript illuminations are striking examples of early medieval painting. As an official court art, book illumination was promoted by the king, his relatives, associates, and officers of state. One exemplary product of the time was the Gospel Book of Godescale (Fig. **7.24**). The models for this work were probably Byzantine: the evangelists have lean, bearded faces, and the cloth of their garments reveals a rudimentary attempt at modeling, with light and dark stripes representing the highlight and shadow of the folds. Unlike the Gospel Book of Godescale (GOHD-uhs-kal), the Gospel Book of Saint Médard of Soissons (san-may-DARD; swah-SAWN; see Fig. **7.4**) displays a definite classicism in its arches complete with columns, intricate architecture, and frames adorned with pictures containing tiny figures. Nonetheless, there is confusion in the plethora of detail and a crowded nervousness characteristic of medieval work.

Sculpture

The works of the palace school at Charlemagne's court also reflect an effort to revive classical style by copying sculpture from the late antique period. Classical influence continued to be nurtured, perhaps because Charlemagne's political opposition to the Byzantine Empire led him to reject its artistic style as well. The so-called *Statuette of Charlemagne* (see Fig. **7.7**), for example, clearly imitates a classical model.

It is, however, the ivories of this period that most clearly show both the classicizing trend and the artistry of the time. Although derived from antique models, these works are highly individual. The ivory covers of the Dagulf Psalter (Fig. **7.25**) bear a close resemblance to Roman work. Commissioned as a gift for Pope Adrian I, the figures and ornamentation on this cover are stilted and lifeless. There is little attempt at creating three-dimensional space, although the figures themselves appear in high relief. Composition in each panel appears to be organized around a central area, to which interior line directs the viewer's eye. This focus is reinforced by the direction in which the figures themselves are looking. The scenes are crowded, but not frenetic. The figures have strange proportions, almost dwarf-like, with heavy rounded heads, long torsos, and short legs. Hairstyles reflect the late Roman Imperial period.

The ivory cover of the ninth-century Lorsch (lohrsh) Gospels (Fig. **7.26**), on the other hand, is an exact replica of a sixth-century design. The images in the upper register, the layout, and the rounded faces in the figure depiction clearly show its kinship with the *Barberini Ivory* (see Fig. **6.15**). The Roman arches in each of the three middle panels testify to the classical derivation of the Lorsch Gospels. In the center panel sits the Virgin Mary, enthroned, with the infant Christ and surrounded by saints. The face of the Christ child is that of a wise adult, a common medieval practice. The risen Christ appears encircled in the top register and flanked by heraldic angels. The lower register shows scenes from the nativity. So the Gospel cover reads chronologically from birth to Resurrection in *hierarchical* fashion (see Chapter 6).

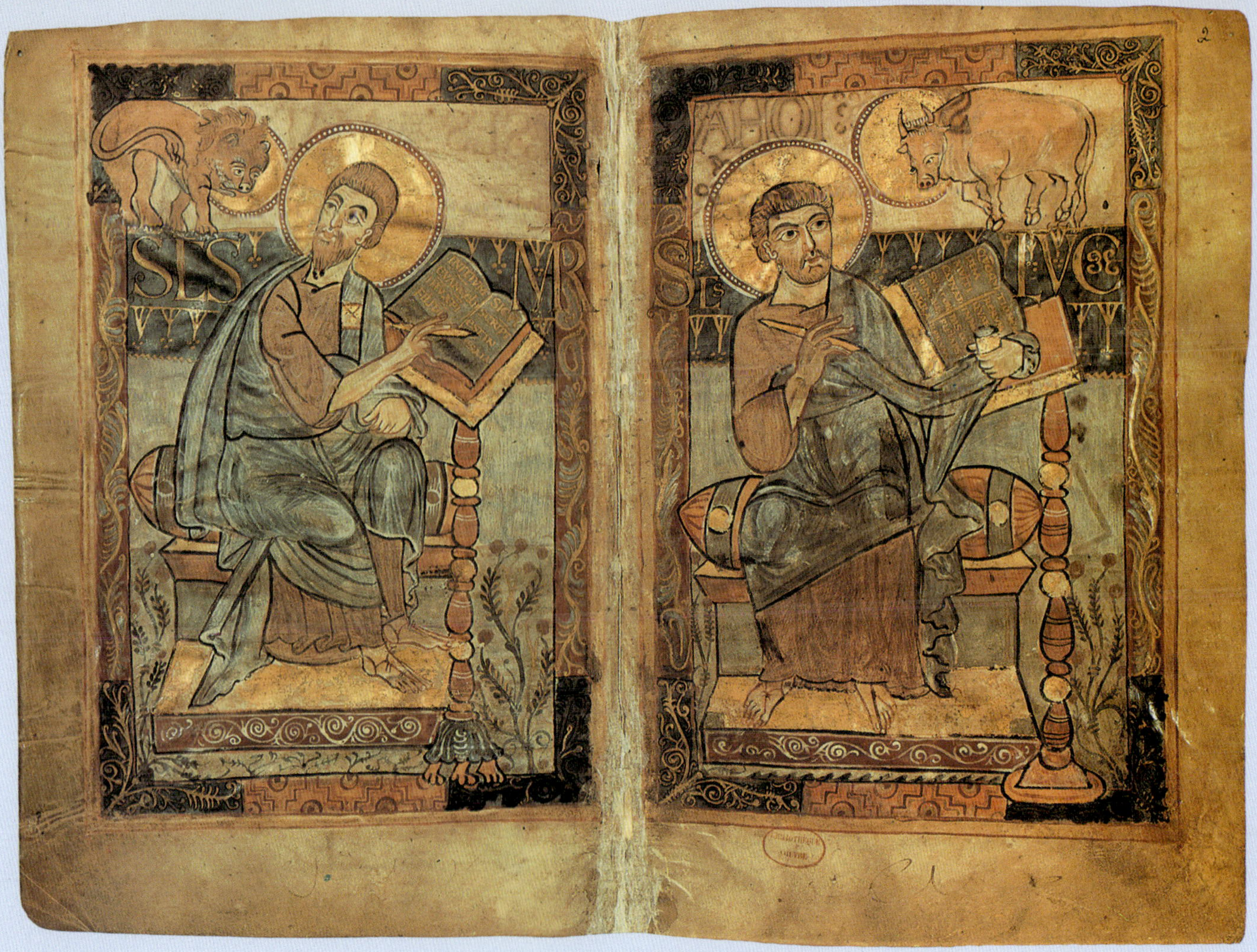

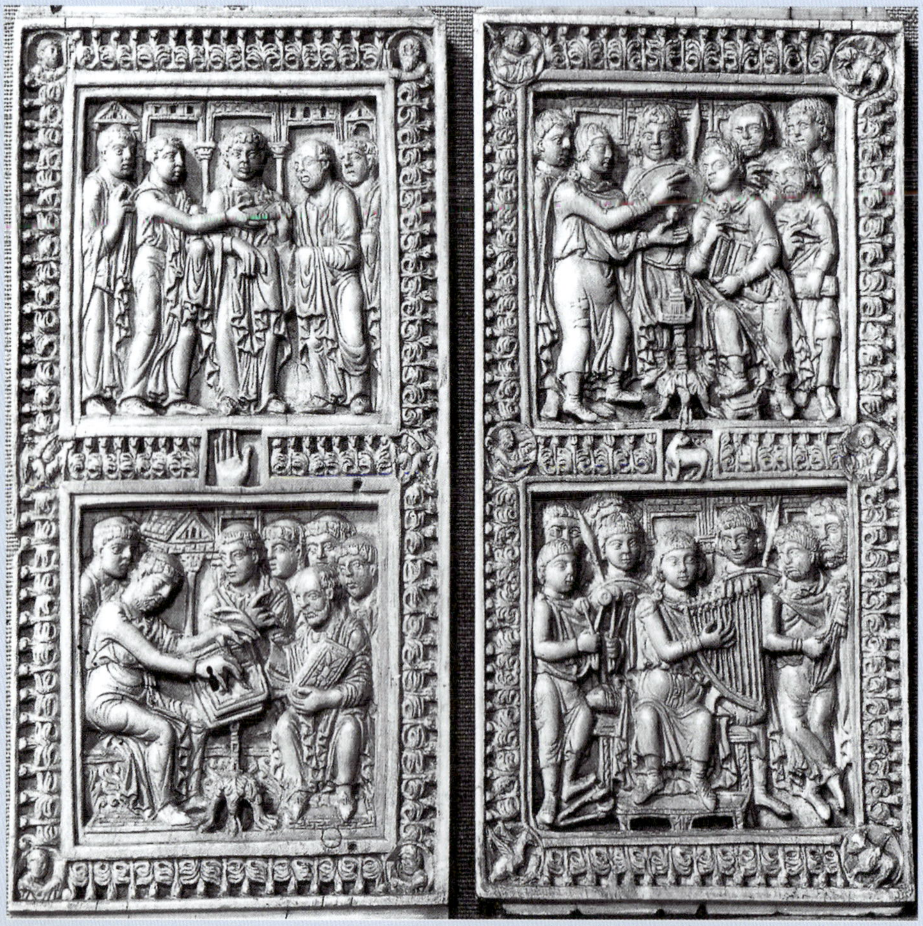

7.24 St Mark and St Luke, from the Gospel Book of Godescale, 781–3. Vellum, $12\frac{1}{4} \times 8\frac{1}{4}$ ins (31.3×21 cm). Bibliothèque Nationale, Paris.

7.26 (*opposite*) Back of the Lorsch Gospels, showing the Virgin and Child between Zacharias and John the Baptist, c. 810. Ivory, $15\frac{1}{8} \times 10\frac{5}{8}$ ins (38.4×27 cm). Victoria & Albert Museum, London.

7.25 Cover of the Dagulf Psalter, showing David in various scenes, 783–95. Ivory, each leaf $6\frac{5}{8} \times 3\frac{1}{4}$ ins (16.8×8.3 cm). Louvre, Paris.

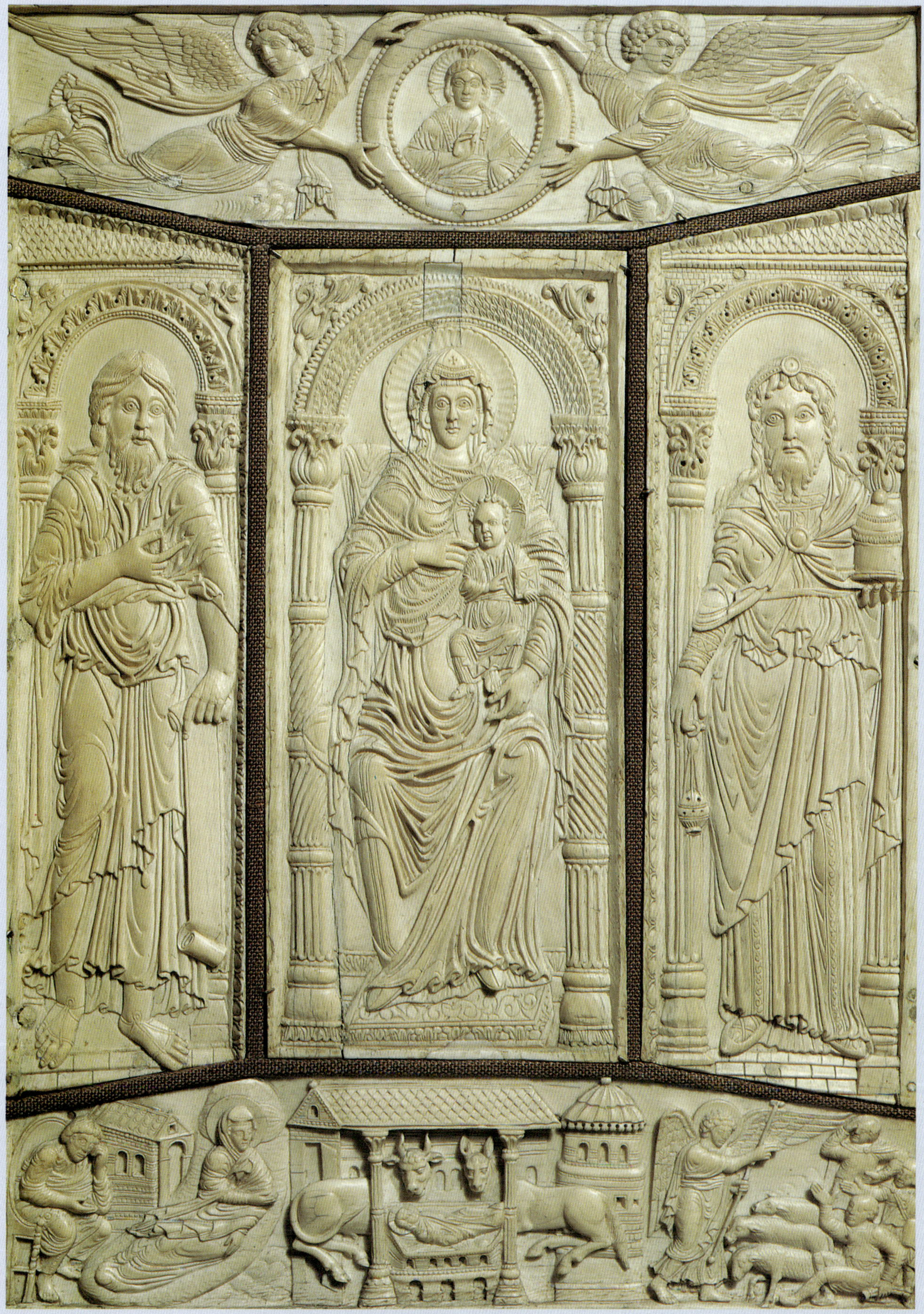

Architecture

Architecture, like painting and sculpture, was ruled by the political goals of the Carolingian court. Charlemagne carefully chose bishops for his kingdom who would assist in the building program he envisaged, and almost immediately new construction began across the empire.

He returned to his capital, Aachen, or Aix-la-Chapelle, from visits to Italy not only with visions of Roman monuments, but also with a belief that majesty and permanence must be symbolized in impressive architecture.

The realization of these dreams, however, was tempered by some of the difficult architectural facts of life. Charlemagne took as his model the church of San Vitale in Ravenna (see Figs **6.26**, **6.27**, and **6.31**), built by Justinian in the Byzantine style. All Charlemagne's materials, including columns and bronze gratings, had to be transported over the Alps from Italy to Aachen in Germany. Skilled stonemasons were few and far between, but the task was, nevertheless, accomplished.

The Palatine Chapel at Aachen (Fig. 7.27), built to be Charlemagne's tomb-house, became the jewel in his crown. The interior reveals the grandeur and style of this building. Designed by a Frankish architect, Odo of Metz, the Palatine Chapel has very little of the spatial subtlety of San Vitale, however. There is less mystery, and the space itself seems more constricted, with the emphasis on verticality rather than openness. The rounded arches and thick, rectangular pillars supporting the dome create massiveness, which cannot be offset by slender, decorative columns. Part of the building's sense of massiveness comes from its material: rubble faced with stone for the vault. Charlemagne's throne was placed in the first gallery above the door and looked down and across the central space to the altar.

During Charlemagne's reign, then, we find a true renaissance, modified as it may have been to serve the grand design and political ambitions of the emperor. The recreation of antiquity in the arts and humanities made visible and intelligible the dream of a resurrected Roman Empire, with Charlemagne at its head.

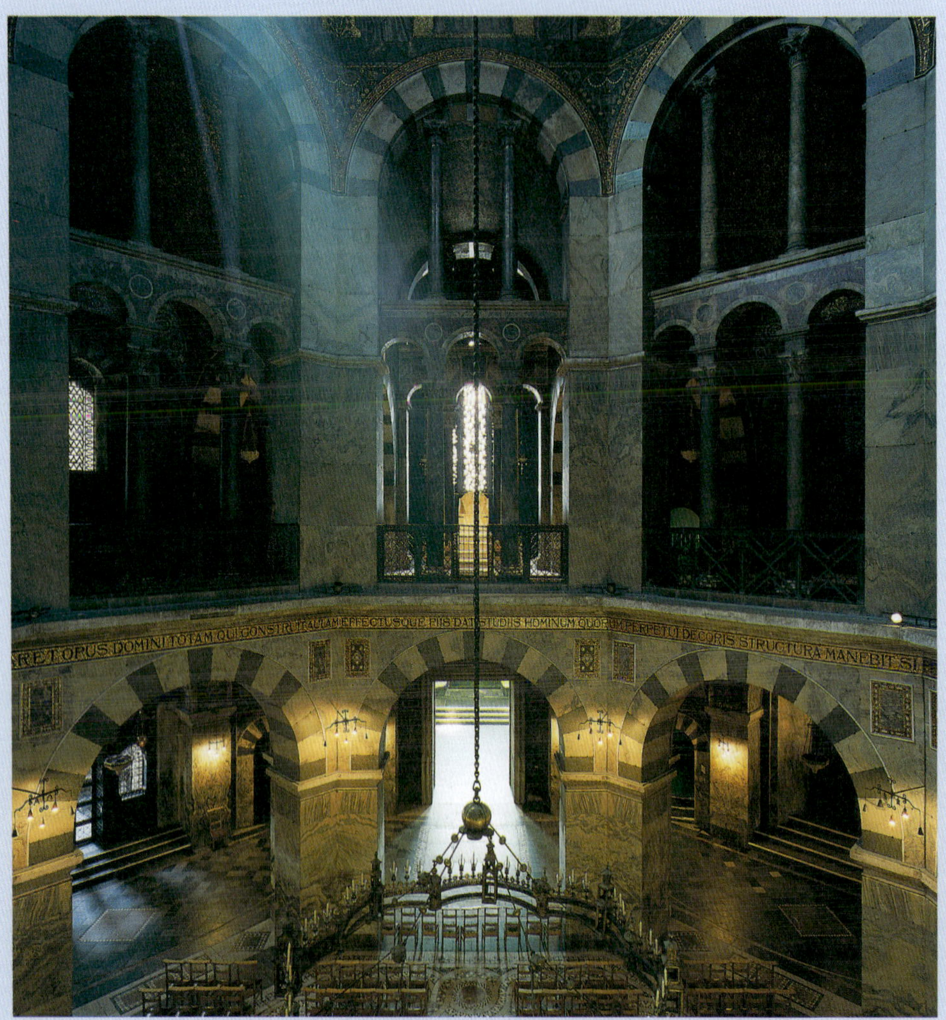

7.27 Palatine Chapel of Charlemagne, Aachen, Germany 792–805. Photo: © Steffans/SOA Photo Agency, London.

CHAPTER REVIEW

❖ CRITICAL THOUGHT ❖

Debates often arise about questions such as these: Does art really mirror its times, or is it purely a result of some internal necessity of the artist? Should it be useful or does it exist for its own sake? In this chapter we have made more than a little of the relationships between the barricaded mentality of the political times and the nervous and crowded spaces of the visual art and the heavy fortress-like nature of architecture. Can you think of examples of how visual art, music, drama, and architecture of our time make similar statements? What is your viewpoint on art as a reflection of society?

◆ SUMMARY ◆

After reading this chapter, you will be able to:

- Identify and define the divisions of the Middle Ages.
- Describe the role of the Christian Church and monasticism in the life of the times.
- Characterize the music of the early Middle Ages, identify its forms, and discuss the role of Pope Gregory I in its development.
- Understand how the Carolingian renaissance affected politics, religion, and the arts and architecture of the period.
- Discuss feudalism as a social system.
- Explain the nature of theatre, dance, and literature and cite specific writers and works with regard to literature.
- Characterize the Romanesque style in visual art and architecture.
- Apply the elements and principles of composition to analyze and compare specific works of art and architecture illustrated in this chapter.

CYBERSOURCES

http://www.mcad.edu/AICT/html/medieval/march_rom.html
http://www.geocities.com/Athens/Parthenon/8063/norman.html
http://www.bc.edu/bc_org/avp/cas/fnart/arch/romanesque_arch.html
http://web.kyoto-inet.or.jp./org/orion/eng/hst/romanesq.html

8 THE HIGH MIDDLE AGES

THE GOTHIC AGE

OUTLINE

VIEW

INDIVIDUALISM

We all desire to be thought of as individuals of worth and to have some semblance of control in our lives. In the twelfth century, humankind found a new interest in themselves as individuals: individuals who had some further purpose on earth than merely getting through this "vale of tears" and into the eternal happiness of heaven beyond the grave. People began to see themselves as being important and as having a relationship with the world of the past. New "personalist" elements entered devotion, philosophy, theology, and literature. Individualism meant a degree of control over one's existence and the sphere around it. Such drift was especially true of the ongoing conflict between the Church and secular leaders, but it had an interesting twist. In our society, we find the issue of separation of Church and state essentially one of keeping the Church out of the affairs of state. In the Middle Ages, the reverse was true: the local secular rulers wanted to oversee the Church.

KEY TERMS

Some of the basic terms and concepts we will encounter in this chapter include the following:

CHIVALRY
A more feminine point of view in ethics and personal conduct as compared to feudalism.

REALISM
A belief, as held by Abelard, that objects have real individuality that makes each a substance in its own right.

STIGMATA
The appearance of wounds, from no discernible cause, that resemble the crucifixion wounds of Jesus Christ.

ALLEGORY
Expression by means of symbols to make a more effective generalization or moral commentary about human existence than could be achieved by direct or literal means.

GOTHIC STYLE
A synthesis of medieval intellect, spirituality, and engineering—in architecture characterized by the pointed arch.

MEASURED RHYTHM
Music employing definite time values and precise meters.

MYSTERY PLAY
A medieval religious play produced by occupational guilds.

8.1 Salisbury Cathedral, England, from the southwest, begun 1220.

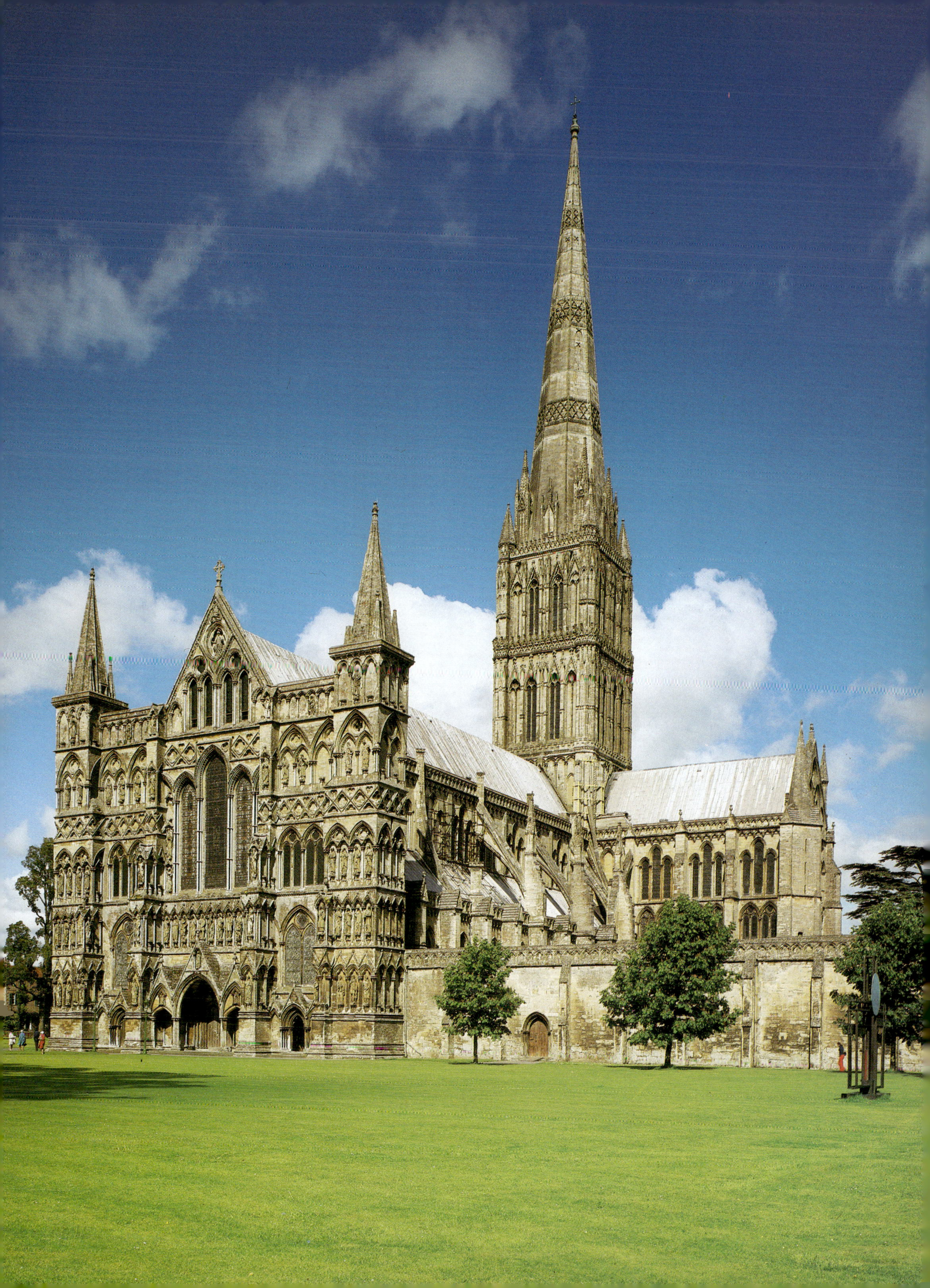

Universals—"Sam's" Story

Many years ago a colleague laid on my desk a very expensive book about architecture. "From a student," he said. "Before or after grades?" I replied in my usual, insensitive, flip manner. After a pregnant pause and a bit of glaring, he told me "Sam's" story.

Sam was a construction worker taking "Introduction to the Arts" as a night course. After the semester ended (and after grades were posted!) Sam brought the book to my colleague, who had taught the course. At that time, such a book probably cost at least a fourth of Sam's weekly salary.

"Why?" asked my colleague.

"Because you changed my life," Sam replied. "Before this course I poured concrete day in and day out. It was concrete—you know, cement, sand, stone etc.—just concrete. After taking this course, I can't see just bland concrete anymore. Whenever I walk onto a job site, I see patterns, colors, lines, and forms. Whenever I look at a building, I see history. I go places I'd never dreamed of going before, and I can't believe how dull my life really was without all the things I now hear and see. I just never knew there was so much out there."

My colleague said, "You know, this construction worker—'Joe Sixpack' we might have called him—a man's man, had tears in his eyes; he was so taken by what he'd found out about life through art."

I have to admit, that brought a certain dewy sting to my own eyes.

Is art relevant? You bet. Just ask Sam.

HOW ART WORKS

UNIVERSALS I:
Letting Light into Lives

Does the art of the past have any relevance to the twenty-first century? One answer is that the relevance of at least some art—"great art," some would say—lies in its delving into "universals"—that is, those significant questions whose answers remain as elusive or vexing today as they were at the beginning of humankind: Who am I? Why am I here? Is there a God? What is He/She like? Is there life after death? How should I treat my neighbor? Some art just has the ability to penetrate into us in such a way that it makes a profound difference in the way we react, think, and feel. The ability to touch us "where we live" is one of the talents no one can really explain, and brilliant people, dolts, the educated, the illiterate, the sane, and the insane have had this talent in every age. Knowing about art—past and present—gives us a shot at having life-changing experiences. Another answer is that art gives us a chance to develop the right side of the brain, which sound scientific evidence suggests determines certain ways of responding, thinking, and feeling. In short, we all have two halves to our brain. Who, in their right mind would want to meet life's challenges with only half the tools available to them? Does it stand to reason that not developing the right half of the brain leaves one a half-wit?

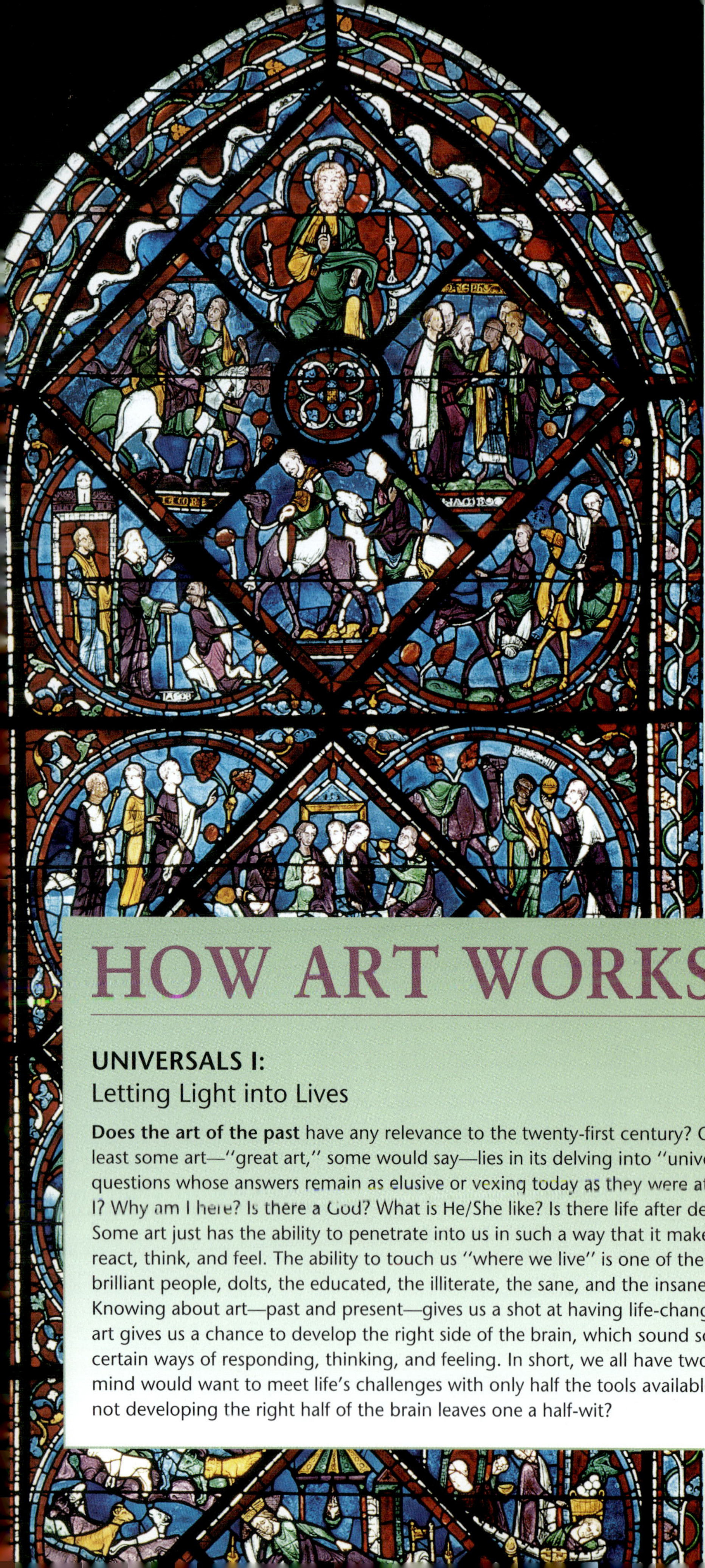

8.2 Chartres Cathedral, France, St. Joseph Window, 13th century. See also Figs **8.22–8.28**.

CONTEXTS AND CONCEPTS

The Social Order of the High Middle Ages

The Rise of Cities

Humanity in the late Middle Ages seemed to undergo a spiritual and intellectual revival that had a profound influence on the creative spirit.

In the year 1000 C.E., Europe consisted of stone fortresses on hills and muddy huts in cramped villages. Two centuries later, the world had been transformed. This transformation of medieval society sprang largely from the resurgence of cities, for which three main factors were responsible—agricultural improvements, population growth, and the revival of trade.

Primitive as the manor system of feudalism was, it did produce important agricultural improvements. One of these was a three-field system of crop rotation. After the year 1000, the amount of land under cultivation increased tremendously. An increase in the food supply meant an increase in the population of Europe.

However, the primary cause of the rebirth of cities was revival of trade in the eleventh, twelfth, and thirteenth centuries. Soldiers returning from the Crusades brought tales of the East and of marvelous goods that caught the fancy of nobles and commoners alike.

Merchant and craft guilds—that is, trade associations of dealers in, or makers of, products from cloth to metals—dominated trading cities. Gradually, cities developed independent political authorities—for example, magistrates and city councils—although these political authorities were elected only by business people. At the heart of the city lay the doers of business—crafts guilds, their masters, assistants, and apprentices; merchants who required stevedores, porters, and muleteers, and so on. In addition, priests, students, lawyers, runaway serfs, and others were drawn to the city in search of protection and employment. The city offered a new hope of escape from slavery to the land, and thousands flocked there.

The Middle Class

As the commercial class grew richer, it also gained power, filling a vacuum between nobility and peasantry. However, no order gives up power easily, and struggles, sometimes violent, pitted burgher against nobleman. The Crusades ruined many feudal landholders, and a taste of potential power and wealth strengthened the resolve of the "middle-class" citizens. They needed a more dynamic society than feudalism could offer, so they threw their

	900–1050	1050–1100	1100–1150	1150–1200	1200–1300
GENERAL EVENTS	Monastic reform, 910	Norman conquest of England, 1066; Investiture Controversy, 1075–1122; First Crusade, 1095	Cistercians founded, 1115; Eleanor of Aquitaine, 1122–1204; Second Crusade, 1147	Muslims conquer Jerusalem, 1187; Third Crusade, 1189	Fourth Crusade, 1202; Franciscans founded, 1209; Louis IX, 1215–70; Dominicans founded, 1216
PAINTING & SCULPTURE			Tympanum, Saint-Denis (**8.10**)		Cimabue (**8.6**), Manuscript illumination (**8.7, 8.8, 8.9**)
ARCHITECTURE			Abbey Church of Saint-Denis (**8.10, 8.13, 8.16**)		Salisbury Cathedral (**8.1**),Chartres Cathedral (**8.2, 8.22–8.28**), Notre Dame (**8.17**), Amiens Cathedral (**8.18**)
THEATRE			Mystery, miracle, and morality plays		
MUSIC & DANCE				Léonin, Pérotin	
LITERATURE & PHILOSOPHY		Anselm	Abelard, St Bernard of Clairvaux	Chrétien de Troyes	Psalter of St Louis, Douce Apocalypse, St Francis of Assisi, Thomas Aquinas, Dante

Timeline 8.1 The High Middle Ages.

TECHNOLOGY

A Better Horse Collar

In the Middle Ages, the horse came into its own as a technological tool. Horsepower was the most universally available source of power known to humankind, although in the medieval period, the horse was seen primarily as a means of carrying knights and their retinue. However, the horse offered potential for both transportation and agriculture. The first horse harnesses unsuccessfully used the ox yoke as a model, but horses do not have the prominent and powerful shoulders of the ox. The next step consisted of a breast-band, which held the harness down by means of a strap passing between the legs to a girth-band. This device chafed the horse, and, when heavy loads were pulled, the breast-band caused choking pressure on the horse's neck and windpipe. Even the ingenious Romans had not been able to invent a useful means for hitching a horse to wagon or plow. In the twelfth century, however, three main improvements occurred. Shafts, which could be attached well down the breast-band, came into common use. Next, traces—that is, side straps or chains to connect the animal to what it is pulling—served in the same way as shafts to bring the pressure to the middle of the breast-band, and made it possible to use horses in file, as opposed to side by side. However, the most important invention was that of the padded horse collar. This stiff apparatus replaced the breast-band and made it possible for the horse's power to be multiplied by as much as five times over the old method. Thus, the horse came into its own as a technological device. Modern horse carts were developed in France, and the horse replaced the ox for pulling plows and carriages. As a result, effective agriculture and land-based trade were just a step away.

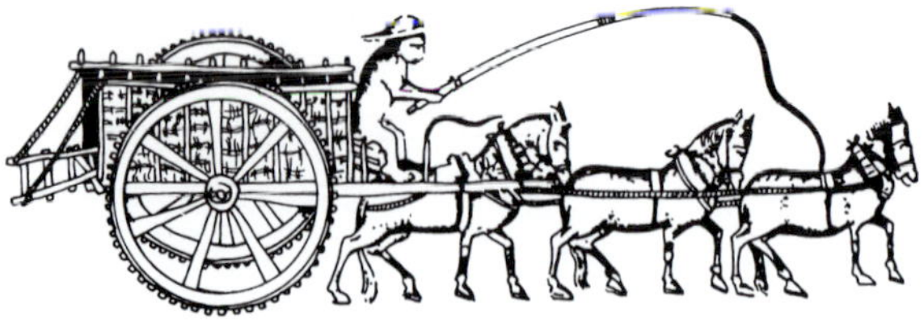

8.3 Two-wheeled cart, from the Luttrell Psalter.

weight and power into strengthening monarchies that favored them. Thus, an emerging middle class played a vital role in a changing social order that would see more centralized administration, stabilization, and rudimentary democracy.

Feudal Monarchs and Monarchies

The explosion of economic activity led to the reestablishment of centralized power in the hands of medieval kings. Under their aegis a new form of government itself evolved. The basic problem for the medieval monarch was the need to replace feudal law with royal law and to tax what amounted to a nation. For such problems to be solved, compromises had to be made, and where the monarchies were most successful—in England and France—the monarchs paid for their growing power by granting rights to representative bodies that spoke for the primary classes of medieval society—that is, the nobility, the Church, and the wealthy new cities and towns.

Some monarchs were more successful than others at statecraft. Probably the most notable of the medieval monarchs was Duke William, the Bastard of Normandy, who invaded and conquered England in 1066, thus gaining for himself the name William I the Conqueror (1066–87). As king of England, he gave the country greater centralized government than it had ever known, and under his successors, Henry I and Henry II, England developed its system of common law, the royal council, and the exchequer (treasury). By the end of the twelfth century, England had the strongest monarchial government in Europe.

France had two significant monarchs during the High Middle Ages. The first was Philip Augustus (1180–1223). Although not particularly inspiring physically, Philip proved to be France's most successful medieval monarch. He used his position to gain power over the nobility and to develop an effective, independent royal administrative system that included a strengthened legal system. Unlike William I of England, Philip Augustus did not conquer any foreign lands. However, he did conquer rebellious feudal barons in the south of France, and he won from Henry II of England parts of western France that had been under English rule since the time of William the Conqueror. Thus, under his rule, France tripled in size and replaced the Holy Roman Empire as the most powerful entity in Europe.

The strong but pious Louis IX (1215–70), who reigned from 1226, gave France the prestige of a saint in its royal lineage. Although Louis did not hesitate to increase royal power, to issue royal edicts without consultation, or to tamper with the legal system, he possessed great strength of character and medieval Christian virtue. He had such a reputation for justice, which he often meted out sitting under an oak tree, that he was known as Louis the Just. Among the acts for which he was canonized only thirty years after his death was the washing of lepers' feet. His saintly life did much to solidify his power.

Chivalry

At the same time, another medieval phenomenon was born of a change in attitude that permeated society and the arts. Feudalism was a masculine, "men-at-arms" code of behavior. But by the twelfth century, a distinctly feminine point of view ruled ethics and personal conduct—that of *chivalry* and the courtly tradition. Men were away from their homes or castles for long periods of time, whether they were off trading or off warring, and it fell to women to run their households and control domestic matters and manners. If Eleanor of Aquitaine (AH-kwih-tayn; 1122–1204) is a representative example, women managed this very well. Society thus took on a gentler, more civil tone than under the rough code of feudalism, and elaborate codes of conduct and etiquette emerged, which culminated in "courts of love," and gave rise to a literary form called the romance (see p. 252), whose subject matter treated chivalric adventure and religious allegories.

The courtly tradition had an important impact on religious philosophy. The early Middle Ages were fixated on devils and death, faith notwithstanding. As time passed, however, we find a warmer feeling, a quality of mercy. Christ the Savior and Mary, his compassionate mother, became the focal points of the faith. This change in viewpoint is reflected very clearly in the arts of the time.

Although chivalry introduced a "feminine" ethos into the High Middle Ages, and although some important women such as Eleanor of Aquitaine emerged, in general, women lost many of the independent opportunities and positions of authority they had earlier enjoyed.

In its earliest formulation, chivalry meant mostly the virtues of war—that is, courage, skill with weapons, fairness to one's foes, and loyalty to one's liege lord (Fig. 8.4). However, under the guidance of medieval women,

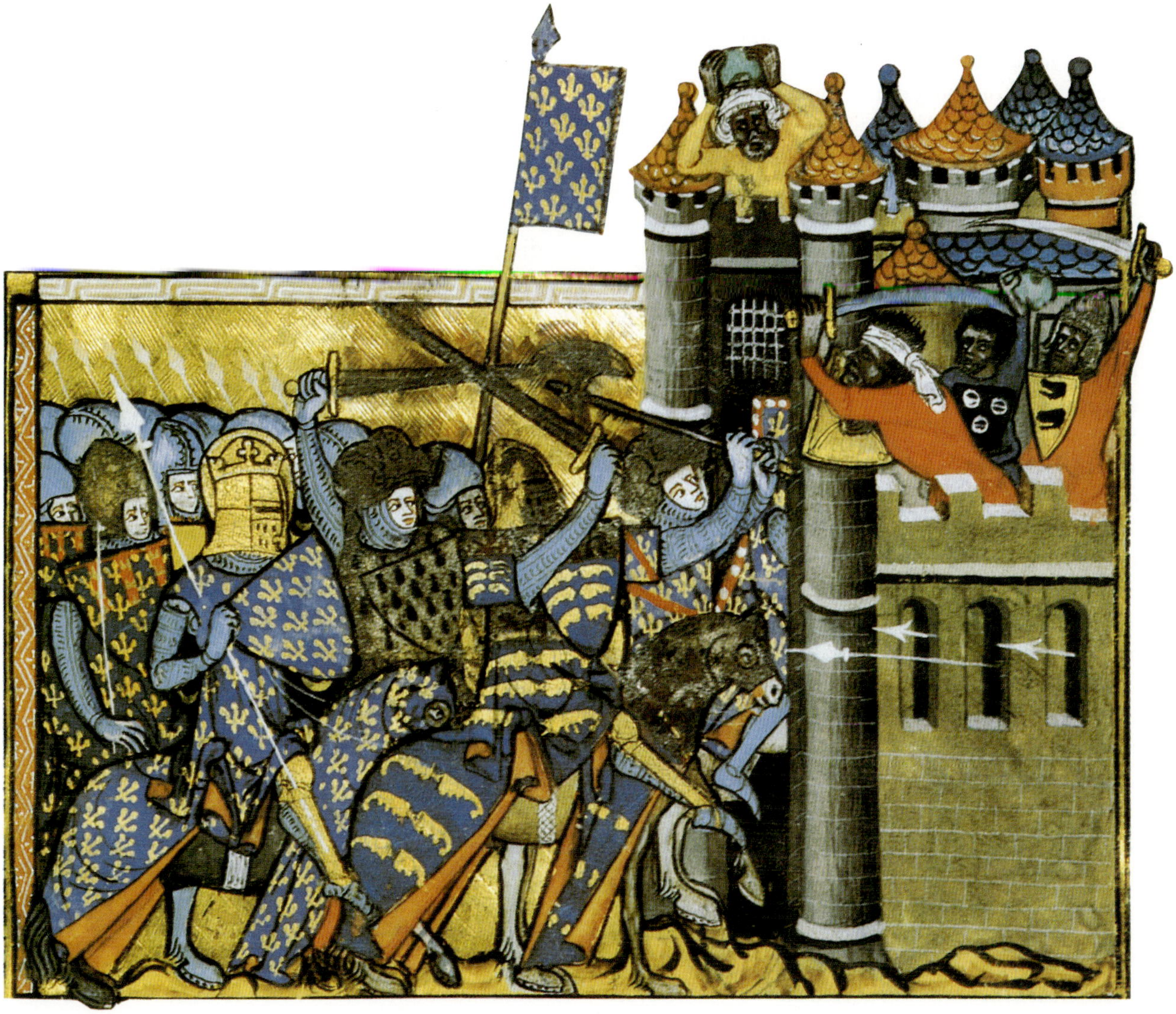

8.4 French knights, commanded by King Louis XI, taking the Egyptian city of Damietta during the Seventh Crusade (1249). MS Fr. 13568. Fol. 83. Bibliothèque Nationale, Paris.

the chivalric code, as we have just noted, turned to a code of courtly love. The truly chivalrous knight was encouraged to protect women *and* to love, serve, and revere a particular lady, although from afar. Women paid for the services of minstrels and troubadours, and these wandering entertainers were suited to the tastes of their benefactresses. They composed and sang songs of love, praising knights who served their ladies well.

The Christian Church

Reform in the Christian Church

The development of Western culture, including its artistic institutions in the late Middle Ages, was profoundly affected, if not controlled, by the Christian Church. By the middle of the eleventh century, the Church had become extremely powerful.

Although the tenth-century Church had become feudalized and corrupt, with many of its secular clergy seeking only wealth and power, this corruption did not go unchallenged. Cries for reform came loudest from the monasteries. The founding of the Abbey of Cluny by William of Aquitaine in 910 signaled the start of a major reform movement. The strict discipline and high moral standards of Cluny's Benedictine monks and abbots made Cluny a model of reform, and its influence spread across Europe.

While monastic life was successfully reformed to its original standards, however, the secular clergy changed their behavior very little. Feudal lords and the lesser nobility appointed priests and bishops, often choosing the highest bidder. Bishoprics were treated as family property, and the secular clergy, many of whose priests were married, did not place a high priority on their religious duties.

Conditions were ripe for reform, and the reformers vehemently attacked the evils of the secular clergy. Circumstances changed in 1046 under Emperor Henry III of Germany. Henry championed the cause of the reformers, and in 1049 he appointed Pope Leo IX, who ruled until 1054. During those five years, Leo introduced a brilliant ecclesiastical reorganization, including the creation of a body of cardinals. Creation of the rank of cardinal made it possible for the papacy to exercise control over those bishops who had been named by lay rulers. After a series of synods in Rome, Leo made a personal tour of the empire, during which he publicized his reforms. As he put them into practice, he both consolidated his program and rid the clergy of many of its most offensive bishops.

Conflict between papacy and laity over the investiture of ecclesiastical office was not solved so easily, however. At the heart of the matter lay the issue of the basis of royal authority. The resulting struggle became known as the "Investiture conflict." Through a series of negotiated settlements with the various monarchs of Europe, the relationships between nobility and clergy, and clergy and papacy, were stabilized. The outcome was a compromise in which kings gave up their ancient claims to represent God's will in appointing senior clergy. They did continue to nominate bishops, but they had greater difficulty in presenting candidates considered unsuitable by the Church. From the twelfth century onward, the quality of ecclesiastical appointments improved substantially.

The papacy emerged from the conflict with greatly enhanced prestige, and the importance of the Church in medieval affairs, artistic and otherwise, continued to grow.

St Bernard of Clairvaux and Mysticism

Many new religious orders were founded during this period. The Virgin Mary assumed a new importance in religious life, and the cult of Mary Magdalene spread through Europe. A key figure in the changing religious thought was a young nobleman, Bernard of Clairvaux (klair-VOH; 1090–1153), who entered the order of Cîteaux (sih-TOH), or the Cistercians, the most influential new monastic movement of the twelfth century.

Bernard was an enthusiast, perhaps even a fanatic, having no doubt in his own mind that his views were correct. He entered into eager combat with anyone who disagreed with him, and those individuals included the most influential clerics and philosophers of the times, men such as the scholar and theologian Peter Abelard (AB-uh-lahrd), the monk and abbot Suger (soo-ZHAY), of Saint-Denis, and the entire order of Cluny. At the same time, Bernard could show great patience and common sense. He treated his monks with patience and forgiveness, and reportedly turned down the duke of Burgundy's request to become a monk by saying that the world had many virtuous monks but few pious dukes.

His religious teaching set a new tone for twelfth-century Christianity through its emphasis on a more mystical and personal sense of piety than had existed previously. In his writings he described a way of "ascent to God," consisting of four stages of love by which a soul could gain union with God. In his sermons for the common people, he treated more ordinary themes and vividly retold familiar stories from the New Testament. Rather than treating Jesus, Mary, and the apostles as remote images, Bernard described them as living personalities. Bernard's preaching was an important stimulant for the spread of the Mary cults.

The Crusades

Many have the notion that the Crusades featured knights in shining armor setting out on glorious quests to free the Holy Land from Infidels. The Crusades were far from a romantic quest, however. Instead, they illustrate clearly a new and practical energy and optimism in Europe in a new millennium and a new era.

As early as the tenth century, popes had led armies against the Saracens in Italy. By the end of the eleventh century, the Church was able to put forward several reasons why a Christian army might march against the Muslims. Constantinople had been rescued from the Turks, and a healing of the east–west schism seemed possible. Furthermore, pilgrimages to the Holy Land as a form of penance had become increasingly popular in this age of religious zeal, and the safety of these pilgrims was ample reason for interference by the popes. A more practical benefit closer to home was the removal of troublesome nobles from the local scene. An opportunity came in 1095 at the Council of Clermont. When envoys of the eastern emperor Alexius Comnenus supposedly asked Pope Urban II for aid, Urban set about mounting a crusading army. The response to his call was astonishing. Thousands came forward to take up the cross. Men, women, and children—even those who were disabled—clamored to take part, and the aforementioned nobles also went riding off to war.

The reasons for the First Crusade went beyond its

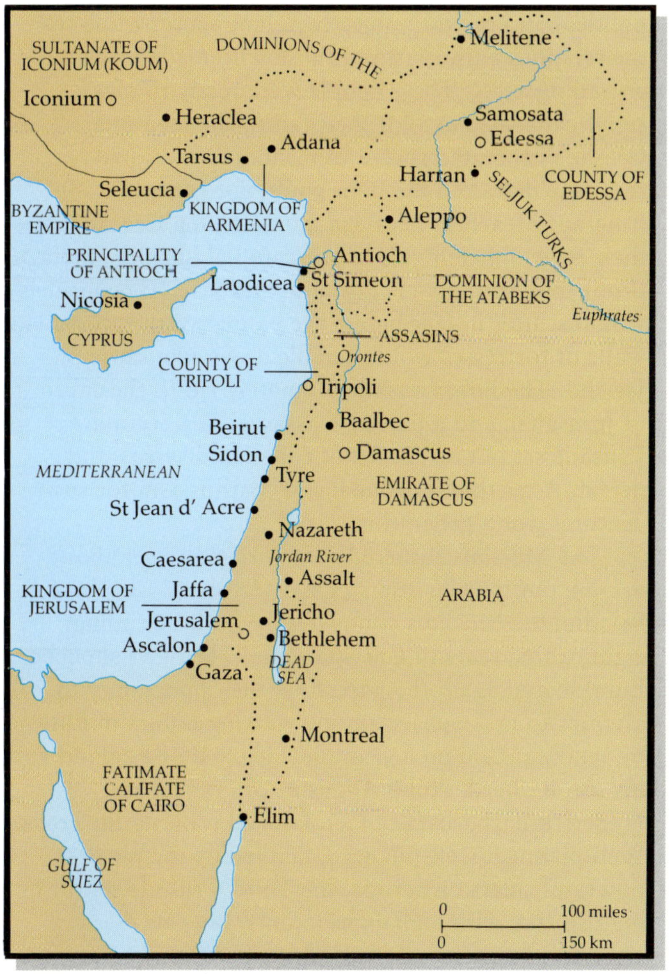

Map 8.1 (*right*) Areas of the Crusades.

Map 8.2 (*below*) The Crusades.

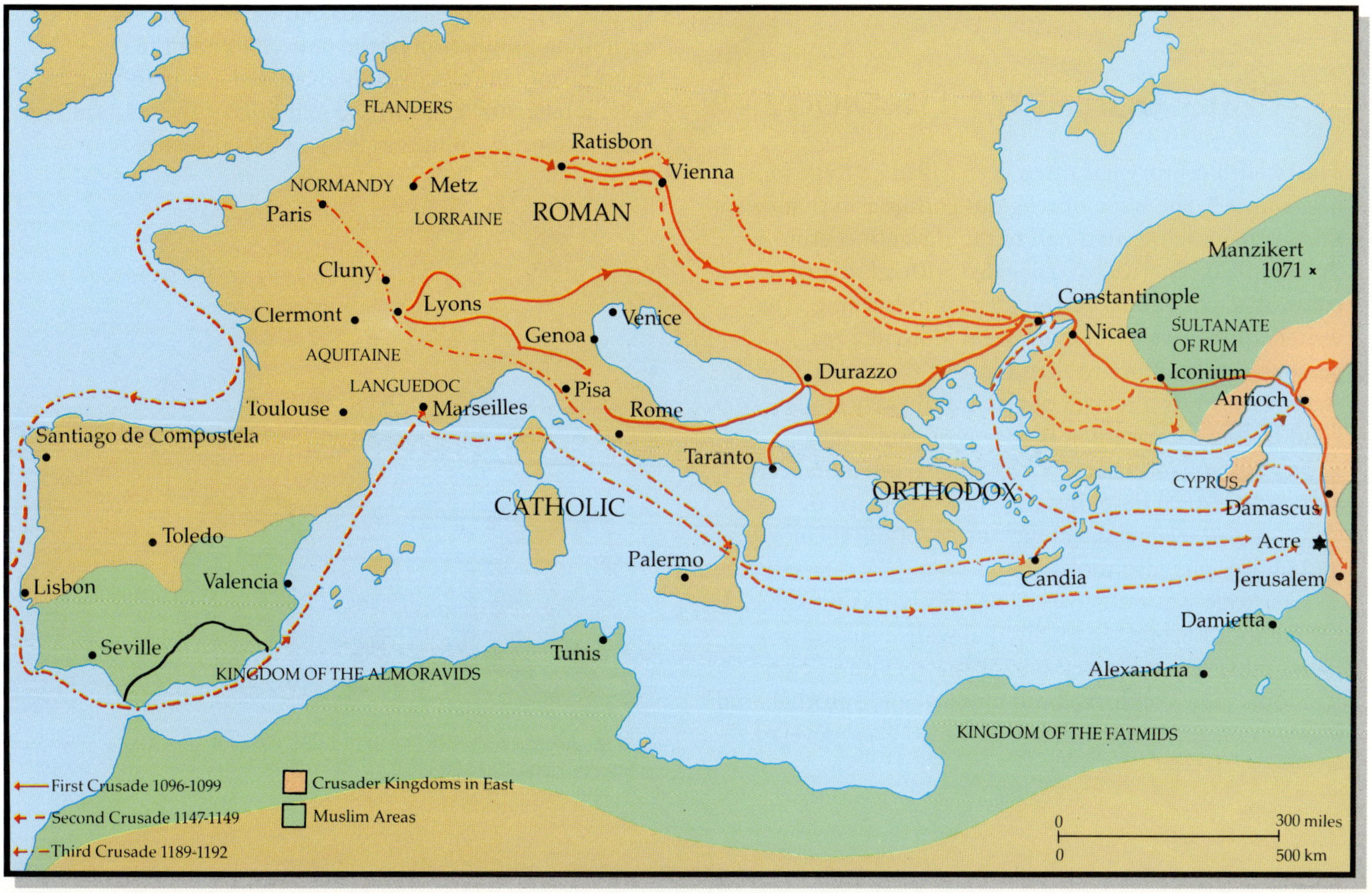

political and military objectives. Its impetus came from the religious enthusiasm of those who made up the crusading army. These people were ready to make significant sacrifices for their faith. The idea of a Crusade generated such a tremendous emotional response that even the Pope could not control it. Itinerant preachers heralded an upcoming Crusade in their revival meetings. No one cared about the practical problems—it was an act of faith and piety. The infidels would scatter in fear before the banner of the cross. The walls of fortresses would tumble down like those of Jericho. The First Crusade ultimately led to the capture of Jerusalem and a bloody massacre. The Second Crusade set out in 1147, but ended in disarray and defeat. After that, Europe lost its enthusiasm for such ventures, for a generation.

The Muslims gathered their forces and set about driving out the Christians. On 3 October 1187, led by Saladin, the Muslims conquered Jerusalem, ending eighty-three years of Christian rule. The news shocked Europe, and again the pope took the opportunity to attempt to make peace among warring nobles in Europe by sending them on a Crusade. Henry II of England and his son Richard, Philip Augustus of France, and Frederick Barbarossa of Germany all took up the cross. Well-planned, well-financed, and led by the most powerful rulers of Europe, the Third Crusade set off in high spirits, with high expectations. But one disaster after another befell the crusaders. Their major accomplishment was the capture of Acre after a two-year siege.

Philosophy and Theology

The twelfth century has often been called an "age of humanism." The wave of religious enthusiasm that swept Europe from the second half of the eleventh century to the middle of the twelfth coincided with a burst of cultural activity and a zestful interest in learning. The writers of the twelfth century seem more like real persons—much more so than those of the earlier Middle Ages. There was a revival of classical literary studies, a vivid feeling for nature in lyric poetry, and a new naturalism in Gothic art. With these exciting intellectual and ecclesiastical developments, new humanist or "personalist" elements in religious devotion, theology, and philosophy also took hold.

Aristotle was rediscovered and his works introduced throughout Europe. As intellectual walls broke down, light and fresh air flooded into Western culture. New freedoms, new comforts, both physical and spiritual, and a new confidence in the future pervaded every level of society.

The Rise of Universities

Many universities gained their charters in the twelfth and thirteenth centuries—for example, Oxford University in England, the University of Salamanca in Spain, the University of Bologna in Italy, and the University of Paris in France. Many had existed previously in association with monasteries, but their formal chartering made the public more aware of them.

Medieval universities were not like today's institutions. They had no buildings or classrooms; instead, they were guilds of scholars and teachers who gathered their students together wherever space permitted. Students came from all over Europe, for example, to hear the lectures at the University of Paris by teachers such as William of Champeaux (1070–1121) and, later, Peter Abelard. University life spawned people with trained minds who sought knowledge for its own sake and who could not accept a society that walled itself in and rigidly resisted any questioning of authority. In Paris, by the late twelfth century, the arts became a prelude to the study of theology.

The rise of universities at this particular time came as a result of a number of factors. This was a time of rediscovery and publication of many of the texts of the classical world, especially the works by Aristotle, which came to the West through Muslim sources in Spain (Fig. 8.5). There was also a large amount of mathematical and scientific material coming to the attention of European scholars, again, largely through contact with Muslim scholars. In addition, for example in Bologna, legal studies received new impetus. All of this, coupled with the exploding population of the new cities and the consequent complexity of life, created a demand for a new, intellectual class who could bolster the cultural and socioeconomic foundations of medieval society.

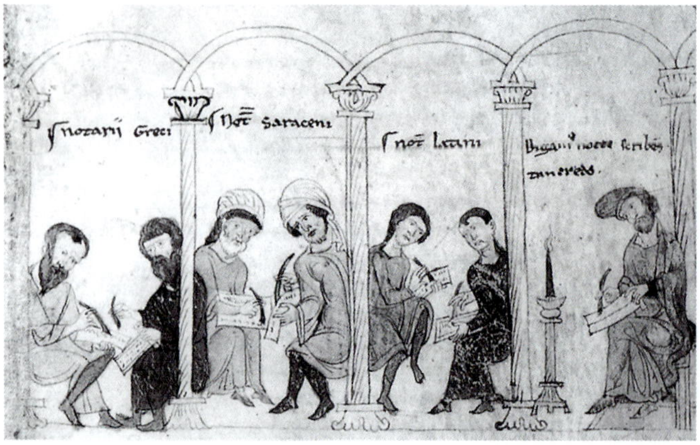

8.5 Medieval scholars studying in Latin, Hebrew, and Arabic at a school in Sicily, c. 1200.

Abelard and Realism

One member of such a class was Peter Abelard (1079–1142), a figure of both philosophy and romance. His lifelong correspondence and late-in-life love affair with Héloïse accounts for the romantic element. As for the philosophy, Abelard denied that objects are merely imperfect imitations of universal ideal models to which they owe their reality. Instead, he argued for the concrete nature of reality. That is to say, objects as we know them have real individuality which makes each object a substance "in its own right."

Abelard went beyond this, to argue that universals do exist, and comprise the "form of the universe" as conceived by the mind of God. These universals are patterns, or types, after which individual substances are created and which make these substances the kinds of things they are.

Abelard has been called a "moderate realist," or, sometimes, a "conceptualist," even though that term is usually applied to later teaching. His views were adopted and modified by St Thomas Aquinas, and in this revised form they constitute part of Roman Catholic Church dogma today. Abelard believed that philosophy had a duty to define Christian doctrine and to make it intelligible. He also believed that philosophers should be free to criticize theology and to reject beliefs that are contrary to reason.

Abelard regarded Christianity as a way of life, but he

PROFILE

St Francis of Assisi (1181/2-1226)

Francis (Fig. **8.6**) was baptized Francesco di Pietro di Bernardone (fron-CHAY-scoe dee pee-AY-troe dee bur-nahr-DOE-nay), the son of a cloth merchant. He learned to read and write Latin as a child and later learned to speak some French. In 1202 he participated in the war between Assisi and Perugia, was taken prisoner, and held for nearly a year. On his release, he was seriously ill, but he recovered and sought to serve in the army again in late 1205. However, after a vision told him to return to Assisi and await a call to a new kind of knighthood, he devoted himself to solitude and prayer in order to know the will of God. This began his conversion, which consisted of a number of episodes. He renounced material goods and family ties and embraced a life of poverty.

Although he was a layman, he began to preach the gospel. He attracted a number of disciples and devised a rule of life for them, based on the Gospel of Matthew: "Take no gold, nor silver, nor money in your belts, no bag for your journey" (Matthew 10:9–11). When the number of disciples, called friars, reached twelve, they went to Rome, where Pope Innocent III gave his blessing to their rule of life. This event, on 16 April 1209, marked the formal beginning of the Franciscan order. The Franciscans preached in the streets and, gradually, the order grew and spread throughout Italy.

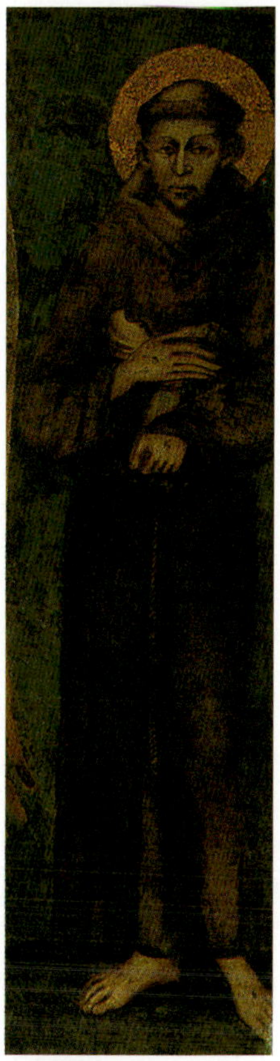

8.6 Cimabue, *Enthroned Madonna with St Francis* (detail), 1280. Fresco, lower church of San Francisco, Assisi, Italy.

Perhaps the most powerful experience of Francis' life occurred in the summer of 1224, when he went to the mountain retreat of La Verna to celebrate the feast of the Assumption of the Virgin and to prepare for St Michael's day with a forty-day fast. He prayed that he might know how best to please God. Opening the Gospels to find an answer, he came three times to the Passion of Christ. Then, as he prayed, he saw a figure coming toward him from heaven. It had the form of a seraph and smiled at him. Francis felt both joy and deep sorrow because of Christ's crucifixion. He understood that by God's providence he would be made like the crucified Christ through conformity of mind and heart. After the vision was over, Francis was marked with the *stigmata* of the Crucified—Francis' body actually showed marks resembling the wounds on the body of Christ. Francis tried to hide the marks for the remainder of his life. He lived for only another two years, and was blind and in constant pain. After his death, his stigmata were announced to the order by letter. One of the most venerated religious figures of his time, he was made a saint on 15 July 1228.

was very tolerant of other religions as well. He considered Socrates and Plato to have been "inspired." The essence of Christianity was not its dogma, but the way Christ had lived his life. Those who lived prior to Jesus were, in a sense, already Christians if they had lived the kind of life Christ did. An individual act should be understood as good or evil "solely as it is well or ill intended," he argued in his treatise *Know Thyself*. However, lest anyone excuse acts on the basis of "good intentions," Abelard insisted that there should be some sort of standard for judging whether intentions were good or bad. Such a standard existed in a natural law of morality, "manifested in the conscience possessed by every man, and founded upon the will of God." When opinions differed over the interpretation of the law of God, he said, each person must obey his or her own conscience. Therefore, "anything a man does that is against his own conscience is sinful, no matter how much his act may commend itself to the consciences of others."[1]

St Thomas Aquinas and Aristotelianism

The rediscovery of Aristotle in the thirteenth century marked a new era in Christian thought. With the exception of Aristotle's treatises on logic, called the *Organon*, his writings were inaccessible to the West until the late twelfth century. Their reintroduction created turmoil. Some centers of education, such as the University of Paris, forbade Aristotle's metaphysics and physics. Others championed Aristotelian thought. These scholars asserted the eternity of the world and denied the existence of divine providence and the foreknowlege of contingent events. In the middle were thinkers such as Albertus Magnus, who, though orthodox in their acceptance of the traditional Christian faith, regarded the rediscovery of Aristotle in a wholly positive light. Magnus' first pupil was Thomas Aquinas (1227–74).

In his youth, Aquinas joined the newly formed mendicant Order of Preachers, the Dominican Order. This led him to Paris to study with Magnus, who was the master teacher of the Dominicans. A prolific writer, Aquinas produced philosophical and theological works and commentaries on Aristotle, the Bible, and Peter Lombard. Aquinas, like Magnus, was a modernist, and he sought to reinterpret the Christian system in the light of Aristotle—in other words, to synthesize Christian theology and Aristotelian thought. He believed that the philosophy of Aristotle would prove acceptable to intelligent men and women, and further, that if Christianity were to maintain the confidence of educated people, it would have to come to terms with and accommodate Aristotle. Nonetheless, Aquinas was a very devout and orthodox believer. He had no wish to sacrifice Christian truth, whether to Aristotle or any other philosopher.

In dealing with God and the universe, Aquinas carefully defined the fields of theology and philosophy. Philosophy was limited to whatever lay open to argument, and its purpose was to establish such truth as could be discovered and demonstrated by human reason. Theology, on the other hand, was restricted to the "content of faith," or "revealed truth," which is beyond the ability of reason to discern or demonstrate, and "about which there can be no argument." There was, nonetheless, an area of overlap.

Aquinas concentrated upon philosophical proofs of God's existence and nature. The existence of God could be proved by reason, he thought, and Aristotle had inadvertently done just that. The qualities, to which Aristotle reduced all the activities of the universe, become intelligible "only on the supposition that there is an unmoved . . . self-existent . . . form of being whose sheer perfection sets the whole world moving in pursuit of it."

THE ARTS OF THE HIGH MIDDLE AGES

Painting

In the twelfth and thirteenth centuries, traditional fresco painting returned to prominence. Manuscript illumination also continued. Two-dimensionality flowed from one style into another without any clearly dominant identity emerging. Because this period is so closely identified with Gothic architecture, and because painting found its primary outlet within the Gothic cathedral, however, we need to ask what qualities identify a Gothic style in painting. The answer is not as readily apparent as it is in architecture and sculpture, but several characteristics can be identified. One is the beginnings of three-dimensionality in figure representation. Another is a striving to give figures mobility and life within three-dimensional space. Space is the essence of Gothic style. Gothic painters and illuminators had not mastered perspective, and their compositions do not exhibit the spatial rationality of later works. But if we compare these painters with their medieval predecessors, we discover that they have more or less broken free from the frozen two-dimensionality of earlier styles. Gothic style also exhibits spirituality, lyricism, and a new humanism. In other words, it favors mercy over irrevocable judgment. Gothic style is less crowded and frantic—its figures are less entangled with each other. It was a changing style with many variations.

The Gothic style of two-dimensional art found magnificent expression in manuscript illumination. The Court Style of France and England is represented by some truly exquisite works. The Psalter of St Louis (Fig. 8.7)

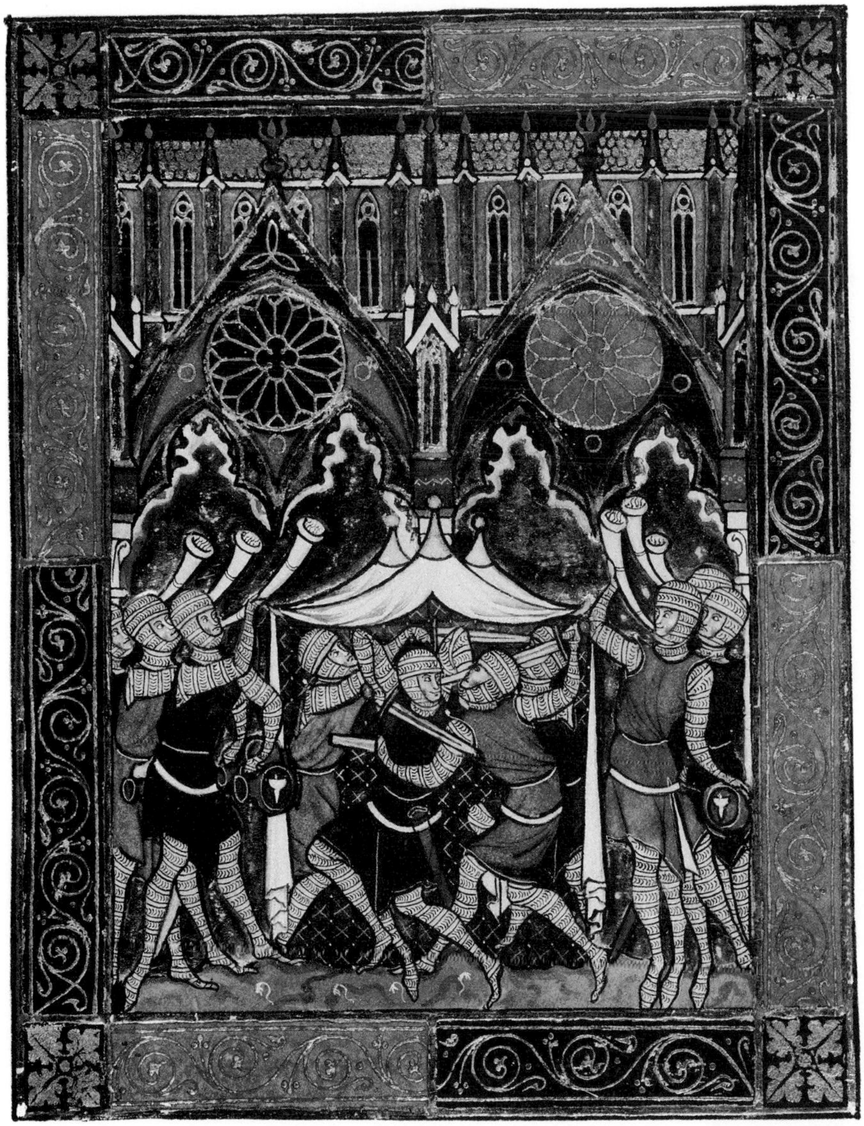

8.7 *Gideon's Army Surprises the Midianites,* from the Psalter of St Louis, c. 1250. 4¾ × 3⅝ ins (12.1 × 9.2 cm). Bibliothèque Nationale, Paris.

was produced for King Louis IX of France in about 1250. It was a lavish book containing seventy-eight full-page pictures of scenes from the Old Testament. The figures are gracefully elongated and delicate. Set against gold backgrounds, the compositions are carefully balanced and, while somewhat crowded, show a relaxed comfort in their spatial relationships. Precision and control characterize the technique. Colors are rich. Human figures and architectural details are blended in the same manner that church sculpture both decorated and became a part of its architectural environment.

The artists who made these works were professionals living in Paris. They were influenced by Italian style, and they clearly had a new interest in pictorial space, which begins to distinguish them from their predecessors. This Parisian style, in turn, influenced English manuscript illumination. Figure **8.8** of *St John on Patmos* was painted for Edward, son of Henry III, and his wife Eleanor of Castile. The elongated figures and small heads reflect the French court influence, as does the heavy drapery. The English painters, however, frequently differed from their French models, by treating drapery folds with greater angularity and giving human subjects exaggerated poses.

The same characteristics can be seen in Figure **8.9**, *David Harping*. The curious proportions of face and hands, as well as the awkward linear draping of fabric juxtaposed against the curved forms of the harp and chair, create a sense of tension. The layout of the background screen is almost careless. The upward curving arcs at the top are intended to be symmetrical, despite the imprecise diamond shapes. A touch of naturalism appears in the curved harp string which David is plucking. A rudimentary use of highlight and shadow gives basic three-dimensionality to cloth and skin, and although it is out of balance in its interior space, the figure does not appear to crowd the borders. It has space

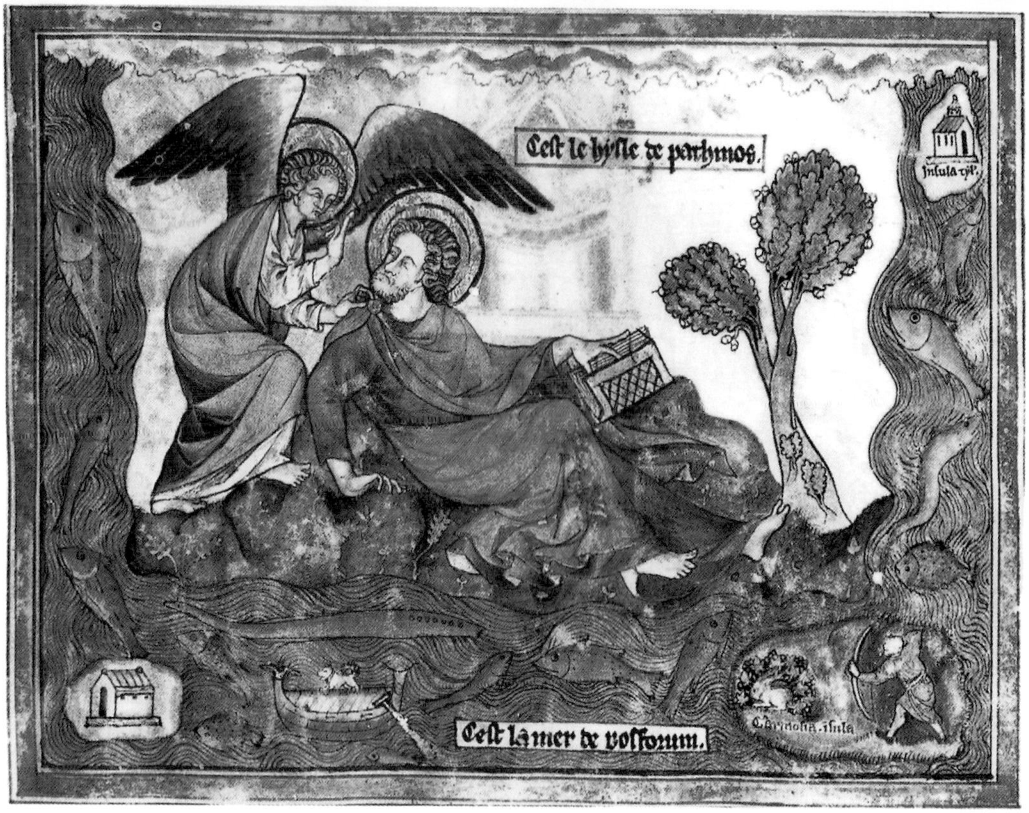

8.8 *St John on Patmos*, from the Douce Apocalypse, before 1272. 12½ × 8⅝ ins (31.75 × 21.9 cm). Bodleian Library, Oxford, England.

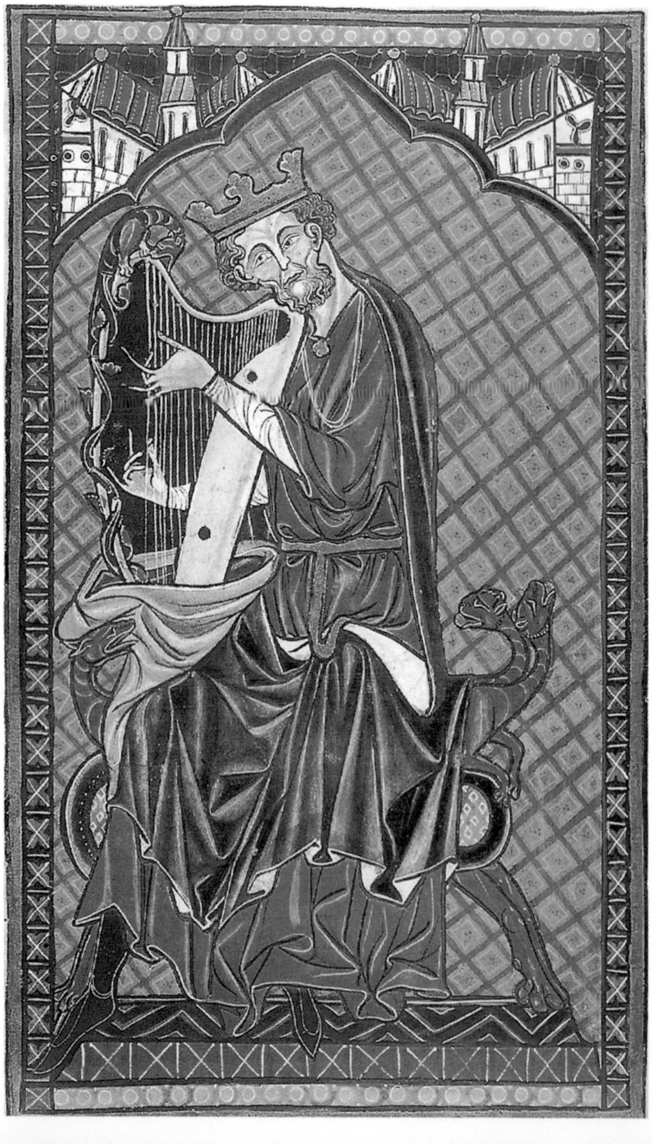

in which to move. More information on Gothic painting with excellent examples is found at http://www.geocities.com/Athens/Parthenon/8063/gothic7.html.

Sculpture

Gothic sculpture again reveals the changes in attitude of the period. It portrays serenity, idealism, and simple naturalism. Gothic sculpture, like painting, has a human quality. Life now seems to be more valuable. The vale of tears, death, and damnation are replaced by conceptions of Christ as a benevolent teacher and of God as awesome in his beauty rather than in his vengeance. There is a new order, symmetry, and clarity. Visual images carry over a distance with greater distinctness. The figures of Gothic sculpture are less entrapped in their material and stand away from their backgrounds.

Schools of sculpture developed throughout France. Thus, although individual stone carvers worked alone, their links with a particular school gave their works the character of that school. The work from Reims, for example, had an almost classical quality; that from Paris was dogmatic and intellectual, perhaps reflecting the role

8.9 *David Harping*, from the Oscott Psalter, c. 1270. 7⅞ × 4⅜ ins (20 × 11.1 cm). British Library, London.

of Paris as a university city. As time went on, sculpture became more naturalistic. Spiritual meaning was sacrificed to everyday appeal, and sculpture increasingly reflected secular interests, both middle-class and aristocratic.

Compositional unity also changed over time. Early Gothic architectural sculpture was subordinate to the overall design of the building. Later work began to claim attention on its own.

The content of Gothic sculpture is also noteworthy. Like most church art, it was *didactic*, or designed to teach. Many of its lessons are straightforward. The Last Judgment tympanum above the central western door of Saint-Denis illustrates this (Fig. **8.10**).

Christ the Judge dominates everything. He reveals his two natures as Son of God and Son of Man. As judge, Christ summons the dead to appear from the grave, which is depicted in the lintel below his feet. He is also depicted at the moment of his crucifixion with outstretched arms and his right side bared showing the mark of the spear. Surrounding the central figure are angels, trumpeting the awakening of the dead, scenes of heaven and hell awaiting the blessed and the damned, and the Apostles, seated together to represent the Last Judgment. They are conversing with each other in their role as teachers.

Other lessons of Gothic cathedral sculpture are more complex and less obvious. According to some scholars, much of this art was created according to specific conventions, codes, and sacred mathematical calculations. These formulas govern positioning, grouping, numbers, and symmetry. For example, the numbers three, four, and seven (which often appear as groupings in compositions of post-Gothic periods) symbolize the Trinity, the Gospels, the sacraments, and the deadly sins (the last two both number seven). The placement of figures around Christ shows their relative importance with the position on Christ's right being the most important. These codes and symbols, consistent with the tendency toward mysticism, and finding allegorical and hidden meanings in holy sources, became more and more complex. More information with excellent examples is found at http://www.geocities.com/Athens/Parthenon/8063/gothic6.html.

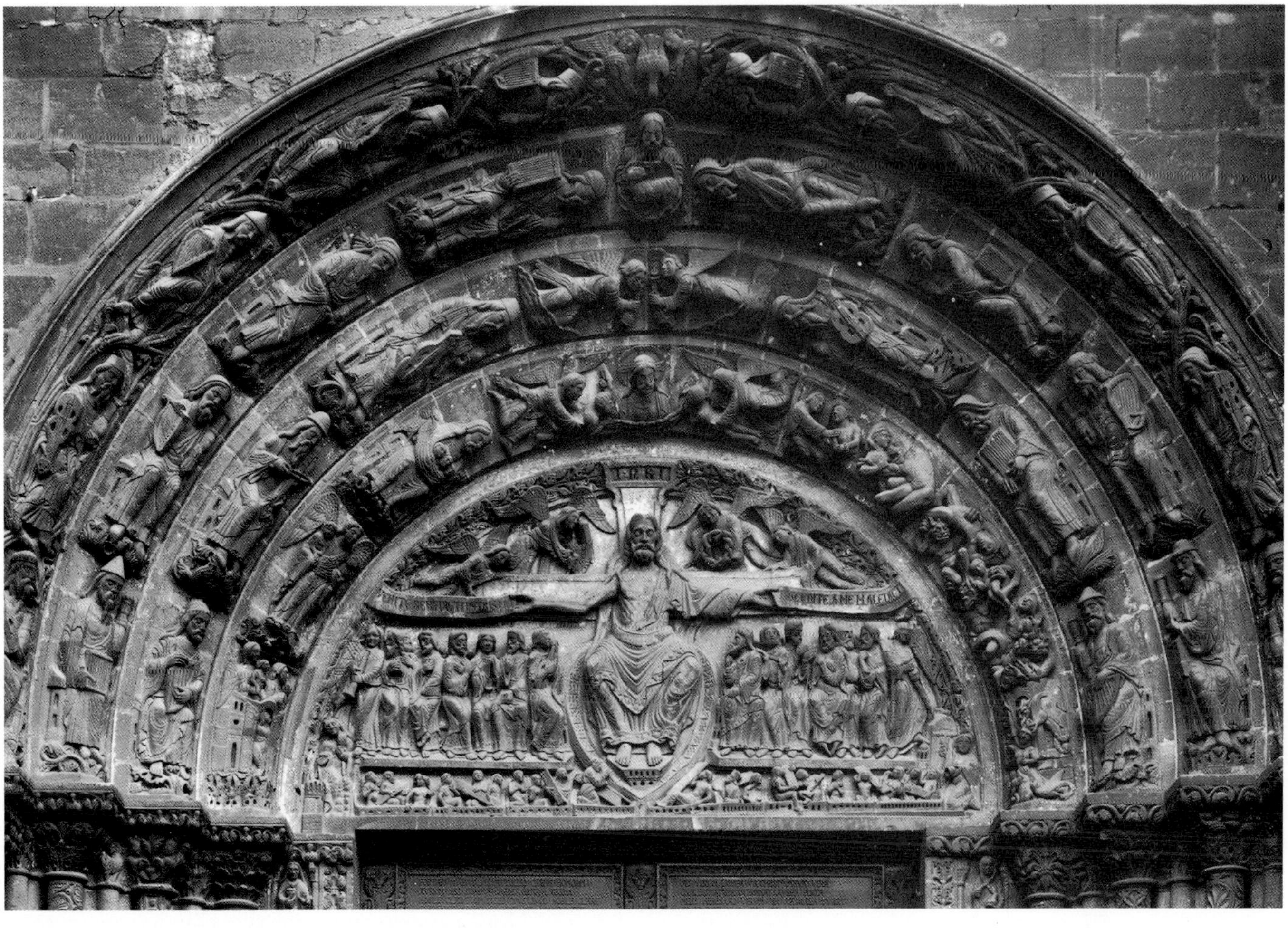

8.10 The tympanum of the west portal, west façade, Saint-Denis. (All heads are nineteenth-century restorations.)

A DYNAMIC WORLD

JAPANESE SCULPTURE

In contrast to European sculpture, in the thirteenth century in Japan, sculpture reached a new maturity, turning to simple works that stressed strength and virility. A series of civil wars had led to the military dictatorship of the shoguns and their samurai (warriors) and to a wider-based feudal regime. This was reflected in the works of sculptors, such as Unkei, whose demonic and colossal wooden Buddhist deities (Fig. **8.11**) guard the entrance to the Todaiji Temple at Nara. We are drawn both by the statue's power, expressed in the fierce facial expression and forbidding hand, and by its simplicity, through the clean lines of the swirling fabrics.

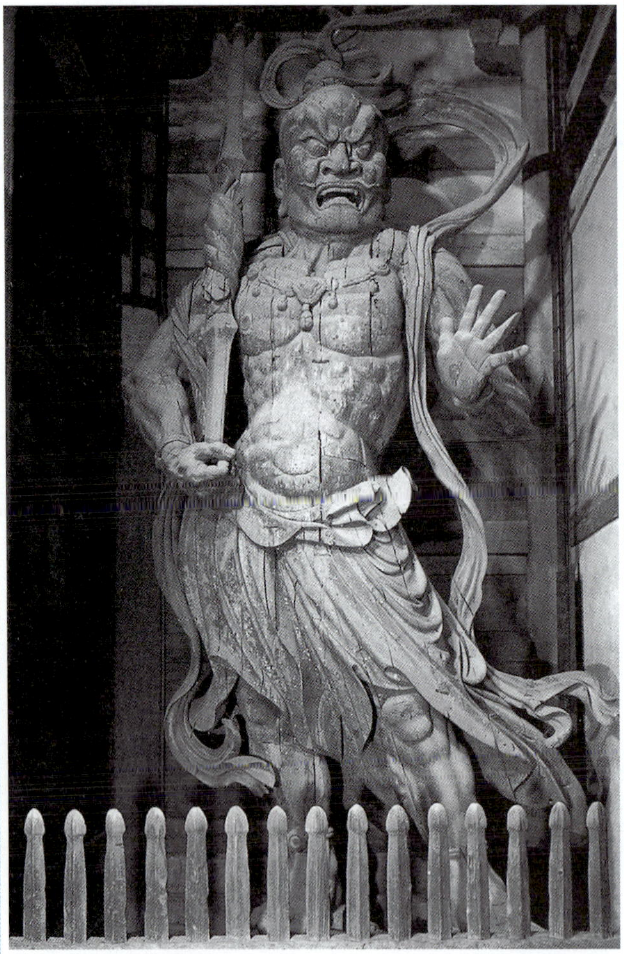

8.11 Unkei, *Nio*, 1203. Wood, 26 ft 6 ins (8 m) high. Todaiji Temple, Nara, Japan.

Architecture

Gothic style in architecture took many forms, but we know it best through the Gothic cathedral. In its synthesis of intellect, spirituality, and engineering, the cathedral perfectly expresses the medieval mind. Gothic style was widespread in Europe, but, like the other arts, it was not uniform in application, nor was it uniform in date. Initially a very local style on the Île de France (eel duh frahns) in the late twelfth century, it spread outward to the rest of Europe. It had died as a style in some places before it was adopted in others.

The cathedral was, of course, a church building whose purpose was the service of God. However, civic pride as well as spirituality inspired the cathedral builders. Local guilds contributed their services in financing or in building the churches, and guilds were often memorialized in special chapels and stained-glass windows. The Gothic church occupied the central, often elevated, area of the town or city—like the acropolis of ancient Greece. Its position symbolized the dominance of the universal Church over all human affairs, both spiritual and secular. Probably no other architectural style has exercised such an influence across the centuries. The story of the Gothic church is an intricate and fascinating one, only a few details of which we can highlight here.

Gothic cathedrals use refined, upward-striving lines to symbolize humanity's upward striving to escape the bounds of earth and enter the mystery of space (the kingdom of heaven). The pointed arch is the most easily identifiable characteristic of this style. It represents not only a symbol of Gothic spirituality, but also an engineering practicality. The round arch of the previous eras places tremendous pressure on its keystone (see Chapter 7), which then transfers thrust outward to the sides, but the pointed arch redistributes the thrust of downward force in more equal, controllable directions. It controls thrust by sending it downward through its legs, and it makes design flexibility possible. The Gothic arch also increases the sense of height in its vaults. Some have said that Gothic structure actually made increased heights possible, but this is not quite correct. Some Romanesque churches had vaults as high as Gothic churches. It is the possibility of changing the proportion of height to width that increases the apparent height of the Gothic church.

Engineering advances implicit in the new form made possible larger clerestory windows, which let in more light (Fig. **8.12**). And more slender ribbing placed greater emphasis on space as opposed to mass. On the exterior, the outward thrust of the vaults is carried gracefully to the ground through a delicate network of ribs, vaults, and **flying buttresses**. Every detail of the decorative tracery is carefully integrated into a system that emphasizes mysterious space.

The beginnings of Gothic architecture can be pinpointed to between 1137 and 1144, in the rebuilding of the royal Abbey Church of Saint-Denis, near Paris (Figs **8.13**, **8.14**, **8.15**, **8.16**).

In preparing for the reconstruction of Saint-Denis, Abbot Suger visited artists throughout Europe. He believed that the church should offer attainment of outward splendor, spectacles offered to God and humankind, and light to lead the dull mind from the material to the immaterial, and that he was translating a godly philosophy into stone, glass, precious metals, and jewels. He summoned the best artists and artisans, and his administrative skills made it possible to handle the finances to attract the best. He guaranteed funds that put no limitations on their work, so an international gathering of artists and craftsmen translated Suger's ideas.

The façade at Saint-Denis, unlike that of many churches, is not merely an exterior embellishment. The Norman towers are set back on the entrance bays so that they become an integral part of the western structure (see Fig. **8.15**). The bays have two stories with upper chapels, which function independently from the rest of the building. This is symbolic of royal, secular authority, as distinct from the authority of the Church, which is presided over by the clergy at the high altar and chapels at the eastern end of the building.

The four-square power of Notre Dame de Paris (Fig. **8.17**) reflects the strength and solidity of an urban cathedral in Europe's greatest city of the age. Its careful design is highly mathematical—each level is equal to the one below it, and its three-part division is clearly symbolic of the Trinity. Arcs (whose radii are equal to the width of the building) drawn from the lower corners meet at the top of the circular window at the second level. The effect of this design is to draw the eye inward and slowly upward. Many more details of Notre Dame Cathedral in Paris are found at http://www2.art.utah.edu/cathedral/paris.html.

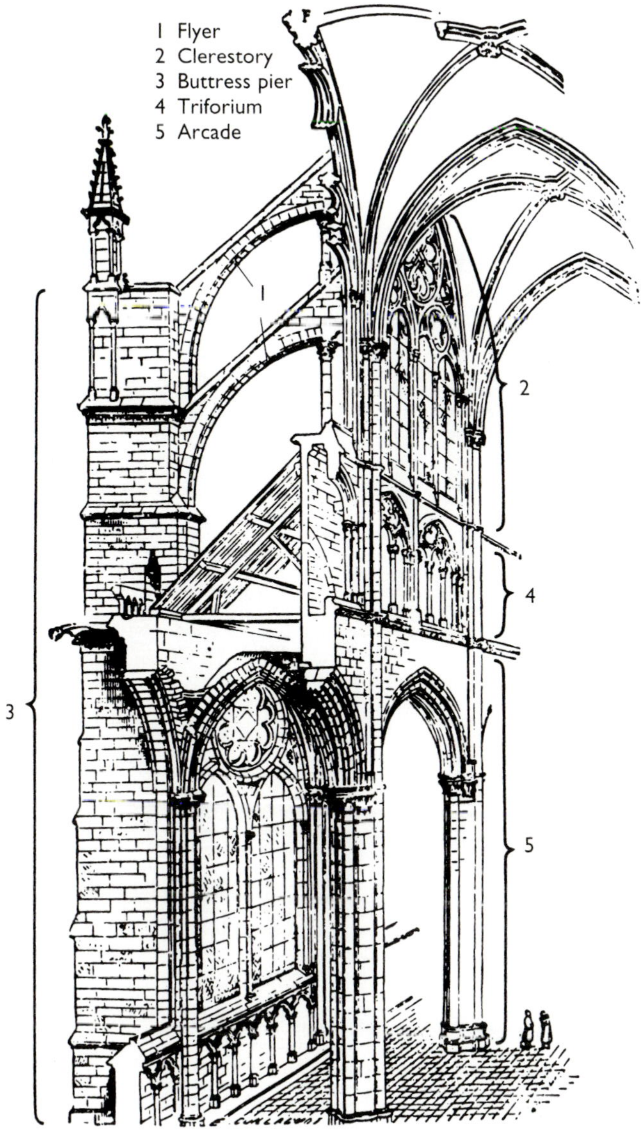

8.12 Principal features of a typical Gothic church.

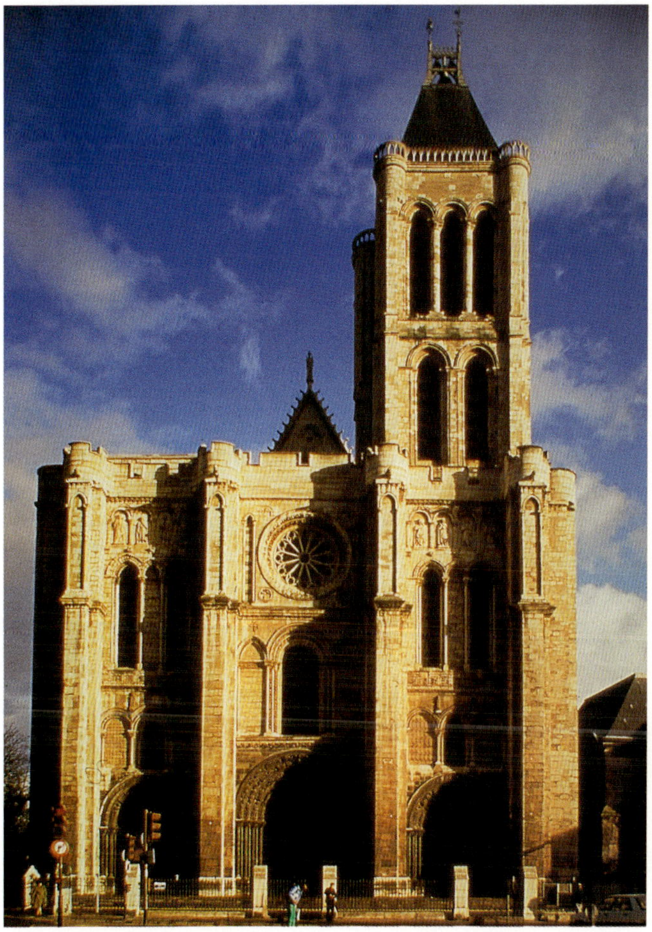

8.13 Exterior of the Abbey Church of Saint-Denis, near Paris, 1137–44.

The Cathedral at Amiens (ah-mee-EN; Fig. 8.18) is similar to Notre Dame in scale and proportion. Rather than creating a sense of power, however, it has a delicate feel. Amiens Cathedral illustrates late developments in Gothic style and also provides, in contrast with Notre Dame, an important lesson in the ways design can be used to elicit response. Amiens is less stolid than Notre Dame, and this feeling is enhanced by the greater detail that focuses our attention on space rather than flat stone. Both cathedrals are divided into three very obvious horizontal and vertical sections of roughly the same proportion. Notre Dame appears to rest heavily on its lowest section, the proportions of which are apparently diminished by the horizontal band of sculptures above the portal. Amiens, on the other hand, carries its portals upward to the full height of the lower section. In fact, the lines of the central portal, which is much larger than the central portal of Notre Dame, combine with the lines of the

MASTERWORK

Suger and the Abbey Church of Saint-Denis

Between 1135 and 1137, Suger, abbot of Saint-Denis, began to rebuild the royal abbey church. That undertaking changed architecture for all time. The ancestry of every Gothic church in the world owes its existence to it. Unlike any other artistic style, the beginning of Gothic style can be pinpointed to the planning and construction of this one building.

Suger, a man blessed with personal charm and great talent, was abbot of Saint-Denis from 1122 to 1151. He was born in 1081 in humble circumstances, but by the time he died, he was known as "father of his country."

Suger was a champion of the monarchy, which he invested with religious significance. The Abbey Church of Saint-Denis benefited from Suger's politics and from its own history. It was the shrine of the apostle of France, the sacred protector of the realm, and the chief memorial of the Carolingian dynasty: Charlemagne and his father, Pepin, had been consecrated there, and it was the burial place of Charles Martel, Pepin, and Charles the Bald. Suger wanted to make the abbey the spiritual center of France, a center of pilgrimage and the center of religious and patriotic emotion. To meet such ends, the church needed to be enlarged. His chronicles of the planning and goals of that project have given us a clear picture of the nature and scope of Gothic architecture itself.

8.14 Plan of the ambulatory and radiating chapels of choir at Saint-Denis, Paris, 1140–44.

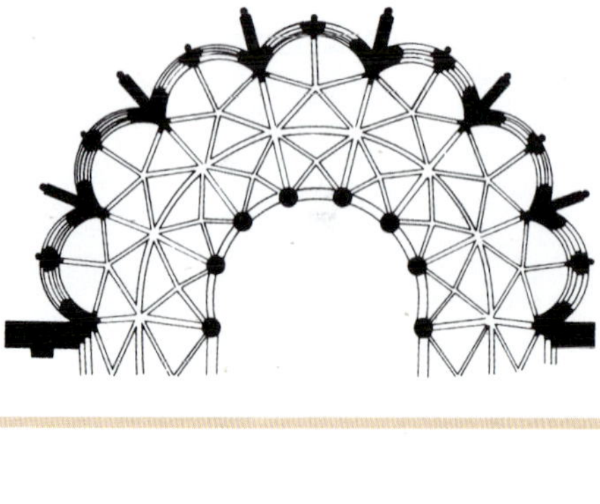

8.15 Reconstruction of the west façade of Saint-Denis as envisaged by Abbot Suger. Drawn by Gregory Robeson.

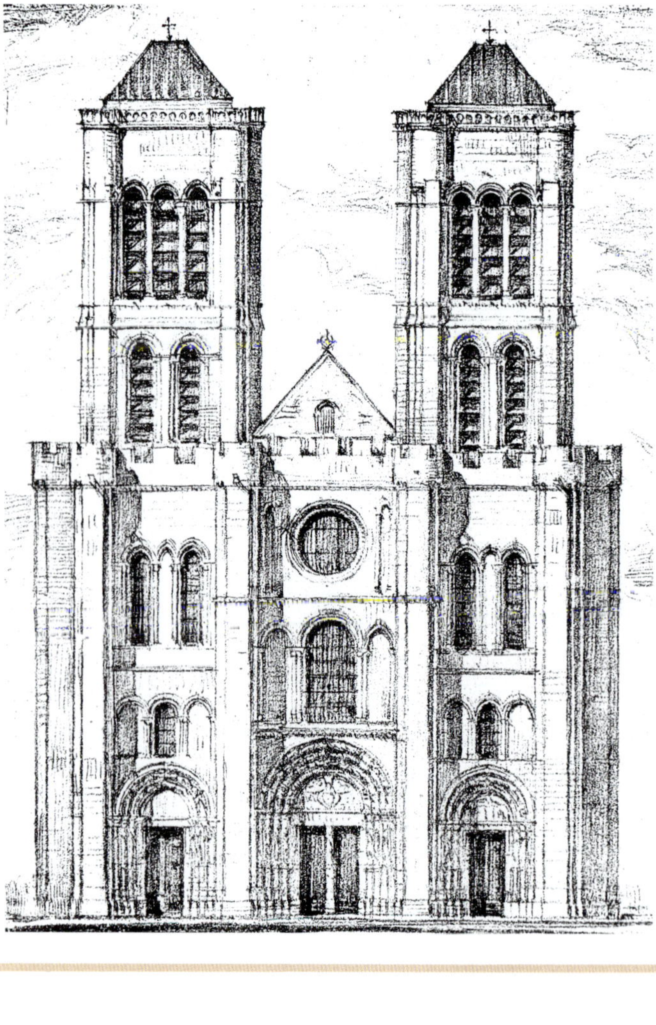

side portals to form a pyramid whose apex penetrates into the section above. The roughly similar size of the portals of Notre Dame reinforces its horizontality, and this is what gives it stability. Every use of line, form, and proportion in Amiens reinforces lightness and action. Everything about the appearance of Notre Dame reinforces stability and strength. One design is no better than the other, of course. Nevertheless, both cathedrals are unquestionably Gothic, and the qualities that make them so are easy to identify.

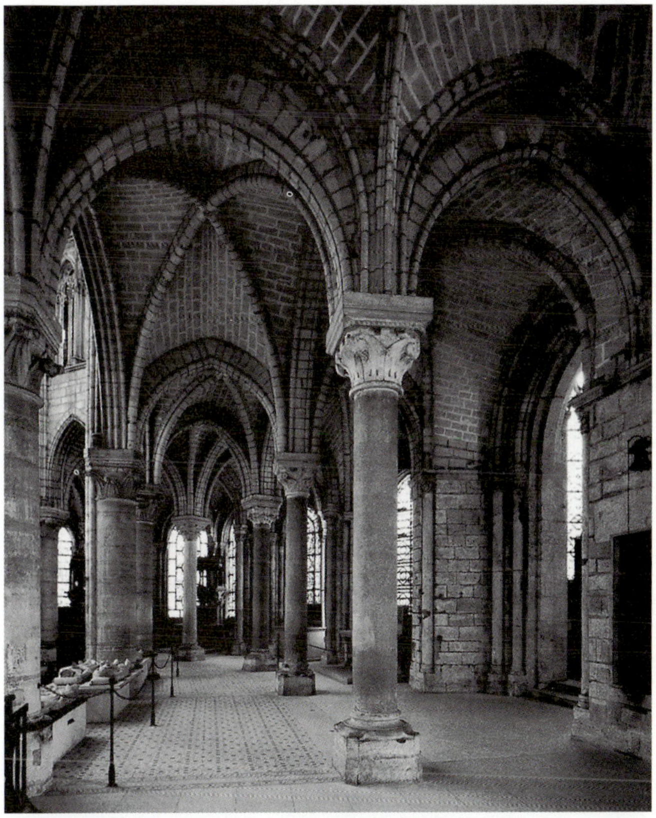

8.16 Interior of the Abbey Church of Saint-Denis.

In reality, none of the individual elements of Saint-Denis was completely new. Apses with radial chapels had been built as early as St Sernin (see Figs **7.18** and **7.19**). However, at Saint-Denis, the plan allowed space to flow around them, uninterrupted by walls (Fig. **8.14**). Pointed arches and ribbed vaults also had been used before, but never in such a way that the heaviness of Romanesque style was transformed into the lightness of slender supports and bearing walls that occurred here. The revolution represented at Saint-Denis was one of structural relationships rather than of forms. It took existing ideas and transformed them into something new and enduring.

An additional revolution occurred in the transformation of the interior. As Suger wrote, the entire church shone "with the wonderful and uninterrupted light of most luminous windows, pervading the interior beauty." The architectural forms seem graceful and weightless, and the windows cease to be openings and become translucent walls in themselves. All this is possible because of the accommodation of the active thrust of the high arches through buttresses. The weight of the whole structure is transferred through them, and, thus, the interior space becomes open and clean, and the structural system is visible only from outside.

The result is a new dimension, a new spirit. Suger's emphasis was on strict geometric planning and a search for luminosity. Suger continually insists that his design placed the highest value on harmony—that is, the perfect relationship among parts in terms of mathematical proportions—as the source of beauty. Harmony for Suger represents the "Divine Reason" by which the universe has been constructed. The light that floods the interior is "Light Divine," a mystic revelation of God's spirit.

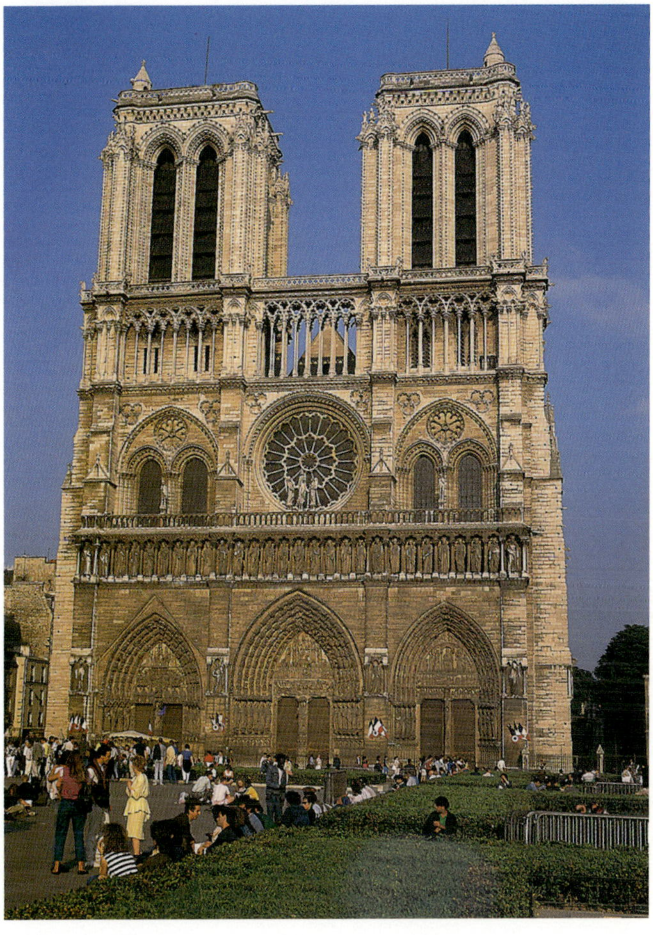

8.17 Notre Dame, Paris, west front, 1163–1250.

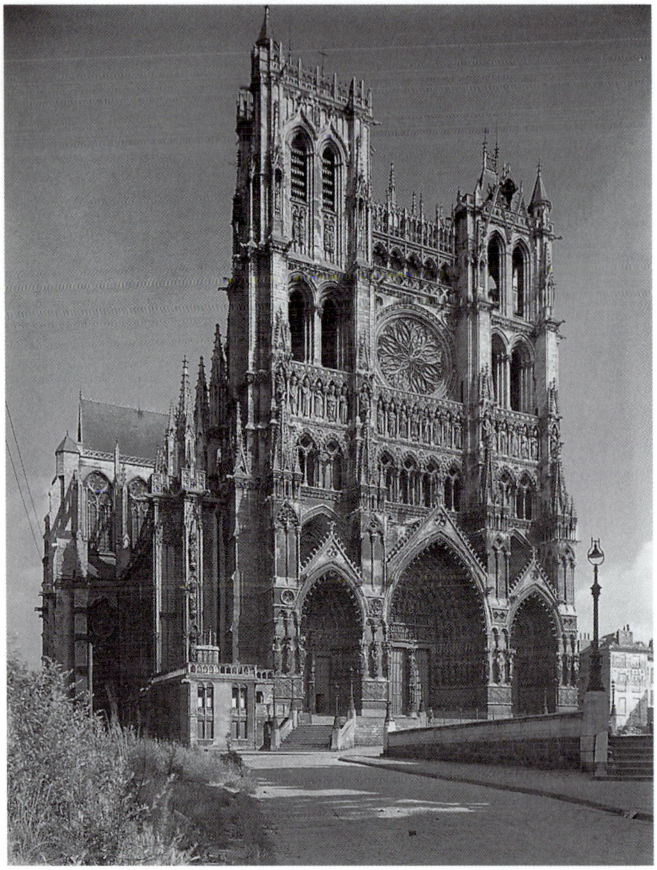

8.18 Amiens Cathedral, France, west front, c. 1220–59.

Theatre

As the Middle Ages progressed, drama associated with the Church followed the example of painting and included more and more Church-related material. Earliest Church drama, that is, the *trope*, was a simple elaboration and illustration of the Mass. The subject matter of later drama included Bible stories (mystery plays), lives of the saints (miracle plays), and didactic allegories (morality plays), which had characters such as Lust, Pride, Sloth, Gluttony, and Hatred.

Mystery plays take their name from the Latin word meaning "service" or "occupation" rather than from the word for "mystery." The designation probably refers to the production of religious plays by the occupational guilds of the Middle Ages rather than the "mysteries" of revelation. Dating from the twelfth century, *The Representation of Adam* is the oldest known French mystery play. There were three parts, each with written dialogue: The Fall of Adam and Eve, the Murder of Abel, and the Prophecies of Christ. Latin instructions, which indicated scenery, costumes, and even actors' gestures, were written into the play: "Paradise shall be situated in a rather prominent place, and is to be hung all around with draperies and silk curtains."

Miracle plays presented a real or fictitious account of the life, miracles, or martyrdom of a saint. Almost all the surviving miracle plays concern either the Virgin Mary or St Nicholas, the fourth-century bishop of Myra in Asia Minor, both of whom had active cults during the Middle Ages. The Mary plays consistently involve her coming to the aid of all who invoke her, be they worthy or wanton. The Nicholas plays are similar, usually chronicling the deliverance of a crusader or the conversion of a Saracen king. We will discuss morality plays in the next chapter (see p. 276).

Tropes were performed in the church sanctuaries, using niches around the church as specific scenic locations. On special occasions, cycles of plays were performed, and the congregation moved to see different parts of the cycle. These dramatizations quickly became very popular.

Over the years, production standards for the same plays changed drastically. At first, only priests performed the roles; later, laymen were allowed to act in liturgical drama. Female roles were usually played by boys, but some evidence suggests that women did participate occasionally. The popularity of Church drama soon made it impractical, if not impossible, to contain the audience within the church building. Evidence also suggests that as laymen assumed a greater role, certain vulgarities were introduced. Comedy and comic characters appeared, even in the Easter tropes. For example, on their way to Jesus' tomb, the three Marys stop to buy ointments and cloths from a merchant. This merchant developed into one of the earliest medieval comic characters. The most popular comic character of all, of course, was the devil.

Church drama eventually moved outside the sanctuary. As medieval drama moved out of the church—first to the west porch of the church and then to the city squares—various production practices developed. In France and Italy, the stationary stage decoration of the church interior became a *mansion stage* (Fig. **8.19**), so-called because the different areas represented "mansions," or houses. The specific configuration of the mansion stage differed from location to location. In Italy, it was rectangular and linear, designed to be viewed from one or two sides. In some parts of France, *arena staging*, in which the audience completely surrounded the stage area, was introduced. Whatever the specific application, the mansion stage had a particular set of aesthetic conventions. The individual mansions depicted their locations realistically. At the same time, areas between the mansions could serve as any location. When the action of a play moved away from a specific mansion, the aesthetic became conventional, just as we saw in classical Greek theatre. That is, the stage could represent any place, as opposed to the representation of place found in the mansion. The text of the play told the audience where the action was supposed to occur, and the audience then imagined that locale.

The most interesting depiction on the medieval stage was that of hell, or hellmouth—the mouth of hell into which sinners were cast. Audiences demanded more and more realism and complexity in the depiction of hellmouth. Descriptions of devils amid smoke and fire, pulling sinners into the mouth of hell, often the jaws of a dragon-like monster, are common (Fig. **8.20**). One source describes a hellmouth so complicated that it took seventeen people to operate it. Some plays, *Antecriste* and *Domes Daye*, for example, were clearly intended to be frightening. But in the late Middle Ages, even vividly depicted hellmouths seem to have been comic in their intentions, rather than fearsome. Plays of the period are humorous and compassionate, clearly reflecting the cultural change in attitude.

In England and parts of France and the Netherlands, another staging style developed. Rather than move the audience or set up all the locations in different places on a mansion stage, theatre was brought to the audience on a succession of pageant wagons, like the floats of a modern parade. Each wagon carried the set for a specific part of the play cycle. Many of these wagons were very elaborate, two stories tall, and curtained for entrances and exits like a modern theatre. In some cases, a flat wagon was combined with an elaborate background wagon to provide a playing area. This type of production was mostly used in cities where narrow wagons were needed to negotiate narrow streets. At intersections where there was more space, wagons were coupled and crowds gathered to watch a segment of the play. When the segment finished, the wagon moved on, and was shortly replaced by another wagon, which served as the setting for another short play in the cycle.

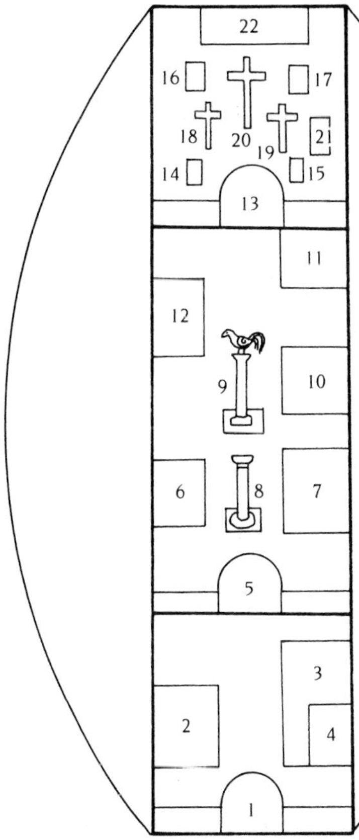

8.19 Plan of a medieval mansion stage, showing the mansions in the Donaueschingen Mystery Play, Germany.

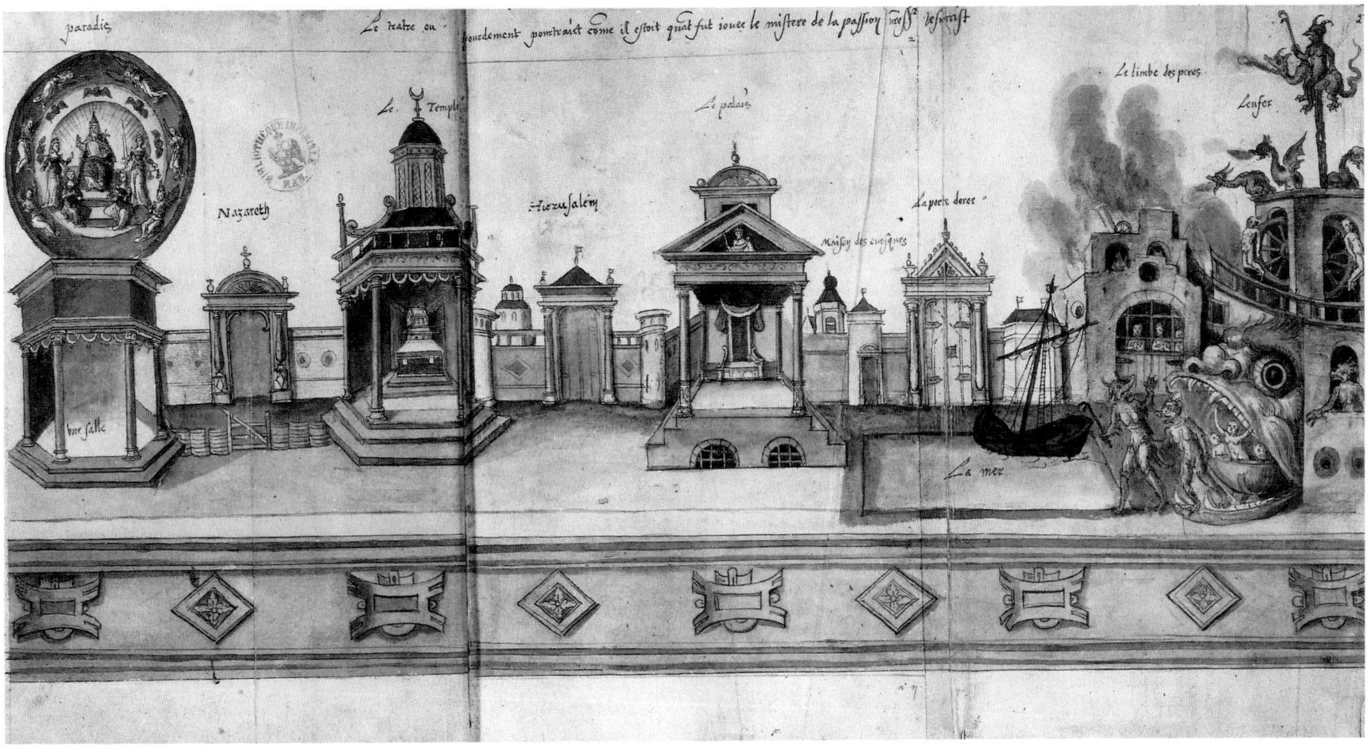

8.20 The Valenciennes Mystery Play, 1547. Contemporary drawing. Bibliothèque Nationale, Paris.

Music

Perhaps in response to the additional stability and increasing complexity of life, music gradually became more formal in notation and in structure, and also increased in textural complexity. Improvisation had formed the basis of musical composition. Gradually musicians felt the need to write down compositions—as opposed to making up each piece anew along certain melodic patterns every time it was performed.

Usually, music was transmitted from performer to performer or from teacher to student. Standardized musical notation, however, made it possible for the composer to transmit ideas directly to the performer. The role of the performer thus changed, making him or her a vehicle of transmission and interpretation in the process of musical communication.

In the twelfth century, as Gothic architecture spread out from the Île de France, composers in Paris developed innovations in rhythm. Two composers who were associated with the cathedral of Notre Dame in Paris employed *measured rhythm*, which had definite time values and precise meters. The first of these, Léonin (lay-oh-NEHN; c. 1135–1200) used a type of chant for two voices called *organum duplum*, in which the lower voice, called the *tenor* (meaning "to hold"—and not associated with today's tenor, male voice) slowly moved over long held notes, while a higher voice, called the *duplum*, moved more quickly with more notes through the text.

A generation later, Pérotin (pay-roh-TEHN: c. 1170–1236) was the first known composer to use more than two voices in his compositions. In Pérotin's, as in Léonin's, work we find the use of a *cantus firmus*, or fixed melody—a chant used as the basis for polyphony. Above the fixed melody (*tenor*), in Pérotin's case, might be found two or three additional voices—*organum triplum* or *organum quadruplum*.

Music was affected by the same change of attitude as two-dimensional art and sculpture—a more rational, as opposed to emotional, underlying approach and feeling. Alongside sacred music existed secular songs such as **ballades** (bahl-LAHD) and **rondeaux** (rohn-DOH). These were vernacular songs in set forms, usually easy to listen to and direct in appeal. Some were dancelike, often in triple meter. The tradition of the troubadour and the wandering entertainer continued, and the courtly approach found in music and poetry an exquisite forum for its love-centered philosophy.

Literature

Courtly Romances

The change in outlook that accompanied the code of chivalry brought with it a new, popular form of poetry called the *romance*. These romances were long narratives whose subjects were knights and ladies. The name itself, like Romanesque, comes from a later age that mistakenly thought that these poems sought to imitate Roman literary forms. Chivalric and sentimental, the romance often drew its subjects from classical legends, from Celtic myths of King Arthur and the knights of the Round Table, and the exploits of Charlemagne and his knights.

Perhaps the first treatment of Arthur and Camelot came from Chrétien de Troyes (krayt-YEN duh TWAH-yuh; c. 1148–90). In this prototype, the simple story we know from the musical *Camelot* is elaborated through many episodes and complicated with religious and courtly themes. In the end, Lancelot rescues Guinevere but, *en route*, suffers through misadventure after misadventure, from which he learns humility in order to love Guinevere with absolute obedience. The fact that Chrétien clearly parallels Lancelot's adventures with the suffering and death of Jesus, gives the work a disturbing character that borders on sacrilege. Also troubling for many is the moral neutrality with which the author treats Guinevere's adultery—a deadly sin in the eyes of the medieval Church. That Chrétien's perspective was unacceptable to some can be seen in a later, English, version of the story, Thomas Malory's *Le Morte d'Arthur*, in which the collapse of Arthur's court is blamed directly on Lancelot and Guinevere's passions.

Dante and the *Divine Comedy*

Undoubtedly, the greatest poet of the age was Dante Alighieri (ah-lee-GYAY-ree; 1265–1321). Dante wrote a few lyric poems and told the story of his passion for his unattainable love, Beatrice, in *La Vita Nuova*, but the *Divine Comedy* was the major work of his life. Its description of heaven, hell, and purgatory is a vision of the state of souls after death told in an **allegory**—that is, a dramatic device in which the superficial sense is accompanied by a deeper or more profound meaning. It works on several levels to demonstrate the human need for spiritual illumination and guidance. On a literal level, it describes the author's fears as a sinner and his hopes for eternal life. On deeper levels, it represents the quandaries and character of medieval society faced with, for example, balancing classicism and Christianity. Part of Dante's significance lies in the fact that he elevated vernacular Italian to the status of a rich, expressive language that was suitable for poetry. It was no longer necessary for writers to use Latin.

Dante, an aristocrat, was educated in both classical and Christian works. As with many Florentine office-holders and literati, Dante suffered exile when his political allies fell from power. In 1301 he was banished from Florence for life. During the years of his exile, in which he suffered deprivation and poverty, he composed *The Comedy* (*Commedia*). Actually, Dante gave the work a particularly personal title: *The Comedy of Dante Alighieri, A Florentine by Birth but not in Behavior*. He called it a comedy because, according to him, it had a happy ending and was written in the language of the people. Recognition of the superb character of the work caused later admirers to affix the word "Divine," which has remained since. The poem is divided into three book-length parts, detailed in Figure **8.21**.

In the *Comedy*, Dante narrates his fictional travels through three realms of the Christian afterlife, beginning on Good Friday 1300. For the first two parts of the journey, he is accompanied by the Roman poet Vergil, from whose work *The Aeneid* Dante drew considerable inspiration. Vergil represents human reason and the classical culture. In the first part, Dante descends into Hell, where he hears the damned tell of their sins against God and moral law. In the second part, Dante stands in Purgatory, where lesser sinners do penance while awaiting their entrance into heaven. In Purgatory, Vergil turns over Dante's guidance to Beatrice (Italian for "blessing"), Dante's symbol of the eternal female and of spiritualized love and Christian culture. She also represents divine revelation, and is, therefore, superior to Vergil. She guides Dante into Paradise, where he finds the souls of the saved divided into three groups: lay people, the active, and the contemplative. Nine categories of angels inhabit the closest circles to the throne of God.

As occurs often in medieval arts, Dante's *Comedy* contains symbolic numbers. The structure of the work breaks into one hundred cantos. The first canto serves as an introduction, and the three major parts each have thirty-three cantos. Three is a common symbol for the Christian Trinity (Father, Son, and Holy Spirit). The poem is written in a three-line verse form called *terza rima*, which uses an interlocking rhyme scheme in three-line stanzas—for example *aba*, *bcb*, *cdc*, *ded*, and so on, ending in a rhymed couplet. Multiples of three occur in the nine regions, plus a vestibule of Hell and Purgatory. Paradise contains nine heavens plus the highest heaven (*Empyrean*; ehm-PEER-ee-ahn). In Hell, the damned are divided into three groups: those who sinned by incontinence, by violence, or by fraud. In Purgatory, those who wait are divided in three ways depending on how they acted in relation to love. Paradise contains nine categories of angels. Here is a short selection from *Inferno*:

(Circle Two) Canto V

The Carnal

So we went down to the second ledge alone;
a smaller circle of so much greater pain
the voice of the damned rose in a bestial moan.

There Minos sits, grinning, grotesque, and hale.
He examines each lost soul as it arrives
and delivers his verdict with his coiling tail.

That is to say, when the ill-fated soul
appears before him it confesses all,
and that grim sorter of the dark and foul

decides which place in Hell shall be its end,
then wraps his twitching tail about himself
one coil for each degree it must descend.

Read Dante's entire *Divine Comedy* at http://www.tonykline.free-online.co.uk/Danthome.htm.

DANTE'S *COMEDY*

HELL
The Anteroom of the Neutrals
Circle 1: The Virtuous Pagans (Limbo)
Circle 2: The Lascivious
Circle 3: The Gluttonous
Circle 4: The Greedy and the Wasteful
Circle 5: The Wrathful
Circle 6: The Heretics
Circle 7: The Violent against Others, Self, God/Nature/and Art
Circle 8: The Fraudulent
Circle 9: The Lake of the Treacherous against kindred, country, guests, lords, and benefactors

PURGATORY
Ante-Purgatory: The Excommunicated/The Lazy/The Unabsolved/Negligent Rulers
The Terraces of the Mount of Purgatory
1. The Proud
2. The Envious
3. The Wrathful
4. The Slothful
5. The Avaricious
6. The Gluttonous
7. The Lascivious

The Earthly Paradise

PARADISE
1. The Moon: The Faithful who were inconstant
2. Mercury: Service marred by ambition
3. Venus: Love marred by lust
4. The Sun: Wisdom; the theologians
5. Mars: Courage; the just warriors
6. Jupiter: Justice; the great rulers
7. Saturn: Temperance; the contemplatives and mystics
8. The Fixed Stars: The Church Triumphant
9. The Primum Mobile: The Order of Angels
10. The Empyrean Heavens: Angels, Saints, The Virgin, and the Holy Trinity

8.21 The structure of Dante's *Divine Comedy*.

FOCAL POINT

Chartres Cathedral

Chartres (SHAHRT-ruh) Cathedral (Figs 8.22–8.28) is a country cathedral that rises above the center of a small city. Its sculptures illustrate a progression of style (Figs 8.25 and 8.27), and so does its architectural design. At first glance, we wonder why its cramped entry portal is so small in comparison with the rest of the building. The reason is that Chartres was not built all at once. Rather, it was built cumulatively over many years, as fire destroyed one part of the church after another. The main entry portal and the windows above it date back to its Romanesque beginnings. The porch of the south transept (Fig. 8.23) is much larger and more in harmony with the rest of the building.

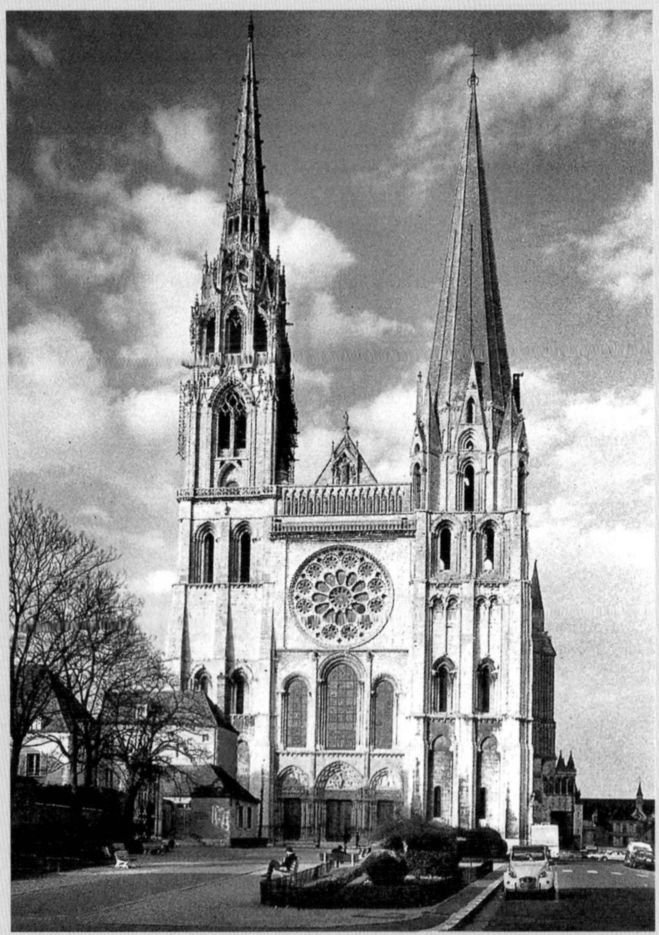

8.22 Chartres Cathedral, France, west front, 1145–1220.

Our biggest question, however, concerns the incongruity of the two unmatched spires. Again, fire was responsible. The early spire, on the right, illustrates faith in its simple upward lines rising, unencumbered, to disappear at the tip into the ultimate mystery of space. The later spire is more ornate and complex—the eye travels up it with increasing difficulty, its progress halted and held by decoration and detail.

A major difference between the Gothic style and the Romanesque lies in the **fenestration** (fen-uh-STRAY-shuhn). Gothic-style walls are pierced by windows that take the form of sparkling jewels of stained glass, such as the *Notre Dame de Belle Verrière* ("Our Lady of the Beautiful Window"; Fig. 8.24). Stained-glass windows replaced the wall paintings of the Romanesque and the mosaics of the Byzantine style. Their ethereal, multicolored light further mysticized the spiritual experience of the medieval worshipper. Light now became an additional property for artistic manipulation and design. The loveliness and intricacy typical of the art of medieval stained glass can also be seen in the magnificent rose window of the north transept of Chartres Cathedral (Fig. 8.26). In the center, the Virgin Mary sits with the Christ Child on her knee. Around her, panels are grouped together in series of twelve, an important symbolic number in the Middle Ages. Angels, archangels, and four white doves represent the gospel and the Holy Spirit. In the squares appear the kings of Israel, named by St Matthew as the ancestors of Joseph, while the prophets sit on the outer edge of the window. Every element in the design leads the eye to the focal center, the Virgin and Child, and, thereby, draws together the Old and New Testaments.

The importance of stained-glass windows in Gothic cathedrals cannot be overemphasized. They carefully control the light entering the sanctuary, and the quality of that light reinforces a marvelous sense of mystery. With the walls of Romanesque style replaced by the space and light of the Gothic style, these windows take the place of wall paintings in telling the story of the Gospels and the saints.

The sculptures of Chartres Cathedral, which bracket nearly a century from 1145 to 1220, illustrate clearly the transition from early to High Gothic. The attenuated figures of the **jamb** statues in Figure 8.25, from the middle of the twelfth century, display a relaxed serenity,

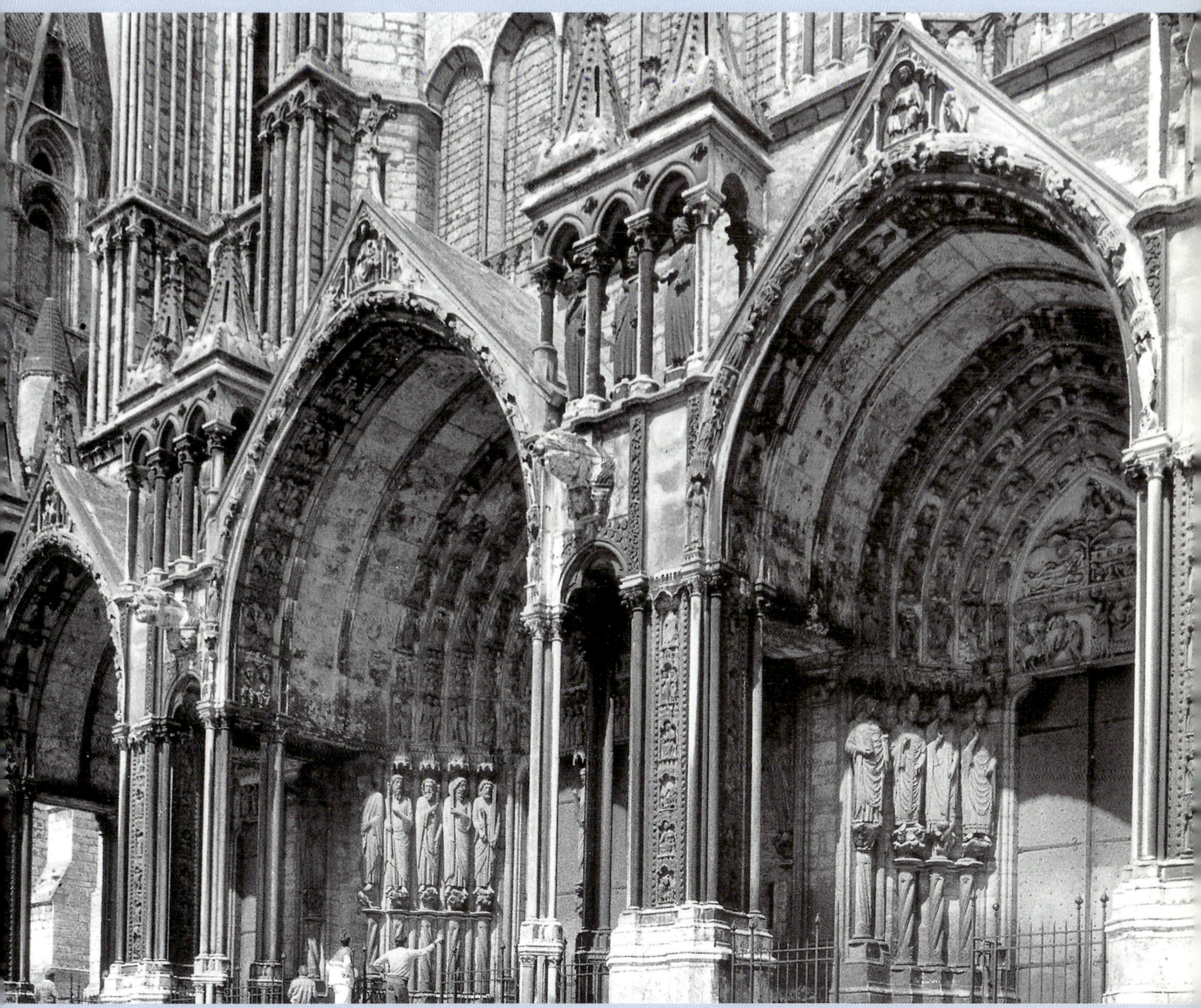

8.23 Chartres Cathedral, France, south transept porth, c. 1205–50.

idealism, and simple naturalism. They are an integral part of the portal columns, but they also emerge from them, each in its own space. Each figure has a particular human dignity despite its idealization. Cloth drapes easily over the bodies. Detail is somewhat formal and shallow, but we now see the human figure beneath the fabric, in contrast to the previous use of fabric merely as surface decoration.

As human as these figures may appear, this quality is even more pronounced in the figures from less than a century later (Fig. **8.27**). Here we see the characteristics of the High Gothic style, or Gothic classicism. These figures have only the most tenuous connection to the building. Proportions are more lifelike, and the figures are carved in subtle S-curves rather than as rigid perpendicular columns. The drape of the fabric is much more natural, with deeper and softer folds. In contrast to the idealized portraits of the earlier period, these figures

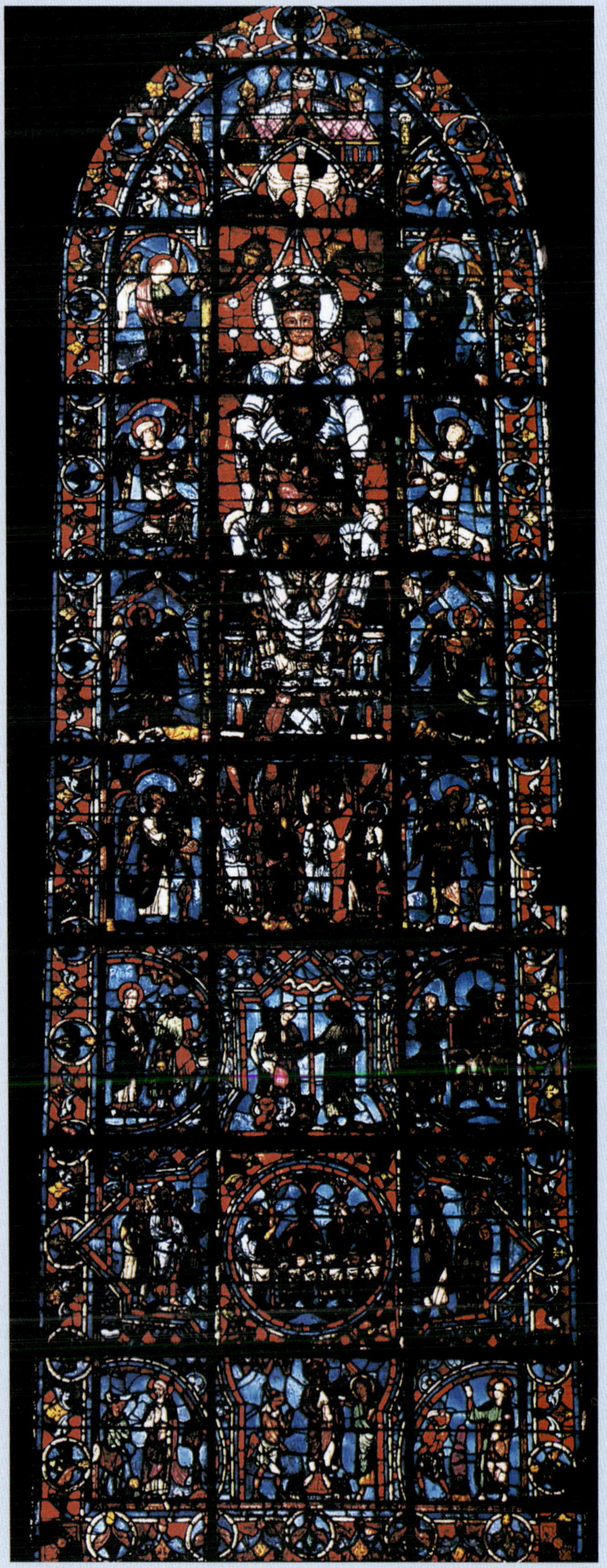

8.24 *Notre Dame de Belle Verrière*, Chartres Cathedral, France.

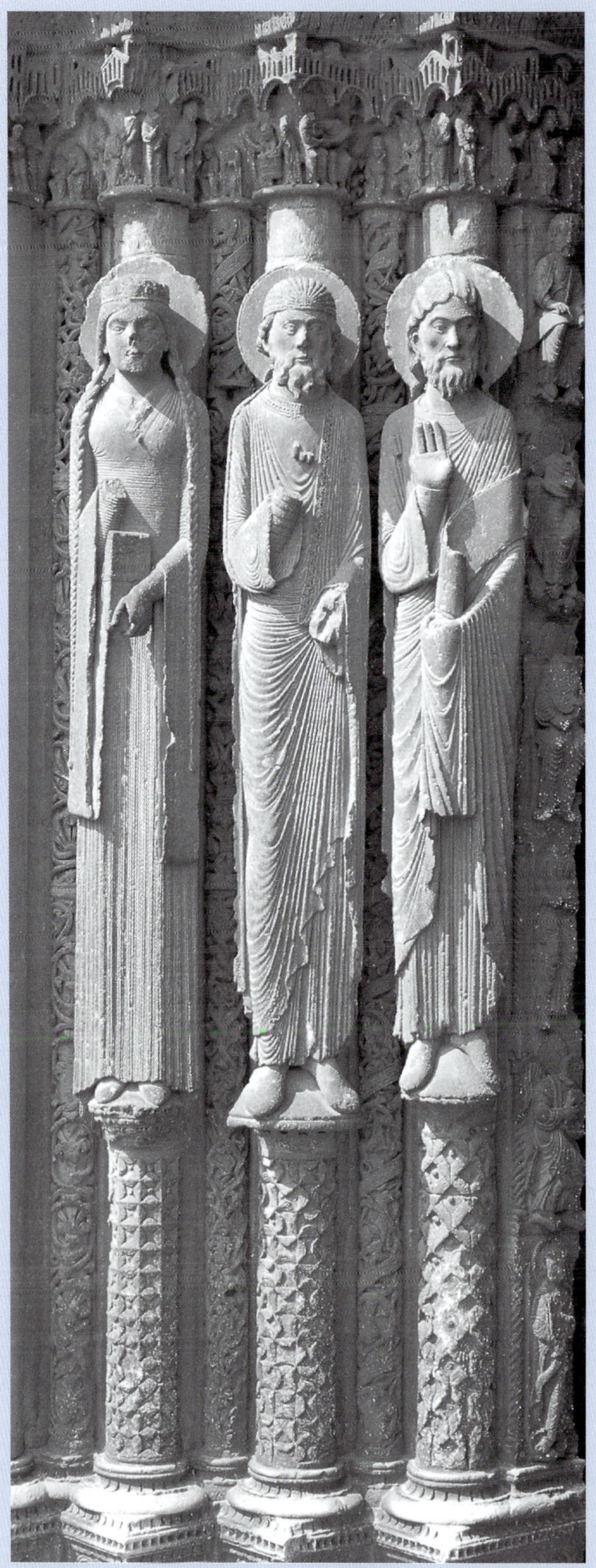

8.25 Chartres Cathedral, France, jamb statues, west portal, c. 1145–70.

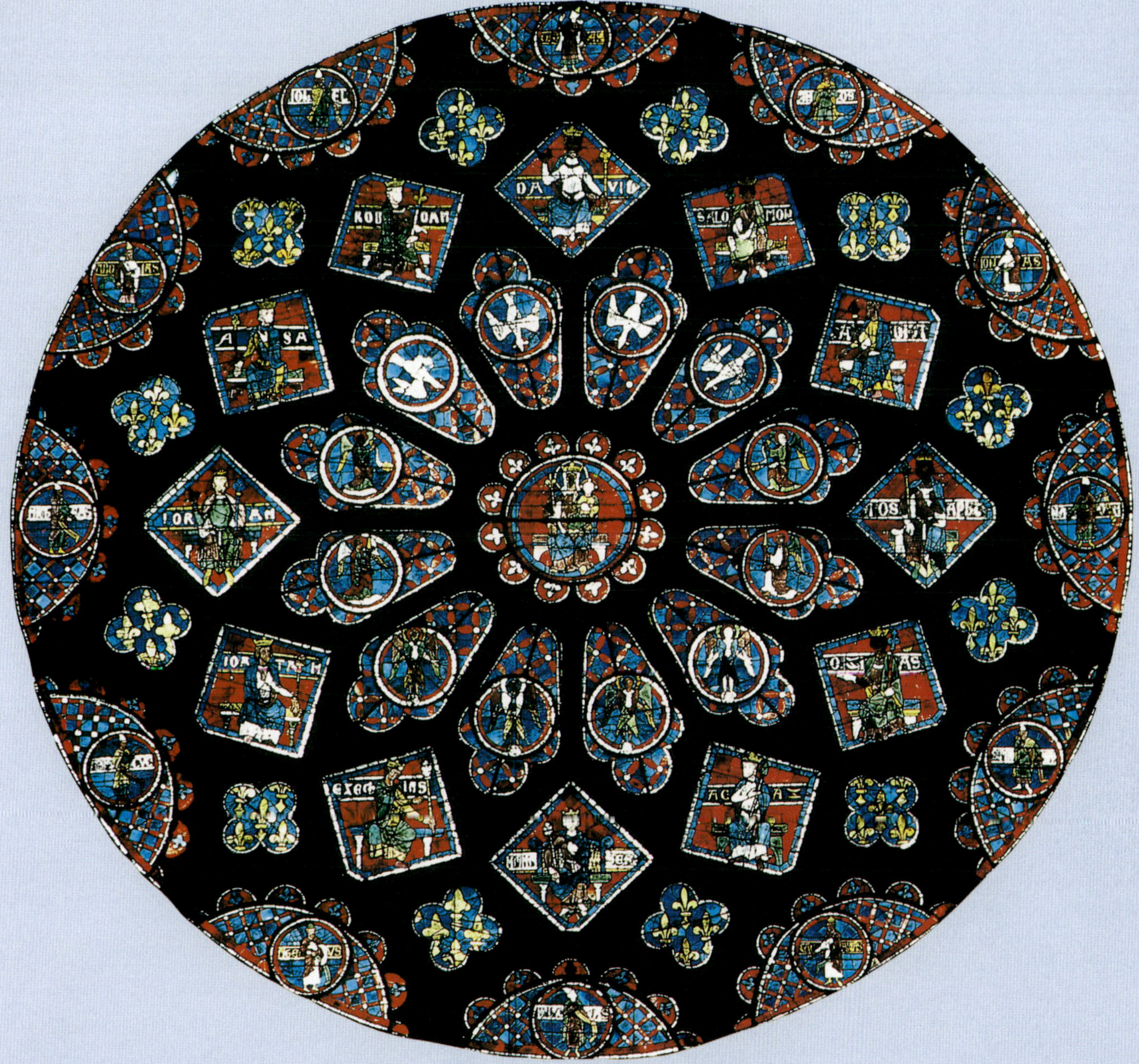

8.26 Chartres Cathedral, France, rose window, north transept, c. 1230. 42 ft 8 ins (13 m) in diameter.

have the features of specific individuals, and they express qualities of spirituality and determination.

The didactic quality of Gothic sculpture is present here as well. The façade's three doorways, sometimes called the Royal Portal (the central arch of which is shown in Figure **8.28**), draws attention to its sculptures. Christ enthroned in royal majesty as ruler and judge of the universe dominates the tympanum. He is surrounded by a host of symbols of the apostles and others. The figures of Figure **8.27** form a segment of the monumental column statues that flank the Royal Portal. They are part of a depiction of twenty-two Old Testament figures seen as precursors of Christ. Other biblical references with which the builders of Chartres identified themselves symbolically included Solomon, who built the first Temple in Jerusalem. The depiction of Old Testament kings and queens ties the Church closely together with the French royal house and proclaims the harmony of secular and spiritual rule, thus suggesting that the kings of France are spiritual descendants of biblical rulers. During the French Revolution, this association, still strong after 600 years, caused the demolition of most of such figures at other churches in France.

Building Chartres Cathedral required a vast

expenditure of resources, including money, materials, and skilled labor. Many common people and nobles were opposed to cathedral building because of the tremendous tax burden placed on them to support the project. Chartres' construction began during a rather flat economic period. To help support the cost, the holy relics of the cathedral were sent on tour as far as England in order to raise funds. The cathedral's officials pledged part of their incomes for three to five years. As work progressed, costs rose, and money dried up. An attempt to levy new feudal and commercial taxes to support the project resulted in the bishop and clergy of the cathedral being driven into exile for four years.

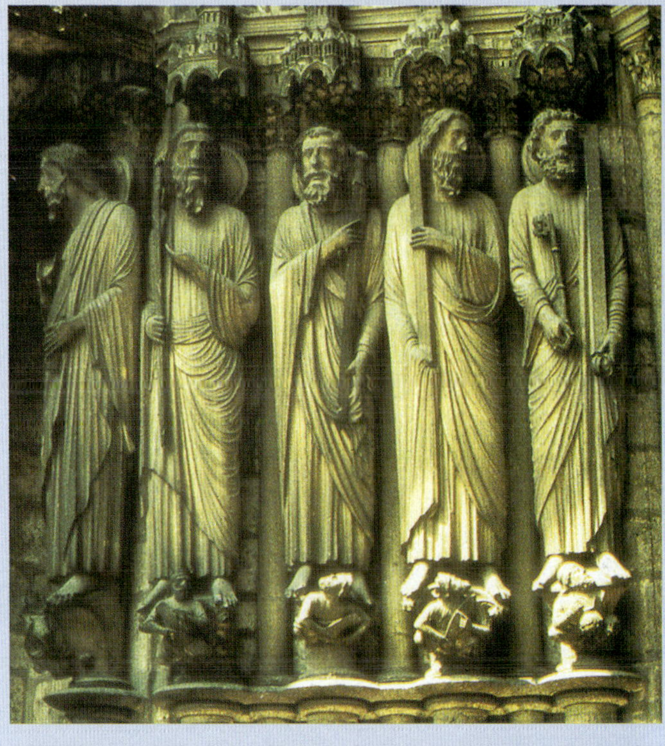

8.27 Chartres Cathedral, France, jamb statues, south transept portal, c. 1215–20.

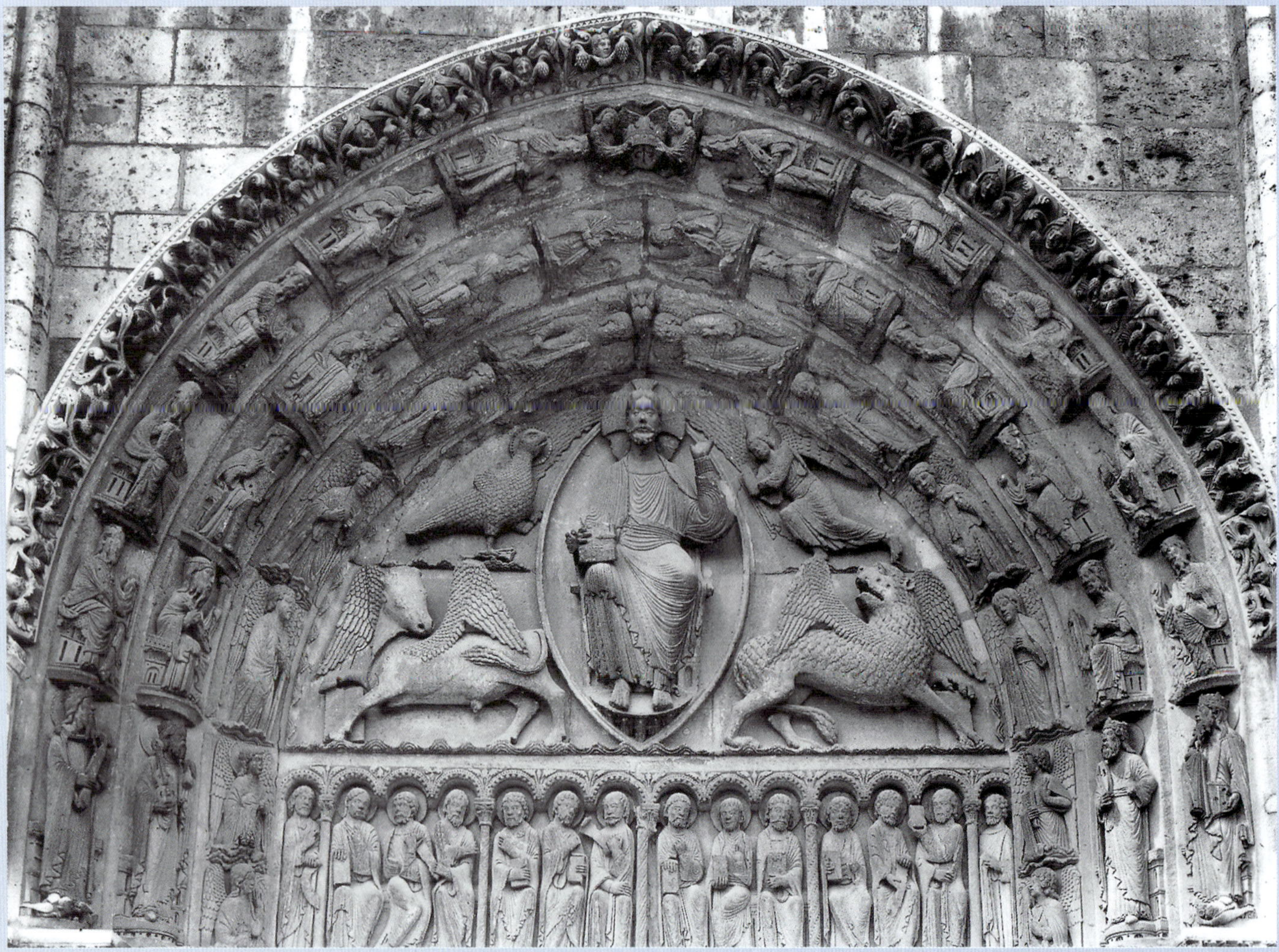

8.28 Chartres Cathedral, France, central tympanum, west portal, c. 1145–70.

Chapter Review

Critical Thought

During the High Middle Ages, profound changes took place in Europe, not only in its institutions but also in the way it viewed matters both earthly and eternal. As we have seen, several reforms affected the Christian Church: the rise of mysticism and the Crusades. Philosophy, theology, and literature shaped the ideas and directions of intellectual and cultural life even as they do today. This was a time of flux. Barricades were coming down and light flowed into every corner of human existence. Universities were born, and people such as Abelard and St Thomas Aquinas remolded and shaped the tenets of Christian faith. Literature gave birth to a new genre, called "courtly romance," and a major poet, named Dante.

Like the Greek temple, Gothic architecture—particularly the Gothic cathedral—has come to symbolize an entire era and to form an important prototype for building not only churches but also other structures in our contemporary world. With similar characteristics in line, form, balance, and unity, Gothic sculpture and two-dimensional art mirror their architectural kindred. Music and theatre embarked on new paths as well, as the "old" gave way to the "new."

Summary

After reading this chapter, you will be able to:

- Explain the changes affecting secular and religious life in the High Middle Ages by citing specific individuals, trends, and conditions.
- Compare and contrast the philosophies of Abelard and St Thomas Aquinas.
- Describe the literature of the period, including the courtly romance and Dante's *Divine Comedy.*
- Understand and discuss the attitudes, reflections, and general characteristics of Gothic architecture, painting, and sculpture, including how Gothic style differs from Romanesque and how Gothic style changed from early to late.
- Characterize the theatre and music of the High Middle Ages, including their forms and presentation.
- Apply the elements and principles of composition to analyze and compare works of art and architecture illustrated in this chapter.

Cybersources

http://witcombe.sbc.edu/ARTHmedieval.html#Gothic
http://www.artcyclopedia.com/history/gothic.html

9 The Late Middle Ages

OUTLINE

VIEW

LEADERS AND DISAPPOINTMENT

The condition of the Christian Church and political Europe in the fourteenth century may remind us of the all-too-human nature of those who undertake leadership in any institution. The nobility or goodness of the institution itself seems irrelevant when humans struggle for power, and the person in "control" often appears to be more important—especially to him- or herself—than the institution. When abuse becomes virulent, cries for "reform" are heard throughout the land. However, the cries often turn into cynicism when the cost of "doing the right thing" is realized; then the cycle begins again.

If the foregoing paragraph sounds like a reflection on a particular event in today's political or religious life, it is only because such comments really do reflect the nature of humankind. So, when it seems as if all our leaders have "gone south" when it comes to showing courage and moral fiber, it's nothing new.

KEY TERMS

Some of the basic terms and concepts we will encounter in this chapter include the following:

Secularism
The rejection of religion and religious considerations.

Schism
A separation into divisions or factions, especially within a Church.

Humanism
A philosophy concerned with human beings, their achievements, and interests, as opposed to abstract beings and problems of theology.

Duomo
The Italian word for cathedral: usually the central architectural feature of a city or town.

Pietà
A sculpture or painting of the dead Christ supported by Mary.

Ars Nova
"New Art," referring to changes in music occurring in the fourteenth century.

Hallenkirche
A German interpretation of Gothic style in which the aisles and nave are the same height.

9.1 Giovanni Pisano, Pulpit, begun 1297. Marble, Sant'Andrea, Pistoia, Italy.

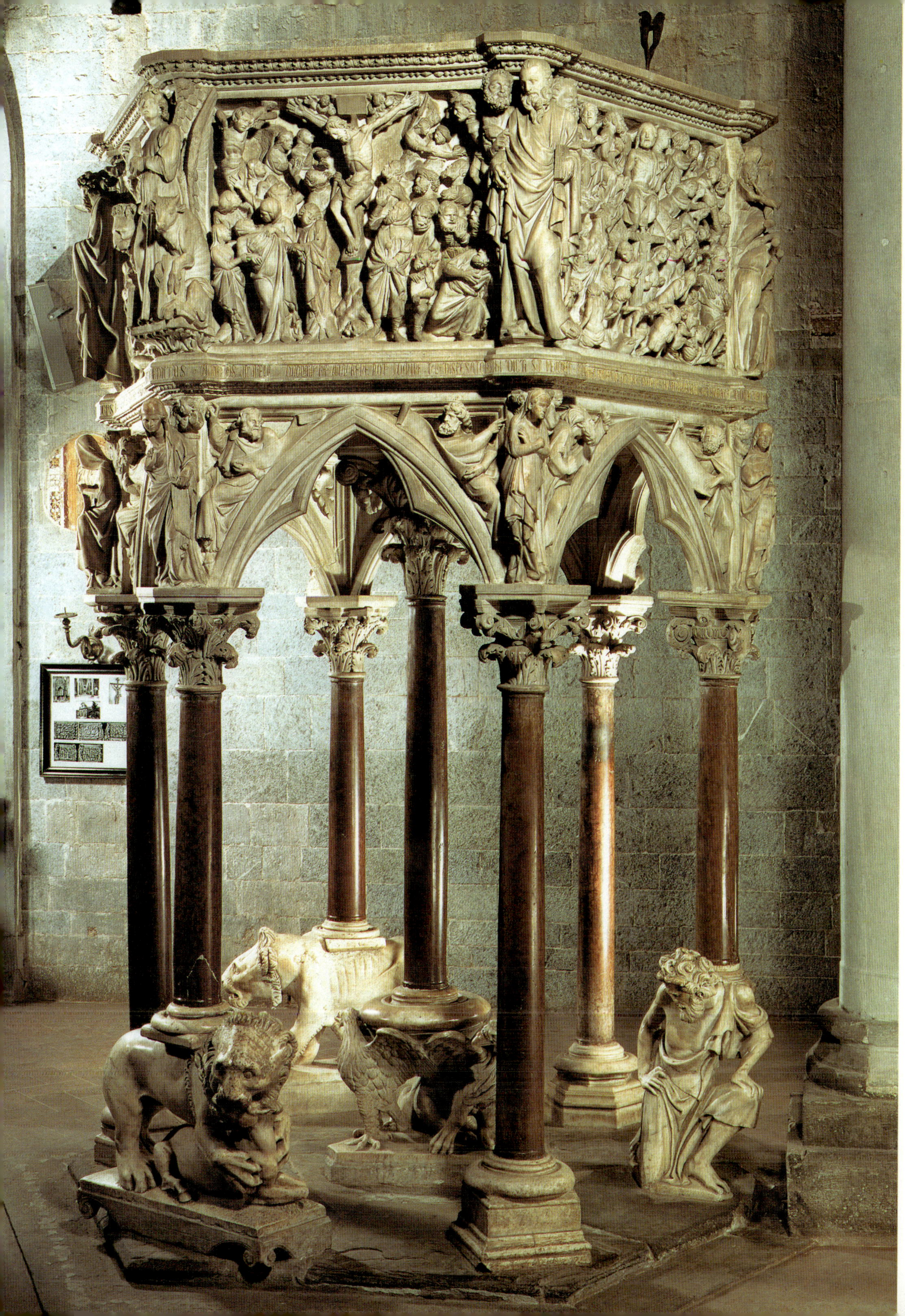

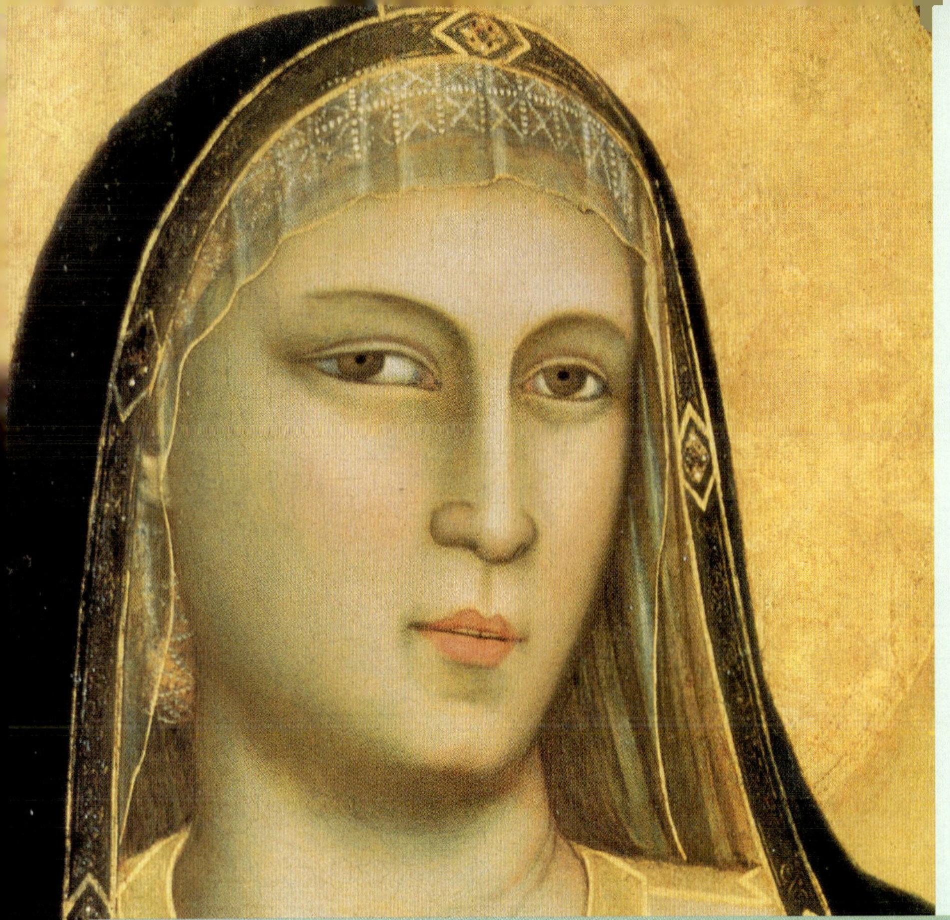

HOW ART WORKS

UNIVERSALS II:
Revealing Reality

In this space in the last chapter we spoke of universals in art as qualities that were capable of touching the lives of a variety of people. Beyond that meaning, "universals" has a more technical, philosophical, meaning that draws together information presented in Chapter 3 and resurfacing in subsequent chapters. It begins with Plato's Theatre of Ideas, that every individual thing has an ideal model—a universal. The philosophical concept of universals also draws on Aristotle's conception that the reality of material objects is contained in their intrinsic properties. The question of the nature (or even the existence of) universals was the subject of a major debate in the Middle Ages. On one side of the question were the *realists*, like St Anselm (1033–1109), Archbishop of Canterbury, for whom universals constituted the only true reality, and *nominalists*, such as William of Ockham (early fourteenth century), who denied the reality of universals altogether. Between the two extremes stood *conceptualists* or "modified realists," as we have defined Peter Abelard (p. 241). Abelard accepted the idea of universals, but considered them as primarily constructs of the mind. On this continuum, realists would argue that the abstract quality of "chairness" has a reality that is independent of the existence of actual chairs; the conceptualists would identify the idea of a chair as the mind's generalization from its experience of particular chairs; and the nominalist would argue that "chair" is merely the name used to classify a group of objects and has nothing to do with their actual reality.

Twenty-first century analytical philosophy would focus on the relation between universals and particulars and concentrate on the relations and paradoxes in categorized groups of things (classes). This would put them more in the camp of the conceptualists, by dispensing with considerations of metaphysical importance, such as "chairness," and considering whether the statement "There are no flying chairs" can be logically, rather than empirically, validated.

All this is relevant to art because it forms the basis for much of what we call "style" and contributes directly to artistic presentation in "realistic" or "abstract" terms, both of which recur constantly throughout our study.

9.2 Giotto, *Madonna Enthroned*, c. 1310 (detail). Tempera on panel, 10 ft 8 ins × 6 ft 8 ins (3.3 × 2 m). Uffizi Gallery, Florence, Italy. See also Fig. **9.10**.

CONTEXTS AND CONCEPTS

The End of the Middle Ages

Secularism and Transition

By the fourteenth century, revelation and reason, and God and the State, were considered to be separate spheres of authority, neither subject to the other. Such a separation, of what had previously been the full realm of the Church, was the beginning of secularism—that is, a rejection of religion and religious considerations. Individual nations—rather than feudal states or holy empires—had arisen throughout Europe, although it would be misleading to say that religion and matters of State were entirely divorced. As we shall see, they intermingled freely when it was convenient; but they clashed severely when questions of power and authority were at stake. However, amid the conflict of secular and Church interests, two events had a catastrophic impact on Europe. The year 1338 marked the beginning of what came to be known as the Hundred Years' War, and, early in that, the plague (1348–51) further disrupted the relative prosperity of the High Middle Ages. During this time, secular arts gradually gained prominence, respectability, and significance, reflecting a shifting emphasis rather than an outright reversal of values.

The Hundred Years' War

The Hundred Years' War really lasted more than one hundred years. It consisted of an intermittent struggle between England and France which involved periodic fighting over the question of English fiefs in France, fighting that had begun in the twelfth century. The series of ongoing battles concerning a number of issues, including the rightful succession to the French crown, traditionally began in 1337 and lasted until 1453.

In the medieval world, one king might, in fact, be the vassal of another king if the first king inherited land that lay within the claim of the second king. Such was the condition of Europe, and such was the situation that had existed in England and France since William I, the Conqueror, who was duke of Normandy, had conquered and become king of England in 1066. William's successor English kings laid claim to portions of France, and

	1290	1350	1375	1400–1500
GENERAL EVENTS	Papacy to Avignon, 1309; Hundred Years' War begins, 1337	Black Death (or Plague) in Europe, 1348–50; Battle of Poitiers, 1356; Ming dynasty in China, 1368–1644; Hanseatic League controls Baltic, 1370	Great Schism, 1378; Mechanical clocks, 1380	Joan of Arc, 1412–31; Wars of the Roses, 1485–1509
PAINTING & SCULPTURE	Pisano (**9.1, 9.14**), Giotto (**9.2, 9.9, 9.10**), Cimabue (**9.7**), Duccio (**9.8**), Lorenzetti (**9.11**)		Sluter (**9.13**)	
ARCHITECTURE	Florence Cathedral (**9.16**), Doge's Palace (**9.18**)	Hallenkirchen, St Sebold (**9.15**)	Milan Cathedral (**9.17**)	
THEATRE				*Everyman*
MUSIC & DANCE	Philippe de Vitry	*Danse macabre*, de Machaut	*Ars nova*, Francesco Landini	
LITERATURE & PHILOSOPHY	Marguerite Porète	Petrarch, Boccaccio, St Catherine of Siena	Froissart, Chaucer, Julian of Norwich, Margery Kempe	Christine de Pisan

Timeline 9.1 The late Middle Ages.

marriages and other alliances complicated the picture. The ensuing conflict was called the Hundred Years' War.

As in modern warfare, medieval wars occasionally consisted of massed armies pitted in battles, a victory in which might prove decisive. More often, however, they consisted of lengthy and expensive sieges of important fortified cities (Fig. 9.3). For approximately twenty-seven years from 1337, the English kept a military presence in France, but did not gain much territory in the process, although they won some battles—for example, at Crécy (kray-SEE) in 1346 and Poitiers (pwah-tee-AY) in 1356. The French then offered a settlement to the English granting full sovereignty over lands formerly held.

In 1429, inspired by Joan of Arc, the French broke the English siege of Orléans (see Profile, p. 266). When the English became embroiled in the War of the Roses at home, France conquered Normandy and Aquitaine, and by 1453, Calais remained as the only English territory in France, and that was relinquished in 1458. The end of the Hundred Years' War heralded the end of English adventurism on the Continent and contributed to a new sense of national identity in western Europe.

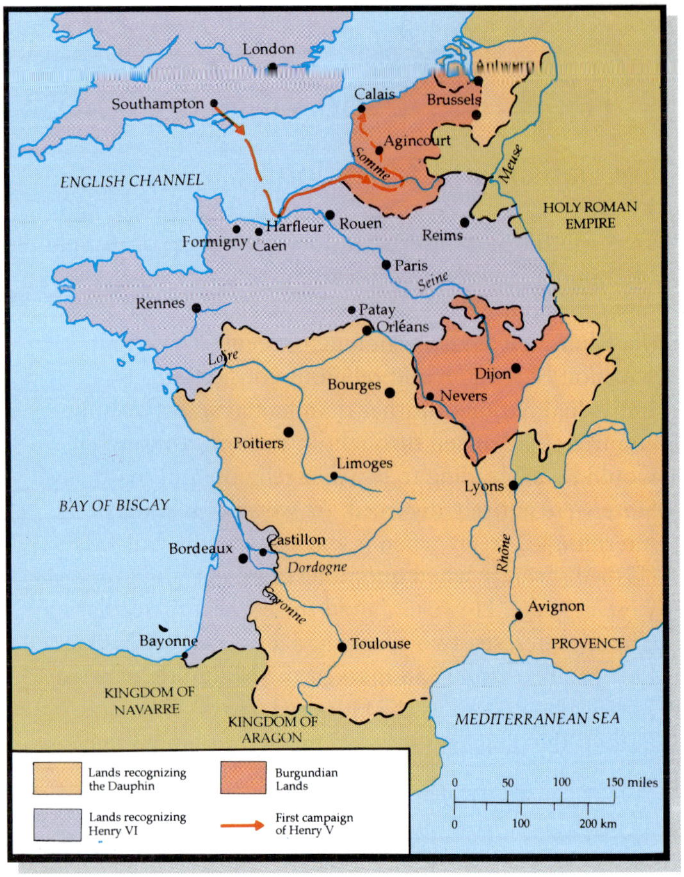

Map 9.1 France in 1429.

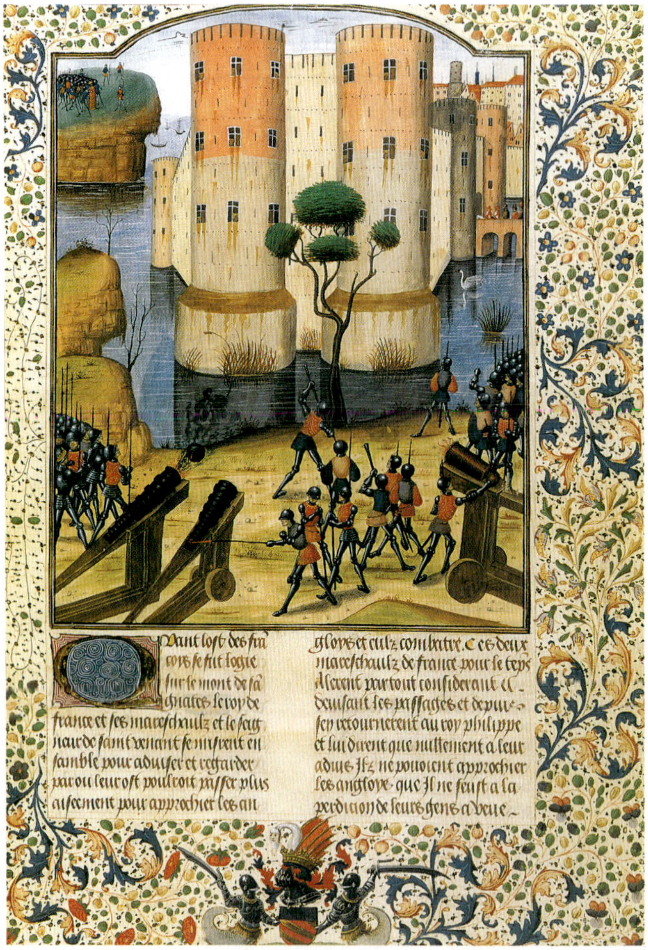

9.3 Jean de Wavrin, *Chroniques d'Angleterre*, showing cannons used as siege weapons, fifteenth century. Bibliothèque Nationale, Paris.

The Secular Monarchies

Amazingly, both France and England seem to have emerged as more stable countries as a result of the Hundred Years' War. In France, the period following the war saw the establishment of a strengthened absolute monarchy, which reached its zenith under Louis XIV in the seventeenth century (see Chapter 13).

In England at this time there were disputes and a power struggle between the kings and an increasingly influential Parliament. In 1485, after the Wars of the Roses, a new dynasty, the Tudors, founded by Henry VII (1485–1509), placed the king and Parliament in less of an adversarial relationship, and managed to avoid most of the issues that had caused friction between previous kings and the legislative body. As a result, England experienced a new centralization of monarchial power, and Henry's political acumen moved Parliament to an increasingly peripheral role. In the end, England emerged with as strong a central monarchy as had been established in France.

The Plague

Known as the Black Death, the catastrophic plague that ravaged Europe between 1348 and 1350 was a combination of bubonic and pneumonic plagues. The epidemic, which eventually claimed more than 25 million lives, originated in China and spread to Europe probably by traders. The first cases of the disease occurred in the Crimea, then in Mediterranean ports in Sicily, north Africa, Italy, Spain, and France, before engulfing the European continent and England. Although it officially came to an end after three years, outbreaks recurred for the next fifty years.

There seemed to be no logic to the disease's devastation. Some areas—for example, Milan and Flanders—suffered little, while others, such as Tuscany and Aragon, were decimated. Those areas with the densest populations—for examples, large cities and monasteries—suffered most. Neither rank nor station offered sanctuary—kings, queens, princes, and archbishops felt the sting of the plague's effects as much as peasants and merchants. In total, nearly one-third of the entire population of Europe died from the disease in the three-year period. By 1400, for example, the population of England had declined to one-half of what it had been a century before, and chroniclers estimated that a thousand English villages were completely wiped out.

The effects of the plague were many. Commerce slumped temporarily, but more importantly, the death of so many people made cultivation of land nearly impossible. In order to stay afloat, many landowners had to begin to pay wages and to substitute money rents in lieu of labor services. The shortage of workers thus led to an increase in wages for both peasants and artisans and tended to break down the previous stratification of society.

Economics and Industrialization

The drastic reduction of population resulting from wars and the plague changed the basic shape of the European economy. Wages rose, production declined, and the cost of goods spiraled upward. Consumers and landowners suffered from inflationary pressures, encouraging many landowners to turn to less labor-intensive use of their lands, such as raising sheep rather than growing crops. Governments across Europe attempted to control the situation by imposing price and wage controls.

The precarious living conditions fomented violent class struggles, conflicts between peasants and landowners, clashes between craft guilds and merchants, and anticlerical outbursts as well. The Church occupied a privileged position—not only did it pay no taxes, but the clergy benefited through the payment of tithes—and was widely resented. Although social unrest accomplished little—those protesting had little power and were easily subdued by a well-armed officialdom—the unheavals ultimately created a better standard of living for everyone. Workers earned higher wages, merchants benefited from higher prices, and landowners profited from new uses of their resources. A new class of entrepreneurs also emerged, who established more effective business practices and encouraged innovation and mechanization (Fig. **9.4**). The textile industry, for example, changed significantly. Previous textile centers, such as Flanders, were cut off from their sources and faced new competition from Germany and Poland, while England stopped exporting raw wool and began to export finished cloth.

In many spheres—mining, metallurgy, printing (Johann Gutenberg—d. 1468—introduced the printing press with movable type around 1450), and shipbuilding, for example—industry became more efficient because of the switch from labor-intensive practices to technology. Demand for iron products—especially weapons, armor, and horseshoes—provided a spur to that industry. Rag paper, which had been invented by the Chinese and

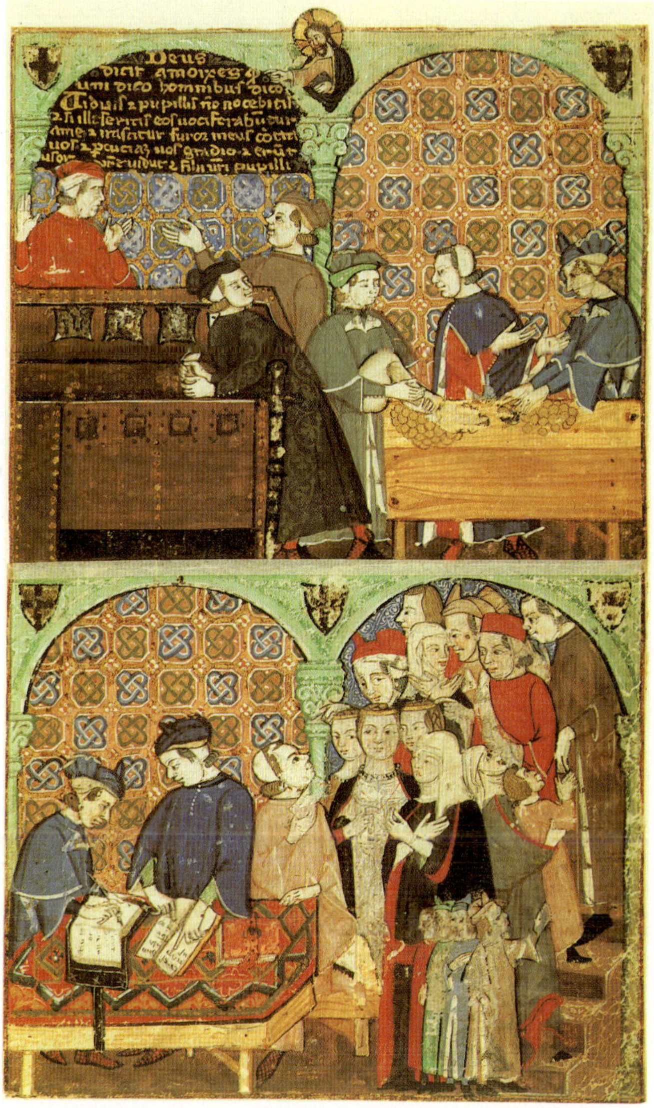

9.4 Banking scenes, miniature from *De septem vitiis*, Italian, late fourteenth century. British Museum, London.

PROFILE

JOAN OF ARC (1412–31)

It is fair to say that Christianity was the heart of medieval European culture, and the life and death of Joan of Arc (Fig. **9.5**) illustrate that circumstance poignantly. Born in a small village in northeastern France, St Joan was a pious but illiterate woman growing up in the middle of the Hundred Years' War. When she was seventeen years old, she began to hear heavenly voices telling her to save her country from the unending ravages of war. With childlike belief and obedience, she left home and family and traveled to the court of King Charles VII. The king was a particularly uninspiring presence—and, at the time, uncrowned—but somehow Joan was able to pick him out of the hundreds of his courtiers. Her simple faith and straightforwardness convinced the unhappy monarch that she should be allowed to join the French army, which was massing for a major battle with the English.

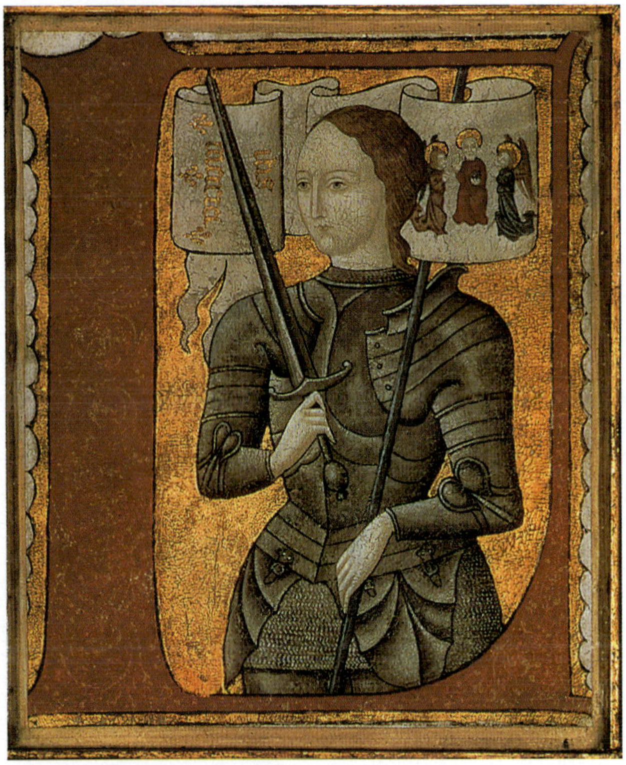

9.5 Joan of Arc (1412–31).

Her presence among the troops lifted their morale and inspired them to victory after victory, from breaking the siege at Orléans to the battle of Reims. After the victory at Reims, Charles was formally crowned at the cathedral there in 1429. Victories inspired by The Maid, as she was universally called, provided a focus for the French, who rallied to the support of the newly crowned and anointed king. After Charles' coronation, Joan ceased hearing her voices. That, for her, meant that her mission had ended, and she wished to return home. The king, however, recognized the powerful symbol she represented and kept her in his service, sending her to lead the French troops marching on Paris, which was still held by the English. The attack failed, and Joan was captured by England's Burgundian allies and sold to the English. She was tried for witchcraft by an ecclesiastical court subservient to the English, found guilty, and burned at the stake in Rouen in 1431.

Although her public career lasted only two years, half of which was spent in prison after her capture, Joan remains one of the most potent symbols of the age: mystical, charismatic, faithful, courageous, and enigmatic. Although she did not actually command troops, she knew exactly when and where to make her appearance felt in order to inspire and turn the tide of battle. She believed completely in her voices—St Catherine and the archangel Michael—and obediently followed their commands, regardless of the circumstances. In many ways, this obedience to the faith was typical of the times. She said that her voices called her a "daughter of God," and no one questioned the powers that drove her, although the English called her "a disciple and limb of the Fiend."

TECHNOLOGY

KEEPING TIME

The measurement of time presented humankind with tremendous difficulties until the late Middle Ages. Records of time were among the earliest uses of writing, and the Egyptians had established a relatively accurate calendar by 3500 B.C.E., but for primitive people, work began at sunrise and ended at dusk, and the divisions of time between were of little interest. A seasonal calendar, on the other hand, was of prime importance. The first attempt to divide daylight into units was probably the shadow-clock, which was developed in Egypt around 1450 B.C.E., with later developments including water clocks and sandglasses. It was not until the thirteenth century, however, that mechanical clocks were invented to bring consistent accuracy into the telling of time. The first mechanical clocks (Fig. **9.6**) were driven by falling weights, and spring-driven mechanisms, which made watches possible, came into being in the fifteenth century.

The accurate measurement of time must be based on some repetitive movement that occurs with complete regularity. The earliest mechanism, called a verge, had a pair of pallets attached to an oscillating arm, which engaged alternately with cogs on a wheel rotated by a falling weight. The earliest surviving clock of this type, in Salisbury Cathedral, dates from around 1386. Although it worked perfectly satisfactorily, the verge was friction-driven and not, therefore, wholly accurate. The spring made it possible to construct more compact mechanisms, but required a device to compensate for the diminishing force of the spring as it uncoiled. This problem did not exist with weight-driven mechanisms, because the force exerted by the weight at the end of the descent is the same as at the beginning. To compensate, spring-driven mechanisms employed a fuse—that is, a conical drum with a helical groove—cut so that, as the spring uncoiled, the connecting cord exerted greater pressure on the shaft.

Early clocks often had only a single hand to indicate the hours. Soon, however, a face to indicate quarter hours became common, as did a minute hand.

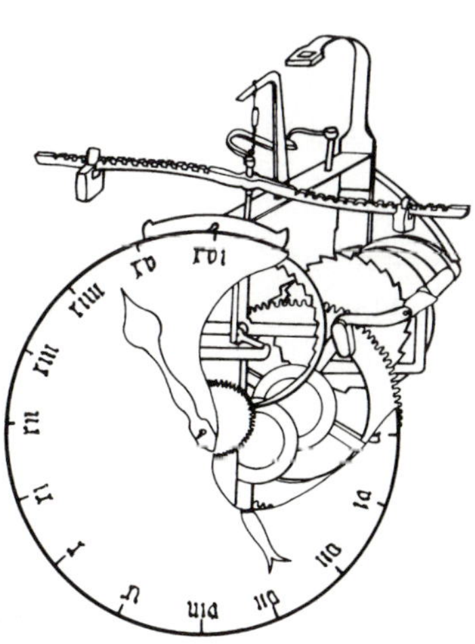

9.6 Early alarm clock, c. 1390.

perfected by the Arabs, was manufactured in Spain and distributed widely. All these conditions drastically changed the course of events in Europe. Printing and publishing industries arose, profoundly changing literature and education. Of course, these developments depended on the extent of the plague's devastation. In some places—for example, Germany and eastern Europe—the plague had little impact, and the old feudal order remained as strong as it had ever been.

Religion and the Great Schism

By the end of the Black Death, it was not uncommon to find religious penitents walking along the roads, flagellating each other and prophesying the end of the world. It was the time of the *dance of death* (see p. 278), with skeletal figures leading knights, burghers, and peasants to the grave. The increasing secularism in government, which separated the Church from the European monarchies, did not diminish the weight of medieval Christianity on the lives of individuals. The simple faith of someone like St Joan stood side by side with the fanaticism of the Inquisition and the burning of witches and heretics. Pogroms against Jews and the persecution of all individuals believed to be in league with Satan were common. Charged with maintaining the purity of Christian thought, the Holy Office of Inquisition used any means necessary—including torture—to obtain confessions from all those accused of heresy. Anyone found to be an enemy of Christ and unrepentant was given over to the civil authorities to be burned alive.

These excesses went hand in hand with sincere and deep, mystical faith among the laity. By this time, the creeds of the Christian Church were well established and much more elaborate than the simple virtues of Pauline Christianity (faith in Christ, hope of salvation, and charity towards one's fellow human beings). The medieval Church recognized seven deadly sins: pride, greed, envy, sexual self-indulgence, violence, laziness, and gluttony. Religious duties were essential. The sacraments brought the Church into the events of everyday life. They also provided penance and absolution for sins, conferred spiritual powers on ordained clergy, and celebrated the communion of believers with their savior in the central Christian mystery of the Mass.

In the fourteenth century, the papacy fell to its nadir. The once mighty and independent popes came under the influence of the French kings, who moved the papal see to Avignon (ah-veen-YOHN) in southern France. The office of pope was humiliated under the force of the French monarchs and further weakened by what is called the Great Schism in 1378. During the Schism, groups supporting diverse claimants to the papal throne fought each other, and for several decades, there were two and even three aspirants to the papacy, each excommunicating the others in what bewildered lay people saw as a complete degradation of the Church. In 1417 the Council of Constance, convened by the Holy Roman Emperor, deposed three pretenders and reunified the papal see at Rome.

The tragedy of what was called the Babylonian Captivity—a term paralleling the Avignon papacy with the Hebrews' captivity in Babylon—and the Great Schism brought increased demands for reform, especially to free the papacy from the control of French monarchs. In England between approximately 1320 and 1384, the reformer John Wycliffe (WY-klif) sought to cleanse the Church of its worldliness. He argued for abolition of all Church property, the subjugation of the Church to secular authority, and the denial of papal authority, although his greatest achievement was the inspiration of a scholarly translation of the first Bible in English. Wycliffe's followers were branded as heretics and were persecuted and punished by the secular authorities. Wycliffe's influence extended as far as Bohemia via reformers in the Holy Roman Empire who had met him at Oxford. In the hands of pietistic Christians and evangelical preachers and theologians such as John Huss (huhs; c. 1369–1415), the reform movement spread. Huss, to whom modern-day Moravian Brethren trace their heritage, accepted some of Wycliffe's teachings and rejected others. He was present at the Council of Constance, but his ideas were viewed as heretical and condemned, and he was burned at the stake. His martyrdom inspired his followers, many of whom were wealthy nobles, and they, in turn, used his beliefs as a vehicle for Czech nationalism against the German emperors and the Roman Church.

THE ARTS OF THE LATE MIDDLE AGES

Painting

The end of the thirteenth century produced an outburst of creative activity in Italy destined profoundly to influence future painting. When the Fourth Crusade sacked Constantinople in 1204, it reinvigorated Byzantine influence in Italian painting that had stayed alive throughout the medieval period, although never straying further north. The "neo-Byzantine" style, or "Greek manner," prevailed in Italy throughout the thirteenth century, and when the Gothic style of northern Europe mixed with the "Greek manner," it produced a revolutionary approach exemplified by Giotto, as we shall see momentarily.

Cimabue

Among the artists of the Greek manner, one of the most famous was Cimabue (chee-mah-BOO-ay), who may have been Giotto's teacher. Cimabue (c. 1250–1302) created very large tempera panels. Tempera is a painting medium in which egg yolk acts as a binder for the pigment, and it was usually applied to panels that had been prepared with a coating of gesso, a smooth mixture of ground chalk or plaster and glue. An application of gold leaf and an underpainting in green or brown preceded the application of the tempera paint. Cimabue's panels were larger than anything that had been attempted in the East, and they further differed from Byzantine works in the severity of their design and expression. The very form of *Madonna Enthroned* (Fig. 9.7) embodies an upward-striving monumentality, and the gabled shape is quite unlike anything done in Byzantium. Designed for the high altar of the church of Santa Trinità, the work rises over 12 feet (3.7 meters) in height. Its *hierarchical* design places the Virgin Mary at the very top center, surrounded by angels, with the Christ Child supported on her lap. Below her elaborate throne, four half-length prophets display their scrolls.

The verticality of the composition is reinforced by rows of inlaid wood in the throne and by ranks of angels rising, one behind the other, on either side. The figures in the top rank bend inward to reinforce both the painting's exterior form and the focus on the Virgin's face. The delicate folds of the blue mantle and dark red robe, which are highlighted with gold, encircle the upper torso, drawing attention to the Madonna's face and to the Child. In a convention appropriate to the theology of the time, the Christ Child is depicted as a wise and omniscient presence, with a patriarchal face older than his infant years. The clean precision of the execution gives the work a fineness and lightness that recall the

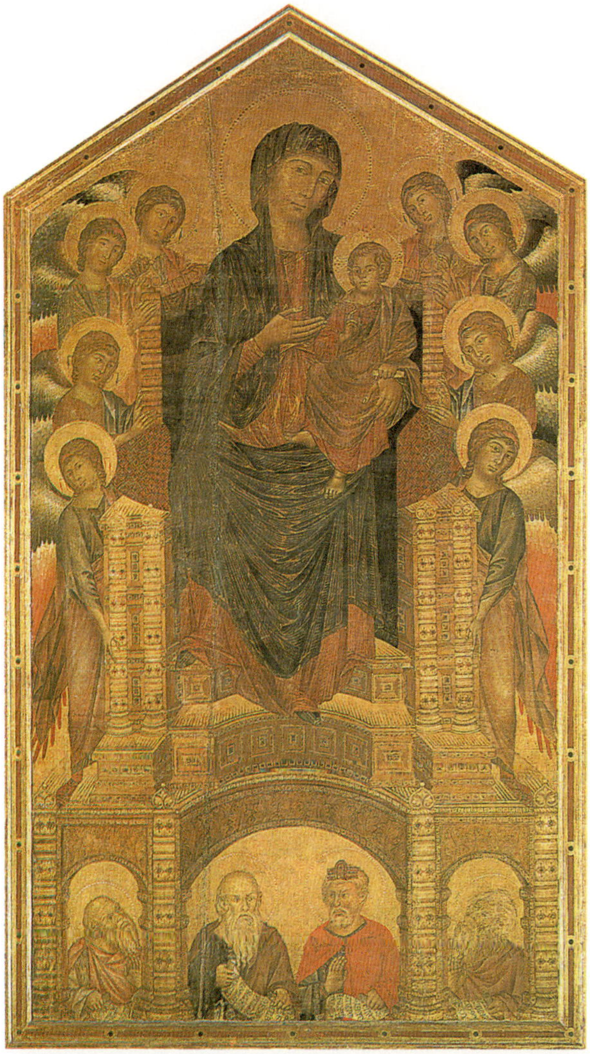

9.7 Cimabue, *Madonna Enthroned*, c. 1280–90. Tempera on wood, about. 12 ft 7½ ins × 7 ft 4 ins (3.84 × 2.24 cm). Uffizi Gallery, Florence, Italy.

exquisiteness of Byzantine mosaics. Find more about Cimabue and his works at http://www.artcyclopedia.com/artists/cimabue.html.

Duccio

A quarter century later, the Italian artist Duccio (c. 1255–1319) portrayed the same subject matter in a similar scheme but with significant differences (Fig. **9.8**). Duccio (DOOT-choh) softens the frozen, Byzantine linearity of Cimabue—his roundness of form and treatment of fabric reflecting Roman characteristics—and gives it a Gothic three-dimensionality. The tender emotion exchanged between mother and child stands in contrast with Cimabue's formal, outward stares of the principal figures. The Sienese called this painting the *maestà* or "majesty," thus identifying the Virgin's role as Queen of Heaven. Unlike Cimabue's vertical composition, Duccio's work flows outward in a horizontal format, increasing the size of the celestial court and adding small compartments with scenes from the lives of Christ and the Madonna. The composition itself reflects a new treatment of space, giving us the sense that the figures are enveloped by space rather than sitting on the front edge of a two-dimensional plane. Find more

9.8 Duccio, *Madonna Enthroned*, center of the *Maestà* altar, 1308–11. Tempera on panel, 6 ft 10½ ins (2.1 m) high. Museo dell' Opera del Duomo, Siena, Italy.

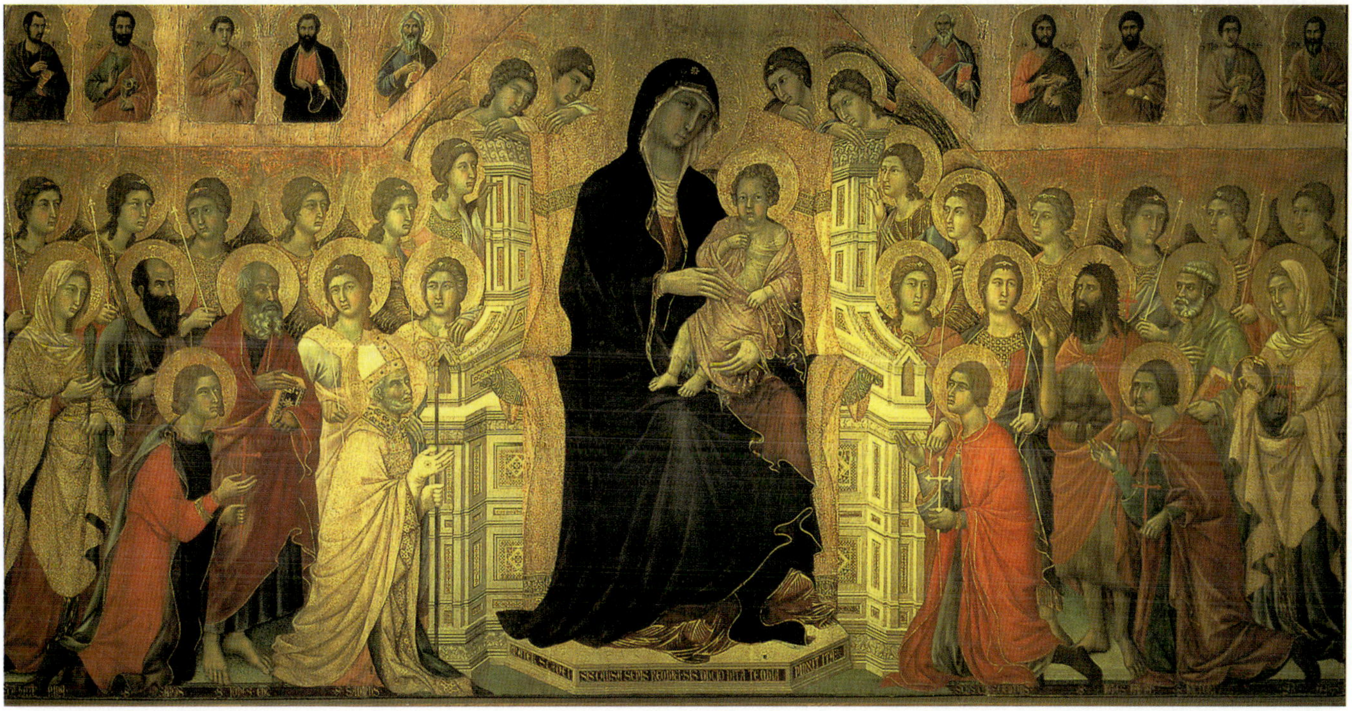

MASTERWORK

GIOTTO—*THE LAMENTATION*

A new sense of space, three-dimensionality, and mobility are clear in Giotto's masterpiece *The Lamentation* (Fig. **9.9**). The figures are skillfully grouped in a simple, coherent scene. Giotto's fabrics retain a decorative quality from an earlier time, but they also show an increased realism. Although the figures are crowded, they still seem free to move within the space. For all its emotion and intensity, the fresco remains human, individualized, and controlled. What makes the fresco so compelling is Giotto's unique mastery of three-dimensional space. He employs **aerial perspective**—that is, the use of haze and indistinction to create a sense of distance—for the background, but unlike other painters, who created deep space behind the primary focal plane, Giotto brings the horizon to our eye-level. As a result, we can move into a three-dimensional space that also moves out to us.

In summary, Giotto was a radical innovator whose dramatic departures made him among the giants of visual art and overshadowed those who followed immediately in his footsteps.

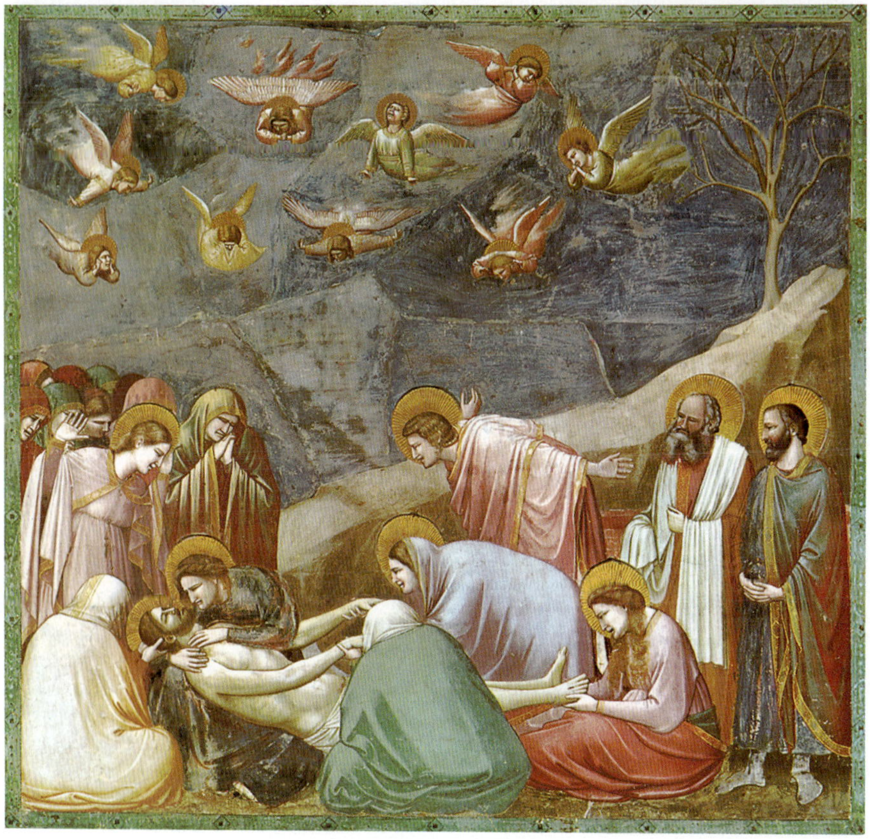

9.9 Giotto, *The Lamentation*, 1305–06. Fresco, 7 ft 7 ins × 7 ft 9 ins (2.31 × 2.36 m). Arena Chapel, Padua, Italy.

about Duccio and his works at http://www.artcyclopedia.com/artists/duccio_di_buoninsegna.html.

Giotto

Despite the advances of Cimabue and Duccio, it remained for Giotto (c. 1266–1336/7) to take far bolder and more dramatic steps. Perhaps less close to the Greek manner than his predecessors, Giotto (JAH-toe) undertook wall painting on a monumental scale. He also painted in tempera on panel. Giotto's treatment of the same subject as Duccio and Cimabue—that is, *Madonna Enthroned* (Fig. **9.10**)—gives us another means by which we can learn to identify the subtleties of style that differentiate one artistic vision from another. In the first place, we find in Giotto's treatment a greater simplification of the subject matter and supporting details. The central focus is even more human, warm, and three-dimensional than in the two earlier works, and it has a sense of drama, heightened by the fact that Giotto's viewpoint is lower than Duccio's or Cimabue's—that is, the viewpoint of the observer relative to the space in the painting. Giotto innovates by defining the actual confines of the painting more by the figures than by the architectural details, and although such a perspective tends to lessen depth of space, it nevertheless gives a more dynamic quality to it. The figures come to life for the viewer, as Giotto's genius

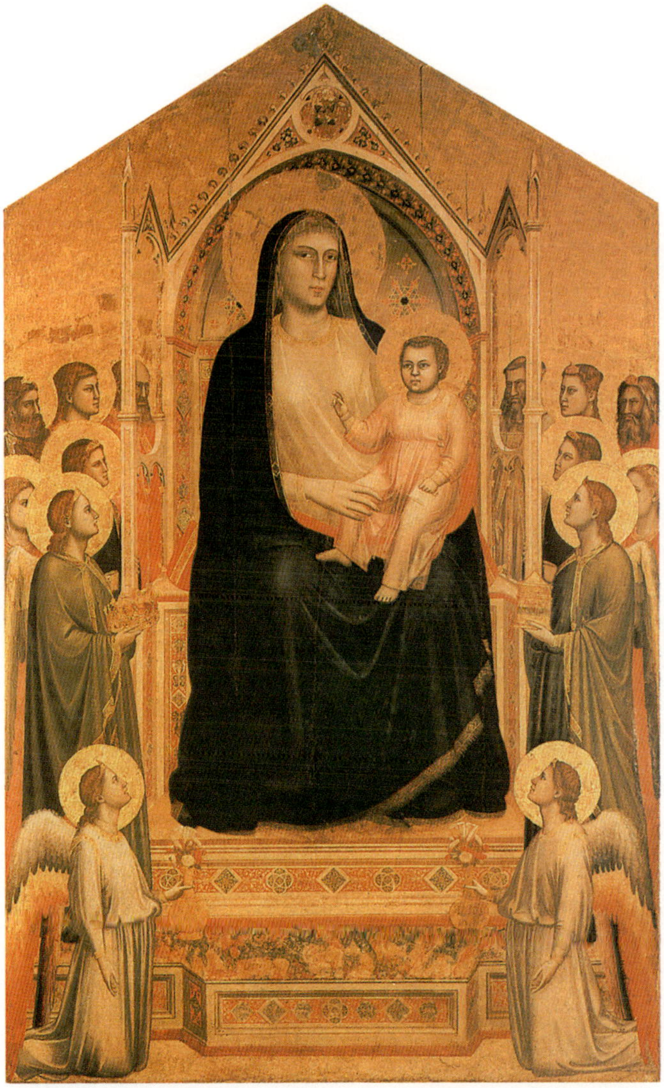

9.10 Giotto, *Madonna Enthroned*, c. 1310. Tempera on panel, 10 ft 8 ins × 6 ft 8 ins (3.25 × 2.04 m). Uffizi Gallery, Florence, Italy.

gives painting a previously unknown liveliness and brings painting to a par with sculpture.

Giotto did not attempt merely to transfer Gothic sculpture into paint. Rather, by creating what amounted to an entirely new treatment of space, he gave the surface of the painting a new appearance. In the past, composition tended to lead the eye from one specific detail to another. Giotto, on the other hand, takes our eye and allows us to grasp the entire work at one time, and the composition has an inner unity achieved by strong, simple groupings of figures. The throne, based on Italian Gothic architecture, encloses the Madonna and cuts her off from the background. In another innovation, Giotto takes great pains to create a fake texture in the colored marble surfaces. The creation of false textures had not been used in painting since early Christian times, and Giotto's reintroduction of this approach attests to his familiarity with ancient Roman wall paintings, similar to those we studied in Chapter 4. Find more about Giotto and his works at http://www.artcyclopedia.com/artists/giotto_di_bondone.html.

Pietro Lorenzetti

One of those who followed Giotto and succeeded in creating his own revolutionary approach to space was Pietro Lorenzetti (pee-AY-troh loh-rehn-ZEHT-ee; d. c. 1348). *The Birth of the Virgin* (Fig. **9.11**) is a bold attempt to solve the problems of space and to create a unified and flowing compositional picture. In contrast to Giotto's sculptural space, we find a new sense of architectural picture space. The figures are lifelike, and highlight and shadow flesh out their faces and garments, with the treatment of draping fabric in the gowns in the right panel showing precise attention to detail. We have a sense of looking in on a scene in progress, rather than at a flat, frozen rendering. The scene has a relaxed atmosphere, and the eye is drawn across the work in a lyrical sweep. The groups of figures are spaced comfortably, and the whole picture, which continues behind the columns separating the panels, spreads throughout the triptych—that is, a devotional picture with a central panel and two flanking hinged wings. Find more about Lorenzetti and his works at http://www.artcyclopedia.com/artists/lorenzetti_pietro.html.

Sculpture

In general, we may say that Gothic sculpture took the traditional themes of Christian art and gave them emotional appeal, and toward the end of the thirteenth century, that tendency was applied to objects designed to enhance private worship. This type of object is often called *Andachtsbild* (AHN-dahkts-bihlt), because Germany played a leading role in its development, and it was best exemplified by the **pietà**, which derives from the Latin word *pietas*, meaning both "pity" and "piety"; its main visual representation was a grieving Virgin Mary holding the dead Christ in her arms. The pietà offers a symmetrical balance to the Madonna and Child depictions that were always popular, although nothing in scripture suggests that the Virgin Mary ever held the body of the crucified Christ in her arms. This tragic scene—full of deep emotion—is a complete invention of the time. The emotion typical of this genre of sculpture stands out poignantly in a German pietà from the early fourteenth century (Fig. **9.12**). In a move away from the emerging naturalism we have seen previously, this work subordinates lifelikeness to powerful emotion, which is achieved through stylization and exaggeration. The forms of Mary and Jesus look remarkably like puppets, and Christ's wounds are

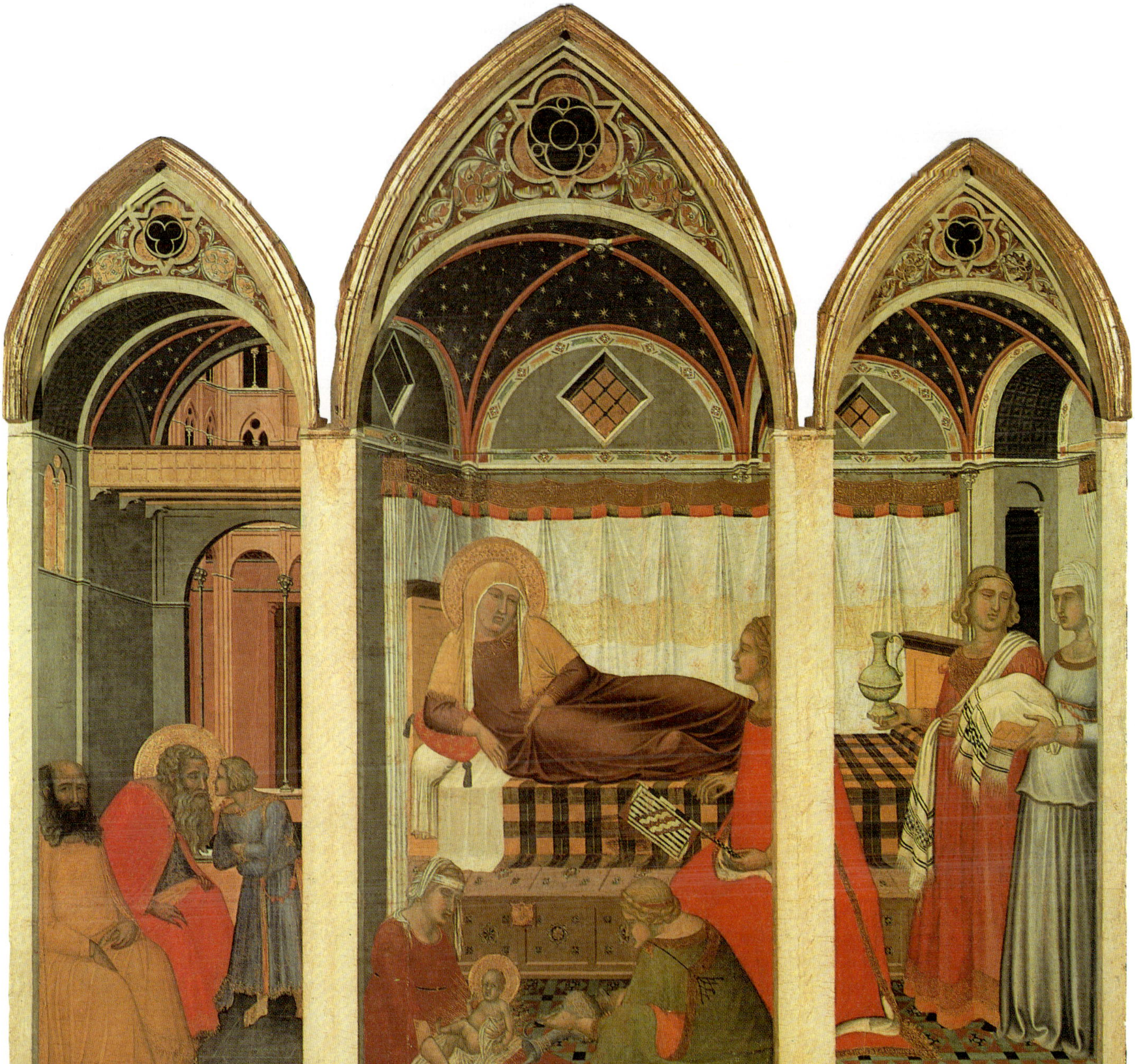

9.11 Pietro Lorenzetti, *The Birth of the Virgin*, 1342. Panel painting, 6 ft 1½ ins × 6 ft ½ in (1.87 × 1.84 m). Museo dell'Opera Metropolitana, Siena, Italy.

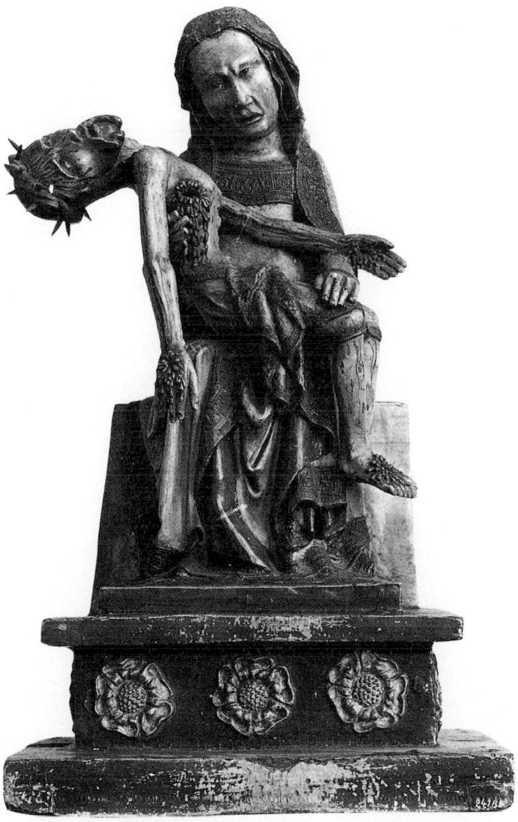

9.12 *Pietà*, early fourteenth century. Wood, 34½ ins (87.5 cm) high. Provinzialmuseum, Bonn, Germany.

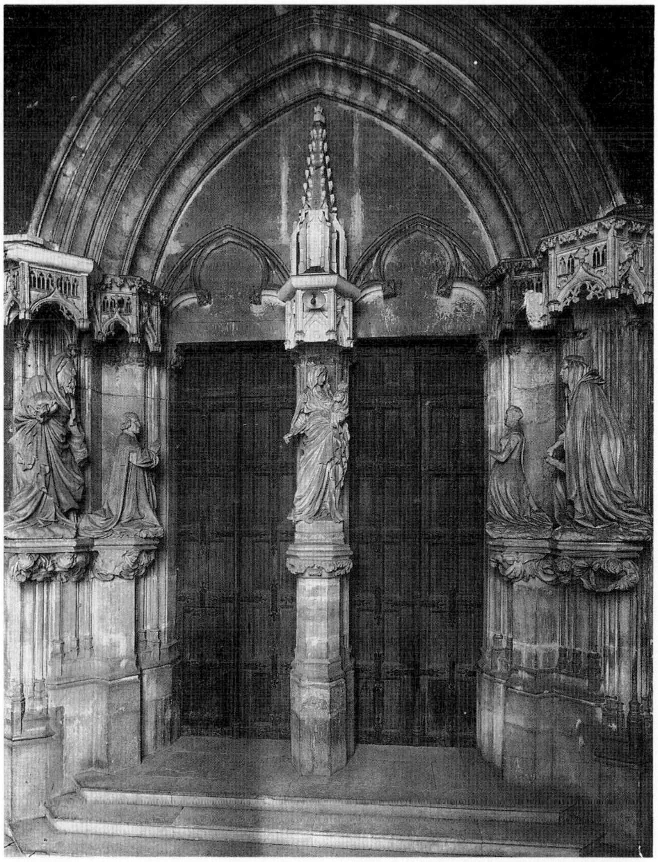

9.13 Claus Sluter, portal of the Chartreuse de Champmol, Dijon, France, 1385–93. Stone.

exaggerated to grotesque proportion for emotional effect. The work clearly asks the viewer to identify with the horror and grief felt by the Mother of God.

In the north of Europe, reaching a climax around the year 1400, the *International style* found its greatest exponent in the Flemish sculptor Claus Sluter (SLOO-tur; c. 1350–1405), who worked for the duke of Burgundy in Dijon. Sluter's work, as evidenced by the portal of the Chartreuse de Champmol at Dijon (Fig. **9.13**) commands the space, seeming to be affixed to the portal rather than growing from it as did earlier medieval sculptures such as those at Chartres (see Figs **8.25** and **8.27**). The figures are large, bold, and nearly full-round. The dynamic quality of the work is intensified by the fact that the figures of Duke Philip the Bold and his wife, who are accompanied by their patron saints, turn inward to direct attention to the central figure of the Madonna. Thus, rather than a series of separate jamb statues, like those at Chartres, this grouping forms a single statement—it is a single work composed to highlight a central focal area.

In sculpture as in architecture, Italy stood apart from the Gothic style found in the rest of Europe. Although the Gothic emotionalism we have previously noted is present, the figures of Italian Gothic sculpture have a more classical sense than their northern counterparts. Figures have a roundness that has been tied not only to classicism but also to Byzantium. We can see this tendency in the work of Giovanni Pisano (c. 1250–1320), the son of the famous Tuscan sculptor, Nicola Pisano (pee-ZAHN-oh; c. 1225–84) whose works reflect the same tendencies. On visits to the Cathedral at Pisa, care must be taken to note which Pisano's works one is viewing. Nicola carved a pulpit in the Baptistery; his son, a pulpit in the cathedral proper, and it is this work that draws our attention here (Fig. **9.14**). Done in marble, Giovanni's figures reflect delicacy and a flowing line. The young Pisano's work reflects the elegance found earlier in Gothic sculpture in Paris. Giovanni's figures have great depth in their dimensionality, in which space becomes as important as the forms themselves (see Fig. **9.1**).

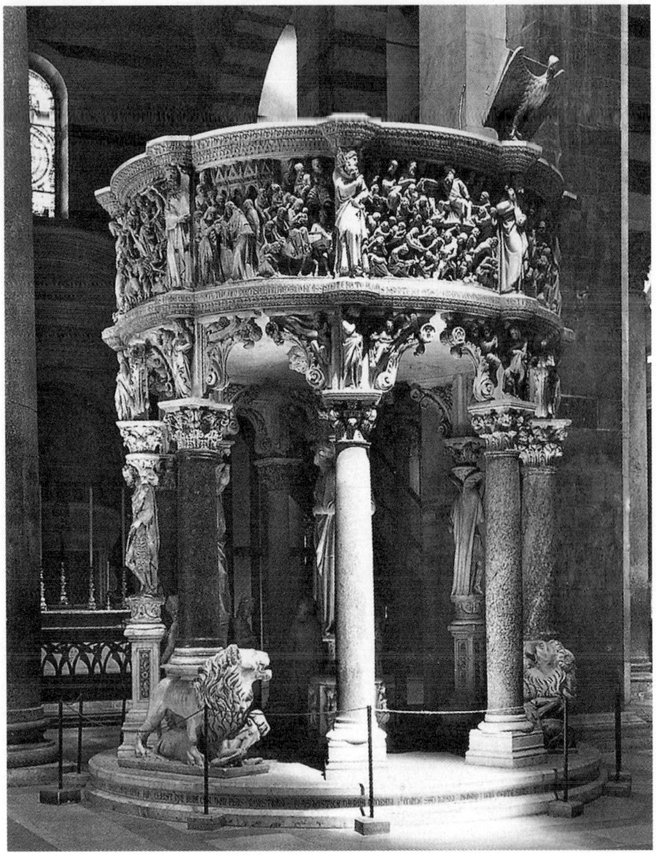

9.14 Giovanni Pisano, pulpit, 1302–10. Marble. Pisa Cathedral, Italy.

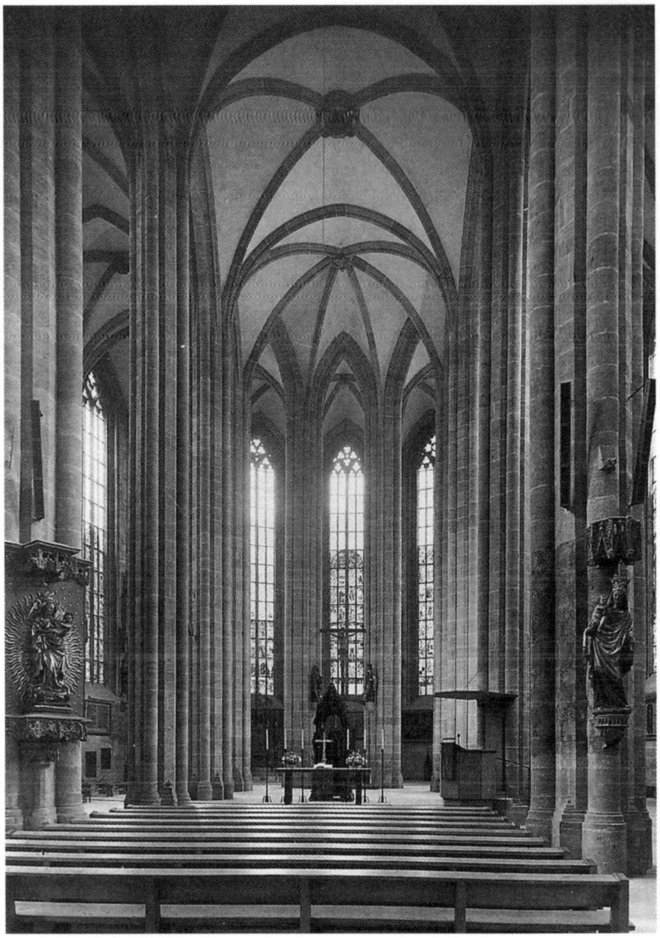

9.15 Choir of church of St Sebald, Nuremberg, Germany, 1361–72.

Architecture

We should be aware by now that generalizations about places as diverse as Europe and timespans as broad as two hundred years do not always apply uniformly. In Germany, for example, Gothic style in architecture took much longer to gain a foothold than in other parts of Europe, and most characteristic of the German interpretation of Gothic style is a form known as the hall church or Hallenkirche (HAHL-ehn-kersh), in which the aisles and the nave are the same height, unlike the more traditional Gothic style, in which the nave is high and the aisles lower in order to allow for clerestory windows in the nave. The *Hallenkirche* approach is, in reality, similar to Romanesque. The large hall choir added to the church of St Sebald in Nuremberg (Fig. **9.15**) is a typical example. Here graceful bundles of columns rise toward pointed arches, flaring outward at the last second into a series of ribs. Space is light and airy, with tall lancet windows adding delicacy to the feeling of openness that results from the slender columns and seemingly unimpeded space. The tone of the design is simple. Nothing interrupts the eye as it travels up the unadorned vertical line to narrow vaults that belie the unencumbered expanse below.

In Italy we find another variation on the Gothic theme in the Florence Cathedral or *Duomo* (Fig. **9.16**). Although the architect's primary concern was an impressive interior, our view of this church tends to focus on the impressive dome (see Fig. **10.23**), which was added later by the Renaissance architect Brunelleschi (broo-nel-LES-kee) in an imitation of classical forms.

As we look at Florence Cathedral from any angle on the exterior, we recognize little that would identify it with the Gothic style—there are no flying buttresses, and rather than great stained-glass windows, we find only solid walls inlaid with geometric marble patterns that match a Romanesque baptistery, a separate building that sits just

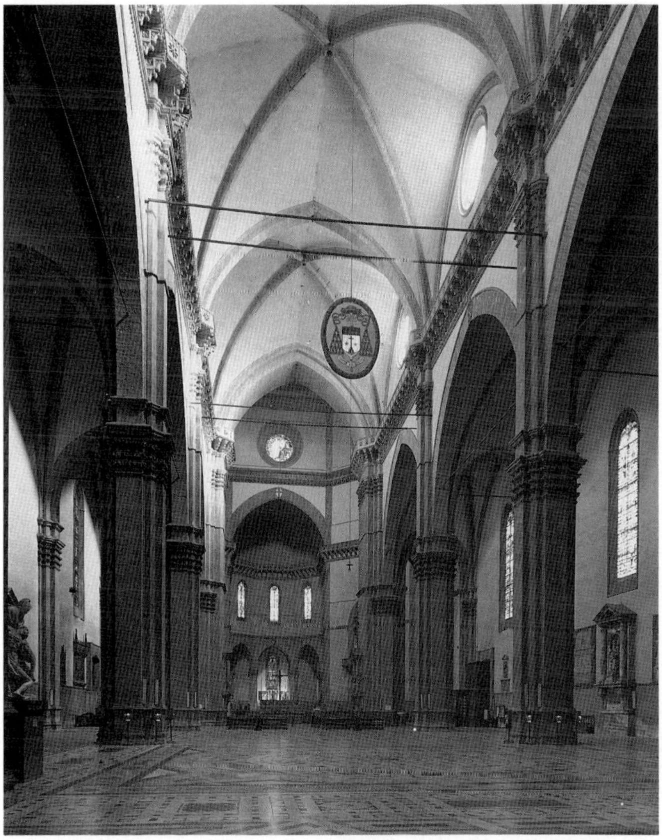

9.16 Nave and choir, Florence Cathedral, Italy, begun 1296.

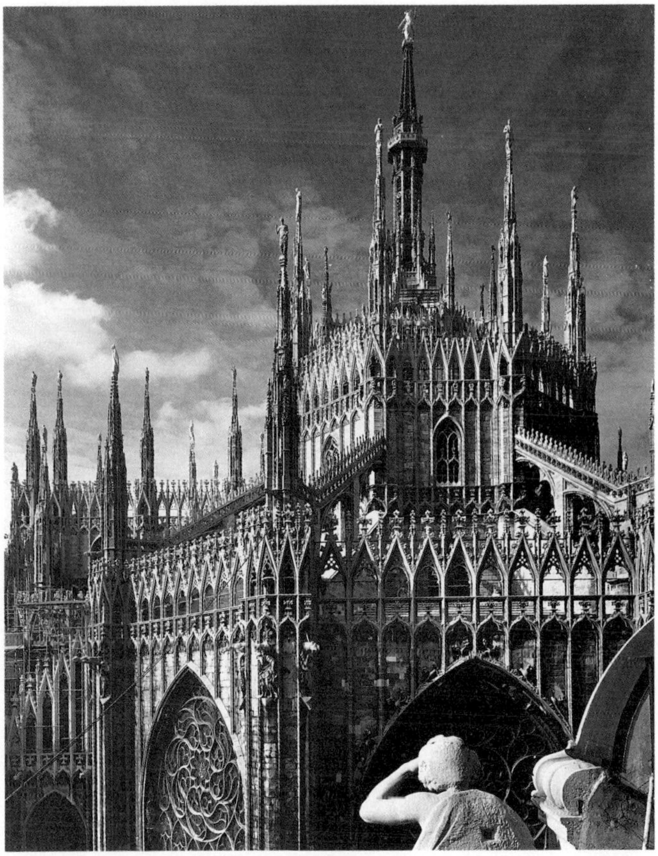

9.17 Apse of Milan Cathedral, Italy, begun 1386.

opposite the main entrance. However, as we move inside, we are greeted by Gothic arches (Fig. **9.16**), perhaps less serene than we have become accustomed to, but Gothic nonetheless. There is a sense of coldness and decorative solemnity here. Horizontal banding breaks the clean flow of line up the supporting columns, separating the design into what seem almost awkward proportions. The sense of space becomes horizontal rather than vertical.

On the other hand, Milan Cathedral (Fig. **9.17**), the largest of Italy's Gothic churches, is, with its delicate traceries, pure late Gothic. Although it was begun in 1386, it was completed only in 1910. Its flamboyance lends the façade a lightness that the somewhat horizontal sprawl of the building would not otherwise achieve. Needlelike spires reach above the roof line to lift the spirit from earth into the mystery of space.

Gothic style was also used in secular buildings, and we capture glimpses of this late application, typical of the spirit of the age, in Venice, where a unique version of the style developed in the fourteenth century and was used in particular for nonreligious buildings. One of the most delightful examples is the Doge's (dohzh) Palace (Fig. **9.18**), which represents a direction in architecture developed specifically for the palaces of the rich and powerful merchant class. Begun in the 1340s, the palace was designed to serve as a large meeting hall for the *Maggior Consiglio*, the elective assembly of the Republic of Venice. Remarkable for this period is the building's sense of openness and tranquility, and the absence of features for fortification reflects the relative peace that the republic enjoyed at the time. The solidity of the upper stories above the open colonnades and an apparent lack of mathematical proportion between upper and lower stories give an almost top-heavy appearance, and the rather squat proportions of the lower arcade detract from the delicacy of the overall design. The curious asymmetry of the facade's **fenestration** draws attention and piques curiosity. Eastern influences join gracefully with Gothic arches in the patterned brickwork. The result illustrates a particularly Venetian inventiveness seen often in the city, as European and Moorish influences intermix.
Find more about Late Gothic architecture at http://ps.theatre.tulane.edu/lester/text/Gothic/Late.Gothic/Late.Gothic.html.

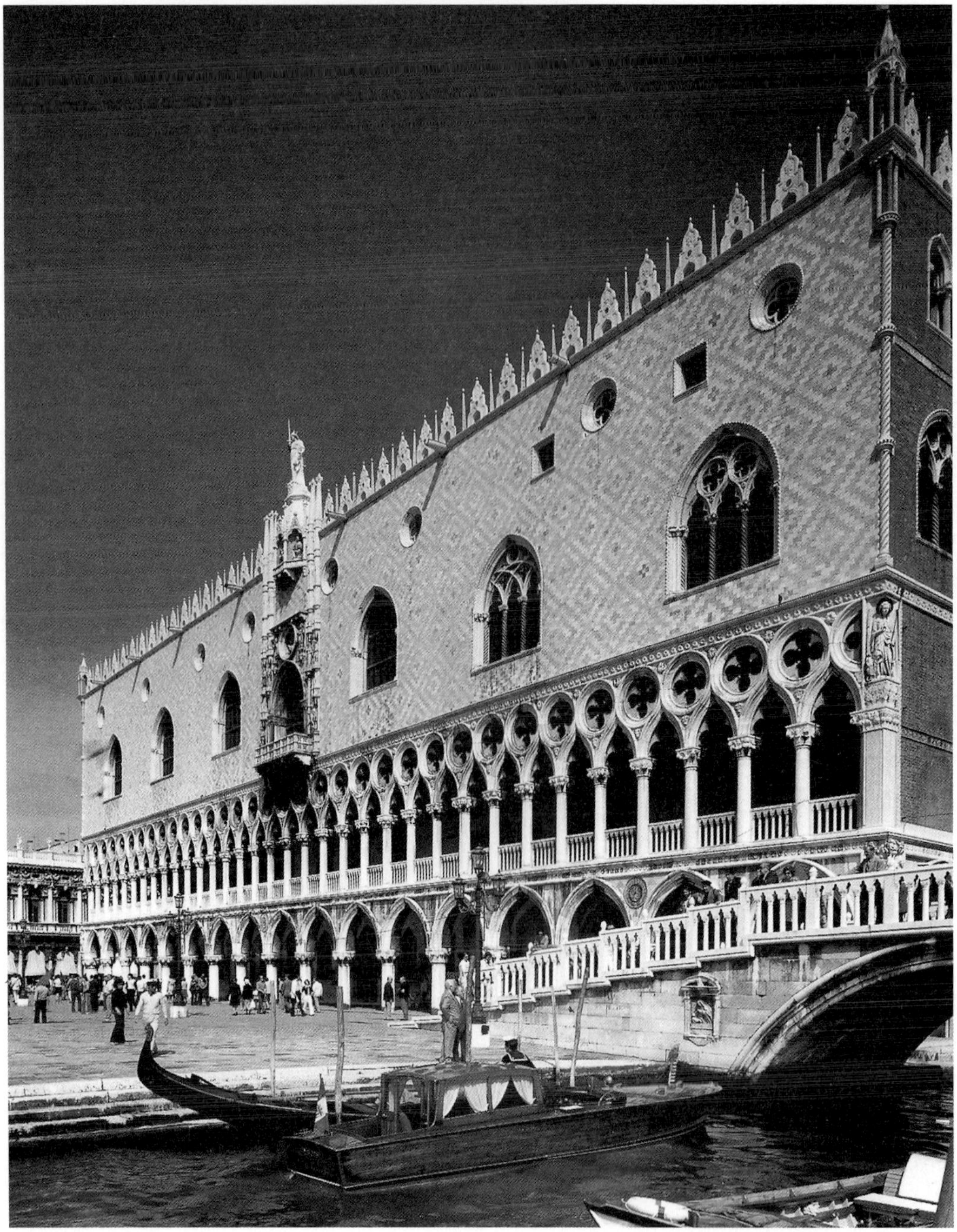

9.18 The Doge's Palace, Venice, Italy, c. 1345–1438

Theatre

The characteristics of theatre we noted in the last chapter (see p. 250) continued throughout the late medieval period. Theatre is often a static art, far more resistant to change than the other arts, which tend to evolve around the vision of a single artist. Theatre, more a group expression, gets caught in its own inertia, and that, certainly, was the case in the late Middle Ages. However, one of the most enduring plays, which is still performed and enjoyed in modern times, came out of this era. No one knows for certain when it originated, because it circulated through the oral tradition before it was finally put into print. Nonetheless, the most famous play of this era—indeed, of the entire Middle Ages—is *Everyman*, an anonymous morality play.

Death summons Everyman to his final judgment. Everyman then seeks, as companions on his journey to judgment, the qualities (characters) of Fellowship, Kindred, Cousin, and Goods. Each refuses to join him. He finally asks Good Deeds, but Good Deeds is too weak from neglect to make the journey. Seeking advice from Knowledge, Everyman is told to do penance—an act that revives Good Deeds, who then takes up the journey with

A Dynamic World

Noh Theatre of Japan

Japanese Noh drama came of age in the fourteenth century. Buddhist monks used it as a teaching tool in much the same way as the Christian Church used medieval miracle, mystery, and morality plays. Slowly it became more and more secularized.

Noh drama is performed on a simple, almost bare stage and, like classical Greek tragedy (see Chapter 3), uses only two actors. Also, as in classical Greek drama, actors wear elaborate masks and costumes, men play women's roles (Fig. **9.19**), and a chorus functions as a narrator. Actors chant the highly poetic dialogue to orchestral, musical accompaniment. All the actions suggest rather than depict, which gives the drama its sense of stylization and conventionality, and symbolism and restraint characterize both acting and staging.

The tone of the plays tends to be serious. The plays are usually short, and an evening's performance encompasses several plays interspersed with comic burlesques called *Kyogen* ("crazy words").

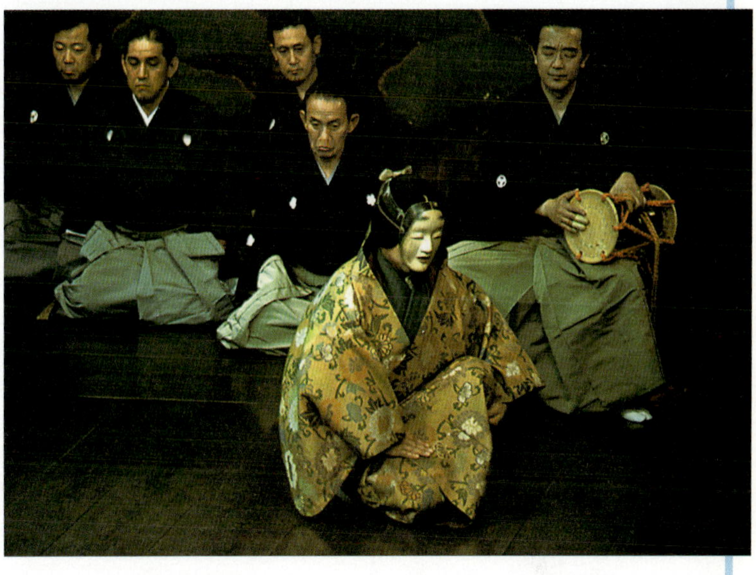

9.19 Performance at the Noh Theatre of the Kongo School, Kyoto.

Everyman. Along the way, Five Wits also deserts him as he nears the grave. Good Deeds, however, stays with him until the end, and so is welcomed to Heaven.

Music

The fourteenth century witnessed a distinct change in musical style. This new style was called *ars nova* or "new art," from the title of a book by Philippe de Vitry (1291–1361). Music of the *ars nova* was more diverse than past music in its harmonies and rhythms. By the early fourteenth century, a new system of musical notation had emerged that allowed a composer to specify nearly any rhythmic pattern. Beats could be subdivided into two as well as three, and **syncopation** took on an important role.

Ars nova was primarily a secular movement. The characteristics of its rhythmic vibrancy did not meet the Church's expectations for worship, and early in the century, the Church forbade any musical elaboration of the Mass that might alter the character of the chant, and this had the effect of stifling polyphonic development in sacred music.

Guillaume de Machaut

Nonetheless, the first great exponent of *ars nova* was the French composer Guillaume de Machaut (gee-YOHM-duh mah-SHOH; 1300–77), priest, poet, and composer, who served King John of Bohemia. Machaut's music in the new style had a smoothness and sweetness, and made increasing use of polyphony. He also used a new structural form that gave his compositions unity of style. One of the features Machaut used to achieve unity was *isorhythm*, in which phrases are repeated in their rhythm, but not necessarily in their melody. He also used short fragments of melody to create unity. This technique provided the structural underpinnings for his *Notre Dame* Mass for four voices, written c. 1364. It is the first complete polyphonic setting of the Mass ordinary by a known composer.

In addition, because his music had a fundamental smoothness and consonance, Machaut was able to use dissonance as an emotional effect. For example, as the words of the Mass describe the crucifixion, the composer underscores them with discordant notes, thereby creating not only beauty but emotional expressiveness.

Machaut also wrote secular poems, often with music. His characteristic texture was that of a solo voice with

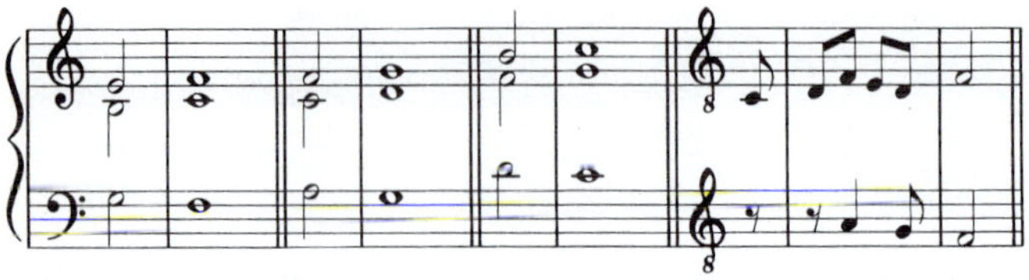

9.20 Examples of cadences.

two instrumental parts forming an accompaniment. Each of his phrases comes to a definite end, called a *cadence*. Some of these are simple, and some are quite ornamental, as an example from one of his *virelais* illustrates (Fig. 9.20).

Machaut was an inventive craftsman and the sound of the music mattered as much to him as its structure. His watchwords were beauty and feeling, and he once indicated that words and music without true feeling were merely false.

Francesco Landini

The most celebrated Italian composer of the fourteenth century was Francesco Landini (lan-DEE-nee; d. 1397). Blind from childhood, he was a famous organist, poet, and scholar. Landini illustrates the new secular impetus of the time. His compositions are exclusively Italian songs for two or three voices that deal with subjects as diverse as nature, love, morality, and politics. His composition *Ecco la primavera* (Spring has Come) is a *ballata*, an Italian poetic and musical form that originated as a dance-song. The text speaks of the joys of springtime, and its lively rhythms result from the use of syncopation.

Dance

Dance was part of medieval religious and secular activity, but with the exception of pantomime, examples of which have perished, theatre dance was less important than forms of group dancing. Fascinating illustrations survive of the "ring dance," for example, in which twelve dancers representing the apostles and the zodiac danced in a circle. Amid the ravages of the plague, the *danse macabre* (dahns mah-CAHB), or dance of death, appeared. Whipped by hysteria, people danced in a frenzy until some dropped dead of exhaustion. *Choreomania*, an English version of the *danse macabre*, seems to have expressed a kind of group psychosis in the throes of which the participants engaged in all kinds of demented behavior, including self-flagellation. Numerous folk and court dances also existed.

Within the courtly tradition, theatre dance was reborn. Dances done at court were performed to instrumental accompaniment. A certain degree of expressiveness and spontaneity marked these court dances, but increasingly they conformed to specific rules. Dance that was performed in the course of court theatricals employed professional entertainers. These performances depended to a large degree upon the guiding hand of the dancing master, who was perhaps more like a square-dance caller than a ballet master or choreographer.

Literature

Petrarch and Boccaccio

It is fair to say that the late Middle Ages—especially the fourteenth century—provided a transition between medieval thought and the Renaissance that was to come. In literature, especially, occurred stirrings of ideas that are more Renaissance than medieval. In the fourteenth century, Italian writers such as Petrarch (PEE-trahrk) and Boccaccio (boh-KAH-choh) began to take the works of ancient writers in a new direction. They borrowed ideas, stories, figures of speech, and general style, and tried to recreate ancient poetic and prose styles. In so doing, they provided a more penetrating investigation and analysis of ancient literature and art than their medieval predecessors had achieved, and achieved an ordered plan, integrated structure, symmetry, and lofty style, which fourteenth-century writers believed represented classical beauty. Various rules emerged—for example, the epic must begin in the middle of the plot, must contain supernatural elements, and must end with a victory for the hero.

Petrarch

The Italian poet Petrarch (1304–74) wrote in both Latin and his native Tuscan dialect and is a key figure in the transition from medieval to Renaissance thought. His writings are very different from those of Dante, for example, and are filled with complaints about "the dangers and apprehensions I have suffered." Contrary to what he wrote, however, he enjoyed the favor of the great men and women of his day. He flourished at the papal court at Avignon. Petrarch was unable to reconcile his own conflicting aspirations and interests into a workable existence: he desired solitude and quiet, but was continually active. Although he adored being a celebrity, he attacked the superficiality of the world around him and longed for the monastic life.

He is well known for his love poems to Laura, written over a period of about twenty years. Petrarch wrote more than 300 Italian *sonnets* to Laura (the sonnet is a fixed verse form consisting of fourteen lines), as well as other short lyrics and one long poem. They treat a variety of moods and subjects, but particularly his intense psychological reactions to his beloved. As he wrote in

PROFILE

Geoffrey Chaucer (c. 1340–1400)

Born in London, Geoffrey Chaucer (CHAW-sir) came from a prosperous family of vintners who were occasionally connected to the King's court (Fig. **9.21**). We know little of his education, although we do know that he learned Latin and French. Although we know him as a writer, he appears mainly to have been a successful government employee with a long career as courtier, diplomat, and public servant. In 1359 he was captured and held for ransom while on a military expedition to France. He married in 1366. He traveled in Spain, and entertained in song, stories, and music at the court of the king of England. Traveling to Italy on the king's business he encountered the works of Dante and Boccaccio, and these probably influenced his poetry, especially *The Canterbury Tales.*

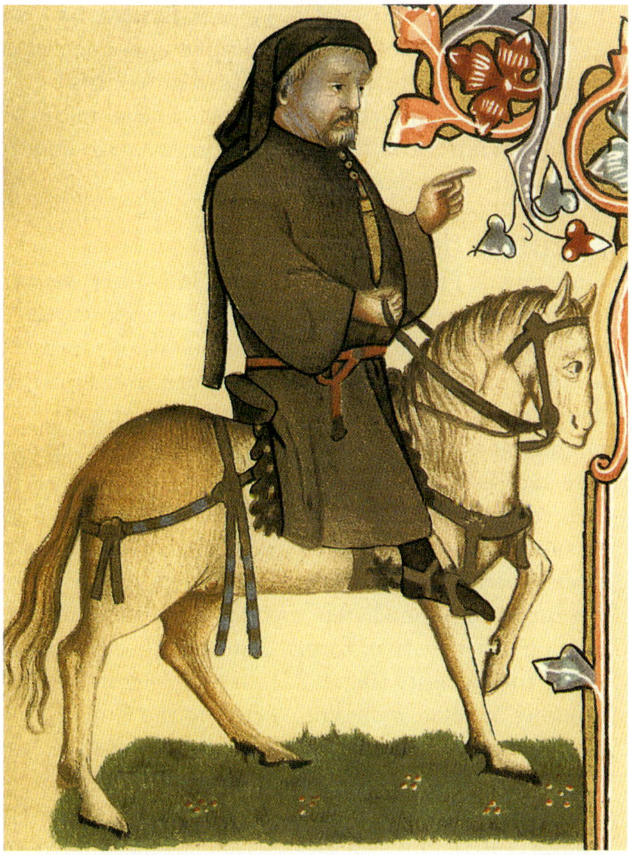

Between 1374 and 1386, he created three major works: *The House of Fame, The Parliament of Fowls,* and *Troilus and Criseyde.* His best-known work, *The Canterbury Tales,* was written over a period of years, mostly after 1387. The large scheme for this work included a band of thirty pilgrims on a journey from the Tabard Inn in Southwark, a suburb of London, to the shrine of Thomas à Becket in Canterbury and back again. Each pilgrim was to tell two stories when going and two while returning, but the final work included only twenty-four stories, some of which remain unfinished. The tales are funny, satirical, ironic, insightful, and individualistic in character development; some are philosophical, some are thoughtful, and others are serious. Altogether, they paint a broad portrait of fourteenth-century life and expectations. The framework resembles that of Boccaccio's *Decameron,* with which Chaucer was familiar, but Chaucer's cultivated irony and robust comedy are unprecedented. Read the *Canterbury Tales* at www.Litrix.com/canterby/cante 001.htm.

9.21 Geoffrey Chaucer (c. 1340–1400).

Sonnet CCXXV, Canzone XXI, To Laura in Life: "I know and love the good, yet, ah! The worst pursue." The Petrarchan sonnet (also called Italian sonnet) is a poem of fourteen lines divided into eight lines rhymed *abbaabba* and six lines with a variable rhyme scheme. Usually, the first eight lines present the theme or problem of the poem, and the final six present a change in thought or resolution of the problem. The sonnet form developed in Italy in the thirteenth century and reached its highest expression in Petrarch. The Italian sonnet was imported into England where it was adapted to create the form now called a Shakespearean sonnet (see p. 376).

Canzone VI

So Wayward is the madness of Desire

Petrarch

Translated by Joseph Auslander

So wayward is the madness of desire
In following her who turns from me in flight,
And who, at liberty, like air or light,
My love-encumbered chase eludes like fire,

That when the more I call, the more aspire
To point the safer path by left or right,

The less it heeds; to curb or to excite
Avails not: Love drives faster, fiercer, higher!

Thus, the triumphant bit between its teeth,
I must remain incapable and mute,
That while against my will it speeds my death

Straight to that laurel whose most fatal fruit,
Instead of healing, spreads its bitter breath
And nourishes the pain it should uproot.

Petrarch's real love was learning, for which he earned the title "Father of Humanism," and he made a significant impact on those who followed. He rejected medieval philosophy and also found science wanting as a way toward a "happy life." He had a passion for classical literature and Roman antiquity, but although he was a classical scholar, his religious thought was thoroughly medieval. He felt guilty about admiring the things learned from pagan philosophers, and he could not accept Dante's connection between the good of this world and that of the next. He rejected the intellectual tradition of the Middle Ages but clung tenaciously to its moral code.

Boccaccio

Giovanni Boccaccio (1313–75), a lifelong friend of Petrarch, was, in contrast, a man of the world. Much of his early work was inspired by, and dedicated to, his consuming passion, Fiammetta, but this was completely overshadowed by the *Decameron*, which was completed in 1358. In the framing tale, ten young people flee from the plague in Florence in 1348 to sit out the danger in the countryside. To amuse themselves, they tell one hundred stories. The first tale from Day One tells of a lively day spent in witty conversation. Days Two and Three are tales of adventure. Day Four presents unhappy love, and Day Five treats the same subject in a somewhat lighter vein. Day Six returns to the happiness of Day One, and Days Seven, Eight, and Nine cover laughter, trickery, and license. Day Ten ties the foregoing themes together in a conclusion. In total, the *Decameron* extols the virtue of humankind, proposing that to be noble, one must accept life as one finds it, without bitterness. Above all, one must accept the responsibility for, and consequences of, one's own actions. Read *The Decameron* at http://www.brown.edu/Departments/Italian _Studies/dweb/dec_ov/dec_ov.html.

Froissart's Chronicles

A popular genre of literature during this period was the *medieval chronicle*. A chronicle is history told in a "romantic" way, and in the contemporary language of the country. The *Chronicles of England, France, and Spain* by the French writer Jean Froissart (fwah-SAHR; c. 1333–1400) is an outstanding example of this genre. Froissart's work covers the history of the fourteenth century and the wars between England and France. It was not written as a factual account but, in the words of its author, "to encourage all valorous hearts and to show them honorable examples."

Froissart loved the ideals of knighthood and its heroic deeds, and his sympathies were always with the lordly knights. In his "history," however, he allowed his imagination free rein to fill in details where facts were missing. He never let accuracy stand in the way of a good story. To collect his tales, he wandered on horseback throughout Europe, his trusty greyhound tagging along behind. He talked to squires, knights, heralds, and pages, gathering their recollections and sometimes fanciful tales of the court and the battlefield. Read Froissart's *Chronicles* at http://etext.lib.virginia.edu/cgibin/browse-mixed?id=FroChro&tag=public&images=images/modeng&data=/1v1/Archive/eng-parsed.

Christine de Pisan

Christine de Pisan (pee-ZAHN; c. 1365–1463) was a prolific and versatile French poet and author whose diverse writings include numerous poems of courtly love and several works championing women. Her father was astrologer to Charles V, and Christine spent her childhood at the French court. She was married at age fifteen to Estienne de Castel, who became court secretary. Ten years later, after his death, she began writing in order to support herself and her three young children. Her first poems were ballades of lost love written in memory of her husband. Immediately successful, she continued writing in a variety of forms, expressing her feelings with grace and sincerity (Fig. 9.22). In total, she wrote ten volumes in verse, including "Letter to the God of Loves" (1399), in which she defended women against the attacks of Jean de Meun in his satire *Roman de la Rose*.

Christine's prose works include *The Book of the City of Ladies* (1405), in which she described women known for their heroism and virtue. Another prose work, *The Book of Three Virtues* (1405), was a sequel to *The Book of the City of Ladies*, which classified women's roles in medieval society and detailed moral instructions for women in various social circumstances. Her life's story, *L'Avision de Christine* (1405), was an allegorical reply to her detractors. At the request of the regent, she wrote a biography of the deceased king (*Book of the Deeds and Good Morals of the Wise King Charles V*). It was a first-hand view of the king and his court. This and her eight other prose works revealed her outstanding breadth of knowledge.

Her final work, written in 1429, was a lyrical and joyous piece inspired by the victories of Joan of Arc. It is the only such French-language work written during Joan's lifetime.

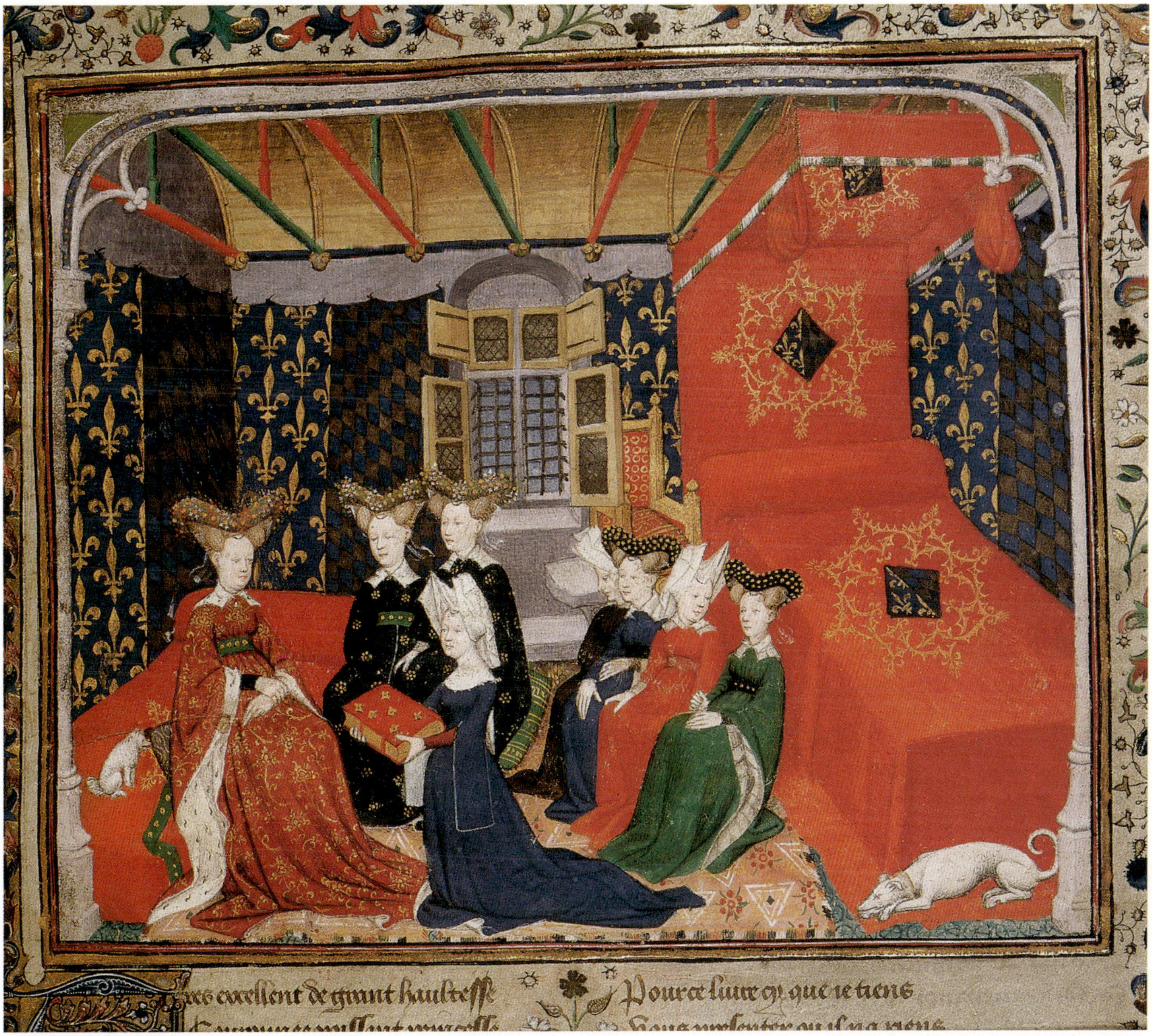

9.22 Illuminated manuscript of Christine de Pisan presenting her poems to Isabel of Bavaria. MS. Harl. 4431 fol. 3. Min. The British Library.

FOCAL POINT

WOMEN MYSTICS OF THE LATE MIDDLE AGES

Despite a growing secularization in society, the mysticism of the earlier Middle Ages remained very much alive, as Joan of Arc demonstrated, and we can see it clearly in the lives and works of four women.

Marguerite Porète (d. 1306) wrote *Le Miroir des simples âmes* (*Mirror of Simple Souls*) sometime between 1296 and 1306. Her verse and commentary form a dialogue between Love, Reason, and the Soul and suggest that the individual moves through seven stages of spiritual growth as it progresses toward union with God. Porète argues that in the last stage the soul need not concern itself with Masses, penance, sermons, fasts, or prayer. Her book was condemned in 1306 and was burned in her presence.

Two years later, she was accused of continuing to make copies of her book available to others. She was imprisoned in Paris, tried for heresy, and burned at the stake.

The Mirror of Simple Souls is sprawling and episodic, changing quickly from narrative to dialogue. The main speakers, personifications of "Love," "Reason," and "the Soul," discuss sublime matters as one might hear lively discussions on the street: "Oh, for god's sake, love, what are you saying?"; "Reason, you'll always be half-blind"; "Oh, you sheep, how crude is your understanding!"

The Mirror of Simple Souls (excerpt)

Introduction:

You who would read this book,
if you indeed wish to grasp it,
think about what you say,
for it is very difficult to comprehend;
humility, who is keeper of the treasury of
knowledge
and the mother of the other Virtues,
Must overtake you.

Theologians and other clerks,
you will not have the intellect for it,
no matter how brilliant your abilities,
if you do not proceed humbly
and make Love and Faith, together,
cause you to rise above Reason
[since] they are the ladies of the house.

...

Humble, then your wisdom
which is based on Reason,
and place all your fidelity
in those things which are given
by Love, illuminated through Faith.
And thus you will understand this book
which makes the Soul live by love.

Margery Kempe (c. 1373–1440) was one of the Middle Ages' most profound mystics and visionaries. Born in Bishop's Lynn, in Norfolk, England, she saw herself as a saint who claimed to be on terms with God. Her writings, however, indicate that she had normal conversations with her neighbors and friends.

She was a pilgrim and made numerous trips abroad. Although she was illiterate and did not keep any notes or diaries until the end of her life, she possessed an incredible memory, but sometimes she would mistake the sequence of certain events. Her writings contain valuable insights into the details of everyday life in medieval Europe.

The England Margery knew was economically and politically corrupt. The aristocracy lived in incredible luxury while the remainder of English society dwelt amid filth and rubbish. The plague was endemic, and everyone, including the wealthy, suffered the ills of lice, fleas, mites, bedbugs, internal parasites, and rats.

Margery lived during the period of Chaucer and Froissart, but there is no evidence she had even heard of them. When she was about twenty, she married the burgess of Lynn, John Kempe, also in his twenties. John Kempe was the son of a successful merchant and public official. He was also said to be very charming and affectionate. She bore him fourteen children.

Margery was a pilgrim who made numerous contacts with notable people throughout Europe. People began to hear about her visions and ideologies. She had even been accused of heresy, but her powerful friends backed her during heresy trials. As time passed, Margery was continually harassed as a heretic. She and her husband spent much time moving around and enduring one heresy trial after another. This all changed during the Great Fire of Lynn in 1421. The town was threatened with total destruction. Priests and other religious figures said that if Margery was indeed under the care of God, then she could save Lynn. Three days later a blizzard came, putting the fire out. She was no longer persecuted after this miracle.

In 1431, Margery followed the news of the trial of Joan of Arc, and only the illness of her husband kept her from going to Joan's aid.

Catherine of Siena (1347–80; Fig. **9.23**) was an Italian Dominican, mystic and diplomat, Doctor of the Church. In response to a vision she entered public life and in 1376 influenced Pope Gregory XI to end the Babylonian Captivity of the papacy (see p. 268) and return to Rome. She was later papal ambassador to Florence. Catherine caused a spiritual revival almost everywhere she went, and her mysticism contains an overwhelming love of God and humanity. *The Dialogue* is a remarkable mystical work.

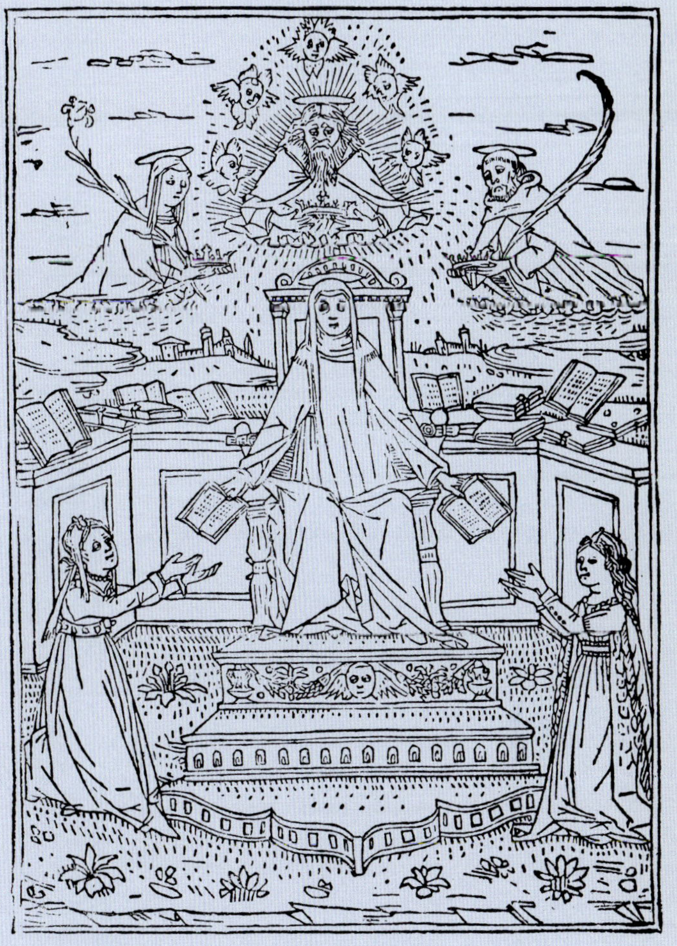

9.23 St Catherine of Siena (1347–80).

The Dialogue of the Seraphic Virgin Catherine of Siena

Dictated by her, while in a state of ecstasy, to her secretaries, and completed in the year of our lord 1370

Translated by Algar Thorold and modernized by Harry Plantinga

A Treatise of Prayer

Of the means which the soul takes to arrive at pure and generous love; and here begins the Treatise of Prayer. "When the soul has passed through the doctrine of Christ crucified, with true love of virtue and hatred of vice, and has arrived at the house of self-knowledge and entered therein, she remains, with her door barred, in watching and constant prayer, separated entirely from the consolations of the world. Why does she thus shut herself in? She does so from fear, knowing her own imperfections, and also from the desire, which she has, of arriving at pure and generous love. And because she sees and knows well that in no other way can she arrive thereat, she waits, with a lively faith for my arrival, through increase of grace in her. How is a lively faith to be recognized? By perseverance in virtue, and by the fact that the soul never turns back for anything, whatever it be, nor rises from holy prayer, for any reason except (note well) for obedience or charity's sake. For no other reason ought she to leave off prayer, for, during the time ordained for prayer, the Devil is wont to arrive in the soul, causing much more conflict and trouble than when the soul is not occupied in prayer. This he does in order that holy prayer may become tedious to the soul, tempting her often with these words: 'This prayer avails you nothing, for you need attend to nothing except your vocal prayers.' He acts thus in order that, becoming wearied and confused in mind, she may abandon the exercise of prayer, which is a weapon with which the soul can defend herself from every adversary, if grasped with the hand of love, by the arm of free choice in the light of the Holy Faith."

Julian of Norwich (1342–1416) was a celebrated mystic, whose *Revelations of Divine Love* provide one of the most remarkable insights into the medieval religious experience. According to her report, on 13 May 1373, she was healed of a serious illness after experiencing a series of visions of Christ's suffering and of the Blessed Virgin, about which she wrote two accounts; the second version was composed twenty or thirty years after the first. *The Revelations* treats some of the most profound mysteries of Christianity: predestination, foreknowledge of God, and the existence of evil. Clear and deep in its perception, the work possesses beautiful sincerity and expression.

Revelations of Divine Love

Recorded by Julian, anchoress at Norwich
Anno Domini 1371

In lumine tuo videbimus lumen.

First Revelation—Of His precious crowning with thorns; and therewith was comprehended and specified the Trinity, with the Incarnation, and unity betwixt God and man's soul, with many fair shewings of endless wisdom and teachings of love: in which all the Shewings that follow be grounded and oned.

Second Revelation—The changing of colour of His fair face in token of His dear worthy Passion.

Third Revelation—That our Lord God, Almighty Wisdom, All-Love, right as verily as He hath made everything that is, all-so verily He doeth and worketh all-thing that is done.

Fourth Revelation—The scourging of His tender body, with plenteous shedding of His blood.

Fifth Revelation—That the Fiend is overcome by the precious Passion of Christ.

Sixth Revelation—The worshipful thanking by our Lord God in which He rewardeth His blessed servants in Heaven.

Seventh Revelation—[Our] often feeling of weal and woe; with ghostly understanding that we are kept all as securely in Love in woe as in weal, by the Goodness of God.

Eighth Revelation—Of the last pains of Christ, and His cruel dying.

Ninth Revelation—Of the pleasing which is in the Blissful Trinity by the hard Passion of Christ and His rueful dying: in which joy and pleasing He willeth that we be solaced and mirthed with Him, till when we come to the fulness in Heaven.

Tenth Revelation—Our Lord Jesus sheweth in love His blissful heart even cloven in two, rejoicing.[1]

The Book of Margery Kempe (1436)

(Transcribed by John F. Tinkler)

On a night, as this creature [i.e. Margery] lay in her bed with her husband, she heard a sound of melancholy so sweet and delectable, that she thought she had been in Paradise, and therewith she started out of her bed and said:

Alas, that ever I did sin! It is full merry in Heaven.

This melody was so sweet that it surpassed all melody that ever might be heard in this world, without any comparison, and caused her, when she heard any mirth or melody afterwards, to have full plenteous and abundant tears of high devotion, with great sobbings and sighings after the bliss of Heaven, not dreading the shames and the spites of this wretched world. Ever after this inspiration, she had in her mind the mirth and the melody that was in Heaven, so much, that she could not well restrain herself from speaking thereof, for wherever she was in any company she would say oftentimes: It is full merry in Heaven.

And they that knew her behaviour beforetime, and now heard her speaking so much of the bliss of Heaven, said to her:

Why speak ye so of the mirth that is in Heaven? Ye know it not, and ye have not been there, any more than we. And were wroth with her, for she would not hear nor speak of worldly things as they did, and as she did beforetime.

And after this time she had never desired to commune fleshly with her husband, for the debt of matrimony was so abominable to her that she would rather, she thought, have eaten or drunk the ooze and the muck in the gutter than consent to any fleshly communing, save only for obedience.

CHAPTER REVIEW

❖ CRITICAL THOUGHT ❖

The struggle between Church and State that occurred in the late Middle Ages broke the hold of the Roman Catholic Church on the general social order and created an increasingly secular society. At the same time, war, disease, and economics changed the basic conditions of human life. Society in Europe moved into a new era, with national interests rising. Several interesting personalities emerged, and feudalism and Church authority took a back seat to emerging secular monarchs who ruled large, nationally homogeneous populations that were beginning to approximate what we recognize today as "countries." All this occurred while nearly half the population of Europe and England succumbed to the plague.

However bleak it may have been, life under the monolithic control of feudal lords and a central Church must have been fairly simple and straightforward. As society changed during the late Middle Ages, things got more complicated, and, as if to mirror the life around it, art reflected that increased complication with an emerging ornateness and emotionalism. The theme of increased complication permeated painting, sculpture, architecture, literature, theatre, and dance. All the while, humankind kept its good humor—perhaps the best solution of all to all the affairs of life.

◆ SUMMARY ◆

After reading this chapter, you will be able to:

- Explain how theatre, dance, and painting reflected their social and religious contexts.
- Characterize late Gothic sculpture and architecture including specific characteristics such as *Andachtsbild.*
- Describe *ars nova* and its principal exponent.
- Identify the major writers of the time and their works, including general characteristics and themes.
- Discuss the effects of the plague and the Hundred Years' War, the rise of secular monarchies, and the Great Schism on European society, commerce, and religion.
- Apply the elements and principles of composition to analyze and compare individual works of art illustrated in this chapter.

CYBERSOURCES

http://witcombe.sbc.edu/ARTHmedieval.html#Gothic
http://witcombe.sbc.edu/ARTHLinks2.html#LateGothic
http://www.artcyclopedia.com/history/gothic.html

Glossary

a cappella. Choral music without instrumental accompaniment.

abacus. The uppermost member of the capital of an architectural column; the slab on which the architrave rests.

absolute music. Music that is free from any reference to nonmusical ideas, such as a text or program.

abstract, abstraction. Nonrepresentational; the essence of a thing rather than its actual appearance.

absurdism. A style dealing with life's apparent meaninglessness and the difficulty or impossibility of human communication.

academy. From the grove (the Academeia) where Plato taught; the term has come to mean the cultural and artistic establishment which exercises responsibility for teaching and the maintenance of standards.

accent. In music, a stress on a note. In the visual arts, any device used to highlight or draw attention to a particular area, such as an accent color. See also *focal point.*

action theatre. A contemporary phenomenon in which plays, happenings, and other types of performance are strongly committed to broad moral and social issues with the overt purpose of effecting a change for the better in society.

aerial perspective. The indication of distance in painting through use of light and color. Also called atmospheric perspective.

aesthetics. A branch of philosophy dealing with the nature of beauty and art and their relation to human experience.

affective. Relating to feelings or emotions, as opposed to facts. See *cognitive.*

aleatory. Chance or accidental. A term used for twentieth-century music in which the composer deliberately incorporates elements of chance.

allegory. Expression by means of symbols to make a more effective generalization or moral commentary about human experience than could be achieved by direct or literal means.

altarpiece. A painted or sculpted panel placed above or behind an altar to inspire religious devotion.

ambulatory. A covered passage for walking, found around the apse or choir of a church.

amphitheatre. A building, typically Roman, that is oval or circular in form and encloses a central performance area.

amphora. A two-handled vessel for storing provisions, with an opening large enough to admit a ladle, and usually fitted with a cover.

antiphonal. A responsive style of singing or playing, in which two groups alternate.

anthropomorphic. With human characteristics attributed to nonhuman beings, or things.

apse. A large niche or niche-like space projecting from and expanding the interior space of an architectural form such as a basilica.

arcade. A series of arches side by side.

arch. In architecture, a structural system in which space is spanned by a curved member supported by two legs.

archetype. An original model or type after which other similar things are patterned.

architrave. In post-and-lintel architecture, the lintel or lowest part of the entablature, resting directly on the capitals of the columns.

aria. An elaborate solo song found primarily in operas, oratorios, and cantatas.

Art Deco. An individual decorative art style that emerged between World War I and World War II. Its name was coined from the title of a Paris exhibit of 1925, the Exposition Internationale des Arts Décoratifs et Industriels Modernes. Art Deco style is characterized by slender forms, straight lines, and a sleekness expressive of modern technology.

art song. A solo musical composition for voice, usually with piano accompaniment.

articulation. The connection of the parts of an artwork. In music or speech, the production of distinct sounds.

artifact. An object produced or shaped by human workmanship.

Art Nouveau. A style of decoration and architecture first current in the 1890s, characterized by curvilinear floral forms.

atonality. The avoidance of tonal centers or keys in musical compositions.

atrium. An open courtyard within or related to a building.

avant-garde. A term used to designate innovators, the "advanced guard," whose experiments in art challenge established values.

balance. In composition, the equilibrium of opposing or interacting forces.

ballade. A verse form usually consisting of three stanzas of eight or ten lines each, with the same concluding line in each stanza, and a brief final stanza, ending with the same last line as that of the preceding stanzas. In musical composition, either a medieval French song, or a lyrical piano piece from the nineteenth century.

baroque. A seventeenth- and eighteenth-century style of art, architecture, and music that is highly ornamental.

barrel vault, tunnel vault. A series of arches placed back to back to enclose space.

basilica. In Roman times, a term referring to building function, usually a law court; later used by Christians to refer to church buildings and a specific form.

bel canto. An Italian baroque style of operatic singing characterized by rich tonal lyricism and brilliant display of vocal technique.

binary form. A musical form consisting of two sections.

biomorphic. Representing life forms as opposed to geometric forms.

bridge. A musical passage of subordinate importance played as a link between two principal themes.

buttress. A support, usually an exterior projection of masonry or wood, for a wall, arch, or vault.

cadence. In music, the specific harmonic arrangement that indicates the closing of a phrase.

canon. A body of principles, rules, standards or norms; a criterion for establishing measure, scale, and proportion. In music, a composition for two or more voices or instruments, where one enters after another in direct imitation of the first.

cantata. A type of composition developed in the baroque period, for chorus and/or solo voice(s) accompanied by an instrumental ensemble.

cantilever. Part of a beam or structure that projects beyond its support. A beam that is fixed at only one end.

capital. The transition between the top of a column and the lintel.

caryatid. A sculpted female figure standing in the place of a column.

catharsis. The cleansing or purification of the emotions through the experience of art, the result of which is spiritual release and renewal.

cella. The principal enclosed room of a temple; the entire body of a temple as opposed to its external parts.

chamber music. Vocal or instrumental music suitable for performance in small rooms.

chiaroscuro. Light and shade. In painting, the balance of light and shade across the whole picture. See also *modeling.* In theatre, the use of light to enhance plasticity of human and scenic form.

chorale. A Protestant hymn, for voices or organ.

chord. Three or more musical tones played at the same time.

choreography. The composition of a dance work; the arrangement of patterns of movement in dance.

citadel. A fortress or a fortified place.

city-state. A sovereign state consisting of an independent city and its surrounding territory.

civilization. The advanced state of human development wherein cities emerge, along with corresponding social, political, and cultural complexity, including the arts and sciences.

classical. Adhering to traditional standards. May refer to Greek and Roman art in which simplicity, clarity of structure, and appeal to the intellect are fundamental.

clerestory. A row of windows in the upper part of a wall.

cloister. A covered walk with an open colonnade on one side, running along the inside walls of buildings that face a quadrangle. A place devoted to religious seclusion.

coffer. A recessed panel in a ceiling.

cognitive. Facts and objectivity as opposed to emotions and subjectivity. See *affective.*

collage. An artwork constructed by pasting together various materials, such as newsprint, to

create textures, or by combining two- and three-dimensional media.
colonnade. A row of columns usually spanned or connected by lintels.
colonnette. A small column-like vertical element or narrow, engaged column; colonnettes are usually attached to piers in buildings such as Gothic cathedrals. Colonnettes are decorative features.
color. In visual design, the hue or wavelength of light or pigment. In sound, the characteristic of an individual tone.
column. A cylindrical post or support which often has three distinct parts: base, shaft, and capital.
comedy. A theatre genre of complex qualities involving humor. Comedy may or may not involve laughter and may or may not end "happily"; compare *tragedy*.
commedia dell'arte. A type of comedy developed in Italy in the sixteenth century, characterized by improvisation from a plot outline and by the use of stock characters.
composition. The arrangement of line, form, mass, color, and so forth, in a work of art.
compression, compressive strength. In architecture, stress that results from two forces moving toward each other.
concerto. A composition for one or more solo instruments, accompanied by an orchestra, typically in three movements.
concerto grosso. A baroque composition for a small group of solo instruments and a small orchestra.
conjunct melody. In music, melody comprising neighboring notes in the scale. The opposite of *disjunct melody*.
consonance. The feeling of a comfortable relationship between elements of a composition. Consonance may be both physical and cultural in its ramifications. The opposite of *dissonance*.
content. The subject matter, meaning, and/or message in and communicated by works of art, including emotional, symbolic, thematic, and narrative qualities.
continuo, basso continuo. In baroque music, a bass line played on a low melodic instrument, such as a cello, while a keyboard instrument (or other chord-playing instrument) also plays the bass line and adds harmonies.
contrapposto, counterpoise. In sculpture, the arrangement of body parts so that the weight-bearing leg is apart from the free leg, thereby shifting the hip/shoulder axis.
Corinthian. A specific order of Greek architecture employing an elaborate leaf motif in the capital.
cornice. A crowning, projecting, architectural feature.
counterpoint. In music, two or more independent melodies played in opposition to each other at the same time.
crosscutting. In film, alternation between two independent actions that are related thematically or by plot to give the impression of simultaneous occurrence.
cross section. A view or graphic representation of an object formed by cutting through the object (figuratively or literally) usually at right angles to an axis.
crossing. The area in a church where the transept crosses the nave.
cruciform. Arranged or shaped like a cross.
crypt. A vaulted chamber, wholly or partly underground, that usually contains a chapel. Found in a church under the choir.
cubism. A revolutionary art form from the early decades of the twentieth century involving the use of geometric shapes to represent objects and figures.
curvilinear. Formed or characterized by curved line.
cutting within the frame. Changing the viewpoint of the camera within a shot by moving from a long or medium shot to a close-up, without cutting the film.
Deism. A belief, based solely on reason, that God created the universe and, after setting it in motion, abandoned it, assuming no control over life or natural phenomena and giving no supernatural revelation.
dénouement. The section of a play's structure in which events are brought to a conclusion.
deposition. A painting or sculpture depicting the removal of the body of Christ from the cross.
design. A comprehensive scheme, plan or conception.
diatonic. Referring to the seven tones of a standard major or minor musical scale.
diptych. A painting on two hinged panels.
disjunct melody. In music, melody characterized by skips or jumps. The opposite of *conjunct melody*.
dissonance. The occurrence of inharmonious elements in music or the other arts. The opposite of *consonance*.
Doric. A Greek order of column having no base and only a simple slab as a capital.
dynamics. The various levels of loudness and softness of sounds.
echinus. In the Doric order, the round, cushion-like element between the top of the shaft and the abacus.
eclecticism. A combination of several differing styles in a single composition.
empirical. Based on experiments, observation, and practical experience, without regard to theory.
engaged column. A column, often decorative, which is part of and projects from a wall surface.
entablature. The upper portion of a classical architectural order above the column capital.
entasis. The slight convex curving on classical columns to correct the optical illusion of concavity which would result if the sides were left straight.
ephemeral. Transitory, not lasting.
epic. A long narrative poem in heightened style about the deeds and adventures of a hero.
étude. Literally, a study, a lesson. An instrumental composition, intended for the practice or display of some technique.
exposition. The introductory material or opening section of a play or a musical composition.
expressionism. A style of painting that seeks to express the artist's emotions rather than accurately represent line or form.
façade. The front of a building, or the sides, if they are emphasized architecturally.
fan vaulting. An intricate style of traceried vaulting, common in the late English Gothic style, in which ribs arch out like a fan from a single point such as a capital.
farce. A theatrical genre characterized by broad, slapstick humor and implausible plots.
fenestration. Windows or window-like openings in an architectural structure.
ferro-concrete. Concrete reinforced with rods or webs of steel.
fluting. Vertical ridges in a column.
flying buttress. A semi-detached buttress.
focal point, focal area. A major or minor area of visual attraction in pictures, sculpture, dance, plays, films, landscape design, or buildings.
foreground. The area of a picture, usually at the bottom, that appears to be closest to the viewer.
form. The shape, structure, configuration, or essence of something.
found object. An object taken from life that is presented as an artwork.
four-part harmony. A standard musical texture, where four tones fill out each chord.
framing tale. Overall unifying story within which one or more tales are related.
fresco. A method of painting in which pigment is mixed with wet plaster and applied as part of the wall surface.
frieze. The central portion of the entablature: any horizontal decorative or sculptural band.
fugue. Originated in the baroque period from a Latin word meaning "flight." A musical composition in a fixed form in which a theme is developed by counterpoint.
full-round. See *sculpture*.
genre. A category of artistic composition characterized by a particular style, form, or content.
geometric. Based on man-made patterns such as triangles, rectangles, circles, ellipses, and so on. The opposite of *biomorphic*.
Gesamtkunstwerk. A complete, totally integrated artwork; associated with the music dramas of Richard Wagner in nineteenth-century Germany.
gesso. A mixture of plaster of Paris and glue, used as a base for low relief or as a surface for painting.
Greek cross. A cross in which all arms are the same length.
Gregorian chant. A medieval form of monophonic church music, also called plainchant or chant, sung unaccompanied, and named for Pope Gregory I.
groin vault. The ceiling formation created by the intersection of two tunnel or barrel vaults.
half cadence. A type of harmonic ending to a musical phrase which does not have a feeling of finality because it does not end on the home or tonic chord.
hamartia. The "tragic flaw" in the character of the protagonist of a classical tragedy.
harmony. The relationship of like elements such as musical notes, colors, and patterns of repetition. See *consonance* and *dissonance*.
Hellenistic. Relating to the time from the reign of Alexander the Great to the first century B.C.
heroic. Larger than lifesize.
hierarchy. Any system of persons or things that has higher and lower ranks.
hieratic. A style of depicting sacred persons or offices, particularly in Byzantine art.
hieroglyph, hieroglyphic. A picture or symbol of an object standing for a word, idea, or sound; developed by the ancient Egyptians into a system of writing.
homophony. A musical texture characterized by chordal texture supporting one melody. See *monophony* and *polyphony*.
horizon line. A real or implied line across the picture plane which, like the horizon in nature, tends to fix the viewer's vantage point.
hubris. Pride; typically the "tragic flaw" found in the protagonist of a classical tragedy. See *hamartia*.
hue. The spectrum notation of color; a specific, pure color with a measurable wavelength. There are primary hues, secondary hues, and tertiary hues.
humanism. A philosophy concerned with human beings, their achievements, and interests, as opposed to abstract beings and problems of theology; a cultural and intellectual movement occurring during the Renaissance focusing on humans and their capabilities.
humanitarianism. The ideas and philosophies associated with people who are concerned about human need and the alleviation of human suffering.
hymnody. The singing, composing, or study of hymns; the hymns of a particular period or church.
hypostyle. A building with a roof or ceiling

supported by rows of columns, as in ancient Egyptian architecture.

icon. A Greek word meaning "image." Used to identify paintings which represent the image of a holy person.

iconography. The meanings of images and symbols.

idealization. The portrayal of an object or human body in its ideal form rather than as a true-to-life portrayal.

idée fixe. A recurring melodic motif representing a nonmusical idea; used by, among others, the composer Berlioz.

illumination. The practice of decorating the pages of books—especially medieval manuscripts—with colorful pictures or motifs.

improvisation. Music or other art produced on the spur of the moment, spontaneously.

intensity. The degree or purity of a hue. In music, theatre, and dance, that quality of dynamics denoting the amount of force used to create a sound or movement.

interval. The difference in pitch between two tones.

intrinsic. Belonging to a thing by its nature.

Ionic. A Greek order of column that has a scroll-like capital with a circular base.

jamb. The upright piece forming the side of a doorway or window frame.

key. A system of tones in music based on and named after a given tone—the tonic.

kouros. An archaic Greek statue of a standing, nude youth.

krater. A bowl for mixing wine and water, the usual Greek beverage.

kylix. A vase turned on a potter's wheel; used as a drinking cup.

lancet window. A tall, narrow window whose top forms a lancet or narrow arch shaped like a spear.

lantern. A relatively small structure on the top of a dome, roof, or tower, frequently open to admit light into the area beneath.

Latin cross. A cross in which the vertical arm is longer than the horizontal arm, through whose midpoint it passes.

leitmotif. A "leading motif" used in music to identify an individual, ideal, object, and so on; associated with Wagner.

lekythos. An oil flask with a long, narrow neck adapted for pouring oil slowly; used in funeral rites.

Lied. German secular art song.

line. The basic building block of visual design; may be a thin mark, a color edge, or implied.

linear perspective. The creation of the illusion of distance in a two-dimensional artwork through the convention of line and foreshortening. That is, the illusion that parallel lines come together in the distance.

linear sculpture. See *sculpture*.

lintel. The horizontal member of a post-and-lintel structure in architecture, or a stone bridging an opening.

loggia. A gallery open on one or more sides, sometimes with arches or with columns.

lost-wax (cire-perdue). A method of casting sculpture in which the basic mold is created by using a wax model, which is then melted to leave the desired spaces in the mold.

low relief. See *sculpture*.

lyric. A category of poetry differentiated from dramatic or narrative. In music, the use of sensual sound patterns.

madrigal. An unaccompanied musical composition for two to five independent voices using a poetic text.

masonry. In architecture, stone or brickwork.

mass. Actual or implied physical bulk, weight, and density. Also, the most important rite of the Catholic liturgy, similar to the Protestant communion service.

medium (pl. media). The process employed by the artist. Also the binding agent used to hold pigments together.

melismatic. Music where a single syllable of text is sung on many notes.

melodrama. A theatrical genre characterized by stereotyped characters, implausible plots, and an emphasis on spectacle.

melody. In music, a succession of single tones; a tune.

metaphor. A figure of speech in which one object is used to represent another in order to imply characteristics.

microtone. A musical interval smaller than a half-step.

miniature. An artwork, usually a painting, done in very small scale.

mobile. A constructed structure whose components have been connected by joints to move by force of wind or motor.

mode. A particular form, style, or manner. In music, a scale; often used with reference to non-Western music.

modeling. The shaping of three-dimensional forms. Also the suggestion of three-dimensionality in two-dimensional forms.

modulation. The changing from one key to another in a musical composition.

monody. A style of musical composition in which one melodic line predominates; a poetic form expressing personal lament.

monolithic. Architecture or sculpture using a single large block of stone.

monophony. In music, a texture employing a single melody line without harmonic support.

monotheism. The belief that there is only one God.

montage. The process of making a single composition by combining parts of others. A rapid sequence of film shots bringing together associated ideas or images.

monumental. Works actually or appearing larger than lifesize.

mosaic. A decorative work for walls, vaults, floors, or ceilings, composed of pieces of colored material set in plaster or cement.

motet. A polyphonic musical composition based on a sacred text and usually sung without accompaniment.

motif, motive. In music, a short, recurrent melodic or rhythmic pattern. In the other arts, a recurrent element.

mural. A painting on a wall, usually large.

musique concrète. A twentieth-century musical approach in which conventional sounds are altered electronically and recorded on tape to produce new sounds.

narthex. A portico or lobby of an early Christian church, separated from the nave by a screen or railing.

naturalistic. Carefully imitating the appearance of nature.

nave. The great central space in a church, usually running from west to east, where the congregation sits.

negative space. Any opening in a work of sculpture.

neo-Attic. Literally, "new Greek." A reintroduction of the classical Greek and Hellenistic elements of architecture and visual art.

neoclassicism. Various artistic styles that borrow the devices or objectives of classical art.

niche. A recess in a wall in which sculpture can be displayed.

nimbus. The circle of radiant light around the head or figures of God, Christ, the Virgin Mary, and the saints.

nonobjective. Without reference to reality; may be differentiated from "abstract."

nonrepresentational. Without reference to reality; including abstract and nonobjective.

obelisk. A tall, tapering, four-sided stone shaft with a pyramidal top.

octave. In music, the distance between a specific pitch vibration and its double; for example, concert A equals 440 vibrations per second, the A one octave above that pitch equals 880, and the A one octave below equals 220.

oculus. A circular opening in the top of a dome.

oligarchy. Government by a small, select group.

opera. A lengthy work combining music and drama, fully staged with scenery and costumes.

opus. A single work of art.

oratorio. A large choral work for soloists, chorus, and orchestra, developed in the baroque period.

orchestra. A large instrumental musical ensemble; the first-floor seating area of a theatre; the circular playing area of the ancient Greek theatre.

organum. Singing together. Earliest form of polyphony in Western music, with the voices moving in parallel lines.

ornament. Anything used as a decoration or embellishment.

palette. In the visual arts, the composite use of color, including range and tonality.

palmette. A decoration taking the form or abstracting the form of a palm branch.

pantheon. A Greek word meaning all the gods.

pantomime. A genre of Roman drama in which an actor played various parts, without words, with a musical background.

pathos. The "suffering" aspect of drama usually associated with the evocation of pity.

pediment. The typically triangular roof piece characteristic of classical architecture.

pendentive. A triangular part of the vaulting which allows the stress of the round base of a dome to be transferred to a rectangular wall base.

performing arts. Music, theatre, and dance; in contrast to *visual arts*—painting and sculpture.

perspective. The representation of distance and three-dimensionality on a two-dimensional surface. See also *linear perspective* and *aerial perspective*.

picaresque. An artwork referring to the environment of rogues and adventurers.

piers. Upright architectural supports—usually rectangular.

pietà. A painting or sculpture of the dead Christ supported by Mary.

pigment. Any substance used as a coloring agent.

plainsong, plainchant. Medieval liturgical music sung without accompaniment and without strict meter.

plan. An architectural drawing that reveals in two dimensions the arrangement and distribution of interior spaces and walls, as well as door and window openings, of a building as seen from above.

plaque. A decorative or informative design placed on a wall.

plasticity. The capability of being molded or altered. In film, the capacity to be cut and shaped. In painting and theatre, the accentuation of dimensionality of form through chiaroscuro.

pointillism. A style of painting in which the paint is applied to the surface by dabbing the brush so as to create small dots of color.

polyphony. Literally, "many voiced." See *counterpoint*.

polyrhythm. The use of contrasting rhythms at the same time in music.

post-and-lintel. An architectural structure in which horizontal pieces (lintels) are held up by vertical columns (posts).
program music. Music that refers to nonmusical ideas through a descriptive title or text. The opposite of *absolute music.*
proportion. The relation, or ratio, of one part to another and of each part to the whole with regard to size, height, width, length, or depth.
proscenium. A Greek word meaning "before the skene." The plaster arch or "picture frame" stage of traditional theatres.
prototype. The model on which something is based.
psalmody. A collection of psalms.
putti. Nude male children—usually winged—especially shown in Renaissance and later art.
pylon. A gateway or a monumental structure flanking an entranceway.
quatrefoil. A carved ornament with four leaflets or lobes arranged around a common center.
rake. To place at an angle. A raked stage is one in which the floor slopes slightly upward from one point, usually downstage, to another, usually upstage.
realism. A style of painting, sculpture, and theatre based on the theory that the method of presentation should be true to life.
recitative. Sung monologue or dialogue, in opera, cantata, and oratorio.
reinforced concrete. See *ferro-concrete.*
relief. See *sculpture.*
repetition. How various elements are duplicated or alternated in a design.
representational. Art showing objects that are recognizable from real life.
requiem. A mass for the dead.
rhythm. The relationship, either of time or space, between recurring elements of a composition.
rib. A slender architectural support projecting from the surface in a vault system.
ribbed vault. A vault to which slender, projecting supports have been added. A structure in which arches are connected by diagonal as well as horizontal members. See *vault.*
rite. A customary form for conducting religious or other solemn ceremonies.
ritornello form. A baroque musical form in which a recurrent orchestral theme alternates with solo passages.
rondeau. A medieval French secular song based on a poetic form.
rondo form. A predominantly classical form of musical composition based around recurrence of the main theme, alternating with contrasting themes.
sarcophagus (plural **sarcophagi**). A stone coffin.
saturation. In color, the purity of a hue in terms of whiteness; the whiter the hue, the less saturated it is.
scale. In music, a graduated series of ascending or descending musical tones. In architecture, the mass of the building in relation to the human body.
schema. A summarized or diagrammatic representation.
sculpture. A three-dimensional art object. Among the types are 1. *cast*: created from molten material utilizing a mold. 2. *relief*: attached to a larger background. 3. *full-round*: freestanding. 4. *linear*: emphasizing linear items such as wire or tubing.
semidome. A roof covering a semicircular space; half a dome.
serial music. A twentieth-century musical style utilizing the tone row; can also employ serialization of rhythms, timbres, and dynamics.
sfumato. A smoky or hazy quality in a painting, with particular reference to Leonardo da Vinci's work.
shaft. The main trunk of a column.
shape. A two-dimensional area or plane with distinguishable boundaries.
silhouette. A form as defined by its outline.
skene. The stage building of the ancient Greek theatre.
skyphos. A two-handled ancient Greek drinking pot with an open top, tapering bowl, and flat, circular base.
sonata. Instrumental composition of the seventeenth through twentieth centuries, consisting of several movements.
statuary. Freestanding, three-dimensional sculpture.
still life. In the visual arts, an arrangement of inanimate objects used as a subject of a work of art.
strainer arch. An arch in an internal space that prevents the walls from being pushed inward.
stream of consciousness. A style of writing in which the author reveals character and event by expressing a continuous flow of a character's thoughts.
strophic form. Form of vocal music in which all stanzas of the text are sung to the same music.
stucco. A plaster or cement finish for interior and exterior walls.
style. The characteristics of a work of art that identify it with an artist, a group of artists, an era, or a nation.
stylized. A type of depiction in which verisimilitude has been altered for artistic effect.
stylobate. The foundation immediately below a row of columns.
suite. A grouping of musical movements, usually unrelated except by key.
symbol. A form, image, or subject standing for something else.
symmetry. The balancing of elements in design by placing physically equal objects on either side of a center line.
symphony. A lengthy orchestral composition, usually in four movements.
syncopation. In a musical composition, the displacement of accent from the normally accented beat to the offbeat.
synthesis. The combination of independent factors or entities into a compound that becomes a new, more complex whole.
synthesizer. An electronic instrument that produces and combines musical sounds.
temperament. In music, a system of tuning. Equal temperament—the division of the octave into twelve equal intervals—is the most common way of tuning keyboard instruments.
tempo. The rate of speed at which a musical composition is performed. In theatre, film, or dance, the rate of speed of the overall performance.
tensile strength. The ability of a material to resist bending and twisting.
text painting. See *word painting.*
theatricality. Exaggeration and artificiality; the opposite of *verisimilitude.*
theme. The subject of an artwork, whether melodic or philosophical.
timbre. The characteristic of a sound that results from the particular source of the sound. For example, the difference between the sound of a violin and the sound of the human voice, also called tone color.
toccata. A baroque keyboard composition intended to display technique.
tonality. In music, the specific key in which a composition is written. In the visual arts, the characteristics of value.
tondo. A circular painting.
tonic. In music, the root tone (*doh*) of a key.
tragedy. A serious drama or other literary work in which conflict between a protagonist and a superior force (often fate) concludes in disaster for the protagonist.
tragicomedy. A drama combining the qualities of tragedy and comedy.
transept. The crossing arm of a cruciform church, at right angles to the nave.
travertine. A creamy-colored type of calcium carbonate used as a facing in building construction.
triforium. The section of the nave wall above the arcade and below the clerestory windows.
triptych. An altarpiece or devotional picture composed of a central panel and two wings.
trompe l'oeil. "Trick of the eye" or "fool the eye." A two-dimensional artwork so executed as to make the viewer believe that three-dimensional subject matter is being perceived.
trope. A medieval dramatic elaboration of the Roman Catholic mass or other offices.
tunnel vault. See *barrel vault.*
twelve-tone technique. A twentieth-century atonal form of musical composition associated with Arnold Schoenberg.
tympanum. The space above the door beam and within the arch of a medieval doorway.
value, value scale. In the visual arts, the range of tonalities from white to black.
vanishing point. In linear perspective, the point on the horizon toward which parallel lines appear to converge and at which they seem to vanish.
variation. Repetition of a theme with small or large changes.
vault. An arched roof or ceiling usually made of stone, brick, or concrete.
verisimilitude. Lifelikeness or nearness to truth. The opposite of *theatricality.*
virtuoso. Referring to the display of impressive technique or skill by an artist or performer.
volute. A spiral architectural element found notably on Ionic and other capitals, but also used decoratively on building façades and interiors.
woodcut. A block of wood with an engraved design; a print made from such a piece of wood.
word painting. The use of language by a poet or playwright to suggest images and emotions; in music, the use of expressive melody to suggest a specific text.

Notes

See Further Reading for full bibliographical details of all cited works.

Chapter 3
1. Hofstadter and Kuhns, *Philosophies of Art and Beauty*, p. 4.
2. *Ibid.*
3. Fuller, *A History of Philosophy*, p. 172
4. Snell, *Discovery of the Mind: The Greek Origins of European Thought*, p. 247
5. *Ibid.*
6. Hamilton, trans. in *Three Greek Plays*
7. Hamilton, *op. cit.*
8. Arrowsmith, trans. in *The Complete Greek Tragedies*, vol. VI, New York: Random House, 1858

Chapter 4
1. Fuller, *op. cit.*, p. 266
2. From material provided by Alan Pizer
3. "Rings around the Pantheon," *Discover*, March, 1985, p. 12
4. Vergil, *The Aeneid*, trans. Theodore C. Williams, New York: Houghton Mifflin Co., 1938, p. 1
5. Andreae, *The Art of Rome*, p. 109

Chapter 5
1. McGiffert, *A History of Christian Thought*, p. 7
2. Fuller, *op. cit.*, p. 353
3. *Ibid.*
4. Hofstadter and Kuhns, *op. cit.*, p. 172
5. Barclay, *The Gospel of Luke*, pp. 15–16

Chapter 6
1. Roberts, *History of the World*, p. 321
2. Nicoll, *The Development of Theatre*, p. 48
3. Mango, *Byzantium*, p. 235

Chapter 8
1. Fuller, *op. cit.*, p. 377

Chapter 9
1. Transcribed by John Ockerbloom. A version from the MS in the British Museum edited by Grace Warrack, London: Methuen & Co. Ltd., 1901

Chapter 10
1. Hartt, *Italian Renaissance Art*, p. 187

Chapter 11
1. Hartt, *op. cit.*, p. 592
2. Campos (ed.), *Art Treasures of the Vatican*, p. 7

Chapter 13
1. Père Menestrier, in Vuillier, *A History of Dance*, New York: D. Appleton and Co., 1897, p. 90

Chapter 14
1. Helm, *Music at the Court of Frederick the Great*, p. 94

Chapter 15
1. Hofstadter and Kuhns, *op. cit.*, p. 381
2. Maas, *Victorian Painters*, p. 10

Chapter 16
1. Hamilton, *Nineteenth and Twentieth Century Art: Painting, Sculpture, Architecture*, p. 211

Chapter 17
1. Zitkala-Sa (Gertrude Bonnin), "The Soft-Hearted Sioux," (copyright 1989 The Arizona Board of Regents). Reprinted from *The Singing Spirit*, edited by Bernd C. Peyer, 1990
2. Giannetti, *Understanding Movies*, p. 360
3. Gropius, *The New Architecture and the Bauhaus*, pp. 51–5

Chapter 18
1. Valerie-Anne Giscard d'Estaing and Mark Young (eds.), *Inventions and Discoveries 1993*, New York: Facts on File Inc., 1993, p. 220
2. Wilkins and Schultz, *Art Past Art Present*, p. 506
3. Otto G. Ocvirk *et al.*, *Art Fundamentals* (7th ed.), p. 309
4. *New York Times*, 30 May 1997
5. *Ibid.*
6. Kernodle and Pixley, *Invitation to the Theatre*, pp. 287–8
7. Arkin and Shollar (eds.), *Longman Anthology of World Literature by Women*, p. 1039

Further Reading

General

Bentley, Eric (ed.), *The Classic Theatre*, (4 vols), Garden City, NY: Doubleday Anchor Books, 1959
Braider, Christopher, *Refiguring the Real: Picture and Modernity in Word and Image: 1400–1700*, Princeton, NJ: Princeton University Press, 1993
Brockett, Oscar G., *History of the Theatre*, Boston: Allyn and Bacon, Inc., 1968
Chadwick, Whitney, *Women, Art, and Society*, New York: Norton, 1991
Clough, Shepard B. *et. al.*, *A History of the Western World*, Boston: D.C. Heath & Co., 1964
De la Crois, Horst, Tansey, Richard G., and Kirkpatric, Diane, *Gardner's Art Through the Ages* (9th ed.), San Diego, CA: Harcourt, 1991
Drinkwater, John, *The Outline of Literature*, London: Transatlantic Arts, 1967
Fuller, B.A.G., *A History of Philosophy*, New York: Henry Holt and Company, 1945
Garraty, John, and Gay, Peter, *A History of the World* (2 vols), New York: Harper & Row, 1972
Giscard d'Estaing, Valerie Anne, and Young, Mark (eds.), *Inventions and Discoveries 1993*, New York: Facts on File, Inc., 1993
Grout, Donald Jay, *A History of Western Music* (rev. ed.), New York: W.W. Norton & Co., Inc., 1979
Hartt, Frederick, *Art* (2 vols). Englewood Cliffs, NJ, and New York: Prentice Hall, Inc. and Harry N. Abrams, Inc., 1979
Hofstadter, Albert, and Kuhns, Richard, *Philosophies of Art and Beauty*, Chicago: University of Chicago Press, 1976
Honour, Hugh, and Fleming, John. *The Visual Arts: A History* (3rd ed.), Englewood Cliffs, NJ: Prentice Hall, Inc., 1992
Kamien, Roger, *Music: An Appreciation* (5th ed.), New York: McGraw-Hill, 1995
Kernodle, George and Portia, and Pixley, Edward, *Invitation to the Theatre* (3rd ed.), San Diego: Harcourt Brace Jovanovich, 1985
McNeill, William H., *The Shape of European History*, New York: Oxford University Press, 1974
Nicoll, Allardyce, *The Development of the Theatre* (5th ed.), London: Harrap & Co. Ltd, 1966
Ocvirk, Otto G., *et al.*, *Art Fundamentals* (7th ed.), Madison, WI: Brown & Benchmark, 1994
Pfeiffer, John E., *The Creative Explosion*, New York: Harper & Row, 1982
Roberts, J.M., *History of the World*, New York: Alfred A. Knopf, Inc, 1976
Sadie, Stanley (ed.), *The New Grove Dictionary of Music and Musicians*, Washington, D.C.; London: Macmillan, 1980
Sperry, Roger, *Science and Moral Priority: Merging Mind, Brain, and Human Values*, New York: Columbia University Press, 1983
Sporre, Dennis J., *The Art of Theatre*, Englewood Cliffs, NJ: Prentice Hall, 1993
Sporre, Dennis J., *Perceiving the Arts*, 5th ed. Englewood Cliffs, NJ: Prentice Hall, Inc., 1997
Vidal-Naquet, Pierre (ed.), *The Harper Atlas of World History*, New York: Harper & Row, 1986
Wilkins, David G., and Schultz, Bernard, *Art Past Art Present*, Englewood Cliffs, NJ, and New York: Prentice Hall Inc. and Harry N. Abrams, Inc., 1990

The Ancient World

Bataille, Georges, *Lascaux*, Switzerland: Skira, n.d.
Engel, Carl, *The Music of the Most Ancient Nations*, Freeport, NY: Books for Libraries Press, 1970
Frankfort, Henri, *Kingship and the Gods*, Chicago: University of Chicago Press, 1948
Graziosi, Paolo, *Palaeolithic Art*, New York: McGraw-Hill, 1960
Lange, Kurt, and Hirmer, Max, *Egypt*, London: Phaidon, 1968
Lloyd, Seton, *The Archaeology of Mesopotamia*, London: Thames & Hudson, 1978
Lommel, Andrea, *Prehistoric and Primitive Man*, New York: McGraw-Hill, 1966
Marshack, Alexander, *The Roots of Civilization*, New York: McGraw-Hill, 1972
Montet, Pierre, *Lives of the Pharaohs*, Cleveland: World Publishing Co., 1968
Moortgat, Anton, *The Art of Ancient Mesopotamia*, London: Phaidon, 1969
Murray, Margaret, *Egyptian Sculpture*, New York: Charles Scribner's Sons, 1930
Oppenheim, A. Leo, *Ancient Mesopotamia*, Chicago: University of Chicago Press, 1964
Powell, T.G.E., *Prehistoric Art*, New York: Frederick Praeger Publishers, 1966
Sachs, Curt, *The Rise of Music in the Ancient World*, New York: W.W. Norton & Co., 1943
Sandars, N.K., *Prehistoric Art in Europe*, Baltimore: Penguin Books, 1968
Smith, Hermann, *The World's Earliest Music*, London: W. Reeves, n.d.
Smith, W. Stevenson, *The Art and Architecture of Ancient Egypt*, Baltimore: Penguin Books, 1958

Archaic Greece and the Aegean

Beye, C.R., *Ancient Greek Literature and Society*, Ithaca: Cornell University Press, 1987
Boardman, J., *The Greeks Overseas*, Baltimore: Penguin, 1973
Boardman, J., Jasper, G., and Murray, O. (eds.), *The Oxford History of the Classical World*, Oxford: Oxford University Press, 1986
Finley, M.I., *Early Greece: The Bronze and Archaic Age*, New York: Norton, 1981
Graves, R., *The Greek Myths*, Garden City, NY: Doubleday, 1981
Groenewegen-Frankfort, H.A., and Ashmole, Bernard, *Art of the Ancient World*, Englewood Cliffs, NJ, and New York: Prentice Hall, Inc. and Harry N. Abrams, Inc., 1972
Janson, H.W., *A Basic History of Art* (4th ed.), Englewood Cliffs, NJ, and New York: Prentice Hall, Inc. and Harry N. Abrams, Inc., 1991
Snell, Bruno, *Discovery of the Mind: The Greek Origins of European Thought*, New York: Harper, 1960

Greek Classicism and Hellenism

Arnott, Peter D., *An Introduction to the Greek Theatre*, Bloomington, IN: Indiana University Press, 1963
Bieber, M., *The Sculpture of the Hellenistic Age*, New York: Columbia University Press, 1955
Boardman, J., *et al.*, *Greek Art and Architecture*, New York: Abrams, 1967
Burcket, W., *Ancient Mystery Cults*, Cambridge, MA: Harvard University Press, 1987
Grant, M., *From Alexander to Cleopatra: The Hellenistic World*, London: Weidenfeld & Nicolson, 1982
Hamilton, Edith, *Three Greek Plays*, New York: W.W. Norton & Co., Inc., 1965
Kjellberg, Ernst, and Saflund, Gosta, *Greek and Roman Art*, New York: Thomas Y. Crowell Co., 1968
Morford, M.P.O., and Lenardon, P.J., *Classical Mythology*, New York: Longman, 1977
Richter, Gisela, *Greek Art*, Greenwich, CT: Phaidon, 1960
Robertson, Martin, *A Shorter History of Greek Art*, Cambridge, UK: Cambridge University Press, 1981

The Roman Period

Andreae, Bernard, *The Art of Rome*, New York: Harry N. Abrams, Inc., 1977
Balsdon, J.P.V.D., *Rome: The Story of an Empire*, New York: McGraw Hill, 1970
Brendel, O.J., *Etruscan Art*, Baltimore: Penguin, 1978
Crawford, M., *The Roman Republic*, Cambridge, MA: Harvard University Press, 1982
Grant, M., *Roman Literature*, New York: Penguin, 1964
Henig, Martin (ed.), *A Handbook of Roman Art*, Ithaca, NY: Cornell University Press, 1983
Kjellberg, Ernst, and Saflund, Gosta, *Greek and Roman Art*, New York: Thomas Y. Crowell Co., 1968
Ward-Perkins, J.B., *Roman Imperial Architecture* (2nd ed.), New York: Penguin, 1981

Judaism and Early Christianity

Achtemeier, Paul (ed.), *Harper's Bible Dictionary*. San Francisco: Harper & Row, 1985
Anderson, Bernhard, *Understanding the Old*

Testament, Englewood Cliffs, NJ: Prentice Hall, 1975
Andreae, Bernard, *The Art of Rome*, New York: Harry N. Abrams, Inc., 1977
Barclay, William, *The Gospel of Luke*, Philadelphia: Westminster Press, 1975
Bevan, G.M., *Early Christians of Rome*, London: Society for Promoting Christian Knowledge, 1927
Brown, P., *Augustine of Hippo*, London: Faber, 1967
Chadwick, H., *The Early Church*, New York: Penguin, 1967
Epstein, Isidore, *Judaism*, Middlesex, UK: Penguin Books, 1968
Frend, W.H.C., *The Rise of Christianity*, Philadelphia: Fortress Press, 1983
Henig, Martin (ed.), *A Handbook of Roman Art*, Ithaca, NY: Cornell University Press, 1983
Johnston, Leonard, *A History of Israel*, New York: Sheed & Ward, 1963
McGiffert, Arthur, *A History of Christian Thought*, New York: Charles Scribner's Sons, 1961
Milburn, Robert, *Early Christian Art and Architecture*, Berkeley: University of California Press, 1988
Wheeler, Robert Eric Mortimer, *Roman Art and Architecture*, New York: Frederick Praeger Publishers, 1964

Byzantium and the Rise of Islam

Armstrong, Karen, *Muhammad: A Western Attempt to Understand Islam*, San Francisco: HarperCollins, 1992
Bovini, G., *Ravenna Mosaics*, Greenwich, CT: New York Graphic Society Publishers, Ltd., 1956
Diehl, Charles, *Byzantium*, New Brunswick, NJ: Rutgers University Press, 1957
Dunlop, D.M., *Arab Civilization to A.D. 1500*, London: Longman, 1971
Esposito, John, *Islam: The Straight Path*, New York: Oxford University Press, 1991
Grabar, Andre, *The Art of the Byzantine Empire*, New York: Crown Publishers, Inc., 1966
MacDonald, William, *Early Christian and Byzantine Architecture*, New York: George Braziller, 1967
Mango, Cyril, *Byzantium*, New York: Charles Scribner's Sons, 1980
Rice, David Talbot, *The Art of Byzantium*, New York: Harry N. Abrams, Inc., n.d.
Sherrard, Philip, *Byzantium*, New York: Time Inc., 1966
Watt, W.M., *Muhammad: Statesman and Prophet*, New York: Oxford University Press, 1974

The Early Middle Ages

Beckwith, J., *Early Medieval Art*, New York: Praeger, 1973
Brondsted, Johannes, *The Vikings* (trans. Kalle Skov), New York: Penguin Books, 1960
Hoppin, Richard, *Medieval Music*, New York: W.W. Norton & Co., Inc., 1978
Jackson, W.T.H., *Medieval Literature: A History and a Guide*, New York: Collier Books, 1966
Knowles, David, *Christian Monasticism*, New York: McGraw Hill, 1969
Rorig, F., *The Medieval Town* (trans. D.J.A. Matthew), Berkeley: University of California Press, 1969
Strayer, Joseph, and Munro, Dana, *The Middle Ages*, Pacific Palisades: Goodyear Publishing Co., 1970
Tierney, Brian, and Painter, Sidney, *Western Europe in the Middle Ages*, New York: Alfred A. Knopf, 1974
Zarnecki, George, *Art of the Medieval World*, Englewood Cliffs, NJ: Prentice Hall, Inc., 1975

The High Middle Ages

Barraclough, G., *The Medieval Papacy*, New York: Harcourt, Brace, & World, 1968
Bony, Jean, *French Gothic Architecture of the Twelfth and Thirteenth Centuries*, Berkeley: University of California Press, 1983
Bruzelius, Carline A., *The 13th-Century Church at St-Denis*, New Haven, CT: Yale University Press, 1985
Crosby, Sumner McKnight, *The Royal Abbey of Saint Denis*, New Haven: Yale University Press, 1987
Daly, Lowric, *The Medieval University: 1200-1400*, New York: Sheed & Ward, 1961
Esser, Kajetan, *Origins of the Franciscan Order* (trans. Aedan Daly and Irina Lynch), Chicago: Franciscan Herald Press, 1970
Hoppin, Richard, *Medieval Music*, New York: W.W. Norton & Co., Inc., 1978
Jackson, W.T.H., *Medieval Literature: A History and a Guide*, New York: Collier Books, 1966
Rorig, F., *The Medieval Town* (trans. D.J.A. Matthew), Berkeley: University of California Press, 1969
Singleton, Charles, *The Divine Comedy of Dante Alighieri* (6 vols), Princeton: Princeton University Press, 1972
Strayer, Joseph, and Munro, Dana, *The Middle Ages*, Pacific Palisades: Goodyear Publishing Co., 1970
Tierney, Brian, and Painter, Sidney, *Western Europe in the Middle Ages*, New York: Alfred A. Knopf, 1974
Zarnecki, George, *Art of the Medieval World*, Englewood Cliffs, NJ: Prentice Hall, Inc., 1975

The Late Middle Ages

Aston, M., *The Fifteenth Century: The Prospect of Europe*, New York: Harcourt, Brace, & World, 1968
Barraclough, G., *The Medieval Papacy*, New York: Harcourt, Brace, & World, 1968
Bishop, M., *Petrarch and His World*, Bloomington, Indiana University Press, 1963
Gottfried, Robert S., *The Black Death: Natural and Human Disaster in Medieval Europe*, New York: Free Press, 1983
Hofstatter, H.H., *Art of the Late Middle Ages* (trans. R.E. Wolf), New York: Abrams, 1968
Hoppin, Richard, *Medieval Music*, New York: W.W. Norton & Co., Inc., 1978
Hubert, J., Porcher, J., and Volbach, W.F., *The Carolingian Renaissance*, New York: George Braziller, 1970.
Jackson, W.T.H., *Medieval Literature: A History and a Guide*, New York: Collier Books, 1966
Janson, H.W., *A Basic History of Art* (4th ed.), Englewood Cliffs, NJ, and New York: Prentice Hall, Inc. and Harry N. Abrams, Inc., 1991
Kane, George, *Chaucer*, New York: Oxford University Press, 1984
Strayer, Joseph, and Munro, Dana, *The Middle Ages*, Pacific Palisades: Goodyear Publishing Co., 1970
Tierney, Brian, and Painter, Sidney, *Western Europe in the Middle Ages*, New York: Alfred A. Knopf, 1974
White, John, *Art and Architecture in Italy 1250–1400*, Baltimore: Pelican, 1966
Zarnecki, George, *Art of the Medieval World*, Englewood Cliffs, NJ: Prentice Hall, Inc., 1975

The Early Renaissance

Artz, Frederick, *From the Renaissance to Romanticism*, Chicago: University of Chicago Press, 1962
Brucker, Gene, *Renaissance Florence*, New York: Wiley, 1969
Burckhardt, Jakob, *The Civilization of the Renaissance in Italy*, New York: Harper Torchbooks, 1958
Cronin, Vincent, *The Florentine Renaissance*, New York: E.P. Dutton & Co., 1967
Fletcher, Jefferson, B., *Literature of the Italian Renaissance*, New York: The Macmillan Co., 1934
Gilbert, Creighton, *History of Renaissance Art Throughout Europe: Painting, Sculpture, Architecture*, New York: Harry N. Abrams, Inc., 1973
Hale, J.R., *Florence and the Medicis*, London: Thames & Hudson, 1977
Hartt, Frederick, *Italian Renaissance Art* (3rd ed.), Englewood Cliffs, NJ, and New York: Prentice Hall, Inc. and Harry N. Abrams, Inc., 1987
Keutner, Hubert, *Sculpture: Renaissance to Rococo*, Greenwich, CN: New York Graphic Society, 1969
King, Margaret, *Women of the Renaissance*, Chicago: University of Chicago Press, 1991
Kristeller, P.O., *Renaissance Thought: The Classic, Scholastic, and Humanist Strains*, New York: Harper Torchbooks, 1955
Staley, Edgcombe, *Famous Women of Florence*, London: Archibald Constable & Co., 1909

The High Renaissance and Mannerism

Artz, Frederick, *From the Renaissance to Romanticism*, Chicago: University of Chicago Press, 1962
Brown, Howard M., *Music in the Renaissance*, Englewood Cliffs, NJ: Prentice Hall, 1976
Campos, D. Redig de (ed.), *Art Treasures of the Vatican*, Englewood Cliffs, NJ: Prentice Hall, Inc., 1974
Cochrane, Eric, *The Late Italian Renaissance, 1525–1630*, New York: Harper Torchbooks, 1970
Fletcher, Jefferson, B., *Literature of the Italian Renaissance*, New York: The Macmillan Co., 1934
Gilbert, Creighton, *History of Renaissance Art Throughout Europe: Painting, Sculpture, Architecture*, New York: Harry N. Abrams, Inc., 1973
Hartt, Frederick, *Italian Renaissance Art* (3rd ed.), Englewood Cliffs, NJ, and New York: Prentice Hall, Inc. and Harry N. Abrams, Inc., 1987
Hay, Denys, and Law, John, *Italy in the Age of the Renaissance, 1380–1530*, London: Longman, 1989
Levey, Michael, *High Renaissance*, New York: Penguin, 1975
Oman, Sir Charles, *The Sixteenth Century*, Westport, CT: Greenwood Press, 1975
Plumb, J.H., *The Italian Renaissance*, New York: Harper Torchbooks, 1961
Stinger, Charles, *The Renaissance in Rome*, Bloomington: Indiana University Press, 1985

Renaissance and Reformation in Northern Europe

Artz, Frederick, *From the Renaissance to Romanticism*, Chicago: University of Chicago Press, 1962
Bainton, Roland, *Here I Stand: A Life of Martin Luther*, New York: New American Library, 1950
Brion, Marcel, *Dürer, His Life and Work*, New York: Tudor Publishing, 1960
Brown, Howard M., *Music in the Renaissance*, Englewood Cliffs, NJ: Prentice Hall, 1976

Fenlon, Iain (ed.), *The Renaissance*, Englewood Cliffs, NJ: Prentice Hall, 1989
Gilbert, Creighton, *History of Renaissance Art Throughout Europe: Painting, Sculpture, Architecture*, New York: Harry N. Abrams, Inc., 1973
Hall, A. Rupert, *The Revolution in Science 1500–1750*, London: Longman, 1983
Oman, Sir Charles, *The Sixteenth Century*, Westport, CT: Greenwood Press, 1975
Smart, Alastair, *The Renaissance and Mannerism in Northern Europe and Spain*, London: Harcourt, Brace Jovanovich, Inc., 1972
Snyder, J., *Northern Renaissance Art*, Englewood Cliffs, NJ: Prentice Hall, 1985
Spitz, Lewis (ed.), *The Protestant Reformation*, Englewood Cliffs, NJ: Prentice Hall, Inc., 1966
Thompson, S. Harrison, *Europe in Renaissance and Reformation*, New York: Harcourt, Brace & World, 1963

The Baroque Age

Bazin, Germain, *The Baroque*, Greenwich, CN: New York Graphic Society, 1968
Boyd, M., *Bach*, London: Dent, 1983
Braider, Christopher, *Refiguring the Real: Picture and Modernity in Word and Image: 1400–1700*, Princeton, NJ: Princeton University Press, 1993
Friedrich, C.J., *The Age of the Baroque: 1610–1660*, New York: Harper Torchbooks, 1961
Grimm, Harold, *The Reformation Era*, New York: Macmillan Co., 1954
Hall, A. Rupert, *The Revolution in Science 1500–1750*, London: Longman, 1983
Held, Julius, and Posner, D., *Seventeenth and Eighteenth Century Art*, New York: Harry N. Abrams, Inc., n.d.
Ogg, D., *Europe in the Seventeenth Century* (rev. ed.), New York: Collier Books, 1968
Van Der Kemp, Gerald, *Versailles*, New York: The Vendome Press, 1977
Willey, B., *The Seventeenth-century Background*, New York: Columbia University Press, 1967
Wolf, J.B., *Louis XIV*, New York: Norton, 1968

The Enlightenment

Conisbee, P., *Painting in Eighteenth-century France*, Ithaca, NY: Cornell University Press, 1981
Hampson, N., *A Cultural History of the Enlightenment*, New York: Pantheon, 1968
Held, Julius, and Posner, D., *Seventeenth and Eighteenth Century Art*, New York: Harry N. Abrams, Inc., n.d.
Helm, Ernest, *Music at the Court of Frederick the Great*, Norman, OK: University of Oklahoma Press, 1960
Hubatsch, Walther, *Frederick the Great of Prussia*, London: Thames & Hudson, 1975
Keutner, Hubert, *Sculpture: Renaissance to Rococo*, Greenwich, CN: New York Graphic Society, 1969
Pignatti, Terisio, *The Age of Rococo*, London: Paul Hamlyn, 1969
Schonberger, Arno, and Soehner, Halldor, *The Rococo Age*, New York: McGraw-Hill, 1960
Waterhouse, E., *Painting in Britain 1530–1790* (4th ed.), New York: Penguin, 1978

The Romantic Age

Booth, Michael, *Victorian Spectacular Theatre 1850–1910*, Boston: Routledge & Kegan Paul, 1981
Glasstone, Victor, *Victorian and Edwardian Theatres*, Cambridge, MA: Harvard University Press, 1975
Goethe, Johann Wolfgang von, *Faust: Part I* (trans. Philip Wayne), Baltimore: Penguin Books, 1962
Hamilton, George Heard, *Nineteenth and Twentieth Century Art: Painting, Sculpture, Architecture*, New York: Harry N. Abrams, Inc., 1970
Henderson, W.O., *The Industrialization of Europe, 1780–1914*, London: Thames & Hudson, 1969
Hewett, Bernard, *Theatre USA*, New York: McGraw-Hill Book Company, 1959
Hitchcock, Henry-Russell, *Architecture: Nineteenth and Twentieth Centuries*, Baltimore: Penguin, 1971
Katz, Bernard, *The Social Implications of Early Negro Music in the United States*, New York: Arno Press and *The New York Times*, 1969
Keck, George R., and Martin, Sherrill V., *Feel the Spirit*, New York: Greenwood Press, 1988
Krehbiel, Henry Edward, *Afro-American Folksongs*, New York: G. Schirmer, n.d. (c. 1914)
Maas, Jeremy, *Victorian Painters*, New York: G.P. Putnam's Sons, 1969
Muthesius, Stefan, *The High Victorian Movement in Architecture 1850–1870*, London: Routledge & Kegan Paul, 1972
Read, Benedict, *Victorian Sculpture*, New Haven: Yale University Press, 1982
Rowell, George, *The Victorian Theatre* (2nd ed.), Cambridge, UK: Cambridge University Press, 1978

From Realism to Modernism

Bohn, T.W., Stomgren, R.L., and Johnson, D.H., *Light and Shadows, A History of Motion Pictures* (2nd ed.), Sherman Oaks, CA: Alfred Publishing Co., 1978
Goldwater, R., *Symbolism*, New York: Harper & Row, 1979
Hamilton, George Heard, *Nineteenth and Twentieth Century Art: Painting, Sculpture, Architecture*, New York: Harry N. Abrams, Inc., 1970
Hayes, C.J.H., *A Generation of Materialism*, New York: Harper & Row, 1963
Henderson, W.O., *The Industrialization of Europe, 1780–1914*, London: Thames & Hudson, 1969
Hitchcock, Henry-Russell, *Architecture: Nineteenth and Twentieth Centuries*, Baltimore: Penguin, 1971
Leish, Kenneth W., *Cinema*, New York: Newsweek Books, 1974
Ostransky, Leroy, *Understanding Jazz*, Englewood Cliffs, NJ: Prentice Hall, Inc., 1977
Robinson, David, *The History of World Cinema*, New York: Stein & Day Publishers, 1973
Salzman, Eric, *Twentieth Century Music: An Introduction*, Englewood Cliffs, NJ: Prentice Hall, Inc., 1967
Tirro, Frank, *Jazz: A History*, New York: W.W. Norton & Co., Inc., 1977

Modernism

Arnason, H.H., *History of Modern Art*, Englewood Cliffs, NJ: Prentice Hall, Inc., 1977
Barrett, W., *Time of Need: Forms of Imagination in the Twentieth Century*, New York: Harper & Row, 1972
Giannetti, Louis, *Understanding Movies* (7th ed.), Englewood Cliffs, NJ: Prentice Hall, Inc., 1996
Golding, John, *Visions of the Modern*, Berkeley, CA: University of California Press, 1994
Griffiths, Paul, *A Concise History of Avant-Garde Music*, New York: Oxford University Press, 1978
Gropius, Walter (ed.), *The Theatre of the Bauhaus*, Middletown, CT: Wesleyan University Press, 1961
Gropius, Walter, *The New Architecture and the Bauhaus*, Cambridge, MA: M.I.T. Press, 1965
Hamilton, George Heard, *Nineteenth and Twentieth Century Art: Painting, Sculpture, Architecture*, New York: Harry N. Abrams, Inc., 1970
Hitchcock, Henry-Russell, *Architecture: Nineteenth and Twentieth Centuries*, Baltimore: Penguin, 1971
Knight, Arthur, *The Liveliest Art: A Panoramic History of the Movies* (rev. ed.), New York: Macmillan, Inc., 1978
Liddell Hart, B.H., *History of the Second World War*, New York: Putnam, 1971
Lippard, Lucy R., *Pop Art*, New York: Oxford University Press, 1966
Nyman, Michael, *Experimental Music: Cage and Beyond*, New York: Schirmer Books, 1974
Robinson, David, *The History of World Cinema*, New York: Stein & Day Publishers, 1973
Roters, Eberhard, *Painters of the Bauhaus*, New York: Frederick Praeger Publishers, 1965
Salzman, Eric, *Twentieth Century Music: An Introduction*, Englewood Cliffs, NJ: Prentice Hall, Inc., 1967
Shirer, William L., *The Rise and Fall of the Third Reich*, New York: Simon & Schuster, 1960

From a Modern to Postmodern World

Arkin, Marian, and Shollar, Barbara (eds.), *Longman Anthology of World Literature by Women*, New York: Longman, 1989
Arnason, H.H., *History of Modern Art*, Englewood Cliffs, NJ: Prentice Hall, Inc., 1977
Brindle, Reginald Smith, *The New Music: The Avant-Garde Since 1945*, London: Oxford University Press, 1975
Coryell, Julie, and Friedman, Laura, *Jazz-Rock Fusion*, New York: Delacorte Press, 1978
Dallmayr, Fred R., *Critical Encounters: Between Philosophy and Politics*, Notre Dame, IN: University of Notre Dame Press, 1987
Ernst, David, *The Evolution of Electronic Music*, New York: Schirmer Books, 1977
Golding, John, *Visions of the Modern*, Berkeley, CA: University of California Press, 1994
Griffiths, Paul, *A Concise History of Avant-Garde Music*, New York: Oxford University Press, 1978
Hitchcock, Henry-Russell, *Architecture: Nineteenth and Twentieth Centuries*, Baltimore: Penguin, 1971
Knight, Arthur, *The Liveliest Art: A Panoramic History of the Movies* (rev. ed.), New York: Macmillan, Inc., 1978
Nyman, Michael, *Experimental Music: Cage and Beyond*, New York: Schirmer Books, 1974
Robinson, David, *The History of World Cinema*, New York: Stein & Day Publishers, 1973
Salzman, Eric, *Twentieth Century Music: An Introduction*, Englewood Cliffs, NJ: Prentice Hall, Inc., 1967

Index

Bold numbers refer to picture and map captions.